D0782566

DATE DUE

BRODART, CO.

Cat. No. 23-221

HISTORICAL DICTIONARY *of* AMERICAN PROPAGANDA

HISTORICAL DICTIONARY
of AMERICAN
PROPAGANDA

Martin Manning

with the assistance of

Herbert Romerstein

James S. Olson
Advisory Editor

Greenwood Press
Westport, Connecticut • London

Library of Congress Cataloging-in-Publication Data

Manning, Martin J.
  Historical dictionary of American propaganda / Martin Manning with
the assistance of Herbert Romerstein.
    p. cm.
  Includes bibliographical references and index.
  ISBN 0-313-29605-7 (alk. paper)
  1. Propaganda, American—History—Dictionaries. I. Romerstein, Herbert. II. Title.
E183.7.M325 2004
303.3'75'097303—dc22   2004052650

British Library Cataloguing in Publication Data is available.

Copyright © 2004 by Martin Manning

All rights reserved. No portion of this book may be
reproduced, by any process or technique, without the
express written consent of the publisher.

Library of Congress Catalog Card Number: 2004052650
ISBN: 0-313-29605-7

First published in 2004

Greenwood Press, 88 Post Road West, Westport, CT 06881
An imprint of Greenwood Publishing Group, Inc.
www.greenwood.com

Printed in the United States of America

∞™

The paper used in this book complies with the
Permanent Paper Standard issued by the National
Information Standards Organization (Z39.48–1984).

10 9 8 7 6 5 4 3 2 1

Disclosure:

Much of the material used in this book is found in the files of the Public Diplomacy
Historical Collection, Bureau of Public Diplomacy, U.S. Department of State,
Washington, DC. The opinions expressed in this book are those of the authors and not
those of the U.S. Department of State or any other agency of the U.S. government.

ACC Library Services
Austin, Texas

Contents

List of Terms

Abolitionist Propaganda

Active Measures Working Group

Adams, Samuel

Advancing American Art

Afghan Media Project

Agitprop

AIDS Disinformation Campaign

"America First" Committee

American Centers and American Corners

American Colonization Society

American Council Against Nazi Propaganda

American Forces Network, Europe (AFN)

American National Exhibition, Moscow

American Nazi Party

American Republics

Amerika Haus

Amerika Illustrated

Analysis of Communist Propaganda

Anti-Imperialist League

Anti-Semitic Propaganda

Appendix Nine

Art Exhibitions

Atoms for Peace

Atrocity Propaganda

Axis Propaganda

Baby Parts

Barnes, Harry Elmer

Benét, Stephen Vincent

Bernays, Edward L.

Big Lie

Binational Centers

Biological and Chemical Weapons Warfare

Birth of a Nation

Bittman, Ladislav

Black Propaganda

Blankenhorn, Heber

Book Fairs

Books

Boston Gazette

Boston Massacre

Boston News-Letter

Boston Tea Party

Braddock II

Brainwashing

Brecht, Bertolt

Brussels Universal and International Exposition (EXPO 1958)

Buenos Aires Convention for Promotion of Inter-American Cultural Relations

Bunker Hill

Bureau of Public Diplomacy and Public Affairs (U.S. Department of State)

Byoir, Carl R.

Guide to Related Topics

ART

Advancing American Art
Art Exhibitions
Family of Man
Federal Arts Project
Four Freedoms

CAMPAIGNS

Afghan Media Project
Boston Massacre
Boston Tea Party
Braddock II
Campaign of Truth
Chesapeake Affair
Darlan Interlude
Farewell Address (Washington)
Henry Ford and *The International Jew*
Holocaust Denial
Katyn Forest Massacre Incident
Lusitania Incident
Marshall Plan
Operation Magic Carpet
Operation Mincemeat
Operation Veto
Panel on International Information, Education, and Cultural Relations
Prestige Project
Project Troy

U.S. Cultural and Information Programs
World Cruise of the U.S. Navy

COUNTRIES

American Republics
Cuba
France
Germany
Great Britain
Iraq
Italy
Japan
Occupied Countries and Territories

DISINFORMATION

AIDS Disinformation Campaign
Baby Parts
Biological and Chemical Weapons Warfare
Disinformation
Gulf War Disinformation
Soviet Active Measures

EXHIBITIONS AND FAIRS

Advancing American Art
American National Exhibition, Moscow
Art Exhibitions

U.S. Cultural and Information
Programs
U.S. Department of Agriculture
U.S. Department of State
U.S. Film Service
U.S. Government
U.S. Information Agency
Vietnam. Joint United States Public
Affairs Office (JUSPAO)

LEGISLATION

Buenos Aires Convention for Promotion
of Inter-American Cultural Relations
Domestic Dissemination
Foreign Agents Registration Act
(FARA)
House Resolution 199
Mutual Educational and Cultural
Exchange Act
OP-16W (Directive)
Postal Regulations (Communist Political
Propaganda)
Stamp Act
U.S. Information and Educational
Exchange Act

LIBRARIES AND CENTERS

American Centers and American
Corners
Amerika Haus
Binational Centers
German Library of Information
Libraries
Propaganda Collections

METHODS AND TECHNIQUES

Agitprop
Brainwashing
Cultural Diplomacy
Cultural Exchanges
Public Opinion
Public Relations

MUSIC

Disney Image
Music
National Anthems

ORGANIZATIONS

"America First" Committee
American Colonization Society
American Council Against Nazi
Propaganda
American Nazi Party
Anti-Imperialist League
Catholic Church
Century Group
Congress for Cultural Freedom
Crusade for Freedom
Cuban Freedom Committee
Fight for Freedom Committee (FFF)
Front Organizations
German-American Bund
Institute for Historical Review
Institute for Propaganda Analysis (IPA)
Institute of Pacific Relations
Inter-Allied Propaganda Commission
John Reed Clubs
Ku Klux Klan
League of American Writers
Liberty Lobby
National Board for Historical Service
National Electric Light Association
Sons of Liberty
War Advertising Council

PEOPLE

Adams, Samuel
Barnes, Harry Elmer
Benét, Stephen Vincent
Bernays, Edward L.
Bittman, Ladislav
Blankenhorn, Heber

PROPAGANDA TYPES

SLOGANS AND TERMS (USAGE)

TELEVISION BROADCASTING

TIME PERIODS

WAR PROPAGANDA

Preface

The *Historical Dictionary of American Propaganda* puts U.S. propaganda into a historical perspective. There are many interpretations of propaganda, but a simple one might be that it is one-sided communication designed to influence people's thinking and actions.

PURPOSE

This book includes two forms of propaganda: (1) any efforts created by the U.S. government and directed toward a foreign country or its people, for example, World War II radio and leaflet propaganda; and (2) propaganda created by foreign countries and aimed at the United States, for example, Axis propaganda that targeted the United States and its Allies in World War II and Soviet propaganda during the Cold War.

An introduction provides an overview on U.S. official propaganda, and there are 353 entries on people and events from the period of the War of American Independence to the Iraqi conflict. Entries range in size from approximately 75 to 1,500 words. This work looks at government campaigns and noted propagandists, bringing together in one concise volume persons, events, themes, and other information on U.S. propaganda.

STRUCTURE

Despite the ever-increasing bibliography on propaganda, including several classic works, the *Historical Dictionary of American Propaganda* is, we believe, the first dictionary work. The 353 entries are arranged alphabetically with appropriate cross referencing ("see also" and "see" references). The front of the book includes an alphabetical list of all the dictionary entry names; a listing by broad subject of all the entry names; an introductory overview of the subject; and a general chronology of American propaganda, highlighting the major dates and events that are further defined in the dictionary. Bibliographic resources are provided with most entries. The bibliography at the back of the book includes general and topical works. An annotated guide provides information on research collections that maintain propaganda-related material. Bold terms in the entries refer the reader to related entries. Although there are cross references throughout the dictionary for further access to information, in addition, an index provides more specific entry to names, publications, and events described within the entries.

SCOPE

The Historical Dictionary of American Propaganda came about from the authors' own experiences at the United States Information Agency (USIA), from which co-author Herb Romerstein retired in 1989 as the Soviet Disinformation Officer. Martin Manning continues as a research librarian in USIA's successor (since 1999), the Bureau of Public Diplomacy, under the U.S. Department of State. There, among other duties, he maintains the Bureau's Public Diplomacy Historical Collection, which was created at the suggestion of then USIA Director Edward R. Murrow (1961–1964) to answer questions on the history of USIA, its successors, and its functions.

The authors explore the historical role of American propaganda and its significance in U.S. history from the French and Indian War (1754) with Benjamin Franklin's Join, or Die cartoon to the aftermath of the terrorist attacks on 9/11/2001. The book is not intended as a comprehensive treatise on American propaganda. Because the focus of this book is U.S. official propaganda, international propaganda is included only as it applies to the United States.

The entries were compiled from both primary and secondary sources after a thorough search of books, articles, documents, dissertations and personal papers, many from the Public Diplomacy Historical Collection, formerly the USIA Historical Collection.

This dictionary tries to be inclusive in its coverage of persons and events that the authors considered to be important in U.S. propaganda history. The authors include all the major publications, people, countries, and events, especially those that are well known from such sources, such as the Committee on Public Information, Office of War Information, United States Information Agency, that were created as propaganda agencies. Also included are such individuals as Thomas Paine, "Axis Sally" (Mildred Gillars), "Tokyo Rose," Harriet Beecher Stowe and her abolition novel, *Uncle Tom's Cabin,* and many more. However, no attempt was made to list everyone who worked in American propaganda.

The selection process for the list of entries was not easy, but an attempt was made to cover topics and people the authors thought were important. General subject areas include front organizations, Soviet disinformation, prominent propagandists, and significant materials in the subject of propaganda (books, exhibitions and fairs, films, newspapers, pamphlets, periodicals, posters). Certain categories were omitted because they are not significant to the book's intent and purpose: (1) activist movements, such as domestic advocacy, or the homosexual liberation movement, a controversial but minor propaganda issue except in its importance in Soviet disinformation regarding AIDS; and (2) morale builders, such as Clara Barton and the Red Cross or the United Service Organizations (USO), which are not really propagandists or propaganda organizations.

Several essays were combined under a more common term rather than treated as individual essays, for example, **U.S. Congressional Investigations of**

Propaganda. This term includes such committees as the Dies Committee, House Special Committee to Investigate Communist Propaganda in the United States, Overman Committee, and Senate Committee on the Investigation of Propaganda. There are appropriate cross references in the text. However, there is a separate entry for the best known of these committees, the House Un-American Activities Committee.

Introduction

PURPOSE

This book came from the authors' experiences at the **United States Information Agency** (USIA), now the **Bureau of Public Diplomacy and Public Affairs** (**U.S. Department of State**), where, among other duties, Martin Manning maintains the Bureau's Public Diplomacy Historical Collection. This collection was created between 1962 and 1999 to answer questions on the history of USIA, its successors, and its functions, specifically propaganda, and to maintain material that both agency staff and outside researchers could consult. It is from the resources in this collection that much of the research on this book was drawn. USIA's once-substantial Propaganda Collection was eventually shipped to the Library of Congress in the early 1980s, after its research use declined and USIA felt that it was too prohibitive to continue maintenance of an operation that required immense physical space and staff time. There was an attempt to resurrect a propaganda collection during the Reagan administration, under USIA Director Charles Z. Wick, but it never got past the planning stage, partly due to the work the original collection entailed.

This propaganda library started during World War II in the **Office of War Information**, one of USIA's predecessors, from **Axis propaganda** (books and posters) that OWI correspondents sent to the New York headquarters. However, a more complete propaganda collection was maintained by its immediate successor, the U.S. Department of State. In 1953, both collections were combined in the newly established USIA. The aim of the collection was to provide a primary source of Free World propaganda samples intended for foreign readership and to make such material available for use in agency lectures, budget hearings, and exhibits. The kinds of material included in the collection included books, pamphlets, posters and periodicals received from Communist bloc countries (USSR, People's Republic of China, Albania, Bulgaria, Czechoslovakia, East Germany, Hungary, Poland, Romania, Yugoslavia, North Korea, North Vietnam, and Cuba) along with offerings from international front organizations and local Communist groups.

The Propaganda Collection was first part of the International Information Administration, U.S. Department of State, then it was transferred to the newly created USIA in 1953 where it was maintained by the Agency Library; it was probably the most extensive, if not the only one, of its kind at the time. Along with USIA staff members, the Propaganda Collection served other government agencies as well. However, administrative files on the Propaganda Collection, in the custody of coauthor Manning, indicate that the material had to be scrutinized through the Bureau of Customs, U.S. Treasury Department, when it entered through New York. Because it was designated as political propaganda sent from the Soviet bloc countries to the United States with its source in the Soviet government and in Soviet bloc countries' governments, this material came under the provisions of the **Foreign Agents Registration Act** (FARA). For years, Irving Fishman, Assistant Deputy Commissioner, Bureau of Customs, in the U.S. Custom House, New York City, screened and monitored the bags of books, newspapers, pamphlets and films of propaganda that entered through the Port of New York en route to Washington, under special contract with USIA. A description of this collection is:

Joseph J. White, *Sino-Soviet Bloc Periodicals Published in Free World Languages* (MSLS, Catholic University, 1964). Mr. White was the propaganda librarian at the time he submitted his master's thesis. This document and a sample of the monthly accessions lists (Acquisitions; Periodicals) remain the best description of this collection's contents.

FORMATS OF PROPAGANDA MATERIAL

Most of American propaganda is ephemeral: leaflets, broadsides, banners, posters, pamphlets, broadcasts, commercials, motion pictures, television, and now the Internet. The study of propaganda is important to serious historical research of U.S. history. To accomplish this, there are archives, libraries, museums and personal collections throughout the United States and in other countries that contain American propaganda materials in their collections. This list is not complete, as there are hundreds of propaganda sources still undocumented.

HISTORY OF PROPAGANDA

What exactly is propaganda that this dictionary tries to explore? How can we begin to understand it? According to John Brown, a retired USIA and State Department Foreign Service Officer, few words in the English language evoke more disdain than propaganda. Like so many *p* words, such as pedophilia, pornography, and prostitution, Americans associate it with the worst in human nature. Its Latin roots, foreign to Anglo-Saxon ears, make it sound un-American. We believe our enemies shamelessly use propaganda to discredit and hurt us. "Terrorism," RAND expert Brian Jenkins said after the terrorist attacks of 9/11/2001, "is fundamentally propaganda, a bloody form of propaganda." To answer this question, the reader needs to go back to the birth of public opinion in Europe. The European revolutions beginning in the seventeenth century gave rise to beliefs held by society or parts of it that could influence government and politics. When the United States declared its independence, it appealed to "the opinions of mankind." By the late nineteenth century, democratization, mass education, increased newspaper circulation, and rapid communications (from the telegraph to motion pictures) made public opinion a major force in political life.

When war broke out in Europe in 1914, nation–states had no choice but to galvanize public opinion to pursue their domestic and foreign interests. Their tool was propaganda, derived from the ancient Greek art of persuasion ("rhetoric") modernized and amplified by new communications techniques.

Chinese strategist Sun Tzu wrote *The Art of War* more than 2500 years ago about the military importance of manipulating information while the famed Greek philosopher Plato connected the foundations of ancient democracy with the emergence of professional communicators skilled in using language to move other people to action. In *Phaedrus,* he defined the practice of rhetoric as "a universal art of winning the mind by arguments both in public councils and in private conference." Plato's pupil, Aristotle, penned *Rhetoric,* a still valuable guide to propaganda techniques, despite the passage of time. The Greeks were among the first to select spokesmen (rhetors) to represent and to argue for various interest groups in the community.

In the Middle Ages, the development of the printing press in Europe and the spread of literacy encouraged greater use of books and tracts published to sway public opinion. Much of this was religious, particularly those designed by independent Protestants trying to distribute Biblical scriptures and doctrinal commentaries to the common people; many of these reformers were tortured and executed for their publishing activities as threats to royal governments and state religious unity.

The term *propaganda* was first widely used by the Catholic Church in 1622 when the Congregatio de Propaganda Fide (Congregation for the Propagation of the Faith) was founded during the Counter-Reformation by a body of cardinals who directed the foreign missionary work of the Roman **Catholic Church**, at the same time that the Inquisition was censoring Galileo for questioning church doctrines. Gradually, the word meant any effort to spread a belief. A guide to the records was published as *Inventory of the Historical Archives of the Sacred Congregation for the Evangelization of Peoples or "De Propaganda Fide"* (3rd enl. ed., 1988).

Lenin combined "propaganda" and "agitation" into "agitprop." Goebbels carried on a "war of nerves" before each of Hitler's aggressions. The activities of the U.S. Office of War Information and **Office of Strategic Services** were coordinated with those of the Psychological Warfare Division at Supreme Headquarters in Europe during **World War II**. During the **Vietnam Conflict**, billions of leaflets were airdropped by the United States in Vietnam, calling on enemy soldiers to defect, telling civilians that their area had been declared a free-fire zone and warning them to move.

Propaganda sometimes evokes indignation and protest. "Hearst papers in Boston are notorious for 'making' of the news," wrote George Seldes in 1938. "Public opinion frequently is influenced by stories which originate not in events but in the minds of editors."

Private groups, such as political action committees (PACs), education and trade groups, and foundations use propaganda for national access to political decision makers and to other sources of mass distribution to accomplish objectives; today new opportunities for propagandists are achieved through direct mail and new information technology. Prerequisite conditions for successful propaganda were discussed by Jacques Ellul in his book *Propaganda: The Formation of Men's Attitudes* (1965; reprint 1973).

World War I, the first total war involving not just the military but populations as a whole, should be considered modern propaganda's launching pad. Both sides in this global struggle made use of it, especially the Allies, who were much better at the craft than the self-righteous Germans, unable, with some exceptions, to understand why persuasion was needed to justify their deeds. In April 1917, shortly after declaring war on Germany, the Woodrow Wilson administration established the **Committee on Public Information** (CPI), the first official U.S. propaganda agency since Abraham Lincoln sent propagandists and **pamphlets** to Europe during the Civil War to sell the Union side. At its peak, CPI employed 150,000 people to convince foreign publics that America, reliable, honest, and invincible, would defeat German militarism and make the world safe for democracy.

Propaganda experts in the postwar period saw Wilson as a master of the trade, "the great generalissimo of the propaganda front" whose "eloquence was the most powerful battering ram of the Allied and American propaganda against Germany." Adolph Hitler wrote in *Mein Kampf* that "the war propaganda of the English and Americans was psychologically correct." After four and one-half years a revolution broke out in Germany, whose slogans came from the enemy's propaganda but the American public turned against it after the war. They had had enough of it. Even during the war, Congress had been critical of **George Creel** and his methods.

By the mid-1930s, brutal propaganda by the Nazis and fascists gave added evidence to arguments that it was undemocratic. Foreign propaganda was considered to be dangerous to American democracy, and the House Committee on Un-American Activities was created in reaction to these fears. Later in the century, Soviet propaganda reinforced these suspicions (some bordering on the hysterical) of the word and the activities it entailed. Despite this widespread popular hostility toward propaganda, both foreign and homemade, the U.S. government continued to use it, arguing at one point, in the words of Assistant Secretary of State George V. Allen (1949), that "propaganda on an immense scale is here to stay. We Americans must become informed and adept at its use, defensively and offensively, or we may find ourselves as archaic as the belted knight who refused to take gunpowder seriously 500 years ago."

At the end of the decade, the dismissive "it's all propaganda anyway" had become widespread in the American idiom. Propaganda had fallen into disrepute. It had come to mean lies, falsehood, and deception. This critical attitude began among American troops in Europe, where naive doughboys sent abroad to make the world safe for democracy discovered that "atrocity stories had been false concoctions and that the Germans had behaved no worse than any other combatants," according to the scholar J. Michael Sproule. U.S. soldiers concluded that propaganda had been misleading and untrue. Ernest Hemingway, who served in the ambulance corps during World War I, witnessed the horrors of that "war to end all wars"; he had enough of what Bertrand Russell calls "the foul literature of glory." The antihero in *A Farewell to Arms* laments: "Abstract words such as glory, honor, courage, or hallow were obscene behind the concrete names of villages, the numbers of roads, the names of rivers, the numbers of regiments and the dates."

In the interwar period, advertising and publicity, which by their very nature are propaganda, were not held in high regard by Americans, who believed that the truth was often lost in the drive to sell and to promote new goods. Aware the public had soured on both propaganda and advertising, **Edward Bernays,** the father of public relations and Viennese-born nephew of Sigmund Freud as well as a CPI graduate, wrote in his *Propaganda* (1928) that "intelligent men must realize that propaganda is the modern instrument by which they can fight for productive ends and help bring order out of chaos."

Government officials after World War I were far more cautious about using propaganda than the Wilson administration. When he established the Office of War Information (OWI) in 1942 to support the war effort both at home and aboard, President Roosevelt took care that it not to repeat the excesses of Creel's CPI. **Voice of America** broadcasts during the war years avoided atrocity stories, even omitting reports on the Holocaust, for fear that they would not be believed or to play down the more serious charge that Roosevelt stalled in helping the Jews. Maybe both reasons. In 1948, the Smith-Mundt Act forbade the **domestic dissemination** of U.S. government materials intended for foreign audiences. In 1999, when the United States Information Agency (USIA), created to spare the State Department from being the major U.S. propaganda agency during the Cold War, was abolished and consolidated into that same State Department, with its exchanges and information functions absorbed into a new Bureau of Public Diplomacy, Secretary Madeleine Albright praised its work of over 45 years as "an anti-propaganda agency," making sure the hated P-word had the right negative prefix before it. Since the events of 9/11/2001, the Bureau of Public Diplomacy has been thrust into a war on terrorism that has commanded incredible resources and staff; this was heightened in 2003 when military operations in Iraq increased public diplomacy efforts in the always volatile Middle East, with new Web pages, publications (especially *Hi,* aimed to Arab youth) and broadcasts (e.g., Radio Sawa). In October of that year, the Advisory Group on Public Diplomacy in the Arab and Muslim World, at the request of the House Committee on Appropriations, released *Changing Minds, Winning Peace: A New Strategic Direction for U.S. Public Diplomacy in the Arab and Muslim World* (popularly, Djerejian Report, for its chairman, Edward P. Djerejian).

ACKNOWLEDGMENTS

First, a special thanks to the authors' families. Other nods of appreciation to colleagues (some now retired) and friends who offered assistance and advice: John Brown, retired Foreign Service Officer who allowed the authors permission to use quotes from the history of propaganda he prepared for his public diplomacy seminar at Georgetown University; Todd Leventhal, Herb's disinformation colleague in the USIA Policy Guidance Office and valued friend to both authors who reviewed parts of the manuscript; Helen Crossley and Dr. Leo Crespi, pioneers in public opinion search who recommended pertinent studies; Dr. Nicholas Cull for his input throughout the writing stages; Dr. Caroline Page for sharing her own research on Vietnam; Allen Hansen, another USIA colleague who constantly asked about the status of the manuscript; Dr. Nancy Gwinn, Dr. Sidney Hart, Katherine Krile, David Ward, and Kathleen Williams of the Smithsonian Institution for guidance and advice; State Department colleagues Cynthia Borys, Mary Boone, Eileen Deegan, Ann Holland, Hugh Howard, Carol Norton, William Reinckens, Miriam Rider, Dr. Judith Siegel, Valerie Wheat, and Mark

Taplin, who shared his own publishing experiences; and John Findling, who first put us in touch with Greenwood Publishing Group. Gratitude also to Eugene and Linda Abbondelo, Frederick Augustyn, Jane and Joseph Keady, Joyce Franklin, Mary and Andrew James, Benjamin and Terry Lowe, John and Cathy Kronebusch, Yvonne Condon, Roberta Zonghi, and Frank and Lee Ann Hoffmann. The authors owe especial thanks to their editors at Greenwood Publishing Group, Cynthia Harris and Anne Thompson, for their endless patience waiting for the manuscript to appear.

List of Abbreviations

ABSIE	American Broadcasting Station in Europe
AFHQ	Armed Forces Headquarters (North Africa)
ANB	American National Biography
BBG	Broadcasting Board of Governors
BNC	Binational Center
CFR	Council on Foreign Relations
CIA	Central Intelligence Agency
CIAA	Coordinator of Inter-American Affairs
COI	Coordinator of Information
CPI	Committee of Public Information
CPUSA	Communist Party of the United States of America
DAB	Dictionary of American Biography
FARA	Foreign Agents Registration Act
FBIS	Foreign Broadcast Intelligence Service
FRUS	*Foreign Relations of the United States*
FTP	Federal Theater Project
HICOG	High Commissioner of Germany (U.S.)
HUAC	House Un-American Activities Committee
IBB	International Broadcasting Bureau
IHR	Institute for Historical Research
JUSPAO	Joint U.S. Public Affairs Office (Vietnam)
KKK	Ku Klux Klan
NARA	National Archives and Records Administration
NSC	National Security Council
OCB	Operations Coordinating Board
OFF	Office of Facts and Figures
OMGUS	Office of the Military Governor for Germany (U.S.)

OSS	Office of Strategic Services
OWI	Office of War Information
PAO	Public Affairs Officer
PD	Public Diplomacy
PSB	Psychological Strategy Board
PSYOPS	Psychological Operations
PSYWAR	Psychological Warfare
PWB	Psychological Warfare Board
PWD	Psychological Warfare Division, SHAEF
PWT	Psychological Warfare Team
RFE	Radio Free Europe
RIAS	Radio in American Sector (Berlin)
RL	Radio Liberation/Radio Liberty
RM	Radio Marti
SACB	Subversive Activities Control Board
SHAEF	Supreme Headquarters Allied Expeditionary Forces
UN	United Nations
USIA	United States Information Agency
USIS	United States Information Service
VOA	Voice of America

Chronology of Important Events in American Propaganda, 1622–2003

1622—Vatican's Pontifical Congregation for the Propagation of the Faith (Propaganda Fide) founded to oversee the expansion of the Catholic Church. This term is generally believed to be the source of the word *propaganda.*

1720s—Arguments for political liberty put forth in *Cato's Letters* by John Trenchard and Thomas Gordon; they proved highly successful and are widely cited in the pamphleteer literature of colonial America.

1754—Political cartoon, Join, or Die, by Benjamin Franklin, with its symbol of a divided snake, appeared in *Pennsylvania Gazette* and urged British colonies to fight in the French and Indian war.

1757–1762, 1765–1775—Benjamin Franklin, the first uncredited Public Affairs Officer (PAO), represented the American colonies in London, where he pamphleteered Europe in support of American revolutionary cause. He later went to France, promoting the American cause at the Court of Louis XVI.

1770 (March 5)—Frightened British troops fired on angry crowd in Boston, later popularized in broadsides as the Boston Massacre. To ignite American reaction, *Short Narrative of the Horrid Massacre in Boston,* with its depositions from eyewitnesses, became a highly effective propaganda piece in minimizing the affair in British eyes.

1773 (December 16)—Radicals disguised as Indians protest new parliamentary tax by tossing British imports into harbor in staged event, later known as Boston Tea Party, to publicize colonial grievances.

1775 (April 19)—Battles of Concord and Lexington and "the shot heard round the world" sparked War of American Independence.

1775 (November 29)—Committee of Secret Correspondence established to fund propaganda activities and conduct covert operations abroad.

1776—Thomas Paine published *Common Sense.*

1776 (July 4)—Declaration of Independence signed in July with its "decent respect for the opinions of mankind."

1776—Psychological warfare operation, formulated by Thomas Jefferson and Benjamin Franklin (Jefferson–Franklin Plan) to cause Hessian desertions, with the promise of free land, through the use of appealing handbills and pamphlets distributed by Army of the Revolution.

1782—Forged copy of a British newspaper, complete with actual advertisements and local news, used by Franklin to stir up public opinion in England with an article that said the British Royal Governor of Canada was paying his Indian Allies for each American scalp provided to him.

1787–1788—Publication of series of newspaper articles, the *Federalist Papers*, by "Publius" (John Jay, Alexander Hamilton, James Madison) to rally support for the new Constitution.

1796 (September 19)—Washington's Farewell Address, in which he warned against "entangling political alliances," published.

1798—John Robison's lurid *Proofs of a Conspiracy Against All the Religions and Governments of Europe, Carried on in the Secret Meetings of Free Masons, Illuminati, and Reading Societies, Collected from Good Authorities* harbored American fears of secret societies.

1800—First presidential campaign (John Adams against the eventual winner, Thomas Jefferson) that used propaganda attacking private lives and character of the candidates; this soon became a staple of American politics.

1810 (August 5)—Jean, Duc de Cadore, French Foreign Minister, delivered a diplomatic note to U.S. Minister John Armstrong in which Napoleon I promised to revoke the Berlin and Milan Decrees in November 1810 if the British Orders-in-Council were repealed or if the United States reinstated sanctions against Great Britain. The Cadore letter turned out to be a forgery.

1812 (June 18)—United States declared war on Great Britain, as Uncle Sam became the symbol of the United States. Its image stirred American feelings against the British.

1827 (March 16)—*Freedom's Journal* began publication with an editorial policy attacking the "return to Africa" colonization program favored by many government leaders.

1829 (September)—Abolitionist David Walker published a widely circulated pamphlet, *David Walker's Appeal, in Four Articles; Together with a Preamble to the Colored Citizens of the World, But in Particular, and Very Expressly, to Those of the United States of America*, that urged slaves to use violence to gain their freedom.

1832 (January 6)—New England Antislavery Society (soon the American Antislavery Society) founded; it quickly launched its successful propaganda campaign.

1835—Anti-Catholicism promoted with joint publications of Rebecca Reed's *Six Months in a Convent* and Samuel F. B. Morse's *Imminent Dangers to the Free Institutions of the United States Through Foreign Immigration*.

1836—Maria Monk published *Awful Disclosures*, another attack on Roman Catholicism.

1844—First telegraph message sent from Washington, D.C., to Baltimore opened faster method for transmitting propaganda.

1851—Harriet Beecher Stowe's *Uncle Tom's Cabin* published and immediately becomes a popular tract on the evils of slavery, although Stowe's plot was criticized as rather naive and simplistic.

1854 (February 28)—"Black Warrior" incident in Havana, in which American naval captain James Bulloch was arrested after his ship docked when Cuban authorities discovered his voyage was to "liberate" the country, contributed to anti-Spanish attitude in the United States.

1857 (March 6)—Dred Scott decision released by U.S. Supreme Court after intense pro-slavery propaganda campaign.

1861 (April 12)–1865 (May 12)—American Civil War (also called the "War between the States" or "The War Against Northern Aggression") fought; President Lincoln mandated first official U.S. government censorship and heavy propaganda campaigns are initiated by both the North and the South.

1863 (January 1)—Emancipation Proclamation by President Lincoln became effective propaganda against the slaveholders in the South.

1860s—Henry Hotze, an effective propagandist, arranged publication in London press of editorials favorable to South's cause in Civil War.

1867—Ku Klux Klan founded in Nashville, Tennessee.

1882—Johan Most, a German radical, arrived in the United States to preach "the propaganda of the deed" and communist anarchism.

1882—President Grover Cleveland began practice of meeting with reporters to influence public opinion.

1893 (May)—World Columbian Exposition, Chicago, opened as observance (one year late) of Columbus's discovery of America.

1898 (February 9)—Letter by Enrique Dupuy de Lome, Spanish minister to the United States, to a friend in Havana that criticized President McKinley as "weak and a bidder for the admiration of the crowd"; the letter was published in William Randolph Hearst's *New York Journal* (February 9, 1898). The publication of the letter ignited public opinion toward future Cuban intervention.

1898 (February 15)—USS *Maine* sunk at Havana; war declared on Spain. "Remember the *Maine*" introduced as rallying cry to American people along with short films that stirred Americans to patriotic fervor for the brief military conflict, such as "The Spanish-American War" and "Tearing Down the American Flag," the first commercial war movie.

1898—Introduction of newspapers as yellow journalism, which brought the casualties down to the level of the average reader with lurid front-page headlines and pictures of real and supposed Spanish horrors.

1900—First public relations firm, the Publicity Bureau, founded in Boston "to do a general press agent business."

1907 (December 16)–1909 (February 22)—Great White Fleet of sixteen battleships sent on world cruise by President Theodore Roosevelt to show U.S. naval power.

1907—Public relations pioneer Ivy Lee published famous article in November issue of *Moody's Magazine* that praised the importance of the railroad industry.

1914 (April)—Ivy Lee humanized John D. Rockefeller, Jr., as caring, sociable and philanthropic, after Colorado coal strike in which 53 people were killed by strike breakers employed by Rockefeller family.

1915—League to Enforce Peace organized.

1915 (February 8)—Premiere of D. W. Griffith's *The Birth of a Nation*, a film that popularized the Ku Klux Klan.

1916—Henry Ford established newspaper, *Dearborn Independent*, which initiated an ongoing education series shortly after World War I to "tell all" about the Jewish Question; much of this disinformation had its roots in *Protocols of the Meetings of the Learned Elders of Zion*, a discredited anti-Semitic hoax that became a centerpiece of anti-Semitic literature.

1917 (April 13)–1919 (June 30)—Committee on Public Information (CPI; Creel Committee) created by President Wilson, the first U.S. propaganda agency, to coordinate official U.S. information effort during World War I.

1917 (February 24)—Zimmermann telegram, from Germany to Mexico, which was intercepted by the United States, was made public; its contents stir up public opinion against German actions.

1917—Poster of Uncle Sam by artist James Montgomery Flagg with its "I Want You" message became one of the most recognizable pieces of art in American history and a classic in military recruiting that was used again in World War II.

1918 (February 8)—*The Stars and Stripes*, newspaper of the American Expeditionary Force in World War I, began publication and continued for sixteen months. It was revised and published in European and in Pacific editions during World War II.

1918 (September 15)—U.S. government released to the press a collection of documents that purported to show that the Bolsheviks had received money both before and after the Russian Revolution. In October 1918, the Committee on Public Information (CPI) released a pamphlet, *The German-Bolshevik Conspiracy*, which contained translations of 68 documents and reproductions of many of them. The documents had been obtained in Russia by Edgar Sisson, the CPI representative, and came to be known as the "Sisson Documents."

1919—CPI started four reading rooms in Mexico City, an unsuccessful experiment that was the predecessor of the Biblioteca Benjamin Franklin that the U.S. government established in April 1942.

1923—Edward Bernays, who called himself the "public relations counsel," published *Crystallizing Public Opinion*, which is considered the first public relations book.

1926 (May)—*New Masses* published as "popular front" for liberal and radical thought, but over time the publication became more doctrinaire Marxist.

1929 (October)—First John Reed Club formed in New York by writers and artists associated with the journal *New Masses* to promote revolutionary art and literature.

1929—Document purporting to be a memorandum from the Japanese Prime Minister Tanaka to the Emperor Hirohito found its way into the Western press. This document, written in 1927, laid out a Japanese plan for world conquest. The Tanaka Memorandum was clearly a forgery. It contained errors of fact about Japan and even about Baron Tanaka, but it was widely circulated until the end of World War II. The forgery originally surfaced in China in 1929 and in the United States in 1930.

1930s—Michigan priest Fr. Charles Coughlin reached the height of his popularity with his weekly radio broadcasts and his newspaper, *Social Justice*, that were effectively anti-Semitic and anti-New Deal.

1930s—New Deal of Franklin Roosevelt (inaugurated March 4, 1933). Federal arts programs created to offer government patronage to the arts placed in four projects (for visual artists, theater workers, musicians, and writers), established in the Works Progress Administration (WPA).

1930 (May 2)—U.S. Congress planned to establish a committee to investigate Communist propaganda. Shortly before it was formed, the New York City police department received copies of a set of documents purporting to be letters from the Communist International instructing Amtorg to carry out Communist propaganda in the United States. The documents were released to the press on May 2, 1930; they appeared in print the next day. They were released by police Commissioner Grover Whalen and came to be known as the Whalen Documents.

1932 (February 24)—Open letter from Secretary of State Henry Stimson to Senator William Borah released; it is used to incite American public opinion toward the Chinese in the Sino-Japanese controversy. Letter was written on February 23.

1934—House Resolution 1999 introduced to provide for the investigation of Nazi propaganda activities in the United States and related questions. Congressional investigations of propaganda continued until 1954 by various committees.

1935 (March 30)—First "Radio Bulletin," precursor of today's "Washington File," sent via Morse Code by State Department to keep diplomatic missions abroad.

1935 (April)—First American Writers' Conference held in which revolutionary symbolism of "the people" versus "the worker" as effective propaganda debated. Also, League of American Writers developed from this meeting.

1936—Federal Theater Project (FTP), most controversial of the federal arts projects created under auspices of Works Progress Administration, began but many of its productions, such as *The Cradle Will Rock,* an agitprop musical produced in 1937, are labeled as "Communist" and "propaganda" by Congressional members. At its funding hearings (1939), Congress abolished the FTP.

1937–1942—Institute for Propaganda Analysis published *Propaganda Analysis* as an aid to student and adult groups.

1937—Emergency Peace Campaign started.

1938—Fr. Charles Coughlin introduced the *Protocols of the Learned Elders of Zion* as an extensive series of articles in his newspaper, *Social Justice,* by invoking the authority of Henry Ford in the authenticity of the writings.

1938 (July)—Division of Cultural Relations established in U.S. Department of State to handle official propaganda directed at Latin Americans. In conjunction with this, Interdepartmental Committee on Scientific and Cultural Cooperation (SCC) and Division of Cultural Cooperation created, also in U.S. Department of State.

1938—Foreign Agents Registration Act passed to restrict distribution of foreign films and publications into the U.S., mostly to counter the growing influence of propaganda from Communist, Fascist and National Socialist (Nazi) governments.

1938 (August)—Roosevelt administration began documentary film program, U.S. Film Service, to coordinate production of motion pictures about national social problems that were neglected by the commercial film industry.

1940–1942—British Secret Intelligence Service carried out various covert operations and propaganda activities in United States.

1940 (May)—Committee to Defend America by Aiding the Allies (CDAAA) established.

1940 (June)—America First, major noninterventionist group, created. One of its prominent members was Charles Lindbergh. In the same year, Century Group, pro-interventionist group, founded.

1940 (August 16)—Office of the Coordination of Commercial and Cultural Relations Between the American Republics, later the Office of Coordinator of Inter-American Affairs (CIAA), established with Nelson A. Rockefeller as the coordinator, to counter Nazi propaganda in the American Republics.

1941 (January 6)—Four Freedoms speech by President Roosevelt published as pamphlet by Office of War Information and translated into four very popular pictures by artist Norman Rockwell for 1942 *Saturday Evening Post* covers. These were used successfully by U.S. government as home front propaganda during World War II to sell war bonds and as inspiration for a 1943 symphony, *Four Freedoms,* by Robert Russell Bennett.

1941 (April 19)— Fight for Freedom Committee established to arouse the American people into fighting Hitler.

1941 (September 8)—U.S. Senate Subcommittee of the Committee on Interstate Commerce began investigation of pro-British and anti-German war propaganda in Hollywood films. The hearings are published as: *Propaganda in Motion Pictures* (Washington, DC: Government Printing Office, 1942).

1941 (July 11)—Coordinator of Information (COI) established to collect, analyze, and coordinate information bearing on national security and to make such data available to the president and to any other officials determined by the president. William B. Donovan ("Wild Bill") was named Coordinator. Foreign Information Service (FIS), headed by playwright and Roosevelt speechwriter Robert Sherwood, created later that summer. Voice of America started under FIS.

1941 (December 7)—Attack on fleet at Pearl Harbor ("a day that will live in infamy") on December 7; rallying cry "Remember Pearl Harbor" reverberates throughout country. The next day, Congress declared war on Japan, and the United States entered World War II. The war officially ended in August 1945 with the surrender of the Japanese on board the USS *Missouri.*

1941 (October 24)—U.S. Office of Facts and Figures founded as propaganda monitoring agency under direction of Archibald MacLeish. In June 1942, its functions were transferred to the Office of War Information.

1941—Frank Capra commissioned to produce Why We Fight documentary series as Hollywood mobilized its resources, putting all its talent, especially directors, writers, producers, and actors, to the war effort. One of Capra's creative talents was future children's author Theodor Seuss Geisel (Dr. Seuss).

1942 (February 24/25)—Voices of America, later the Voice of America (VOA), began shortwave broadcasts in German, in French, in Italian, and in English; first VOA broadcast to Germany takes place evening of February 24/25. By 2001, there were 53 languages, including English, broadcast via medium wave (AM) and shortwave broadcast, and on local AM and FM stations around the world.

1942 (April)—First U.S. government-sponsored library opened in Mexico City. By 2001, there were 170 (now designated as Information Resource Centers) in operation throughout the world. By the end of World War II, others followed in London, Calcutta, Wellington and other pro-Allied cities.

1942 (June)—U.S. Office of War Information (OWI) established as World War II propaganda agency with Elmer Davis as its director; its information functions were transferred from the COI while the Office of Strategic Services (OSS) was created from COI's nonin-formation functions of Coordinator of Information, under direction of William "Wild Bill" Donovan, to coordinate covert operations and to engage in spying and spacecraft.

1942—Anglo-American Psychological Warfare Branch, Allied Force Headquarters, in Algiers, established as a Mediterranean-wide domestic propaganda and tactical PW orga-nization under Colonel H. B. Hazeltine.

1942 (November)—Brigadier General Robert A. McClure appointed chief of the Information and Censorship Section, Allied Force Headquarters (AFHQ) in its Psychological Warfare Branch (PWB). On April 13, 1944, PWB became part of the Psychological Warfare Division (PWD), Supreme Headquarters, Allied Expeditionary Forces (SHAEF). SHAEF was officially dissolved on July 13, 1945.

1943 (April 30)—Operation Mincemeat carried out to deceive the Germans with the location where Allies would make an assault on the European continent with "the man who never was," the corpse of a young man who just died of pneumonia who was dressed as a British officer and dropped off the coast of Spain with papers indicating that an attack on Sicily would not be the real thing but that the real objective was Sardinia and Greece.

1943 (July 25)—OWI broadcast, in which Italy's king, Victor Emmanuel III, is called a "moronic little king" and his prime minister, Marshal Badoglio, is referred to as a "Fascist," embarrassed the Roosevelt administration but insinuations by the *New York Times* about the broadcast are proved to be untrue.

1943—Warner Bros. released controversial film, *Mission to Moscow*, based on the mem-oirs of Joseph E. Davies, former U.S. Ambassador to the Soviet Union, which was criti-cized, among other charges, as a piece of Communist propaganda sympathetic to the Roosevelt administration.

1944 (November 24)—Law No. 191 and its de-Nazification directives (close Nazi media, censor resurgent neo-Nazi ideologies) issued by Allied Control Council.

1944—Captain James Monroe developed cheap, propaganda bomb to disseminate leaflets in an acceptable pattern. Monroe's discovery revolutionized leaflet operations in the European Theater of Operations.

1944 (June 6)—Operation Neptune/Overlord (D-Day) planned by staff of Psychological Warfare Division, OWI, as greatest propaganda show ever staged, especially in its use of radio broadcasts and leaflets.

1944—Operation Nest Egg, leaflet campaign jointly planned by PWD/SHAEF and British military intelligence to bring about the surrender and evacuation of the German garrison on Guernsey in the British Channel, failed due to poor planning and not enough leaflets.

1944–1945—Operation Annie, a strategic clandestine Allied propaganda station operated out of Luxembourg by the Psychological Warfare Branch, U.S. Army, instituted to develop an audience among German troops by broadcasting news with a pro-German bias.

1945 (December)—OWI abolished; foreign information activities transferred to U.S. Department of State. To handle them, an Office of International Information and Cultural Affairs and International Press and Publications Division are created.

1945—Operation Cornflakes initiated by Allies to place anti-Nazi propaganda letters into German mailbags to be delivered punctually at breakfast time ("cornflakes") by the mailman.

1945–1952—First version of *America Illustrated* is published under agreement first conceived at Yalta by Roosevelt and Stalin in an exchange-of-information agreement.

1946 (August 1)—Fulbright Act (PL 79-584) signed; it mandated peacetime international exchange program. It is administered principally by the U.S. Department of State with the Department of Education handling a smaller program for Americans only. Abroad, it is administered by 51 binational Fulbright Commissions and by the U.S. Embassy in countries without Commissions.

1946—Office of Military Governor of United States (OMGUS) established in occupied Germany. One of its mandates was to provide cultural and information programs (books, libraries, film showings, distribution of pamphlets). In 1949, U.S. Office of High Commissioner for Germany (HICOG) replaced OMGUS.

1946 (February 7)—Radio in the American Sector created in Berlin.

1946 (March 5)—Winston Churchill's "Iron Curtain" speech in Fulton, Missouri, warned against Soviet expansionism. Term first coined by German propaganda minister Josef Goebbels.

1947 (May 7)—U.S. House Committee on Un-American Activities begins hearings on alleged un-American activities and propaganda, including Communist influence in motion picture industry, which culminated in trial of "Hollywood Ten." Testimony heard from individuals, such as Gerhard Eisler, Whittaker Chambers, Bertolt Brecht, Gerald L. K. Smith, and organizations, including the Office of Price Administration and the Joint Anti-Fascist Refugee Committee. Hearings continued sporadically through 1953.

1948 (April 3)—President Truman signed the Foreign Assistance Act that established the Marshall Plan (European Recovery Program) that provided U.S. aid for the financial reconstruction of Europe.

1948–1953—Multimedia information programs to promote and to document European Recovery Program conducted by Marshall Plan agencies (Economic Cooperation Administration and Mutual Security Agency). One of the first was the Informational Media Guaranty (IMG) program in which producers of various informational media (books, magazines, films, musical recordings) could sell their products in countries short of hard-currency foreign exchange.

1948 (January 27)—Smith-Mundt Act (PL 80-402) enacted; it chartered peacetime overseas program. Section 501 forbids domestic dissemination of program materials in the United States. Legislation still effective mandate for U.S. information and cultural programs.

1948—National Security Directive NSC 10/2 issued; it authorized covert action and propaganda by U.S. intelligence services.

1948—Harold Lasswell created the "who says what to whom with what effect?" model of communication.

1949–1952—Massive reorientation and reeducation programs conducted in countries under U.S. Occupation forces. Major resources spent in Germany and in Japan, but Korea and Italy also were the beneficiaries of U.S. information programs.

1949 (June 21)—Central Intelligence Agency (CIA) Act signed.

1949 (August 5)—U.S. Department of State issued a white paper that disclaimed any responsibility for the Communist conquest of mainland China.

1950 (April)—President Truman gave Campaign of Truth speech then asked Congress for supplemental appropriation to finance a "campaign of truth" program to counteract Radio Moscow's propaganda broadcasts.

1950 (January–April)—NSC-68, drawn up by National Security Council, has among its provisions the effective use of propaganda to win over the Russian people.

1950 (June 25)—Korean Conflict began, initiating a major Soviet disinformation campaign in which a biological and chemical warfare campaign was started by American soldiers against the Korean population. Conflict ended in 1953.

1950—*Red Channels: The Report of Communist Influence in Radio and Television* published by American Business Consultants, Inc., who also published *Counterattack: The Newsletter of Facts to Combat Communism*.

1950 (July 4)—Radio Free Europe began its shortwave broadcasts from a small mobile transmitter near the woods of Lampertheim, Germany. Originally, its funding came from the CIA but this changed in 1973 when the U.S. Congress established the Board for International Broadcasting, which provided authorizations for RFE and its sister station, Radio Liberty.

1951—Warner Brothers film, *I Was a Communist for the FBI* that supported the activities of the House Committee on Un-American Activities, released. It was based on a three-part series by Matt Cvetic, as told to Pete Martin, "I Posed as a Communist for the FBI," *Saturday Evening Post* (July 1950). It later became a long-running radio series.

1952–1954—Claims of Communist infiltration of U.S. propaganda programs conducted by U.S. Congress.

1952 (January 16)—International Information Administration (IIA) established in State Department from previous information programs created in 1946 after the end of World War II.

1952—*Problems of Communism* launched as a Cold War weapon against the Soviet Union but it ceases publication with the fall of the Soviet Union. The last issue is dated May–June 1992.

1952 (August 25)—Operation Magic Carpet did much to counter Soviet anti-American propaganda among the Moslems as U.S. air forces airlifted thousands of Muslims stranded in Beirut, Lebanon, hundreds of miles from Mecca (Holy City), shortly before the Mecca city gates were to be closed.

1952—*I Led Three Lives: Citizen, "Communist," Counterspy* by Herbert Philbrick, based on his adventures, became a TV series. Premise of both book and series was that someone close to you could be a traitor and not to be trusted.

1953 (March 1)—Radio Liberation, later Radio Liberty, began broadcasts to the Soviet Union from Munich, Germany. Like Radio Free Europe, its funding originally came from the CIA, but this changed in 1973 when the U.S. Congress established the Board for International Broadcasting, which provided authorizations for RFE and Radio Liberty.

1953 (April)—Grace Lumpkin testified before U.S. Senate Permanent Committee on Investigations, chaired by Senator Joseph McCarthy, that she put Communist party propaganda into her 1935 novel, *A Sign for Cain*. Same committee also held several weeks of televised hearings on VOA after alleged false charges of Communist influence at the radio station appeared.

1953 (August 1)—United States Information Agency (USIA) created by Reorganization Plan No. 8; it merged the U.S. information and cultural programs overseas where it is called the United States Information Service (USIS) in many countries, although the word was actually in effect in the 1930s to designate similar programs under the U.S. Department of State.

1954—Vietnamese Conflict began as North Vietnam struggled for control over South Vietnam. United States sent military advisors and began propaganda campaign, which culminated in creation of JUSPAO (Joint U.S. Public Affairs Office, Vietnam) in 1965 to coordinate these activities, including massive leaflet campaigns and field research surveys.

1954—President Eisenhower received from U.S. Congress five million dollars appropriated to the President's Emergency Fund for cultural presentations; these include sports exchanges and the performing artists program. Also, the U.S. Department of Commerce, in cooperation with USIA, announced U.S. participation in trade fairs, something the U.S. had not previously done

1954 (April 29)—Operation Veto, first sustained effort to reach the population of an Iron Curtain country satellite by both printed (balloon leaflets) and spoken word (Radio Free Europe broadcasts) on a closely coordinated saturation basis, began over Czechoslovakia in April and extended into that autumn.

1954 (May)—USIA established a Committee on Books Abroad to advise on problems in publishing and library fields, including book selection policies. The committee was a subcommittee of the U.S. Advisory Commission on Information.

1954 (June 15)—Atoms for Peace exhibit, based on speech by President Eisenhower, to show peaceful use of atoms (medicine, industry and agriculture), began its showings abroad to emphasize American leadership in peaceful uses of atomic energy.

1955—First original USIA television programs shown overseas as the number of overseas TV stations receiving USIS programs increased from 24 to 29 in 21 countries.

1955 (January)—Edward Steichen's Family of Man photographic exhibit began worldwide showings, with the initial showings in Guatemala and in Germany. Within five years, a global audience of almost nine million people saw the exhibit.

1956—Second version of America Illustrated published and distributed in Soviet Union under a second cultural agreement between the United States and the USSR; USSR (later Soviet Life) distributed in the United States in reciprocity. Publication ceased in 1994.

1956 (November)—Hungarian Revolution proved effectiveness of Voice of America (VOA) and of Radio Free Europe in bringing balanced message to captured Hungarians of events going on in their country.

1957 (February 15)—Eisenhower–Rockefeller Letter released, an extensive forgery presented as a private letter from Nelson A. Rockefeller to President Dwight D. Eisenhower, in which Rockefeller was portrayed as the advocate of a "bolder program of aid to underdeveloped countries." This was a cover for what the East Germany press called "supercolonialism" ("superkolonialismus"). Its aim was to discredit the U.S. commitment to the removal of the old colonial powers from their involvements in Africa and in Asia.

1958 (January 27)—First U.S.–USSR cultural exchange agreement signed.

1958 (April 17–October 19)—Brussels Universal and International Exposition (Expo 1958) opened. During its six-month run, Cold War tensions between the United States and the Soviet Union were reflected in the exhibitions in their respective pavilions. Opposition in

U.S. Congress to Unfinished Business exhibit on segregation forces its closure before end of exposition.

1959 (July 25–September 4)—American National Exhibition held in Moscow's Sokolniki Park; "kitchen debate" between Vice-President Nixon and Soviet Premier Khrushchev took place in exhibition's model American home. A reciprocal exhibition, on a smaller scale, was held by the Russians in New York City.

1960 (May 17)—Radio Swan, CIA's first major anti-Castro radio station, began broadcasting to Cuba and to the Caribbean; the station was located on a tiny island off the coast of Honduras. Radio Swan became Radio Americas in 1961.

1960 (November 26)—Three VOA programs broadcast by Radio Moscow and provincial Soviet stations, first such broadcasting activity under 1958 U.S.–USSR cultural exchange agreement.

1961 (September 21)—Fulbright-Hays Act (Public Law 87-256) signed; it consolidated educational and cultural exchange activities. In 1962, an amendment to the act (Public Law 87-565) gave presidential authority to provide for U.S. participation in fairs and expositions held abroad.

1961—Newly inaugurated Kennedy administration kept up pressure against Cuba's revolutionary government with continued propaganda operations.

1962 (November)—U.S. Government Advisory Committee on Book and Library Programs, established by Secretary of State Dean Rusk, under authority of Fulbright-Hays Act, to ensure effective distribution abroad of American books, both in English and in translation. It was abolished in 1977.

1965 (July 1)—U.S. Joint Public Affairs Office (JUSPAO) established under direction of USIA to coordinate U.S. information efforts in Vietnam. It was deactivated in 1975 when the U.S. withdrew troops.

1967—Congress for Cultural Freedom, later renamed International Association for Cultural Freedom, discovered to be a European CIA front organization; it began in June 1950 from a Berlin conference to "inoculate the world against the contagion of Communism and to ease the passage of American foreign policy interests abroad" by countering a worldwide Soviet propaganda campaign.

1968 (January)—Seizure of USS *Pueblo*, an intelligence-gathering ship, by North Korean forces ignited public opinion when film of its capture is broadcast on American television.

1973 (October 19)—Board for International Broadcasting (BIB) created by Public Law 93-129 to oversee Radio Free Europe and Radio Liberty. BIB was repealed by the United States International Broadcasting Act of 1994 (Public Law 103-326).

1975—U.S. Senate Select Committee to Study Governmental Operations with Respect to Intelligence Activities (Church Committee) began extensive hearings. Its final report, issued 1976, found covert action programs being used to disrupt and to discredit lawful political activities and revealed over 200 CIA publishing front organizations in U.S. and abroad.

1976 (July 12)—Voice of America charter signed into law (Public Law 94-350); it authorized VOA to present balanced, objective, and reliable news. VOA also began transmitting via international satellite circuits, replacing shortwave, and introduced "New Sound" in worldwide English broadcasts with more diverse mixture of news and music.

1976 (September)—Photocopy of U.S. Army Field Manual, FM 30-31B, also known as "Stability Operations-Intelligence," appeared on the bulletin board of the Philippine Embassy in Thailand together with a letter addressed to President Marcos. The forgery said that the United States planned to use leftist terrorist groups in Western countries to promote U.S. objectives. It reappeared in 1978 in two Spanish publications, where it had been planted by a Spanish Communist and a Cuban intelligence officer. The forged field manual had worldwide distribution in the late 1970s.

1978 (April 1)—U.S. information and cultural programs reorganized as independent U.S. International Communication Agency (USICA) by merger of USIA and of State's Bureau of Educational and Cultural Affairs, but name change causes confusion overseas because it is abbreviated CIA in some languages. USIA name restored in August 1982.

1978—Institute for Historical Review founded "to investigate the true causes and nature of war and to disseminate those findings" through "scholarship in the promotion of peace" but its contention that the Holocaust was the work of Jewish propagandists caused controversy.

1980 (September 17)—White House press spokesman Jody Powell announced that an unidentified group had sought to sow racial discord by circulating a forged Presidential Review Memorandum on Africa that suggested a racist policy on the part of the United States. The first surfacing on the forgery was San Francisco black newspaper, *Sun Reporter* (September 18, 1980). The forgery was replayed by the Soviet news agency TASS on September 18, 1980, and distributed worldwide.

1981 (June 9)—Charles Wick sworn in as USIA's longest-serving director. His contacts to President Reagan allow him to refocus agency's mission to enhance "public diplomacy" functions and to try to restore a tarnished agency image.

1981—Reagan administration created the Active Measures Working Group in 1981 to bring together the information the various agencies had to counter Soviet disinformation and forgery. It served as a clearinghouse to expose such information, and it had permission to use classified documents and any other resources that were required to meet this goal. The Working Group was chaired by the State Department with representatives from State, Central Intelligence Agency, Defense Intelligence Agency, Arms Control and Disarmament Agency, United States Information Agency, and the Defense and Justice Departments. It ended in 1991.

1982 (January 31)—Expensive USIA TV production *Let Poland be Poland,* hosted by Frank Sinatra, was televised on January 31 to support Polish people under martial law. Fifteen world leaders, among them British Prime Minister Margaret Thatcher, came together to offer courage and concern. Under H.J. Resolution 382, Congress allowed the film to be shown in the United States.

1982—*Soviet Propaganda Alert*, a monthly publication based on information transmitted by USIA officers abroad, issued to expose Soviet disinformation around the world.

1982 (September 9)—President Reagan designated USIA to lead an interdepartmental effort to counter Soviet propaganda and disinformation.

1983 (February 6)—Pro-Soviet Indian weekly, *Link,* published the text of a supposed speech by UN Ambassador Jeane Kirkpatrick outlining a plan for the Balkanization of India. The speech was never given but this forgery was replayed many times by Soviet-controlled propaganda outlets.

1983 (October)—After the invasion of Grenada, U.S. Army psychological warfare operations began against Cuban personnel on island, including the use of surrender leaflets, which were replicas of Cuban currency.

1983 (October 4)—Radio Marti created by the Radio Broadcasting to Cuba Act (Public Law 98-111) to provide Spanish-language news and programming to Cuba; its first broadcasts began May 15, 1985.

1983 (November 3)—Worldnet, USIA's global satellite television network, went on the air with its own satellite television network to link Washington with U.S. embassies and USIS posts as well as to television stations in up to 100 major cities on six continents.

1983 (November)—Fulbright-Hays Act amended to give USIA authority to conduct educational and cultural affairs in nonpolitical fashion and according to highest academic and artistic standards.

1984 (January 26)—Helene von Damm was the U.S. Ambassador to Austria during the Reagan administration. To damage relations between the United States and Austria, the KGB created a forged letter, dated January 26, 1984, and purportedly signed by von Damm, which appeared on authentic but out-of-date U.S. Embassy letterhead and was designed to be insulting to American neutrality. After Viennese newspapers received copies, the Austrian Defense Ministry exposed it as a forgery.

1985—Afghan Media Project, a Reagan administration initiative funded by USIA but administered through Boston University's School of Media and Communications, was appropriated $500,000 from Supplemental Appropriations Act of 1985 (Public Law 99-88) to focus world attention on the Soviet invasion of Afghanistan; it included VOA broadcasts and editorials, publications, and TV programs distributed by USIA.

1985—AIDS disinformation campaign started by KGB with placements in both Soviet and foreign newspapers; by September 1986 it became a major campaign when an English language "paper," that actually originated in East Berlin, "AIDS: Its Nature and Origin," was distributed at the Non-Aligned Movement Summit in Harare.

1985—Radio Caiman, a new CIA clandestine radio station targeting young Cubans, began broadcasting in the summer.

1985 (July)—Italian journalist found a copy of a letter signed with the name of General Robert Schweitzer, the head of the Inter-American Defense Board. The letter was a forgery addressed to President Pinochet of Chile asking him to provide troops to fight on behalf of the United States in Central America. The journalist contacted the U.S. Embassy and within the day received evidence that the letter was a forgery.

1985–1987—Media Alliance in San Francisco published *Propaganda Analysis Review*.

1986— During the summer of 1986, West European journalists received a copy of the text of a supposed speech by U.S. Secretary of Defense Casper Weinberger on the Strategic Defense Initiative. No such speech was ever made. The Weinberger forgery was intended to assist the Soviet active measures campaign. However, it was exposed by the U.S. government.

1987—Soviet Union ceased jamming VOA broadcasts to the USSR and to the Baltic Republics but continued against other Western broadcasters, including Radio Free Europe and Radio Liberty.

1987 (June)—Information USA exhibit, produced by USIA's Exhibits Service, opened in Moscow, the beginning of what was a very successful nine-city tour of the Soviet Union.

1987 (January)—Rumors started, widespread in world media, that children are being kidnapped to be used as unwilling donors in organ transplants but no credible evidence has ever been produced by governments, international bodies, nongovernmental organizations, or investigative journalists to substantiate these stories.

1988—Under court order, USIA created new interim rules that certified documentaries that want duty-free distribution status in foreign markets and allowed government officials to still impose "propaganda" warnings on "unacceptable" films.

1990 (February)—President Bush signed the Foreign Relations Authorization, Fiscal Years 1990 and 1991 (Public Law 101-246) on February 19, with its amendment to the domestic dissemination section of the 1948 Smith-Mundt Act. With the new law, USIA program materials over twelve years old that are also in the custody of the National Archives may be made available for research in the United States.

1990 (February 19)—Television Marti created under Section 241 (Television Broadcasting to Cuba) of the Foreign Relations Authorization Act, Fiscal Years 1990 and 1991 (Public Law 101-246). Fidel Castro denounced TV Marti and its "propaganda broadcasts" as unlawful interference in Cuban domestic affairs and jammed it from its first broadcast on March 27.

1991 (January 19)—Voice of the Gulf radio network, operated by members of the U.S. Special Forces psychological operations (PSYOPS), began broadcasting as part of a propaganda effort that also included loudspeaker operations and literature drops.

1993—Public Affairs Section, U.S. Embassy Moscow, set up a network of public access libraries across Russia, including five American Centers, with large reference and circulating collections, and twelve American Corners, with a focus on electronic resources.

1993 (April 19)—Roper Organization conducted public opinion survey for American Jewish Committee that found more than one in five Americans believed Holocaust never happened.

1994 (April 30)—United States International Broadcasting Act (Public Law 103-236) signed; it established an International Broadcasting Bureau (IBB), composed of VOA, Radio and TV Marti, and Worldnet, within USIA; created a nine-member, bipartisan Broadcasting Board of Governors (BBG) with oversight authority over all civilian U.S. government international broadcast services; and funded a new surrogate, Asian Democracy Radio Service (later called Radio Free Asia). The BBG's oversight extends to Radio Free Europe, Radio Liberty and Radio Free Asia.

1994 (October 1)—USIA reorganization refocused Clinton administration mandate as post–Cold War organization; Bureau of Information created from former Bureau of Programs and from nonexchange elements of Bureau of Educational and Cultural Affairs as part of Vice President Gore's "reinvention of government" plan.

1994—Several USIA-produced magazines, including *America Illustrated, Dialogue*, and *Problems of Communism*, ceased publication as Cold War ends but *Span* and *English Teaching Forum* continue.

1994—"The Child Organ Trafficking Rumor: A Modern 'Urban Legend': A Report Submitted to the United Nations Special Rapporteur on the Sale of Children, Child Prostitution, and Child Pornography by the United States Information Agency," compiled by Todd Leventhal, is released.

1996 (April)—Omnibus appropriations act passed by Congress and signed by President Clinton mandated the move of Radio and TV Marti operations from Washington, DC, to Miami, Florida. Move completed by August 1998.

1996 (March)—Radio Free Asia began broadcasting in Mandarin to China, quickly followed by broadcasts in Tibetan, Vietnamese, Burmese, Korean (to North Korea), Khmer (to Cambodia), and Lao. It has offices in Hong Kong, Tokyo, Taipei, Phnom Penh, Dharamsala, Bangkok, and Seoul.

1998 (October 21)—Foreign Affairs Reform and Restructuring Act (Public Law 105-277), signed by President Clinton; it abolished USIA, consolidated its cultural and educational functions into the State Department, and established the BBG as an independent federal entity with supervisory authority over all U.S. publicly funded, nonmilitary overseas broadcasting.

1999 (October 1)—USIA abolished, and its programming functions (information, educational exchanges, cultural) are transferred to the new Bureau of Public Diplomacy in the U.S. Department of State. Evelyn Lieberman, former VOA director, is appointed the first Under Secretary of Public Diplomacy and Public Affairs. BBG inaugurated new independence of U.S. government civilian international broadcasting.

2001 (January 31)—Gulf War disinformation began when a South African minister was speaking to the media about the "genocide" caused by depleted uranium. The disinformation started by Doug Rokke in a presentation to members of the South African Parliament on January 31, 2001, when he made a number of assertions about depleted uranium.

2001 (September 11)—Terrorist attacks on the World Trade Center (New York) and the Pentagon (outside Washington, DC) caused Bureau of Public Diplomacy to refocus its public diplomacy efforts in the Muslim world in the aftermath of the attacks as U.S. embassies worldwide countered heavy anti-Americanism while the Defense Department created a short-lived Office of Strategic Influence to oversee military propaganda and other information-related operations. State Department unveils a response to terrorism Web site that includes policy materials, electronic journals, links, and a publication, *Network of Terrorism* (Web site: usinfo.state.gov).

2001 (September)—After the terrorist attacks, disinformation campaign originated as a conspiracy theory that 4,000 Jews did not show up for work on that day, a harmless conspiracy theory or a virulent new anti-Semitism? This was the first recorded account of an urban legend that has swept the Arab world. Within a matter of days it was no longer 4,000 Israelis who were supposed not to have turned up to work, but 4,000 Jews; then reports appeared that "not a single Jew" died on September 11.

2001—As part of its response to terrorism, VOA increased its broadcasts to Afghanistan. A news report, aired September 25, with a segment of an interview with Mullah Mohammed Omar, leader of Afghanistan's Taliban militia, is broadcast over State Department objections.

2001 (October)—Hearings held on effectiveness of public diplomacy in handling the U.S. response in countering negative opinion toward the terrorism attacks. One of its key witnesses is Charlotte Beers, new Under Secretary of Public Diplomacy and Public Affairs, only one week after she is sworn into office. Another witness is Nick Nathanson, chairman, Broadcasting Board of Governors, International Broadcasting Bureau.

2001—U.S. planes dropped propaganda leaflets over parts of Afghanistan to undermine support for the radical Islamic militia that rules that country as part of a coordinated psychological warfare effort that included radio broadcasts on three frequencies.

2002—U.S. government intensifies its propaganda campaign as Israeli–Palestinian conflict continues in the Middle East. Efforts include placement of U.S. Department of State policy papers on its terrorism Web site.

2002 (June)—Follow-up hearings by the Senate Foreign Relations Committee on broadcasting and outreach to Moslem audiences through radio and television, the American Room concept, expanded youth exchange programs, and other initiatives as Under Secretary Beers requests "more resources if we are to reverse negative feelings about America and Americans."

2002 (August)—U.S. government countered allegations that Abdul Salem Zayef, the former ambassador to Pakistan, had been tortured and killed in captivity at Guantanamo. After the

U.S. Embassy, Islamabad, alerted the Department of State that the story was appearing in the Urdu press and that allegations were "being broadcast as fact on state-controlled media," State Department worked with elements in the Department of Defense to track how the disinformation was being disseminated and to prepare guidance.

2003 (March)—Iraqi war makes use of propaganda campaigns on both sides, including leaflets and media broadcasts. Both State and Defense departments initiate propaganda operations. A Strategic Planning Office is set up in the Bureau of International Information Programs, State Department, to coordinate State's efforts.

2003—White House issued *Apparatus of Lies: Saddam's Disinformation and Propaganda, 1990–2003* (Washington, DC: U.S. Department of State, 2003), compiled by State and Defense departments disinformation specialist Todd Leventhal, to highlight the apparatus used by Saddam Hussein and his cadres to deceive the Iraqi people and the international community.

2003 (October)—Advisory Group on Public Diplomacy for the Arab and Muslim World released its report, *Changing Minds Winning Peace*; the report was prepared at the request of the House Committee on Appropriations.

2003 (October)—Former U.S. Ambassador to Morocco Margaret Tutwiller confirmed as the third Under Secretary of Public Diplomacy and Public Affairs, replacing Charlotte Beers, who resigned earlier in March, after only seventeen months in the position. She resigns in June 2004.

2003 (November)—Stuart Holliday, who spearheaded the State Department's U.S. propaganda campaign against Iraq as Coordinator, Bureau of International Information Programs, confirmed as Alternate Ambassador to the United Nations for Political Affairs. He is replaced by Alexander Feldman.

Bibliography of sources consulted in chronology:

Files in the Public Diplomacy Historical Collection, Bureau of Public Diplomacy, U.S. Department of State; William E. Daugherty, *Psychological Warfare Casebook* (Baltimore, MD: Johns Hopkins; published for Operations Research Office, Johns Hopkins University, 1958); John E. Findling, *Dictionary of American Diplomatic History,* 2d ed., rev. (Westport, CT: Greenwood, 1989); Richard A. Nelson, *A Chronology and Glossary of Propaganda in the United States* (Westport, CT: Greenwood, 1996); U.S. Congress, *Legislation on Foreign Relations Through 1999,* v. 2 (Washington, DC: Government Printing Office, 2000); U.S. Dept. of State, *Foreign Relations of the United States* (Washington, DC: Government Printing Office, 1945–). (Various volumes).

HISTORICAL
DICTIONARY
of AMERICAN
PROPAGANDA

A

ABOLITIONIST MOVEMENT. *See* Abolitionist Propaganda

ABOLITIONIST PROPAGANDA. The abolition of slavery was one of the earliest causes in American history. Advertisements appeared in newspapers as early as 1704 in the *Boston News-Letter*, and the American Antislavery Society was established in 1832 (originally New England Antislavery Society) to spearhead the antislavery movement. Early abolitionist propaganda periodicals included *Anti-Slavery Reporter* and *Freedom's Journal*, the first newspaper published by blacks in the United States, which began publication in March 1827 and ceased two years later (March 1829). It attacked the "return to Africa" colonization programs favored by many prominent politicians. The antislavery movement soon repudiated this policy for assimilation. It was considered the first newspaper published by blacks in the United States. Some issues had the subtitle: Devoted to the promotion of colored people.

The organization and development of antislavery societies displayed continuing communication efforts to win over public opinion by activists such as William Lloyd Garrison and **Theodore Dwight Weld** (1803–1895), who was considered one of the most effective of the early abolitionists. Others included Augusta Jane Evans Wilson (1835–1901), author of *Beulah*, published just before the Civil War (1859), and *Macaria; or, Altars of Sacrifice* (1864), a persuasive defense of Confederate policy, which predicted horrible consequences if the slaves were freed. It was popular in both the North and in the South but was banned by some Union commanders because of its adverse effect on morale. However, the most famous abolitionist author was **Harriet Beecher Stowe**, whose classic antislavery novel, **Uncle Tom's Cabin,** was credited by Abraham Lincoln with starting the Civil War. There were abolitionist societies such as Indian Society of Anti-Slavery Friends (1821–1857) and the American Society for the Colonization of People of Color (**American Colonization Society**), founded 1816, to assist former slaves to return to Africa. The country of Liberia was formed under its auspices (1822).

Later there was the emergence of partisan activity in the Liberal Party that led "Free-Soilers" to consolidate their interests by forming the Republican Party.

Joel Sibley later developed a revisionist theory that slavery was not the most important issue in American politics in the period prior to the outbreak of the Civil War. The Ostend Manifesto (October 18, 1854), drafted in that Belgian city, declared the right of the United States to control Cuba. Its purpose was to preserve slavery and to aid the "manifest destiny" of the United States.

In the famous *Dred Scott* decision, a victory for proslavery propagandists, the U.S. Supreme Court ruled that slaves were chattel, owned by their masters, not free blacks who could vote. In this atmosphere, books appeared that supported the proslavery cause. *Cannibals All, or Slaves Without Masters*, by George Fitzhugh, a Virginian, highlighted the master–slave relationship as a most positive way of life, whereas the controversial *Slavery Ordained of God*, by Presbyterian minister Frederick A. Ross, put slavery on the same level as the treatment of women.

FURTHER READING: Patricia Bradley, *Slavery, Propaganda, and the American Revolution* (Jackson: University Press of Mississippi, 1998); Eugene Henry Mayer, *All on Fire: William Lloyd Garrison and the Abolition of Slavery* (New York: St. Martin's, 1998); Richard Newman, Patrick Rael, and Phillip Lapsansky, eds., *Pamphlets of Protest: An Anthology of Early African-American Protest Literature, 1790–1860* (New York: Routledge, 2001); Janet Wilson, "The Early Anti-Slavery Propaganda," *More Books: The Bulletin of the Boston Public Library* (November 1944): 343–359; (December 1944): 393–405; and (January 1945): 51–67.

ACQUIRED IMMUNODEFICIENCY SYNDROME. *See* AIDS Disinformation Campaign

ACTIVE MEASURES. *See* Soviet Active Measures

ACTIVE MEASURES WORKING GROUP. On September 9, 1982, President Reagan designated the **U.S. Information Agency** (USIA) to lead an interdepartmental effort to counter Soviet propaganda, and the administration created the Active Measures Working Group in 1981 to bring together the information the various agencies had to counter Soviet disinformation and forgery. It served as a clearinghouse to expose such information, and it had permission to use classified documents and any other resources that were required to meet this goal. The Working Group was chaired by the State Department with representatives from State, Central Intelligence Agency, Defense Intelligence Agency, Arms Control and Disarmament Agency, United States Information Agency, and the Defense and Justice Departments. It ended in 1991. After the collapse of the Soviet Union in 1989, meetings continued into the Bush administration but as there was no longer a Soviet Union, the group dealt with other problem areas and continued into late 1993.

FURTHER READING: File on the Active Measures Working Group, Public Diplomacy Historical Collection, Bureau of Public Diplomacy, U.S. Department of State.

ADAMS, SAMUEL (1722–1803). Samuel Adams was a major propagandist and tenacious, uncompromising leader of the independence movement, an agitator, mass organizer, and political manipulator. As a radical leader of the common people, he effectively employed mass demonstrations and economic boycotts and created an infrastructure for the revolutionary movement. He capitalized on authorities' errors and blunders to reach his goal. When opponents failed to provide errors, Adams created them and colored the facts. He understood the appeal of the common people. For twenty years, Adams wrote newspaper articles and pamphlets encouraging independence from Great Britain. He believed that no man was the subject of a commonwealth except "by positive engagement and express promise or compact." Under various names (Determinatus, A Layman, A Tory, Populus, An Impartialist, A Son of Liberty, A Chatterer), he contributed to various political weeklies, including *Public Advertiser*, which he founded (1748) and continued until 1775. Adams was a propagandist of revolution who started in opposition to restrictive laws and hereditary rights, listed grievances, and ended up inciting rebellion. He was cunning and cautious and able to change his writing style with each pen name. Adams helped organize the Sons of Liberty (1765) in opposition to the Stamp Act and later the **Committees of Correspondence**, directed the **Boston Tea Party**, was a delegate to the first Continental Congress, evaded arrest by British troops, and supported immediate independence. At the second Continental Congress, Adams signed the Declaration of Independence, but his success came at a cost. He failed at business, cared little for money, and depended on the generosity of friends. He was a delegate to the Constitutional Convention (1788), served as lieutenant governor of Massachusetts (1789–1794), and then served as governor (1794–1797). John Adams was his second cousin.

According to Cass Canfield, it was primarily Sam Adams who fanned the flames of rebellion, and he was more effective than any other major American leader. Without his spirit, American independence could not have been declared in 1776. Adams was considered the "father of the American Revolution," but he was neither as extreme nor as violent as his biographers often portrayed him.

See also War of American Independence Propaganda

FURTHER READING: Cass Canfield, *Samuel Adams' Revolution, 1765–1776* (New York: Harper and Row, 1976); John C. Miller, *Sam Adams: Pioneer Propagandist* (Stanford, CA: Stanford University, 1967, 1936).

ADVANCING AMERICAN ART. In spring 1946, J. LeRoy Davidson, visual arts specialist, Office of International Information and Cultural Affairs, U.S. Department of State, bought seventy-nine oil paintings for the collection, Advancing American Art. Thirty-eight watercolors were purchased by the American Federation of Arts under a contract to supplement the oils. That October, an exhibition with the seventy-nine oil paintings from Advancing American Art opened at the Metropolitan Museum of Art, New York. When the exhibition closed at the end of October 1946, the paintings were divided into two groups and shipped to Europe and to Latin America to begin overseas showings but Albert Reid, vice president of the American Artists Professional League (AAPL), wrote a letter (November 6, 1946) of protest concerning Advancing American Art to U.S. Secretary of State James F. Byrne, in which Reid deplored the "radicalism" of the stylistic trends demonstrated in the collection's paintings.

The Hearst press and *Look* magazine published full-page articles (November 19 and 26; December 3, 1946) that reproduced some of the collection's works in its syndicated newspapers as direct attacks on Advancing American Art and modern painting and made alleged attacks on the leftist political leanings of several of the artists, which included Ben Shahn, Philip Guston, Romare Bearden, Philip Evergood, and William Gropper. In February 1947, John Taber, chairman of the House Appropriations Committee, wrote Byrne's successor, George Marshall, requesting a full account of the Advancing American Art project. After a backlash of negative criticism in the press, Secretary Marshall ordered the paintings to be held in Prague, Czechoslovakia, and Port-au-Prince, Haiti, until further action was decided. It came on May 5, 1947, when the House Committee on Appropriations recommended the abolition of the State Department's cultural relations program after Assistant Secretary William Benton testified about the Advancing American Art collection. Benton's testimony was published in U.S. Congress, *House Hearings Before the Subcommittee of the Committee on Appropriations on the Department of State Appropriation Bill for 1948*, 80th Cong., 1st sess., 1947 (Washington, DC: Government Printing Office, 1948): 412–419.

Rallies were organized by the American art community to support the exhibition, but with no money to fund the art tours and continuing criticism from Congress, who leveled such charges that several of the paintings were "subversive" and "un-American," the exhibition was effectively canceled, and Secretary Marshall ordered the paintings returned to the United States, where they were stored in a New York warehouse. In May 1948, 117 paintings from the Advancing American Art collection were placed on view at the Whitney Museum of American Art prior to their sale by auction by the War Assets Administration.

FURTHER READING: Gary O. Larson, *The Reluctant Patron: The United States Government and the Arts, 1943–1965* (Philadelphia: University of Pennsylvania, 1983); Jane DeHart Mathews, "Art and Politics in Cold War America," *American Historical Review* 81 (October 1976): 762–787; Virginia M. Mecklenburg and Margaret L. Ausfield, *Advancing American Art: Politics and Aesthetics in the State Department Exhibition, 1946–1948; Essays* (Montgomery, AL: Montgomery Museum of Fine Arts, 1984); Frank A. Ninkovich, "The Currents of Cultural Diplomacy: Art and the State Department, 1938–1947," *Diplomatic History* 1 (July 1977): 215–237.

ADVISORY COMMITTEE ON GOVERNMENT ORGANIZATION. *See* President's Advisory Committee on Government Organization

AFGHAN MEDIA PROJECT. The Afghan Media Project was an initiative of President Ronald Reagan's administration. It was funded by the **U.S. Information Agency** through the Supplemental Appropriations Act of 1985 (Public Law 99-88), which allocated $500,000 for the project, but it was administered through Boston University's School of Media and Communications. The project came about as the result of a Task Force on Afghanistan that USIA established (1981) to focus world attention on the Soviet invasion of Afghanistan. Task Force activities included: VOA broadcasts and editorials; the USIA-produced pamphlet,

Afghanistan: The Struggle to Regain Freedom; Afghanistan Week programs at seventy-four USIS country posts; inauguration of the agency's *Afghanistan Digest*, whose first issue was relayed to twelve countries and air-shipped to an additional forty-five for television placement; and programs acquired and distributed by USIA's Television Service for posts worldwide and to commercial network programs, such as a MacNeill/Lehrer report, "Afghan Update," and an NBC Magazine program, "Inside Afghanistan." In 1982, Kirk Douglas visited refugee camps in Pakistan, and it was filmed as "Thanksgiving in Peshawar." The Afghan Media Project ended with the Reagan administration.

FURTHER READING: Sarah Boxer, "When Afghanistan Collapsed," *New York Times*, October 2, 2001; United States Information Agency, *United States Information Agency, 1981–1988: Years of Progress* (Washington, DC: Unpublished, 1989).

AFGHAN MEDIA RESOURCE CENTER. *See* **Afghan Media Project**

AFRICA. *See* **AIDS Disinformation Campaign**

AFRICAN AMERICANS. *See* **AIDS Disinformation Campaign**

AGITATION PROPAGANDA. *See* **Agitprop**

AGITPROP. This word is a combination of agitation and propaganda. All Communist Parties had an Agitprop Department (the American Communist Party after World War II called it an Education Department) on every level down to the local cells. Modeled after the Soviet Agitprop, it handled agitation (themes and slogans to achieve immediate goals) and propaganda (themes and slogans to promote long-term goals). The Soviet Communist Party, in the postwar period, called it the Propaganda Department and in the last few years before the collapse of the Communist regime, the Ideology Department. Traditionally, each Communist Party unit included a unit that specialized in agitprop to ensure that slogans and propaganda followed the "party line." In the United States, agitprop theater was particularly active during the Depression of the 1930s, best exemplified by the **Federal Theater Project,** with its political plays, such as the Living Newspaper Project and the Marc Blitzstein musical, *The Cradle Will Rock.* Another period of agitprop demonstrations was during the American opposition to U.S. involvement in Vietnam, in plays, such as *MacBird*, and in sometimes-violent demonstrations against the government.

FURTHER READING: Lorraine Brown, ed., *Liberty Deferred and Other Living Newspapers of the 1930s Federal Theater Project* (Fairfax, VA: George Mason University, 1989).

AIDS (ACQUIRED IMMUNODEFICIENCY SYNDROME). *See* **AIDS Disinformation Campaign**

AIDS DISINFORMATION CAMPAIGN. Controversial topic that had its basis as a Soviet disinformation campaign. It complemented the disinformation that the homosexual lobby created the AIDS myth with the U.S. government, mainly to raise money. It has been a sensational disinformation story with allegations that the United States deliberately created AIDS in the laboratory to use it as a weapon. The KGB started the story in 1985 with placements in both Soviet and foreign newspapers; by September 1986 it became a major campaign when an English-language "paper," that actually originated in East Berlin, "AIDS: Its Nature and Origin," was distributed at the Non-Aligned Movement Summit in Harare; it contained pseudoscientific verbiage but the only "evidence" linking the origin of AIDS to U.S. military laboratories was the statement: "The first appearance of AIDS exactly coincides with the opening of a P-4 laboratory at Fort Detrick [Maryland]—taking into account the incubation period. This is also indicated by the fact, that the spreading of AIDS to the world emanated from New York, a city in the neighbourhood [sic] of Fort Detrick. The assumtion [sic] that AIDS is a product of the preparation of biological warfare can therefore be quite plainly be expressed."

The Soviet disinformation campaign accused the U.S. government of creating the AIDS virus as a weapon against black people, and the story quickly appeared worldwide, despite U.S. protests that Fort Detrick, in Maryland, was hundreds of miles from New York. In April 1987, U.S. Surgeon General C. Everett Koop, M.D., advised the Soviets that if this campaign continued, "direct U.S.–Soviet collaboration on AIDS research would be impossible." When it became clear that the U.S. was serious, the KGB began winding down the worldwide campaign, but other countries continued to endorse the disinformation. In Africa, stories circulated for years that the United States created the AIDS virus. U.S. Information Service (USIA overseas) staff responded with accurate information that countered these charges and defused the situation. In Pretoria, South Africa, and in Lilongwe, Malawi, USIS information was able to refocus the media on AIDS prevention rather than blame.

FURTHER READING: Douglas Crimp and Adam Rolston, *AIDS Demo Graphics* (Seattle: Bay Press, 1990); Nat Hentoff. "The Evil Empire's Last Hurrah," *Village Voice* (February 2, 1993): 22–23; Herbert Romerstein, "Disinformation as a KGB Weapon in the Cold War," Prepared for a Conference on Germany and Intelligence Organizations: The Last Fifty Years in Review, sponsored by Akademie fur Politische Bildung Tutzing, June 18–20, 1999; Herbert Romerstein, *Soviet Active Measures and Propaganda: "New Thinking" and Influence Activities in the Gorbachev Era* (Toronto, Canada: Mackenzie Institute for the Study of Terrorism, Revolution, and Propaganda; Washington, DC: National Intelligence Book Center, 1989).

ALBRECHT, RALPH G. *See* "Norden, Commander Robert Lee"

AMERICA FIRST COMMITTEE. An isolationist organization that opposed American entry into World War II. It was founded in June 1940 by R. Douglas Stuart, a Yale law student; Robert E. Wood, board chairman of Sears, Roebuck; William E. Regnery, a wealthy publisher; and other prominent Americans, ranging from conservatives such as John T. Flynn and Charles Lindbergh, to socialists such as Norman Thomas. America First wanted the country to keep out of the European war by building a strong defense and by avoiding "aid short of war." Members lobbied the public and in Congress against measures such as Lend-Lease, convoying, and repeal of the Neutrality Acts. America First tried to unify noninterventionist sentiment to force President Franklin D. Roosevelt to cautiously approach American involvement in the war. The America First Committee had a publicly announced policy to exclude from its ranks anyone who was pro-Nazi. This did not prevent interventionist organizations from falsely accusing them of supporting Hitler. The committee published pamphlets, such as *Can Hitler Invade America?* and *The Proposition is Peace*, and newsletters to publicize its cause, but after the attack on **Pearl Harbor**, America First disbanded, and most of its members supported the war effort.

FURTHER READING: Wayne S. Cole, *America First: The Battle Against Intervention, 1940–1941* (New York: Octagon, 1971 [1953]); Wayne S. Cole, *Charles A. Lindbergh and the Battle Against American Intervention in World War II* (New York: Harcourt Brace Jovanovich, 1974); Bill Kauffman, *America First* (Amherst, NY: Prometheus Books, 1995); *Register of the America First Committee Records, 1940–1942* (Stanford, CA: Hoover Institution Archives, Stanford University, 1998).

AMERICA HOUSES. *See* **Amerika Haus**

AMERICA ILLUSTRATED. See AMERIKA ILLUSTRATED

AMERICAN ANTISLAVERY SOCIETY. *See* **Abolitionist Propaganda**

AMERICAN BUSINESS CONSULTANTS. *See Counterattack*; **Red Channels**

AMERICAN CENTERS AND AMERICAN CORNERS. American Corners are sponsored jointly by a U.S. Embassy and a host-country organization; they serve as an information outpost similar to a public library reference service. Initially, American Corners were established in host-country **libraries** but posts are now considering other local institutions as partners. The multimedia, book, and periodical collections of an American Corner are open and accessible to self-selecting audiences not usually reached through targeted **public diplomacy** outreach. American Corner collections can be developed to also attract a young adult readership. Where possible, associated reading or meeting rooms are made available to host program events and activities. Although an individual American Corner reflects local circumstances, all share a fundamental function: They are programming platforms that make information about the United States available to foreign publics at large.

The concept of American Corners started as a network of five public-access libraries across Russia (Moscow, Nizhniv Novgorod, Rostov-na-Donu, Tomsk, and Yekaterinburg), which opened in 1993–1994; the libraries are operated by the Public Affairs Section (PA) of the U.S. Embassy in Moscow to promote Americana. They have large English-language reference and circulation collections,

CD-ROMs, subscriptions to periodicals, and access to online databases. There are also twelve American Corners, conceived as mini-American Centers, with a focus on electronic resources, Internet access, and a print collection with a long shelf life. Both the centers and the corners are designed to support ongoing public diplomacy and other Mission programs throughout Russia, serving as a focal point for U.S. government activities in Russia's regions. Also part of this network are the Information Resource Centers (IRCs) in St. Petersburg and in Vladivostok, which are colocated with consulates general and currently offer limited public access. Start-up costs for each Center are about $100,000 and require $10,000 annually to maintain, whereas each Corner requires approximately $35,000 to set up.

With the success of the American Corners in Russia, the State Department opened centers in the Ukraine, Kosovo, Kenya, Namibia, Rwanda, and Mongolia, but their success has not yet been determined; not all countries are suited for an American Corner. In 2003, American Corners were expected to open in Turkey, Yugoslavia, Eritrea, Malawi, Uganda, Bosnia, and Mexico. In other countries, such as in Germany, or in most of the Latin American countries, similar programs are already in place, such as the German American Institutes and the Binational Centers (BNCs).

FURTHER READING: "American Centers, American Corners: A Program of the U.S. Embassy in Moscow" (Fact sheet on Web site, Office of International Information Programs, U.S. Department of State); David Grimes, "Turning Corners: American Librarians in Post-Soviet Russia," American Libraries (October 2003): 56, 58.

AMERICAN COLONIZATION SOCIETY. Meetings of the American Colonization Society were held in Washington, D.C., as early as December 1816 to discuss forming a colonization society, the American Society for Colonizing Free People of Colour of the United States, with Bushrod Washington as president, to buy slaves and return them to Africa. In 1821, Eli Ayres and Robert Stockton purchased land for a colony at Cape Mesurado on the west coast of Africa, which was first settled the next year, and in 1824, the new colony was named Liberia with a settlement called Monrovia. Thirteen years later, the American Colonization Society (ACS) was incorporated into the state of Maryland.

During the decades prior to the Civil War, the society tried to implement its solution to the slavery problem, colonization of Negroes in Africa, by raising money to support and transport emigrants and to appeal to all sections of the country through such media as its journal, *African Repository*, first published in 1825. However, there was also heavy attack from critics, especially William Lloyd Garrison and other abolitionists, who termed it proslavery. *Freedom's Journal*, which began publication in 1827, attacked the "return to Africa" colonization programs favored by the society and many prominent politicians. The American Colonization Society's support of emigration ended in 1912–1913, and it ceased all its activities by March 1963.

See also Abolitionist Propaganda

FURTHER READING: Early L. Fox, *American Colonization Society* (Baltimore, MD: Johns Hopkins, 1919); U.S. Library of Congress, *American Colonization Society; A Register of Its Records in the Library of Congress* (Washington, DC: The Library, 1979).

AMERICAN CORNERS. *See* American Centers and American Corners

AMERICAN COUNCIL AGAINST NAZI PROPAGANDA. Established in New York City in 1939, the American Council Against Nazi Propaganda published a newsletter called *The Hour.* The first editor was Dr. Albert Parry. Although it was actively anti-Nazi, it was generally friendly to the Soviet Union. In 1940, Albert E. Kahn, a Soviet agent, became first the business manager, then the managing editor, and finally the editor. Parry had been driven out by Kahn, and the publication became increasingly pro-Soviet. It attacked a number of noncommunist anti-Nazis as Nazi agents. The Anti-Defamation League of B'nai B'rith, which had earlier supplied the newsletter with information and support, broke relations with them. Parry reported this information to the **Office of Strategic Services,** and his reports are now in the U.S. National Archives as part of the OSS/CIA collection. *The Hour* continued to be published until May 1943. Kahn was identified as a Soviet agent by the former KGB courier Elizabeth Bentley and in Venona, the Soviet intelligence communications intercepted by the United States during World War II.

FURTHER READING: Issues of *The Hour*; U.S. Congress. House, Special Committee on Un-American Activities, *Investigation of Un-American Propaganda Activities in the United States*, April 6, 1943 (Washington, DC: Government Printing Office, 1939), v.7: Executive Hearings.

AMERICAN EXHIBITION, MOSCOW. *See* American National Exhibition, Moscow (1959)

AMERICAN EXHIBITION, NEW YORK. *See* American National Exhibition, Moscow (1959)

AMERICAN FORCES NETWORK, EUROPE (AFN). With the end of World War II, many American soldiers remained in Germany with the occupation forces. The American Forces Network, Europe, was created during the war (1943) in London. It accompanied advancing forces after D-Day, and it was transmitted to occupied territories of Belgium and France but was expanded (1945) as a news information service to American servicemen and their families to counter the pervasive postwar propaganda bombarded on other radio stations in Western Europe. The programs offered both entertainment and current news programming. Unlike other international broadcasting services, AFN carefully avoided programming to European audiences, broadcast only in English, and devoted the largest portion of its programming to popular entertainment. Newscasts and discussion programs, compiled from U.S. sources, were relatively open on American political and social problems, a situation that many in its audience found to be a rather positive and appealing image of the United States.

AFN continues to operate today, airing music, news, and other information around the clock on the network's studio stations that produce both radio and television programming.

FURTHER READING: R. Stephen Craig, "American Forces Network in the Cold War: Military Broadcasting in Postwar Germany," *Journal of Broadcasting and Electronic Media* 32, no. 3 (Summer 1988): 307–321; Patrick Morley, *"This is the American Forces Network": The Anglo-American Battle of the Air Waves in World War II* (Westport, CT: Praeger, 2001); David Reynolds, *Rich Relations: The American Occupation of Britain, 1942–1945* (New York: Random House, 1995).

AMERICAN INDEPENDENCE, WAR OF. *See* **War of American Independence**

AMERICAN NATIONAL EXHIBITION, MOSCOW (1959). The American Exhibition in Moscow, with a Soviet counterpart in New York, was one of the results of a general agreement reached in 1958 covering a wide range of American–Soviet contacts in the cultural, scientific, and educational fields. The event in Moscow's Sokolniki Park, held from July 25 to September 4, 1959, and a major landmark in the U.S.-Soviet cultural exchange program, was produced by the **U.S. Information Agency** and other government agencies in cooperation with private organizations and firms. It is probably best remembered as the site of two Nixon–Khrushchev confrontations. The first, less-publicized incident, occurred at the opening, July 24, 1959, when Nixon escorted the Russian premier around the exhibition and tried to interest Khrushchev in examining the voting machine and to persuade him to register his opinion on the overall impression of the exhibition but was rudely rebuffed. The more publicized incident, the famous "kitchen debate," took place later in the tour when the Soviet premier was visiting the Moscow exhibit of a model American kitchen and made disparaging remarks about the "silly" U.S. exposition and the United States. Today, the rhetoric seems harmless, but at the time it was controversial. Nixon poked his finger at Khrushchev's chest and told the Soviets not to make unilateral demands at the upcoming Four Power Conference in Geneva. In turn, the Soviet premier accused the American vice president of threatening him. No television cameras were present but newspaper accounts and still photographs solidified Nixon's image as an anti-Communist crusader.

Besides the voting machine exhibit, the fair included a Disney-produced film, *Circarama* and the **Family of Man** presentation. USIA prepared some 3,000 answers in Russian to questions about the United States for Ramac, the "electronic brain," which visitors plied with queries. Nearly three million visitors saw the exhibition during its six-week run, but it was criticized daily in the Soviet press as a propaganda display that did not represent the United States.

The most important gain from the Moscow exhibition was probably the chance for a large group of Russian-speaking Americans to have direct access to the Soviet people. It changed previously held images of America, fostered by Soviet propaganda, and intensified a desire for American consumer goods. On the negative side, the exchange of exhibitions (Moscow and New York) allowed Soviet leaders some propaganda gains by appearing to relax U.S.–Soviet tensions without diminishing the Cold War atmosphere.

By reciprocal agreement for the exhibition to the American National Exhibition in Moscow, the USSR Exhibition of Achievements in Science, Technology and Culture, was held in the New York Coliseum, New York City, from June 30–August 10, 1959. It was considered the largest show ever put on by one nation up to that time, but American newspapers attacked the exhibition as "the most highly infectious propaganda campaign" ever, whereas similar critical reports and attacks on the exhibition led to similar reprisals in Soviet newspapers on the U.S. show in Moscow. The Soviet exhibit in New York emphasized Russian industrial potential and advances in science, industry, and culture, but its major aim was to break down the U.S. government's restrictions on trade with the Communist world and expand the exchange of industrial goods.

FURTHER READING: Walter L. Hixson, *Parting the Curtain: Propaganda, Culture, and the Cold War, 1945–1961* (New York: St. Martin's, 1997); Lou Schneider, "Russians Invade N.Y., Open All-Out Propaganda War," *Atlanta Constitution* (July 8, 1959); John R. Thomas, *Report on Service with the American Exhibition in Moscow* (Santa Monica, CA: Rand Corporation, 1960).

AMERICAN NAZI PARTY. Neo-Nazi organization founded by **George Lincoln Rockwell** in 1959; in 1966 he changed the party's name to the National Socialist White People's Party. After Rockwell's murder (1967), the party's organizational direction was taken over by Frank Collin, who planned a Nazi parade in Skokie, Illinois, the most Jewish populated city in the United States. The march shocked the Jewish community, who maintained a strong attack defense against the Nazis coming to their community. When Collin couldn't get a march permit, he went to the American Civil Liberties Union; his Jewish lawyer, David Goldenberger, was opposed to Collin and his Nazi beliefs but took the case to defend Collin's freedom of speech rights, despite much criticism from the Jewish Defense League. The Skokie Case (as it came to be called in the media) ended up in the U.S. Supreme Court. Also, the U.S. Justice Department offered another venue for the march away from Skokie, which was accepted. However, Collin was ousted shortly after this incident and jailed on child molestation charges.

A prominent American neo-Nazi is Gary Lauck, who supplied hate literature, armbands, and other paraphernalia to Germans of the far right for two decades. He was convicted in Hamburg, Germany, on August 22, 1996, of inciting racial hatred and distributing propaganda that violated the constitution. He was sentenced to four years in prison.

Since its establishment, the American Nazi Party has heavily promoted its white supremacy theories and hate campaign against targeted ethnic groups, especially Jews and blacks, and the denial that the Holocaust atrocities ever existed with a heavy propaganda campaign (newspapers, media, clothing, publications) and hate literature.

In the late 1990s, Richard Butler and his Aryan Nation organization continued the work of Rockwell and his associates in their goal of completing the "final solution" and ethnic cleansing.

See also German-American Bund

FURTHER READING: "Notes from 'Nazi America: A Secret History'" (TV documentary on The History Channel, 1/21/00); "U.S. Neo-Nazi Sentenced in Germany to Four Years," *New York Times* (August 23, 1996).

AMERICAN REPUBLICS. The American Republics cover areas also known as Central America, Latin America, and South America. Earliest propaganda efforts began as early as the **Spanish-American War**. Later efforts were formalized by the Interdepartmental Committee for Scientific and Cultural Cooperation and Division of Cultural Cooperation, which was formed to counteract German and Italian propaganda in Latin America in the 1930s, followed by an institutional framework to counter such dangers, which was started by President Roosevelt with his creation of the Office of the **Coordinator of Inter-American Affairs** (CIAA) and its successors. Nelson Aldrich Rockefeller was appointed coordinator of commercial and cultural affairs between U.S. and American Republics (exchange of persons, **libraries**, and **binational centers**).

See also Buenos Aires Convention for Promotion of Inter-American Cultural Relations; Comics and Comic Strips; Cuban Freedom Committee; Radio Marti; Television Marti

AMERICAN REVOLUTION. *See* War of American Independence Propaganda

AMERICAN SOCIETY FOR COLONIZING FREE PEOPLE OF COLOUR OF THE UNITED STATES. *See* Abolitionist Propaganda; American Colonization Society

AMERICAN WRITERS CONGRESS. *See* League of American Writers

AMERIKA HAUS. After World War II, the U.S. government funded cultural programs in countries under U.S. occupation. These included Austria, Germany, Japan, and Korea. Funded by millions of dollars by the State Department for cultural and educational programs, U.S. information officers were advised to set up cultural programs that would have an impact on the occupied country. In Austria and in Germany, one of the most long-lasting was a series of libraries and cultural centers, designated as Amerika Haus (America Houses), which were used for cultural activities, such as lectures and film showings, and English language classes and as libraries and binational centers.

After the breakup of the Soviet Union, **American Centers and Corners** were established in many Information Resource Centers (IRCs) in Russia and in other countries comprising the Newly Independent States.

FURTHER READING: Henry Dunlap oral history, USIA Alumni Association Oral History Program; Henry Kellermann, *Cultural Relations as an Instrument of U.S. Foreign Policy: The Educational Exchange Program Between the United States and Germany, 1945–1954* (Washington, DC: Bureau of Educational and Cultural Affairs, U.S. Department of State; for sale by the U.S. Government Printing Office, 1978); Henry P. Pilgert, *History of the Development of Information Services Through Information Centers and*

Documentary Films (Bonn, Germany: Historical Division, Office of the Executive Secretary, Office of the U.S. High Commissioner for Germany, 1951).

AMERIKA ILLUSTRATED. A monthly magazine published by the **U.S. Information Agency** (USIA) to counter Soviet propaganda during the Cold War; it ceased in 1994 because "the job was finished." For generations of Russians, *Amerika Illustrated* was one of the few sources of information about life outside the Communist orbit. The first agreement for an exchange of magazines was part of a broader agreement for the exchange of information between the United States and the Soviet Union reached at the Yalta Conference in early 1945. The magazine, designed to win the hearts and minds of Soviets with vivid pictures of American life and culture, was first published in 1945 as an outgrowth of *USA* and *Victory*, World War II periodicals produced by the **Office of War Information** for worldwide distribution. As circulation problems worsened and the Cold War escalated, the magazine was discontinued in 1952. After Stalin died in 1953, President Eisenhower decided to try again to "lower the barriers which now impede the interchange of information and ideas between peoples." An agreement was proposed in a note from the American Embassy in Moscow on September 9, 1955, and it was accepted by the Soviet Foreign Office on December 16. Soviet acceptance made possible a revival of the magazine. *Amerika* (which also had a Polish edition, *Ameryka*) was distributed in the Soviet Union (through subscriptions and sales), and in return, the United States agreed to distribute the Soviet government publication *USSR* (later *Soviet Life*). *Amerika Illustrated* presented a mostly optimistic picture of American life, with a visual format similar to *Life*, but it also touched on some of America's troubles, though with a light hand. As an example of a nonpolitical, propaganda publication, *Amerika* served as a model for many other USIA publications.

FURTHER READING: First and last issues of *Amerika Illustrated*; Howard Oiseth, *Way It Was: USIA's Press and Publications Service, 1935–77* (Washington, DC: United States Information Agency, 1977); U.S. Dept. of State, "Revival of Russian Language Magazine *Amerika* [press release] with texts of notes, December 23, 1955.

AMERIKA-DEUTSCHER VOLKSBUND. *See* **German-American Bund**

"ANALYSIS OF COMMUNIST PROPAGANDA." Intelligence reports prepared by the U.S. Department of State at the height of the Cold War in the early 1950s from information available by the Coordinator of Psychological Intelligence. Each report, which focused on a specific country, had chapters on major propaganda themes, appeals and psychological devices, factors affecting Communist propaganda and its effectiveness, and target groups. Appendices usually included information on the exchange of persons, press and publishing programs, motion pictures, and radio. Reports on countries considered especially important, such as France and India, delved further into the Communist political situation, party membership, and front organizations.

FURTHER READING: Issues of *Analysis of Communist Propaganda*.

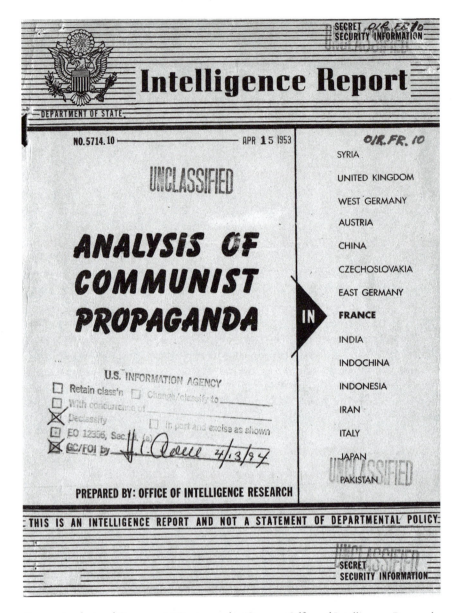

Cover: *Analysis of Communist Propaganda*. (*Source*: Office of Intelligence Research, U.S. Department of State)

ANDERSON, JANE. *See* U.S.A. Zone of the Overseas Service (North American Service)

ANGLO-AMERICAN EMERGENCY PROPAGANDA COMMITTEE FOR PACIFIC, EUROPEAN, AND SOUTH-EAST ASIAN THEATRES. *See* Propaganda Committees

ANTI-CATHOLIC PROPAGANDA. *See* Catholic Church

ANTI-CATHOLICISM. *See* Catholic Church

ANTI-COMMUNIST PROPAGANDA. *See various subjects, e.g.,* U.S. Congress. House. Committee on Un-American Activities; U.S. Congressional Investigations of Propaganda

ANTI-IMPERIALIST LEAGUE. A political organization of about 1898 to 1900, composed primarily of Democrats with a few Republicans also participating. It was begun in late 1898 in several eastern cities by moderate reformers and anti-imperialists, such as Carl Schurz, E. L. Godkin, Edward Atkinson, and Charles Eliot Norton. In 1899, local organizations were joined in a single American Anti-Imperialist League, which propagandized the country and the Congress by holding conferences, sponsoring speakers, and publishing pamphlets and articles opposing America's colonial policy, such as bitter denunciations of the U.S. Army's use of torture to suppress rebellion in the Philippines. Andrew Carnegie funded much of the campaign with much active support from labor, agricultural, and ethnic leaders. The league disbanded in 1920, but the same name was used later in the 1920s by a Communist front organization, All-American Anti-Imperialist League.

FURTHER READING: Robert L. Beisner, *Twelve Against Empire: The Anti-Imperialists, 1898–1900* (New York, McGraw-Hill, 1968); David Healy, *U.S. Expansionism: The Imperialist Urge in the 1890s* (Madison: University of Wisconsin, 1970).

ANTI-SEMITIC PROPAGANDA. Anti-Semitism has often been used as a propaganda vehicle. It is the belief or behavior hostile toward Jews just because they are Jewish. It may take the form of religious teachings that proclaim the inferiority of Jews, for instance, or political efforts to isolate, oppress, or otherwise injure them. It may also include prejudiced or stereotyped views about Jews.

Earliest Times

In the nineteenth century, anti-Semites turned to the new "racial science," an attempt by various scientists and writers to "prove" the supremacy of non-Jewish whites. The opponents of Jews argued that Jewishness was not a religion but a racial category, and that the Jewish "race" was biologically inferior, a belief that later became Germany's justification for seeking to kill every Jewish person in lands Germany occupied during World War II, whether the person practiced Judaism or not. The Holocaust, as this systematic mass extermination between 1939 and 1945 is known, resulted in the death of six million Jews, more than one-third of the world's Jewish population.

Post–World War II

Since World War II, stereotypes about Jews remain common. The hatred of Jewishness and the conspiracy beliefs of past eras are for the most part shared only by tiny numbers of those on the fringes of society, although as the World Trade Center and Oklahoma bombings showed, even a handful of extremists can carry out acts of great violence. There are exceptions. Disagreement over policy toward the state of Israel has created opportunities in which the expression "Zionist," support for Israel as the Jewish homeland, is often used as an anti-Semitic code word for "Jew" in mainstream debate. **Holocaust denial** and other recent rewritings of history, such as the false claim that Jews controlled the Atlantic slave trade, present unfounded information about the events of the past to make Jews seem underhanded and evil.

In discussing the U.S.-led campaign to oust Saddam Hussein, **newspapers** in the Muslim and Arab world turned to classic anti-Semitic conspiracy theories, suggesting that Israel and the Jews were the "invisible hand" behind America's foreign policy toward Iraq. Editorial cartoons appearing in popular daily newspapers, including those of America's strategic allies in the region, Qatar and Saudi Arabia, recycled classical anti-Semitic canards in depicting Jews and Israel to suggest that Jews were steering American foreign policy. Others published cartoons that suggested that the U.S. war was a diversion manufactured by Israel to turn international attention away from its treatment of the Palestinians. **Cartoons** often appeared on Web sites viewed by Muslim communities all over the world that were especially dangerous in societies where there was a high rate of illiteracy and where the image carried more power then the printed word.

Disinformation Campaign

After the terrorist attacks of September 11, 2001, a **disinformation** campaign originated as a conspiracy theory that 4,000 Jews did not show up for work on that day. Was this a harmless conspiracy theory or virulent new anti-Semitism? This was the first recorded account of an urban legend that has swept the Arab world. Not a single fact in it has ever been substantiated. It appears to be based on concern expressed by the Israeli government for the fate of 4,000 Israelis resident in New York, a small number of whom worked at the World Trade Center. Within a matter of days, it was no longer 4,000 Israelis who were supposed not to have turned up to work, but 4,000 Jews; then reports appeared that "not a single Jew" died on September 11. It was easy to rebut as the list of victims were printed on many reputable Web sites. A quick scan showed about one out of every dozen names was Jewish. That matched U.S. Census Bureau data, which showed 9 percent of New York's population is Jewish. If 4,000 Jews didn't go to work that day, far fewer than one out of twelve would be on the lists. In fact, many American Jews died in the attack, as well as four Israeli citizens, two in the World Trade Center and two on hijacked planes, according to the Israeli Foreign Ministry. President Bush's erroneous assertion in his September 20 speech to Congress that "more than 130 Israelis" had perished has yet to be explained, but the source was most likely not the intelligence agents in Tel Aviv but overwhelmed authorities in New York.

See also Coughlin, Charles Edward; Henry Ford and "The International Jew"; *Protocols of the Learned Elders of Zion*

FURTHER READING: Information from Anti-Defamation League of B'nai B'rith Web site (http://www.adl.org); Norman Cohn, *Warrant for Genocide: The Myth of the Jewish World Conspiracy and the "Protocols of the Elders of Zion"* (London: Eyre and Spottiswoode,

1967); Abraham H. Foxman, *Never Again? The Threat of the New Anti-Semitism* (San Francisco: HarperSanFrancisco, 2003); Stephen J. Whitfield, "The Politics of Pageantry, 1938–1946," *American Jewish History* 84, no. 3 (September 1996): 221–251.

ANTISLAVERY PROPAGANDA. *See* Abolitionist Propaganda

APPEAL TO THE COLORED PEOPLE OF THE WORLD. See Walker, David

APPENDIX NINE. Officially entitled *Communist Front Organizations with Special Reference to the National Citizens Political Action Committee; Fourth Section*, it became known as Appendix Nine because it was the ninth addendum to the House Special Committee on Un-American Activities series of reports for the year. A seven-volume collection of documents, the appendix was actually a compilation of letterheads and other documents from organizations, helpful in understanding the heyday of American Communism in the 1930s. The volumes were released in 1944. There were 245 sections in six volumes that described alleged Communist front organizations, with text and documents ("exhibits") from committee files; the seventh volume was an index of approximately 22,000 names. Publication of the documents in Appendix Nine was motivated by the fear of certain committee members that this material would be destroyed when the committee was disbanded in December 1944. In fact, in January 1945, it was reestablished as a permanent committee of Congress.

See also **U.S. Congressional Investigations of Propaganda**

FURTHER READING: U.S. Congress. House. Special Committee on Un-American Activities, *Investigation of Un-American Propaganda Activities in the U.S. Special Committee on Un-American Activities*, 78th Cong., 2nd sess., *on H. Res. 282 ... Committee Print, Appendix-Part IX: Communist Front Organizations with Special Reference to the National Citizens Political Action Committee; Fourth Section* (Washington, DC: Government Printing Office, 1944).

ART. *See* Advancing American Art; Art Exhibitions; Federal Arts Project

ART EXHIBITIONS. Art exhibitions sponsored by the U.S. government started as early as 1927 when the State Department unofficially sent them to the American Republics, but there was no real official sponsorship until after the 1938 Buenos Aires Convention, which established U.S. cultural and educational exchanges. In 1940, there was an Art Committee in the Cultural Relations Division of the Office of the **Coordinator of Inter-American Affairs** (OIAA), which worked with the State Department in commissioning artists to visit countries in the American Republics, in subsidizing the showing of exhibits of Latin American art, and in funding various organizations that promoted Latin American art in the United States. Artists had special passports and, in some instances, letters of introduction from President Roosevelt. The Arts Committee also produced art exhibitions that were displayed in various countries in Latin America.

The first major art exhibition funded in this way was a 1941 tour of contemporary American paintings throughout Latin America. The program had its congressional critics, who tried to scrap it, but overall the art program was considered a powerful "antidote" to Axis propaganda contention that Americans were "cultural Bolshevists" with no interest in the region. In 1943, these exchanges were handled by the **U.S. Department of State**, then were transferred in 1953 to the **U.S. Information Agency** (USIA), which worked with private museums and artists to loan out the work of "representative American art." In 1965, USIA transferred the program to the Smithsonian Institution, who administered it, while it continued to fund the exhibitions in conjunction with the State Department, who directed policy.

In November 1965 the Smithsonian Institution and the USIA agreed that the Smithsonian would assume the responsibility for an international exchange program of art exhibitions; support American entries in international art exhibitions, in particular, the Venice and Sao Paulo biennials; and service the U.S. Information Services' field requests when possible. The USIA would continue to be responsible for national exhibitions presented in the Soviet Union and East European countries.

Between 1965 and 1970, exhibition budgets were directed at large international shows, most notably the Biennales. After the threatened boycott of American artists at the 1970 Venice Biennale, the Smithsonian reconsidered its role in international art shows, not wanting to get involved in politics and with the consequences of such activity in its relations with artists. At the same time, USIA no longer felt that international shows were the best way to reach foreign audiences, so it started to produce smaller exhibitions, approximately six a year. The Smithsonian, which continued its assistance to American entries in the larger international shows until 1981, encouraged private-sector support for them. The art program came back to USIA in 1978 to be administered by its Arts America program but was scaled down to almost nothing in 1997, a victim of budget cuts. Another official program is the State Department's Art-in-Embassies Program, which displays the work of American artists in U.S. embassies abroad, sometimes loaning private exhibitions by museums and collectors.

The United States continues to participate in the international art festival, Venice Biennale, but with the end of the Cold War and the fall of the Soviet Union, the strictly art shows were replaced by more technological presentations, such as **Information USA**.

Art exhibitions were most effective as counterpropaganda to the Soviet influence by creating an "awareness of the American presence" in otherwise difficult situations, such as the immensely successful 1947 exhibition, Advancing American Art, in the Prague embassy, which caused the Russians to mount their own art collection but with less popular acclaim from the Czechs. Art masterpieces from foreign collections often tried to alter individual political views, whereas certain international loan exhibitions attempted to exploit American museums for this purpose. The U.S. government conceived such shows then sold them to the museum community.

See also **Advancing American Art; Federal Arts Project**

FURTHER READING: Grace Glueck, "Are Art Exchanges a Game of Propaganda?" *New York Times*, Section 2 (September 26, 1976); Frank Ninkovich, "The Currents of Cultural Diplomacy: Art and the State Department, 1938–1947," *Diplomatic History* (Summer 1977): 215–237.

ATOMIC WEAPONS. *See* Atoms for Peace

ATOMS FOR PEACE. Theme based on President Eisenhower's speech of December 8, 1953, before the United Nations General Assembly in which he emphasized the constructive potentialities of atomic energy and proposed an international pool of atomic energy materials for peaceful uses. From this, the **U.S. Information Agency** designed a series of mobile exhibits that demonstrated the atom's use (medicine, industry, and agriculture) as part of an all-out effort to emphasize the United States' leadership in the peaceful uses of atomic energy. The Atoms for Peace exhibit, which was shown worldwide over the next few years, first opened in Rome in June 1954 to much enthusiasm, although the Communist press tried to turn it into a propaganda weapon for the Soviet Union with a "me, too" approach that credited them with the progress achieved by the United States in the development of atomic energy. The United States countered this with film showings on atomic energy, extensive distribution of pamphlets and posters, weekly stories on the daily press files, extensive radio and television coverage, and special collections of books and materials on the subject in overseas information centers.

FURTHER READING: "Preliminary Report on the Mobile Exhibit 'Peaceful Uses of Atomic Energy,'" *Foreign Service Despatch*, June 18, 1954; U.S. Information Agency, "Former D.C. Newspaperman Describes Red Propaganda Failures in India" [SR-964/330; Undated press release, 1955?]

ATROCITY PROPAGANDA. Material of this sort was exposed after World War I as being usually untrue. As a result, it became more difficult for people to believe the truth of stories of atrocity during World War II. Films in World War I showed brutal treatment of captured or occupied peoples, usually by the Germans. It was most effective in visual format. The public reaction to learning that much of the World War I anti-German propaganda was false found it hard to believe the truth about the Nazi atrocities in World War II. It was only after the death camps were invaded and Americans saw newsreels of the horrors that they were able to understand the nature of the Nazi regime. According to James Read, atrocity stories published as propaganda fed the public's appetite for a Carthaginian peace, which in turn limited the flexibility of negotiations at the peace conference.
  See also War Propaganda

FURTHER READING: Arthur Ponsonby, *Falsehood in Wartime* (New York: E. P. Dutton, 1928); James M. Read, *Atrocity Propaganda, 1914–1919* (New York: Arno, 1972 [1941]).

AUSTRIA. *See* Helene Von Damm Forgery Letter; Occupied Countries and Territories

AWARE INC. *See Counterattack*; Red Channels

AWFUL DISCLOSURES OF MARIA MONK. See Catholic Church

AXIS PROPAGANDA. During World War II, the three major Axis countries were Germany, Italy, and Japan. Other countries within its orbit were under Nazi domination, including those in Eastern Europe (Czechoslovakia, Hungary, Poland, etc.). The name came from the Anti-Communist International (Comintern) Pact. There were marked differences between U.S. propaganda and that of the Axis powers, who proved more adept at using the latest advances in technology until battlefield losses hampered their effectiveness. National Socialist magazines, such as *Signal*, an extremely sophisticated propaganda organ unlike many of the others, were published in lavish color versions in all major European languages, including English. Well-produced German newsreels and documentaries were masterful propaganda devices screened widely not only in the German Fatherland and in occupied Europe but also in many neutral countries, including the United States prior to 1942. However, most of the enemy effort depended on radio for its effectiveness. The sarcastic broadcasts of "Lord Haw Haw" (**William Joyce**) and "Axis Sally" (**Mildred Gillars**) from Germany, "Tokyo Rose" and "The Zero Hour" from Japan, and American expatriate poet **Ezra Pound** from Italy were listened to widely by U.S. servicemen.

See also **German Library of Information; Goebbels and His Propaganda Efforts Against the Allies; "Moronic Little King" Incident; U.S.A. Zone of the Overseas Service (North American Service); Viereck, George Sylvester**

FURTHER READING: William E. Daugherty, *Psychological Warfare Casebook* (Baltimore, MD: Johns Hopkins Press; published for Operations Research Office, Johns Hopkins University, 1958).

"AXIS SALLY." *See* **Gillars, Mildred Elizabeth**

B

BABY PARTS. Since January 1987, rumors have been widespread in world media that children are being kidnapped to be used as unwilling donors in organ transplants, but no credible evidence has ever been produced by a government, international body, nongovernmental organization, or investigative journalist to substantiate these stories. Instead, there is every reason to consider the child organ trafficking rumors as a modern "urban legend," a false story that is commonly believed because it encompasses, in story form, widespread anxieties about modern life. In 1987 and 1988, the Soviet Union and its international front organization, the International Association of Democratic Lawyers, adopted the story and gave it widespread circulation. When it was first alleged that Americans were adopting children for the purpose of organ transplantation, several U.S. agencies, including the Justice Department, the **Federal Bureau of Investigation** (FBI), Food and Drug Administration, National Institutes of Health, Department of Health and Human Services, and the Immigration and Naturalization Service, investigated their records and stated that they found no evidence of alleged organ trafficking. Still, rumors entered the world press and its adverse effects; it attained unprecedented credibility in 1993–1994. Lifesaving organ contributions in countries decreased as a result of the stories, and international adoptions were disrupted.

"The Body Parts Business" (British/Canadian TV program) was broadcast in Britain (November 21, 1993) and in Canada the next day. It was funded by the British Broadcasting Corporation, Canadian Broadcasting Corporation, and Canadian National Film Board and examined alleged organ and tissue trafficking abuses in Guatemala, Honduras, Argentina, and Russia. "Organ Snatchers" ("Voleurs d'organes"), a French TV documentary, was broadcast in late 1993 and alleged to show evidence of child organ trafficking. It was shown in several countries and at the U.N. Center for Human Rights, Geneva, by the International Association of Democratic Lawyers (IADL), who claimed that the film presented irrefutable evidence of "criminal trafficking of organs removed from destitute children."

On September 14, 1993, the European Parliament adopted a "Resolution on Prohibiting Trade in Transplant Organs" that gave credence to allegations of worldwide child organ trafficking, whereas Eric Sottas of the World Organization

"Voleurs d'Organes" (Organ Parts). (This is one if 81 slides in the custody of the U.S. Department of State. Some are title pages of official documents; others are newspaper headlines.)

Against Torture presented a paper on trade in organs and torture at the Eurosciences Media Workshop in March 1994, described in the European media as the "Sottas report," that found increasing evidence of a network that trafficked in human beings for organ transplants. Sottas's conclusions were covered heavily in the Latin American press, but none of them were substantiated; some were repudiated before his paper was written.

In May 1994, the book *Ninos de Repuesto* (Spare-Parts Children) was published; it relied heavily on media accounts that included numerous misstatements between 1988 and 1994. From July 24 to July 31, 1994, a series of articles on alleged child organ trafficking appeared in the Brazilian newspaper *Correio Braziliense* that demonstrated the journalistic hazards of relying on secondary sources. The author, Ana Beatriz Magno, interviewed many people but did not consult sources in Argentina or in Colombia. The articles, which gave credence to the child organ trafficking charges, appeared reliable and authoritative to an unfamiliar Brazilian audience but were factually inaccurate and out of date.

One of the strongest arguments against child organ trafficking is the impossibility of concealing clandestine organ trafficking rings. In many countries, the sale or purchase of organs for transplants is illegal, and the medical procedures involved are too sophisticated and technical for the average criminal to even comprehend.

FURTHER READING: Ladislav Bittman, *The KGB and Soviet Disinformation* (Washington: Pergamon-Brassey's International Defense Publishers, 1985); Herbert Romerstein, "Disinformation as a KGB Weapon in the Cold War," Prepared for a Conference on Germany and

Intelligence Organizations: The Last Fifty Years in Review, sponsored by Akademie fur Politische Bildung Tutzing, June 18–20, 1999; Herbert Romerstein, *Soviet Active Measures and Propaganda: "New Thinking" and Influence Activities in the Gorbachev Era* (Toronto, Canada: Mackenzie Institute for the Study of Terrorism, Revolution, and Propaganda; Washington, DC: National Intelligence Book Center, 1989); U.S. Congress. Senate. Committee on Foreign Relations. Subcommittee on European Affairs, *Soviet Active Measures*; hearings. 99th Cong., 1st sess. (Washington, DC: GPO, 1985); U.S. Information Agency, *Child Organ Trafficking Rumor: A Modern "Urban Legend,"* prepared by Todd Leventhal (Washington, DC: USIA, 1994).

BADOGLIO, PIETRO. *See* **Moronic Little King Incident**

BALLOONS. *See* **Leaflets**

BARNES, HARRY ELMER (June 15, 1889–August 25, 1968). Historian and sociologist. During World War I, Barnes was a strong interventionist who contributed propaganda for such extremist prowar groups as the Nationalist Security League and the American Defense Society. Among his efforts was *The American Revolution in Our School Textbooks* (1917), coauthored with Charles Altschul, which proposed the rewriting of texts to stress a common Anglo-American heritage; a pamphlet, *America's Peril from Germany's Aggressive Growth* (1917); and an article, "Democracy," *Encyclopedia Americana* (1918), which accused Germany of launching an aggressive war. Barnes recanted his World War I positions by the mid-1920s when he published articles and reviews in *New Republic, Current History, American Mercury,* and *Christian Century,* in which he found the war's origins rooted in France's desire to avenge the Franco-Prussian War and Russia's quest to control the Turkish straits. In *Genesis of the World War* (1926), he absolved Germany of any war responsibility. To counter criticisms of his positions, Barnes published *In Quest of Truth and Justice: DeBunking the War-Guilt Myth* (1928).

As a foe of U.S. intervention in World War II before Pearl Harbor, Barnes offered a revisionist critique in the 1950s that accused President Franklin Roosevelt of deliberately withholding crucial intelligence from the U.S. military command at Pearl Harbor. In this period, Barnes supported the work of other revisionist historians and espoused "the New History" movement that centered on the rewriting of all history in light of contemporary problems and that stressed the social and economic roots of particular events. He coined terms *blackout boys* and *court historians* as derogatory terms against progovernment historians, positions he clarified in *The Struggle Against the Historical Blackout.*

FURTHER READING: Robert H. Barnes, *Harry Elmer Barnes As I Knew Him* (Worland, WY: High Plains Publishing, 1994); Arthur Goddard, ed., *Harry Elmer Barnes, Learned Crusader; the New History in Action* (Colorado Springs, CO: R. Myles, 1968).

BELGIUM. *See* **Occupied Countries and Territories**

BENELUX COUNTRIES. *See* **Occupied Countries and Territories**

BENÉT, STEPHEN VINCENT (July 22, 1898–March 13, 1943). Stephen Vincent Benét, poet, novelist, and short story writer, was born in Bethlehem, Pennsylvania, son of James W. Benét and Frances Neill (Rose). He performed civilian service during World War I as a cryptographer for military intelligence then completed his studies at Yale (1919). He published several volumes of verse, and his first novel, *The Beginning of Wisdom* (1921), was followed by others; his last novel was *James Shore's Daughter* (1934), a comment on the American rich. During the outbreak of World War II, Benét wrote propaganda against the Axis powers, which he justified as both an art and a necessary task. These works included *Dear Adolf,* a series of six radio letters written each week that were based on actual letters written to Hitler by representative Americans and delivered over the National Broadcasting Company in cooperation with the Council for Democracy. These included: Letter from a farmer, June 21, 1942; Letter from a business man, June 28, 1942; Letter from a working man, July 5, 1942; Letter from a housewife and mother, July 12, 1942; Letter from an American soldier, July 26, 1942; and Letter from a foreign-born American, August 2, 1942 and a collection of radio scripts, *We Stand United,* a declaration written by Benét and read by Raymond Massey at an American United Rally sponsored by the Council for Democracy at Carnegie Hall, Wednesday evening, November 6, 1940. It was published posthumously as *We Stand United, and Other Radio Scripts* (New York and Toronto: Farrar and Rinehart, 1945). In 1943, he wrote *America* for the **Office of War Information** that was distributed throughout liberated Europe and Asia. Benét died unexpectedly in New York City. His epic poem, *Western Star,* book one of what was to be a narrative poem, was published posthumously in 1943; it won a Pulitzer Prize.

FURTHER READING: Charles A. Fenton, *Stephen Vincent Benét: The Life and Times of an American Man of Letters, 1898–1943* (Westport, CT: Greenwood, 1978/1960); David G. Izzo and Lincoln Konkle, eds., *Stephen Vincent Benét: Essays on His Life and Work* (Jefferson, NC: McFarland, 2003).

BERNAYS, EDWARD L. (November 22, 1891–March 9, 1995). Edward Bernays was a publicist credited with creating the concept of the public relations counselor; he is universally considered as one of the major figures in the development of public relations in the United States. Bernays was born in Vienna, Austria, the maternal nephew of psychoanalyst Sigmund Freud, and raised in New York. After jobs as an ad writer and as a publicity impresario, Bernays joined the Foreign Press Bureau of the **Committee on Public Information** during World War I; he directed *Latin American News,* utilizing American corporations' overseas offices to promote the Allied cause. In 1919 he was part of the CPI mission to the Paris Peace Conference, but a growing backlash against CPI director George Creel prevented Bernays from handling American publicity there.

After his war work, he opened a public relations office with his future wife, Doris Fleischman (1891–1980), to represent governmental, industrial, business, and professional clients, and he was the first to make full use of the survey as a data-gathering tool. In 1929, he achieved national prominence when he promoted the Golden Jubilee of Light in Dearborn, Michigan, attended by Thomas Edison and other dignitaries, to much praise. Another celebrated publicity campaign was the Lucky Strike campaign for the American Tobacco Company, which refocused the issue of women smoking to that of sex discrimination ("Light another torch for freedom! Fight another sex taboo!"). Bernays's considerable publications include *Crystallizing Public Opinion* (1923), considered the first public relations book; *Propaganda* (1928); *The Engineering of Consent* (1955); *Your Future in Public Relations* (1961); his autobiography, *Biography of an Idea* (1965); and *The Later Years: Public Relations Insights, 1956–1986*. He died in Cambridge, Massachusetts. Bernays rejected individual psychotherapy to concentrate on linking psychological principles to practical mass applications. He helped focus attention on how meaningful public relationships might be collectively managed ("engineering of consent"), and he firmly believed that "you have to know your public and figure out how to make it respond." Bernays properly measured his target audience then sought creative ways to make them respond to his lifelong dictum that everything is a matter of public relations, whether the individual knows it or not.

FURTHER READING: Scott M. Cutlip, *The Unseen Power: Public Relations, a History* (Hillsdale, NJ: Lawrence Erlbaum Associates, 1994); Keith A. Larson, *Public Relations, the Edward L. Bernayses and the American Scene: A Bibliography* (Westwood, MA: F. W. Faxon, 1978).

BEST, ROBERT HENRY. *See* **U.S.A. Zone of the Overseas Service (North American Service)**

BIG LIE. Term associated with Adolf Hitler, who argued that lies by one's opponents had to be countered by still bigger lies, and that the larger and more widely repeated the lie, the more believable it became to the masses. The actual quote was, "Lie often enough and boldly enough, and people will find it difficult not to believe you," since history never questions the victor.

FURTHER READING: William E. Daugherty, *Psychological Warfare Casebook* (Baltimore, MD: Johns Hopkins Press; published for Operations Research Office, Johns Hopkins University, 1958).

BINATIONAL CENTERS. A Binational Center (BNC) is an autonomous, cultural institution governed by a locally selected board of directors. They have been established on three continents by host-country citizens and resident Americans that are dedicated to the promotion of mutual understanding between the United States and the host country through cultural, educational, and informational activities, especially English-teaching programs. The first one was established in Buenos Aires, Argentina. Since then, the BNC concept has appeared in over thirty-one countries. The majority are located in the American Republics with the remainder in Africa, Europe, the Near East, and Asia. The U.S. government first began to assist BNCs in 1941. Now they are operated under the auspices of the Bureau of Educational and Cultural Affairs, U.S. Department of State, which provides assistance through American personnel, program materials, and cash grants. The BNC is one of the most successful elements in U.S. cultural programming overseas with its emphasis on classes in English as a second language along with other cultural programs (lectures, film showings, dramatic presentations, exhibitions, musical performances, etc.), but BNCs are not expected to be propaganda mills for the U.S. government but conduits of American culture.

There is a board of directors for each BNC with citizens appointed from the host country, whereas the U.S. government has at least one person on the board. USIA assistance is granted after a BNC meets certain criteria, such as sponsorship by U.S. citizens, sound fiscal procedures, a legal entity (nonprofit, nonpolitical, nonsectarian) recognized by the host government, an open library, and physical facilities adequate for effective cultural programming. Three BNC classifications determine levels of U.S. funding, ranging from Class A (direct media, personnel, and financial support) to Class C (occasional support, e.g., equipment, publications, teaching, and program materials). The ACAO (Assistant Cultural Affairs Officer) or the CAO (Cultural Affairs Officer) is usually BNC director; overall authority is vested in the U.S. Department of State.

FURTHER READING: U.S. Information Agency, *Binational Center Handbook* (Washington, DC: The Agency, 1970).

BIOLOGICAL AND CHEMICAL WEAPONS WARFARE. This was a major Soviet, Chinese, and North Korean **disinformation** campaign in Korea that generated lots of media attention. The Americans were accused of going into Korean villages during the Korean conflict (1950–1953) and shooting villagers and killing them with biological weapons and chemical warfare. The KGB assisted the North Koreans and Chinese with this campaign. An attempt now underway with the Cold War History Project at the Woodrow Wilson International Center for Scholars, Smithsonian Institution, in Washington, D.C., has published material to expose this false propaganda, especially through the work of Katherine Weathersby, who discovered the Soviet documents through a Japanese researcher that put the lie to these accusations. The issue resurfaced in the book *United States and Biological Warfare: Secrets of the Early Cold War and Korea* (Bloomington: Indiana University Press, 1999) by Stephen Endicott and Edward Hagerman. Endicott is the son of one of the men who helped to disseminate the disinformation campaign, James Endicott, a major player in this campaign, who won the 1953 Stalin Peace Prize for his efforts. Another important disseminator was Australian journalist Wilfrid Burchett.

FURTHER READING: Milton Leitenberg, *Korean War Biological Warfare Allegations Resolved* (Stockholm: Center for Pacific Asia Studies at Stockholm University, 1998); Herbert Romerstein, "Disinformation as a KGB Weapon in the Cold War," Prepared for a Conference on Germany and Intelligence Organizations: The Last Fifty Years in Review, sponsored by Akademie fur Politische Bildung Tutzing, June 18–20, 1999; Kathryn Weathersby, *New Evidence on the Allegations of the Use of Biological Warfare During the Korean War* (Washington, DC: Woodrow Wilson Center, Smithsonian Institution, 1998).

BIRTH OF A NATION (FILM). Controversial 1915 silent film by David W. Griffith based on Thomas Dixon's novels, *The Klansman* (1905) and *The Leopard's Spots* (1902), it was produced at a cost of $110,000 and became a technical landmark with a cast that was a "who's who" of the early movie industry. The film was originally released as *The Klansman* in Los Angeles in February 1915, but Dixon, a fundamentalist preacher who was the grandson of a **Ku Klux Klan** member, suggested changing the title to *The Birth of a Nation* for its New York release. Dixon tried to get an endorsement of the film's historical authenticity from his former classmate, President Woodrow Wilson, who saw the film and allegedly saw it as "viewing history written with lightning," a quote widely used to publicize the film, even though it was actually created by Griffith after he received only a lukewarm reply from Wilson. In its epic portrayal of Southern African Americans in the Reconstruction era and of the white supremacy movement, *Birth of a Nation* was an important propaganda tool that helped revive the Ku Klux Klan in 1915 as a powerful nationalist and nativist political force. Despite a protest by the NAACP, the film was a popular success, but today it is considered a violently racist comment of the period in which it was produced. However, in 2003, artist and musician DJ Spooky decided to "remix" the film by rearranging offensive scenes to alter their content and adding new scenes with lyrics of original music and effects laid on top.

FURTHER READING: Thomas Cripps, *Slow Fade to Black: The Negro in American Film, 1900–1942* (New York: Oxford University, 1977); M. Paul Holsinger, ed., *War and American Popular Culture; A Historical Encyclopedia* (Westport, CT: Greenwood, 1999).

BITTMAN, LADISLAV (1931–). Ladislav Bittman was a Czech intelligence officer before he defected from the Czech Intelligence Service in 1968. He had served as deputy head of the disinformation department. He is the author of a number of books on the subject of disinformation, such as *Deception Game: Czechoslovak Intelligence in Soviet Political Warfare* (1972), based on his personal experiences working in cooperation with the Soviet KGB, and *New Image Makers: Soviet Propaganda and Disinformation Today* (1987), which he edited. He recently retired from Boston University, where he used the name Lawrence Martin. He headed the Program for the Study of Disinformation in the College of Communication.

FURTHER READING: Ladislav Bittman, *The KGB and Soviet Disinformation: An Insider's View* (Washington: Pergamon-Brassey's International Defense Publishers, 1985); Sharon McDonnell, "In From the Cold," *American Journalism Review* (June 1995): 16–17.

BITTMAN, LAWRENCE MARTIN. *See* Bittman, Ladislav

BLACK PROPAGANDA. Black propaganda refers to falsely attributed propaganda. Sometimes practitioners of this form pretend that the information is being published by the enemy to deceive the reader or listener as to the origin of the information, which may be true or false. The results are usually quite ingenious and rather intriguing. Samples include fake newspapers, broadsides, leaflets, booklets, postage stamps, radio broadcasts, currency, and even army discharge forms requiring only the name of the soldier to be filled in. During World

War II, the British were extremely successful with their black propaganda campaign, whereas the Germans were often unsuccessful, too obvious in their message, with fake stories unsubtle in their lies and poor printing. Black propaganda was often created to undermine the enemy's morale.

See also Gray Propaganda; White Propaganda

FURTHER READING: Garth Jowett and Victoria O'Donnell, *Propaganda and Persuasion* (London: Sage, 1992).

BLACKOUT BOYS. *See* **Barnes, Harry Elmer**

BLANKENHORN, HEBER (1884–1956). Labor journalist and industrial economist who played an important role in army psychological warfare efforts during World War I. As Captain Heber Blankenhorn from the American Expeditionary Force (AEF), he commanded the Propaganda Subsection, G-2D, General Headquarters, U.S. Army (Pershing's Headquarters) in World War I, which distributed over 2,000 copies of the first U.S. propaganda leaflet of World War I. His final *Report on Propaganda Against the Enemy* was issued only days after the Armistice was signed (1918), and his wartime experiences became *Adventures in Propaganda; Letters From an Intelligence Officer in France* (1919). After the war, Blankenhorn worked on labor issues and prepared research studies, such as *The Strike for Union* (1924), a study of the nonunion question in coal mining and the problems of a democratic movement based on the record of the 1922–1923 Somerset County, Pennsylvania, strike, for the Bureau of Industrial Research. Blankenhorn was a member of the Commission of Inquiry of the Interchurch World Movement of North America on the Steel Strike of 1919 that resulted in *Report on the Steel Strike* (1920), and he was chairman of the first and second National Labor Relations Boards. Blankenhorn returned as a psychological warfare officer in World War II, where he spearheaded a leaflet campaign in North Africa to convince the Italians that the Germans were willing to let them be slaughtered in hopeless campaigns. Blankenhorn gave his reminiscences to the Columbia University Oral History Collection (microfilmed in 1979).

FURTHER READING: Clayton D. Laurie, "'The Chanting of Crusaders': Captain Heber Blankenhorn and AEF Combat Propaganda in World War I," *Journal of Military History* (July 1995): 457–481; Paul M. A. Linebarger, *Psychological Warfare* (Washington, DC: Combat Forces, 1954).

BOARD FOR INTERNATIONAL BROADCASTING. *See* **Radio Free Europe; Radio Liberty**

BOOK FAIRS. United States participation at foreign book fairs is chance for American booksellers to display what they consider their most important books ("Americanism on display"). Also, fairs give American publishers an opportunity to show off superior technical quality of book production in the United States, although the displays by American publishers are usually modest compared to the lavish presentations mounted by European organizations, such as the British

Kiosks at the fourth International Book Fair, Buenos Aires, 1978. (*Source:* USIA)

Council. Book fairs are of many distinct kinds: genuine trade fairs, rights fairs, selling fairs, or a combination of all these types. The major annual fall event is considered to be the Frankfurt International Book Fair, with other important ones in Eastern Europe (e.g., Budapest, Prague), an area that is gaining predominance in the book fair market. The other major international book fair is the Bologna Children's Book Fair. It is unlikely in the post–Cold War atmosphere that the Moscow fair, once one of the biggest events in the publishing world, will ever be significant again. Regional, national, or language-specific fairs, although less significant than the international event in Frankfurt and with higher impact, are held in Cairo, New Delhi (biennial in one of the largest book-producing countries), Belgrade (point in bilateral cultural talks), Karachi or Calcutta, and Buenos Aires (most important Latin American bookselling event). Frankfurt is the most challenging, difficult, and promising of the book fairs and the largest in the world with representatives from over 5,000 publishing houses and 100 countries. It is an international rights fair, booksellers' convention, and national fair for rights, promotion, and selling of books in all languages. U.S. official participation is coordinated by the U.S. Department of State's Bureau of Public Diplomacy, successor to the **U.S. Information Agency** (USIA); it now operates at book fairs with fewer resources, due to budget cuts, than it had in the 1960s and early 1970s, when USIA had a half dozen programs aimed at sending books abroad, all aimed at promoting American culture. State Department facilitates the translation of serious American works, then places them in locales and in circumstances in which the agency is active with related programs.

FURTHER READING: William M. Childs and Donald E. McNeil, eds., *American Books Abroad: Towards a National Policy* (Washington, DC: Helen Dwight Reid Educational Foundation, 1986); Herbert R. Lottman, "World Trade and World Fairs, 1996: King Frankfurt and His Minions," *Bowker Annual: Library and Book Trade Almanac*, 42nd edition (New Providence, NJ: R. R. Bowker, 1997): 216–219; U.S. Information Agency, "USIA Participation in International Book Fairs" [Background Paper, 1983].

BOOKS. Books are basic tools for communicating information and to counter a worldwide disinformation industry that confuses and misleads others about the American way of life. The U.S. government has a legitimate interest to ensure that books communicating a fair picture of America are available abroad. Books, educational exchange, and now the Internet are the foremost tools of modernization.

Serious American books in English or in translation on themes that emphasize U.S. society and values are considered. Books have unique qualities that provide foreigners substantive perceptions and insight into American society and government policies that they can get in no other way. However, distribution and readership have declined steadily in the Third World, one of the major targets, for many years whereas other nations, especially the former Soviet Union, have increased significantly the distribution of their books and, subsequently, their philosophies.

The U.S. government uses a variety of methods for publishing and distributing books abroad: promotion of titles selected by the State Department for translation by foreign publishers (usually supported through guaranteed purchase of a certain number of copies for the department), direct publication by State of important titles unavailable from other sources, the assemblage of book exhibits on appropriate themes, efforts to encourage donations of relevant books from the American publishing industry for use with appropriate institutions and individuals abroad, and surveys of American books published by U.S. and foreign publishers and their acquisition for use in public diplomacy programming.

Major U.S. assistance programs of the past included: Informational Media Guarantee (IMG) program (1948–1968), USIA donated book programs (1960s–1980s), USIA low-priced books in translation (1956–1960), USIA low-priced books in English (1956–1964), Ladder books in low-priced editions (1957–1975), and USIA French for Africa Program (1962–1979). Of the private-sector programs, the best known was probably the Franklin Book Program (1952–1979), which was established by the International Information Administration in the State Department to manage its projected overseas publishing ventures. Others were the Philippines' U.S. Textbook Production Project (TPP, 1961–1966), which operated under the auspices of the U.S. Agency for International Development (USAID); Third Education Project for Indonesia (1973–1978/79); Joint Indo-American Textbook Program (1960s–1981); and Association of American University Presses (AAUP), which jointly founded and operated (1965–1976) with the National University of Mexico a program in Mexico City known as Centro Interamericano de Libros Academicos (CILA), or Inter-American Scholarly Book Center. Finally, there was the Government Advisory Committee on Book and Library Programs (GAC), which was established in November 1962 by Secretary of State Dean Rusk, under authority of the

Fulbright-Hays Act, to ensure effective distribution abroad of American books, both in English and in translation. It was abolished in 1977 by the Carter administration. The types of U.S. books exported include trade, religious, professional, book clubs, mail order, mass market paperbacks, university press, school, college, subscription, and reference. Besides the State Department, other government agencies that offer U.S. assistance programs are the Peace Corps, the National Library of Medicine, and the Library of Congress.

Timeline of Important Developments Since World War II

1949—State Department issued directive against use of books and other materials by persons affiliated with subversive or Communist organizations.

1950—Small group of leading American publishers established the American Book Publishers Council (ABPC), a trade association, to promote books, reading, and libraries.

1950s—Censorship when private groups and public officials throughout the United States made attempts to remove books from sale, to censor textbooks, to distribute lists of "objectionable" books or authors, and to purge libraries overseas.

1953—Hearing by the Senate Permanent Committee on Investigations for its Committee on Government Operations held over several months into the conduct of State Department libraries overseas and the contents of books on library shelves by authors deemed unsuitable to represent the United States. (U.S. Congress. [Hearing released as: *State Department Information Program: Information Centers*; hearing, 83d Congress, 1st Session (Washington, DC: Government Printing Office, 1953)].)

1954–1974—National Book Committee existed to encourage use of libraries and lifelong reading habits.

1955—Commission on the Freedom to Read established.

1962–1977—Government Advisory Committee on International Book and Library Programs (GAC) was established in 1962 (under the Fulbright-Hays Act) with a panel of publishers, booksellers, and librarians, who met with government officials to provide advice about federal book policies and programs.

1977—U.S. Congress created the Center for the Book in the Library of Congress "to heighten public interest in the role of books and printing in the diffusion of knowledge."

1990s—Foreign owners buy American book publishing houses. German firm, Holtzbrinck, owns Farrar Straus Giroux, Henry Holt, and St. Martin's; British conglomerate Pearson takes control of Viking, Penguin, Dutton, and Putnam; and in March 1998, the German conglomerate Bertelsmann A.G. bought Random House, a move that gave a foreign entity control of at least one-tenth of American book publishing.

The biggest promoter of American books abroad are the programs of the Bureau of Public Diplomacy, U.S. Department of State, which includes its libraries and reading rooms in almost one hundred countries. It also organizes exhibits of American books for major international fairs (e.g., Frankfurt Book Fair), reprints or translates popular books into some fifteen languages, and assembles exhibits of appropriate American publications for overseas professional events, seminars, libraries, and scholarly institutions. In many countries, translations by the U.S. Information Service (USIS) of popular and classic American books are essential, as are the printing of "ladder books," which are English-language editions of

American classics with glossaries that explain many of the harder words in the text. Other government agencies that offer U.S. assistance programs are the Peace Corps, the Library of Congress, and the National Library of Medicine.

Sabre Foundation

An important source of donated books has become the Sabre Foundation, founded in 1969 as a small foundation, based in Cambridge, Massachusetts, whose principal activity since 1986 has been the donation of new books. It presently gives away three million books a year, drawing on a diverse inventory of elementary and secondary school books, college, reference, and professional materials, to free institutions. The first donations originally went to Eastern Europe and the former Soviet Union. In 1996, it expanded its programs into Bosnia-Herzegovina, Brazil, Grenada, and Romania; a year later, it initiated work in India, Mongolia, Tanzania, the West Bank, and Zambia. A small group of employees try to get American publishers to donate any extra stocks of new books from their lists, such as dictionaries, medical handbooks, and engineering manuals, to the developing countries that request them. Sabre sends the books to East Africa, computer texts to Mongolia and Lithuania, and whole law libraries to a university in the Ukraine. Sabre gets renewed support from private and public sources, such as the Peace Corps, the Asia Foundation, Books for Africa, the World Bank Book Project, USIA, the U.S. Agency for International Development, and other distributing partners to carry out its always expanding programs.

PUBWATCH

PUBWATCH, which was established in 1990, is the only American organization to date that promotes assistance to the book sector in Central and Eastern Europe, in the Baltic countries, and in the Commonwealth of Independent States, the former Soviet Union. PUBWATCH activities include in-country professional educational programs, international research programs, U.S. and West European workshops and seminars, and resource publications. The programs bring eminent Western publishing professionals together with publishers, booksellers, librarians, and policy makers of Eastern Europe and the former Soviet Union. PUBWATCH works closely with organizations such as the American Booksellers Association, USIA, Library of Congress's Center for the Book, Frankfurt Book Fair, World Bank, and the British Council's Libraries, Books and Information Division.

FURTHER READING: Curtis G. Benjamin, *U.S. Books Abroad: Neglected Ambassadors* (Washington: Library of Congress, 1984); William M. Childs and Donald E. McNeil, eds., *American Books Abroad: Towards a National Policy* (Washington, DC: Helen Dwight Reid Educational Foundation, 1986); Rosemary N. Mokia, "Publishers, United States Foreign Policy and the Third World, 1960–1967," *Publishing Research Quarterly* 11, no. 2 (Summer 1995); *Pubwatch, About Pubwatch, 1990–1994* (New York: Pubwatch, 1994); Christine Spolar, "Romance by the Book in Poland," *Washington Post*, 8/28/95); U.S. Congress. Senate. Committee on Government Operations. Permanent Subcommittee on Investigations, *State Department Information Program: Information Centers*; hearing, 83d Cong., 1st sess. (Washington, DC: Government Printing Office, 1953).

BORAH, WILLIAM E. *See* Stimson-Borah Letter

BOSTON COMMITTEE OF CORRESPONDENCE. *See* Committees of Correspondence

BOSTON GAZETTE. The second newspaper published in the American Colonies, it first appeared from 1719–1741 then again from 1755—1798, when it was branded "an infamous weekly" by British authorities after it assailed the 1765 Stamp Act . Its first publisher was **Benjamin Franklin**'s brother, James. Samuel Adams was a major contributor, who shrewdly used it to ignite patriotic fervor. For example, he expanded a story in the *Boston Gazette* into the **Boston Massacre** then calculated that other colonial newspapers would publish his story and he commissioned Paul Revere to make an "eyewitness" engraving that was published in the *Boston Gazette* on March 12, 1770. Also, the *Gazette* deliberately misguided readers regarding the 1772 decision in which the American slave James Somerset was freed by a British court.

FURTHER READING: Patricia Bradley, "*The Boston Gazette* and Slavery as Revolutionary Propaganda," *Journalism and Mass Communication Quarterly* 72, no. 3 (Autumn 1995): 581–596.

BOSTON MASSACRE. Soldier–civilian tensions in Boston started as early as October 1768 when British troops, poorly paid and housed, arrived to maintain order in that city. On March 5, 1770, a group of frightened British soldiers of the Twenty-ninth Regiment opened fire on a "threatening" crowd of demonstrators (actually a mob of men and boys who had been taunting them and throwing stones); they killed five men and wounded seven. Captain Thomas Preston, commander of the British contingent, and six of his men were charged with murder. Ironically, they were defended in court by John Adams and Josiah Quincy although it is still unclear why. All were acquitted but two soldiers, who were found guilty of manslaughter. Four civilians, accused of firing from the customhouse windows, were tried in December 1770, but were quickly acquitted from lack of evidence. Anti-British opinion was inflamed with broadsides and pamphlets, such as '**A Short Narrative of the Horrid Massacre in Boston**,' first published in 1770 by a partisan committee chaired by James Bidden, along with Joseph Warren and Samuel Pemberton; it was "a particular account of the massacre" along with observations on the state of things prior to the shootings. The document included eyewitness interviews of military men, citizens, and others who testified about their experiences on that day. **Samuel Adams**, one of the most ardent propagandists of the American Revolution, expanded the deaths into a massacre in a story in the *Boston Gazette* then shrewdly estimated that other colonial newspapers would publish his story. He commissioned Paul Revere to make an "eyewitness" engraving that was published in the *Boston Gazette* on March 12. An hour of street rioting became Revere's famous propaganda piece, "The Boston Massacre," and the Douglas Chandler painting that contributed to a lasting impression of that rather minor event as a "major" occasion in the American colonies' march to revolution and independence from

Great Britain. Media coverage of the "massacre" had little impact in the American colonies outside Massachusetts, but it was commemorated for many years afterward on its anniversary. The site of the event is now marked by a plaque. There are also monuments on Boston Common and in the Old Granary Burial Ground.

FURTHER READING: Philip Davidson, *Propaganda and the American Revolution, 1763–1783* (New York: Norton, 1973 [1941]); Paul Foley and Oscar de Mejo, *Fresh Views of the American Revolution* (New York: Rizzoli, 1976); Harry Hansen, *Boston Massacre* (New York: Hastings House, 1970); Hiller B. Zobel, *Boston Massacre* (New York: W. W. Norton, 1996, 1970).

BOSTON NEWS-LETTER. The *Boston News-Letter,* which started publishing on April 24, 1704, was the first continuously published newspaper in the American colonies. Along with the news, it carried advertisements for the slave trade. Publication was suspended for eight months in 1707, due to poor circulation, but then resumed. In 1763, the paper was renamed *Massachusetts Gazette and Boston News-Letter* after the governor and Executive Council authorized the publication in the paper of all official sources. It ceased publication with its last issue on February 22, 1776.

FURTHER READING: "Ask the Globe," *Boston Globe* (October 18, 1999); Frederic B. Farrar, *This Common Channel to Independence: Revolution and Newspapers, 1759–1789* (Garden City, NY: Farrar, 1975).

BOSTON TEA PARTY. Staged event in which Bostonians rejected English tea then planned town meetings that culminated in what was designated the Boston Tea Party. On the evening of December 16, 1773, a group of men dressed as Indians boarded three British ships at Griffin's Wharf in Boston Harbor and threw 342 chests of tea, worth 18,000 pounds, into the water. The action was the climax of growing colonial opposition to the Stamp Act, a protest against British taxes, especially on tea (no "taxation without representation"). Participants met at the house of newspaper publisher **Benjamin Edes** to don their disguises prior to boarding the ships for their "tea party." The event was heavily publicized in colonial newspapers, especially in the *Pennsylvania Gazette,* which printed over a thousand copies, but the "patriots" were equally adept at publicizing their actions through other major organs of public opinion, such as broadsides, pamphlets, and music, that discredited the loyalist opposition. Today, a replica of one of the ships stands in an identical spot as a living museum with reenactments of the actual event. At Our National Heritage Museum, Lexington, Massachusetts, the event is depicted as it would have been if television had been there in 1773. On two opposite televisions, a British newscaster and his American counterpart give their versions of events. There was also another "tea party," but less well-known than the 1773 event. It took place on March 28, 1774, in Weston, outside Boston, when an angry mob of one hundred patriots, disguised and painted, raided the Golden Ball Tavern of Tory innkeeper Isaac Jones after the *Massachusetts Spy* reported he had "a considerable quantity of tea for sale." Jones observed the first tea boycott but ignored the resolution calling for total abstinence.

FURTHER READING: Frederic B. Farrar, *This Common Channel to Independence: Revolution and Newspapers, 1759–1789* (Garden City, NY: Farrar, 1975); Wesley S. Griswold, *The Night the Revolution Began: The Boston Tea Party, 1773* (Brattleboro, VT: S. Greene Press, 1972); Peter D. G. Thomas, *Tea Party to Independence: The Third Phase of the American Revolution, 1773–1776* (Oxford: Clarendon Press; New York: Oxford University, 1991).

BRADDOCK II. Operation undertaken by psychological warfare personnel to threaten German internal security by the millions of foreign workers in **Germany** by dropping four to five million "small powerful time fuse incendiaries" in those areas (Germany and Austria) where foreign workers were concentrated. Each fuse package carried a "how to use" instruction card in nine languages with a folder marking likely targets, and the operation was supported by nightly broadcasts on "**Soldatensender Calais**," an Allied station that didn't identify itself as Allied, and by "white" (official) leaflets carrying General Eisenhower's signature. Braddock II had two purposes: to profit by whatever actual sabotage was committed by the foreign workers and to strain the enemy's security forces to the limit. The sabotage objective ended in the early weeks of 1945 when a speedy conclusion of the war seemed unlikely but not before official reports showed evidence that Nazi officials were watching the operation. The second objective of "stretching the German security service by keeping them in a constant state of apprehension and watchfulness" was continued until April 1945, when the end of World War II was inevitable. Overall, Braddock II was unsuccessful because Allied propagandists underestimated foreign workers and their willingness to sabotage the working conditions of their factories and, subsequently, their livelihoods.

FURTHER READING: Daniel Lerner, "Braddock II," in *Psychological Warfare Casebook*, ed. William E. Daugherty (Baltimore, MD: Johns Hopkins Press; published for Operations Research Office, Johns Hopkins University, 1958).

BRAINWASHING. A related technique to **psychological warfare**, brainwashing is most often used against prisoners. It combines political propaganda with harsh treatment to reduce a prisoner's resistance. The best weapons to use for brainwashing the enemy are good intelligence and an intimate understanding of the way the human mind works.

FURTHER READING: Laura Spinney, "Mindwars," *New Scientist* (November 4, 1995): 20–21.

BRECHT, BERTOLT (February 10, 1898–August 14, 1956). Very important propagandist. Eugen Berthold Friedrich Brecht was a German playwright who used his art to promote Communist propaganda themes. He wrote his first play, *Baal,* while studying medicine in Munich (1918), but his first play to reach the stage, *Trommeln in der Nacht (Drums in the Night,* 1922), won the coveted Kleidt Prize, and two years later he started working at the Deutsches Theater in Berlin. Over the next decade, he produced plays such as *Die Dreigroschenoper (The Threepenny Opera,* 1928), a collaboration with composer Kurt Weill, and

Die Massnahme (*The Measures Taken,* 1930) with Hanns Eisler, the first of Brecht's plays with a communist theme.

Brecht went into exile in Finland (1933) during the Nazi years, where he waited for a U.S. visa and wrote some of his best-known plays, including *Mutter Courage und ihre Kinder* (*Mother Courage and Her Children,* 1941); *The Resistable Rise of Arturo Ui* (1941) on Adolf Hitler's rise to power; *Leben des Galileo* (*The Life of Galileo,* 1943); *Der gute Mensch von Sezuan* (*The Good Woman of Sezuan,* 1943); and *Der Kaukasische Kreidekris* (*The Caucasian Chalk Circle,* 1948). He contributed to **Federal Theater Project** productions, worked in Hollywood as a scriptwriter, and served on the **Voice of America**'s German desk in the **Office of War Information**. He left the United States the day after he was called to give testimony before the House Un-American Activities Committee on October 30, 1947; this was broadcast on radio as it was held, and it was preserved as an aural record, "Brecht Before the Un-American Activities Committee" (Folkways, FD5531), which allows comparison of the spoken record against the stenographer's transcript. Brecht's carefully rehearsed appearance was so congenial that committee chairman J. Parnell Thomas thanked him for being a "good example" to future witnesses. Brecht spent his last years in East Berlin, where he established his own theater, the Berliner Ensemble, and completed his development of epic theater, which exploited the artificial nature of theatrical productions.

FURTHER READING: Eric Bentley, ed., *Thirty Years of Treason: Excerpts from Hearings Before the House Committee on Un-American Activities, 1938-1968* (New York: Viking, 1971); Michael Denning, *The Cultural Front: The Laboring of American Culture in the Twentieth Century* (London and New York: Verso, 1997); U.S. Congress. House. Committee on Un-American Activities, *Hearings Regarding Communist Infiltration of the Motion Picture Industry*; 80th Cong., 1st sess. (Washington, DC: Government Printing Office, 1947).

BROADCASTING, RADIO. *See* **Clandestine Radio Stations; "Debunk" (Radio Station); Lorient; Radio Free Europe; Radio in the American Sector; Radio Liberty; Radio Marti; Radio Sawa; "Soldatensender Calais"; Voice of America**

BRUSSELS UNIVERSAL AND INTERNATIONAL EXPOSITION (EXPO 1958). The United States endeavored to show the American way of life at the expo, officially the Brussels Universal and International Exposition, the first major world's fair held since World War II, which ran from April 17 to October 19, 1958. Originally intended to promote Belgian economic growth, the fair was remembered for the Cold War tensions that developed, especially between the Americans and the Russians, who built rival pavilions, literally across from each other, that propagandized their different political systems. The Soviet pavilion was a high-tech tribute to Communism, but the U.S. effort was not up to the Russian level, and its pavilion was considered a front for American intelligence agencies, a charge never effectively proved, while representatives from other countries tried to determine what this would mean for international relations.

U.S. Pavilion, Brussels International Exposition, 1958. (*Source*: USIA)

U.S. participation came with difficulty. President Eisenhower requested special funds for the expo in his budget message to Congress, but Congress reduced the fair's budget to $13 million compared to the $50 million the Soviets spent on their participation. One controversial reason was the U.S. exhibit, "Unfinished Business," about U.S. social problems, including segregation, which angered southern congressmen ("gross insult in the South"), who forced budget cuts. This reduced the U.S. scientific exhibits in the International Hall of Science and allowed the Russians to take over the space, an action that increased American anxieties toward the Soviet Union, and gave the Russians more space to emphasize their scientific and technological progress, such as a Soviet display on the peaceful uses of atomic energy, which contrasted to their view of Americans' use of nuclear power "for the undoing of mankind." Culturally, both countries offered a wide variety of art and music to their visitors, but the Soviet Union overwhelmed with the range and amount of its artistic and musical offerings. When the exposition ended, the United States was criticized for its poor showing in what was primarily a Cold War propaganda battle with the Soviet Union.

FURTHER READING: Walter L. Hixson, *Parting the Curtain: Propaganda, Culture, and the Cold War, 1945–1961* (New York: St. Martin's, 1997); Robert W. Rydell, *World of Fairs: The Century of Progress Expositions* (Chicago: University of Chicago, 1993).

BUENOS AIRES CONVENTION FOR PROMOTION OF INTER-AMERICAN CULTURAL RELATIONS. Officially, the Inter-American Conference for the Maintenance of Peace, this meeting was held in Buenos Aires, Argentina, December 1–23, 1936, as a cooperative effort to counter the "threat to the hemisphere" by the Axis Powers. It resulted in the agreement that established an official U.S. educational exchange program, Convention for the Promotion of Inter-American Cultural Relations, approved December 23, 1936. Representatives from twenty American Republics and the United States met "for the promotion of inter-American cultural relations" that provided for the exchange between each signatory government of two graduate students annually and one professor every two years. Also, five treaties and several resolutions were approved by the United States dealing with cultural relations, as were three other conventions dealing with the exchange of publications, the holding of art exhibits, and educational films. The resolutions favored revision of textbooks, use of radio broadcasts for peace, reading rooms, bibliographical exchanges, intellectual property protection, education conferences, and cooperation of private organizations. The report of the U.S. delegation was released as: *Report of the Delegation of the United States of America to the Inter-American Conference for the Maintenance of Peace, Buenos Aires, Argentina, December 1–23, 1936* (Washington, DC: GPO, 1937).

FURTHER READING: J. Manuel Espinosa, *Inter-American Beginnings of U.S. Cultural Diplomacy, 1936–1948* (Washington, DC: U.S. Department of State, 1976); U.S. Dept. of State, *Foreign Relations of the United States, 1936: vol. V, The American Republics* (Washington, DC: Government Printing Office, 1954).

BUND (FRITZ KUHN). *See* **German-American Bund**

BUNKER HILL. On June 17, 1775, the day George Washington accepted command of the Continental Army, General Artemas Ward, in Boston, ordered Bunker Hill, a quarter-mile from Breed's Hill, the actual battle site, fortified. There the British launched three frontal attacks. Historians still cannot agree on who actually said, "Don't fire 'til you see the whites of their eyes," as British redcoats marched up Breed's Hill, but a soldier who misinterpreted the command fired the first shot that started the shooting. The battle was reported on both sides of the Atlantic. London's *Monthly Magazine* published both American and British reports together, but in the American version Breed's Hill became Bunker Hill. The propaganda value of this event in the United States did much to stir up American resistance to the British occupation in New England. However, it was also debated that because someone incorrectly identified the hill, it can logically be argued that there never was a Battle of Bunker Hill but instead the Battle of Breed's Hill.

FURTHER READING: Frederic B. Farrar, *This Common Channel to Independence: Revolution and Newspapers, 1759–1789* (Garden City, NY: Farrar, 1975).

BURCHETT, WILFRID. *See* **Biological and Chemical Weapons Warfare**

BUREAU OF CUSTOMS (TREASURY DEPARTMENT). *See* Postal Regulations (Communist Political Propaganda); Propaganda Collections

BUREAU OF PUBLIC DIPLOMACY AND PUBLIC AFFAIRS (U.S. DEPARTMENT OF STATE). New bureau within the U.S. Department of State that was created after a 1999 consolidation of public diplomacy functions. On October 1, 1999, the **U.S. Information Agency** (USIA) was abolished, and its three program operations were separated. The International Broadcasting Bureau, under the policy direction of its Broadcasting Board of Governors, became an independent agency; it includes the **Voice of America, Radio Marti, Radio Free Europe,** and **Radio Liberty.** The rest of USIA became part of the **U.S. Department of State.** The Foreign Press Centers and Worldnet TV were placed in the new bureau. The exchange programs, including the Fulbright Program, and the information programs, with its libraries, book programs, Washington File, and speaker programs, were designated as the Bureau of Public Diplomacy and Public Affairs under the authority of an Under Secretary of Public Diplomacy and Public Affairs who answered directly to the Secretary of State. The first Undersecretary of Public Diplomacy and Public Affairs was Evelyn Lieberman, who was Voice of America director, 1997–1999, during the Clinton administration. Her successor was Charlotte Beers, a public relations executive in New York City, who was nominated by President George W. Bush in 2001. She resigned in March 2003 after increasing attacks on the manner in which she handled public diplomacy efforts after the events following the 9/11 terrorist attacks. The most recent undersecretary was Margaret Tutwiller, who was sworn in December 16, 2003, but left in June 2004 for the private sector.

FURTHER READING: Bureau of International Information, U.S. Department of State Web site: http://usinfo.state.gov; U.S. Advisory Commission on Public Diplomacy, *Consolidation of USIA Into the State Department: An Assessment After One Year* (Washington: The Commission, 2000).

BURGMAN, HERBERT JOHN. *See* U.S.A. Zone of the Overseas Service (North American Service)

BYOIR, CARL R. (June 24, 1888–February 3, 1957). Public relations counsel Carl R. Byoir was born June 24, 1888, in Des Moines, Iowa and was a reporter for *Iowa State Register* and *Waterloo (Iowa) Times-Tribune.* He attended the University of Iowa and received a law degree (1912) from Columbia University Law School. Four years later, he became circulation director for *Cosmopolitan.* He purchased rights to Maria Montessori kindergarten training methods, introduced it to America, and reportedly made a profit. He was associate chairman, **Committee on Public Information,** and was a delegate at the peace conference at Versailles. Byoir persuaded President Hoover (1932) to use propaganda techniques to create jobs at no cost to the government by mobilizing public opinion in support of expanded production and the free enterprise system ("War Against Depression"), but he was indicted (1942) for violating the Sherman Anti-Trust Act.

Byoir went to **Germany** allegedly, he claimed, to promote German tourism, but his meeting with Hitler drew suspicions of his real activities, and he was called before a Congressional committee to investigate Nazi propaganda to explain his actions. He founded Carl Byoir and Associates, one of the largest public relations firms in the United States, which counseled clients whose products ranged from ballpoint pens to photographic supplies and greeting cards and influenced an estimated one hundred industries. "We will be judged by public opinion," he told his associates, "by the job we do." Byoir's firm continued to flourish, and in March 1978, it was merged with the advertising firm of Foote, Cone and Belding Communications but continued to operate independently and to retain its own name. Carl Byoir died in New York City on February 3, 1957.

FURTHER READING: Scott Cutlip, *The Unseen Power: Public Relations, a History* (Hillsdale, NJ: Lawrence Erlbaum Associates, 1994).

C

CADORE LETTER. On August 5, 1810, Jean, Duc de Cadore, French Foreign Minister, delivered a diplomatic note to U.S. Minister John Armstrong. In it, Napoleon I promised to revoke the Berlin and Milan Decrees in November 1810 if the British Orders-in-Council were repealed or if the United States reinstated sanctions against Great Britain. The latter happened, and nonintercourse against the British resumed on February 28, 1811. The Cadore letter turned out to be a forgery. American ships continued to be seized, and President James Madison refused to change his decision with regard to the British embargo.

See also Forgeries

FURTHER READING: Clifford L. Egan, *Neither Peace nor War: Franco-American Relations, 1803–1812* (Baton Rouge: Louisiana State University Press, 1983).

CAMPAIGN IN CUBA. *See* Spanish-American War

CAMPAIGN OF TRUTH. On April 20, 1950, President Harry Truman gave a foreign policy speech to the American Society of Newspaper Editors in which he recognized that the U.S. government was not doing enough in the international information field and called upon his audience "to meet false propaganda with truth all around the globe" with a much greater and more militant "campaign of truth." After his speech, Truman requested the Departments of State and of Defense to reappraise the position of the United States in world affairs and to recommend a course of action. After extensive discussion and analysis in both departments, a program was developed for reference to the National Security Council (called NSC 68), approved, and put into effect. A program was mapped out country by country, target group by target group, and area by area. From the propaganda aspect, this plan was particularly significant in that for the first time the U.S. government officially recognized psychological activities as one of the four basic means of influencing foreign affairs; the other three were military, economic, and diplomatic. It was specifically stated that all of these four means were to be used together. The five basic objectives were: multiply and intensify psychological deterrents to aggression by Soviet Communism; intensify the growth of confidence among the

Cover: "Stalin's Red Dove of Peace." (*Source:* Leaflet distributed to posts by State Department's Division of International Press and Publications as part of the "Campaign of Truth")

people and the governments of the free world, especially in Western Europe; combat extremist tendencies, especially in Southeast Asia, that threaten the stability of the free world; continue hope of ultimate liberation among peoples held captive by Soviet Communism; and maintain a continued recognition of mutual interdependence, particularly in Latin America.

A propaganda campaign was developed to portray the Soviets as a group of blunderers rather than as an enormously efficient and evil machine and to induce Titoism within communist groups in Western Europe. Its minor campaign was "to make the satellite [country] leaders" jittery and "to revive the concept of

America as an 'arsenal of democracy.'" There was a need for an interplay of psychological warfare and political leadership for maximum effectiveness and the need to employ psychological warfare methods and concepts. Along with this, there was a proposal for the establishment of a United States Information Administration (USIA) within the State Department to administer an expanded Campaign of Truth.

FURTHER READING: U.S. Dept. of State, *The Campaign of Truth: How You Can Help* (Washington, DC: Department of State, 1950?); U.S. Dept. of State, *Suggested Answer to the Frequently Asked Question of Whether We Have a Basic Plan for the "Campaign of Truth?"* (Office Memorandum, November 28, 1951).

CANTRIL, ALBERT HADLEY (June 16, 1906–May 28, 1969). Public opinion researcher and social psychologist who established the Office of Public Opinion Research, Princeton University in 1940; later renamed Institute for International Social Research. His first attempt to use surveys for policy research was to analyze propaganda coming into Latin America for Nelson A. Rockefeller, **Coordinator of Inter-American Affairs**, and President **Franklin D. Roosevelt**. Cantril was probably the most important source of polls reaching the White House. He was a liberal, loyal to the president, and determined to make the polls serve Roosevelt. To accomplish this, Cantril designed his polls for maximum political utility and conducted many of his surveys at the president's suggestion. He employed a special technique that produced fairly accurate preliminary findings, compared to his competition, and provided data for trend charts that Cantril constantly updated. During World War II, Cantril was an expert consultant to the secretary of war and to the **Office of War Information**.

Cantril was the founding associate editor, *Public Opinion Quarterly*. His many publications include *General and Specific Attitudes* (1932), a study for the Harvard Psychological Laboratory; the classic **Psychology of Radio** with G. W. Allport (1935), which examined the formation of public opinion; *Psychology of Social Movements* (1941); *How Nations See Each Other; a Study in Public Opinion* (1953); *Politics of Despair* (1958); *Pattern of Human Concerns* (1966); *Human Dimension: Experiences in Policy Research* (1967); and *Political Beliefs of Americans; a Study of Public Opinion* (1967). He edited *Gauging Public Opinion* (1944); *Tensions That Cause War* (1950), a common statement with individual papers by a group of social scientists brought together by UNESCO; and *Public Opinion, 1935–1946* (1951), opinion poll results collected from 23 organizations in 16 countries. He also contributed to *Public Opinion in a Democracy* (1947), a series of articles written by Dartmouth men for their alumni magazine. In 1948, he headed a UNESCO project, "Tensions Affecting International Understanding" ("Tensions Project") and served as a consultant to President Eisenhower.

Hadley Cantril tried to induce the consideration of psychological factors in the making of crucial government decisions through several presidential administrations. Beginning with World War II, he tried to use public opinion to shape important policy announcements, to get the public to understand certain domestic policies, and to improve international relations. Cantril's son, Albert Hadley, became a public opinion analyst.

FURTHER READING: Hadley Cantril, *Psychology, Humanism, and Scientific Inquiry: The Selected Essays of Hadley Cantril* (New Brunswick, NJ: Transaction Books, 1988); Richard W. Steele, *Propaganda in an Open Society* (Westport, CT: Greenwood, 1985).

CAPRA, FRANK. *See* "Why We Fight" Series

CARICATURES. *See* Cartoons

CARROLL, JOHN WALLACE (December 15, 1906–July 28, 2002). John Wallace Carroll was born in Milwaukee, Wisconsin, son of John F. Carroll and Josephine Meyer. He graduated from Marquette University (1928), then worked as a foreign correspondent for United Press International, 1928–1941. Carroll covered the Spanish Civil War, was a diplomatic correspondent in London, and witnessed the first two years of World War II from the Russian front. During World War II, he directed psychological operations from the London office for the **Office of War Information,** 1942–1943, and he was a psychological warfare adviser to General Dwight D. Eisenhower. However, Carroll and three of his top assistants resigned suddenly in December 1943 because of the lack of support he received from OWI's Overseas Branch, but he returned as Deputy Director, Overseas Branch, OWI (for Europe), 1944–1945. Carroll supported the theory of President Roosevelt that unconditional surrender did not mean the destruction of Germany, Italy, or Japan. In the spring of 1944, Carroll argued that Josef Goebbels, Germany's propaganda minister, would persuade the Germans that unconditional surrender meant "slavery, castration, the end of Germany as a nation." He considered propaganda "a weapon of a definite but limited utility" that could occasionally produce visible results under favorable conditions.

After the war, Carroll was a consultant to the **U.S. Department of State's Psychological Strategy Board** (PSB) and to other U.S. government agencies in 1947–1952. Carroll became an editor at the *Winston-Salem (N.C.) Journal and Sentinel* (1949–1955) and then at the *New York Times,* 1955–1963, then returned to the *Journal* as editor and publisher before retiring in 1973. A highlight was a frequently reprinted editorial, "Vietnam—Quo Vadis?" that first appeared in the *Winston-Salem Journal and Sentinel* (March 17, 1968); Carroll argued that the Johnson administration was wrong about Vietnam, wasting valuable resources on a minor country while ignoring the real threat of Soviet expansion.

He was the author of *Inside Warring Russia: An Eye-witness Report on the Soviet Union's Battle, Compiled From Dispatches, Censored and Uncensored* (New York: United Press Associations, 1942), *We're in This With Russia* (Boston: Houghton Mifflin, 1942), and *Persuade or Perish* (Boston: Houghton Mifflin, 1948). Carroll married Margaret Sawyer in 1938; they had four children.

FURTHER READING: Richard Pearson, "Wallace Carroll Dies; Journalist's Editorial Turned Vietnam Policy," *Washington Post,* July 30, 2002: B4; Allan M. Winkler, *Politics of Propaganda: The Office of War Information, 1942–1945* (New Haven, CT: Yale University, 1978); *Who's Who in America, 1974–1975,* 38th ed. (Wilmette, IL: Marquis Who's Who, 1974).

CARROLL, WALLACE. *See* Carroll, John Wallace

CARTER, BOAKE (HAROLD THOMAS HENRY) (September 28, 1898–November 16, 1944). Born in Azerbaijan, Baku, part of the Russian Empire, of English parents, Boake Carter moved to England as a child, was educated at Cambridge, and served in the Royal Air Force in World War I. He worked for dailies in London, in Mexico City, and in Philadelphia and became an American citizen in 1933. He broke into radio in 1930 and came into national prominence two years later through covering the Lindbergh kidnapping case and became one of the most famous political commentators of the late 1930s. He was affiliated with the Columbia Broadcasting System after 1932, where he was an influential commentator with a distinctive, English-accented voice punctuated by American idioms and a sign-off, "Cheerio," that was nationally known.

Carter interviewed prominent personalities and caused some controversies by not checking his facts before broadcasting his stories. He was a strong isolationist who believed that U.S. involvement abroad was interference and not in the national interest. His persuasive radio voice strengthened extreme isolationist sentiment in the mid-1930s and led to accusations that he favored totalitarianism and was sympathetic to Father **Charles E. Coughlin**; he also spoke at meetings of the right-wing Christian Front. He supported President Roosevelt's reelection in 1936, but turned against him the next year with such vehemence that government investigators began checking his background. CBS tried to restrain him but until the fall of 1938, when the Munich crisis stirred up public interest in radio newscasts, Carter was the only newscaster who had a significant audience.

In 1938, his sponsor, General Foods, refused to renew his contract, which effectively silenced him, but he continued with his newspaper column and returned to the air the next year on the Mutual Broadcasting System but with fewer stations and a new religious zeal ("biblical Hebrew"). Carter married Beatrice Olive Richter (1924); he died in Hollywood. Carter was a pioneering news analyst and commentator and the author of *Black Shirt, Black Skin* (1935), a popular account of the Italo-Ethiopian War; *"Johnny Q. Public" Speaks! The Nation Appraises the New Deal* (1936); *I Talk As I Like* (1937); *This is Life* (1937), a compilation of his broadcasts; *Made in U.S.A.* (1938); *Why Meddle in the Orient?* (1938); and *Why Meddle in Europe?* (1939).

FURTHER READING: David H. Culbert, *News for Everyman: Radio and Foreign Affairs in Thirties America* (Westport, CT: Greenwood, 1976); *Current Biography 1942*; Richard W. Steele, *Propaganda in an Open Society* (Westport, CT: Greenwood, 1985).

CARTO, WILLIS. *See* Institute for Historical Review

CARTOONS. An important propaganda tool, cartoons represent one of the earliest and most popular forms of American propaganda because they are visual and easy to understand. They are both animated and print images. American editorial cartooning probably began in 1747 with "Non Votis" or "The Wagoner and Hercules," usually attributed to **Benjamin Franklin**, who is also associated with another early political cartoon, "**Join, or Die,**" which appeared in the *Pennsylvania Gazette.* The engraver was Paul Revere, whose 1770 engraving, "The Boston Massacre," was widely circulated for its propaganda value. The satirical thrust of these cartoons continued through the War of American Independence, with some, such as "Magna Britannia: Her Colonies Reduced," for distribution in England to sway the English Parliament toward a more lenient colonial policy. However, few cartoons actually appeared in this period.

The next phase started with the developments in lithography, a process that was much faster than woodcuts and engravings. The first lithographed cartoon appeared in 1829, and a major producer of these cartoons was Currier and Ives, who marketed cartoons for both sides of a controversial issue, slavery, through the campaigns of 1856 and 1860, and then into the Civil War. In the post–Civil War years, now called the Gilded Age, the outstanding cartoonist or caricaturist to judge by his drawings and sketches was the German-born Thomas Nast (1840–1902), who became famous for his scathing attacks on Boss Tweed and his ring of political corruption in Tammany Hall from the pages of *Harper's Weekly*. In the first decade of the twentieth century, a popular target for cartoonists was President Theodore Roosevelt, who with his distinct features (glasses, mustache, teeth) kept cartoonists active for years, as did World War I, which provided a rich lode for cartoonists, as they were able to lampoon "the Hun," especially the Kaiser (Wilhelm II), but other cartoons promoted the image of Uncle Sam. The **Committee on Public Information**, set up by President Wilson to promote the war effort on the home front, made full use of cartoons in its many publications and posters.

The 1920s and its high-living image after the deprivations of World War I offered another fertile field with boot-legging and the Jazz Age, but all crashed with the Great Depression and the real poverty it initiated. Cartoons became sharp and bitter as thousands of Americans fell into poverty and the government tried to help them while restoring the financial equilibrium.

The 1930s saw the development of Walt Disney's animated cartoons, which began with Mickey Mouse and the Silly Symphonies. Their success encouraged Disney to try a full-length feature animated film, *Snow White and the Seven Dwarfs* (1937), with its vividly drawn characters of good (Snow White) and bad (Stepmother), followed by *Pinocchio*, *Fantasia*, and *Bambi*. The markets for these films, and other Hollywood features, in Latin America and Europe closed off as war approached.

When President Franklin Roosevelt created the Works Progress Administration (WPA), he made it possible for artists and musicians to work during a period when the arts suffered. Although some of its components, such as the **Federal Theater Project**, were closed by Congress after controversial productions, the **Federal Arts Project** managed to turn out much work that still has value today. Many cartoonists became artists and illustrators on WPA projects and continued this service with the **Office of War Information** in World War II, another rich lode of opportunity for cartoonists. Besides the unparalleled opportunities it offered to lampoon the easily caricatured Axis leaders, Hitler, Hirohito, and Mussolini, and the Nazis, there was also the simple heroism of Bill Maudlin's "Willy and Joe" characters, a salute to the American GI. Maudlin continued his work with the *St. Louis Post-Dispatch* after the war, when he lampooned the Russian Cold War hysteria and targeted the civil rights struggles. During World War II, the Hollywood studios enlisted cartoon characters, such as Mickey Mouse and Donald Duck, to help the war effort. These cartoons were used as morale builders in the

Cartoons from the World's Free Press. (*Source*: USIA-Regional Publication Center, Manila; photo by Lorin Reeder, USIA overseas)

United States and to explain dated references ("Is this trip really necessary?" for conserving gasoline). A popular one was "Die Fuehrer's Face" with Donald Duck that satirized the Axis leaders, introduced a catchy title song, and won an Oscar.

The 1950s introduced two other important cartoonists, Herbert Block ("Herblock") and the Australian-born Patrick Oliphant. Herblock became one of the best-known cartoonists of the last part of the twentieth century. Beginning with his first major phase, McCarthyism, and carrying through to the 1990s, Herblock stroked deftly and accurately the Cold War; Lyndon Johnson, Nixon, Reagan, and Clinton presidencies; and the false steps of these administrations. His images moved profoundly (his portrait of slain President Kennedy, the moon landing) and lashed sharply (Vietnam, Watergate). Oliphant was influenced by the style of British cartoonist Ronald Searles, and he is considered a true satirist.

The Cold War also provided opportunities for the artists in the Press and Publications Service at the **U.S. Information Agency**. Perhaps the best known was "Little Moe: His Life Behind the Iron Curtain" by Philip Brady, who depicted the beleaguered Little Moe as he outwitted the Soviets, but USIA published comic books on American history (*Eight Great Americans*), science (*The Atom*) and the political situation (*When the Communists Came* and *Cartoons From the World's Free Press*).

Today, graphic satire has changed considerably since the golden age of political cartooning at the close of the nineteenth century and the heyday of Thomas Nast, Joseph Keppler, and Bernarn Gilliam, among others. Cartoon artists now use the "mother lodes" of popular culture, especially films, television programs, animated cartoons, and comic strips, to attack political figures and movements, but there has been little linkage between genius and fairness.

FURTHER READING: Eberhard Damm, "Propaganda and Caricature in the First World War," *Journal of Contemporary History* 28, no. 1 (January 1993): 163–192; Michael

Denning, *The Cultural Front: The Laboring of American Culture in the Twentieth Century* (London and New York: Verso, 1997); Roger A. Fischer, *Them Damned Pictures: Explorations in American Political Cartoon Art* (North Haven, CT: Archon Books, 1996); Maurice Horn, ed. *World Encyclopedia of Cartoons*, 2d ed. (New York: Chelsea House, 1999); Guy Lamolinara, "Savage Glee: A Pictorial Satire of the Gilded Age," *Library of Congress Information Bulletin* 54, no. 4 (February 20, 1995): 68–75).

CATHOLIC CHURCH. Anti-Catholicism, a concerted and coordinated opposition on principle to the Roman Catholic Church, has made it one of the most heavily propagandized religious groups; it began as early as 1700s. Its origins are lost in obscurity, but its modern development was one of the fruits of the Reformation. The rise of the modern secular state has intensified the conflict.

The assistance given by Canadian and by French Catholics in the American Revolution softened Americans toward the Catholic Church, but in 1779, John Adams warned the Continental Congress not to send an envoy to the Papal States because he feared the pope "would send to Washington a Catholic legate or nuncio; in other words, an ecclesiastical tyrant, which, it is to be hoped, the United States will be too wise ever to admit into their territories."

Anti-Catholicism remained more of a religious sentiment than an active political agenda for the first few decades of the United States. There was economic competition with a heavily Catholic immigrant population willing to take almost any job. To attack this, literature was published that implied immorality and scandal among Catholic priests, nuns, and lay members. Then there were the anti-Catholic "exposes," such as *Priestcraft Unmasked and Priestcraft Exposed*, the first of many books to offer unsubstantiated rumors of Catholic "scandals," which were profitable for their authors. George Bourne published his novel, *Lorette: the history of Louise, daughter of a Canadian nun, exhibiting the interior of female convents* (1833). The next year, the Reverend Lyman Beecher heightened anti-Catholic fears with his reactionary *Plea for the West*, three incendiary sermons in which he claimed that the pope was orchestrating a massive influx of Catholics into the Mississippi valley region to "overrun" Protestants and force Americans to return to "feudal institutions." Following this, a mob led by John Buzzell burned the Ursuline convent on Mount Benedict in Charlestown, Massachusetts, on August 11, 1834.

In 1835, Rebecca Theresa Reed, an "escaped" nun, published *Six Months in a Convent*, her tales of dreadful happenings when she lived at the Ursuline convent in Charlestown, Massachusetts, and a probable counterattack to support Buzzell's 1834 arson trial. Her book proved only that convent life was boring but hardly immoral or lascivious. However, the "revealing" bestseller came the next year when Maria Monk published her notorious *Awful Disclosures of the Hotel Dieu Nunnery of Montreal*, in which she "revealed the secrets of the black nunnery" and many other incidents "never before published." Monk evidently worked with William L. Stone, whose own falsehoods against the convent were soon rebutted, but her book was an immediate commercial success. The Protestant press found the work a "frank and credible exposition of the tawdry corruptions rampant throughout the Catholic Church," and sales continued at a record pace to make Monk's "disclosures" an enormous best seller. An impartial inspection of the Hotel Dieu convent by two Protestant clergyman proved all the allegations groundless and provided evidence of Monk's questionable character, but this did nothing to kill public enthusiasm for this outrageous anti-Catholic propaganda. Then, in 1868, Hiram Mattison contributed to the anti-Catholic furor with his book about the abduction of Mary Ann Smith by the Roman Catholics and her imprisonment in a nunnery. Alleged evil doings in convents also appeared later in Julia Wright's *Secrets of the Convent and Confessional* (1872). *Trials and Persecutions of Miss Edith O'Gorman: Otherwise Sister Teresa de Chantal of St. Joseph's Convent Hudson City N.J.* (1871) proved to be another hoax.

Some early nineteenth-century forms of anti-Catholicism included five sermons against popery by Thomas Secker in 1827, a continuing antebellum Protestant encounter with Catholicism. Then in 1830, a group of Protestant ministers launched the *Protestant*, an anti-Catholic weekly, which spearheaded the nativist movement that targeted many racial and ethnic groups, including Roman Catholicism, one of its most consistent targets. According to John Higham, there were four major periods of anti-Catholic nativism. The first took place prior to the American revolution when the "papal anti-Christ" cry rallied colonists against Catholic France and, later, the king of England, who was head of the papal-like Anglican Church. The second period, more intense than the first, came in the mid-1800s with the massive Catholic immigration from Ireland and from Germany, which incited fears of subversion from foreign powers and stimulated the emergence of the Know-Nothing Party.

Anti-Catholic developments in this pre-Civil War period included Edward Beecher's "expose" of a papal conspiracy (1854) and publication of William Hogan's controversial three-volume work, *Popery! As it was and as it is: also, Auricular confession and popish nunneries* (1856). The next year, Justin Dewey added to the anti-Catholic controversy with his book, *The Roman Catholic Element in American History.*

In the late 1880s, a third period ensued in a period of rapid growth, labor strife, and economic difficulty. The American Protective Association (APA) revived anti-Catholic images of the "Catholic Beast," blamed hard times on Irish Catholic labor leaders, "uncovered" a secret papal plot to massacre American Protestants, and refused to vote for a Catholic, hire one if Protestants were available ("No Irish Need Apply"), or join Catholics in a strike.

The fourth outbreak was directed from rural areas against urban Catholic political power and new immigrant groups. It existed sporadically between 1905 and 1930 in such publications as *Tom Watson's Magazine*, in the resurgence of the Ku Klux Klan, and in the emergence of fundamentalist thinking that imagined satanic conspiracies in the Catholic menace to keep the "papal anti-Christ" in proper perspective.

In 1949, tensions increased with publication of secularist Paul Blanshard's *American Freedom and Catholic Power* (1949); the author believed that America had a "Catholic problem" with a Church that was an "undemocratic system of alien control" and a laity enslaved by the "absolute rule of the clergy." The book went through six printings in as many months and sold hundreds of thousands of copies in the 1950s. In 1950, Blanshard published *Communism, Democracy, and Catholic Power*, which attacked Catholic patriotism and labeled Moscow and Rome as "two alien and undemocratic" centers of "thought control" and the "management of truth." During the 1960 presidential campaign, when the Catholic John F. Kennedy defeated Richard M. Nixon, Maria Monk's *Awful Disclosures* was reissued.

In 1990, anti-Catholicism was the subject of Steven Watt's Mid-America American Studies Association's presidential address, "Saving the West from the Pope," which focused on the roots of nativist sentiment on the American cultural landscape. Today, anti-Catholicism in the United States is neither gone nor forgotten.

FURTHER READING: Wilfred J. Bisson, *Countdown to Violence: The Charlestown Convent Riot of 1834* (New York: Garland, 1989); Lynn Dumenil, "The Tribal Twenties: 'Assimilated' Catholics' Response to Anti-Catholicism in the 1920s," *Journal of American Ethnic History* 11, no. 1 (Fall 1991): 21–49; Robert C. Fuller, *Naming the Antichrist: The History of an American Obsession* (New York and Oxford: Oxford University Press, 1995); Andrew Greeley, *An Ugly Little Secret: Anti-Catholicism in North America* (Kansas City: Sheed Andrews and McMeel, 1977); Bryan LeBeau, "'Saving the West from the Pope': Anti-Catholic Propaganda and the Settlement of the Mississippi River Valley," *American Studies International* 32, no. 1 (Spring 1991): 101–114, the author's response to Steven Watt's 1990 Mid-America American Studies Association's presidential address that focused on the roots of anti-Catholicism that bore fruit over time across the American cultural landscape; Michael Schwartz, *The Persistent Prejudice: Anti-Catholicism in America* (Huntington, IN: Our Sunday Visitor, 1984).

CATO'S LETTERS. These documents were first printed in the 1720s in the London and British journals as *Cato's Letters: or, Essays on Liberty, Civil and Religious, and Other Important Subjects.* They were a series of letters, actually written by John Trenchard and Thomas Gordon, and "first printed weekly in the London and British journals," but issued "without any name, from Bath, as letters to the author of the London journal, who sign'd them Cato, and by that name they afterwards went." They were printed in the eighteenth-century English press as treatises on political liberty, representative government, and freedom of expression. The essays were reprinted in American newspapers, retaining the pen name "Cato" that was first used with the *Independent Whim* (1720–1721) and in the *London Journal* and in the *British Journal* between 1720 and 1723; in 1724 they were published in four volumes. American papers that reprinted them included James Franklin's *New England Courant*, Andrew Bradford's *American Weekly Mercury*, and John Peter Zenger's *New York Weekly Journal*. The letters strongly influenced the movement of the colonies toward revolution and independence.

CENTRAL AMERICA. *See* **Binational Centers; Buenos Aires Convention for Promotion of Inter-American Cultural Relations; Comics and Comic Strips; Coordinator of Inter-American Affairs (CIAA); Cuban Freedom Committee; Libraries; Radio Marti; Television Marti**

CENTRAL INTELLIGENCE AGENCY (CIA). The evolution of an official intelligence-gathering operation began in 1882 when the Navy created the nation's first spy service, the Office of Naval Intelligence, to determine the ability of foreign countries to engage U.S. ships at sea. Three years later, the Army set up an analogous service, the Military Information Division.

The shortcomings of these early spy operations became evident during World War I, when the Army set up a more sophisticated spy group, known as MI-8, to detect enemy agents, primarily by intercepting and decoding German correspondence. After the war, the Army disbanded MI-8, but the group's work continued to be carried out by the so-called "Black Chamber," the country's first civilian spy agency. Soon after its founding in 1919, the small and highly secretive **U.S. Department of State** operation had broken the diplomatic codes of most of America's allies and foes alike.

Intelligence activities were controversial from the start. Newly appointed Secretary of State Henry L. Stimson unceremoniously disbanded the Black Chamber in 1929, noting that, "Gentlemen do not read each other's mail." The business of gathering intelligence on other countries was handed over to the State Department's normal diplomatic channels. As Europe edged closer to World War II, President Franklin D. Roosevelt called on World War I hero **William J. Donovan** to help improve the quality of intelligence reaching Washington. Over the strong objections of FBI Director J. Edgar Hoover and the heads of military spy groups fearful of losing power, the president in 1941 appointed Donovan to head the new office of the **Coordinator of Information**, which was to collect and analyze all data of interest to national security.

In 1942, after the U.S. entry into the war, Donovan's fledgling group was renamed the **Office of Strategic Services** (OSS), with responsibility for both military and diplomatic intelligence. The agency received valuable help in perfecting its methods from the respected British secret service, MI-6.

Despite its successes during the war, President Harry S Truman bowed to public pressure from Hoover and congressional critics and disbanded the OSS in 1945, but less than a year later, Truman reversed his OSS decision to deal with the sudden onset of the Cold War. Closed out of the Soviet Union in the aftermath of World War II, American policy makers had no reliable information on which to base U.S. policy toward the wartime ally turned adversary. By contrast, covert action had been an integral part of Soviet foreign policy since the USSR was founded in 1922. To counter Stalin's KGB, Truman decided the United States needed a permanent, peacetime intelligence capability.

The CIA formally began in 1947 with a mission to coordinate the intelligence collection by various government agencies as needed for conducting U.S. foreign policy. Its first chief was Rear Admiral Roscoe M. Hillenkdetter (1947–1950), who launched the agency's first covert operation, financing the Christian Democrats in Italy by using, among other techniques, a leaflet campaign to defeat their opposition.

Propaganda activities undertaken by the CIA are complex, and they are organizationally part of the covert action cadre. Its propaganda tools have covered a wide spectrum, including the spread of "white" (openly distributed), "gray" (of lightly concealed origin), and "black" (of completely concealed origin), balloon leaflet campaigns, decals and wall-painting, press placement, rumor, radio, motion pictures, and data for political speeches. The CIA supported **Radio Free Europe** and **Radio Liberty** until they were exposed in the 1960s and were then publicly funded by Congress. At the beginning of the Carter administration and then expanded during the Reagan administration, the CIA made publicly available information on Soviet active measures, which led the United States to upgrade its own propaganda efforts.

See also **Congress for Cultural Freedom; Front Organizations**

FURTHER READING: Arthur B. Darling, *Central Intelligence Agency: An Instrument of Government, to 1950* (University Park, PA: Pennsylvania State University, 1990); U.S.

Dept. of State, *Foreign Relations of the United States, 1945–1950: Emergence of the Intelligence Establishment* (Washington, DC: Government Printing Office, 1996).

CENTURY GROUP. Interventionist group (1940–1941) formed in July 1940 by Lewis W. Douglas, Herbert Agar, Bishop Henry Hobson, Francis P. Miller, Whitney Shephardson, and Admiral William Standley. The organization took its name from the Century Association, a private club in New York City where the group, which soon had twenty-eight members, held its meetings. The group believed that the United States should declare war immediately to halt **Germany**'s march toward world domination, which would become most likely if Britain fell under German control. Aware of the need to change public opinion, the group used endorsements, personal influence, news releases, and lobbying tactics to show the folly of isolationism and the desirability of war. Through Douglas's liaison work, the Century Group established close relations with the **Committee to Defend America by Aiding the Allies,** but the group was actually more militant. They came with the idea of the destroyers-for-bases deal at a time when Congress was objecting because the British asked for the destroyers without offering anything in return.

FURTHER READING: Mark L. Chadwin, *Warhawks: The Interventionists of 1940–1941* (Thesis—Columbia University, 1966); Robert A. Divine, *The Reluctant Belligerent; American Entry into World War II* (New York: Wiley, 1965).

CHAMBERS, WHITTAKER (April 1, 1901–July 9, 1961). Born in Philadelphia, Pennsylvania, as Jay Vivian Chambers, Whittaker Chambers joined the infant Communist Party in 1925, which used his writing talent for its propaganda. He was praised for his "authentic" portrayals of the working-class struggle. In 1931, he joined an underground group in Washington, D.C., that passed classified documents to Soviet military intelligence. In 1937, horrified by the Soviet purge trials, he broke with the Communists and went into hiding. During the Soviet-Nazi Pact, 1939–1941, he became a fervent anti-communist. Chambers went to work for *Time* magazine, where he was a favorite of its publisher, Henry R. Luce. By 1944, Chambers was a foreign news editor who began a tireless campaign to expose Stalinist Russia, then a wartime ally, as an oppressive regime determined to spread communism throughout the world; he was largely correct, but few paid attention. In 1948, he was summoned as a witness before the House Un-American Activities Committee. He described a "Communist cell" in Washington and named Alger Hiss, then head of the Carnegie Endowment for World Peace, as one of its key members. He avoided revealing that the group was involved in espionage. He claimed that it was merely to influence policy. When Hiss was summoned by the HUAC, he lied under oath and sued Chambers for calling him a Communist on national radio. Chambers retrieved a "life preserver" of documents and of microfilm ("pumpkin papers") that showed that Hiss and others supplied secret documents to Soviet intelligence. Hiss was convicted of perjury.

After the trial, Chambers retired to his Westminster, Maryland, farm, wrote his autobiography, *Witness* (1952), and was an editor of William F. Buckley's *National Review* (1957–1959). After his death, he was awarded a posthumous Medal of Freedom by President Ronald Reagan in 1984. On his death, Arthur Koestler wrote: "The witness is gone, the testimony will stand."

FURTHER READING: Patrick Swan, ed., *Alger Hiss, Whittaker Chambers, and the Schism in the American Soul* (Wilmington, DE: ISI Books, 2003); Sam Tanenhaus, *Whittaker Chambers* (New York: Random House, 1997); Allen Weinstein, *Perjury: The Hiss-Chambers Case* (New York: Random House, 1997).

CHANDLER, DOUGLAS. *See* **U.S.A. Zone of the Overseas Service (North American Service)**

CHANGING MINDS, WINNING PEACE. This report, subtitled *A New Strategic Direction for U.S. Public Diplomacy in the Arab and Muslim World*, was issued in October 2003 by the Advisory Group on Public Diplomacy for the Arab and Muslim World, a subcommittee of the U.S. Advisory Commission on Public Diplomacy, at the request of the House Committee on Appropriations. Its chair was Edward P. Djerejian. The report recommended dramatically increased funding for public diplomacy in the Arab and Muslim world and for specific public diplomacy programs, with additional resources and staff to carry out these efforts. Specific programs included increased English-language training programs, expanded **American Corners**, and a new initiative, American Knowledge Library, that would translate thousands of the best American books in many fields of education into local languages and make them available to libraries, American Studies centers, universities, and American Corners.

FURTHER READING: Advisory Group on Public Diplomacy for the Arab and Muslim World, *Changing Minds, Winning Peace: A New Strategic Direction for U.S. Public Diplomacy in the Arab and Muslim World* (Washington, DC: The Group, 2003).

Cover: *Changing Minds, Winning Peace: A New Strategic Direction for U.S. Public Diplomacy in the Arab and Muslin World.* (*Source:* Advisory Group on Public Diplomacy for the Arab and Muslim World)

CHAPLIN, CHARLES SPENCER (April 16, 1889–December 25, 1977). Charlie Chaplin, who was one of America's most beloved film stars, grew up in the East End of London. He started as a music hall comedian, then came to Hollywood, where he quickly became a famous star; his creations included "The Little Tramp" character. During World War I, he supported the Allied cause by giving public speeches to encourage Americans to buy government bonds. Chaplin did not have the same success in talkies as he did in silent films but his film, *Great Dictator* (1940), a satire on Adolf Hitler and the Nazi regime in Germany, was an important propaganda film that attacked the Axis leaders (Hitler and Mussolini), but before its release, Chaplin added an oration expressing pacifist sentiments, as this was during the Soviet–Nazi Pact. During World War II, he made several speeches praising the Soviet military effort on the Eastern Front. In the postwar climate, his procommunist sympathies made him suspect, and he was subpoenaed by the House Un-American Activities Committee in 1947. After three postponements, he was never asked to testify, but his political stance cost him public support. In 1952, he moved to Switzerland to avoid an investigation by the U.S. Department of Justice and to avoid paying U.S. taxes; these actions received heavy media criticism. Chaplin did not return to the United States until 1972, when he was awarded an honorary Oscar. He was knighted in 1975.

FURTHER READING: Jerry Epstein, *Remembering Charlie: A Pictorial Biography* (New York: Doubleday, 1989); Georgia Hale, *Charlie Chaplin: Intimate Close-ups*, ed. by Heather Kiernan (Metuchen, NJ: Scarecrow, 1995); David J. LeMaster, "The Pathos of the Unconscious: Charlie Chaplin and Dreams, *"Journal of Popular Film and Television* 25, no. 3 (Fall 1997): 110–117; Kenneth S. Lynn, *Charlie Chaplin and His Times* (New York: Simon and Schuster, 1997); David Robinson, *Chaplin: His Life and Art* (New York: Da Capo, 1994); Jeffrey Vance, *Chaplin: Genius of the Cinema* (New York: Harry N. Abrams, 2003).

CHESAPEAKE AFFAIR (1807). Naval incident that was used as propaganda. The U.S.S. *Chesapeake*, a frigate, was fired upon June 22, 1807, in the Atlantic Ocean off Norfolk, Virginia, by the British warship *Leopard*, resulting in three deaths and eighteen wounded. A boarding party from the *Leopard* removed four deserters from the British Navy, three of whom were American. This event caused a great public outcry against Great Britain in the United States, and many Americans urged war. However, President Thomas Jefferson moved the country toward the Embargo Act instead.

FURTHER READING: Reginald Horsman, *The Causes of the War of 1812* (New York: Octagon Books, 1972; reprint of the 1962 ed.); Bradford Perkins, *Prologue to War, England and the United States, 1805–1812* (Berkeley: University of California Press, 1968); Burton Spivak, *Jefferson's English Crisis: Commerce, Embargo, and the Republican Revolution* (Charlottesville: University Press of Virginia, 1979).

CHILD ORGAN TRAFFICKING. *See* **Baby Parts**

CHINA. *See* **China White Paper; Smedley, Agnes; Strong, Anna Louise**

CHINA WHITE PAPER. Originally issued in August 1949 by the State Department as *United States Relations with China, with Special Reference to the Period*

1944–1949. This was an important statement that defended U.S. policy toward China, but it was an unsuccessful propaganda move by the U.S. government. In his introduction, Secretary of State Dean Acheson claimed that nothing the U.S. did would have prevented a Communist victory in the Chinese civil war, but his statements and those presented in the White Paper were highly criticized as a falsified record that omitted important documents, which, if printed, would have materially altered the facts. It was insinuated that the White Paper was not "the full historical record," and charges were made by Congressman Walter Judd of the House Foreign Affairs Committee that the State Department suppressed materials, including a report on the Chinese Communists prepared by the Military Intelligence Division of the War Department (1945). In a rebuttal to sixteen charges of "dishonesty" in the White Paper by Judd, the State Department defended its position and the integrity of the research.

FURTHER READING: "Department of State Answers Criticism on China Policy," *Department of State Bulletin* (September 5, 1949): 350–352, 359; Francis R. Valeo. *The China White Paper: A Summary; with Commentary of the Department of State's "United States Relations with China"* (Washington, DC: The Department, 1949; also published in: *Public Affairs Bulletin*, no. 77 [1949]).

CHURCHES AND PROPAGANDA. *See* Anti-Semitic Propaganda; Catholic Church

CIVIL WAR PROPAGANDA. The American Civil War initiated propaganda campaigns from both the North and the South. President Lincoln imposed the first official U.S. government censorship of news media during wartime and issued an executive order, based on national emergency, that punished journalists for disloyalty, such as reporting unfavorable or inaccurate battle news. Lincoln also dispatched special agents to European countries to counter propaganda gains made by the Confederacy. As sectional differences became more pronounced and war became inevitable, leaders from both the Union and the Confederacy appreciated the importance of propaganda to the conflict. In the North, the war remained unpopular, as emphasized by draft riots in New York (1863) and by the rise of the "Copperhead movement" that fielded peace candidates; as late as 1864, propaganda mobilized public opinion both at home and abroad. On the battlefields, military leaders instituted press conferences, press passes, and author bylines to censor battle reportage unfavorable to the Union. In the North, private organizations, such as the Loyal Publication Society and the Union League Board of Publications, began unceasing pamphleteering efforts.

The Loyal Publication Society, established 1863, sent publications to Europe that tried to promote the Union side during the Civil War. George P. Putnam (1814–1872) was one of the society's editors. For the North, there was Abraham Lincoln's moving letter to working men of Manchester, England's cotton mills, asking them to shun alliances with plantation slaveholders. The president also dispatched about one hundred special agents to Great Britain along with a ship of foodstuffs for unemployed English cotton-textile workers to counter the propaganda attacks made by the Confederacy. The federal government also distributed pamphlets to European countries asking for Union support.

The Great Rebellion had the advantage as the first major war fought in the United States with a general literacy. With strong philosophical and ideological differences between the Northern and the Southern leaderships, the increasing presence of large numbers of foreign-born immigrants who needed to be "Americanized," and the lack of support for the war among large segments of the nonsecessionist population, pamphlets and broadsides proliferated as both sides prepared for what all realized would be an extended and bloody conflict.

Confederate propaganda in Europe was mostly directed to England and to France under the expertise of **Henry Hotze**, but there was also Southern activity in Ireland and in Germany as well as Confederate sympathizers in the North who distributed leaflets and other publications of Confederate sympathizers. There were serious Confederate attempts to win British support, including the publication of *The Index*, the pro-Confederate organ that generated support for its cause. Hotze went there to generate favorable public opinion toward the Confederacy, often without adequate financial resources or capable colleagues; he achieved outstanding success in England, where he went to generate favorable public opinion toward the Confederacy, whereas his Federal opponent, **Edwin De Leon**, with a much larger budget, proved to be a misfit in France. It is still debated among Civil War scholars whether the "battle between the states" was a British empire-sponsored insurrection coordinated through a coalition of proslavery secret societies, Latin American expansionists, and financial interests that sought to weaken U.S. competition with English interests.

Along with Hotze and De Leon, probably the best known, there were other propagandists of considerable talent. Sarah Jane Clarke Lippincott (1823–1904), known as Grace Greenwood, wrote famous Washington political letters for the *New York Times*. She was born in Pompey, New York; at 21, she contributed verse to Nathaniel P. Willis's magazine, *New Mirror*, and later, pieces to his *Home Journal*. She joined *Godey's Lady Book* in 1849 but lost her job when she wrote an antislavery article for the *National Era*; she then began her Washington letters, which appeared for the next 50 years in papers in various American cities. From 1873 to 1878, Lippincott wrote for the *New York Times*, commenting on government and attacking corruption. During the Civil War, she lectured to patriotic groups and in army camps and hospitals, and President Lincoln called her "Grace Greenwood, the Patriot."

John Reuben Thompson (1823–1873), a staunch secessionist, supported the Confederacy through his editing, his poems ("Music in Camp," "The Burial of Latane," "Lee to the Rear," and "Ashby"), and his work as a propagandist in England, where he wrote for *The Index* while James Williams (1796–1869) was a journalist and diplomat who had a distinguished career before the Civil War when he returned to Europe as a Confederate propagandist and minister at large. In London he assisted Henry Hotze, where he effectively presented the history of the sectional struggle between North and South and explained the slavery question in articles to various British newspapers. Some of his essays on slavery were published as *Letters on Slavery from the Old World* (1861), revised as *The South Vindicated*. Hotze had it translated into German and circulated among the German people. In 1863, Williams published *The Rise and Fall of the Model Republic*. While trying to promote European public opinion toward the Southern cause, he kept in touch with Confederate diplomats and maintained a secret correspondence with President Jefferson Davis.

Augusta Jane Evans Wilson (1835–1901), author of *Beulah*, was published just before the Civil War (1859). In 1864, she published *Macaria; or, Altars of Sacrifice*, a persuasive defense of Confederate policy that predicted horrible consequences if the slaves were freed. It was popular in both the North and in the South but was banned by some Union commanders because of its adverse effect on morale.

See also Abolitionist Propaganda

FURTHER READING: Charles P. Cullop, *Confederate Propaganda in Europe, 1861–1865* (Coral Gables, FL: University of Miami, 1969).

CIVIL WAR TOKENS. During the Civil War, coins were in short supply and as there was no law against people issuing unofficial coins, penny-sized tokens were issued by merchants with their advertising slogans and by others with patriotic or unpatriotic slogans. One of the patriotic slogans quoted General John Dix: "The flag of our Union if anyone attempts to tear it down, shoot him on the spot." One of the unpatriotic tokens read "Millions for contractors not one cent for the widows." There are at least 12,000 different varieties of these tokens. In 1864, unofficial coins were outlawed.

FURTHER READING: Grover C. Criswell and Herb Romerstein, *The Official Guide to Confederate Money and Civil War Tokens, Tradesmen and Patriotic* (New York: HC Publishers, 1971).

CLANDESTINE RADIO STATIONS. Clandestine radio stations should not be confused with pirate radio stations, which are also unlicensed. Clandestine stations are usually operated by revolutionary groups or by intelligence agencies that usually leave behind no documentary evidence of their existence, and unlike printed propaganda, there are no artifacts left behind. A clandestine station often pretends to come from within the country it serves while actually coming from someplace else, often hundreds or even thousands of miles away. Much of what is known about clandestine radio stations is usually no more than educated guesswork.

The first known evidence of clandestine stations appeared in the 1930s, when radio receivers became widely available. In 1931, the Czech post office, which oversaw telecommunications in the country, asked for police assistance in locating a "secret Communist broadcasting station" that evaded detection by moving its operation from one location to another to avoid seizure. The station broadcast to Communist sympathizers in Czech, German, and Hungarian and could be heard throughout the country, according to a report in the *New York Times* (March 19, 1931, p. 11). In the same period, the Irish Republican Army (IRA) broadcast clandestine programs in Northern Ireland; a clandestine station briefly surfaced during an uprising against Cuban dictator Machado in 1933; and there was Radio Free Spain in existence during the Spanish Civil War, which continued to broadcast until the mid-1970s, operating largely from the Soviet Union and Romania.

After Hitler came to power in Germany, several clandestine stations appeared, operated by anti-Nazi dissidents, and during World War II, clandestine radio stations became routine with both the Allied and the Axis powers to complement other propaganda campaigns, such as Radio 1212, which claimed to be a German-based and German-operated anti-Nazi station but was actually transmitted behind

Allied lines by the Psychological Warfare Bureau, U.S. Army. Most of these World War II clandestine stations disappeared by the end of the war.

The earliest clandestine station operated by the United States seems to have broadcast to Morocco from the naval battleship *Texas*. A 10-kilowatt transmitter aboard the ship broadcast pro-Allied programs on a wavelength next to that occupied by Radio Morocco while Radio Moscow reportedly warned its listeners to "beware" of the clandestine broadcasts. For the **Central Intelligence Agency**, clandestine stations were another part of their covert operations that were discovered years after the fact. Free Voice of Iran broadcast reports on corruption and opposition to the regime of the Ayatollah Khomeini that were first carried by American newspapers as accurate sources of information. Later it was discovered that the CIA was operating the radio station. During the Cultural Revolution in China, the CIA operated clandestine stations on Taiwan that claimed to broadcast from within the People's Republic of China to increase the turmoil within that country. This covert operation was so successful that its real origin was not discovered by the U.S. press, academics, State Department analysts, and other parts of the U.S. intelligence community for many years. U.S. clandestine stations continued to operate through operations in Cambodia and in Vietnam and were part of military operations in European countries.

Clandestine stations are classified as either black or gray. Gray radio refers to clandestine stations attributed to or allegedly operated by dissident groups within a country. Voice of the Revolution, a station operated by the Caribbean Legion, which tried to overthrow Rafael Trujillo (1949), and Free Voice of Iran are examples of gray stations. Black stations are "broadcasts by one side that are disguised as broadcasts by another." The Soviet version of Radio Beijing and the CIA-operated version of the Vietnamese Liberation Radio, the clandestine actually operated by the NLF (National Liberation Front) of South Vietnam, are black broadcasting stations; they claim to be stations of the opposition when they are not. Stations that operate legally, openly identify themselves, and whose purpose is to propagandize, such as **Radio Free Europe** and **Radio Liberty**, are "white" radio stations.

See also Debunk; Operation Annie; Radio Broadcasting by the U.S. Government; Radio Caiman; Radio Swan; Soldatensender Calais

FURTHER READING: Donald R. Browne, *International Radio Broadcasting: The Limits of the Limitless Medium* (New York: Praeger, 1982); Lawrence C. Soley and John S. Nichols, *Clandestine Radio Broadcasting: A Study of Revolutionary and Counterrevolutionary Electronic Communication* (New York and Westport, CT: Praeger, 1987).

COBBETT, WILLIAM ("PETER PORCUPINE") (March 9, 1763–June 18, 1835). Born in England, William Cobbett was a political journalist and pamphleteer and a founder of the partisan press in America. He viewed a newspaper as a "cut and thrust weapon," and he wrote in a vituperative, vitriolic, and violent style while using the first-person singular. Cobbett attacked Jeffersonian Republicans, called for an alliance with England and war against France, and vilified **Thomas Paine**, which he later regretted and tried to redeem. During the 1797 yellow fever epidemic in Philadelphia, he claimed that Dr. Benjamin Rush was killing his patients through excessive bloodletting, a charge that proved true, but Rush sued for libel and won a $5,000 award. Cobbett

William Cobbett. (*Source:* Library of Congress, Prints and
Photographs Division)

published *Porcupine's Gazette and the Daily Advertiser*, a Federalist, pro-British
newspaper (1797–1799). He twice exiled himself from the United States. The
first time, in 1792, he exposed British army corruption and quickly fled England;
he returned home in 1800. Cobbett spent two years in prison (1810–1812) for
criticizing the practice of flogging and again left after the "Gagging Bills" of
1817. He returned two years later to England to agitate for parliamentary reform. From 1802 to 1835, Cobbett published irregularly the *Political Register*, a
reform journal, and was tried in July 1831 in the Court of King's Bench, London, for libel. He was elected to Parliament (1832); wrote books, such as
Grammar of the English Language (1818), *A Year's Residence in the United
States* (1818–1819), and *Rural Rides* (1830); and wrote pamphlets, including *A
Bone to Knaw for the Democrats* and *A Kick for a Bite* (both 1795). Cobbett's
pamphlets were compiled and published as *Peter Porcupine in America* (1994).

Cobbett's detractors were savage in their counterattacks. *The Last Confession
and Dying Speech of Peter Porcupine: With an Account of His Dissection* (1797)

was a political lampoon on Cobbett, as was James Carey's various attacks, including *A Pill for Porcupine: Being a Specific for an Obstinate Itching Which that Hireling Has Long Contracted for Lying and Calumny* (1796), which contained "a vindication of the American, French and Irish characters against his scurrilities"; *A Nosegay, for the Young Men from 16 to 24 Years of Age* (1798), which was dedicated to the "hireling skunk Porcupine, with his petition to the corruption, of the city of Philadelphia"; and *Anticipation! Peter Porcupine's Descent into Hell* (1797). Carey was rebutted with *Tit for Tat; or A Purge for a Pill: Being an Answer to a Scurrilous Pamphlet, Entitled "A Pill for Porcupine"* (1796). Other critics published the weekly *Anti-Cobbett* (February–April 1817) to counteract what they considered his "dangerous errors." Cobbett died in England.

FURTHER READING: George D. H. Cole, *The Life of William Cobbett* (New York: Russell and Russell, 1925; reprinted: Westport, CT: Greenwood, 1971); Ian Dyck, *William Cobbett and Rural Popular Culture* (Cambridge, England, New York: Cambridge University, 1992); Leonora Nattrass, *William Cobbett: The Politics of Style* (Cambridge, England, New York: Cambridge University, 1992/1995); David A. Wilson, *Paine and Cobbett: The Transatlantic Connection* (Kingston: McGill-Queen's University Press, 1988).

COLD WAR. Important term and concept (*cold war* as opposed to *hot war*) that represents the thinking of that time. Common term that describes the state of relations between the United States and its allies and the Soviet Union and its allies after World War II. It unofficially ended with the fall of the Berlin Wall in 1989. The origin of the term is usually credited to Winston Churchill's March 1946 speech in Fulton, Missouri, when he declared that the Cold War had begun and that the United States must give up its dream of Big Three unity in the United Nations. What is certain is the intense propaganda war campaign that both sides waged against each other in an effort to influence international opinion and to gain allies, especially among Third World nations. This was highlighted by an event that has come to symbolize the definitive Cold War rivalry, the **Brussels Universal and International Exposition**, which is remembered for the Cold War tensions that developed, especially between the Americans and the Russians, who built rival pavilions, literally across from each other, that propagandized their different political systems. The Soviet pavilion was a high-tech tribute to Communism, whereas the U.S. pavilion was considered a front for American intelligence agencies, a charge never effectively proved. When the exposition ended, the United States was criticized for its poor showing in what was primarily a Cold War propaganda battle with the Soviet Union.

FURTHER READING: Kenneth M. Jensen, ed. *Origins of the Cold War: The Novikov, Kennan, and Roberts "Long Telegrams" of 1946* (Washington, DC: U.S. Institute of Peace, 1991); U.S. Library of Congress, *Drawing the Iron Curtain: Cold War Cartoons, 1946–1960* (Washington, DC: The Library, 1996); Bernard A. Weinberger, *Cold War Cold Peace: The United States and Russia Since 1945* (Boston: Houghton Mifflin, 1984).

COMBAT PROPAGANDA. *See* **Psychological Warfare**

COMIC BOOKS. *See* **Comics and Comic Strips**

COMIC STRIPS. *See* Comics and Comic Strips

COMICS AND COMIC STRIPS. Throughout the twentieth century, comic strips have been one of the prime conveyors of popular American images and effective propaganda weapons, especially in Europe. Early syndicated comic strips, such as Winsor McCay's *Little Sammy Sneezes* and Richard Felton Outcault's *Buster Brown*, were translated and published in book form in France at the beginning of the twentieth century, but it was not until the 1930s that American comics became really popular in Europe. Not surprisingly, it started with the marketing of Walt Disney comics in hardbound collections and in weekly magazines. Later, European publishers printed American comic strips, such as Hal Foster's *Prince Valiant*, George McManus's *Bringing Up Father*, Phil Davis's *Mandrake the Magician*, Ray Moore's *The Phantom*, and Alex Raymond's *Flash Gordon*. These comic characters became quite familiar images to many European children in the pre–World War II period. In the late 1940s, the State Department saw comic books and comic strip art as an exciting and effective new means of fighting Communist propaganda. Between 1948 and 1950, the U.S. government actively solicited comic books from various sources to reach mass audiences worldwide with the American message of freedom and of democracy. In the 1950s and 1960s, the **U.S. Information Agency** distributed its message in the format of comic books (e.g., *Eight Great Americans, The United Nations, The Atomic Bomb*) that were visually attractive and easy to understand. In Latin America, the **U.S. Information Agency** produced several comic books that, although humorous, addressed serious issues for that region, such as birth control and literacy.

However, U.S. comic strips were not popular in all European countries, at least by their governments. Germany, Italy, and Spain were experiencing political difficulties, and the Catholic Church still controlled juvenile entertainments in Belgium and in the Netherlands, so they were not receptive to an art form that highlighted Protestant America. Comic books maintained a growing popularity in Great Britain and in France, but it was really in France that U.S. comics were most enjoyed by children who didn't seem to have the parental and institutional control prevalent during the late 1930s as in the rest of Europe. Ironically, this control of U.S. comic strips led to the emergence of the European comic strip, especially in Belgium, which saw the rise of comic publishers and the great comic strip artist Herge (Georges Remi) and his creation, "Tintin," and in France, which passed a 1949 law that regulated material in children's magazines, specifically too much action and violence, a definite anti-American measure. By the 1950s, Franco-Belgian comics established credibility of the comic book art and marginalized U.S. comics, which still appeared but as cheaply made black-and-white pamphlets. The influence of U.S. comics on their European counterparts came from American movies and popular literature, especially science fiction and westerns.

During World War II, the *Joe Palooka* comic strip by Hammond Fisher was used by the war effort for recruitment, the promotion of hygiene, instruction in languages, and custom guides. Fisher put his boxer into uniform, and the strip followed the American GI into all the major battle zones and then returned with him to civilian life. At the end of World War II, the U.S. military used *Joe Palooka* as an educational comic book to help soldiers readjust to their postwar

Six language versions of the USIA publication, *When the Communists Came!* (*Source:* USIS-Regional Publication Center, Manila; photo by Lorin Reeder)

lives as civilians. German propaganda minister Josef Goebbels called *Palooka* "the most vicious of anti-Nazi propaganda." During the Nazi regime, U.S. and foreign comic strips were strictly forbidden, and Goebbels' propaganda directory never relied heavily on comics as a means of propaganda. Germany never had a chance to develop a comics-making tradition relying on national products because the Americans flooded the existing market with their own products after World War II. Until the fall of the Berlin Wall and the opening of democratic traditions, the only comic strips available in German bookstores were translations of Franco-Belgian material and a few Spanish and Italian comic strips. Now there are a few German-created strips available in bookstores, but comics sales figures in Germany are much lower than in other European countries.

During the 1950s, the comic strip *Little Moe: His Life Behind the Iron Curtain*, created by USIA artist Philip Brady, became a satirical but funny attack on the Soviet dictatorship as the little character engaged in all types of activities to outwit "Big Brother Russia" and the Communist regime to make his life more comfortable. His frustrations, miseries, and subtle triumphs over his oppressors were depicted in pantomime cartoon strips understandable even to the world's illiterates. Within one year of its debut, it reached an estimated 100 million persons weekly through 850 newspapers overseas. The strip was abolished in 1961. In the late 1960s and early 1970s, during the turbulent Cold War years, Europe was inundated with translations of Marvel comic strips, such as *Batman*, while the *Peanuts* characters, including Charlie Brown, Lucy, Linus, and Snoopy, created by Charles Schultz, enchanted readers worldwide with their simple morals in a humorous but nonpreachy format. Always very popular with religious groups, exhibitions of the *Peanuts* characters have been displayed at the Louvre, in Paris, among other internationally known art palaces.

FURTHER READING: Jean-Paul Gabilliet, "A Comics Interlude," in *European Readings of American Popular Culture*, ed. John Dean and Jean-Paul Gabilliet, 23–42 (Westport, CT: Greenwood, 1996); Kenneth W. Heger, "Rich Foreign Relations Ore: The Department of State Office Files," *The Record* 4, no. 2 (November 1997): 14–16; Howard Oiseth, *Way It Was: USIA's Press and Publications Service, 1935–77* (Washington: United States Information Agency, 1977); Roger Sabin, *Adult Comics: An Introduction* (New York: Routledge, 1993).

COMMISSION ON ORGANIZATION OF THE EXECUTIVE BRANCH OF THE GOVERNMENT (HOOVER COMMISSION). Commission that suggested the establishment of an independent information agency to handle propaganda. Chaired by former President Herbert Hoover, the Commission on Organization of the Executive Branch of the Government was established by Public Law 162 (July 7, 1947) to investigate and to recommend a possible reorganization of the Executive Branch. The Task Force Report on Foreign Affairs was appointed in January 1948 by the Commission to investigate organizational policy and principles. In its January 1949 report, *Organization of the Government for the Conduct of Foreign Affairs*, it found it desirable to separate the bulk of the operational responsibility of the information and cultural activities from the State Department. In another report, *Foreign Affairs*, the Hoover Commission called on the Department to free the Assistant Secretary for Public Affairs from the day-to-day management of the information program by creating a General Manager to operate it. It was further recommended that the Assistant Secretary concentrate on serving as a high-level staff adviser on domestic and foreign public opinion and as chief of press relations for the State Department. Finally, the Commission called for the merger of all personnel involved in foreign affairs into a unified personnel system.

The State Department issued *An Organizational Plan for the Office of the Assistant Secretary of Public Affairs* in April 1949 with its proposed implementation of the recommendations by the Hoover Commission. At the request of the U.S. Bureau of the Budget, the Brookings Institution prepared this study as an attempt by the Executive Branch to carry out the recommendations of the Commission, which had proposed a survey of overseas administration be made. The staff and witnesses were primarily drawn from the staff of the Hoover Commission or from persons long associated with the information and cultural program. The 1951 report, *Administration of Foreign Affairs and Overseas Operations*, recommended that the information program in the Economic Cooperation Administration should be merged with that in the State Department.

FURTHER READINGS: Brookings Institution, *Administration of Foreign Affairs and Overseas Operations* (Washington, DC: The Institution, 1951); Commission on Organization of the Executive Branch of the Government. Task Force Report on Foreign Affairs,

Organization of the Government for the Conduct of Foreign Affairs (Washington, DC: Government Printing Office, 1949); U.S. Dept. of State, *An Organizational Plan for the Office of the Assistant Secretary of Public Affairs* (Washington, DC: The Department, 1949).

COMMITTEE FOR FOREIGN AFFAIRS. *See* **Committee of Secret Correspondence**

COMMITTEE FOR NATIONAL MORALE. Private organization, affiliated with the interventionist Council for Democracy, founded in 1940 as a forum for psychologists, sociologists, political scientists, and other public opinion experts to diagnose and suggest remedies for morale problems. Members included experts such as Gordon Allport, Ruth Benedict, Hadley Cantril, Leonard Doob, Erik Erikson, Erich Fromm, Geoffrey Gorer, George Gallup, and Margaret Mead. They collected data, formulated basic principles, and published their findings on morale and propaganda. In their report to the White House, the committee concluded that, among other issues, propaganda could not be left to speech makers, journalists, politicians, or others associated with it in the past but should be handled by practical experts who knew how to manipulate the public. President **Franklin D. Roosevelt**, who supported the importance of psychological warfare, agreed with this recommendation and provided White House funds for the committee to compile a list of experts for a proposed super morale agency. This agency was supported by Roosevelt advisor Harold Ickes but strongly opposed by Lowell Mellett, head of the Office of Government Reports, who argued that such an agency would have difficulty getting its messages accepted; there could be no national propaganda policy until there was a consensus for an interventionist policy. After weak attempts at a compromise, the Office of Civilian Defense was created.

FURTHER READING: Committee for National Morale, *White Book of the United States Foreign Policy, 1932–1942* (New York: Authentic Publications, 1942); Ladislas Farago, ed., *German Psychological Warfare* (New York: G. P. Putnam's Sons for the Committee for National Morale, 1942); Richard W. Steele, *Propaganda in an Open Society: The Roosevelt Administration and the Media, 1933–1941* (Westport, CT: Greenwood, 1985).

COMMITTEE OF SECRET CORRESPONDENCE. Formed November 29, 1775, by the Continental Congress, this committee, the first U.S. intelligence agency, was to correspond "with our friends in Great Britain, Ireland and other parts of the world." Its first action was to direct Arthur Lee in London to send secret information to America regarding the attitudes of foreign nations toward the rebellious colonies. After April 1777, it was the Committee for Foreign Affairs, and in 1781, the secretary of foreign affairs for the Continental Congress assumed the responsibilities of the Committee for Foreign Affairs. Following the adoption of the U.S. Constitution (1789), the **U.S. Department of State** handled foreign affairs.

FURTHER READING: Samuel F. Bemis, *The Diplomacy of the American Revolution* (Westport, CT: Greenwood, 1983/1957).

COMMITTEE ON INFORMATION ACTIVITIES ABROAD. *See* **President's Committee on International Information Activities.**

COMMITTEE ON INTERNATIONAL INFORMATION ACTIVITIES. *See* President's Committee on International Information Activities

COMMITTEE ON PUBLIC INFORMATION. The United States was the last major power to enter World War I, but it was the first to establish an open, fully coordinated propaganda unit. American propaganda was coordinated by the Committee on Public Information (CPI), the first official propaganda agency in American history, established by President Woodrow Wilson on April 13, 1917, one week after the United States entered the war, by Executive Order No. 2594 with the staggering task of "holding fast the inner lines" by encouraging and then consolidating the revolution of opinion that changed the United States from an antimilitaristic democracy to an organized war machine. Advertising executive **George Creel** was appointed the civilian chairman "to sell the war to America" with the assistance of the secretaries of state, of war, and of navy.

To help attain its goals, CPI (or the Creel Committee, as it became known) established a national speakers' bureau of "four-minute men" who stirred audiences with carefully timed short propaganda messages supporting Liberty Bond sales drives. Creel also recognized the importance of films and arranged for cooperation between the private motion picture industry, including newsreel companies, and the military.

Another effective war item was the **poster;** individual governments flooded their countries with millions of propaganda posters designed to encourage public support for total victory. American artists who volunteered their talents to the war effort included Norman Rockwell, James Montgomery Flagg (whose "I Want You For U.S. Army" **Uncle Sam** recruiting poster was the best known of the period), and Charles Dana Gibson (creator of the Gibson girl). CPI distributed more than 100 million of these patriotic posters and other publications, including *Official Bulletin*, first published in May 1917, to increase support for the war, and it was the first U.S. large-scale entry into information activities abroad. It conducted anti-Bolshevik propaganda campaign in Russia following the collapse of the Czarist regime and effectively used various media to cooperate with educators, labor organizations, and corporate leaders to create an effective internal propaganda campaign, as well as "the fight for the mind of mankind" overseas. With the end of the war, most Americans desired a return to normalcy, and CPI was quickly abolished in 1919 along with a limited use of U.S. government propaganda efforts. There was a congressional attempt to suppress Creel's 1920 public report, *How We Advertised America*, describing the true nature of CPI's propaganda activities, but the CPI director was proud of his wartime activities and detailed the history of the CPI's foreign and domestic sections with an account of the tumultuous period of postwar demobilization. Creel's publications included *What Have Women Done With the Vote?* (1914), *Wilson and the Issues* (1916), and *The War, the World and Wilson* (1920), created in April 1917 to guide and shape public attitudes about the war while avoiding direct censorship and interference with the press. CPI focused its attention on both its domestic and foreign audience. The committee instituted voluntary press censorship, produced films, hired speakers (especially the "Four Minute Men" who gave speeches of that length), distributed literature that praised the nations allied with the United States, commissioned posters, bought newspaper ads, and sent agents to

Cover: Pamphlet, *How the War Came to America*. Original copy issued by Washington: Government Printing Office, 1917. (*Source:* Committee on Public Information; Red, White and Blue Series)

targeted countries. Leaflets were attached to hydrogen balloons and dropped from airplanes and shot from guns to get the American message to the German people, what CPI head George Creel called "the world's largest adventure in advertising."

FURTHER READING: George Creel, *How We Advertised America: The First Telling of the Amazing Story of the Committee on Public Information that Carried the Gospel of Americanism to Every Corner of the Globe* (New York: Arno Press, 1972); James R. Mock and Cedric Larson, *Words That Won the War: The Story of the Committee on Public Information, 1917–1919* (Princeton: Princeton University Press, 1939); Stephen Vaughn, *Holding Fast the Inner Lines: Democracy, Nationalism, and the Committee on Public Information* (Chapel Hill: University of North Carolina, 1980).

COMMITTEE ON UN-AMERICAN ACTIVITIES, HOUSE. *See* U.S. Congressional Investigations of Propaganda

COMMITTEE TO DEFEND AMERICA BY AIDING THE ALLIES. Interventionist organization, 1940–1941, created by William Allen White and Clark Eichelberger after the German offensive in May 1940. The Committee to Defend America by Aiding the Allies (CDAAA; commonly called the "White Committee") became a national organization with over 300 local chapters to lobby and influence public opinion in favor of aid to Britain and to other allies in the European war to ensure an Axis defeat. CDAAA cooperated with the **Century Group** and other internationalist organizations, such as **Fight for Freedom Committee**, to support measures such as the bases-for-destroyers deal, Lend-Lease, and American convoys. During the campaign for Lend-Lease, for example, the committee distributed a pamphlet outlining the situation if Germany attacked the Western Hemisphere and a movie, *It Could Happen Here*, on the vulnerability of the United States to a Nazi attack. By 1941, the committee edged toward supporting intervention and was credited, along with European events, in forcing a major shift in American public opinion concerning aid to Britain and in making entry into the war more acceptable. Sentiment quickly shifted to the Fight for Freedom Committee.

FURTHER READING: Richard W. Steele, *Propaganda in an Open Society: The Roosevelt Administration and the Media, 1933–1941* (Westport, CT: Greenwood, 1985).

COMMITTEES OF CORRESPONDENCE. Several types of committees have been designated Committee of Correspondence, including committees appointed by colonial legislatures to correspond with colonial agents in England. During the Revolutionary period, local Committees of Correspondence, Safety and Inspection, became the vehicles of colonial protest. These committees were formed between November 1772 (the first was in Boston, the famous committee through which **Samuel Adams** and his colleagues stirred up opposition to British colonial rule) and 1774 to serve as communications link and to ignite public opinion toward independence from Great Britain. The complete plan for unifying the action of these colonial assemblies came from Thomas Jefferson and Richard Henry Lee, who in March 1773 secured the appointment of a standing committee of eleven members, all anti-British Whigs, by the Virginia House of Burgess. By 1774, every assembly except Pennsylvania established a standing committee of correspondence, which was supposed to be free from decisions of the royal governors. An example of this was when bitterness over the Tea Act and passage of the Intolerable Acts required united action. The Massachusetts assembly ordered the Boston Committee of Correspondence to draft a pamphlet stating the rights of the colonists and their grievances and to send copies of the Boston Port Act to other assemblies with requests for support. These letters contained the basics of propaganda for stirring up public opinion for the "insulted, beseiged [sic] capital of Massachusetts Bay."

FURTHER READING: Edward D. Collins, "Committees of Correspondence of the American Revolution," *Annual Report of the American Historical Association* (1902): 243–271; Philip Davidson, *Propaganda and the American Revolution, 1763–1783* (New York: Norton, 1973, 1941).

COMMUNIST FRONT ORGANIZATIONS WITH SPECIAL REFERENCE TO THE NATIONAL CITIZENS POLITICAL ACTION COMMITTEE. *See* **Appendix Nine**

CONCORD, BATTLE OF. *See* Lexington and Concord, Battle of

CONFEDERACY. *See* Civil War Propaganda

CONFEDERATE MONEY. *See* Civil War Tokens

CONGRESS, U.S. *See* U.S. Congress. House. Committee on Un-American Activities; U.S. Congressional Investigations of Propaganda

CONGRESS FOR CULTURAL FREEDOM. The Congress for Cultural Freedom (CCF) was an important propaganda organ that began in June 1950 from a Berlin conference to "inoculate the world against the contagion of Communism and to ease the passage of American foreign policy interests abroad" by countering a worldwide Soviet propaganda campaign. It was widely considered one of the CIA's more daring and effective Cold War covert operations. It published literary and political journals, such as the influential *Encounter* (United Kingdom), *Preuves* (France), and *Quest* (India); hosted dozens of international conferences that brought together some of the most eminent Western thinkers; created music festivals and jazz concerts; and did what it could to help intellectuals behind the Iron Curtain. In 1967, CIA sponsorship of the Congress for Cultural Freedom was exposed. CCF was renamed International Association for Cultural Freedom in 1977.

The idea for the CCF began in March 1949 at New York's Waldorf-Astoria Hotel, the setting for the pro-Soviet Cultural and Scientific Conference for World Peace, a peace conference that included over 800 literary and artistic figures, including Lillian Hellman, Aaron Copland, Arthur Miller, and Norman Mailer, who met in the Waldorf to repudiate "U.S. warmongering." One of the participants, Sydney Hook, editor of *New Leader*, and his mentor, John Dewey, had earlier founded a controversial group called the Committee for Cultural Freedom, which attacked both Communism and Nazism. Hook now organized a similar committee to expose the peace conference in the Waldorf-Astoria, Americans for Intellectual Freedom.

In August 1949, a crucial meeting took place in Frankfurt. American journalist Melvin J. Lasky, together with a pair of ex-Communists, Franz Borkenau and Ruth Fischer, hatched a plan for an international conference of the non-Communist Left in Berlin the following year. With the backing of several prominent Berlin academics, a committee of American and European thinkers organized the event and invited participants, selecting them on the basis of their political outlook, international reputation, and popularity in Germany. The congress was used to bring about the creation of some sort of permanent committee, which, with a few interested people and a certain amount of funds, could maintain the degree of intellectual and rhetorical coordination expected to be achieved in Berlin. The answer was covert funding.

Michael Josselson stepped forward to promote the proposal late in 1949. Josselson had witnessed the shaky beginnings of the anti-Communist counteroffensive in New York and Paris that spring while he was still working as a cultural officer for the American occupation government in Germany. He told his composer friend Nicolas Nabokov that Berlin needed something similar. At some point that autumn, Josselson talked with Melvin Lasky about the Berlin conference idea. The Josselson proposal reached Washington in January 1950. The Congress for Cultural Freedom convened in Berlin's Titania Palace on June 26, 1950. American delegates Hook, James Burnham, James T. Farrell, playwright Tennessee Williams, historian Arthur Schlesinger, Jr., actor Robert Montgomery, and chairman of the Atomic Energy Commission David Lilienthal were greeted on arrival with the news that troops of North Korea had launched a massive invasion of the South, an event that heightened the sense of apprehension in the hall. The congress's opening reflected this mood. Lord Mayor Reuter asked the almost 200 delegates and the 4,000 other attendees to stand for a moment of silence in memory of those who had died fighting for freedom or who still languished in concentration camps.

U.S. Department of Defense representative Gen. John Magruder deemed it "a subtle covert operation carried out on the highest intellectual level" and "unconventional warfare at its best" in a memo to Secretary of Defense Louis Johnson. U.S. occupation officials in Germany sensed that the CCF boosted the morale of West Berlin, but they believed the event's most important effect would be felt by Western intellectuals who had been politically adrift since 1945.

FURTHER READING: Peter Coleman, *The Liberal Conspiracy: The Congress for Cultural Freedom and the Struggle for the Mind of Postwar Europe* (New York: Free; London: Collier Macmillan, 1989); Frances S. Saunders, *Cultural Cold War: The CIA and the World of Arts and Letters* (New York: New Press, 2000); Hugh Wilford, "Playing the CIA's Tune? The New Leader," *Diplomatic History* 27, no. 1 (January 2003): 15–34.

CONSTITUTION, U.S. *See The Federalist*

COORDINATOR OF INFORMATION. As Europe edged closer to World War II, **William J. Donovan** was working in 1940–1941 with senior analysts in the British Secret Intelligence Service, including Sir William Stephenson, who helped Donovan develop a relationship with British intelligence that would frustrate Axis operations in the Western Hemisphere to help bring the United States into World War II and ensure Allied victory. The foundation of an official U.S. intelligence service originated from this Anglo-American liaison.

President **Franklin D. Roosevelt** called on World War I hero Donovan to improve the quality of intelligence reaching Washington. Donovan passed on the idea to President Roosevelt who established the Office of the Coordinator of Information (1941) with Donovan at its head. Earlier drafts of the presidential order mentioned a Coordinator of Strategic Information and a Coordinator of Defense Information.

Donovan was appointed by President Franklin D. Roosevelt as the Coordinator of Information on July 11, 1941, and was to collect and analyze all data of interest to national security. COI was established over the strong objections of FBI Director J. Edgar Hoover and officials in the **U.S. Department of State**, the Army, and the Navy, who were fearful of losing power, and a bitter dispute with **Office of Coordinator of Inter-American Affairs** (CIAA) director Nelson Rockefeller eliminated Latin America from Donovan's propaganda responsibility.

The forerunner of CIA, the Office of the Coordinator of Information (COI) was established by presidential order (July 11, 1941) "to collect and analyze all information and data, which may bear upon national security; to correlate such information and data; and to make such information and data available to the President and to such departments and officials of the Government as the President may determine." Propaganda functions were performed through its Foreign Information Service (FIS) Branch. The **Voice of America** (VOA) began in FIS as did the U.S. information program; both became part of **Office of War Information** in June 1942. Secret intelligence stayed with OSS.

FURTHER READING: Arthur B. Darling, *Central Intelligence Agency: An Instrument of Government, to 1950* (University Park: Pennsylvania State University, 1990); Thomas F. Troy, *Wild Bill and Intrepid: Donovan, Stephenson and the Origin of the CIA* (New Haven, CT: Yale University, 1996); U.S. Dept. of State, *Foreign Relations of the United States, 1945–1950: Emergence of the Intelligence Establishment* (Washington, DC: Government Printing Office, 1996).

COORDINATOR OF INTER-AMERICAN AFFAIRS. In 1938, a Division of Cultural Relations was established in the **U.S. Department of State** to handle official propaganda directed at Latin Americans. In conjunction with this, an Interdepartmental Committee on Scientific and Cultural Cooperation (SCC) and Division of Cultural Cooperation were established in the State Department. President Franklin Roosevelt created the Office of the Coordination of Commercial and Cultural Relations Between the American Republics (OCCCRBAR) by Council of National Defense order on August 16, 1940. Nelson A. Rockefeller was appointed the coordinator. It was abolished by Executive Order 8840 (July 30, 1941), and its functions were transferred to the **Office of Coordinator of Inter-American Affairs** (CIAA).

CIAA was primarily concerned with commercial and financial problems of the Latin American countries. However, an increase in defense preparations and the creation of the Board of Economic Warfare made it essential that CIAA increasingly identify with cultural relationships, primarily to counter Nazi propaganda in that region. Under CIAA auspices, there were exchange of persons programs, binational centers and libraries; in 1942, the first U.S. government-sponsored library opened in Mexico City.

Its Motion Picture Division, set up in October 1940, was directed by John Jay Whitney, vice president of the Museum of Modern Art and president of the Film Library. CIAA's film activities were notable for educational cartoons by Walt Disney and its vigorous exhibition policy carried on with traveling shows. An agreement on part of U.S. distributors to withdraw all U.S. films from theater operators who showed Axis films was a major achievement in an informational war. Immediate effects resulted in an increased showing of newsreels. Except in Argentina, German and Japanese newsreels ceased to be generally shown, but it became necessary for CIAA to provide other materials.

It was a war information agency. If Rockefeller had not made strenuous efforts to keep the American Republics separate as an area of cultural exchange, the Budget Bureau would have combined the agency with the others that formed the **Office of War Information** in June 1942. During World War II, Rockefeller

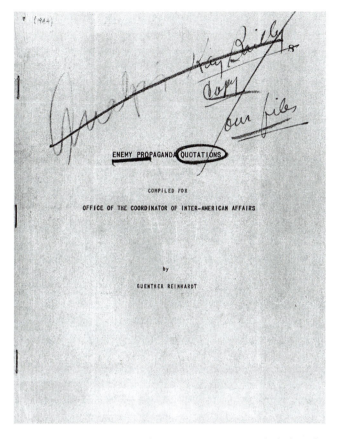

Cover: Enemy Propaganda Quotations, compiled for the Office of the Coordinator of Inter-American Affairs, by Guenther Reinhardt.

promoted a favorable U.S. image in this region. CIAA became the Office of Inter-American Affairs in 1945 but was abolished in 1946 when it transferred its functions into the State Department. Its cultural activities were absorbed into the **U.S. Information Agency** in 1953.

See also **Office of Strategic Services**

FURTHER READING: J. Manuel Espinosa, *Inter-American Beginnings of U.S. Cultural Diplomacy, 1936–1948* (Washington, DC: Bureau of Educational and Cultural Affairs, U.S. Department of State, 1976); Alton Frye, *Nazi Germany and the American Hemisphere, 1933–1941* (New Haven, CT and London: Yale University, 1967); Richard D. MacCann, *The People's Films: A Political History of U.S. Government Motion Pictures* (New York: Hastings House, 1973).

COUGHLIN, CHARLES EDWARD (October 25, 1891–October 27, 1979). Charles Coughlin was the "radio priest" who commanded an audience of millions with anti-Communist and anti-Semitic broadcasts over a forty-seven-station hookup in the 1930s that advocated neutrality and sometimes used propaganda themes promoted by the Nazis. He was born in Hamilton, Ontario, and educated at the University of Toronto. After ordination, Coughlin taught school for ten years before being assigned to his Royal Oaks parish. In 1926, he started broadcasting over WJR, Detroit; four years later, eighteen stations were carrying his speeches in which he attacked "international bankers" and doomed democracy. By 1934, he was heard over twenty-eight stations, held huge rallies in several cities, and received thousands of letters and contributions supporting his cause. Coughlin was a strong supporter of President Franklin Roosevelt until 1936, the year he formed the Union Party, which ran its own presidential candidate, excoriated Roosevelt as "anti-God," and sponsored the anti-Semitic Christian Front in 1939. A. B. Magil, a Communist party propagandist, wrote in *New Masses* that "the American Hitler may have died with Huey Long but the Paul Joseph Goebbels of Royal Oaks believes his successor will come."

Coughlin published the weekly magazine *Social Justice* "in the interest of the National Union for Social Justice," his organization, from March 13, 1936–April 20, 1942; it was criticized as anti-Semitic (it published a series of articles updating the classic forgery, *Protocols of the Learned Elders of Zion*) and antiwar. The newspaper was virulently anti-Communist ("You Can't Compromise with a Rattlesnake" was one reference) and sponsored various educational competitions, such as Christian Front and America Today, whose proceeds went to the Radio League of the Little Flower (later the Broadcasting Fund) to defray the cost of Coughlin's broadcasts. From 1926 until his retirement forty years later, he was pastor of the Shrine of the Little Flower, Royal Oaks, Michigan, outside Detroit. After the United States entered World War II, Coughlin's influence quickly diminished, church pressure forced him off the air, and *Social Justice* was banned from the mails by the U.S. Post Office. He returned to his pastoral duties but refused to take back any of his inflammatory pronouncements. He died at his home near Detroit.

FURTHER READING: Mary C. Athans, *The Coughlin-Fahey Connection: Father Charles E. Coughlin, Father Denis Fahey, C.S.Sp., and Religious Anti-Semitism in the United States, 1938–1954* (New York: P. Lang, 1991); Alan Brinkley, *Voices of Protest: Huey Long, Father Coughlin, and the Great Depression* (New York: Knopf, 1982); Ronald H. Carpenter, *Father Charles E. Coughlin: Surrogate Spokesman for the Disaffected* (Westport, CT: Greenwood, 1998); Alfred M. Lee and Elizabeth B. Lee, eds., *The Fine Art of Propaganda: A Study of Father Coughlin's Speeches*; prepared for the Institute for Propaganda Analysis (1939); Charles J. Tull, *Father Coughlin and the New Deal* (Syracuse, NY: Syracuse University, 1965); Donald I. Warren, *Radio Priest: Charles Coughlin, the Father of Hate Radio* (New York: Free Press, 1996).

COUNTERATTACK. Newsletter started in 1947 by three former agents of the **Federal Bureau of Investigation** to counter Communist propaganda. Information was based on public propaganda releases and its **front organizations**, Congressional reports, and information from former Communists; the newsletter identified publications and organizations used for propaganda by the Communist Party. *Counterattack* was part of a venture known as American Business Consultants (ABC). Funding came partly from Alfred Kohlberg. Three years later, ABC published **Red Channels**, a list of people in the entertainment industry who had been involved in Communist front activities.

FURTHER READING: Issues of *Counterattack*.

COURT HISTORIANS. *See* **Barnes, Harry Elmer**

COVERT ACTION INFORMATION BULLETIN. Covert Action Information Bulletin was an anti-CIA publication in Washington, D.C., that often carried Soviet disinformation. It occasionally reproduced Soviet forgeries as if they were authentic documents. The journal was published between 1978 and 1992; it became *Covert Action Quarterly* with the Winter 1992–1993 issue. It continues as a quarterly.

FURTHER READING: Issues of *Covert Action Information Bulletin*.

COVERT ACTION QUARTERLY. See Covert Action Information Bulletin

CREEL, GEORGE (December 1, 1876–October 2, 1953). A journalist and government official, Creel was born in Lafayette County, Missouri. He worked on newspapers in New York, Kansas City, and Denver; starred in a cowboy film; married Blanche Bates, a popular stage actress, in 1912; wrote a book on child labor, *Children of Bondage*; engaged in reform politics; served as Denver police commissioner; and campaigned for Woodrow Wilson as president. In 1917, Wilson appointed Creel to direct the **Committee on Public Information**, the U.S. government's official "propaganda agency" during World War I, a post he held until it was disbanded in 1919. Creel believed he was fighting "for the minds of men, for the conquest of their convictions, and the battle-line ran through every home in the country." While "holding fast the inner lines," Creel "advertised" America abroad: its aims, its ideals, its struggles, and its achievements. To assist him, he hired Will Irwin, **Carl Byoir,** and other prominent journalists; supervised a system of newspaper and magazine censorship that fell into three categories (dangerous, questionable and routine); operated a twenty-four-hour-a-day news bureau that distributed press releases, communiqués, casualty lists, and interviews; and directed patriotic advertising campaigns ("Don't talk . . . spies are listening"; "Halt the Hun"). Creel's salesmanship was criticized by writers such as H. L. Mencken and I. F. Stone, but he was also defended for his honesty and efficiency. Creel wrote about his CPI experiences in *How We Advertised America: The First Telling of the Amazing Story of the Committee on Public Information that Carried the Gospel of Americanism to Every Corner of the Globe* (New York: Arno Press, 1972) and *War, the World and Wilson* (1920).

After CPI was abolished, Creel wrote books on popular history, such as *War Criminals and Punishment* (1944), edited a column for Collier's in the 1930s, and was appointed chairman, National Advisory Board, Works Progress Administration (1935), and U.S. Commissioner for the Golden Gate International Exposition, San Francisco (1939–1940). He married Alice Rosseter in 1943, two years after his first wife died, and published his autobiography, *Rebel at Large: Recollections of Fifty Crowded Years* (1947). He died in San Francisco.

FURTHER READING: James R. Mock and Cedric Larson, *Words That Won the War: The Story of the Committee on Public Information, 1917–1919* (Princeton, NJ: Princeton

University Press, 1939); Stephen Vaughn, *Holding Fast the Inner Lines: Democracy, Nationalism, and the Committee on Public Information* (Chapel Hill: University of North Carolina, 1980).

CREEL COMMITTEE. *See* **Committee on Public Information**

CRUSADE FOR FREEDOM. This was a CIA covertly funded international organization that was an operation of the National Committee for a Free Europe, Inc. (NCFE). The Crusade for Freedom (CFF) was dedicated to keeping the Western democracies in contact with the inhabitants of Eastern Europe. It tried less-threatening forms of propaganda to achieve its goals. One of the first was the ten-ton "freedom bell" constructed in 1950 and sent on a tour of the United States before it was installed in the Rathaus Tower, West Berlin, just across the border from East Germany. The bell rang for the first time on October 24, 1950 (United Nations Day); its "peals for peace" were broadcast by **Radio Free Europe** (RFE). Near the bell were "freedom scrolls" with the signatures of millions of Americans. Another campaign was a propaganda balloon assault on Czechoslovakia that started in a wheat field in Bavaria, where CFF officials, such as columnist Drew Pearson, released several thousand balloons filled with propaganda leaflets with messages that emphasized the importance of truth on the front and a list of wave lengths and schedules for RFE broadcasts on the back.

FURTHER READING: Peter Coleman, *The Liberal Conspiracy: The Congress for Cultural Freedom and the Struggle for the Mind of Postwar Europe* (New York: Free; London: Collier Macmillan, 1989); Frances S. Saunders, *Cultural Cold War: The CIA and the World of Arts and Letters* (New York: New Press, 2000); Hugh Wilford, "Playing the CIA's Tune? The New Leader," *Diplomatic History* 27, no. 1 (January 2003): 15–34.

CUBA. The first attempt at propaganda toward the island of Cuba was in 1492, when Christopher Columbus landed there, thinking he was in Japan. The earliest official propaganda efforts that the United States made toward Cuba began indirectly with the explosion of the *Maine*, a second-class battleship, in Havana harbor on February 15, 1898, which ignited the **Spanish-American War**. The incident became a sensation in the American press, who laid the blame on the Spanish, with whom the U.S. was then having bad relations, and it served as a rallying point to the American people to "Remember the Maine," a highly effective propaganda slogan. The most important propaganda tool was newspapers, the "yellow press," which brought the casualties down to the level of the average reader with lurid front-page headlines and pictures. One of the major factors given for the initiation of U.S. hostilities against Cuba was the propagandistic efforts of Joseph Pulitzer and William Hearst and their respective newspapers, which exerted a strong influence on America's decision to go to war by stirring up interventionist enthusiasm. The publishers were helped in their efforts by highly patriotic films, such as *Tearing Down the Spanish Flag*, and phony pictorial "news" accounts, typified by *The Campaign in Cuba* (actually filmed in New Jersey). Between 1898 and 1959, the United States supported a series of Cuban republics and dictatorships, which only targeted the United States as an enemy of Cuban independence.

HOW YOU CAN HELP DRIVE COMMUNISM FROM CUBA

The Cuban Freedom Committee plans daily broadcasts of powerful messages over a Caribbean radio station.

These messages will reach Cuban multitudes starving for news and facts of the democratic world from which they were so cruelly wrenched by the Castro dictatorship.

Serving news, facts, and truth to our millions of friends in Cuba is vital to offset the iron chants and jibes of the Reds.

HELP NOW!

Support the Cuban Freedom Committee
JOHN B. McCLATCHY, *Chairman*

Send checks to: The Christianform
1737 H Street; N.W., Washington 6, D. C.

A non-profit organization • Contributions are tax-deductible.

Ad from the *Wall Street Journal* (November 29, 1960) for the Cuban Freedom Committee, which was set up by the CIA to sponsor anti-Castro broadcasts similar to those of Radio Swan. (*Source:* CIA)

When Fidel Castro, a master propagandist, took power in 1959, he declared Cuba a communist state, declared his allegiance to the Soviet Union, and heightened anti-American propaganda efforts by promising land reform and economic independence from the United States while identifying his movement with the image of Cuba's great poet and leader, Jose Marti. To counter Castro's efforts, the United States supported anti-Communist regimes. An early effort was the **Cuban Freedom Committee**, established by the **Central Intelligence Agency** in late 1960 to sponsor anti-Castro broadcasts similar to those of **Radio Swan**. The **Voice of**

America continued to transmit to the Cuban people, but these broadcasts were usually jammed, a situation that did not change in 1982 when President Ronald signed the Radio Broadcasting to Cuba Act of 1983 (Public Law 98-111) to focus on Cuban domestic and international news and information that is not reported by the government-controlled media. The law created **Radio Marti** and **Television Marti** under the direction of the Office of Cuba Broadcasting.

See also Front Organizations

FURTHER READING: Nicholas J. Cull, David Culbert, and David Welch, *Propaganda and Mass Persuasion: A Historical Encyclopedia, 1500 to the Present* (Santa Barbara, CA and Denver, CO: ABC-Clio, 2003); Karen C. Lund, "The Motion Picture Camera Goes to War," *Library of Congress Information Bulletin* 57, no. 3 (March 1998): 48–49, 53; Lawrence C. Soley, *Radio Warfare: OSS and CIA Subversive Propaganda* (New York: Praeger, 1987).

CUBAN FREEDOM COMMITTEE. The CIA set up the Cuban Freedom Committee in late 1960 to sponsor anti-Castro broadcasts similar to those of **Radio Swan**. The committee appeared as a private activist group that solicited donations for the operation through Christianform, later identified as a funding conduit for CIA domestic operations. It produced Free Cuba Radio, a stridently anti-Castro program that was broadcast before, during, and after the Bay of Pigs invasion by licensed stations in the United States and overseas.

See also Front Organizations

FURTHER READING: Jon Elliston, ed., *Psywar on Cuba: The Declassified History of U.S. Anti-Castro Propaganda* (Melbourne, Vic.; New York: Ocean, 1999); Lawrence C. Soley, *Radio Warfare: OSS and CIA Subversive Propaganda* (New York: Praeger, 1987).

CUBAN PSYCHOLOGICAL OPERATIONS. *See* Cuban Freedom Committee; Radio Marti; Radio Swan; Television Marti

CULT PROPAGANDA. *See* Hate Propaganda; Terrorism

CULTURAL AND SCIENTIFIC CONFERENCE FOR WORLD PEACE. *See* Congress for Cultural Freedom

CULTURAL DIPLOMACY. Type of diplomacy that best defines the work of the **Bureau of Public Diplomacy, U.S. Department of State** (formerly the **U.S. Information Agency**) abroad. Information officers in overseas posts (U.S. Information Service) promote American culture and prestige abroad through various methods and forms, such as art exchanges and educational exchanges, to achieve such goals as the popularity of motion pictures and television in foreign markets or the respect gained by the Fulbright Scholarship Program. American culture as part of diplomacy was not fully explored until the middle 1930s when the Roosevelt administration decided that cultural and educational exchanges were important to U.S. foreign policy and pursued a more active cultural policy to counterattack the spread of German and of Italian influence in Latin America. The United States launched a series of cultural and educational programs to promote Latin America's loyalty to its northern neighbor. In 1936, the American delegation agreed to a government-sponsored exchange of professors, graduate students, and teachers at the Inter-American Conference for the Maintenance of Peace in Buenos Aires. Two years later, the **U.S. State Department** formed a **Division of Cultural Relations** to supervise these programs in Latin America and to operate libraries and cultural centers in the capital cities. This beginning was followed in World War II by the introduction of the **Voice of America** in 1942 and by the establishment of the **Office of War Information** to sell America's war effort both at home and abroad through motion pictures, books and magazines, posters and pamphlets, and art exhibitions, among other programs.

After World War II, cultural diplomacy was heavily targeted toward the Communist bloc countries during the Cold War. After the tensions of the 1958 Brussels exposition, a breakthrough was the signing of the 1958 U.S.–USSR Cultural Agreement, which opened the way for the exchange of American and Soviet cultural presentations. In 1959, the Bolshoi Ballet toured the United States and the American National Exhibition opened in Moscow's Sokolniki Park while its Russian counterpart was displayed in New York City. Since then, the United States has had mixed successes in its attempts to undermine Communism and to reach détente through the exhibition of Western consumer culture, but cultural diplomacy has always been a most effective anti-Communist propaganda weapon.

White House Conference

On November 28, 2000, President and Mrs. Clinton hosted, and Secretary of State Madeleine Albright chaired, the first (and to date only) White House Conference on Culture and Diplomacy; it was organized by the U.S. Department of State in cooperation with the Office of the First Lady, the White House Millennium Council, and the National Security Council. The participants, from the fields of the arts, business, and government, addressed a wide variety of issues, especially the vital role culture plays in diplomacy. In her remarks at the end of the one-day conference, Secretary Albright noted that the consolidation of USIA into the State Department provided new opportunities for funding cultural programs. Other recommendations included: Cultural factors are inseparable from foreign policy; the United States must do a better job of explaining American culture to the world; funding for programs of cultural exchange, understanding, and collaboration must be increased; and culture is not elitist but the way the people of a country express themselves.

See also **Advancing American Art; American National Exhibition, Moscow; Art Exhibitions; Atoms for Peace; Brussels Universal and International Exposition; Bureau of Public Diplomacy, U.S. Department of State; Cultural Exchanges; Family of Man; International Expositions; Music; U.S. Information Agency**

FURTHER READING: Helena K. Finn, "The Case for Cultural Diplomacy: Engaging Foreign Audiences," *Foreign Affairs* 82, no. 6 (November/December 2003): 15–20; Walter L. Hixson, *Parting the Curtain: Propaganda, Culture, and the Cold War, 1945–1961* (New York: St. Martin's Press, 1997); Richard Pells, *Not Like Us: How Europeans Have Loved, Hated, and Transformed American Culture Since World War II* (New York: Basic Books, 1997); Cynthia P. Schneider, *Diplomacy That Works: "Best Practices" in Cultural Diplomacy* (Washington, DC: Center for Arts and Culture, 2003); White House Conference on Culture and Diplomacy, November 28, 2000. [Final Report] (Washington, DC: U.S. Department of State, 2001).

CULTURAL EXCHANGES. Type of exchanges that best defined the work of the **U.S. Information Agency** overseas (U.S. Information Service) and now administered by the **Bureau of Public Diplomacy, U.S. Department of State,** it is one of the most effective tools of U.S. diplomacy because it is the work of information officers in overseas posts to promote American culture and prestige abroad through various methods and forms (art, education, language, literature, motion pictures, music, sports, and theater) to achieve U.S. cultural influence, such as the popularity of American films and television shows in foreign markets or the respect gained by the Fulbright Scholarship Program. U.S. cultural exchanges were aimed toward the Communist bloc during the Cold War. After the tensions of the **Brussels Universal and International Exposition (Expo 58),** a breakthrough was the signing, in the same year, of the 1958 U.S.–USSR Cultural Agreement, which opened the way for the exchange of American and Soviet cultural presentations. In 1959, the Bolshoi Ballet toured the United States and the **American National Exhibition** opened in Moscow's Sokolniki Park (with its Russian counterpart in New York City).

Although the United States was not always successful in its attempts to undermine Communism and to reach détente through the exhibition of Western consumer culture, at the height of the Cold War, cultural propaganda provided the main contact with the Russians and was the most effective of the anti-Communist propaganda. Although it's debatable whether more cultural programs might possibly have led to an earlier resolution of the East-West détente despite being undercut by foreign policy blunders (e.g., U-2 incident, Cuban missile crisis, "star wars"), cultural propaganda was a significant factor in the defeat of Communism in the Soviet bloc countries.

See also Art Exhibitions; Atoms for Peace; Family of Man; International Expositions

FURTHER READING: Robert Cole, *Propaganda in Twentieth Century War and Politics* (Lanham, MD: Scarecrow Press; Pasadena, CA: Salem Press, 1996); Helena K. Finn, "The Case for Cultural Diplomacy: Engaging Foreign Audiences," *Foreign Affairs* 82, no. 6 (November/December 2003): 15–20 Walter L. Hixson, *Parting the Curtain: Propaganda, Culture, and the Cold War, 1945–1961* (New York: St. Martin's, 1997); U.S. Dept. of State, *Foreign Relations of the United States, 1955–1957; v. IX: Foreign Economic Policy; Foreign Information Program* (Washington, DC: Government Printing Office, 1987).

CULTURAL PROPAGANDA. *See* **Cultural Exchanges**

CUSTOMS LAWS. *See* **Postal Regulations (Communist Political Propaganda)**

D

D-DAY. *See* Normandy Invasion

DAMM, HELENE VON. *See* Helene von Damm Forgery Letter

D'AQUINO, IVA IKUKO TOGURI. *See* Tokyo Rose

DARLAN AGREEMENT. *See* Darlan Interlude

DARLAN INTERLUDE. The so-called Darlan Interlude dealt with American collaboration with a Vichy French leader and its psychological warfare implications with overall political and military strategy. It exemplified how significant military requirements put propagandists in a disadvantaged, though temporary, position and created conflicts with psychological warriors. U.S. involvement dealt with issues such as the continued suspension (then resumption) of an economic aid program and negotiations and policies regarding possible American assistance to the resistance movement in French North Africa. During the period 1940–1942, the U.S. government, through the State Department and its agencies overseas, maintained diplomatic relations with the pro-Nazi Vichy French government, headed by Marshal Petain, a policy strongly attacked by anti-Nazi elements, both in the United States and abroad, who were concerned about the treatment of American nationals of Jewish origin, with rumored U.S. collaboration in North Africa and with the question of cooperation with Allied causes.

Admiral Jean Louis Alexander Xavier Francois Darlan was Vichy Vice President of the French Council of Ministers, Minister for Foreign Affairs, Navy and Defense, Marine, and commander-in-chief of French fighting forces; he was then residing in Algiers. In the United States and throughout the British Commonwealth, Darlan was known for his anti-British sentiments and pro-German sympathies, as a violent Anglophobe, and as largely responsible for the Nazi-like policies put into effect against the civilian populations of France and North Africa. He was assassinated on December 24, 1942; General Henri Honore Giraud was quickly installed as High

Commissioner in North French Africa. De Gaulle continued as president of French National Committee, which assumed administration of all French territory under Allied control. Allied psychological warfare officers were concerned that Americans in North Africa were unable to put effective pressure on Darlan and his followers to terminate the Nazi-like Vichy policies in the area under nominal American control, changes promised by President Roosevelt. There was also grave concern that compromises with Vichy leaders in North Africa would cause American supporters in all occupied countries to lose faith in the United States as liberators and compromise Allied support for General Charles de Gaulle as the leader of free French.

FURTHER READING: William E. Daugherty and Morris Janowitz, "The Darlan Story," in *Psychological Warfare Casebook*, ed. William E. Daugherty (Baltimore: Johns Hopkins Press; published for Operations Research Office, Johns Hopkins University, 1958); U.S. Dept. of State, *Foreign Relations of the United States, 1942*, vol. II (Washington, DC: Government Printing Office, 1962).

DAVIS, ELMER HOLMES (January 13, 1890–May 18, 1958). Elmer Davis was a radio news commentator, author, and director of the **Office of War Information** (OWI) during World War II. He was born in Aurora, Indiana, educated at Franklin College, and awarded a Rhodes scholarship to Oxford. He started with the *New York Times* as an editorial writer, wrote *History of the New York Times* (1921), and published several novels, including *Friends of Mr. Sweeney* (1925), a newspaper story. He became a popular CBS commentator in 1939, noted for his calm, humorous, and practical approach to events. In 1942, Davis was appointed head of the **Office of War Information** by President **Franklin D. Roosevelt** without the unlimited authority enjoyed by his World War I predecessor, **George Creel**. This was largely due to Roosevelt's experience as Assistant Secretary of the Navy in World War I, when he had a chance to observe closely the power that Creel and his **Committee on Public Information** (CPI) wielded over wartime propaganda policy, often at odds with President Wilson. Subsequently, OWl was curtailed by President Franklin Roosevelt, who was determined not to have another CPI, and it came under constant Congressional attack, often with Davis caught in the middle of policy battles with both the White House and the U.S. Congress over propaganda dissemination in both the domestic and foreign divisions. After the war, Davis became an ABC broadcaster and published *But We Were Born Free* (Garden City, NY: Garden City Books, 1954), an attack on Senator Joseph McCarthy. Davis died in Washington.

FURTHER READING: Roger Burlingame, *Don't Let Them Scare You* (Philadelphia: J. B. Lippincott, 1961; reprinted 1974); Elmer Davis, "War Information," in *War Information and Censorship* (Washington, DC: American Council on Public Affairs, 1943); R. L. Davis, ed., *By Elmer Davis* (Indianapolis, IN: Bobbs Merrill, 1964).

DAY, DONALD. *See* **U.S.A. Zone of the Overseas Service (North American Service)**

DEBUNK. Debunk—The Station of All Free Americans was an Axis "clandestine" radio station that used news flashes, slogans, stories in the Walter Winchell manner (anecdotes and interviews with American farmers, officers, etc.), and wild fantasies.

Broadcasts suggested the formation of listeners' clubs, which would disseminate the contents of the broadcasts, and encouraged the writing of chain letters to spread mostly anti-Semitic propaganda. The form of the broadcasts appeared as rumors, one of the major functions of Debunk, which paralleled Axis propaganda statements (e.g., the U.S. government exaggerated every little victory, high-ranking Naval officers gave away secret information, British troops were fighting badly, the Canadians hated the British, Washington was withholding true information on the state of the war, Winston Churchill and Franklin Roosevelt were cousins, savings accounts in the banks would soon be paid in war bonds, black cadets were being admitted to officer training schools while white men will do the menial tasks, and promiscuity, venereal disease, and prostitution were prominent in Army camp regions).

The station used the call sign D-E-B-U-N-K (i.e., the station that debunks the war, debunks war propaganda); it began its broadcasts on March 12, 1942, with Herbert John Burgman, a former employee at the U.S. Embassy in Berlin, who used the name Joe Scanlon, a fictitious figure associated with the isolationist, anticommunist Christian Front movement. He broadcast regularly to North America as the host. The broadcasts ceased operations before the Nazi government fell, and Burgman, who was accused of treason, died in prison.

FURTHER READING: Horst J. P. Bergmeier and Rainer E. Lotz, *Hitler's Airwaves: The Inside Story of Nazi Radio Broadcasting and Propaganda Swing* (New Haven, CT: Yale, 1997); John P. Kishler, Kenneth W. Yarnold, et al., "The Use of Rumor in Psychological Warfare," in *Psychological Warfare Casebook*, ed. William E. Daugherty (Baltimore: Johns Hopkins; published for Operations Research Office, Johns Hopkins University, 1958): 657–666.

DECEPTION. Deception, also called feinting, is the process of influencing the enemy by supplying or withholding information to make decisions disadvantageous to the enemy. It is also a purposeful attempt by the deceiver to manipulate the perceptions of the targets' decision makers to gain a competitive advantage. It is often a means to achieve surprise.

See also Disinformation

FURTHER READING: Robert Cowley and Geoffrey Parker, eds., *Reader's Companion to Military History* (Boston: Houghton Mifflin, 1996); Morris Janowitz, "Propaganda for Strategic Deception," in *Psychological Warfare Casebook*, ed. William E. Daugherty (Baltimore: Johns Hopkins; published for Operations Research Office, Johns Hopkins University, 1958): 657–666.

DELANEY, EDWARD LEOPOLD. *See* U.S.A. Zone of the Overseas Service (North American Service)

DE LEON, EDWIN (May 4, 1818–December 1, 1891). Diplomat and propagandist Edwin De Leon was born in Columbia, South Carolina. He was a newspaper editor in Savannah, Georgia, and in Washington, DC, until President Franklin Pierce appointed him Consul General and Diplomatic Agent in Egypt in 1854, a position he held until 1861, when he became a publicity agent in Europe for the Confederacy. He was not as successful a propagandist as his Union counterpart, **Henry Hotze.** De Leon spent considerable money bribing the French press, but his most important contribution was a pamphlet, *La Verite sur les Etats Confederes d'Amerique*, which tried to ignite French public opinion for the Confederate cause, but he destroyed his career when he opened a secret document of Confederate diplomat John Slidell (1863) and gave a speech (1864) that criticized the French government. De Leon spent the rest of his life abroad, mostly in Egypt and in Europe, but he died in New York City. He wrote two books on Egypt and published his autobiography, *Thirty Years of Life on Three Continents* (1886).

FURTHER READING: Charles P. Cullop, "Edwin De Leon, Jefferson Davis' Propagandist," *Civil War History* 8, no. 4 (December 1962): 386–400.

DE LOME LETTER. Written by the Spanish minister to the United States, Enrique de Lome, to a friend in Havana, the letter was published in William Randolph Hearst's *New York Journal* (February 9, 1898). It characterized President William McKinley as "weak and a bidder for the admiration of the crowd" and questioned his political integrity. This private letter was stolen by a Cuban rebel sympathizer from the Havana mails and returned to New York. The publication of the letter uncovered the false promise of Spain's foreign policy toward the United States. In its wake, de Lome immediately resigned, Spain sent a not-too-sincere apology, and McKinley let the incident pass, but it ignited American opinion toward future Cuban intervention.

FURTHER READING: U.S. Dept. of State, *Diplomatic Papers of the Foreign Relations of the United States, 1898* (Washington, DC: Government Printing Office, 1901): 1007–1022.

DIES, MARTIN. *See* **U.S. Congressional Investigations of Propaganda**

DIES COMMITTEE. *See* **U.S. Congressional Investigations of Propaganda**

DIPLOMATIC PROPAGANDA. *See* **Buenos Aires Convention for Promotion of Inter-American Cultural Relations; Bureau of Public Diplomacy (U.S. Department of State); Committee of Secret Correspondence; Coordinator of Inter-American Affairs; Cultural Exchanges; Division of Cultural Relations (U.S. Department of State)**

DIRECTIVE FOR PSYCHOLOGICAL WARFARE AND CONTROL OF GERMAN INFORMATION SERVICES. *See* **Libraries; Occupied Countries and Territories**

DISINFORMATION. Disinformation is false information targeted to an individual, group or country, created by governments in wartime for military purposes and by totalitarian governments at other times for political purposes. Even the

United States has been accused of using disinformation, although it has been harder to find. **Rumors,** lies, and other forms of disinformation were put out by the Soviet Union to discredit the United States, the latter being the context in which the word is generally applied. The KGB coined the Russian word *dezinformatsiya*; it came into the English language as disinformation. One of the classic disinformation campaigns, and a notorious forgery, was **Protocols for the Learned Elders of Zion,** which was distributed by the czarist secret police in 1905, but the techniques of disinformation increased after World War I. Disinformation as a KGB weapon began in 1923 when I. S. Unshlikht, Deputy Chairman of the GPU, then the name of the KGB, proposed the establishment of a "special disinformation office to conduct active intelligence operations . . ." It is an important element of **Soviet active measures.**

During the 1980s, the Reagan administration monitored disinformation activities in three annual reports: U.S. Department of State, *Active Measures: A Report on the Substance and Process of Anti-U.S. Disinformation and Propaganda Campaigns* (Washington, DC: The Department, 1986); U.S. Department of State, *Report on Active Measures and Propaganda, 1986–87* (Washington, DC: The Department, 1987); U.S. Department of State, *Report on Active Measures and Propaganda, 1987–1988* (Washington, DC: The Department, 1989).

See also **Active Measures Working Group; AIDS Disinformation Campaign; Anti-Semitic Propaganda; Baby Parts; Biological and Chemical Weapons Warfare; Gulf War Disinformation; Iraq; Terrorism**

FURTHER READING: Dennis Kux, "Soviet Active Measures and Disinformation: Overview and Assessment," *Parameters, Journal of the U.S. Army War College* 15, no. 4 (1985): 19–28; Herbert Romerstein, "Disinformation as a KGB Weapon in the Cold War." Prepared for a Conference on Germany and Intelligence Organizations: The Last Fifty Years in Review, sponsored by Akademie fur Politische Bildung Tutzing, June 18–20, 1999; Herbert Romerstein, *Soviet Active Measures and Propaganda: "New Thinking" and Influence Activities in the Gorbachev Era* (Toronto, Canada: Mackenzie Institute for the Study of Terrorism, Revolution, and Propaganda; Washington, DC: National Intelligence Book Center, 1989); Richard H. Shultz and Roy Godson, *Dezinformatsia* (Washington: Pergamon-Brassey's International Defense Publishers, 1984); U.S. Congress. House. Permanent Select Committee on Intelligence, *Soviet Active Measures;* hearings. 97th Congress, 2d Session. (Washington, DC: Government Printing Office, 1982).

DISNEY, WALTER ELIAS. *See* Disney Image

DISNEY FILMS. *See* Disney Image

DISNEY IMAGE. Since 1928, Walt Disney's creations have been a part of our culture. From the first simple animation to the elaborate, computer-enhanced feature films of the 1990s, the Disney image continues to be magical. Generations have grown up on Donald Duck and Mickey Mouse. King Hassan of Morocco claimed that the mouse was one of his favorite characters as a boy. The image that Disney always projected was one of wholesomeness and family. In France, the incredible success of Euro-Disney, after its disastrous first year, has seen the proliferation of Disney characters along the Champs ds Elysee. The characters are also on French telephone charge cards. The Disney name includes films, television productions, records, resorts, theme parks, book publishing, stage shows, stores, and an international merchandising campaign of Disney characters. There is now a growing impact of these Disney products in the world. Disney's major overseas businesses include distribution of the company's films and TV products as well as consumer products of every description. Its publications are among the most popular worldwide, and the Disney logo that accompanies it is instantly recognizable everywhere. In 1984, Disney's revenues from countries outside the United States totaled $142 million, or about 8.4 percent of the company's consolidated revenues of nearly $1.7 billion. Ten years later, overseas revenue totaled approximately $2.4 billion, or 23 percent of total Disney revenues of $10.1 billion. This was a growth of 30 percent for revenues outside the United States and includes revenues from Tokyo Disneyland but not Disneyland Paris (Euro-Disney).

In China, the Disney organization has jeopardized its potentially vast and growing market with its release of the Martin Scorsese-directed film, *Kundun*, about the Dalai Lama, a Tibetan religious leader the Chinese consider an agent of subversion out to undermine China's 46-year domination of Tibet. Chinese officials have warned the company that its role in the movie could have unspecified consequences for Disney's planned expansion into China. At the Vatican, the seat of Roman Catholicism, the Disney company had to make amends for its release of *Priest*, which was considered anti-Catholic and which was heavily criticized by Catholic organizations, who threatened a boycott of all Disney films and products.

The creator of this image, Walter Elias Disney (1901–1966), was known for his family-friendly films, but he had a darker side that was revealed after his death. He was accused of practicing forms of censorship in his adaptations of materials from other sources, and he was an official FBI informant (Special Agent in Charge) in Hollywood who reported several of his colleagues and workers as possible Communist sympathizers. During World War II, Disney produced films that showed him to be a great propagandist. Films represented "perfect" America to American fighting personnel overseas and were great morale boosters, as were the Disney insignia that appeared on planes, trucks, and other military property. This image is still practiced by Walt Disney Corporation. After the war started, Disney turned his film production over to the war effort, and many of his films were propaganda and war-training productions. The studio made several films for U.S. government agencies, most for distribution to a home front America audience, but he also used his stockpile of well-known cartoon characters to sell the war. His best-known animated short from this period was *Der Fuhrer's Face* (1943), which won an Oscar for its depiction of Donald Duck's horrifying life in wartime Nazi Germany and for its catchy title song, which became a popular hit in the United States; the Nazis retaliated by banning Mickey Mouse cartoons. By the end of the war, most of the Disney animated characters were used in the war effort, selling war bonds, serving in the armed forces, and exhorting citizens on the home front to conserve vital materials for the war effort.

The earliest characters to be used as propaganda were the dwarfs (*Snow White and the Seven Dwarfs*, 1937), who were commissioned by the National

Film Board of Canada in *The Seven Wise Dwarfs* (1941) to invest the diamonds from their mine in war savings and in *All Together* (1942), also for the National Film Board. They sold war bonds, but the true wartime Disney star of the war effort was Donald Duck. Along with *Der Fuhrer's Face*, the cranky web-footed aquatic appeared in all manner of short films. For the National Film Board, Donald sold war bonds (*Donald's Decision*, 1942), then performed a similar function for the U.S. Department of the Treasury in *The New Spirit* (1942) and *The Spirit of '43* (1943) by encouraging Americans to support the war effort by paying their income taxes. Along with films that had Donald getting drafted or serving in the U.S. Army, Disney used the character in two full-length features. The first, *Saludas Amigos* (1943), was suggested by the **U.S. Department of State** to discourage pro-Nazi feelings in Latin America. Its success allowed Disney to make *The Three Caballeros* (1945) without the government's offer of financial backing; it also encouraged pro-American feelings and drew on the lucrative South and Central American film markets.

Three Disney short subjects also served as Nazi propaganda, but they did not use the major Disney characters. *Education for Death* (1943) dealt with a little German boy who suffered Nazi indoctrination that destroyed his tolerance. *Reason and Emotion* (1943) argued that reason and emotion are necessary to maintain a humane government. In *Chicken Little* (1943), Foxy Loxy used underhanded methods to convince the barnyard fowls to seek safety outside the chicken coop. *Victory Through Air Power* (1943) had no popular Disney characters, but it did convince Winston Churchill to adopt strategic bombing as a major tool of war.

After World War II, Disney was one of the best-known "friendly" witnesses before the House Un-American Activities Committee, where he publicly named those he suspected of communist intrigue in his testimony of October 24, 1947. These included the Cartoonists' Guild, which went on strike against his studio in 1941, and the League of Women Shoppers, which he confused with the League of Women Voters, for its support of the Guild's strike. He had to apologize to the latter group after they called for a boycott of his movies. In the 1952 presidential election, Disney produced a cartoon for Eisenhower, with a "We Like Ike," soundtrack song, probably the first animated commercial ever made by Disney.

FURTHER READING: Robert Cole, ed., *The Encyclopedia of Propaganda*, v.1 (Armonk, NY: M. E. Sharpe, 1998); Marc Eliot, *Walt Disney: Hollywood's Dark Prince* (New York: Birch Lane, 1993); U.S. Congress. House. Committee on Un-American Activities, *Hearings Regarding Communist Infiltration of the Motion Picture Industry*; 80th Congress, 1st Session (Washington, DC: Government Printing Office, 1947); Steven Watts, *The Magic Kingdom: Walt Disney and the American Way of Life* (Boston and New York: Houghton Mifflin, 1997).

DIVISION OF CULTURAL RELATIONS (DEPARTMENT OF STATE). The Division of Cultural Relations, U.S. Department of State, was formed in 1938 as a result of the **Buenos Aires Convention for Promotion of Inter-American Cultural Relations** as the U.S. was building up its position in Latin America. The division firmly issued propaganda designed to portray the United States as an altruistic benefactor in a common struggle against possible foreign aggression.

After several name changes, the program became part of the Office of the **Coordinator of Inter-American Affairs** (CIAA) during World War II, went back to the State Department in 1946, and became part of the **U.S. Information Agency** in 1953.

FURTHER READING: J. Manuel Espinosa, *Inter-American Beginnings of U.S. Cultural Diplomacy, 1936–1948* (Washington, DC: U.S. Department of State, 1976).

DOCUMENTARY FILMS. The documentary film ("sponsored film") is an important propaganda form that is difficult to define. The first notable American documentary filmmaker was Robert Joseph Flaherty (1884–1951), who is considered the "father of American documentary film." He filmed Eskimo arts and culture during an expedition to northern Quebec in 1913–1914 but he accidentally destroyed the negatives in a fire. With more funding, he returned in 1920, and the result was *Nanook of the North.* A follow-up was *Moana* (1926), filmed in Samoa and depicting everyday life in the South Seas. Under British filmmaker John Grierson's leadership, Flaherty produced *Man of Aran* (1934) about life on the Aran Islands on Ireland's west coast. Back in the United States, Flaherty filmed *The Land* (1941) for the Department of Agriculture and the U.S. Film Service.

The 1930s saw the advent of sound and the beginning of the sponsored film. Another important documentary filmmaker was **Pare Lorentz** (1905–1992) who wrote, directed, and produced films for the U.S. government. When the Roosevelt administration initiated the filming of documentaries with strong social messages to build support for his New Deal policies, Lorentz produced his award-winning *The Plow That Broke the Plains* (Resettlement Administration, 1936), which led to natural resource conservation. His second film, *The River* (Farm Security Administration, 1937), about the Mississippi and the havoc it could wreak, was considered his masterpiece and a "documentary film poem" but labeled "New Deal propaganda" by its critics.

At Lorentz's request, Roosevelt created the U.S. Film Service in 1938 to coordinate production of motion pictures about social problems that were ignored by Hollywood. During this period, when he was head of the U.S. Film Service, Lorentz wrote an outline for a film for the American Institute of Planners, which eventually became the celebrated documentary, *The City.* In *The Fight for Life* (1940), he dramatized the war against the perils of childbirth. World War II stimulated more federal funding as government agencies produced films to help the war effort. Armed Forces documentaries were most popular and productive during World War II, but the documentary films that were used to convince Americans of all races to join together to defeat Hitler were not integrated themselves. These films divided the U.S. into whites and all others, with white America extolled almost without exception as the real America ("It's a white man's war"). One film, *Teamwork*, actually tried to disguise this fact with its portrayal of how blacks and whites worked side by side throughout the war; however, skillful editing disguised the fact that the units in the film were actually segregated. For African Americans, there were films with black celebrities such as world heavyweight champion Joe Louis, who figured prominently in wartime messages that extolled the importance of winning because "we're on God's side." The Japanese were featured as "The

Jap" and as "the yellow menace," one-dimensional characterization that actually vilified them, with great numbers rounded up and placed in concentration camps. Native Americans were usually ignored.

General Marshall commissioned film director Frank Capra to produce the **Why We Fight** series but there was also the rationale of "Information-Education Division" in the War Department, which started as the Morale Services Division to produce health and training films for the Air Force and Navy. The first documentary of the war was the color footage that a Navy photographer took from a pier during the actual attack. This footage has been incorporated into other films, both real and fictional, since then. It formed the basis of John Ford's documentary, *December 7th*, which won an Oscar for best documentary, although Ford padded the film with supplemental footage.

Army documentaries were produced with the U.S. Signal Corps; they included *At the Front in North Africa*, *The Liberation of Rome*, *Report from the Aleutians*, and two films by John Huston: *The Battle of San Pietro*, and *Let There Be Light*, a film about psychiatric cases in a veteran's hospital that was never released to the public. *The True Glory* (1945), a tribute to the campaign in Western Europe, was a joint British-American production from the British Ministry of Information and the **Office of War Information**, commentary by General Dwight Eisenhower. It was considered a priceless film and an enduring artistic monument to men at war. Other major Hollywood directors who made documentaries for the war effort included Joseph von Sternberg and William Wyler.

Between 1943 and 1954, a large repository of documentaries of propaganda were produced or coordinated by the United States Information Service (USIS) in Italian. Material was casually found in the Italian national archives in 1995 or early 1996. In the post-World War climate, John Ford made a film on Korea (1951) at the request of the U.S. Navy, *This Is Korea*, about the Korean War. The noted director didn't view the conflict as a heroic war, so the resulting picture was a somber one. The film was poorly released, and few theater owners distributed it. During this conflict, the U.S. Signal Corps captured film of the North Korean Army, footage it loaned to other government agencies and commercial companies. There was also the "Kingfish" Project (1960–1968), an effort in which USIA funded the Hearst-Metrotone Organization to distribute overseas newsreels.

George Stevens, Jr., with his ties to the Hollywood establishment, who served as director of USIA's Motion Picture Service, 1962–1967, under USIA Director **Edward R. Murrow**, kept a balance among newsreels, special projects supporting foreign policy, and the art of the documentary film. Stevens authorized Charles Guggenheim to produce *Night of the Dragon*, and *John F. Kennedy: Years of Lightning, Day of Drums* (1964), a memorial tribute to the late president that won an Oscar in 1965 as Best Documentary and was given an exemption by Congress from the **domestic dissemination** provision of the 1948 Smith-Mundt Act to be shown in the United States. It was produced by Bruce Herschensohn, who also made other films for USIA and succeeded Stevens as director of the agency's Motion Picture Service in 1967.

Arthur Schlesinger, an adviser to President Kennedy, found the USIA film program under Stevens as not having "so many striking films stimulated in Washington since the days of Pare Lorentz and the U.S. Department of

Agriculture film program a generation ago." However, a highlight was *Nine From Little Rock*, another Oscar winner (1964), while three others won Oscar nominations for best documentary. In this same period, USIA also won awards at international film festivals (Bilbao, Cannes, Venice).

The continuing cooperation between the motion picture industry and the federal government was evident in features and numerous patriotic shorts made by Hollywood studios to demonstrate their patriotism. During the **Vietnam Conflict**, USIA and other filmmakers produced documentaries that displayed viewpoints on both sides of U.S. involvement. *Red Nightmare* (1962; reissued 1965) was made by Warner Brothers as an "educational" film as part of a formal alliance between the Hollywood studios and the Pentagon through such cosponsors as the Department for Defense's Directorate for the Armed Forces and Educational Information. USIA produced *Why Viet Nam?* (1965) and *Vietnam! Vietnam!* (1968), among other documentaries. An Oscar winner with a different viewpoint was *Hearts and Minds* (1974), an anti-Vietnam film.

In 1988, under court order, USIA created new interim rules that certified documentaries for duty-free distribution status in foreign markets and allowed government officials to still impose "propaganda" warnings on "unacceptable" films but the agency came under attack. Film distributors who did not receive this certification accused USIA of blacklisting certain types of film and of being government historians.

Present documentary filmmakers include Michael Moore, with his "in-your-face" attack on American greed and the corporate culture (*Roger and Me, The Big One, Fahrenheit 9/11*), John Sayles, the Coen brothers, Barbara Kopple, Frederick Wiseman, and Ken Burns, who brought documentaries into popular culture with such landmark PBS miniseries as *The Civil War* (1990), *Baseball* (1994), and *The West* (1996).

FURTHER READING: Richard M. Barsam, *Vision of Robert Flaherty: The Artist as Myth and Filmmaker* (Bloomington: Indiana University Press, 1988); Greg Garrett, "It's Everybody's War: Racism and the World War Two Documentary," *Journal of Popular Film and Television* 22, no. 2 (Summer 1994): 70–78; Richard Griffith, *The World of Robert Flaherty* (New York: Da Capo Press, 1972 [1953]); Richard D. MacCann, *The People's Films: A Political History of U.S. Government Motion Pictures* (New York: Hastings House, 1973); Paul Rotha, *Robert J. Flaherty*, ed. Jay Ruby (Philadelphia: University of Pennsylvania, 1983).

DOMESTIC DISSEMINATION. Title V of the 1948 U.S. Information and Cultural Exchange Act [Public Law 80-402, approved January 27, 1948], popularly called the Smith-Mundt Act, authorized "the preparation and dissemination abroad, of information about the United States, its people and its policies, through press, publications, radio, motion pictures, and other information media, and through information centers and instructors abroad." The act prohibited the distribution or dissemination of program materials produced by the U.S. information and cultural programs, first in the **U.S. Department of State** then in 1953, in the **U.S. Information Agency** (USIA), then back to State's **Bureau of Public Diplomacy** in 1999, within the United States "but, on request, shall be available in the English language at the Agency . . . for examination only." The exceptions were English Teaching Forum and **Problems of Communism**.

The law provided for two exceptions. First, Congress itself occasionally exempts specific USIA program materials (usually films or artistic works) to permit their distribution within the United States. A notable example was the release of *Years of Lightning, Day of Drums* (1964) about President John F. Kennedy. Second, Section (b)(1) authorizes distribution by the Archivist of the United States 12 years after initial dissemination of such materials abroad. The second exception was added by an amendment to the Foreign Relations Authorization Act, Fiscal Years 1990 and 1991 (Public Law 101-246, approved February 16, 1990) that allowed the USIA Director to make available to the Archivist of the United States certain program materials, "for domestic distribution, motion pictures, films, videotapes, and other material prepared for dissemination abroad 12 years or, in the case of such material not disseminated abroad, twelve years after the preparation of the material."

The domestic dissemination ban also restricts the Bureau of Public Diplomacy and its employees from taking steps to reach an audience within the United States through the **Voice of America** or other U.S. information programs. It does not directly restrict the right of U.S. residents to view, to hear, or to otherwise use the Agency's information materials, which they might obtain on their own, but it does forbid USIA and its employees from assisting residents of the U.S. to gain access to Agency Internet servers, on which program materials are posted, or to the program materials themselves.

FURTHER READING: Charles F. Gormly, "The United States Information Agency Domestic Dissemination Ban: Arguments for Repeal," *Administrative Law Journal* 9 (Spring 1995): 191–220; John R. Fitzpatrick, "Domestic Availability of Certain United States Information Agency Program Materials," *Virginia Journal of International Law* 11 (1970): 71–96; U.S. Congress. *Legislation on Foreign Relations Through 1999* (Washington, DC: Government Printing Office, 2000).

DONOVAN, WILLIAM J. (January 1, 1883–February 8, 1959). William Joseph Donovan was born and raised in Buffalo, New York, the son of a railroad yards superintendent. He attended Columbia Law School the same time as Franklin Roosevelt, but they did not know each other. Donovan became a decorated World War I hero and won the Medal of Honor for his actions under fire. Donovan won the nickname "Wild Bill" while training recruits in France, pushing them hard. The name stuck to him for life, and Donovan liked it, but it was considered the opposite of his real personality. After the war ended, Donovan returned to his law practice in Buffalo, was appointed U.S. attorney for New York's Western District, and ran unsuccessfully for lieutenant governor (1922) and governor (1932). He was an assistant attorney general in the U.S. Department of Justice but moved back to Buffalo after President Hoover declined to make him attorney general.

As Europe edged closer to World War II, Donovan was working in 1940–1941 with senior analysts in the British Secret Intelligence Service, including Sir William Stephenson, who helped Donovan develop a relationship with British intelligence that would frustrate Axis operations in the Western Hemisphere to help bring the United States into World War II and ensure Allied victory. The foundation of an official U.S. intelligence service originated from this Anglo-American liaison. When President Franklin D. Roosevelt called on Donovan to improve the quality of intelligence reaching Washington, he passed on the idea to the president, who established the Office of the **Coordinator of Information** (COI) with Donovan at its head on July 11, 1941, to carry out research and analysis, propaganda broadcasts, economic warfare, espionage, sabotage, subversion, and commando operations. COI was established over the strong objections of FBI Director J. Edgar Hoover and the heads of military spy groups, who were fearful of losing power, and it initiated a bitter dispute with CIAA director Nelson Rockefeller, which eliminated Latin America from Donovan's propaganda responsibility.

In 1942, after the U.S. entry into the war, Donovan's fledgling group was renamed the **Office of Strategic Services** (OSS), with responsibility for both military and diplomatic intelligence. The agency received valuable help in perfecting its methods from the respected British secret service, MI-6, and Donovan hoped to make it a permanent agency, but his proposal was leaked to the press, and President Harry S. Truman, unsympathetic to Donovan, abolished OSS in October 1945. However, Donovan's plan became the blueprint for the Central Intelligence Agency that Truman established in July 1947 with a mission to coordinate the intelligence collection by various government agencies as needed for conducting U.S. foreign policy. In 1953, Donovan became U.S. Ambassador to Thailand, but resigned a year later. He died in Washington, DC.

FURTHER READING: Robert Cole, ed., *Encyclopedia of Propaganda*, v.1 (Armonk, NY: M. E. Sharpe, 1998); Arthur B. Darling, *Central Intelligence Agency: An Instrument of Government, to 1950* (University Park: Pennsylvania State, 1990); Thomas F. Troy, *Wild Bill and Intrepid: Donovan, Stephenson and the Origin of the CIA* (New Haven, CT: Yale University, 1996); U.S. Dept. of State, *Foreign Relations of the United States, 1945–1950: Emergence of the Intelligence Establishment* (Washington, DC: Government Printing Office, 1996).

"DON'T TREAD ON ME" (SLOGAN). The first flags in colonial America were often symbolic of the struggles of the young country. There were pictures such as beavers, pine trees, rattlesnakes, anchors, and various other insignia affixed to banners, newspapers, paper money, uniform buttons, drums, and on military and naval flags with or without the warning "Don't Tread on Me." Flags with this slogan and a rattlesnake theme gained increasing prestige in the colonies. Examples were the flag designed by Christopher Gadsden (erroneously called "the flag of the South Carolina navy") that was flown in early 1776 as the rank flag of Commodore Esek Hopkins of Rhode Island, first commander-in-chief of the American navy; it had a yellow field with a rattlesnake in a spiral coil, poised to strike, in the center with the motto underneath it. There was also the Culpepper flag, the banner of the Minutemen of Culpepper [now Culpeper] County, Virginia, with a rattlesnake on a white field.

"Don't Tread on Me" represented defiance that, when added to the symbolic rattler, added significance to the design of the flags, which were first used around 1776. There are at least three of these flags still in existence. One is the red standard of the Fifty-Second Independent Battalion (Westmoreland County or Colonel John Proctor's Battalion), which was one of the Pennsylvania volunteer units known as Associators. The other two flags are from Rhode Island: the United Company of the Train of Artillery, an independent charted company from Providence, and the white and blue striped flag carried in 1778 during General Sullivan's siege at Newport, which is now preserved, in fragmentary form, in the Rhode Island Historical Society.

FURTHER READING: William R. Furlong and Byron McCandless, *So Proudly We Hail* (Washington, DC: Smithsonian Institution, 1981); Whitney Smith, *Flag Book of the United States*, rev. ed. (New York: Morrow, 1975).

DOVE, DAVID JAMES (1696?–April 1769). Educator, pamphleteer, and one of the first propagandists in the American colonies, David Dove was born in Portsmouth, England, the son of Mar and David Dove, a tailor. He was a teacher in Chicester before he came to America with his wife in 1750 and settled in Philadelphia, where he taught at the Philadelphia Academy. Benjamin Franklin recognized his talents, and Dove founded a girls' academy in September 1751; he was one of first to offer education to women. Over the next decade, Dove operated other schools, often in opposition to school authorities and local townspeople.

As a "sarcastic and ill-tempered doggerelizer" (as one of his students described him) with the temper of a hawk, and his pen "the beak of a falcon pouncing on innocent prey," Dove pounced on his critics with broadsides and pamphlets. In 1757, he authored *Labour in Vain; or, an Attempt to Wash a Black-Moor White*, a caricature of a judge then under arrest for libel. The next year, he issued a pamphlet, *The Lottery; a Dialogue Between Mr. Trueman and Mr. Humphrey Dude*, that attacked the lotteries then employed by schools to raise funds as "no better than public frauds." As Philopatrius, Dove published *The Quaker Unmask'd; or, Plain Truth, Humbly Address'd to the Consideration of all the Freemen of Pennsylvania* (1764), which slandered the Quakers. Dove's enemies savaged him after this publication appeared; he responded with *The Counter-Medley, Being a Proper Answer to All the Dunces of the Medley and Their Abettors*.

FURTHER READING: Germantown Academy, *A History of the Germantown Academy* (Philadelphia: Press of S.H. Burbank, 1910–1935); Alexander Graydon, *Memoirs of His Own Time; With Reminiscences of the Men and Events of the Revolution*, ed. by John Stockton Littell (Philadelphia: Lindsay and Blakiston, 1846).

DJEREJIAN REPORT. *See Changing Minds Winning Peace*

DR. SEUSS. *See* Geisel, Theodor S.

DRAFT OF A PLAN FOR POST-WAR GERMANY. *See* Morgenthau Plan

DREXEL, CONSTANCE. *See* U.S.A. Zone of the Overseas Service (North American Service)

DURANTY, WALTER (May 25, 1884–October 3, 1957). Important American journalist whose reporting was manipulated by the Soviet Union for propaganda purposes. Walter Duranty was born in Liverpool, England. After he graduated from Emmanual College, Cambridge (1906), he worked various jobs before his persistent inquires to the *New York Times* landed him a job with the Paris Bureau. He became Moscow correspondent for the *New York Times* (1921–1941) after he went there to report on American relief efforts in the Volga famines. He managed to operate successfully in the Soviet Union and to report accurately on events in that country; his reporting was favorable in tone but objective in content. Duranty won the Pulitzer Prize in journalism (1932) for his reporting there. However, his ability to live within the Communist system, to speak the language fluently, and to enjoy the favor of the communist regime, which in turn allowed him to circumvent the Soviet censors, made his reporting more propaganda than objective, and he was harshly criticized for being manipulated by the Soviets, especially after his reports denying the truth of the Ukrainian famine that followed collectivization and of the Stalinist purges. His inability or refusal to question the false treason and sabotage charges that were leveled by Stalin against prominent Bolsheviks, culminating in his misreporting of the major Moscow purge trials, hurt Duranty's credibility; his career declined after he left the Soviet Union. He died in Orlando, Florida.

FURTHER READING: James W. Crowl, *Angels in Stalin's Paradise: Western Reporters in Soviet Russia, 1917 to 1937, a Case Study of Louis Fischer and Walter Duranty* (Washington, DC: University Press of America, 1982); Sally J. Taylor, *Stalin's Apologist: Walter Duranty, the New York Times's Man in Moscow* (New York: Oxford University Press, 1990).

DWIGHT, THEODORE. *See* **Abolitionist Propaganda**

E

___

EDES, BENJAMIN (October 14, 1732–December 11, 1803). A journalist, Edes was one of the most influential and active newspaper editors and political writers of the Revolutionary period. Edes was born in Charlestown (now part of Boston), Massachusetts, son of Peter and Esther (Hall) Edes, and was modestly educated. He and his partner, John Gill, took over publication of the *Boston Gazette and Country Journal*, the "organ" of the colonial patriots, in 1755, and the third newspaper of that name in the city; Paul Revere designed its masthead. Both men were considered of bold and fearless hearts, and their paper was relentless in its opposition to British policy; it fought the political battles of the day in its columns, especially those against the Stamp Act, the tea tax, and the Boston Port Bill; and it published editorials and propaganda of some of the leaders of the American Revolution, including John Hancock and **Samuel Adams**, one of America's first propagandists. The *Gazette*'s office became the gathering place of leading opponents of George III.

Edes was one of the radical Sons of Liberty, a group called "the Loyall Nine" by Samuel Adams. Contemporary evidence reports that the members of the Boston Tea Party assembled at Edes's house on the afternoon of December 16, 1773, before moving to the *Gazette* office at the corner of Court Street and Franklin Avenue to dress in their Indian disguises. Edes was probably one of the "mohawks." He and Gill were assailed by the British authorities as "those Trumpeters of Sedition," and the *Gazette* was characterized by the governor of the colony, Sir Francis Bernard, as an "infamous weekly paper which has swarmed with Libells of the most atrocious kind." Sir Francis tried to obtain a libel indictment against its proprietors but the grand jury refused to indict, and the colony's House of Representatives admonished the governor that "the Liberty of the Press is a great bulwark of the Liberty of the People" and it is the "Duty of those who are constituted the Guardians of the People's Rights to defend and maintain it." Andrew Oliver wrote to England (1768) that the *Gazette* represented "the temper of the people," a fountainhead of patriotic radical propaganda, and the newspaper quickly achieved a circulation of 2,000, a record-breaker for its time. In April 1775, Edes ended his partnership with Gill and fled to Watertown with one old press and a few fonts of type when the British besieged Boston. He resumed printing his paper again, with great difficulty, in June 1775 in partnership with his two sons, Benjamin and Peter. Edes returned to Boston in November 1776 when the British finally evacuated the city and continued printing with his sons until 1794, when he continued the paper by himself. However, it did not regain its former prominence. Its patriotic mission was over, and Edes was unsuccessful in soliciting financial aid from former supporters. The paper bitterly attacked the Federalists, who considered it "contemptible by its grossness and vulgarity," and it finally ceased publication on September 17, 1798. Edes tried to continue his printing business but was unsuccessful. He lost his money in currency depreciations and spent his last years printing in a chamber over a tin-plate worker's shop. He died in poverty in Boston. He married Martha Starr around 1754; besides the two sons, there were several daughters.

FURTHER READING: Charles and Lois Apfelbaum, *Early American Newspapers and Their Printers: 1715–1783* (Valley Stream, NY: Appletree Press, 1980); Frederic Hudson, *Journalism in the U.S. From 1690 to 1872* (London: Routledge/Thoemmes, 2000; reprint of the ed. published: New York: Harper and Brothers, 1873).

EISENHOWER-ROCKEFELLER LETTER. After World War II, the Soviet Union continued to release forgeries that it expected to damage U.S. relations with its allies. Several were important campaigns. One was designated the Eisenhower-Rockefeller Letter, an extensive forgery presented as a private letter from Nelson A. Rockefeller to President Dwight D. Eisenhower in which Rockefeller was portrayed as the advocate of a "bolder program of aid to under-developed countries," as a cover for what the East German press called "supercolonialism" ("superkolonialismus"). Its aim was to discredit the U.S. commitment to the removal of the old colonial powers from their involvements in Africa and Asia.

The document first appeared on February 15, 1957, in the East German daily, *Neues Deutschland*, and circulated throughout the world during what was termed the "Camp David" period of East-West cordiality (1959–1960); it later appeared on Radio Moscow, in *Pravda* (Soviet party organ), on Radio Hanoi, on Radio Beijing, in the Czechoslovak domestic press, and in the official news agency of the People's Republic of China.

In 1961, Richard Helms, Assistant Director of the Central Intelligence Agency, testified before the U.S. Senate. He said, "Long before 1957, the Communists were as skillful as the Nazis in the production and exploitation of forgeries. But in that year, they first began to aim them frequently against American targets, to turn them out in volume, and to exploit them through a wide-flung international network. Then CIA put these fakes under the microscope. We found that each Soviet forgery is manufactured and spread according to a plan. Each is devised and timed to mesh with other techniques of psychological warfare in support of Soviet strategy." During this period, more than 32 forged documents were found.

FURTHER READING: Herbert Romerstein, "Disinformation as a KGB Weapon in the Cold War," paper prepared for a Conference on Germany and Intelligence Organizations: The Last Fifty Years in Review, Akademie fur Politische Bildung Tutzing [Germany] (Washington: Unpublished, 1999).

EISLER, GERHARDT (February 20, 1897–March 21, 1968). Communist international operative and later East German Communist party official, Gerhardt Eisler was a sharp propagandist and effective speaker who would do anything for the Soviet Union. He was born in Leipzig, Germany, son of Rudolf Eisler, a professor of philosophy at the University of Leipzig, and Marie Fischer. Shortly after his birth, his family moved to Vienna; he attended the University of Vienna but quit to enlist in the Austrian army during World War I. After his discharge (1918), he joined the Austrian Communist party but transferred his membership to the Communist party in Berlin, where he worked as an organizer and a propagandist for the party in the 1920s.

In the late 1920s, Eisler went to Moscow then was sent to China in the early 1930s to purge rebellious Chinese Communists. In 1933, Eisler came to the United States, under false passports forged in the name of Samuel Liptzen, where he became the top Comintern agent in America under the name "Edwards." Three years later, he traveled to Europe and worked for the Comintern during the Spanish Civil War. During the Soviet Nazi Pact, he was detained in an internment camp by the government as a suspicious character of German origins. In 1941, he returned to the United States on the way to Mexico but was detained at Ellis Island; he was given a visitor's visa after a ten-week investigation. While living in Queens, New York, Eisler resumed his position as senior advisor to the U.S. Communist party. An October 13, 1946, radio broadcast by Louis Budenz, former managing editor of the *Daily Worker*, who turned anti-Communist, exposed Eisler's activity ("one of the Soviet Union's top agents in America"). He was stopped from leaving the country and then called before the House Committee on Un-American Activities (HUAC) on February 6, 1947, where he claimed that he was "very glad" for the chance to "defend myself against the accusation of having misused the hospitality which the great American people and its government granted me, a German anti-fascist." However, when he appeared, he refused to be sworn in before reading a prepared statement. He got into a shouting match with the committee's chairman, J. Parnell Thomas, and was cited for contempt; his sister, Ruth Fischer, denounced him as "a most dangerous terrorist" both to Americans and to Germans; that September, his brother Hanns, a composer and author of Communist propaganda, was brought before the HUAC as a member of the Communist party. While appealing his convictions, Gerhardt Eisler jumped bond and stowed away to England, where he was arrested, but a London court refused to extradite him back to the United States. He returned to East Germany, where he became a leading Communist propagandist for Ulbricht and the East German regime, a professor at the University of Leipzig, a member of East Germany's Central Committee, and chairman of the state radio and television committee. During his career, Eisler used various aliases, including Hans Burger or Berger and "Edwards." He was married three times. Eisler died in Yerevan, Armenian Soviet Socialist Republic, while negotiating a contract between the East German and Soviet radio networks.

Eisler's publications include *Lesson of Germany: A Guide to Her History* with Albert Norden and Albert Schreiner (1945); *Eisler Hits Back: A Reply to the Rankin Men* (1947) in which Eisler counterattacked the charges brought against him by the House Committee on Un-American Activities; and *My Side of the Story: The Statement the Newspapers Refused to Print* (1947).

FURTHER READING: U.S. Congress. House Committee on Un-American Activities, *Hearings on Gerhart Eisler: Investigation of Un-American Propaganda Activities in the United States*, Transcript of Proceedings, Committee on Un-American Activities, House of Representatives, Eightieth Congress, First Session (Washington, DC: Government Printing Office, 1947).

ELDERS OF ZION. *See Protocols of the Elders of Zion*

ELLUL, JACQUES. *See Propaganda: The Formation of Men's Attitudes*

EMANCIPATION PROCLAMATION. On January 1, 1863, President Abraham Lincoln issued the Emancipation Proclamation as a temporary war measure; it freed slaves only in those states still in rebellion against the Union and not all the slaves in the United States. It was designed as propaganda, scrupulously planned and considered, as potential punishment for the South, who, in return, used it as "anti-North" propaganda. The Emancipation Proclamation was addressed to several specific target groups, and its public release was timed to produce the greatest possible reaction among its several audiences. Lincoln formulated a well-planned attack that would have the most diverse consequences for the progress of the war, depending on what psychological effects it had on several different groups. These included: the white population of the Confederate states, the slave population of the Southern states, the white population in the slave states still on the side of the North ("border" states), the politically influential Northern abolitionists, Northerners opposed to challenging Southern slavery, and the British, who were largely sympathetic to the Southern cause well into 1862. Total emancipation of all slaves was finally accomplished by the 13th Amendment to the U.S. Constitution, which was passed two years later.

FURTHER READING: M. J. [Morris Janowitz], "The Emancipation Proclamation as an Instrument of Psychological Warfare," in *Psychological Warfare Casebook*, ed. William E. Daugherty (Baltimore: Johns Hopkins; for Operations Research Office, Johns Hopkins University, 1958).

ENDICOTT, JAMES G. *See* Biological and Chemical Weapons Warfare

EXHIBITIONS. *See* Advancing American Art; American National Exhibition (Moscow); Brussels Universal and International Exposition; The Family of Man; Information USA; International Expositions

EXPOSITIONS. *See* International Expositions

F

FACTS IN REVIEW. *See* German Library of Information

FAKES. *See* Forgeries

FALSE GERM WARFARE STORY. *See* Biological and Chemical Weapons Warfare

FAMILY OF MAN. Edward Steichen's 1955 optimistic, antiwar, sentimental exhibition appeared in the context of the 1950s emergence of the United States as a world power. It was a most positive image for nearly nine million people in 38 countries with 91 stops over five years. There were two editions; the initial showings in Guatemala and in Germany were a great success, and the exhibition received rave reviews in subsequent programming. Its theme, the oneness of humanity, contrasted with the pessimistic viewpoint portrayed by Robert Frank in his photographic book, *The Americans*, which appeared at the same time The Family of Man was in Moscow (1959) as part of a larger U.S. exhibition. At all of its showings, Steichen's photographs were co-opted as a Cold War weapon by its sponsor, the U.S. Information Agency, as a selling point for its freedom ideology symbolized by the choice of consumer products resulting from U.S. postwar industry and technology. The exhibition's oneness theme, reassuring but dated, was soon replaced by Frank's book, disturbing but current, and the harsher realities of U.S. domestic (e.g., civil rights) and foreign policy (e.g., Cold War, Vietnam).

FURTHER READING: Eric J. Sandeen, *Picturing an Exhibition: 'The Family of Man' and 1950s America* (Albuquerque: University of New Mexico, 1995); Family of Man file in the Public Diplomacy Historical Collection, Bureau of Public Diplomacy, U.S. Department of State.

FAREWELL ADDRESS (WASHINGTON). Message by President George Washington on September 19, 1796, to his officers at Fraunces Tavern, in New York's Wall Street area, was allegedly written by Alexander Hamilton. The address contained what became the fundamental statement of American nationalism until well into the twentieth century: there should be "as little political connection with foreign naitons [sic] as possible." This traditional view was later challenged; Washington foresaw an expanding United States, and his views of "entangling political alliances" were meant for the present in view of the weakness of the newly independent nation.

Washington's remarks were printed by "the hated Tory printer," James Rivington, in his *New York Gazette* and were picked up by the London *Morning Chronicle* (March 2, 1784). Without Rivington's action, Washington's speech might have been lost forever. Although not intended as propaganda but as a statement of basic future principles, it was used to make the point that isolationism has deep roots in American history beginning with Washington's speech. In its time, it was considered a seminal contribution to American political thought along with the Declaration of Independence, the Constitution, and the **Federalist Papers,** but Spalding notes that the warning against "entangling alliances" first appeared in the 1801 Inaugural Address of Thomas Jefferson and that Washington favored an active policy of national independence, rather than noninvolvement in world affairs.

FURTHER READING: Frederic B. Farrar, *This Common Channel to Independence: Revolution and Newspapers, 1759–1789* (Garden City, NY: Farrar, 1975); Burton I. Kaufman, *Washington's Farewell Address: The View From the 20th Century* (Chicago: Quadrangle Books, 1969); Matthew Spalding, "George Washington's Farewell Address," *Wilson Quarterly* (Autumn 1996): 65–71.

FEDERAL ARTS PROJECT. The Federal Art Project (FPA) was one of four programs that were collectively part of the Works Progress Administration's (WPA) Federal Project Number One (Federal One); the others were the Federal Music Project (FMP), the **Federal Theater Project** (FTP), and the Federal Writers' Project (FWP). WPA, the parent agency, was created by President Franklin Roosevelt through Executive Order 7034 ("The Creation of Machinery for the Works Progress Administration"), signed May 6, 1935, under authority vested in the president by the "Emergency Relief Appropriation Act of 1935," approved April 8, 1935, was designated as an aid to white-collar or "professional persons," which included over 3.5 million "employables" (artists, musicians, actors, and writers).

FAP was established in August 1935 as the first major attempt at government patronage of the visual arts in the United States and the most extensive and influential of the visual arts projects conceived during the Great Depression of the 1930s by the Roosevelt administration. In a more humorous vein, FAP was a relief agency that responded to the poverty of America's artists by giving each of them a can of paint and telling them to decorate the walls of America's public buildings. However, FAP should not be confused with the Department of the Treasury art programs (Treasury Section of Painting and Sculpture, Public Works of Art Project, and Treasury Relief Art Project or TRAP), but, unlike the Treasury's endeavors, the Works Progress (later Projects) Administration Federal Art Project (WPA/FAP) employed artists with a wide range of experience and styles, sponsored a more varied and experimental body of art, and had a far greater influence on subsequent American movements. This was chiefly the result of the leadership of its national director, Holger Cahill, a former museum curator and expert on American folk art, who saw the potential for cultural development in what was essentially a work-relief program for artists. Cahill and his staff learned from the Public Works of Art Project of 1933–34, an FAP predecessor, that any relief program faced the problem of attempting to produce art of high quality while trying to help the unemployed, regardless of talent. In the fall of 1935, a range of creative, educational, research, and service projects were organized to preserve the skills of professional artists in mural, easel, sculpture, and graphic art divisions, of commercial artists in the poster and Index of American Design divisions, and of the less experienced in art education and technical jobs. The project developed an audience by establishing more than 100 community art centers and galleries across the country in regions where art and artists were almost unknown.

Cahill stated in 1936 that "the organization of the Project has proceeded on the principle that it is not the solitary genius but a sound general movement which maintains art as a vital, functioning part of any cultural scheme." According to Cahill, art was not a matter of rare, occasional masterpieces, a viewpoint that was in direct opposition to the philosophy of the Department of the Treasury programs, which sought to commission outstanding works rather than to provide work relief. Both Treasury (through TRAP) and FAP provided the State Department with scores of paintings for use in legations around the world and in art exhibitions.

The project's greatest problem was to balance the whims and irregular schedules of the creative process with the rigid timekeeping rules of the WPA bureaucracy. During its existence, FAP employed an estimated 5,000 artists who produced some 2,500 murals, 108,000 easel paintings, 17,700 sculptures, and 11,200 print designs. Another basic problem arose when budget reductions required the WPA to eliminate artists from its rolls; when too many termination notices were received, riots and sit-down strikes often occurred among the artists.

During the depths of the Great Depression of the 1930s and into the early years of World War II, the federal government supported the arts in unprecedented ways, provided work for jobless artists, and promoted American art and culture and to give more Americans access to what President Franklin Roosevelt described as "an abundant life." The projects saved thousands of artists from poverty and despair and enabled Americans all across the country to see an original painting for the first time, attend their first professional live theater performance, or take their first music or drawing class, but the art projects also sparked controversy. Some politicians believed them to be wasteful propaganda and wanted them ended; others wanted them expanded. The controversies that these actions generated, along with the United States' entry into World War II, the decrease in unemployment, and the need for work relief, eventually killed the projects.

After mounting Congressional and public criticism of the WPA projects, the Federal Art Project ended its government funding when Roosevelt signed the Reorganization Act of 1939 (April 25, 1939), which transferred WPA functions to a new Federal Works Agency. FAP ended in September 1939 with instructions for states to assume their supervision along with 25 percent of their cost and stiffer requirements for employment. An artist could be employed for only 18 months before being removed from the FAP rolls. The art project struggled through World War II when many FAP artists and photographers turned their efforts to defense work, such as designing posters for the **Office of War Information** and other wartime agencies or documenting community mobilization in American cities and towns. WPA was finally abolished by presidential letter, December 4, 1942, effective June 30, 1943. After World War II, the U.S. government used the arts for Cold War propaganda, most notably the **U.S. Information Agency** (USIA), which sponsored foreign tours of art exhibitions.

Most New Deal artists were grateful to President Roosevelt for giving them work and enthusiastically supported the New Deal's liberal agenda. Not surprisingly, their art celebrated the progress made under Franklin Roosevelt and promoted the president and his programs. Many politically active artists worked for the New Deal projects. United by a desire to use art to promote social change, these artists sympathized with the labor movement and exhibited an affinity for left-wing politics ranging from New Deal liberalism to socialism to communism.

FURTHER READING: "American Art Abroad: The State Department Collection," *Art News* 45 (October 1946): 20–31; Ray A. Billington, "Government and the Arts: The WPA," *American Quarterly* 13 (1961): 466–479; John Y. Cole, "Amassing American "Stuff": The Library of Congress and the Federal Arts Projects of the 1930s," *Quarterly Journal of the Library of Congress* (Fall 1983) 356–389; Michael Denning, *The Cultural Front: The Laboring of American Culture in the Twentieth Century* (New York and London: Verso, 1997); Kenneth W. Heger, "Diplomats and the Depression: The Department of State and the New Deal," *Prologue* (Summer 1998): 98–108; Jane de Hart Mathews, "Art and Politics in Cold War America," *American Historical Review* 81 (October 1976): 762–777; Francis V. O'Connor, ed. *Art for the Millions: Essays From the 1930s by Artists an Administrators of the WPA Federal Arts Project* (Greenwich, CT: New York Graphic Society, 1973); Marlene Park and Gerald E. Mokowitz, *Democratic Visas: Post Offices and Public Art in the New Deal* (Philadelphia: Temple University, 1984).

FEDERAL BUREAU OF INVESTIGATION. The Federal Bureau of Investigation (FBI) does not use propaganda in any significant way, but the agency was responsible for investigation of propaganda by hostile governments, such as Nazi Germany in World War II or the Soviet Union during the Cold War.

FEDERAL THEATER PROJECT (FTP). The Federal Theater Project (FTP) was established by the U.S. Works Progress Administration in 1935 by an act of Congress, under the direction of Hallie Flanagan (1890–1969), to make work for theatrical professionals idled by the Depression and to create, according to Depression Relief Administrator Harry Hopkins, a standard of "free, adult, uncensored" theater. From its beginnings, it was a controversial venture, as many of its productions were written by activist playwrights to inform and to influence Americans about the causes and possible solutions to the Depression. Productions included creative revivals of old classics through new plays, children's plays, plays in foreign languages, marionette shows, and evenings of dance. An innovation was The Living Newspaper documentaries, a series of New Deal stage productions that used slides, recordings, actual voices, and actors to bring political journalism into the theater through dialogue taken from newspaper articles, speeches, and government documents. However, many of the productions were considered left-wing propaganda pieces, and opposition to the FTP increased.

In August, November, and December 1938, the House Special Committee on Un-American Activities, under the chairmanship of Martin Dies, held hearings on the Federal Theater Project as part of WPA appropriations for 1939–1940. The committee heard testimony from Flanagan and Ellen S. Woodward, WPA assistant administrator; Flanagan defended the project, but the FTP was identified with everything conservative critics hated in the New Deal. The productions were called "putrid" and designed to spread Communist propaganda at the expense of American taxpayers while Congressmen ridiculed even the titles of plays, finding them silly and even immoral. One angry Congressman made news by asking Flanagan if Christopher Marlowe was a Communist! There was considerable support from the theater and film community but the critics outweighed them, and Congress stopped its funding; FTP ended on June 30, 1939. U.S. Congressman J. Parnell Thomas (R-N.J.), later chairman of the House Un-American Activities Committee, stated that almost "practically every play presented under the auspices of the [National Theater] Project is sheer propaganda for Communism or the New Deal."

See also **U.S. Congress. House. Committee on Un-American Activities; U.S. Congressional Investigations of Propaganda**

FURTHER READING: Eric Bentley, ed., *Thirty Years of Treason: Excerpts from Hearings Before the House Committee on Un-American Activities, 1938–1968* (New York: Viking, 1971); U.S. Congress. House. Special Committee on Un-American Activities, *Investigation of Un-American Propaganda Activities in the United States*; hearings, 75th Congress, 3d Session (Washington, DC: Government Printing Office, 1938–1939), v. 4: 2729–2830, 2837–2885; John Y. Cole, "Amassing American Stuff," *Quarterly Journal of the Library of Congress* (Fall 1983): 356–389; Yvonne French, "Theater's Paper Trail," *Library of Congress Information Bulletin* 54, no. 3 (February 6, 1995): 44–49; George Kazacoff, *Dangerous Theatre: The Federal Theatre Project as a Forum for New Plays* (New York: Peter Lang, 1989).

FEDERAL THEATRE PROJECT. *See* Federal Theater Project

THE FEDERALIST. Now considered one of the four "basic documents" of the American political tradition that influenced the constitutional debate, *The Federalist* was originally a series of eighty-five newspaper articles, now known collectively as *The Federalist Papers*, that appeared anonymously at regular intervals in the New York press prepared by "Publius" (Alexander Hamilton, James Madison, and John Jay) between October 1787 and May 1788 to win New York State's support for the recently drafted Constitution of the United States. The essays, eighty-five in all, were effective political propaganda that appeared during the controversial period surrounding adoption of a federal Constitution to replace the Articles of Federation after the American Revolution; one of their main objectives was to persuade the citizens in the thirteen states to accept and to ratify the new document. They proved an effective propaganda instrument among opinion leaders as well as a careful and thoughtful political treatise.

The essays were still appearing serially when the first collected edition, edited with an introduction by Hamilton, appeared in two volumes (March–May 1788) as *The Federalist: A Collection of Essays written in Favour of the New Constitution, as agreed upon by the Federal Convention, September 17, 1787.* Since then, there have been a great many American editions published as well as several foreign translations of the collected papers, but the used reference text is that edited by Clinton Rossiter based on the first edition published in 1788 by J. M'Lean and Company, with all 85 essays. It was in the French edition (1792) that the authorship of the essays was first formally acknowledged.

FURTHER READING: Ed Crews, "The Federalist," *Colonial Williamsburg* 25, no. 2 (Summer 2003): 26–31; John G. Heller, *The Selling of the Constitution: The Federalist Papers Viewed as an Advertising Campaign* (M.A. thesis, University of Florida, 1974); Willmoore Kendall and George W. Carey, "Introduction: How to Read 'The Federalist,'" in *The Federalist Papers* [by] James Madison, Alexander Hamilton [and] John Jay (New Rochelle, NY: Arlington House, 1966).

(Continued)

Albanian translation of *The Federalist Papers* by Albania's then Deputy Minister of Justice Kristaq Traja (on page 102). Also shown (above) is "The Federalist Papers," essay number 22 by Alexander Hamilton, as it appeared in the Albanian newspaper Drita. (*Source:* USIA World, vol. 12, no. 1, pp. 8–9)

FEDERALIST PAPERS. *See The Federalist*

FIFTH COLUMN. The Fifth Column refers to a propaganda or paramilitary group operating behind enemy lines and usually consisting of citizens of the target country. It is also used as a designation for suspected traitors on the home front, willing to assist "the enemy" occupying forces if they come or as covert propaganda spread by people in a country who secretly support its enemies. In the United States, they were people who filled the ranks of the Communist Party, U.S.A., and of the 500 or more Fascist organizations in the United States, the people who led the organizations, and the individuals who swirled around its edges.

Historians place the origin of the term *fifth column* with the Peloponnesian Wars, and there was a fifth column during the Civil War. In modern times, it took on much significance during the Spanish Civil War of the 1930s, when a rebel general declared that he had four columns of troops marching to republican Madrid and a fifth column of citizens awaiting his arrival in that city. Ernest Hemingway's play, *The Fifth Column*, was his political commitment to the Spanish cause. The Fifth Column was an organization of Rebel sympathizers who lived in Loyalist territory and committed acts of sabotage and murder. Franco led rebels or Nationalists. The Loyalists were championed by Hemingway and aided by the Soviets.

During World War II, a fifth columnist became anyone with suspected Nazi sympathies. To counter this, the Veterans of Foreign Wars issued *Fifth Column Facts: A Handbook of Information on Nazi, Fascist, and Communist Activities in the United States* (1940?).

Colonel **William J. Donovan** ("Wild Bill"), World War I Medal of Honor winner, who was appointed by President Franklin Roosevelt as his first director of secret intelligence (**Coordinator of Information**, predecessor of the **Central Intelligence Agency**), warned Americans about the dangers of fifth columnists in *Fifth Column Lessons for America* (1941), which he wrote with Edgar Mowrer. The pamphlet had a foreword by Secretary of the Navy Frank Knox; it was a series of articles that originally appeared in the U.S. press by the authors as an attempt to forewarn Americans against a subtle form of attack then being used successfully in Europe by the Nazis.

A different use of the fifth column was in a covert program that was part of China's Hong Kong policy after 1982. There was to be a secret immigration from mainland China to Hong Kong, which was designed to put in place a classic fifth column of Communist loyalists to be used if all other institution-based arrangements for the power transfer of the British colony to Chinese rule failed.

FURTHER READING: Dan Gilbert, *The Real Fifth Column and How It Is Undermining America* (San Diego, CA: Danielle Publishers, 1942); Harold Lavine, *Fifth Column in America* (New York: Doubleday, Doran and Company, 1940); Francis M. MacDonnell, *Insidious Foes: The Axis Fifth Column and the American Home Front* (New York: Oxford University, 1995).

FIGHT FOR FREEDOM COMMITTEE (FFF). Founded on April 19, 1941, in New York City, the Fight for Freedom Committee (FFF) was an interventionist organization whose members were dubbed "warhawks" for their determination to get an immediate war declaration against Germany. It was established after several months of preliminary meetings with Century Group members. FFF supported complete aid to Great Britain, except for war, and tried to arouse Americans to fight Adolf Hitler by arguing that the United States was already at war against the Axis. FFF was competitive with the **Committee to Defend America by Aiding the Allies** but it became the more important of the two by the summer before **Pearl Harbor** and quickly established local chapters throughout the country that held rallies, placed news stories, sponsored radio programs and public meetings, and agitated against isolationism. The Committee constantly attacked isolationists and their principal organization, **America First Committee**, and tried to discredit isolationists and their cause, especially by pinning certain images on them (e.g., Nazi, Fascist, Axis dupe). On October 19, 1941, FFF placed its famous ad in the *New York Times*, "In Hitler's Own Words: Shut up, Yank—learn to speak NAZI!" FFF had a friendly, sometimes subservient, relationship with the White House. When the United States entered World War II, the Fight for Freedom Committee disbanded.

FURTHER READING: Mark L. Chadwin, *The Warhawks: American Interventionists before Pearl Harbor* (New York: Norton, 1970/1968); Richard W. Steele, *Propaganda in an Open Society: The Roosevelt Administration and the Media, 1933–1941* (Westport, CT: Greenwood, 1985).

FILMS. *See Birth of a Nation*; Disney Image; Documentary Films; Motion Pictures; Spanish-American War; Vietnam Movies; Why We Fight Series

FISH, HAMILTON, SR. *See* U.S. Congressional Investigations of Propaganda

FISHER, HAMMOND EDWARD ("JOE PALOOKA"). *See* Comics and Comic Strips

FLAHERTY, ROBERT. *See* Documentary Films

FLANAGAN, HALLIE. *See* Federal Theater Project

FLEMMING REPORT. *See* President's Advisory Committee on Government Organization

FORD, HENRY. *See* Henry Ford's *The International Jew*

FOREIGN AGENTS REGISTRATION ACT (FARA). The Foreign Agents Registration Act was enacted into law on June 8, 1938 [52 Stat. 631] to restrict distribution of foreign films and publications into the United States, mostly to counter the growing influence of propaganda from communist, fascist, and national socialist (Nazi) governments that circulated within the United States. Section 4 of the act contained the provisions relating to the filing and labeling of political propaganda by persons required to register under the Act. These regulations applied only to political propaganda transmitted in the United States mails or by any means or instrumentality of interstate or foreign commerce for or in the interests of the foreign principal. Individuals and organizations that disseminated propaganda or participated in related activities on behalf of another country had to file public reports with the U.S. Department of Justice's Criminal Division. Although there are exemptions in the legislation (commercial, religious, scientific, artistic, academic), it was mainly used to prohibit unlabeled political propaganda (prints, radio broadcasts, telecasts) from coming in, or to limit access to political materials hostile to the United States.

The act was revised on June 29, 1942, and then amended further on several occasions, the most recent being on July 4, 1966. One of the major purposes of the 1966 amendments was to refocus the Act to protect the public's right to identify sources of foreign political propaganda. During the 1980s, the act was given a new interpretation by the Reagan administration when the U.S.

Department of Justice tried to label three films produced by the National Film Board of Canada as propaganda. The Justice Department ordered the Film Board of Canada to include a disclaimer with the films, two about acid rain and the Oscar-winning *If You Love This Planet*, that the U.S. government considered the films "political propaganda." Under U.S. law, the Film Board of Canada was required to provide the names of the persons and organizations in the United States who ordered the films. The American Civil Liberties Union (ACLU) challenged the "political propaganda" label through the courts, but the Supreme Court upheld the decision to label the three Canadian films as "propaganda."

See also Postal Regulations (Communist Political Propaganda)

FURTHER READING: [U.S. Dept. of Justice] *Foreign Agents Registration Act of 1938, as Amended, and the Rules and Regulations Prescribed by the Attorney General* (Washington, DC: U.S. Dept. of Justice, 1986); Joseph E. Pattison and John L. Taylor, eds., *The Registration of Foreign Agents in the United States: A Practical and Legal Guide* (Washington, DC: District of Columbia Bar, 1981).

FOREIGN INFORMATION SERVICE. *See* **Coordinator of Information**

FORGERIES. The use of forgeries to deceive an enemy or affect public opinion has been a stable of disinformation almost through modern history but they can also be more easily exposed than other types of active measures largely because careful analysis can often demonstrate convincingly that the document is a fake. They are effective in at least two ways:

First, a forgery can be secretly given to a target government ("silent" forgery). This can be the most damaging, for the target does not know that the forgery is being circulated and may never get the opportunity to refute it.

Second, forgeries, when exposed, force the government that created it to spend time, effort, and funds to defend it. However, denial never entirely offsets the damage done, as "when there's smoke there's fire," a doubt that can be compounded by repeated reference to the forgery and to its contents.

Although forgeries are usually considered an invention of the Soviet Union, forgeries have been documented in the United States since its earliest days. These included the **Cadore Letter** and **De Lome Letter**. However, no country has used forgeries as extensively as the Soviet Union; they developed them to a level unparalleled in previous times. For the Soviets, forgeries are a weapon of active measures (i.e., influence operations) that support propaganda themes. KGB has the responsibility for carrying out active measures and producing forgeries. Describing the role of the KGB in influencing attitudes in the West, Yuri Andropov, then head of KGB, said in 1967: "The state security bodies are also actively participating in the fulfillment of this task. The workers of these bodies are aware that peaceful coexistence is a form of class struggle; that it is a bitter and stubborn battle on all fronts, economic, political, and ideological. In this fight, the state security bodies are obliged to carry out their specific duties efficiently and faultlessly." These Soviet state security bodies were built on the activities of the czarist secret police (Okhrana), who produced one of history's classic forgeries.

One of the most widely circulated propaganda tracts and one of the centerpieces of anti-Semitic literature is the infamous **Protocols of the Learned Elders of Zion**, which was created by the czarist secret police. It appeared shortly before the 1905 uprising against Nicholas II of Russia. Six months after seizing power, the Bolsheviks denied charges that Lenin and his comrades were German agents. On September 15, 1918, the U.S. government released to the press a collection of documents that purported to show that the Bolsheviks had received money both before and after the Russian Revolution. The next month, the **Committee on Public Information** (CPI) released a pamphlet to the press entitled *The German-Bolshevik Conspiracy*, which contained translations of 68 documents and reproductions of many of them.

On October 25, 1924, the British Foreign Office released to the press the text of an alleged document of the Communist International ordering the British Communist Party to carry out activities against the Labour government and to organize cells in the army (**Zinoviev Letter**). Ruth Fischer, who was an alternate member of the Executive Committee of the Comintern and a German delegate to the Fifth Congress, claimed that Zinoviev had told her that the letter had indeed been a forgery but had been produced by the GPU (Soviet secret police) to undermine his position in the Party. A Soviet book, *Anti-Soviet Forgeries*, published in Russian (1926) and in English (1927), identified the number of White Russian émigré Druzhelovsky's forgeries. One of these was a supposed letter from the Comintern to the Communist Party of Bulgaria ordering them to organize an insurrection on April 15, 1924. The document had fallen into the hands of the police weeks earlier, and translations and a facsimile of it appeared in Bulgarian newspapers on April 4. The document was clearly a forgery and was soon exposed as such. No one expected the Communists to move on April 15, the day General Gheorghieff was murdered. The next day, during a memorial service at the Sofia Cathedral, an explosion killed more than 200 people and at least 500 were injured. The police cracked down on the Communist Party. The Comintern responded, "It is not the work of a Party. The whole population is conducting the struggle against the bloody reaction."

The liberal American journalist George Seldes shed light on Druzhelovsky's possible true allegiances. He had been taken in by a Druzhelovsky forgery in the 1920s. Writing in 1929, Seldes said, "I had been offered documents and when the agent was approved by the American consulate, I bought them. One was a letter about $25,000 sent by the Third International for Bolshevik work in Buenos Aires. The man who sold me this document confessed forgery (according to the Moscow press), but an American newspaper men [*sic*: man] in Russia say [*sic*: says] Drushieowsky [*sic*: Druzhelovsky], always was and is now a secret agent of the Chekah (*sic*: Cheka). I suppose the documents were his forgeries but I can not understand the excitement in the radical press about them because in open sessions of the Third International Congress of 1922 I heard announcements about the sending of money for Bolshevik enterprises in South America. The document may have been a forgery; the forged words, however, relate historical facts."

Then in 1930, the U.S. Congress was planning to establish a committee to investigate Communist propaganda. Shortly before it was formed, the New York City police department received copies of a set of documents (**Whalen Documents**) purporting to be letters from the Communist International instructing Amtorg to carry out Communist propaganda in the United States. An examination of the documents reveals clearly that they are forgeries. For example, the letterhead reads "Ispolkom Kominterna" (Excom Comintern). An authentic document would spell out "Communist International," rather than using the nickname Comintern. Journalist John L. Spivak, a Communist Party member, exposed the forgeries. His inside information about the forgeries indicated that the Communist Party itself had created them.

Post–World War II Developments

Since World War II, the Soviet Union continued to release forgeries that it expected to damage U.S. relations with its allies. Several were important campaigns. One was designated the **Eisenhower–Rockefeller Letter**, an extensive forgery presented as a private letter from Nelson A. Rockefeller to President Dwight D. Eisenhower in which Rockefeller was portrayed as the advocate of a "bolder program of aid to under-developed countries" as a cover for what the East Germany press called "supercolonialism" ("superkolonialismus"). Its aim was to discredit the U.S. commitment to the removal of the old colonial powers from their involvements in Africa and Asia.

In 1961 Richard Helms, Assistant Director of the Central Intelligence Agency, testified before the U.S. Senate. He said, "Long before 1957, the Communists were as skillful as the Nazis in the production and exploitation of forgeries. But in that year, they first began to aim them frequently against American targets, to turn them out in volume, and to exploit them through a wide-flung international network. Then CIA put these fakes under the microscope. We found that each Soviet forgery is manufactured and spread according to a plan. Each is devised and timed to mesh with other techniques of psychological warfare in support of Soviet strategy." During this period, more than 32 forged documents were found.

In a 1980 report to the U.S. Congress, the CIA revealed that "the KGB provides a non-attributable adjunct to the overt Soviet propaganda network. Service A of the KGB's Foreign Intelligence Directorate plans, coordinates and supports operations which are designed to backstop overt Soviet propaganda using such devices of covert actions as forgeries, planted press articles, planted rumors, and controlled information media. In particular, the number of Soviet forgeries has increased dramatically in recent years. In the early 1970s, this section of the KGB was upgraded from "department" to "service" status, an indication of its increased importance. Service A maintains liaison with its counterparts in the Cuban and the East European services and coordinates its overall program with theirs." A more recent forgery involved the sale of uranium, supposedly sold to Iraq by Niger. That forgery is a complicated and controversial case. Speculation was that it may have been done by a Nigerian diplomat, although no final determination was made, at least publicly. Discussion of the forgery has disappeared, at least in the public arena, perhaps because of political sensitivities. Another one involved George Galloway, the British MP who was found to be on

Saddam's payroll. After true information about that surfaced, a forgery appeared making the same allegation.

Forgery Dissemination

The usual path of a Soviet forgery was from the KGB to a target newspaper. When the target was a legitimate publication it became difficult for the Soviets to succeed in planting the forgery. They often used publications that they could control or influence for the initial surfacing. One publication frequently used this way was the Indian newspaper *Patriot*. In testimony before a British court on March 24, 1987, Ilya Dzhirkvelov, a former officer of the KGB, revealed that in 1962 on KGB orders he participated in setting up this newspaper.

After a forgery appeared in a publication such as the *Patriot*, it was replayed by the Soviet press agencies TASS or Novosti. This provided copies in every language for KGB officers to plant in the world press through their agents but not all forgeries were meant for publication. They were passed by KGB agents of influence to officials of a target government in the hope that they would believe forgeries designed to increase anti-American feeling. Such forgeries were often unknown to American officials, who had no opportunity to refute many of them. With the fall of the Soviet Union and the relaxation of the American–Soviet rivalry, KGB forgeries lessened, but they continue to remain a significant weapon of disinformation stories.

See also Active Measures Working Group; Helene Von Damm Forgery Letter; Kirkpatrick Speech; Ku Klux Klan; Rockefeller Letter; Stimson–Borah Letter; Tanaka Memorandum; U.S. Army Field Manual

FURTHER READING: Neil Baldwin, *Henry Ford and the Jews: The Mass Production of Hate* (New York: Public Affairs, 2001); Herbert Romerstein, "Disinformation as a KGB Weapon in the Cold War," paper prepared for a Conference on Germany and Intelligence Organizations: The Last Fifty Years in Review, Akademie fur Politische Bildung Tutzing [Germany] (Washington: Unpublished, 1999); William E. Daugherty, *Psychological Warfare Casebook* (Baltimore: Johns Hopkins; published for Operations Research Office, Johns Hopkins University, 1958); U.S. Department of State, *Active Measures: A Report on the Substance and Process of Anti-U.S. Disinformation and Propaganda Campaigns* (Washington: The Department, 1986); U.S. Department of State, *Soviet Influence Activities: A Report on Active Measures and Propaganda, 1987–1988* (Washington: The Department, 1989); U.S. International Communication Agency, *Forgeries of U.S. Documents*; prepared by the European Branch, Office of Research (Washington: The Agency, 1982).

FOUR FREEDOMS. President Franklin D. Roosevelt outlined the Four Freedoms at the opening address of the 77th Congress on January 6, 1941. It became a rallying point for U.S. involvement in World War II. The speech expressed what Roosevelt saw as the imperial nature of human freedom in Europe at the Nazis' hands. He used the speech to urge Congress to back his program of lend-lease to the Allies. Freedom from Want and Freedom from Fear (the others are Freedom of Religion and Freedom of Speech) referred to the Atlantic Charter, the statement of principles formulated on August 14, 1941, by Roosevelt and British Prime Minister Winston Churchill. After **Pearl Harbor**, the **Office of War Information** (OWI) used the Four Freedoms to explain military participation in World War II.

In August 1942, the OWI published a pamphlet, *The U.N. Fight for the Four Freedoms: The Rights of All Men—Everywhere*, under the direction of poet and Librarian of Congress Archibald MacLeish. The pamphlet had no byline, but it clearly bore the authority of MacLeish's idealism; the introduction was by Roosevelt. The Four Freedoms received a visual boost from Norman Rockwell, who created four vignettes using his neighbors in Arlington, Vermont, as models. OWI rejected the artist's plans for a series of works illustrating Roosevelt's principles, but *Saturday Evening Post* editor Ben Hibbs embraced them. When the paintings were published in a series of supplements, beginning February 20, 1943, accompanied by an essay of the same title, the popular reaction was so intense that more than 25,000 readers requested reproductions suitable for framing. OWI printed more that 2,500,000 copies of the prints as posters for the war bond effort and toured Rockwell's original paintings and their reproductions in summer 1943 to launch a patriotic bond campaign, which sold almost $133 million at the campaign's end.

FURTHER READING: Notes from Library of Congress exhibition, The Four Freedoms (1996).

FOUR-MINUTE MEN. Volunteer program of speakers, which was organized in Chicago in April 1917 and lasted until the end of World War I, whose sole function was to serve as spokesmen for the U.S. government in World War I by generating home front support for the war effort. The Four-Minute Men organization became a part of the **Committee on Public Information** (CPI), which provided the speakers with slides to introduce themselves, bulletins with suggested speech topics, and plenty of advice on major topics, such as Liberty Loans, military draft, food conservation, the Red Cross, patriotism, and anti-German propaganda, all geared to the home front helping the American war effort.

Speakers gave four-minute speeches in movie theaters, an especially popular place, as well as in other public places, such as churches and lodge meeting halls, to stir up patriotism during the war. It was estimated that four minutes was the amount of time it took movie projectionists to change the reels of film. There were eventually over 75,000 members in every state and some territories who delivered over 750,000 speeches to an estimated 300 million people; the all-male organization added women, schoolchildren, and college students as U.S. involvement in the war continued and more speakers were needed to carry the government's message. As official spokespersons, the speakers were not encouraged to stray from the suggestions and programs outlined in the bulletins, and they were advised to not talk over the four-minute length. Toward the end of the war, four-minute singing of popular and patriotic songs was added.

FURTHER READING: Stephen L. Vaughn, *Holding Fast the Inner Lines: Democracy, Nationalism, and the Committee on Public Information* (Chapel Hill: University of North Carolina, 1980).

FRANCE. Benjamin Franklin's mission in the 1780s to the Court of Louis XVI to sell the American Revolution was probably the first major propaganda effort by the new United States. Since then, France's attitude has been ambivalent; it is one of America's biggest allies and one of its strongest critics. During the post–World War II Fourth Republic, France was one of the European countries targeted for assistance by the **Marshall Plan**; in return for this aid, France was required to open all its markets to American imports and investments; this resulted in an inundation of products and of propaganda, selling the American way of life, like Disney, *Reader's Digest*, and Coca-Cola, which seemed to be the most influential. In opposition to the growth of Coca-Cola bottling plants in their country, groups such as the French Communist party responded with their own propaganda, claiming that the distribution centers were actually spy networks. Others, such as the wine and bottled water interests, were concerned about their domestic markets. This ambivalence from the French toward Americans still seems to exist, most recently with the anti-American opposition that surfaced after President George W. Bush sent troops to Iraq in 2003.

See also **Committee on Public Information; Normandy Invasion (D-Day); Occupied Countries and Territories; Office of War Information; World War I; World War II**

FURTHER READING: William R. Keylor, "'How They Advertised France': The French Propaganda Campaign in the United States During the Breakup of the Franco-American Entente, 1918–1923," *Diplomatic History* 17, no. 3 (Summer 1993): 351–373.

FRANK, BENNO D. (1907 or 1908?–1980). Benno Frank, a naturalized American citizen, was born in Mannheim, Germany, the son of a Polish diplomat. Frank's father, who moved around frequently in the diplomatic service, believed in the virtues of the German culture, and he wanted his son to have an intensive training in his heritage. Being from another country, the father made arrangements to leave his son in the home of General von Kliest while he received his education in Germany during the 1920s. Frank acquired an appreciation of German civilization, which was considered better than many native-born Germans and which helped him later as a propagandist. After he graduated from Marburg University he directed plays and operas and was an assistant to legendary stage director Max Reinhardt. When Hitler came to power, Frank escaped to Israel, where he became general manager and director of the Palestine Opera Company and head of drama and opera at the Palestine Conservatory. He came to the United States in 1938 and worked as a stage director at the American League for Opera, chaired the opera department at the New York College of Music, and directed plays at the 1939–1940 New York World's Fair, the Academy of Vocal Arts, Philadelphia, and in other eastern colleges.

During World War II, Frank enlisted in the U.S. Army and was appointed production chief for radio activities in the Psychological Warfare Division, 12th Army Group, where he improvised new tricks or devices that threw the enemy off psychological balance. He honed these skills in his radio broadcasts to German troops quite effectively to the besieged garrison of **Lorient**, in summer 1944. He encouraged the troops to "live to go back to Germany to assist in its reconstruction" rather than to "die on the battlefield." To the Germans, Frank became "Captain Angers," a soldier who had served in the German army but who later became a captain in the U.S. Army. He spoke on subjects important to his German listeners, commenting on the American way of life, the peculiar differences between American and German ways of doing things, and the value of democracy. A memorable image was his gesticulating Hitlerian fury before the mike.

After Lorient, Frank was transferred to Radio Luxembourg and **Operation Annie**, also known as Radio 1212 because of its broadcasting frequency, the second most powerful commercial transmitter in Europe (1212 meters). As its acknowledged voice and principal broadcaster, with an unmistakable Rhenish accent, Frank put together the distinctive broadcast segments that made the station completely believable. When the war ended, he became deputy director, Film, Theater and Music Control Branch, Information Control Branch, Office of the Military Governor for the U.S. (OMGUS), during the U.S. occupation of Germany, where he tried to de-Nazify German theaters and orchestras. After his military stint, Frank settled in Cleveland, Ohio, as a drama teacher and musical director in municipal theater, including Karamu Theater and the Cleveland Play House, but he also headed the opera department of the Cleveland Music School Settlement and directed plays off-Broadway and in San Francisco. In 1960, the German government awarded him the Officer's Cross of the Order of Merit for reestablishing German theaters and orchestras and for his prewar service as director of the Schiller Opera in Hamburg and for his work in starting cultural exchange programs for OMGUS. Frank moved to Israel in the early 1970s, where he died. In a *New York Times* (April 14, 1990) story about a reunion of Army psychological warriors from Frank's former unit, the author calls him the "patron saint of psych warriors," a group that included future travel expert Eugene Fodor and later CBS chairman William S. Paley.

FURTHER READING: William E. Daugherty, *A Psychological Warfare Casebook* (Baltimore: Johns Hopkins; published for Operations Research Office, Johns Hopkins University, 1958); "The Death of a Maestro," [Cleveland] *Plain Dealer*, April 8, 1980: 5B; Douglas Martin,"About New York: Together Again, These Silly Foes of Nazi Resolve," *New York Times* (April 14, 1990): I, 25; Kathleen McLaughlin, "Report from Berlin," *New York Times* (May 19, 1946): II, 2; Lawrence C. Soley and John S. Nichols, *Clandestine Radio Broadcasting: A Study of Revolutionary and Counterrevolutionary Electronic Communication* (New York and Westport, CT: Praeger, 1987).

FRANKLIN, BENJAMIN (January 17, 1706–April 17, 1790). Benjamin Franklin was born in Boston, Massachusetts. He left school early to learn the printing trade from his brother, James, who published the *New England Courant*, one of America's first newspapers. Franklin moved, first to New York, then to Philadelphia, where he published the *Pennsylvania Gazette* and wrote *Poor Richard's Almanack: Being the choicest Morsels of Wisdom, written during the Years of the Almanack's Publication. By that well-known Savant, Dr. Benjamin Franklin of Philadelphia* (Philadelphia: Published in Mount Vernon, New York. at the Sign of the Peter Pauper Press, with numerous quaint Cuts by an Unknown Hand, c. 1732–1757). In May 1732, he founded *Philadelphische Zeitung, von Allerhand Auswartig-und Einheimischen Merckwurdigen Sachen*, the first foreign-language newspaper in British North America.

Franklin was one of the first renaissance men in the United States; he was a statesman, scientist, writer, and colonial printer. He experimented with electricity, charted the Gulf Stream, invented the glass harmonica, organized America's first police force, and thought up the fire department, the lending library, and a college that became the University of Pennsylvania. He should also be considered, among his other accomplishments, the first American public relations man, one who well knew the power of the press. He was also an agent of influence, manager of covert French aid to the American revolutionaries, and director of American paramilitary activities against the British.

Franklin was a strong pamphleteer in Europe in support of the American revolutionary cause, but one of his earliest propaganda efforts was the "**Join or Die**" political cartoon that urged the colonies to unite. He was in England (1757–1762 and 1765–1775), then was appointed in September 1776 as the first U.S. diplomat. He arrived in Paris on November 29, 1776, as part of a three-man commission charged with gaining French support for American independence; he was, in effect, the first Public Affairs Officer (PAO) and intelligence agent. He stayed until 1784 at the Court of Louis XVI.

In England, Franklin exploited the available media with a mix of materials, such as letters to the editor, books and tracts that highlighted American grievances, political cartoons, and **gray propaganda**. In some of his propaganda letters, he used an imaginative Baron Munchausen type of story. Franklin noticed early on that the British press liked to print misinformation about the colonies to the disadvantage of the Americans. Franklin "attacked" constantly in the English press and with pamphlets from 1757 until the beginning of the American Revolution, mostly with pseudonyms. While he was in France, Franklin set up printing plant near his Paris home and turned out leaflets and brochures to correct false impressions about his country. One of the best was *Information to Those Who Would Remove to America*, which described the benefits of a country with a "good climate, fertile soil, wholesome air, free government, wise laws, liberty, a good people to live among, and a hearty welcome."

One of Franklin's best efforts as a propagandist was the **Jefferson-Franklin Plan**, but another effective one was a forged copy of a 1782 edition of a Boston newspaper complete with actual advertisements and local news; the paper contained an article that said the British Royal Governor of Canada was paying his Indian allies for each American scalp provided to him and that many of the scalps "sold" were from women and children. This story touched off a public uproar in Britain and was used by opposition Whig politicians to attack the conduct of the war. Franklin was the only one of the Founding Fathers who signed all three of the most important documents in early American history: Declaration of Independence, U.S. Constitution, and the treaty of Paris. He died in Philadelphia.

FURTHER READING: Susan M. Alsop, *Yankees at the Court: The First Americans in Paris* (Garden City, NY: Doubleday, 1982); Lyman H. Butterfield, "Psychological Warfare in 1776: The Jefferson-Franklin Plan to Cause Hessian Desertions," *Proceedings of American Philosophical Society* 94 (1950): 233–241; William E. Daugherty, *Psychological Warfare Casebook* (Baltimore: Johns Hopkins; published for Operations Research Office, Johns Hopkins University, 1958); Fitzhugh Green, *American Propaganda Abroad* (New York: Hippocrene Books, 1988); Walter Isaacson, *Benjamin Franklin: An American Life* (New York: Simon and Schuster, 2003); Lisa Rogers, "Our Man in Paris," *Humanities* (July/August 2002): 12–13, 44–45.

FRANKLIN LETTER TO PRUSSIANS. *See* Jefferson-Franklin Plan (1776)

FREE EUROPE COMMITTEE. *See* Radio Free Europe

FREEDOM'S JOURNAL. See Abolitionist Propaganda

FRENEAU, PHILIP MORIN (1752–1832). Freneau was called the "poet of the American Revolution" and the "father of American prose." He edited *United States Magazine* with Hugh Brackenridge. On a trip to the West Indies, he was captured by the British for a second time and, unlike the first time, was not quickly released. This experience and the subsequent illness he suffered made him an inspired critic of British prison methods. In 1781, he became the editor of *Freeman's Journal*, published in Philadelphia by Francis Bailey, where he published lacerating, venomous poems about the British, such as satires on George III, "The British Prison Ship," and "General Gage's Confession." Collections of Freneau's poems were published after his death, such as *Letters on Various Interesting and Important Subjects* (1943), *A Freneau Sampler* (1963), and *A Collection of Poems on American Affairs and a Variety of Other Subjects . . .* (1815; reprint, 1976).

FURTHER READING: Philip Davidson, *Propaganda and the American Revolution, 1763–1783* (New York: Norton, 1973, 1941); Judith R. Hiltner, ed., *Newspaper Verse of Philip Freneau: An Edition and Bibliographical Survey* (Troy, NY: Whitston, 1986); Richard Nickson, *Philip Freneau: Poet of the Revolution* (Trenton: New Jersey Historical Commission, 1980).

FRONT GROUPS. *See* Front Organizations

FRONT ORGANIZATIONS. A front organization is any "agency of influence." It has come to mean Soviet front groups or organizations under the Union of Soviet Socialists Republics (USSR), in non-Communist countries. Front organizations included think tanks, foundations, citizens committees, and coalitions; they were often international in character but actually under the direction and control of (and often financed) by the Communist Party of the Soviet Union (CPSU). There are two major classifications of Communist front organizations in the United States. The first are organizations that either were founded by the Communist Party in the United States of America (CPUSA) to act as fronts or were taken over by the CPUSA. The second are U.S. affiliates of international front organizations.

Since the early 1920s, the Soviet Union has used front organizations as a means of getting worldwide support for its policies. Fronts were designed to appeal to a broad range of opinions and to conceal their links to the former Soviet Union and to international communism. They supported Soviet propaganda themes, attacked the West, and never criticized the Soviet Union. The Comintern ran the pre–World War II fronts from a multinational bureaucracy in Moscow, tightly controlled by the CPSU.

The largest and most important Soviet international front was the World Peace Council, founded 1950 and headquartered in Helsinki, which represented each of the major fronts and some of the minor ones to ensure a unified position in support of Soviet policies and interfront coordination. The three oldest, all established in 1945, were the World Federation of Democratic Youth (WFDY), the World Federation of Trade Unions (WFTU), and the Women's International Democratic Federation (WIDF).

The FBI collected the information on front organizations. Useful data also came from the Bureau of Customs in the U.S. Department of the Treasury, but there was no designated agency that devoted resources to international front organizations until the Central Intelligence Agency began the collection effort.

See also Congress for Cultural Freedom; League of American Writers; Radio Free Europe; Radio Liberty

FURTHER READING: U.S. Congress. House. Permanent Select Committee on Intelligence. Subcommittee on Oversight, *The CIA and the Media: CIA Report on Soviet Propaganda Operations* [Excerpt of April 20, 1978 Hearing] (Washington, DC: Government Printing Office, 1978): 531–627. A detailed source of information on Soviet front organizations was released in three reports, compiled by the U.S. Department of State, with input from other agencies: *Active Measures: A Report on the Substance and Process of Anti-U.S. Disinformation and Propaganda Campaigns* (Washington, DC: The Department, 1986); *A Report on Active Measures and Propaganda, 1986–87* (Washington, DC: The Department, 1987); *A Report on Active Measures and Propaganda, 1987–1988* (Washington, DC: The Department, 1989).

FULBRIGHT-HAYS ACT. *See* Mutual Educational and Cultural Exchange Act

G

GEILENKIRCHEN SALIENT ("ASSAULT" ON). Well-conceived, efficiently coordinated propaganda plan utilizing leaflet barrages and loudspeaker broadcasts to achieve its objectives. Geilenkirchen was a German stronghold that formed the top of a salient that the American XIX Corps tried to capture in November 1944. The 84th Division was charged with taking the town, one of the strongest points in that section of the Siegfried Line. It was tactical propaganda that saved lives.

FURTHER READING: Edward A. Caskey, "Baloney Barrage," *Infantry Journal* (December 1949): 20–23; William E. Daugherty, *Psychological Warfare Casebook* (Baltimore: Johns Hopkins; published for Operations Research Office, Johns Hopkins University, 1958).

GEISEL, THEODOR SEUSS (**March 2, 1904–September 24, 1991**). Theodor S. Geisel was born in Springfield, Massachusetts. As Dr. Seuss, he was one of most popular children's authors, he was the creator of the Cat in the Hat, Horton the Elephant, Thidwick the Moose, and the Grinch. After attending Dartmouth and Oxford, Geisel worked as an advertising cartoonist. From 1940 to 1942, he worked as an editorial cartoonist for *PM* magazine and sketched drawings and posters for the U.S. Treasury Department and for the War Productions Board. Richard H. Minear compiled these as *Dr. Seuss Goes to War: The World War II Editorial Cartoons of Theodor Seuss Geisel* (New York: New Press, 1999). In 1943, he was assigned to the U.S. Army Signal Corps, Information and Educational Division; under director Frank Capra, Geisel worked on propaganda films, including the Why We Fight series. He received the first of three Academy Awards for *Hitler Lives* (originally, *Your Job in Germany*). His second Oscar was for *Design for Death* (1947), which he wrote with his first wife, Helen Palmer; the third came for a cartoon film, *Gerald McBoing-Boing*. After the war, Geisel continued to write his children's books, including one of his most popular titles, *How the Grinch Stole Christmas* (1957) and probably his most popular title, *Green Eggs and Ham* (1960). His books sold more than 200 million copies in some twenty languages and reached an international audience. In 1984, Geisel won the Pulitzer Prize for his contributions to children's literature. He died in La Jolla, California.

FURTHER READING: Thomas Fensch, ed., *Of Sneetches and Whos and the Good Dr. Seuss: Essays on the Writings and Life of Theodor Geisel* (Jefferson City, NC: McFarland, 1997); Judith and Neil Morgan, *Dr. Seuss and Mr. Geisel* (New York: Random House, 1995); Robert Sullivan, "The Boy Who Drew Wynnmphs," *Yankee* (December 1995).

GERM WARFARE STORY. *See* **Biological and Chemical Weapons Warfare**

GERMAN-AMERICAN BUND. Fritz Kuhn (1910–1967) was a native German who emigrated to the United States and set up the Amerika-Deutscher Volksbund, the largest and most influential of all pro-Nazi organizations in the United States, in 1936, during a period of high national stress. He visited Germany at the time of the 1936 Summer Olympics and met Hitler, who didn't express much enthusiasm for Kuhn. Upon his return to America, Kuhn decided to reinterpret the purpose of Nazi message in the spirit of "new" Germany. Central to this were social gatherings, adult camps where Germans could relive the vision of a Nazi America, and the Bund youth camps to turn impressionable youth into little Nazis. There was a responsive audience to Kuhn's movement with the German-American community, but it had its detractors, especially the Jewish war veterans, one of the Bund's most vocal opponents. They protested the mass rallies and the rest of Kuhn's movement as Nazi breeding grounds. In 1938, Congress passed the **Foreign Agents Registration Act**, which put brakes on Kuhn's activities. In February 1939, the Bund organized its largest rally in New York's Madison Square Garden. During Kuhn's speech, a protester rushed the stage while demonstrators smoldered outside. In the press coverage the following day, the media used the Trojan horse analogy to describe these simultaneous events.

Shortly after the New York rally, Kuhn was investigated for embezzlement and sent to prison for grand larceny. From 1938 until 1941, Martin Dies's Special House Committee on Un-American Activities investigated the Bund's activities, but these investigations were ended after **Pearl Harbor**. The Bund dispersed shortly afterward. The History 8mm Documents Project released a film, "German-American Bundists," originally produced by Thorne Films, Boulder Colorado, 1967, that showed Bundist youth camps, meetings, distribution of literature, and the George Washington Day celebration with Kuhn as speaker. It was transferred to videotape by Token Media, Richfield, Minnesota, in 2000.

See also **American Nazi Party**

FURTHER READING: Sander A. Diamond, *Nazi Movement in the United States, 1924–1941* (Ithaca, NY: Cornell University, 1974); Hyman S. Jaben, *The German-American Bund* (M.A. thesis, University of Missouri, Kansas City, 1973); Notes from "Nazi America: A Secret History" (TV documentary on The History Channel, 1/21/2000); Ronald W. Johnson, "The German-American Bund and Nazi Germany, 1936–1941," *Studies in History and Society* 6, no. 2 (1975): 31–45.

THE GERMAN-BOLSHEVIK CONSPIRACY. Drawing on the experience of their Czarist predecessors and their success with the classic forgery, *Protocols of the Learned Elders of Zion*, the Soviet KGB (known earlier as the Cheka,

OGPU, and GPU) continued to use forgeries. Six months after seizing power, the Bolsheviks were concerned about continuing accusations labeling Lenin and his comrades as German agents. There was some logic to this accusation as the Germans had helped send Lenin back into Russia to undermine their wartime enemy. The Bolsheviks denied that they were in the pay of the Germans. On September 15, 1918, the U.S. government released to the press a collection of documents that purported to show the Bolsheviks had received money both before and after the Russian Revolution. In October 1918, the **Committee on Public Information** (CPI) released a pamphlet to the press entitled *The German-Bolshevik Conspiracy*, which contained translations of 68 documents and reproductions of many of them. In addition, the pamphlet contained an analysis of the documents prepared for the National Board for Historical Service by two distinguished scholars. The report concluded that most of the documents were genuine, but some were questionable. The documents had been obtained in Russia by Edgar Sisson, the CPI representative, and came to be known as the "Sisson Documents."

The release of the Sisson Documents was reported in the American press on September 16, 1918, but, on September 21, the *New York Evening Post* challenged their authenticity, citing as their source Santeri Nuorteva, who was described by them as "head of the Finnish Information Bureau in New York," a notorious Soviet propagandist who had been a representative of the short-lived Communist government established in Finland by the Red Army. Nuorteva revealed that the first American to see the documents was Col. Raymond Robins, the Red Cross administrator in Russia, who was later identified as a Bolshevik sympathizer.

The controversial Sisson Documents are consistent with documents proving German financing of the Bolsheviks that were found in the German Foreign Office after World War II. The possibility exists that the Bolsheviks created a set of forgeries that were then mixed with authentic documents and passed to the American government by Robins for the purpose of discrediting the thesis that Lenin and company were on the German payroll. In fact, the exposure of the Sisson Documents created an atmosphere in which any allegation of German financial support to the Bolshevik was treated with distrust. It was only decades later that the German Foreign Office documents became available and proved the point.

FURTHER READING: Herbert Romerstein, "Disinformation as a KGB Weapon in the Cold War," paper prepared for a Conference on Germany and Intelligence Organizations: The Last Fifty Years in Review, Akademie fur Politische Bildung Tutzing [Germany] (Washington, DC: Unpublished, 1999).

GERMAN LIBRARY OF INFORMATION. The German Library of Information, in New York City, was an information center located in and funded by the German consulate. It was a major distribution center for publications that disseminated Nazi propaganda. It published *Facts in Review*, a weekly propaganda newsletter edited by **George Sylvester Viereck**.

FURTHER READING: Alton Frye, *Nazi Germany and the American Hemisphere, 1933–1941* (New Haven, CT and London, UK: Yale University, 1967).

GERMANY. As early as 1910, Germany began an active propaganda campaign to counteract pro-British biases in the leading organs of U.S. opinion. When World War I began, German-American propagandists such as **George Sylvester Viereck** tried to combat more persuasive prointervention views spread by English agents working through a well-organized network of native sympathizers, press contacts, cultural exchanges, and business and banking ties. However, the British view prevailed due to clumsy German diplomacy, American gullibility, and huge investments made in United Kingdom war bonds by U.S. financial interests. This maneuvered the United States into collective hatred of all things German through widespread dissemination of maliciously false but still effective "anti-Hun" atrocity stories and other propaganda.

Nazi Germany's uses of propaganda during the 1930s and its recognition that such activities could help win the war, a theory first advocated by journalists and internationalists and later by influential advisers to government officials, led to the creation of wartime propaganda and psychological warfare agencies. The total impact of Nazi propaganda in Germany was the creation of an image of reality shaped according to the wishes of the leaders of the movement. Hitler's conception was based on control of the reins of government, a point he emphatically stated in *Mein Kampf*. **Paul Josef Goebbels**'s task as Nazi propaganda minister was to see that this power was maintained. He succeeded with such heavy-handed symbols as the swastika, flags, films, and music.

During World War II, Nazi propaganda efforts met with mixed success. Its black propaganda was definitely a failure, although its forged currency was well executed. Leaflets were delivered to Allied soldiers through artillery shells, which could be fired 12,000 yards and would burst 300 feet over the front lines, showering the troops with leaflets. German themes to Allied troops remained the same, such as the image of the Allied soldier risking his life while his wife or girlfriend was at home with Sam Levy, the Jewish war profiteer. Another was the play on "gentlemen prefer blondes," but blondes prefer strong and healthy men, not cripples. Allied leaflets to the Germans focused on simple and direct ideas, recognizing the German soldier's good military qualities and his bravery but emphasizing the impossible situation of the German army. Good conduct passes through Allied lines promised medical care and good treatment as prisoners of war, whereas leaflets illustrated with maps of front-line positions convinced German soldiers of the hopelessness of their cause. By early 1945, leaflets were specific on the hopelessness of the German situation and the need to surrender.

An important Allied propaganda tool was the newspapers dropped on German troops. *Feldpost* and *Sternenbanner* showed their anti-Nazi origins but *Nachrichten* appeared so real that many Germans thought it was of German origin, and 500,000 copies were distributed every day. After the **Normandy Invasion**, news of Allied progress and of German defeats were so demoralizing to German forces that Allied propaganda needed only to report it unembellished. The Nazis' only propaganda attempt in the United States failed. The German-American Bund was unfocused in its propaganda efforts and, for Americans, too anti-Semitic to appeal anyone but extremists.

The U.S. military's postwar de-Nazification efforts at reeducating the German people to support democracy were the major responsibility of the American Information Control Division. U.S. forces tried to reshape the media and cultural

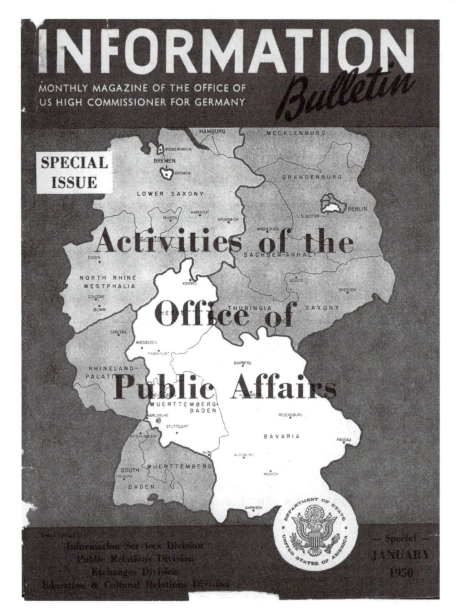

Cover: *Information Bulletin: Monthly Magazine of the Office of U.S. High Commissioner for Germany*; Special Issue: Activities of the Office of Public Affairs (January 1950).

institutions of a defeated Germany. The Western allies slowly abandoned all systematic reeducation attempts and soon resorted to a series of piecemeal measures. After World War II, the United States funded cultural and information programs, first in the Office of the Military Governor for the U.S. (OMGUS) then the Office of the U.S. High Commissioner for Germany (HICOG).

See also Axis Propaganda; Frank, Benno D.; The German-Bolshevik Conspiracy; German Library of Information; Goebbels and His Propaganda Efforts

Against the Allies; Morgenthau Plan; Occupied Countries and Territories; U.S.A. Zone of the Overseas Service (North American Service); Viereck, George Sylvester

FURTHER READING: Clayton D. Laurie, *The Propaganda Warriors: America's Crusade Against Nazi Germany* (Lawrence: University Press of Kansas, 1996); "The Propaganda Theory of the German Nazis," *Four Working Papers on Propaganda Theory* (Urbana: University of Illinois, 1955).

GERMANY IS OUR PROBLEM. *See* Morgenthau Plan

GIBSON, CHARLES DANA. *See* Committee on Public Information

GILLARS, MILDRED ELIZABETH (November 29, 1900–June 25, 1988). Radio broadcaster dubbed "Axis Sally" by American GIs, Mildred Elizabeth Sisk was born in Portland, Maine. In 1907, her parents divorced, and her mother married Robert Gillars; after that the girl was known as Mildred Gillars. After attending Ohio Wesleyan University, she worked at various jobs before moving to Germany (1935) to become an English instructor at the Berlitz School of Languages in Berlin. Possibly to make more money but definitely at the influence of her intimate friend, Max Otto Koischwitz, an official in the German Foreign Office and the top person at the Reich Rundfunk, the German radio system, Gillars went to work for Radio Berlin as an actress and an announcer. With Koischwitz, she cohosted *Home Sweet Home*, which was beamed to American servicemen in North Africa, starting in 1942. The next year, she was hostess of *Midge at the Mike*, which was very popular with GIs in North Africa and Europe, who enjoyed her nostalgic love songs.

Gillars and her propaganda programs were heard all over Europe, the Mediterranean, North Africa, and in the United States "between December 11, 1941, through May 6, 1945," the period in which she was accused of giving aid and comfort to the enemy. In many of her broadcasts, she described in harrowing detail the agonies of wounded American soldiers before they died or taunted the soldiers about what their wives and girlfriends were doing back home. Her most famous broadcast, titled "Vision of Invasion" and written by Koischwitz, was the one that would eventually get her convicted of treason; it was done prior to the D-Day invasion of Normandy (May 11, 1944) and was intended to frighten Americans with grisly forecasts of staggering casualties.

After the defeat of Nazi Germany, Gillars lived as a displaced refugee and sought shelter and medical treatment from Allied forces, but she was arrested while traveling to Frankfurt, detained by the U.S. Army, then incarcerated in Washington, DC, and charged with ten counts of treason, which were reduced to eight to speed her trial. She was tried for treason and pleaded innocent at her trial, but her broadcasts had been monitored and recorded by the U.S. government and were used as damaging evidence at her trial when the prosecution charged that her broadcasts were "sugarcoated propaganda pills" aimed at convincing American soldiers that they were fighting on the wrong side. Gillars was charged with broadcasting Nazi wartime radio propaganda, was convicted of treason on March 10, 1949, and served her time in the Federal Women's Reformatory, Alderson, West Virginia. After her release from prison in 1959, she spent the rest of her life quietly.

FURTHER READING: John C. Edwards, *Berlin Calling: American Broadcasters in Service to the Third Reich* (New York: Praeger, 1991); Dale P. Harper, "American-Born Axis Sally Made Propaganda Broadcasts for Radio Berlin in Hitler's Germany," *World War II* (November 1995).

GOEBBELS AND HIS PROPAGANDA EFFORTS AGAINST THE ALLIES. Paul Joseph Goebbels (October 29, 1897–May 1, 1945) was appointed by Hitler as his Minister for Popular Enlightenment and Propaganda, a position that gave him control of the press, cinema, radio, literature, and art, all areas of communication that could create an extraordinary propaganda campaign to enhance the public image of Der Fuhrer. As the third-ranking Nazi, his ministry was a powerful one; he was subordinate only to Hitler. Goebbels was all powerful in the three propaganda organizations: Propaganda Ministry, Party Propaganda Department, and Reich Chamber of Culture. Every area of Nazi activity and of German life was designed for this purpose, including the swastika (Nazi party symbol), emotional music, and architecture. Policies were carried out or discarded, depending on their propagandistic effort. At one time, Goebbels's ministry had control of propaganda in diplomacy; he successfully placed propaganda attaches into every foreign post. His propaganda approach was extremely flexible, and he became one of the most highly developed examples of the manipulative, amoral propagandist of modern times.

Goebbels's propaganda efforts built on earlier German efforts. As early as 1910, Germany began an active propaganda campaign to counteract pro-British biases in the leading organs of U.S. opinion. When World War I began, German-American propagandists such as **George Sylvester Viereck** tried to combat more persuasive prointervention views spread by English agents working through a well-organized network of native sympathizers, press contacts, cultural exchanges, and business and banking ties. However, the British view prevailed due to clumsy German diplomacy, American gullibility, and huge investments made in United Kingdom war bonds by U.S. financial interests. This maneuvered the United States into collective hatred of all things German through widespread dissemination of maliciously false but still effective "anti-Hun" atrocity stories and other propaganda.

Nazi Germany's uses of propaganda during the 1930s and its recognition that such activities could help win the war, a theory first advocated by journalists and internationalists and later by influential advisers to government officials, led to the creation of wartime propaganda and **psychological warfare** agencies. The total impact of Nazi propaganda in Germany was the creation of an image of reality shaped according to the wishes of the leaders of the movement. Hitler's conception was based on control of the reins of government, a point he emphatically stated in *Mein Kamf*. Goebbels's task as Nazi propaganda minister was to see that this power was maintained. He succeeded with such heavy-handed symbols as the swastika and flags.

During World War II, Nazi propaganda efforts met with mixed success. Its black propaganda was definitely a failure, although its forged currency was well executed. Leaflets were delivered to Allied soldiers through artillery shells, which could be fired 12,000 yards and would burst 300 feet over the front lines, showering the troops with leaflets. German themes to Allied troops remained the same, such as the image of the Allied soldier risking his life while his wife or girlfriend was at home with Sam Levy, the Jewish war profiteer. Another was the play on "gentlemen prefer blondes," but blondes prefer strong and healthy men, not cripples. The Nazis' only propaganda attempt in the United States failed. The German-American Bund was unfocused in its propaganda efforts and, for Americans, too anti-Semitic to appeal anyone but extremists.

Samples of Nazi music propaganda have been preserved on CDs. Recordings by a German jazz band (Charlie and His Orchestra) that were used by Goebbels to espouse the Nazi cause were released in 1988 by historian Rainer Lotz. *Hitler's Airwaves: The Inside Story of Nazi Radio Broadcasting and Propaganda Swing* by Horst J. P. Bergmeier and Rainer E. Lotz (New Haven, CT: Yale University, 1997) has a CD with a collection of original songs and propaganda talks broadcast by the Nazis.

FURTHER READING: William E. Daugherty, *Psychological Warfare Casebook* (Baltimore: Johns Hopkins; published for Operations Research Office, Johns Hopkins University, 1958); Clayton D. Laurie, *Propaganda Warriors: America's Crusade Against Nazi Germany* (Lawrence: University Press of Kansas, 1996); "The Propaganda Theory of the German Nazis," *Four Working Papers on Propaganda Theory* (Urbana: University of Illinois, 1955).

GOVERNMENT AGENCIES. *See* individual agencies

GOVERNMENT PROPAGANDA. *See* Advancing American Art; American National Exhibition, Moscow; Barnes, Harry Elmer; Black Propaganda; Brussels Universal and International Exposition (Expo 1958); Bureau of Public Diplomacy (U.S. Department of State); Central Intelligence Agency; Committee of Secret Correspondence; Committee on Public Information; Coordinator of Information; Coordinator of Inter-American Affairs; Division of Cultural Relations (U.S. Department of State); Documentary Films; Federal Arts Project; Federal Theater Project; Gray Propaganda; International Expositions; Office of Strategic Services; Office of War Information; President's Advisory Committee on Government Organization; President's Committee on Information Activities Abroad; President's Committee on International Information Activities; Publicity Bureau; "Uncle Sam"; U.S. Congress. House. Committee on Un-American Activities; U.S. Congressional Investigations of Propaganda; U.S. Department of State; U.S. Information Agency; White Propaganda; World Cruise of the U.S. Navy; Why We Fight Series

GRAY PROPAGANDA. Form of propaganda located between **white propaganda** and **black propaganda** in which truth and falsehoods are mixed and whose origin is lightly concealed. The true origin can sometimes be determined when the question, "Who benefits?" is asked. The source may or may not be accurately presented, and the correctness of the information is not ascertainable.

Gray propaganda has often been dismissed as nothing more that poorly disguised covert, or black, propaganda that originates from a source other than the true one.

FURTHER READING: William E. Daugherty, *Psychological Warfare Casebook* (Baltimore: Johns Hopkins; published for Operations Research Office, Johns Hopkins University, 1958); Terence H. Qualter, *Opinion Control in the Democracies* (New York: St. Martin's, 1985).

GREAT BRITAIN. Great Britain was the target of the American colonists in the years before the American Revolution with heavy propaganda attacks in broadsides, pamphlets, and newspapers aimed at both the British crown and its officials; these gave additional impact to events such as the **Boston Massacre,** the **Boston Tea Party,** and **Bunker Hill.** During the Civil War, there were several Confederate attempts to win British support. **Henry Hotze** went there to generate favorable public opinion toward the Confederacy. President Lincoln personally dispatched about 100 special agents to Great Britain along with publications to stir up support and a ship of foodstuffs for unemployed English cotton-textile workers to counter the propaganda attacks made by the Confederacy. It is still debated among Civil War scholars whether the "battle between the states" was a British empire-sponsored insurrection coordinated through a coalition of proslavery secret societies, Latin American expansionists, and financial interests that sought to weaken United States' competition with English interests. During the interwar period, Winston Churchill, perhaps the consummate propagandist, who dismissed the importance of propaganda in modern war and politics, was one of the few British speakers who could command a radio audience in the neutral United States, where his broadcasts stirred up much sympathy for the British cause. In the buildup to American involvement in **World War II,** President **Franklin D. Roosevelt** used his Fireside Chats to warn Americans that if England were defeated, the United States would face a serious crisis, with a united Nazi Europe as her enemy. After that, Germany would turn to Latin America for its conquests.

See also Adams, Samuel; *Boston Gazette*; *Boston News-Letter*; Civil War Propaganda; Committee of Secret Correspondence; Committees of Correspondence; "Don't Tread on Me"; "Join, or Die"; Lexington and Concord; *Mrs. Miniver*; *Short Narrative of the Horrid Massacre in Boston*; Sons of Liberty; Stamp Act; War of American Independence Propaganda; Wodehouse, Pelham Grenville

FURTHER READING: Nicholas J. Cull, *Selling War: The British Propaganda Campaign Against American Neutrality in World War II* (New York: Oxford University, 1995); William E. Daugherty, *Psychological Warfare Casebook* (Baltimore: Johns Hopkins; published for Operations Research Office, Johns Hopkins University, 1958); James D. Startt, "American Propaganda in Britain During World War I," *Prologue* (Spring 1996): 16–33.

"GREAT WHITE FLEET." *See* World Cruise of the U.S. Navy

GULAG—SLAVERY, INC. The American Federation of Labor (AFL) prepared an elaborately detailed map (GULAG—Slavery, Inc.; The Documented Map of Forced Labor Camps in Soviet Russia) that gave the location of Russian forced labor colonies and concentration camps. It was part of an effort to create a message that would effectively disseminate the impact of the Russian slave-labor system to larger audiences in a smaller format than either a pamphlet or a book. These maps were in great demand due in part to the heavy play given to them by **Voice of America** (VOA) broadcasts to such areas as Latin America. The map's existence first came to light in a widely publicized September 1951 incident at the San Francisco conference to sign the Japanese peace treaty when U.S. Representative O. K. Armstrong handed Andrei Gromyko a copy who, upon closer inspection of the additional cartographic symbols, threw it to the floor in disgust. Also in the map were pictures of an emaciated child wearing a crucifix, victim of the GULAG system, and photostatic copies of GULAG "passports" (release certificates) given to those fortunate enough to survive their imprisonment.

The GULAG map became one of the most widely circulated pieces of anti-Communist literature. It was distributed in the United States on a request basis then shipped worldwide for dissemination through labor unions and other AFL contacts. The VOA offered the map to its Latin American listeners, but soon the Government Printing Office made copies in Spanish for distribution through United States Information Service (USIS) posts. VOA letters indicated that a majority of requests for the map came from local opinion leaders, a crucially important group. Overall, the GULAG map highlighted the effective use of a private organization in voluntary association with U.S. governmental agencies to support official information objectives.

FURTHER READING: William R. Young, "GULAG—Slavery, Inc.: The Use of an Illustrated Map in Printed Propaganda." in *Psychological Warfare Casebook*, ed. William E. Daugherty (Baltimore: Johns Hopkins; published for Operations Research Office, Johns Hopkins University, 1958).

GULF WAR DISINFORMATION. During the Gulf War, Voice of the Gulf radio network, operated by members of the U.S. Special Forces psychological operations (PSYOPS), began broadcasting in 1991 as part of a propaganda effort that also included loudspeaker operations and leaflet drops. There was also a disinformation campaign that originated with the Gulf military operation. It began when a South African minister was speaking to the media about the "genocide" caused by depleted uranium.

Doug Rokke started the disinformation in a presentation to members of the South African Parliament on January 31, 2001, when he made a number of assertions about depleted uranium (DU). Media reports quoted him saying that he knew only one person from "his team" that "wasn't sick." He was also reported as saying that tests indicated he had 5,000 times the permissible level of uranium in his body. He was presented as the Department of Defense's expert on depleted uranium and the director of the Pentagon's depleted uranium project. His comments resulted in a renewed fear about depleted uranium.

To correct the record, the U.S. Department of Defense, already criticized for restrictions on Gulf War reporting that deliberately withheld information about military operations from the American people during the Gulf crisis, revealed that Rokke was a private citizen and did not represent the Department of Defense. Following the ground war, Rokke was attached for duty to assist technical experts in the recovery and decontamination of radioactive material and equipment. The team of approximately ten people was led, not by Rokke, but by a civilian from the Army Munitions and Chemical Command (AMCCOM). Rokke's primary role was to facilitate the recovery operations by ensuring the team had the proper support. Over the past years, Doug Rokke has reported varying numbers of ill or dead unit members or members of his team.

These claims have been researched and are unsubstantiated. In 1998, OSAGWI staff compiled a list of twenty-nine names of people Rokke reported to be on his team. Staff members were able to interview twenty-two of them. Approximately fifteen of the twenty-nine people Doug Rokke had identified as being on his team actually worked on DU-contaminated vehicles. Two of the twenty-nine had died; however, in interviews with the others, neither of these two veterans was named as having worked with depleted uranium. The interviews also revealed that of the twenty-two interviewed, ten had no or extremely limited exposure to depleted uranium. (Of those ten, one said he was in good health, four made no mention of health concerns, and five had various health concerns.) Of the remaining twelve, four had no health concerns, and eight had a wide variety of health problems. There is no evidence that any of the veterans' ill health resulted from exposure to depleted uranium.

See also Iraq

FURTHER READING: Todd Leventhal, *Apparatus of Lies* (Washington, DC: U.S. Department of State, 2003); Todd Leventhal, *Iraqi Propaganda and Disinformation During the Gulf War: Lessons for the Future* (Abu Dhabi, United Arab Emirates, 1999); John R. MacArthur, *Second Front: Censorship and Propaganda in the Gulf War* (New York: Hill and Wang, 1992).

H

HALE, WILLIAM BAYARD (April 6, 1869–April 10, 1924). Born in Richmond, Indiana, William Bayard Hale was educated at Boston University and at Harvard, then was ordained an Episcopal priest. After serving as a priest in Massachusetts, he became involved in politics and wrote for *Cosmopolitan, Current Literature*, and *World*. In 1907, Hale was Paris correspondent for the *New York Times*. He originally supported President Woodrow Wilson, who sent him as a special agent to Mexico, but turned against him after Wilson ignored his advice to not recognize the Huerta government. During World War I, Hale worked for the German Information Service, where he advised the Germans on propaganda in the United States. As a paid German agent, he spoke out for Germany against Britain and tried to halt munitions shipments to the Allied countries. His pro-German activities ignited much American hatred toward him, especially after his involvement with Berlin was revealed in captured German cables. A damaging criticism was his edit of the so-called Dernberg speech that justified the sinking of the English luxury liner *Lusitania*. When the war ended, Hale was bitterly opposed to President Wilson, and he became persona non grata in the United States. He went to Germany, where he died in Munich, April 10, 1924. His writings include *Week in the White House with Theodore Roosevelt* (1908); a campaign biography, *Woodrow Wilson: The Story of His Life* (1912), and *Story of a Style* (1920), which criticized Wilson.

FURTHER READING: Robert E. Annin, *Woodrow Wilson; a Character Study* (New York: Dodd, Mead and Company, 1924); Johann H. Bernstorff, *My Three Years in America*, by Count Bernstorff. (New York: Charles Scribner's Sons, 1920); George S. Viereck, *Spreading Germs of Hate* (New York: H. Liveright, 1930).

HATE LITERATURE. *See* American Nazi Party; Anti-Semitic Propaganda; Henry Ford and *The International Jew*; Ku Klux Klan; *Mein Kampf*; *Protocols of the Learned Elders of Zion*

HATE PROPAGANDA. One of the oldest hate groups in the United States is the movement for white supremacy. It was never far from the surface from the earliest days of the United States, when white settlers tried and sometimes succeeded in conquering Native Americans already living for centuries on the North American continent when white European exploration first started. It reached its peak during the nativism movements of the late nineteenth century and the 1920s, in which the targets were immigrants and blacks. The purpose of these groups is the preservation of White America. The most recent group in the news is the Council of Conservative Citizens, led by Gordon Baum, which claims its purpose is to "save the white race." Prominent U.S. and state officials, such as former

EMBASSY OF THE
UNITED STATES OF AMERICA
Wien, den 26. Januar 1984

Sehr geehrter Herr Bundesminister,

      Gestatten Sie mir, dass ich Ihnen meine engste Verbundenheit zum Ausdruck bringe. Ich habe die Ehre Ihnen zu versichern, an einer breiten Zusammenarbeit auch weiterhin interessiert zu sein.

      Wie Ihnen ebenfalls bekannt ist, muessen die Laender Westeuropas infolge der Stationierung moderner amerikanischer Mittelstreckenraketen mit russischen Gegenmassnahmen rechnen. Die Sowjets haben nicht nur ihre Absicht bekundet, in der Tschechoslowakei und in Ostdeutschland Atomraketen aufzustellen, sondern diesbezuegliche Arbeiten sind bereits im fortgeschrittenen Stadium. Diese Lage birgt nicht nur fuer die NATO-Laender grosse Risiken in sich, sondern auch fuer alle neutralen Demokratien.

      Um eine solche Gefahr zu vermindern, moechte ich Sie im Namen der Regierung der Vereinigten Staaten dazu veranlassen ueberpruefen zu wollen, in welcher Art und Weise die Republik Oesterreich im Falle eines sowjetischen Atomangriffes den Westen beistehen koennte. Vor allem sollte in Betracht gezogen werden, dass eine wirksame Einschaltung Ihres Luftraum-Ueberwachungssystems in das der NATO offensichtliche Vorteile fuer die gemeinsame Verteidigung in sich birgt. Das von Ihnen verwendete italienische System ist kompatibel und eignet sich ausgezeichnet fuer die Einschaltung in das sueddeutsche oder norditalienische Netz; in gegebenen Fall ist die Regierung der Vereinigten Staaten bereit, die noetigen technischen und finanziellen Mittel aufzubringen.

      Ich darf Sie darueber informieren, dass eine aehnliche Anregung unserseits von zustaendigen Regierungskreisen eines anderen neutralen Landes befuerwortet wurde.

      Erlauben Sie mir, Herr Bundesminister, auch diese Gelegenheit zu benutzen, um Ihnen meine ausgezeichnete Hochachtung zu versichern.

                            Helene von Damm

                              Helene von Damm

Herr Bundesminister fuer Landesverteidigung
Dr. Friedhelm Frischenschlager
Wien

(Continued)

EMBASSY OF THE
UNITED STATES OF AMERICA

Vienna, 26 January 1984

Very respected Mr. Federal Minister:

Permit me to express to you my closest attachment. I have the honor to assure you that I continue to be interested in a broad cooperation.

As is also known to you, the countries of Western Europe, as a result of the stationing of modern American intermediate-range missiles, must expect Russian countermeasures. The Soviets have not only declared their intention to install atomic missiles in Czechoslovakia and East Germany, but the work connected with this is already in an advanced stage. This situation holds great risks not only for the NATO countries but also for all neutral democracies.

In order to diminish such a danger, I would like to have you please examine in what way and manner the Republic of Austria could assist the West in the event of a Soviet atomic attack. Above all, it should be considered that an effective insertion of your airspace surveillance system into that of NATO holds obvious advantages for the common defense. The Italian system used by you is compatible and is excellently suited for insertion into the southern German or northern Italian network; in the given case, the government of the United States is willing to provide the necessary technical and financial means.

I am permitted to inform you that a similar suggestion on our part was endorsed by responsible government circles in another neutral country.

Allow me, Mr. Federal Minister, also to use this opportunity to assure you of my excellent respect.

signature

Helene von Damm

Mr. Federal Minister for National Defense
Dr. Friedhelm Frischenschlager
Vienna

Fabricated letter from U.S. Ambassador to Austria, Helene von Damm, to Austrian Defense Minister Friedhelm Frischenschlager that proposes the integration of Austria's air defense radar system into that of NATO, a flagrant violation of Austrian neutrality. (*Source:* U.S. Department of State, *Active Measures: A Report on the Substance and Process of Anti-U.S. Disinformation and Propaganda Campaigns* [Washington, DC: The Department, 1986])

Senate Majority Leader Trent Lott (R.-Miss.), Mississippi Governor Kirk Fordice (R.), and Representative Bob Barr (R.-Ga.), have spoken before the group. Lott endorsed the group as a "needed" organization to help "protect our flag, Constitution and other symbols of freedom" from the "dark forces." All tried to deny their association with the Council, but the documented record showed otherwise.

See also **American Nazi Party; Anti-Semitic Propaganda; Henry Ford and** *The International Jew*; **Ku Klux Klan;** *Mein Kampf*; *Protocols of the Learned Elders of Zion*

FURTHER READING: Owen M. Fiss, *The Irony of Free Speech* (Cambridge, MA: Harvard University, 1996); Nicholas Wolfson, *Hate Speech, Sex Speech, Free Speech* (Westport, CT: Praeger, 1997).

HELENE VON DAMM FORGERY LETTER. Helene von Damm was the U.S. Ambassador to Austria during the Reagan administration. To damage relations between the U.S. and Austria, the KGB created a fabricated letter, dated January 26, 1984, which was addressed to Austrian Defense Minister Friedhelm Frischenschlager and purportedly signed by von Damm. It appeared on authentic but out-of-date U.S. Embassy letterhead and proposed the integration of Austria's air defense radar system into that of NATO, a flagrant violation of Austrian neutrality, and commented on the increased risk to Europe from the stationing of modernized U.S. missiles. The letter was designed to damage U.S.-Austrian relations on the eve of the Austrian president's state visit to the United States and to affect negatively the American image among other West Europeans, who would question the seeming U.S. manipulation of NATO. After Viennese newspapers received copies, the Austrian Defense Ministry exposed it as a forgery.

FURTHER READING: Herbert Romerstein, "Disinformation as a KGB Weapon in the Cold War," prepared for a Conference on Germany and Intelligence Organizations: The Last Fifty Years in Review, sponsored by Akademie fur Politische Bildung Tutzing, June 18–20, 1999; U.S. Department of State, *Active Measures: A Report on the Substance and Process of Anti-U.S. Disinformation and Propaganda Campaigns* (Washington: The Department, 1986).

HENRY FORD AND *THE INTERNATIONAL JEW.* Henry Ford was one of the most famous Americans in the early decades of the twentieth century as his Ford Motor Company in Dearborn, Michigan, mass-produced inexpensive automobiles for working-class America. Henry Ford published an "educational" series of ninety-one consecutive, unsigned articles in his newspaper, *Dearborn Independent*, between May 22 and October 2, 1920, that were attacks against the Jews. Ford later tried to make amends for his actions. Although he apologized (1927) for republishing the material, some of it was widely circulated as a series of pamphlets in four volumes, *The International Jew; The World's Foremost Problem*, despite Ford's recantation. As an anti-Semitic tract, it was translated into several languages, distributed worldwide, and used by anti-Semitic propagandists, such as **Gerald L. K. Smith.**

FURTHER READING: Neil Baldwin, *Henry Ford and The Jews: The Mass Production of Hate* (New York: Public Affairs, 2001); Nelson Marans, "Ford's Better-Late-Than-Never Idea" [Letter to the Editor], *Washington Post* (March 9, 1997): G2.

HERZ, MARTIN FLORIAN (July 9, 1917–October 5, 1983). Martin Herz had a profound knowledge of the German language and understood and respected all that was good in German culture while rejecting the negative aspects of the training imposed on German youth by Nazism; these characteristics made him an effective combat propagandist in World War II. Because of his general background, he was assigned to psychological warfare operations during the war. He became an authority on surrender, capture, and desertion and wrote a brief study on the possibilities of tactical psychological warfare, one of the first studies of its kind written on the subject in the United States. During the Sicilian campaign, Herz was chief of a propaganda unit in the First Mobile Radio Broadcasting Company, attached to Headquarters, Seventh U.S. Army, that wrote and disseminated the first American leaflets fired from artillery pieces. Yet he was a Foreign Service Officer for over 30 years and U.S. ambassador to Bulgaria (1974–1977).

FURTHER READING: *Preliminary Inventory to the Martin Herz Collection, Propaganda Leaflets* (Stanford, CA: Hoover Institution Archives, Stanford University, 1999).

HISS, ALGER. *See* Chambers, Whittaker

HITLER, ADOLF. *See* Goebbels and His Propaganda Efforts Against the Allies; Henry Ford and *The International Jew*; *Mein Kampf*

HITLER'S AIRWAVES. *Hitler's Airwaves: The Inside Story of Nazi Radio Broadcasting and Propaganda Swing* by Horst J. P. Bergmeier and Rainer E. Lotz (1997) is a masterful study of Nazi radio propaganda and its English foreign propaganda service, including the people and processes that created these radio programs and how the Nazis tried to use elements such as jazz to help their war effort. Most important, the book details the role of an important component of the service, the Americans who served on the **U.S.A. Zone of the Overseas Service** (**North American Service**), which was established by German Propaganda Minister Paul Josef Goebbels as early as 1933 to house the foreign nationals who were broadcasting for the Nazis. The U.S.A. Zone was staffed with American expatriates (called "foreign correspondents"), who were ordered to weaken the United States' resolve to fight and to raise Germany's credibility among Americans at Great Britain's expense. Broadcasters were expected to be patriotic but semidetached Americans who appeared motivated strictly by their country's best interests and an overall sense of fair play.

Germany was the first to employ foreign nationals as propagandists in their respective countries, and it recruited broadcasters from, among other nations, Egypt, France, Great Britain, Italy, Mexico, and South Africa, beside the United States. The dean of the U.S.A. Zone "repatriates" was Frederick W. Kaltenbach. Other notable recruits included Jane Anderson (the "Georgia Peach"), Robert H. Best ("Mr. Guess Who"), Douglas Chandler ("Paul Revere"), Donald Day, Edward Delaney, Constance Drexel, and Max O. Koischwitz ("Mr. O.K.").

The book has an added bonus of a CD featuring twenty-two rare tracks of Charlie and His Orchestra numbers and spoken-word broadcast material, such as "Lord Haw Haw" (**William Joyce**).

FURTHER READING: Horst J. P. Bergmeier and Rainer E. Lotz, *Hitler's Airwaves: The Inside Story of Nazi Radio Broadcasting and Propaganda Swing* (New Haven, CT: Yale, 1997).

HOAXES. *See* Forgeries

HOGAN, WILLIAM. *See* Catholic Church

HOLOCAUST DENIAL. The ongoing debate of Jewish survival writing and recollections against the anti-Semitism of Holocaust deniers has been an important issue since the end of World War II, most notably the case of *Deborah Lipstadt v. David Irving.* In January 2000, David Irving sued historian Deborah Lipstadt and Penguin Books for libel after she called him a Holocaust denier in her book, *Denying the Holocaust: The Growing Assault on Truth and Memory* (New York: Free Press, 1993).

Lipstadt showed that, despite the witnesses and evidence to the contrary, this irrational idea has not only continued to gain adherents but has also become an internationally organized movement. She argued strongly against giving Holocaust deniers a forum in the name of free speech or freedom of the press, and she details the efforts of California revisionist Bradley Smith, who pushed a "Holocaust was a hoax" campaign in college newspapers throughout the United States.

Background

Holocaust denial is an anti-Semitic propaganda movement active in the United States, Canada, and western Europe that seeks to deny the reality of the Nazi regime's systematic mass murder of six million Jews during World War II. It generally depicts historical accounts of this genocide as propaganda, generated by a Jewish, or "Zionist," conspiracy. In the United States, the movement has been known in recent years primarily through the publication of advertisements in college campus newspapers.

The first of these ads claimed to call for "open debate on the Holocaust." Although discussion of historical events is certainly useful and educational, "debating" the Holocaust would be like debating whether American colonists even, in fact, fought for independence from England in 1776. Another ad questioned the authenticity of the U.S. Holocaust Memorial Museum in Washington, D.C. These ads have been published in several dozen student newspapers on campuses across the country. Similar examples of such propaganda have begun to appear on the Internet as well. In addition to creating their own home pages, Holocaust deniers have sometimes crashed the sites of legitimate Holocaust and Jewish discussion groups in an effort to spread false information and harass Jews, and they have advertised their Web sites in classified ads in college and community newspapers.

By attacking the facts of the Holocaust and maintaining that their attack is merely an unorthodox point of view, Holocaust deniers demonstrate their subtle but hateful anti-Semitic beliefs. They try to spread the view that Jews are only using the Holocaust to take advantage of non-Jewish guilt and that Jews control the media and academic world. Some of these beliefs, in fact, are similar to those that helped bring Hitler to power in Germany during the 1930s.

After World War II, former Nazis and their supporters similarly claimed that Hitler's hatred of the Jews had been misinterpreted, and that the numerous confessions of Nazi leaders describing the genocide had been coerced by the Allies. This neo-Nazi movement also dismissed the testimony of survivors from the concentration camps as exaggeration and lies. Other political extremists in the 1960s and 1970s, such as radical anti-Israel groups or fringe conspiracy theorists, echoed the views of these right-wing anti-Semites.

As an organized movement, Holocaust denial began in 1979 with the founding of a group called the **Institute for Historical Review** (IHR), which publishes a magazine (the *Journal of Historical Review*), holds conferences, and distributes a variety of anti-Jewish books, all devoted to the idea that Hitler's record of atrocities is a fraud concocted by a powerful, secret conspiracy of Jews. Among those connected to the IHR is Bradley Smith, the man responsible for most of the Holocaust denial advertisements in college newspapers.

Many proponents of Holocaust denial claim that their propaganda has been misrepresented and that they are victims of yet another conspiracy, also led by Jews, to suppress independent research. In making these claims, Holocaust deniers try to exploit the sympathy of most people, especially students, for academic debate and honest critical thinking. These arguments are false for three main reasons:

1. Holocaust deniers reject all evidence and research that contradicts their views. Rather than promote honest research, these propagandists wish to challenge the historical record with their own views, which have no credibility.

2. The "research" the deniers use comes to conclusions that are false. Among the untruths routinely promoted are the claims that no gas chambers existed at Auschwitz, that only 600,000 Jews were killed rather than six million, and that Hitler had no murderous intentions toward Jews or other groups persecuted by his government.

3. Holocaust deniers conceal the true motivation for their propaganda. Though the deniers often try to assume a scholarly, reasonable tone in their public statements, in their more private newsletters, conferences, and e-mails, they typically display hatred of Jews, admiration for Nazism, and contempt for free speech and democracy.

Holocaust denial, which its propagandists misrepresent as "historical revisionism," has become one of the most important vehicles for contemporary anti-Semitism. It is the invention of a collection of long-time anti-Semites and apologists for Hitler. During the fall semester of 1997, Bradley Smith, "director" of the self-styled "Committee for Open Debate on the Holocaust" (CODOH), launched a new salvo in his continuing propaganda campaign to deny the reality of the Holocaust. He is attempting to place an ad in college newspapers around the country that promises $50,000 to anyone "convincing a national television network to air" a ninety-minute video that attempts to show that the universally accepted account of Nazi genocide is false. The ad is clearly a ploy. Smith must know his money is safe because no TV network would broadcast such a video. Holocaust denial, which deniers such as Smith describe as Holocaust "revisionism," has become one of the most important vehicles for contemporary anti-Semitism. The deniers distort, even fabricate, history and then broadcast their creations. Smith and his cohorts are engaged in what historian Deborah Lipstadt has termed an "assault on truth and memory."

These so-called revisionists have appropriated the name of the post–World War I historical revisionists of the 1920s and 1930s, who challenged successfully the previously dominant view of exclusive German guilt for causing the Great War. They assert that the accepted premise that Nazi Germany engaged in a premeditated campaign of systematic genocide against the Jews of Europe during the period of the Second World War is one that does not stand honest scholarly scrutiny. They do not deny that Hitler's government engaged in persecution of and discrimination against Jews in Germany and German-controlled countries. They even admit the existence of concentration camps. They assert, however, that the anti-Semitic actions of the Nazi government were in large part a legitimate response to Jewish misdeeds and disloyalty during wartime. As such, the measures taken and the use of concentration camps were not qualitatively different from similar wartime and postwar actions of the Western allies and the Soviet Union. Only Germany is singled out for special condemnation, they argue, because it lost the war. What they deny is the existence of any German plan or program to subject the Jews of Europe to genocide.

Holocaust deniers argue that the manufactured guilt and shame over a mythological Holocaust led to Western, specifically United States, support for the establishment and sustenance of the Israeli state, a sustenance that costs the American taxpayer over three billion dollars per year. They assert that American taxpayers have been and continue to be swindled as well as misled and imagine that by showing the American and other Western peoples how and why they have been victimized can the power of this conspiracy be broken. Once they have been shown the "truth," that there was never any legitimate basis for their feeling of guilt, deniers postulate that these good people will rise up in righteous anger and treat the Holocaust myth conspirators in an appropriate manner.

FURTHER READING: Richard J. Evans, *Lying about Hitler: History, Holocaust, and the David Irving Trial* (New York: Basic Books, 2001); Michael Shermer and Alex Grobman, *Denying History: Who Says the Holocaust Never Happened and Why Do They Say It?* (Berkeley: University of California, 2000). This essay also quotes excerpts from a presentation made at the 1995 Symposium of the Northwest Coalition Against Malicious Harassment; it was subsequently published in: *Conspiracies: Real Grievances, Paranoia and Mass Movements, 1996*. It is posted on the Anti-Defamation League Web site with the permission of the Northwest Coalition Against Malicious Harassment at: http://www.adl.org/hate-patrol/holocaust.html

HOLOCAUST MEMORY. *See* **Anti-Semitic Propaganda; Holocaust Denial**

HOLY SEE. *See* **Catholic Church**

HOME FRONT PROPAGANDA. Attempts by the U.S. government to sell the people at home on the war being fought overseas. During World War I, this was the responsibility of the Committee on Public Information (CPI), and during World War II it was handled by the Office of War Information (OWI).

The importance of radio in creating a "wartime culture" was recognized as soon as the United States entered the war after Pearl Harbor. America's favorite radio characters were pressed into service as radio emerged as the central wartime propaganda vehicle because it provided a daily and continuous link with many people and because it was a commercial medium. Bob Hope was dubbed "Radio's No. 1 soldier in grease-paint" for his tours of U.S. Army bases and battlefields, which he continued annually through the Vietnamese conflict. CBS newscaster William Shirer gained fame for his debunking of Nazi propaganda through his *Berlin Diary*. Messages and news items that were carried over the three major national broadcasting networks (NBC, CBS, and ABC) were supplemented by the Network Allocation Plan, which carried material from OWI that could be dropped in to newscasts or soap operas.

The role of the **War Advertising Council** (WAC) was critical to this activity; its message was endorsed by its "A War Message in Every Ad Campaign," which included the creation of posters as one of the most influential means of persuasion on the home front. The Council was a group of national advertisers who worked as liaison between advertising and government agencies. It was created before Pearl Harbor to cooperate with the government in the pending war effort. From this cooperation, the Network Allocation Plan was devised as a propaganda scheme in which the radio industry accepted OWI's Radio Division as the central clearing station for all government propaganda and as the authority on the types and priority of specific propaganda messages. In return, OWI provided every national radio advertiser with a schedule of propaganda themes at least a month in advance of the actual broadcasts.

The most important collaboration of WAC and the government was the national gas rationing effort after the Office of Price Administration (OPA) decided gas rationing was the best way to conserve rubber, a most essential commodity in wartime; there was not a shortage of fuel. Radio comedians, such as Fibber McGee and Molly, used their weekly NBC show to promote the government's message on gas rationing. Another was Jack Benny, whose reputation as a tightwad made him the perfect celebrity to defuse the public's growing resentment against rationing by exploiting its comic possibilities on his radio show.

Networks had probusiness program bias, and advertising played a crucial role. The government allowed businesses to write off up to 80 percent of their advertising costs as long as they participated in the propaganda effort. Advertising and commercial radio became an integral collaboration, helped immeasurably by images such as Rosie the Riveter and, most important of all, by Hollywood films. On a personal level, there were home front symbols, such as gold stars for mothers who lost a child in the war or flags on the lawn indicating that a family member was in the service.

The poster campaign, inexpensive, colorful, and immediate, was the ideal medium for delivering messages about American duties on the home front during World War II; they were seen in schools, in workplaces, and in other public spaces. The posters touched on all aspects of wartime life, from the factory, where workers were instructed to take shorter cigarette breaks and focus on increased production ("KILLING Time Is KILLING Men."), to the home, where conserving scarce resources was essential ("We'll have lots to eat this winter, won't we Mother? Grow your own."), to the farm, where eggs and meat were wartime weapons in their own right ("Our Allies Need Eggs." and "Grow It Yourself—Plan a Farm Garden Now.").

FURTHER READING: William L. Bird and Harry R. Rubenstein, *Design for Victory: World War II Posters on the American Home Front* (Princeton, NJ: Princeton Architectural, 1998); W. Gerd Horten, *Radio Goes to War: The Cultural Politics of Propaganda During World War II* (Berkeley and Los Angeles: University of California, 2002).

HOOVER COMMISSION. *See* **Commission on Organization of the Executive Branch of the Government**

HOTZE, HENRY (September 2, 1833–April 19, 1887). Henry Hotze was born in Zurich, Switzerland, but moved to the United States and became a citizen after a Jesuit college education. By 1855, he was working as a journalist for the *Mobile Register* (Alabama). When the Civil War started, Hotze was appointed public opinion director in Europe for the Confederacy and instructed to persuade the British that the Confederacy was a viable government that could undertake the war and maintain its independence. In London, he wrote editorials for the *London Post* and other papers favoring the Southern cause and published *The Index*, a "Confederate-British" journal, from 1862 to 1865 to promote the Confederacy. By 1863, Hotze favored emancipation of slaves if necessary to win Southern independence.

After the recall of **Edwin De Leon** (1864), Hotze worked in France planting news items in newspapers. Hotze was an accomplished propagandist, probably the best one that the Confederacy had in Europe, who worked hard to gain recognition and support. After the Confederacy's collapse, Hotze stayed in Europe as a journalist and died in Zug, Switzerland.

See also **Civil War Propaganda**

FURTHER READING: Charles P. Cullop, *Confederate Propaganda in Europe, 1861–1865* (Coral Gables, FL: University of Miami, 1969).

THE HOUR. A newsletter, *The Hour*, was published by the American Council Against Nazi Propaganda that attacked those that the council considered subversive. Its chairman was former U.S. ambassador to Germany, William Dodd. His daughter, Martha Dodd, was a Soviet intelligence agent. The editor of *The Hour* was Albert Kahn, also identified as a Soviet intelligence agent. During World War II, the Office of Strategic Services (OSS) concluded that *The Hour* was not a reliable source of information on Nazi activity, in part because the newsletter on a number of occasions had to apologize to people they attacked to avoid lawsuits.

FURTHER READING: Herbert Romerstein and Eric Breindel, *The Venona Secrets: Exposing Soviet Espionage and America's Traitors* (Washington, DC: Regnery; Lanham, MD: Distributed to the trade by National Book Network, 2000).

HOUSE RESOLUTION 199. Legislation introduced by Representative Samuel Dickstein on January 3, 1934, to provide for the investigation of Nazi propaganda activities in the United States. It passed with little difficulty on March 20, with an appropriation of $10,000 supplemented by an additional allocation of $25,000. John McCormack (D-Mass.) chaired the special investigating committee that worked through 1934 and 1935. In its report, it called attention to the budding activities of Nazis and other fascist groups in the United States and their connections with authoritarian movements in Europe.

See also U.S. Congressional Investigations of Propaganda

FURTHER READING: Alton Frye, *Nazi Germany and the American Hemisphere, 1933–1941* (New Haven, CT: Yale, 1967).

HOUSE UN-AMERICAN ACTIVITIES COMMITTEE (HUAC). *See* U.S. Congress. House. Committee on Un-American Activities

HUGHES REPORT. *See* President's Task Force on U.S. Government International Broadcasting

I

I LED THREE LIVES. Anti-Communist book by Herbert Arthur Philbrick (1915–1993), who was a member of the Communist party and a counterspy for the Federal Bureau of Investigation at the same time that he considered himself just an average citizen (his three lives), was published as *I Led Three Lives: Citizen, "Communist," Counterspy* (New York: McGraw-Hill, 1952) and became a popular success as did the television series that was adapted from it. The theme of both the book and the television series, which was shown from 1953 to 1956 with Richard Carlson as Philbrick and loosely based on the author's adventures, was that someone close to you could be a secret Communist and not to be trusted. The FBI reviewed all scripts. The television series dramatized Communist activities in the United States, and it is considered one of the most overt pieces of Cold War propaganda ever broadcast on American television.

FURTHER READING: Robert Cole, ed., *Encyclopedia of Propaganda*, vol. 2 (Armonk, NY: M. E. Sharpe, 1998); U.S. Congress. House. Committee on Un-American Activities, *Expose of Communist Activities in the State of Massachusetts, Based on the Testimony of Herbert A. Philbrick*; hearings held July 23–October 11, 1951; 82d Congress, 1st Session (Washington, DC: Government Printing Office, 1951).

IMPOSSIBLE CERTAINTY. *See* Big Lie

INDEPENDENCE, WAR OF. *See* War of American Independence Propaganda

THE INDEX. The *Index* was a Civil War journal, subtitled *A Weekly Journal of Politics, Literature, and News*, that was created by **Henry Hotze** in Great Britain to support Confederate diplomacy. He tried to make it representative of English journalism, with its three columns, contents that included the latest direct intelligence from the South, foreign correspondence, developments of the Confederate cause in Europe, and two pages of advertisements, mostly of shipping notices, sales of Confederate bonds, and pleas for Southern prisoner-of-war relief.

FURTHER READING: Charles P. Cullop, *Confederate Propaganda in Europe, 1861–1865* (Coral Gables, FL: University of Miami, 1969).

Cover from *Information USA* book distributed at exhibition in USSR; both English and Russian editions. Book was prepared by USIA, 1987, to accompany the exhibition. (*Source:* USIA)

INDOCTRINATION. *See* **Brainwashing**

INFORMATION USA. Information USA, the first official exhibition exchanged between the United States and the Soviet Union since 1979, was presented under the US–USSR cultural exchange agreement signed in Geneva in November 1985. Produced by the **U.S. Information Agency**, the exhibit opened in Moscow on June 4, 1987, and had a very successful run in the Soviet capital city then toured to Kiev, Rostov-on-Don, Thilisi, Tashkent, Magnitogorsk, Irkutsk, Leningrad, and Minsk, where it closed in December 1988. Visitors averaged about 200,000 per city. It was one of the best-attended exhibitions in the history of U.S.–Soviet cultural exchanges, with a total attendance of over two million people, a very successful public diplomacy effort for USIA and one of its last before the breakup of the Soviet Union and the end of the Cold War that so dominated U.S.–USSR cultural exchanges after World War II.

The 1,250-square-meter exhibition, designed by Ralph Appelbaum Associates, New York, was the result of over a year's planning and consultation by USIA's exhibits staff with Soviet-area scholars and experts. There were fifty-six video modules that offered a glimpse into everyday lives of Americans. Visitors could see how Americans benefitted from communication technology and information systems in schools, communities, offices, farms, factories, stores, cultural and recreational pursuits, health care facilities, and homes. Displays included a Plymouth Voyager, a home office with a demonstration of desktop publishing, and a video center that played classic American cartoons from Looney Tunes, such as Bugs Bunny, Elmer Fudd, and Daffy Duck.

FURTHER READING: "American Exhibit in the Soviet Union Is Best Attended Ever; Passes Two-Millionth-Visitor Milestone in Leningrad," *USIA News Release*, October 23,

1988; "Highest Ever Attendance at 'Information USA,'" *USIA World* (Washington, DC: 1988).

INSTITUTE FOR HISTORICAL REVIEW. The Institute for Historical Review (IHR) was founded in Torrance, California (1978) "to investigate the true causes and nature of war and to disseminate those findings" through "scholarship in the promotion of peace." IHR and its parent corporation, Liberty Lobby, were founded by Willis Carto. Its subsequent conferences and publications engendered international controversy, arguing that the Holocaust did not take place but that it was an invention of Jewish propagandists.
  See also Anti-Semitic Propaganda; Holocaust Denial

FURTHER READING: Richard J. Evans, *Lying about Hitler: History, Holocaust, and the David Irving Trial* (New York: Basic Books, 2001); Deborah E. Lipstadt, *Denying the Holocaust: The Growing Assault on Truth and Memory* (New York: Free Press, 1993); Michael Shermer and Alex Grobman, *Denying History: Who Says the Holocaust Never Happened and Why Do They Say It?* (Berkeley: University of California, 2000). Also see the home page for the Institute for Historical Review (Web site: http://www.ihr.org).

INSTITUTE FOR PROPAGANDA ANALYSIS (IPA). The Institute for Propaganda Analysis (IPA) was established in October 1937 in New York City by Clyde Miller, a professor at Columbia University Teachers' College, and other scholars who were concerned with Nazi propaganda. It was a nonprofit, educational institution, helped by a $10,000 grant from The Good Will Fund of the late Edward A. Filene, to analyze "the propagandas of today and to formulate methods whereby American citizens can make their own analyses of attempts to persuade them to do something that they might not do if they were given all of the facts." In the beginning, IPA did not seek to propagandize or to influence legislation or corporations, but it soon created the possibility that traditional views could be rejected. Its critics maintained that it undermined mainstream American institutions in a time of economic and political stress. The ensuing controversy hindered fund-raising, and it ceased operations in January 1942. IPA published its bulletin, *Propaganda Analysis* (October 1937–January 1942), "to help the intelligent citizen detect and analyze propaganda" along with study materials, such as *Group Leader's Guide to Propaganda Analysis* and *Propaganda: How to Recognize It and Deal with It* (both 1938). IPA ceased when World War II started; some of the reasons for its demise included insufficient funding and the Institute's refusal to analyze domestic and foreign wartime propaganda.

FURTHER READING: Institute for Propaganda Analysis, *Propaganda Analysis* (New York: The Institute, 1938); David A. Lincove, "Propaganda and the American Public Library from the 1930s to the Eve of World War II," RQ [Reference Quarterly] (Summer 1994): 510–523.

INSTITUTE OF PACIFIC RELATIONS. Founded in 1925 by officials of the Young Men's Christian Association, the Institute of Pacific Relations (IPR) studied Far East affairs; its purpose was to promote investigation and discussion of the problems and mutual relations of the peoples of the Pacific area. One of its most prominent members was Owen Lattimore, who prepared a **Voice of**

America (VOA) script attacking Emperor Hirohito, which went against VOA policy about criticizing the Japanese emperor.

On July 25, 1951, the Senate Judiciary Committee's Subcommittee to Investigate the Administration of the Internal Security Act and Other Internal Security Laws (commonly known as the McCarran Committee after its chair, Patrick McCarran, D-Nevada) began hearings on the Communist infiltration of IPR and its seven semi-autonomous regional centers; the hearings ended June 20, 1952, and were released in fifteen parts, with considerable material on the Chinese Communist Party.

IPR was accused by the McCarran Committee of placing Communist propaganda in textbooks, among other charges, and it was questioned about its ties with the China Lobby and that it was filled with Soviet agents. IPR's use as a propaganda front to influence U.S. policy in Asia was confirmed by the sub-committee's report (Senate Report No. 2050), issued later in 1952.

FURTHER READING: U.S. Congress. Senate. Committee on Government Operations. *Congressional Investigations of Communism and Subversive Activities: Summary-Index, 1918–1956, United States Senate and House of Representatives* (Washington, DC: Government Printing Office, 1956); U.S. Congress. Senate. Committee on the Judiciary. *Institute of Pacific Relations*, hearings before the Subcommittee to Investigate the Administration of the Internal Security Act and Other Internal Security Laws; 82d Congress, 1st-2d sessions (Washington, DC: Government Printing Office, 1951–1952).

INTER-ALLIED PROPAGANDA COMMISSION. One of the major achievements of World War I propaganda was its effectiveness in the breakup of the Austro-Hungarian Empire in 1918. Once policy agreements were arranged, propaganda operations began with the establishment of an Inter-Allied Propaganda Commission at the Italian General Headquarters with one member designated to represent each of the Allied powers. Additional members representing each of the "oppressed" nationalities that were intended to separate from Austria-Hungary were attached to the commissions. The first step was publication of a newsheet that soon became a weekly publication printed in four languages. These and the pamphlets were distributed by airplane, balloon, rocket, grenade, and infantry patrols. In the same way, religious pictures were distributed that appealed to the piety and latent or active patriotism of the different nationalities, whereas photographs and native songs were employed on the front lines and in no-man's-land. Patrols of mostly deserters were sent on effective propaganda missions, and secret channels were devised to send propaganda into the interior of the country. Soon the propaganda operations in the area were distributing (by their count) over a million copies of leaflets and pamphlets daily. With the war's end and the success of its mission, the Inter-Allied Propaganda Commission turned to "peace propaganda" to influence peace terms.

FURTHER READING: "Psychological Warfare and the Breakup of the Austro-Hungarian Empire in 1918," in *Psychological Warfare Casebook*, ed. William E. Daugherty (Baltimore: Johns Hopkins; published for Operations Research Office, Johns Hopkins University, 1958).

INTER-AMERICAN CONFERENCE FOR THE MAINTENANCE OF PEACE. *See* **Buenos Aires Convention for Promotion of Inter-American Cultural Relations**

INTERNAL SECURITY SUBCOMMITTEE. *See* U.S. Congressional Investigations of Propaganda

INTERNATIONAL ASSOCIATION FOR CULTURAL FREEDOM. *See* Congress for Cultural Freedom

INTERNATIONAL BROADCASTING. *See* Clandestine Radio Stations; Debunk (Radio Station); Lorient; Radio Free Europe; Radio in the American Sector; Radio Liberty; Radio Marti; Radio Sawa; Soldatensender Calais; Voice of America

INTERNATIONAL EXPOSITIONS. These are a combination of national and propaganda events staged by their participants to publicize their country's achievements, to generate tourism, and to expand trade opportunities. The first major international exposition, or exhibition, was the Crystal Palace in London (1851). During the many expositions, also called world fairs, that were held in the late nineteenth century and early years of the twentieth century, the Smithsonian Institution was responsible for the increasing role that the United States achieved at these events.

After World War II, the first international exposition was the Brussels Universal and International Exposition (1958), which showed developments in atomic physics and exhibited an enormous model of a molecule, the symbol of the peaceful use of atomic energy; the same fair heightened the Cold War tensions of the 1950s, as the American and Soviet pavilions, directly located across from each other, tried to outdo each other in their exhibits and in other displays. Expos reached their peak in the 1980s with fairs almost every other year. The nadir was probably 1992, with the universal exhibition at Seville and the specialized event in Genoa, both to honor the quincentenary of Columbus's discovery of the New World. U.S. participation at Seville was almost sunk from poor Congressional funding and little lobbying support from Hispanic groups, which resulted in a U.S. pavilion that was not based on the original plans but that had to serve the purpose, as an American presence was required. Propaganda value of expos includes showing America's "best face," heightening trade relations, and increasing tourism. Expos also operate under the theory: "I went to your country's, you have to come to mine."

The U.S. Pavilion is usually one of the "must-see" sites at the expo, with its high-tech exhibits and popular culture displays. Montreal (Expo 67) had its salute to Hollywood and folk artifacts such as Indian ornaments, dolls, and coats along with a pavilion designed by Buckminster Fuller. At Osaka (1970), there was a U.S. space exhibit containing a moon rock taken from the famous moon landing the year before and a sports corner with Babe Ruth's uniform and locker. In 1986, Vancouver saluted the age of transportation and communication with classic vintage cars on display in the U.S. pavilion that drew thousands of old car enthusiasts and an exhibit that took visitors through the U.S. space program. At Brisbane, two years later, the most popular pavilion was undoubtedly the United States'. Its theme was sports and recreation in the United States; it exhibited memorabilia from several American sports halls of fame (baseball, basketball, football, golf, ice hockey, rodeo, tennis), including Ted Williams's baseball glove and Arnold Palmer's Masters jacket. In front of the pavilion, over 1,500 American athletes performed.

See also American National Exhibition, Moscow; Brussels Universal and International Exposition (Expo 58)

FURTHER READING: Martin J. Manning, "Fairs! Fairs! Fairs! The United States Information Agency and U.S. Participation at World Fairs Since World War II," *Popular Culture in Libraries* 2, no. 3 (1994): 1–32.

THE INTERNATIONAL JEW. See Henry Ford and *The International Jew*

INTERWAR PERIOD (1919–1941). *See* America First Committee; New Deal

INVISIBLE EMPIRE OF THE SOUTH. *See* Ku Klux Klan

IRAQ. During the first Gulf War, which was fought between January and February 1991, the Iraqi regime of Saddam Hussein invaded neighboring Kuwait and took control of its oil fields. As Operation Desert Shield, as the coalition of Western and Middle Eastern countries was designated, got underway, the U.S. government and the commercial media both tended to personalize the campaign as a war against the dictator Saddam. However, unlike the free reporting of the Vietnam conflict, the United States tried to manage reporting from the Gulf War by instituting a system of press pools with its armed forces in which a limited number of journalists became part of the "team." Others enjoyed the briefings from General Norman Schwarzkopf, the commander of U.S. forces, who often displayed images of U.S. "smart weapons" in action, whereas the official view emphasized technology and precision rather than images of bloodshed and death from the U.S. bombardment of Iraq. To create further dissent, the United States created **black propaganda** radio stations like the Voice of Free Iraq and Radio Free Iraq, which pretended to be the voice of opposition groups within Iraq. A **white propaganda** station, the Voice of the Gulf, broadcast war news to the Iraqi front lines while the United States dropped around twenty-nine million leaflets over Iraqi lines between December 1990 and February 1991, which included safe-conduct passes to encourage mass surrender, and employed loudspeaker teams to broadcast instructions on how to surrender. Sixty thousand Iraqi troops did so, which greatly accelerated the progress of the Western campaign and boosted confidence in the power of **psychological warfare**. In December 1998, when U.N weapons inspector Dr. Richard Spertzel became exasperated by Iraqi evasions and misrepresentations, he confronted Dr. Rihab Taha, the woman the Iraqis identified as the head of their biological weapons program, and asked her directly, "You know that we know you are lying. So why do you do it?" She replied: "Dr. Spertzel, it's not a lie when you are ordered to lie."

Gulf War (2003)

When the United States went after Saddam Hussein a second time in March 2003, it built on the successes of its propaganda campaigns in the earlier Gulf War, including some innovations. One of these was the competing information systems, a war in which television reporting of the conflict was a weapon for both Iraq and for the United States and Great Britain, particularly with an eye toward influencing European as well as Arab public opinion. The United States controlled channel 3 of Iraqi state television, broadcasting directly to the Iraqi people. Another innovation was the embedding of reporters and television journalists (Operation Embed), a ploy by the Defense Department to control the news coverage by allowing only those newspeople who were willing to cooperate with the Pentagon's ground rules to actually live among the troops, outfitting the media with gas masks, dispensing anthrax vaccinations, sharing meals, and enduring hardships. In return, the military services promised lots of access and exclusives, with "escorts" for the embedders to make sure they got accurate information; embedded reporters were able to report firefights and other action as they actually took place, but they were forbidden from reporting actual locations. Among the embedded journalists, the United States included the correspondents from Al Jazeera, the Arab television network in Qatar, which provided the Arab world with news programming of considerable independence.

Not all news reporters were cooperative. Peter Arnett, who reported the first Gulf War from Baghdad, a first for television news, was fired by CNN when he appeared on Iraqi state television to state that most Americans opposed the war, a claim that suggested he was giving aid and comfort to Saddam Hussein's forces. Arnett's actions were criticized by viewers, who asked advertisers, such as Nabisco Brands, Sterling Motor cars, and KitchenAid, to pull their advertising from CNN, but the companies refused to do so. There were also charges that TV coverage of the Persian Gulf War was often distorted with much stock footage used to convey very little meaning as well as the propaganda value of not counting bodies.

Early in 2003, the White House issued *Apparatus of Lies: Saddam's Disinformation and Propaganda, 1990–2003* (Washington, DC: U.S. Department of State, 2003) compiled by State and Defense departments disinformation specialist Todd Leventhal on Iraqi disinformation. This report highlighted the apparatus used by Saddam Hussein and his cadres to deceive the Iraqi people and the international community. The oppressive and totalitarian nature of Saddam Hussein's regime enabled his deception and deceit. This regime, which became expert at obfuscation during the 1991 Persian Gulf War, had more than a decade to perfect these practices before the Allied forces finally toppled it in March and April 2003.

Recent U.S. government reports, including *A Decade of Defiance and Deception*, have documented Saddam's deceit regarding UN resolutions and weapons inspections. In order to raise awareness of many of the regime's other forms of deception, particularly those likely to be repeated, *Apparatus of Lies* examined the facts behind Iraqi disinformation and propaganda since 1990.

In discussing the U.S.-led campaign to oust Saddam Hussein, newspapers in the Muslim and Arab world turned to classic anti-Semitic conspiracy theories, suggesting that Israel and the Jews were the "invisible hand" behind America's foreign policy toward Iraq. Editorial cartoons appeared in popular daily newspapers, including those of America's strategic allies in the region, Qatar and Saudi Arabia, regularly turned to classical **anti-Semitic propaganda** in depicting Jews and Israel. With the war against Iraq, newspapers in these and other Arab nations used the classic canard of "Jewish control" to suggest that Jews were steering American foreign policy. Others published cartoons that suggest that the U.S. war was a diversion manufactured by Israel to turn international attention away from its treatment of the Palestinians.

During the Iraqi conflict, which continues to be an ongoing battle as insurgents try to confront problems with self-government, the Americans used leaflets developed by the U.S. Army, printed in both Arabic and in English, and air-dropped them by the thousands to persuade Iraqis to stay at home with their families and to abandon Saddam Hussein. Others directed Iraqis to tune in to evening radio programs originating in Commando Solo psychological warfare planes that broadcasted a mix of Euro-pop, traditional Arabic music, contemporary singers, and a steady stream of U.S. propaganda. These addressed the major concerns the American commanders and policy makers had about a war with Iraq: the use of chemical and biological weapons, the destruction of Iraq's oil wells, the willingness of Iraq's military units to fight, and the use of civilians and national landmarks as shields. A sign that the leaflets were working came from Saddam Hussein, who announced on television, "Do they think they can shake the 11th Division with leaflets?" In December 2003, Saddam was captured in his eight-foot-deep spider hole in al-Dawr, fifteen miles from his hometown of Tikrit by soldiers from the Raider Brigade of the U.S. Army's 4th Infantry Division as part of Operation Red Dawn. In the news conference that followed, U.S. Ambassador L. Paul Bremer told the crowd: "Ladies and Gentlemen, We Got Him!"
See also Terrorism

FURTHER READING: Joel Achenbach, "Mind over Material," *Washington Post* (March 29, 2003): C1, C4; Steven W. Colford, "Protests of CNN Hit Advertisers," *Advertising Age* (February 18 1991): 1, 48; Nicholas J. Cull, David Culbert, and David Welch, *Propaganda and Mass Persuasion: A Historical Encyclopedia, 1500 to the Present* (Santa Barbara, CA: ABC-Clio, 2003); James Dao, "Trying to Win Iraqi Hearts and Minds on the Battlefield," *New York Times*, April 6, 2003: B5; Richard Leiby, "The Hilton's Strange Embed Fellows," *Washington Post* (March 7, 2003): C1, C3; Todd Leventhal. *Apparatus of Lies: Saddam's Disinformation and Propaganda, 1990–2003* (Washington, DC: U.S. Department of State, 2003); Todd Leventhal, *Iraqi Propaganda and Disinformation During the Gulf War: Lessons for the Future* (Abu Dhabi, United Arab Emirates: Emirates Center for Strategic Studies and Research, 1999); David Lieberman, "How Saddam Manipulates TV as a Weapon of War," *TV Guide* (March 9, 1991): 14–16; Vernon Loeb. "With Leaflets and Broadcasts, U.S. Aims to Sway Iraqi Minds," *Washington Post* (March 17, 2003): A11; Emily Wax and Alia Ibrahim, "TV Images Stir Anger, Shock and Warnings of Backlash," *Washington Post* (April 10, 2003): A41. See also the "Response to Terrorism" Web site, Bureau of International Information Programs, U.S. Dept. of State (http://usinfo.state.gov/topical/pol/terror).

ITALY. Official U.S. propaganda efforts in Italy started in World War I when the **Committee on Public Information** established a mission, headed by **Charles Merriam,** to promote the American cause and to keep the Italian public's interest in the war at the highest possible level; CPI distributed films, posters, flags, music, exhibits, photographs, and postcards throughout the country. In the United States, CPI prepared news items that were distributed by the Agenzi Stefani, the largest press association in Italy, and encouraged Italians living in the United States to write letters home that reported the American effort.

During World War II, Axis propaganda was directed toward the Allied countries, including the United States; to counter this, Americans retaliated with embarrassments such as the **"Moronic Little King" Incident.** In 1943, the Allies took over the key organs of Italian mass communications, including Radio Bari, for their own propaganda purposes and introduced Italian journalists to broadcasting freedom; Mussolini had imprisoned many of these same journalists for their political beliefs. Allied propaganda concentrated on anti-Fascist programs intended for German-occupied territories and aimed at winning the approval of the Italian people, such as *Italia Combatte*, famous in its time, which was broadcast by Radio Bari. The program started with the "Bollettino della Guerra Partigiana," which emphasized a policy of unconditional surrender; the more interesting part of the program, following BBC strategy, discredited the enemy through fake intercepted correspondence, offered valuable information about the German army, and revealed espionage activity. In post–World War II Italy, the United States conducted propaganda for the free enterprise system under the **Marshall Plan** and, with Great Britain and the Vatican, played an active role in financing the Democrazia Cristiana (DC), especially in the 1948 elections; these combined forces made it the leading political force in the country and later, as the Cold War intensified, promoted it as the only party that could protect the country against Communism.

See also Committee on Public Information; Merriam, Charles; "Moronic Little King" Incident

FURTHER READING: W. V. Arnold, *The Illusion of Victory: Propaganda and the Second World War* (New York: Peter Lang, 1998); Nicholas J. Cull, David Culbert, and David Welch, *Propaganda and Mass Persuasion: A Historical Encyclopedia, 1500 to the Present* (Santa Barbara, CA: ABC-Clio, 2003); William E. Daugherty, *Psychological Warfare Casebook* (Baltimore: Johns Hopkins; published for Operations Research Office, Johns Hopkins University, 1958); Mario Del Pero, "The United States and 'Psychological Warfare' in Italy, 1948–1955," *Journal of American History* 87, no. 4 (March 2001): 1304–1334.

ITALIA COMBATTE. *See* Italy

J

JACKSON, CHARLES DOUGLAS (C. D.) (March 16, 1902–September 18, 1964). Charles D. Jackson was the publisher of *Fortune* magazine and vice-spresident in the Luce publishing organization, where he was associated with various news collection and publishing activities from 1931 until his death. Jackson took frequent leaves of absence to devote to public service. He organized the Council for Democracy (1940) to counter isolationist opinion, then went on a special mission to Turkey for the State Department and the Bureau of Economic Warfare (1942), where he was successful in offsetting German efforts to monopolize Turkish chrome, which was much needed for industrial war production. In 1943, he was appointed deputy chief of Psychological Warfare Branch, **Office of War Information**. During World War II, Jackson helped organize the **Psychological Warfare Division (PWD)**, **Supreme Headquarters Allied Expeditionary Forces (SHAEF)** before the D-Day invasion. PWD planned and executed propaganda and related activities during combat and de-Nazified information control programs to be used by the Allies in Germany after the war ended. For his contributions, Jackson was awarded France's Legion of Honor and returned to Life, Inc. in 1945. Six years later, he became president of the National Committee for a Free Europe, which created the Crusade for Freedom, which in turn financed **Radio Free Europe**. Jackson went to Europe to establish radio broadcasting to Czechoslovakia and to other Iron Curtain countries.

Jackson was appointed as President Eisenhower's **psychological warfare** adviser on February 16, 1953. He was a member of various special committees and delegations appointed by President Eisenhower, but he resigned on April 1, 1954, after playing an important part in formulating new developments in the role of psychological factors in international relations. Jackson died in New York City.

FURTHER READING: William E. Daugherty, *Psychological Warfare Casebook* (Baltimore: Johns Hopkins; published for Operations Research Office, Johns Hopkins University, 1958).

JACKSON, WILLIAM H. *See* **President's Committee on International Information Activities**

JACKSON COMMITTEE. *See* President's Committee on International Information Activities

JACKSONIAN DEMOCRACY. *See* Kendall, Amos

JAPAN. The visit of Commodore Matthew C. Perry in 1853 opened up Japan to the West and with it, the stereotypical portrayal of Japanese by Westerners. When Japan invaded China in 1931, relations with the United States deteriorated. In China, Japanese posters assailed the American and European powers as China's real enemies. The military-controlled government in Tokyo, which was ready to expand the war, did not try to influence its own citizens. However, it did consider propaganda important for its youth. After the attack on Pearl Harbor, home front propaganda viciously attacked British and Americans as people who idolized materialism, individualism, and utilitarianism, while portraying themselves as spiritual and glorifying the Nazis and the Fascists. The decadence of American society was portrayed by Hollywood gangster films, which the Japanese represented more as documentaries than as entertainment; other campaigns tried to destroy all American and British influence, such as music. The monkey trio ("hear no evil, see no evil, speak no evil") was a popular theme. In their conquered territories, Japanese leaflets depicted the Americans and the British as victors who would carry off their women while the men were off fighting in the war. Japanese propaganda leaflets to the Australians emphasized possible American annexation ("While Aussies shed their precious blood, Ole Man Roosevelt finds his selfish aims going according to schedule"). In their effective radio broadcasts, POW messages describing their excellent treatment were aired with long propaganda pieces. Tokyo Rose, who broadcast to American forces in the Pacific, was the most famous Japanese radio personality.

Japanese propaganda to the United States was a failure, displaying a real lack of understanding of Americans. The Japanese portrayed Americans as morally and physically weak and urged Americans to make peace and recognize Japan's conquests. Through 1942, the Japanese population was not informed of Japanese defeats to keep morale and support of the war effort high; this changed with the fall of Saipan.

American propaganda efforts to the Japanese people remained in abeyance during most of the European and North African campaigns. When it resumed, it stressed the defeat of Germany and of Italy ("Two down and One to go" and "Jap . . . You're Next"). When Japanese soldiers refused to surrender, new safe conduct passes were printed, avoiding the word *surrender*, but they were unsuccessful. American aerial leaflets to the Japanese populace warned of imminent air raids and were printed on the reverse of counterfeit Japanese currency to attract attention. Others pictured Japanese isolation from oil and industrial supplies. Leaflets to Japanese troops were dropped from planes instead of shot by artillery bullets, as in Europe. The message did not belittle Japanese leaders, insult the soldiers, or criticize their equipment. Leaflet campaigns in the Philippines stressed U.S. military progress and the hopelessness of the Japanese situation, while leaflets warning the Filipinos of bombing attacks were used to mislead the Japanese as to the invasion area. When the Japanese executed three captured airmen, however, U.S. propaganda began describing the Japanese as apelike monsters.

The Americans used enormous quantities of aerial leaflets to warn the Japanese of coming bombing raids and, by 1945, the Japanese people were getting their only factual news from American leaflets, as Japan's propaganda agencies warned them of the atrocities they could expect if American forces won; the honorable thing was to die heroically. Japanese propaganda, now at its lowest point, was also extolling the great (but nonexistent) battles Japan was winning and the heavy losses they were inflicting on their enemies.

Many of the U.S. psychological warfare successes in the southwest Pacific during World War II were attributed to Japanese prisoners, who assisted American propagandists in waging an effective campaign against their former comrades.

See also Axis Propaganda; Kobayashi Experiment; Occupied Countries and Territories; Zacharias, Ellis Mark

FURTHER READING: Nancy Brcak and John R. Pavia, "Racism in Japanese and U.S. Wartime Propaganda," *Historian* 56, no. 4 (Summer 1994): 671–684; Allison B. Gilmore, "'We Have Been Reborn': Japanese Prisoners and the Allied Propaganda War in the Southwest Pacific," *Pacific Historical Review* (May 1995): 195–215; Kyoko Hirano, *Mr. Smith Goes to Tokyo: Japanese Cinema Under the American Occupation* (Washington, DC: Smithsonian Institution, 1992); James J. Weingartner, "Trophies of War: U.S. Troops and the Mutilation of Japanese War Dead, 1941–1945," *Pacific Historical Review* (February 1992): 53–67.

JEFFERSON–FRANKLIN PLAN (1776). In November 1775, King George III approved treaties, first suggested by Lord North, that the British government approach the Landgravine of Hesse-Cassell and the Duke of Brunswick to supply troops to serve in America. For the British monarch, this was routine; his relatives on the European continent were used to renting their troops to the British monarch to pay their own debts. When copies of the contracts were received in the American colonies, the Continental Congress ordered them published along with "an adequate reward for the person who brought the intelligence and to prepare an address to the foreign mercenaries who are coming to invade America." A message was written, believed to be by Thomas Jefferson, because it reflects his writing style, and approved by Congress, who directed a committee, augmented by **Benjamin Franklin**, "to take proper measures to have it communicated to the foreign troops." Copies were sent promptly to General George Washington at New York, who reported in August 1776 that the "appealing" handbills addressed to the German troops were instrumental in causing German mercenaries to desert from the British army.

FURTHER READING: Lyman H. Butterfield, "Psychological Warfare in 1776: The Jefferson–Franklin Plan to Cause Hessian Desertions," *Proceedings of American Philosophical Society* 94 (1950): 233–241; William E. Daugherty, *Psychological Warfare Casebook* (Baltimore: Johns Hopkins; published for Operations Research Office, Johns Hopkins University, 1958).

JOE SCANLAN. *See* Debunk (Radio Station)

JOHN REED CLUBS. The first John Reed Club (JRC) was formed in October 1929 in New York by writers and artists associated with **New Masses** to "clarify the principles and purposes of revolutionary art and literature, to propagate them, to practice them." In reality, they recruited "opinion-makers" for the Communist Party USA. They were modeled on literary studios for worker-correspondents created by the Proletcult in the Soviet Union; JRCs were militant, energetic and highly political with a slogan ("Art Is a Class Weapon") and a journal, *JRC Bulletin*. By 1934, there were about thirty John Reed Clubs in the United States, but in 1935 the Communist party that controlled the clubs shut them down to consolidate literary efforts in the **League of American Writers**. Isolated cities retained active clubs for another decade, but the journals mostly stopped publication. One of these, the prestigious *Partisan Review*, was reborn as an anti-Stalinist journal of the Left in 1936.

FURTHER READING: Richard A. Nelson, *Chronology and Glossary of Propaganda in the United States* (Westport, CT: Greenwood, 1996); with additional comments by Herbert Romerstein.

"JOIN, OR DIE." Snake cartoons first appeared in newspapers before the Albany Congress of 1754 then in November 1765 before the Stamp Act went into effect and finally between June 1774 and August 1776, when snake flags were also used, but the most effective was the one by **Benjamin Franklin,** who proposed a rattlesnake as the country's first emblem and its first personification as Hercules. It first appeared in the *Pennsylvania Gazette* (May 9, 1754). The symbol easily conveyed need for political solidarity among the colonies while the strength of the infant Hercules was likened to the mighty young nation. The message urged people of the colonies to unite in fighting the French and Indian War. Franklin consulted several sources to find an appropriate symbol for the union of the colonies. A French one provided the image of a cut snake with the motto that translated as "Join, or Die," whereas an Italian iconography book identified snakes as symbols

"Join, or Die," the first American cartoon. Drawn by Benjamin Franklin and published in the *Pennsylvania Gazette*, May 9, 1754. (*Source:* USIA photo collection)

of democracy. With the snake's negative connotations, however, Franklin and others looked for alternative symbols of union. These included a circular chain of 13 links and a Liberty Column supported by hands and arms that represented the states. After the American Revolution, national political union was embodied in the Great Seal of the United States. During the 1775 crisis of the Boston port closing, the *Pennsylvania Journal* adopted a version of Franklin's snake cartoon with the slogan "Unite or Die."

FURTHER READING: Frederic B. Farrar, *This Common Channel to Independence: Revolution and Newspapers, 1759–1789* (Garden City, NY: Farrar, 1975); Pamela Scott, "'Temple of Liberty': Building a Capitol for a New Nation," *Library of Congress Information Bulletin* (March 20, 1995): 117–126, 134.

JOINT U.S. PUBLIC AFFAIRS OFFICE, VIETNAM. *See* Vietnam. Joint U.S. Public Affairs Office

JOSSELSON, MICHAEL. *See* Congress for Cultural Freedom

"JOURNAL OF OCCURRENCES." After British troops occupied Boston (October 1, 1768) to defend the Townshend Acts, colonial papers reprinted a series of news items that described, from the American viewpoint, Boston's difficulties under the occupation. **Samuel Adams**, the great propagandist of the American Revolution, wrote most of the stories, which were sent to the *New York Journal* (titled "Journal of Occurrences") because Adams didn't believe Bostonians would believe them. Other newspapers quickly printed them as Boston news under the journal's title, and these "news" stories fostered anti-British feeling that culminated in the **Boston Massacre** (1770). After that event, anti-British feeling died down when the troops were removed.

FURTHER READING: Frederic B. Farrar, *This Common Channel to Independence: Revolution and Newspapers, 1759–1789* (Garden City, NY: Farrar, 1975).

JOYCE, WILLIAM BROOKE (April 24, 1906–January 3, 1946). Born in Brooklyn, New York, William Joyce became the best-known English propagandist for the Germans in World War II as "Lord Haw-Haw," but as a British renegade working for the Germans, he was not especially effective. By extraction, he was actually Irish because both his parents were born in Ireland. Legally, he was an American citizen, although his family returned to Ireland in 1906, where Joyce was educated. His father was a naturalized American, and neither father nor son ever acquired British citizenship. The British court that convicted Joyce for treason tried him as an alien owing allegiance to the British crown because his British citizenship could not be established.

While at the University of London, Joyce joined the British Union of Fascist, led by Oswald Mosley, where he learned oratorical agitation; his voice was especially memorable so that in 1945 it led to his instant recognition and arrest by British officers when he was hiding out in a forest in Germany. Joyce made his first broadcasts under German auspices in autumn 1939. These were characterized by a wry humor, which, together with his pseudocultured accents, earned him his nickname, Lord Haw-Haw, although Martin A. Doherty, in *Nazi Wireless Propaganda: Lord Haw-Haw and British Public Opinion in the Second World War* (Edinburgh, Scotland: Edinburgh University, 2000; with a CD of wartime German broadcasts to Britain, many by Joyce), claims that there were, in fact, several individuals identified as "Lord Haw-Haw."

Whatever the strength of this argument, Joyce is still identified as the infamous broadcaster. His broadcasts were popular in Great Britain, where there were no restrictions on listening to enemy broadcasts, but British authorities became concerned when Joyce's speeches provoked rumors, mostly concerned with town clocks, that German spies were everywhere. Joyce tried to flee after the German government collapsed, but was arrested at the Danish frontier in May 1945. He was tried in the Central Criminal Court, London, September 17–19, 1945 and convicted of high treason against Great Britain. On November 7, 1945, the Court of Criminal Appeal dismissed the appeal, which was taken to the House of Lords, where the opinion of the trial court was upheld. He was hanged at Wandsworth prison. Joyce, who was married twice, wrote *Twilight over England* (1940).

FURTHER READING: Horst J. P. Bergmeier and Rainer E. Lotz, *Hitler's Airwaves: The Inside Story of Nazi Radio Broadcasting and Propaganda Swing* (New Haven, CT: Yale, 1997), which has recordings of Lord Haw-Haw's speeches and songs on its accompanying CD; John A. Cole, *Lord Haw Haw—and William Joyce: The Full Story* (New York: Farrar, Straus and Giroux, 1965); John W. Hall, ed., *Trial of William Joyce* (London: W. Hodge, 1946); Rebecca West, *Meaning of Treason*, 2d ed. (London: Macmillan, 1952).

JUDAISM. *See* **Anti-Semitic Propaganda; Holocaust Denial**

JUSPAO. *See* **Vietnam. Joint United States Public Affairs Office**

K

KALTENBACH, FREDERICK WILHELM. *See* U.S.A. Zone of the Overseas Service (North American Zone)

KATYN FOREST MASSACRE INCIDENT. Important propaganda theme for several groups, including Nazis. During the period of the German–Soviet pact (1939–1941), in coordination with the German Wehrmacht, Soviet troops entered Poland on September 17, 1939, advanced rapidly, and captured an estimated 250,000 Polish prisoners of war, who were grouped in some hundred odd camps in Poland's eastern territories and in the western provinces of the Soviet Union. By the end of October 1939, three of these camps became special camps for officers (Kozielsk, Starobielsk, Ostashikov). Approximately 15,000 Polish officers from two of these camps were never located after June 1941; the third camp (Ostashikov) housed police, gendarmerie, and Military Frontier Guards.

Soviet leaders professed themselves unable to account for the disappearance, but the issue was quickly raised by Nazi Germany, who reported the discovery of mass executions and mass graves in Katyn Forest near Smolensk, Russia. Under Nazi propaganda minister Josef Goebbels's direction, the Germans turned this information into a propaganda campaign to disturb Allied unity while British and American psychological warfare agencies were unable to counter the German offensive.

Wallace Carroll, who was then an **Office of War Information** (OWI) psychological warfare adviser, considered the Katyn massacre a "classic of propaganda warfare" greatly assisted by Goebbels's "intelligence on Soviet–Polish relations." It severed Soviet–Polish relations and caused a dissension that was still working to the advantage of a defeated Germany after the war. As anti-Soviet propaganda distributed by the Germans among the Allies, it was one of the first indications of Russian postwar designs in Poland and of German domination of the occupied East European countries. Although the Nazis used it as propaganda, the truth was that the Polish officers were murdered by the Soviet Union. In the last years of the Soviet Union, Gorbachev released evidence of Soviet responsibility.

Congressional hearings were held by the Select Committee to Conduct an Investigation of the Facts, Evidence, and Circumstances of the Katyn Forest Massacre between October 1951 and November 1952. (The hearings were published in seven parts by the Government Printing Office as *The Katyn Forest Massacre*.) Allegations arose during the hearings that despite sympathy for the Polish people, the U.S. government tried to hide the truth to appease the Soviet Union. During World War II, OWI officer Alan Cranston (later U.S. Senator, California) and Soviet agent David Karr directed campaigns to pressure Polish-American groups to deny the Soviet involvement. After the collapse of the Soviet Union, the Russian government released documents showing that the Polish officers were murdered under the direct orders of Stalin.

FURTHER READING: Morris Janowitz and Elizabeth W. Marvick, "The Katyn Incident," in *Psychological Warfare Casebook*, ed. William E. Daugherty, 352–356 (Baltimore: Johns Hopkins; published for Operations Research Office, Johns Hopkins, University, 1958); Allen Paul, *Katyn: Stalin's Massacre and the Seeds of the Polish Resurrection* (Annapolis, MD: Naval Institute Press, 1996); U.S. Congress. Senate. Committee on Government Operations, *Congressional Investigations of Communism and Subversive Activities: Summary-Index, 1918–1956, U.S. Senate and House of Representatives* (Washington, DC: Government Printing Office, 1956).

KENDALL, AMOS (August 16, 1789–November 12, 1869). Journalist and postmaster-general, Amos Kendall was born in Dunstable, Massachusetts, and graduated from Dartmouth (1811). He was Andrew Jackson's chief advisor

Amos Kendall. (*Source:* Library of Congress, Prints and Photographs Division)

and later earned title of "first presidential public relations man." Kendall was a writer and editor who is now considered the first presidential press secretary. His effective publicity techniques are widely credited with Jackson's success. He wrote speeches, state papers, and press releases; conducted public opinion polls to gauge Jackson's popularity; and created the image of Andrew Jackson as a man of the people and the "Second Washington," making a strong appeal for popular democracy.

In 1828, "Old Hickory's" allies in Congress used their power of the frank to mail out quantities of printed propaganda to attack the "effete and corrupt" John Quincy Adams. Jackson won the election, and his strong leadership, aided by Kendall, helped build the modern Democratic Party and the two-party system. As postmaster-general in Jackson's administration, Kendall condoned the illegal exclusion of abolitionist propaganda from the mails by Southern postmasters, but his action was heavily criticized by antislavery supporters. He later represented Western Cherokees (1852) for certain wrongs done them. Kendall wrote *Life of General Andrew Jackson* (1843) and his autobiography, which was published posthumously (1872).

FURTHER READING: Terry L. Shoptaugh, *Amos Kendall: A Political Biography* (Ph.D. thesis, University of New Hampshire, 1984).

KIRKPATRICK SPEECH. Reagan administration officials were the subjects of several forgeries. Jeanne Kirkpatrick has been the target of more than one Soviet forgery. On February 6, 1983, the pro-Soviet Indian weekly, *Link*, published the text of a supposed speech by UN Ambassador Kirkpatrick outlining a plan for the Balkanization of India. The speech was never given, but this forgery has been replayed many times by Soviet-controlled propaganda outlets, including the book, *Devil and His Dart: How the CIA Is Plotting in the Third World*, by Kunhanandan Nair (New Delhi: Sterling Publishers, 1986). The author is the European correspondent of *Blitz*, another pro-Soviet publication.

On November 5, 1982, the British magazine *New Statesman* published a Photostat of a letter supposedly from a South African official to Kirkpatrick. He was allegedly sending her a birthday gift. The U.S. Mission to the U.N. wrote the magazine on November 19, branding the letter a forgery. *New Statesman* countered this by printing another Photostat of the forgery with entirely different spacing between the lines. The magazine claimed that the letter was authentic and that they had received it from a source in the U.S. Department of State. A comparison of this forgery with a letter sent by the South African official to a number of U.S. journalists announcing his appointment as Information Counsellor at the embassy revealed that this letter was the exemplar. The real letter had been typed on a computer. The forgery based on it was typed on a typewriter and contained a number of misspellings.

FURTHER READING: Herbert Romerstein, "Disinformation as a KGB Weapon in the Cold War," paper prepared for a Conference on Germany and Intelligence Organizations: The Last Fifty Years in Review, Akademie fur Politische Bildung Tutzing [Germany] (Washington: Unpublished, 1999).

KITCHEN DEBATE. *See* **American National Exhibition, Moscow**

KOBAYASHI EXPERIMENT. During World War II, Second Lieutenant Kobayashi, Japanese Imperial Navy, was found living in a cave, eating snails, and writing poetry on American V-mail stationery he had salvaged from an Army refuse dump. He was captured by American soldiers, who found him an invaluable American propagandist who understood the Japanese mentality and how to appeal to it. He was an effective worker who was smothered by kindness and attention from his American captors and distracted from his primary interest of persuading other Japanese to desert. As he learned to drink American beverages, to play cards with American soldiers, and to engage in other strictly American pastimes, Kobayashi lost his effectiveness as a psychological warrior against his former Japanese comrades. Instead, he believed that Japan was going to lose the war so a quick defeat was necessary for the country to begin its rebuilding. Kobayashi skillfully delivered eloquent appeals by loudspeaker broadcasts to the Japanese people to surrender; it was the Americans who would lose face because they were obliged by the International Red Cross to provide for their prisoners. He mentioned his own superior care. The more Japanese the Americans had to help, the greater the strain on their resources. However, his effectiveness as a psychological warrior was soon undermined by American personnel, who smothered him with attention and unnecessary favors.

FURTHER READING: Gordon Cotler, "Kobayashi," *New Yorker* (August 26, 1950); reprinted: Gordon Cotler, "Kobayashi," in *Psychological Warfare Casebook*, ed. William E. Daugherty, 198–200 (Baltimore: Johns Hopkins; published for Operations Research Office, Johns Hopkins University, 1958).

KOREAN CONFLICT. *See* **Biological and Chemical Weapons Warfare**

KOREAN GERM WARFARE DISINFORMATION. *See* **Biological and Chemical Weapons Warfare**

KU KLUX KLAN. An organization of white supremacists that was founded in Pulaski, Tennessee, in 1865, during the post–Civil War period as a political and a social movement to control the "black problem." Its influence was soon felt nationally, and it still exists today. Now controlled by legislation, the Ku Klux Klan (KKK) continues to operate with more subtle political methods within mainstream society. Organization mostly existed in rural, fundamentalist areas of South and in the Midwest. KKK publications, cartoons, and posters depicted a vicious, distorted picture of the group's targets (blacks, Catholics, Indians, Jews). By the beginning of the twentieth century, the organization was waning in membership but its revitalization was helped by the 1915 release of D. W. Griffith's *Birth of a Nation*. Many members, not necessarily racist, were taken in by the Klan's propaganda and indirectly gave assent to the bigotry and lawlessness perpetrated by the KKK. Female members were designated Women of the Ku Klux Klan (WKKK). In 1940, the Special Committee on Un-American Activities published hearings exposing the relationship between the Ku Klux Klan and the German-American Bund. In 1965, the House Committee on Un-American Activities (HUAC) held extensive hearings on the Klan, which resulted in eight Klan leaders serving sentences in a federal penitentiary and almost half of the membership leaving the organization. The FBI investigations, after the passage of the Civil Rights Act, resulted in more Klan officials serving prison sentences and a further erosion of the Klan membership.

The Klanwatch Project was established (1979) at Southern Poverty Law Center in Montgomery, Alabama, to monitor and to combat KKK activities and other white supremacist organizations. In 1982, the project produced an award-winning half-hour documentary film, *The Klan: A Legacy of Hate in America.* At the 1984 Olympics in Los Angeles, two bizarre leaflets were mailed to African and Asian participants in the Los Angeles Olympics. Signed by the Klu Klux Klan, they threatened the lives of these athletes. These were Soviet forgeries that were used as payback against the United States for boycotting the 1980 Olympics after the invasion of Afghanistan. It would serve Soviet purposes if some African countries withdrew from the Olympics for "the safety of their athletes," thus the KKK leaflets. With a KKK insignia that wasn't authentic and English that wasn't a first language, the forgeries were quickly exposed, and not a single African Olympic Committee withdrew from the games. When the U.S. government exposed them and pointed out that there is no organization in the United States called simply the Klu Klux Klan, TASS responded on July 12, 1984, by claiming that the leaflets were signed "the Invisible Empire, The Knights of the Klu Klux Klan." TASS was trying to correct the error made by KGB. From 1965 to 1967, HUAC conducted extensive hearings on the Klan, which resulted in eight Klan leaders being convicted and serving jail sentences.

FURTHER READING: David M. Chalmers, *Hooded Americanism: The History of the Ku Klux Klan*, 3rd ed. (Durham, NC: Duke University, 1987); Rebecca McClanahan, "Klan of the Grandmother," *Southern Review* 32, no. 2 (Spring 1996): 344–62; Herbert Romerstein, "Disinformation as a KGB Weapon in the Cold War" (Unpublished, 1999).

KUHN, FRITZ. *See* **German-American Bund**

L

LASSWELL, HAROLD DWIGHT (February 13, 1902–December 18, 1978). Pioneer propaganda analyst and political scientist who wrote studies of power, the individual and politics, propaganda, and political communication, Harold Lasswell is perhaps best known for his development of the "policy sciences," a fusion of law, political science, sociology, and psychology into one discipline dealing with public choice and decision making. Born in Donnellson, Illinois, he received his Ph.D. in political science from the University of Chicago, where he taught (1922–1938). Lasswell was director of war communications research, Library of Congress (1939–1946), and he taught at Yale (1946–1971) and at the City University of New York (1971–1972). He was also codirector of the Policy Sciences Center in New York City. His books include *Propaganda Technique in the [First] World War* (reprint of 1927 ed.: Cambridge, MA: M.I.T. Press, [1971]), based on his doctoral dissertation; *World Politics and Political Insecurity* (1935); *Propaganda and Dictatorship* (1936), with Harwood L. Childs; *World Revolutionary Propaganda* (1939), with Dorothy Blumenstock; *Public Opinion and British-American Unity* (1941); *Public Opinion in War and Peace* (1943); and *Power and Society: A Framework for Political Inquiry* (1950), with Abraham Kaplan, and propaganda bibliographies. He edited the three-volume *Propaganda and Communication in World History* (Honolulu: Published for the East-West Center by the University of Hawaii, 1979–1980) with **Daniel Lerner** and Hans Speier.

Lasswell is often called the father of propaganda study in the United States, who made a number of important contributions toward the development of a comprehensive theory for analyzing propaganda. He argued that propaganda is "the making of a deliberately one-sided statement to a mass audience" and concluded that the propagandist works in a specific culture in which strategies are circumscribed by media availability, value norms of targeted audiences, and other preexisting constraints that are not universal in character. In 1927, he taught the first college course in public opinion and propaganda at the University of Chicago, and in 1948 he designed the "who says what to whom with what effect?" model of communication. Lasswell's work is now heavily outdated, but in its time it influenced later propaganda studies, especially during the revisionist 1930s, but few altered his conclusions. His communications formula, "who says what, in which channel, to whom, with what effect," is still the starting point for most empirical studies.

FURTHER READING: William E. Daugherty, *Psychological Warfare Casebook* (Baltimore: Johns Hopkins; published for Operations Research Office, Johns Hopkins University, 1958); Derek McDougall, *Harold D. Lasswell and the Study of International Relations* (Lanham, MD: University Press of America, 1984).

LATIN AMERICA. *See* Binational Centers; Buenos Aires Convention for Promotion of Inter-American Cultural Relations; Coordinator of Inter-American Affairs (CIAA); Libraries; Zimmermann Telegram

LAUCK, GARY. *See* American Nazi Party

LAW AND PROPAGANDA. *See* Domestic Dissemination; Emancipation Proclamation; Mutual Educational and Cultural Exchange Act; Postal Regulations (Communist Political Propaganda)

LEAFLET PROPAGANDA. *See* Leaflets

LEAFLETS. Leaflets are among most effective propaganda materials. They were sometimes ground distributed, but usually they were dropped from balloons as early as the Civil War and from aircraft during the world wars. The first known instructions on leaflets as propaganda were probably in *Art of War*, written during the fifth and third century B.C.E. and attributed to Sun Tzu, a mystic warrior–philosopher, who described dropping propaganda leaflets from kites to incite the enemy to surrender and the use of noise to paralyze and fool enemy soldiers. Then, between 1500 and 1600, the printing press opened the field of propaganda to mass communications. In the American Revolution, the Bunker Hill propaganda leaflet became a classic example of effective field propaganda. Its appeal was direct, and it made use of the sharp class distinctions then existing between British officers and enlisted men, fear was exploited as an aid to persuasion, and the language was pointed. No source was indicated, but there was no attempt to suggest a false source different from the real one. Wealth ("Three Pence a Day"), food ("Fresh provisions and in Plenty"), health, and economic status ("Seven Dollars a Month") were stressed. During the nineteenth-century wars, balloons were used to distribute leaflets during the Napoleonic wars, a stunt performed later by Union forces to scout Confederate positions in the Civil War. In the Mexican War of 1847, Mexican propaganda offered the appeals of land, honor, and common religious beliefs to American soldiers who doubted their cause.

World War I

World War I was the first international conflict in which full-scale use of leaflet propaganda was employed by all of the governments concerned; it became a major military instrument. From its inception, both Germany and Great Britain tried to get the United States as its ally and geared much propaganda to that effect. From the beginning, all the warring nations organized campaigns to win the support of their own people for the war effort. American propaganda was coordinated by two agencies: **Committee on Public Information** (CPI), the first official propaganda agency in American history, created in April 1917 to guide and shape public attitudes about the war while avoiding direct censorship and interference with the press, and the Propaganda Section (or Psychological Section), **G-2D, General Headquarters, American Expeditionary Forces (U.S. Army),** under Captain **Heber Blankenhorn,** which concentrated on morale and surrender leaflets.

World War II

With World War II, military propaganda came into its own. Along with powerful programs in Nazi Germany and in Fascist Italy, the United States and Great Britain realized that they needed propaganda ministries to help them win the public opinion war as their countries entered the conflict and to counter the Nazis, who were very effective propagandists. For the Allies, psychological warfare reached large proportions, with continuous radio broadcasting, the printing and dissemination of billions of propaganda leaflets, and many covert and deception operations. The "fast-reaction" or tactical situation leaflets and surrender passes were delivered to enemy or occupied territory by bomber aircraft of the U.S. Strategic Air Forces in both England and in the Mediterranean theater, by a special leaflet squadron of the Eighth Air Force based in England, and by training planes and Bomber Command aircraft of the Royal Air Force. In the radio siege of **Lorient,** both leaflets and radio broadcasts were used to deliver the message.

Japanese propaganda used some of the same themes as the Germans. One was a leaflet dropped on Australian troops stationed in remote Pacific Islands while American troops were stationed in Australia. The point was to arouse bad feelings between the Australian and American forces by promoting Australian fears of what was happening to their women "back home." Meanwhile, Allied forces dropped seeds on Asian countries, such as Burma, to show the population that the Japanese forces brought destruction and ruin while the Allies brought prosperity. Information was included on how to sow the seeds.

In 1944, Captain James Monroe developed a cheap, frangible propaganda bomb to disseminate leaflets in an acceptable pattern. Monroe's discovery revolutionized leaflet operations in the European Theater of Operations. Operation Neptune/Overlord (D-Day) was planned by the staff of **Psychological Warfare Division,** OWI, as the greatest propaganda show ever staged, especially in its use of radio broadcasts and leaflets, whereas Operation "Nest Egg," also 1944, was a leaflet campaign jointly planned by PWD/SHAEF and British military intelligence to bring about the surrender and evacuation of the German garrison on Guernsey in the British Channel. This operation failed due to poor planning and not enough leaflets.

Korea

Five years after World War II ended, North Korean Communist troops crossed into South Korea, and the Korean Conflict began with U.S. troops assisting the South Korean forces. North Korean propaganda used quotes from American sources to support statements aimed at destroying American soldiers' willingness to fight and directed appeals to their fears of being victimized and dying for profiteers in the United States. In a divide-and-conquer approach, American leaflets showed the North Korean soldier being pushed to the war front by the Chinese and Russian Communists. Another leaflet pictured a Chinese military hand over a North Korean soldier's eyes to prevent him from seeing United Nations facts on the Korean situation. The leaflets were aimed at splitting up the Chinese and North Korean alliance. Most effective were the baseless accusations that the U.S. initiated germ warfare, charges that were still being debated in 1999.

1950s

During the Malayan Emergency (1948–1960), the British established the Emergency Information Service (1952); by 1954, it had distributed more than 100 million leaflets. **Radio Free Europe** started its first of many "balloon" invasions that carried millions of propaganda pieces inside Poland and Czechoslovakia in August 1951. Soviet planes unsuccessfully tried to shoot them down, but there were 11,000 balloons carrying 13 million leaflets "to boost the morale of the entire non-Communist population" and to fortify "spiritual resistance" until "the day of liberation." In 1954, "Operation Veto," the first sustained effort to reach the population of an Iron Curtain country by both printed (balloon leaflets) and spoken word (Radio Free Europe broadcasts) on a closely coordinated saturation basis, began over Czechoslovakia in April.

Vietnam

The Vietnamese Conflict (1954–1975) drew on the troop strengths of some of America's allies, especially the British and the Australians. The propaganda campaign was fought on two sides: the American military establishment as it tried to sell a very unpopular situation to the people and the antiwar activists, who used sometimes violent methods to show their dissatisfaction with a conflict they were against and to win public opinion for their side. Leaflets and radio broadcasts were the major psychological warfare tools used against the Vietnamese.

After the 1983 invasion of Grenada, U.S. Army psychological warfare operations began against Cuban personnel on the island, including the use of surrender leaflets, which were replicas of Cuban currency. When the 1991 Persian Gulf War ended, U.S. officials determined that leafleting that instructed Iraqi soldiers on how to surrender had been highly effective, with a high percentage of Iraqi war prisoners saying they had been swayed by the leaflets.

In 2001, U.S. planes dropped propaganda leaflets over parts of Afghanistan to undermine support for the radical Islamic militia that ruled that country as part of a coordinated psychological warfare effort that included radio broadcasts on three frequencies. During the short-lived Iraqi war, the Americans used leaflets developed by the U.S. Army, printed in both Arabic and in English, and air-dropped them by the thousands to persuade Iraqis to stay at home with their families and to abandon Saddam Hussein. Others directed Iraqis to tune into evening radio programs originating in Commando Solo psychological warfare planes that broadcasted a mix of Euro-pop, traditional Arabic music, contemporary singers, and

Airdrop of anti-Communist leaflets. (*Source:* USIS-Regional
Publication Center, Manila; photo by Lorin Reeder)

a steady stream of U.S. propaganda. These addressed the major concerns the
American commanders and policy makers had about a war with Iraq: the use of
chemical and biological weapons, the destruction of Iraq's oil wells, the willingness
of Iraq's military units to fight, and the use of civilians and national landmarks as
shields. A sign that the leaflets were working came from Hussein, who announced
on television, "Do they think they can shake the 11th Division with leaflets?"

FURTHER READING: Carl Berger, *An Introduction to Wartime Leaflets* (Washington,
DC: Special Operations Research Office, American University; prepared for U.S. Dept. of
the Army, 1959); William E. Daugherty, "Unconditional Surrender," *Psychological War-
fare Casebook* (Baltimore: Johns Hopkins; published for Operations Research Office,
Johns Hopkins University, 1958); Melvin L. DeFleur and Otto N. Larsen, *Flow of Infor-
mation: An Experiment in Mass Communication* (New Brunswick, NJ: Transaction
Books, 1987/1958); James M. Erdmann, *Leaflet Operations in the Second World War:
The Story of the How and Why of the 6,500,000,000 Propaganda Leaflets Dropped on
Axis Forces and Homelands in the Mediterranean and European Theaters of Operations*

(Denver, CO: Reproduced by Kopy Kats, 1969); Paul M. A. Linebarger, *Psychological Warfare* (Washington, DC: Combat Forces, 1954); Vernon Loeb, "With Leaflets and Broadcasts, U.S. Aims to Sway Iraqi Minds," *Washington Post*, March 17, 2003: A11.

LEAGUE OF AMERICAN WRITERS. Founded in April 1935 out of the first American Writers' Conference, the League of American Writers pledged to "fight against imperialist war and fascism"; defend the Soviet Union against "capitalist aggression"; and work against the persecution of "minority groups and of the foreign-born." The League also promised to fight against "bourgeois distortions in American literature" and for freedom for "imprisoned writers and artists," and it promoted symbolism of the term "the people" as effective propaganda rather than continued references to "the worker." The League was controlled by the Communist Party. During the late 1930s, it promoted Soviet propaganda against so-called Trotskyism and supported the Moscow purge trials. From 1939 to 1941, the League supported the Soviet-Nazi Pact, opposed U.S. aid to Great Britain, and denounced President Roosevelt as a "war monger." The League ceased operation in 1942.

FURTHER READING: Franklin Folsom, *Days of Anger, Days of Hope: A Memoir of the League of American Writers, 1937–1942* (Niwot, CO: University Press of Colorado, 1994).

LEE, IVY LEDBETTER (July 16, 1877–November 9, 1934). Considered the "father of modern **public relations**" and one of the most quotable publicity men who ever lived, Ivy Lee was born in Atlanta and graduated from Princeton. He represented big business with clients such as the Pennsylvania Railroad, the Bethlehem Steel Co., John D. Rockefeller, the Guggenheims, and the International Sugar Council; his main focus was to dispel the image of industry leaders as heartless. Lee called himself "a physician to corporate bodies" and was associated with openness between the corporation and the public. In November 1907, he published a celebrated article in *Moody's Magazine* that extolled the railroads for hiring hundreds of workers, shipping goods to market, and making travel to the West possible. During the long and bitter coal strike (1908), Lee handed out reports to journalists not allowed to attend strike conferences and issued his *Declaration of Principles*, which advocated openness and accuracy in supplying press information. During a 1914 coal miners' strike in Colorado, in which 53 people were murdered by strikebreakers employed by the Rockefellers, Lee "humanized" John D. Rockefeller, Jr., as caring, sociable, and philanthropic. Lee also offered his services free to the United Hospital Fund of New York, Henry Street Settlement, and Cathedral of St. John the Divine. He issued press releases, wrote magazine articles, and gave newspaper interviews and platform presentations. Ivy believed that "the essential evil of propaganda is failure to disclose the source of information" and that nothing was more ridiculous than the idea that "anybody can get the papers to print what he wants them to print."

In 1904, Lee met George F. Parker while working in the press bureau of the Democratic National Committee during the presidential election. Their subsequent partnership, based in New York City, lasted four years but was one of the country's first public relations firms. Lee wrote *Railroad Valuation* (1907), *Is Railroad Regulation Becoming Strangulation?* (1914), *Human Nature and Railroads* (1915), *Publicity: Some of the Things It Is and Is Not* (1925), *Public*

Opinion and International Relations (1927), *The Press Today* (1929), and *The Black Legend* (1929). Another pamphlet, *Problem of International Propaganda: A New Technique Necessary in Developing Understanding Between Nations*, was a reprint of an address he delivered before a private group of persons concerned with international affairs in London, July 3, 1934.

FURTHER READING: Ray E. Hiebert, *Courtier to the Crowd: The Story of Ivy Lee and the Development of Public Relations* (Ames: Iowa State University, 1966).

LERNER, DANIEL (October 30, 1917–May 1, 1980). Daniel Lerner was born in New York City; he received his Ph.D. from New York University (1948) with a thesis on Skyewar, ETO, an account of the psychological warfare campaign against Germany, conducted in the European Theater of Operations from D-Day to VE-Day by PWD/SHAEF (Psychological Warfare Division, Supreme Headquarters Allied Expeditionary Force; it was published as *Skyewar: Psychological Warfare Against Germany, D-Day to VE-Day* (New York: G. E. Stewart, 1949; reissued as: *Psychological Warfare Against Nazi Germany; the Skyewar Campaign, D-Day to VE-Day* (Cambridge, MA: MIT Press, 1971).

Lerner taught at Stanford University, where he was research director of the International Studies project, Hoover Library. Lerner was an intelligence officer during World War II on the staff of **Psychological Warfare Division, Supreme Headquarters, Allied Expeditionary Forces (SHAEF)**. He described the experiences of Americans engaged in **psychological warfare** operations in Europe during World War II and considered the formulation of themes as "possibly the most critical step in the whole Skyewar process."

Lerner wrote *Propaganda in War and Crisis: Materials for American Policy* (New York: Arno, 1972) and with **Harold D. Lasswell** and Hans Speier, he edited the three-volume *Propaganda and Communication in World History* (Honolulu: Published for the East-West Center by the University of Hawaii, 1979–1980). In 1958, Lerner became Ford Professor of Sociology, Massachusetts Institute of Technology. He died in Santa Cruz, California.

FURTHER READING: William E. Daugherty, *Psychological Warfare Casebook* (Baltimore: Johns Hopkins; published for Operations Research Office, Johns Hopkins University, 1958); *Register of the Daniel Lerner Collection, 1914–1949* (Stanford, CA: Hoover Institution Archives, Stanford University, 1998).

LET POLAND BE POLAND. Let *Poland Be Poland* was a major production for the **U.S. Information Agency** during the Reagan administration. It was an international television special, first broadcast on January 31, 1982, to support the Polish Solidarity movement that featured famous Americans, such as Frank Sinatra and Charlton Heston, and it highlighted appearances by 15 world leaders who came together to deliver the same message, outrage and concern at the plight of the people of Poland under martial law. According to USIA research figures, 185 million people in 50 countries saw 30 minutes or more of the program. In addition, 3- to 30-minute highlights were shown in 17 countries, whereas others heard an audio version on the **Voice of America** or on **Radio Free Europe** or **Radio Liberty**. At least 142 PBS affiliates broadcast the program in the United States. With assistance from the VOA, many independent radio networks around the world broadcast the soundtrack, including **Radio in the American Sector**, Deutschlandfunk, and Radio France.

The House and the Senate passed H.J. Resolution 382, which permitted the showing of the film in the United States, to let the "people of Poland . . . know through every possible means that the American public and all-freedom-loving people of the world are deeply concerned about their fate and strongly support the efforts of the Polish people to solve problems in their own way." Through USIA's private-sector program, foundations, companies, and individuals pledged funds to produce *Let Poland Be Poland* totaling more than $550,000.

FURTHER READING: United States Information Agency. *United States Information Agency, 1981–1988: Years of Progress* (Washington: The Agency, 1988?)

LETTERS. *See* **Forgeries**

LEXINGTON AND CONCORD (BATTLE). First skirmish of the War of American Independence (American Revolution) that was used as a propaganda event in stirring up emerging colonial support against the "enemy" British troops. The shot heard round the world on April 19, 1775, and who fired it will never be known. It started when Massachusetts' military governor Thomas Cage sent hundreds of British troops to seize hundreds of caches of guns and ammunition rumored to be hidden there. Instead, the British found armed resistance from the minuteman and in the ensuing conflict bloodshed occurred. The resulting media coverage, including broadsides and pamphlets, sparked public opinion against the British, whereas the newspapers reflected the opposing coverage of the battle, with the expected viewpoints, from both the American and the British side. The American account reported the British troops' "savage barbarity exercised upon the bodies of our unfortunate brethren who fell . . ." and adds that "not withstanding the highest provocations . . . not one . . . cruelty . . . was commit[sic]ed by our militia." In the British version, based on officers' reports, the "cruelty and barbarity of the rebels" was so great that "they scalped and cut off the ears of some of the wounded men. . . ."
See also **War of American Independence**

FURTHER READING: Victor Brooks, *The Boston Campaign: April 1775–March 1776* (Conshohocken, PA: Combined Pub., 1999); Frederic B. Farrar, *This Common Channel to Independence: Revolution and Newspapers, 1759–1789* (Garden City, NY: Farrar, 1975); David H. Fischer, *Paul Revere's Ride* (New York: Oxford University, 1994); Brendan Morrissey, *Boston, 1775: The Shot Heard Around the World* (Westport, CT: Praeger, 2004).

LIBERTY LOBBY. Founded by Willis Carto in 1956, the Liberty Lobby developed into an influential multimillion-dollar political information action organization. It stressed **America First** themes through its periodical, *Liberty Letter* (196?–1972), and its successor, *National Spotlight*, as well as with its revisionist books and various other publications. By the late 1960s, the Liberty Lobby was criticized by more mainstream conservative organizations as being "ultra-conservative," racist, and anti-Zionist. Liberal organizations, such as the Anti-Defamation League of B'nai B'rith, considered it a "neo-Nazi group," which Liberty Lobby strongly denied. Instead, it considered itself an advocate of nationalist constitutional policies, economy in government, low taxes, and non-interventionism. Carto also was a founder of the **Institute of Historical Review**.

See also American Nazi Party

FURTHER READING: Frank P. Mintz, *The Liberty Lobby and the American Right: Race, Conspiracy, and Culture* (Westport, CT: Greenwood, 1985).

LIBRARIES. Although libraries were not an American invention, library practices in terms of public service certainly are. American libraries were the first to establish policies to circulate books, periodicals, and other materials and to promote the openness of library collections; it is these practices that have been successful overseas. For many countries, the most accessible library or Information Resource Center (as they are now called) is the library operated by the U.S. Department of State in its Public Affairs Section by the public diplomacy staff.

The U.S. information program has been an active part of American foreign policy since 1942, but historically it began on July 4, 1776, with the Declaration of Independence and its "decent respect to the opinion of mankind." Its first official venture, however, was during World War I, when the Committee on Public Information (CPI; Creel Committee) was established on April 13, 1917, by President Woodrow Wilson to promote the American war effort.

Post–World War I Efforts

The **Committee on Public Information** (CPI) was the first official propaganda agency in American history. When World War I ended, CPI continued to maintain a small presence in the area by opening four reading rooms (1919) in Mexico City, but these were closed within seven months. Their presence in this region was significant, as Latin America was becoming very important in inter-American relations.

Another post–World War II development, parallel to the reading rooms, was the American Library in Paris, which was created as a legacy of the Library War Service; it was set up by the American Library Association (ALA) to supply books to U.S. troops during World War I. In 1919, ALA decided to give the 25,000-volume library to a local board, if sufficient funds were raised for its support. Both French and American donors responded enthusiastically to the appeal and soon raised the stipulated sum. The American Library became a mecca to French students, journalists, and scholars as well as to the American expatriate community and managed to remain open through the German occupation and after the liberation. The postwar period also witnessed a renaissance of French interest in the United States and brought new readers eager to find works on American science and technology as well as literature and culture.

In the 1930s, many Americans saw the communist and fascist propaganda in the mass media as a threat to American values. The public library community responded by discussions in the profession literature on how propaganda should be handled: censored, avoided, or intentionally provided as another point of view. This stimulated controversial debate about professional values, the role of public libraries and librarians in a democratic society, and reforms in library services. The result was a national Library Bill of Rights, adopted June 18, 1948 (amended February 2, 1961; January 23, 1980; January 23, 1996), which was to reverse the negative impact of library censorship. In the bill's preamble, the American Library Association affirmed that "all libraries are forums for information and ideas." This was followed by six rights:

1. Books and other library resources for all members of the community the library serves;
2. Libraries will provide materials and information presenting all points of view;
3. Libraries will challenge censorship;
4. Libraries will cooperate with all persons and groups who try to abridge free expression and free access to ideas;
5. No one should be denied access to library services because of "origin, age, background, or views";
6. Libraries will make exhibit spaces and meeting rooms available to all "on an equitable basis, regardless of the beliefs or affiliations of individuals or groups requesting their use."

However, after the terrorist attacks on September 11, 2001, these rights have been challenged. Less than two weeks after the tragedy, Congress passed, and President George Bush signed, the USA Patriot Act on October 26, 2001, which restricts some of these points.

Latin American Cooperation

After the Buenos Aires Convention for Promotion of Inter-American Cultural Relations was held in Buenos Aires, Argentina, December 1 to 23, 1936, a cooperative effort began to counter the "threat to the hemisphere" by the Axis Powers. The Convention for the Promotion of Inter-American Cultural Relations, approved December 23, 1936, established an official U.S. educational exchanges program, and five treaties and several resolutions were approved by the United States, including statements that favored revision of textbooks, reading rooms, bibliographical exchanges, and intellectual property protection. To monitor the program in the American Republics, Roosevelt created the Office of the Coordination of Commercial and Cultural Relations Between the American Republics (OCCCRBAR) by Council of National Defense order on August 16, 1940; it later became the **Office of Coordinator of Inter-American Affairs** (CIAA).

The CIAA was primarily concerned with commercial and financial problems of the Latin American countries. However, an increase in defense preparations and the creation of the Board of Economic Warfare made it essential that CIAA increasingly identify with cultural relationships, primarily to counter Nazi propaganda in that region. Under CIAA auspices, there were exchange of persons programs, binational centers, and libraries. In the late 1930s and in 1940, Nazi infiltration in Latin America was a serious threat to U.S.–Latin American relations. President Roosevelt needed an American presence in the region that would be more permanent than the four reading rooms that CPI opened briefly in Mexico City in 1919.

Wartime Libraries

Out of this need, CIAA gave a grant to the American Library Association to establish a library, the Biblioteca Benjamin Franklin (BBF), and the Benjamin

Franklin Library Association was set up to fund BBF, promote books and cultural exchanges, and for other related purposes. The articles of agreement were signed December 8, 1941, and a formal organization of the Board of Directors took place January 8, 1942. Government and administration of the library was vested in this Board of Directors and a Librarian-Director; the first was Harry Miller Lydenberg. The BBF, located at Londres #16, Mexico City, opened its doors on April 13, 1942, an action that prompted the Mexican foreign minister to state that this was "the finest single thing" the United States has done for its country. It began with 4,000 books and periodicals and a large children's library (until 1968); today it contains over 25,000 volumes, with 250 periodicals and newspaper subscriptions, access to various databases, and a growing videotape collection.

Within the year, other libraries opened in Managua, Nicaragua (November 26, 1942) and in Montevideo, Uruguay (August 23, 1943), all by grants to ALA from CIAA. The libraries established outside Latin America were under the administration of the **Office of War Information** (OWI), which coordinated American overt propaganda activities in World War II. OWI strategically opened libraries in areas crucial to the war effort, beginning with Calcutta (September 1942), followed by London (December 1942), the first overseas library directly under U.S. control; Madrid; Sydney, Australia (February 1944); Wellington, New Zealand (August 28, 1944); Manila, The Philippine (September 26, 1945); and Tokyo, Japan (November 26, 1945).

Postwar Developments

When World War II ended, OWI and CIAA were abolished, and their foreign information programs, including the libraries, were transferred to the U.S. Department of State. However, the governmental recognition of libraries came into conflict with ALA. State Department's use of its libraries was political and propagandistic, directed toward achieving foreign policy objectives. ALA continued to maintain its professional standards, but the organization worked actively to pass the Smith-Mundt Act, (Public Law 80-402), officially the **United States Information and Educational Exchange Act** of 1948, which was signed (approved) by President Harry S Truman on January 27, 1948; it legalized overseas libraries in peacetime and ensured that they provided a service of uncompromising integrity.

On April 16, 1945, after the fall of the Third Reich, the Chief of Staff, Supreme Headquarters, Allied Expeditionary Forces (SHAEF), released two documents dealing with the upcoming U.S. occupation Army Groups: "Manual for the Control of German Information Services" and "Directive for Psychological Warfare and Control of German Information Services." In 1946, the Office of Military Governor of United States (OMGUS) was established in occupied Germany. The U.S. government funded cultural programs in countries under U.S. occupation; along with Germany, these included Austria, Japan, and Korea. U.S. information officers were advised to set up cultural programs that would have an impact on the occupied country. In Austria and in Germany, one of the most long lasting was a series of libraries and cultural centers, designated as **Amerika Haus** (America Houses), that were used for cultural activities, such as lectures and film showings, and English language classes, and as libraries and **binational centers**. Examples: Stuttgart opened in January 1946 as an Amerika

Haus. Prior to the fall of the Wall in 1989, two libraries were maintained in Berlin. The Amerika Haus in West Berlin opened in November 1945 as a reading room whereas its counterpart in East Berlin started in September 1977.

Domestic Dissemination

An important mandate for the libraries was Title V of the 1948 U.S. Information and Cultural Exchange Act (Public Law 80-402, January 27, 1948), popularly called the Smith-Mundt Act, which authorized "the preparation and dissemination abroad, of information about the United States, its people and its policies, through press, publications, radio, motion pictures, and other information media, and through information centers and instructors abroad." The act prohibited the distribution or dissemination of program materials produced by the U.S. information and cultural programs, first in the U.S. Department of State then in 1953, in the United States Information Agency (USIA), then back to State's Bureau of Public Diplomacy in 1999, within the United States "but, on request, shall be available in the English language at the Agency . . . for examination only."

Cold War Tensions

The importance of libraries in a rapidly developing Cold War environment was heightened by McCarthyism. In Europe, the Marshall Plan provided desperate financial aid to countries devastated by the destruction of World War II. For U.S. libraries, the period was a particularly unpleasant one, as State Department libraries came under attack in the early 1950s for being the repository of Communist books. There was an investigation at headquarters of the purchase of any books by authors with Communist or other "suspicious" leanings in their background. The libraries were removed from the State Department when President Eisenhower transferred the U.S. information and cultural programs to the U.S. Information Agency (USIA) on August 1, 1953, under Reorganization Plan No. 8, as an independent organization within the executive branch responsible for the U.S. government's information and cultural programs. The new agency was born in the tense, controversial climate of the times. Along with the libraries under attack for holding books by alleged Communist authors, the program was also subjected to repeated calls for burning such books or closing suspicious libraries down completely.

In 1954, USIA established a Committee on Books Abroad to advise on problems in publishing and library fields, including book selection policies. The committee was a subcommittee of the U.S. Advisory Commission on Information.

Undoubtedly, Eisenhower's decision for such an agency was simplified by influential Secretary of State John Foster Dulles's flippant remark that he did not want "any propagandists in the State Department." Another Dulles remark was a reaction to pressure on the State Department to burn unsuitable books, a tailgate to the larger issue of "books, publications and other materials by controversial authors." This was the hot issue in 1953 when Eisenhower took over. Dulles made his statement at a press conference (June 15, 1953) in which he was asked about the administration's book burning of "unacceptable" books in overseas libraries. In his response, he said that "I think that out of two million books, eleven, as far as I can find out, were burned."

Changing Times

The 1960s were an optimistic period for the U.S. information programs, and it was reflected in the budgets and in the programs that USIA continued overseas. In 1962, the U.S. Government Advisory Committee on Book and Library Programs was established under authority of Fulbright-Hays Act to advise libraries on book selection and other issues that reflected directly on the American presence in libraries. The committee was abolished in 1977 at the beginning of the Carter administration when President Carter and his advisors wanted to change the focus of the USIA mandate overseas.

During the 1970s, the U.S. libraries were particularly challenged by the Nixon administration, with its covert operations and secrecy, and the negative public opinion of Vietnam and Watergate. USIA director Frank Shakespeare was particularly hardline in his approach to fighting the Cold War, and the libraries were another part of the USIA information tool to serve this purpose.

With **Charles Z. Wick**, appointed USIA director in 1981, USIA got an administrator with direct contacts to President Reagan; this allowed him to refocus the agency's mission to enhance public diplomacy functions and to restore a tarnished agency image. An important development for the libraries was an amendment to the Fulbright-Hays Act (1961) that included a Bureau of Educational and Cultural Affairs Charter. The libraries became part of this bureau, in effect becoming part of the exchanges programs.

Modern Developments

The 1989 collapse of the Soviet Union political system and the domino events that culminated in the end of the Cold War led to substantial changes in the USIA mission and its programs. Library services for "telling America's story abroad" were replaced by collections that reflected newly emerging democratic processes. In the former Soviet Union, a series of Information Center (Amerika Hauser) libraries, similar to those that began in Germany under the occupation, were reestablished in countries that had to close their libraries due to repressive Communist regimes, especially in East European countries, or begun in places that never had a USIS library (e.g. Tirana, Albania). In 1993, the Public Affairs Section, U.S. Embassy Moscow, set up a network of public access libraries across Russia, including five American Centers, with large reference and circulating collections, and 12 American Corners, with a focus on electronic resources.

American Corners

The concept of American Corners started as a network of five public-access libraries across Russia (Moscow, Nizhniv Novgorod, Rostov-na-Donu, Tomsk, Yekaterinburg), which opened in 1993–1994; the libraries are operated by the Public Affairs Section (PA) of the U.S. Embassy in Moscow to promote Americana. They have large English-language reference and circulation collections, CD-ROMs, subscriptions to periodicals, and access to online databases. There are also 12 American Corners, conceived as mini-American Centers, with a focus on electronic resources, Internet access, and a print collection with a long shelf life. Both the centers and the corners are designed to support ongoing public diplomacy and other Mission programs throughout Russia, serving as a focal point for U.S. government activities in Russia's regions. Also part of this network are the Information Resource Centers (IRCs) in St. Petersburg and in Vladivostok, which are colocated with Consulates Generals and currently offer limited public access. Startup costs for each Center are about $100,000 and require $10,000 annually to maintain, whereas each Corner requires approximately $35,000 to set up.

American Corners are sponsored jointly by a U.S. Embassy and a host-country organization; they serve as an information outpost similar to a public library reference service. Initially, American Corners were established in host-country libraries, but posts are now considering other local institutions as partners.

The multimedia, book, and periodical collections of an American Corner are open and accessible to self-selecting audiences not usually reached through targeted public diplomacy outreach. American Corner collections can be developed to also attract a young adult readership. Where possible, associated reading or meeting rooms are made available to host program events and activities. Although an individual American Corner reflects local circumstances, all share a fundamental function: they are programming platforms that make information about the United States available to foreign publics at large.

With the success of the American Corners in Russia, the State Department opened centers in the Ukraine, Kosovo, Kenya, Namibia, Rwanda, and Mongolia but their success has not yet been determined; not all countries are suited for an American Corner. In 2003, American Corners were expected to open in Turkey, Yugoslavia, Eritrea, Malawi, Uganda, Bosnia, and Mexico. In other countries, such as in Germany or in most of the Latin American countries, similar programs are already in place, such as the German American Institutes and the Binational Centers (BNCs).

Information Resource Centers

In the mid-1990s, in developments parallel to the reinvention in Washington, the USIS libraries evolved into Information Resource Centers (IRCs). Three major factors are given as the impetus for this. First, the changing world political situation upset the global balance as democratic processes replaced Communist regimes. Second, a stronger emphasis on balancing the U.S. budget greatly reduced the funding of U.S. information programs. Third, the explosion of the information age made it possible to get information electronically from commercial databases and the Internet, initiated more access to major U.S. databases, and allowed for extremely sophisticated research that could not be done before.

On October 1, 1999, the Foreign Affairs Reform and Restructuring Act (Public Act 105-277), signed by President Clinton on October 21, 1998, abolished U.S. Information Agency (USIA) and consolidated its cultural and educational functions into the State Department. Libraries, book programs, Washington File, and speaker programs were placed within a new Bureau of Public Diplomacy under the authority of an Under Secretary, who answered directly to the Secretary of State. Today, IRCs vary significantly from country to country, but all provide the most current and authoritative information about official U.S. government policies and serve as a primary source of informed commentary on the origin, growth, and development of American social, political, economic, and cultural values and institutions. They are intended and funded as tools for public diplomacy.

FURTHER READING: John N. Berry, "Open Inquiry vs. Closed Orthodoxy," *Library Journal* (November 15, 1994): 6; Bo Gilliam, "United States Information Agency," *Bowker Annual*, 44th edition, 1999 (New Providence, NJ: R. R. Bowker, 1999): 47–49; Kraske, Gary E., *Missionaries of the Book: The American Library Profession and the Origins of United States Cultural Diplomacy* (Westport, CT: Greenwood, 1985); Paxton P. Price, ed., *International Book and Library Activities; The History of a U.S. Foreign Policy* (Metuchen, NJ: Scarecrow, 1982); David A. Lincove, "Propaganda and the American Public Library From the 1930s to the Eve of World War II," *RQ* [Reference Quarterly] (Summer 1994): 510–23; Henry P. Pilgert, *History of the Development of Information Services Through Information Centers and Documentary Films* (Bonn: Historical Division, Office of the Executive Secretary, Office of the U.S. High Commissioner for Germany, 1951); Stewart W. Smith, "Propaganda and the Library," *Library Journal* (June 15, 1991): S28–S30; U.S. Congress. Senate. Committee on Foreign Relations, *Overseas Information Programs of the United States*; hearings before a subcommittee of the Committee on Foreign Relations, part 2; 82d Congress, 2d Session [and 83rd Congress, 1st Session] (Washington, DC: Government Printing Office, 1953–1954); U.S. Congress. Senate. Committee on Government Information. Permanent Subcommittee on Investigations, *State Department Information Program: Information Centers*; hearing; 83d Congress, 1st Session (Washington, DC: Government Printing Office, 1953).

LILLY, EDWARD PAUL (1910–December 1, 1994). Edward Lilly was born in Brooklyn, New York; he graduated from Holy Cross (1932) and Catholic University (Ph.D., 1936), then taught at various colleges before returning to Catholic University in 1940. During World War II, he took a leave of absence to become a special assistant to **Elmer Davis** in the **Office of War Information**. After the war, he transferred to the Joint Chiefs of Staff, where he became a special consultant on **psychological warfare**. He continued teaching part time at Catholic University and gave lectures on political and psychological warfare at Georgetown (1948–1950). From 1948 to 1951, he taught psychological warfare at several defense colleges and wrote two unpublished studies on American psychological warfare that were used for background briefings. In 1952, Lilly joined the National Security Council and was a planning officer on the **Psychological Strategy Board**. After his retirement from the government (1965), he taught at St. John's University, Queens, New York (1966–1969) then at the Washington Technical Institute, later part of the University of the District of Columbia in 1976. He retired from teaching in 1977 and died in Silver Spring, Maryland. He was the author of *History of Psychological Warfare* (Washington, DC: Historical Section, Organization of the Joint Chiefs of Staff (1975?).

FURTHER READING: Harold D. Langley, "Edward P. Lilly," *Perspectives* (November 1995): 30–31; Obituary, *Washington Post*, December 3, 1994): B4.

LINDBERGH, CHARLES AUGUSTUS. *See* **America First Committee**

LIPPINCOTT, SARA JANE CLARKE. *See* Civil War Propaganda

LITERATURE. *See* Books; Comics and Comic Strips; Henry Ford's *The International Jew*; Libraries; *Mein Kampf*; Propaganda: *The Formation of Men's Attitudes*; Psychology of Radio; Uncle Tom's Cabin

LIVING NEWSPAPER. *See* Federal Theater Project

LORD HAW HAW. *See* Joyce, William

LORENTZ, PARE MᴀcTAGGART (December 11, 1905–1992). Pare Lorentz was a major documentary filmmaker of the 1930s and 1940s who wrote, directed, and produced films for the U.S. government. Before this, he spent time at the University of West Virginia and wrote movie criticism for *McCall's* magazine (1935) and a column, "Washington Sideshow," as well as a book, *The Roosevelt Year* (1934), before he produced movies. Lorentz was a protégée of Rexford G. Tugwell, Undersecretary of Agriculture and administrator of the Resettlement Administration, who hired him as a government filmmaker. When the Roosevelt administration initiated the filming of documentaries with strong social messages to build support for his New Deal policies, Lorentz produced his award-winning *The Plow That Broke the Plains* (Resettlement Administration, 1936), which led to natural resource conservation. His second film, *The River* (Farm Security Administration, 1937), was considered his masterpiece and a "documentary film poem," but labeled "**New Deal** propaganda" by its critics. At Lorentz's request, Roosevelt created the **U.S. Film Service** in 1938 to coordinate production of motion pictures about social problems that were ignored by Hollywood. During this period, when he was head of the U.S. Film Service, Lorentz wrote an outline for a film for the American Institute of Planners, which eventually became the celebrated documentary, *The City*. In *The Fight for Life* (1940), he dramatized the war against the perils of childbirth; his screenplay was adapted from the book of the same title by Paul de Kruif (1890–1971).

FURTHER READING: *Current Biography 1940*; obituary, *Current Biography 1992*; Pare Lorentz, *FDR's Moviemaker: Memoirs and Scripts* (Reno: University of Nevada, 1992); Pare Lorentz, *Lorentz on Film: Movies 1927 to 1941* (Norman: University of Oklahoma, 1986); Richard D. MacCann, *People's Films: A Political History of U.S. Government Motion Pictures* (New York: Hastings House, 1973); Gary P. Seligman, *"Good Art, Good Propaganda": Pare Lorentz and the Golden Age of Government Filmmaking, 1935–1940* (A.B. Honor's Thesis, Harvard University, 1994); Robert L. Snyder, *Pare Lorentz and the Documentary Film* (Reno: University of Nevada, 1994).

LORIENT (RADIO SIEGE). Example of the use of radio broadcasts in tactical operations designed to impair the morale of enemy troops. It was a radio siege in August 1944 of the 28,000-member German garrison, cut off at Lorient in Brittany, with the objective of softening morale in the garrison prior to an American attack. The great advantage of Lorient as a radio target was that radios

Lorient poster, an illustration in Carl Berger, *An Introduction to Wartime Leaflets*. (*Source*: Special Operations Research Office under contract to the U.S. Department of the Army, 1959)

were plentiful to bored German officers and soldiers eager to listen to an American station aimed especially at them, whereas intimate knowledge about Lorient was obtained from deserters. In the four months of their occupation, the Americans got more information than most of the officers in the garrison, in a pleasant little resort town ready to be "attacked," with continual broadcasts that mimicked the characters inside the garrison. It was tactical radio warfare at its best, but no American attack followed. In fact, the Americans blanketed the area with leaflets that directed the Germans to "quit the fight honorably" and "come over before it is to late" as "further shedding of blood is unjustifiable."

The Americans continued to broadcast lists of Germans killed, wounded, and captured, information rarely available to an enemy during warfare, but found their most effective propaganda in reading the besieged men their personal mail, from bags the Americans discovered when the garrison was first cut off. In October 1944, the Americans were ordered to Radio Luxembourg. A questionnaire filled out by the prisoners showed that the broadcasts were successful, with a ratio of 200 Germans for every member of the nine-man crew. Sergeant Benno Frank, the mainspring of the tightly integrated nine-man crew, portrayed Captain Angers; a memorable image was his gesticulating Hitlerian fury before the mike.

FURTHER READING: David Hertz, "The Radio Siege of Lorient," *Hollywood Quarterly* 1 (1946): 291–302; reprinted in William E. Daugherty, *Psychological Warfare Casebook* (Baltimore: Johns Hopkins; published for Operations Research Office, Johns Hopkins University, 1958).

LOW, DAVID. *See Cartoons*

LOYAL PUBLICATION SOCIETY. *See* Civil War Propagandists

LUSITANIA INCIDENT. May 7, 1915, incident in which a German submarine sank the *Lusitania*, a passenger liner, off the Irish coast and took nearly 1,200 lives, including many prominent Americans. In its aftermath, the British government unleashed anti-German propaganda in the United States in an unsuccessful attempt to initiate American intervention in World War I, but this action did stir up intense Germanophobia in the United States. A strong propaganda tool was the British reproduction of the *Lusitania* medal, which was privately issued in Germany after the May 1915 sinking. These were used on posters to demonstrate Germany's heartless insensitivity toward the dead. In a diplomatic note to Secretary of State Bryan, the British ambassador lied by stating that the ship was not armed and Americans were not told about secret munitions on board nor the report commissioned by First Sea Lord Winston Churchill that outlined the public opinion advantages if a passenger line with prominent neutral passengers was sunk by the Germans. Americans believed the British lies, which, combined with poorly executed German propaganda in the United States, quickly destroyed pro-neutrality support.

See also Viereck, George Sylvester

FURTHER READING: U.S. Dept. of State. *Papers Relating to the Foreign Relations of the United States: 1915 Supplement: The World War* (Washington, DC: Government Printing Office, 1928).

LUSITANIA MEDALS. *See Lusitania* Incident

LUXEMBOURG. *See* Occupied Countries and Territories

M

MAGAZINES. Picture magazines were popular in Victorian England with such features as early photos. Americans pioneered the weekly news digest or magazine concept, but they did not develop or invent it. Literary magazines were started in Europe, and children's magazines have a prototype in *Saint Nicholas Magazine*, which was created in Great Britain. The first magazine in the American colonies was *American Magazine and Historical Chronicle*, created in 1743 to discuss a "Variety of Subjects having a certain Quality" printed from a "Collection of the best and most approved Pieces published in Great Britain and the Plantations." This little experiment ceased in 1746. The next mass-market venture was *Niles' Weekly Register*. After that, there was almost a production line of titles to appeal to the ever-changing tastes of the rapidly expanding American populace. Later magazines include the better-known and longest-lasting titles.

During World War II, *Victory* magazine was produced by the U.S. **Office of War Information** in several language versions and in a format that was similar to *Life* and *Look* with its glossy pages and black-and-white photographs. This was continued by one of OWI's successors, **U.S. Information Agency**, with several magazines that it produced for overseas distribution, including *America Illustrated*, *Dialogue*, *Economic Impact*, *Span*, and *Topic*. These magazines were not allowed to be shown in the United States without an act of Congress (domestic dissemination section of the Smith-Mundt Act), but they reprinted articles from many of their better-known counterparts.

Time developed foreign divisions (Time Asia, Time Canada) so the audience became international, whereas *Life* had two foreign editions, *Life International* and *Life en Español*. *National Geographic*, published by the National Geographic Society, represents a symbol of excellence well known internationally by its yellow-bordered cover. It has expanded its foreign editions where the Spanish edition has become the No. 1 subscription magazine in Spain, the Greek edition has achieved the same status in Greece, and the Hebrew edition has become the second-leading magazine in Israel whereas new editions were expected to debut in 1999 in French, German, and Polish versions. The foreign editions have over a million subscribers with expectations for another million, which will offset the losses for the English-language edition. In Abu Dhabi, there was a request for a

Cover of the first issue of *hi* magazine (July 2003), produced by the Bureau of International Information Programs, U.S. Department of State. Language is Arabic, and it is targeted to Arabs ages 18–35 and is sold on newsstands in 22 countries. (*Source:* U.S. Department of State)

similar type of magazine that would be interested in writing stories and reports that pertain to the United Arab Emirates: desertification, saline agriculture, wildlife, and other issues that could improve the image of that country as a tourist destination.

In the 1990s, there was a growth in national magazines that appealed to the newly recognized consumer, an upwardly mobile Hispanic with a good education, a steady job, and money to spend. Unlike ethnic populations that were produced for small enclaves in and around the major cities in the United States, most famously the Irish, the Italians, the Polish, or the African-American community with its own mass-market magazines (e.g., *Ebony, Jet*), many of the major magazines have produced Spanish-language versions of their products within the United States, such as *People* magazine's *People en Español*.

See also *Covert Action Information Bulletin; The Hour; The Index; New Masses; Official Bulletin; Problems of Communism*

FURTHER READING: Marie Arana-Ward, "Magazines, Latinos Find Themselves on the Same Page," *Washington Post*, December 5, 1996; Amy Janello and Brennon Jones, *American Magazine* (New York: Harry N. Abrams, 1991); Alan Nourie and Barbara Nourie, eds., *American Mass-Market Magazines* (New York and Westport, CT: Greenwood, 1990); Howard Oiseth, *Way It Was: USIA's Press and Publications Service, 1953–77* (Washington: USIA, 1977).

MAGIC CARPET (OPERATION). *See* OPERATION MAGIC CARPET

***MAINE*, U.S.S.** *See* SPANISH-AMERICAN WAR

MANUAL FOR THE CONTROL OF GERMAN INFORMATION SERVICES. *See* Occupied Countries and Territories

MARSHALL PLAN. The idea of the Marshall Plan was first unveiled by Secretary of State George Marshall in a commencement address at Harvard University on June 5, 1947. In his remarks, Marshall invited the European countries to draw up a program for economic recovery after the devastation of World War II that would be the basis for further U.S. assistance.

This speech marked the official beginning of the Economic Recovery Program (ERP), better known as "the Marshall Plan," cemented the Allied victory, planted the seeds of European economic integration, and strengthened trans-Atlantic ties. The economic recovery program covered 18 countries in Europe; the exceptions were Spain, which was not asked to join because of the Franco dictatorship, and West Germany, which was under Allied occupation and didn't join the Marshall Plan until 1949, when a significant measure of self-government was restored. In support of this program, ABC TV presented *The Marshall Plan in Action* (1950–53), a series of television documentaries that showed how Marshall Plan aid was used to reconstruct war-devastated Europe. The films were prepared by the federal government. In Europe, many governments produced materials to explain the Marshall Plan to their citizens. Not every American supported the Marshall Plan.

One negative view came from Clarence Batchelor, whose cartoon, "Endle$$ Proce$$ion" (ca. 1953), cynically commented on massive U.S. aid to postwar France by showing marchers with dollar coins as heads endlessly marching through the Arc de Triomphe with the words "Lafayette, we are here," a popular phrase reportedly coined by General John Pershing (1860–1948) at the tomb of the Marquis de Lafayette in 1917. U.S. military assistance was viewed as a return for the help that Frenchmen rendered during the War of American Independence. Batchelor's cartoon suggested that America's post–World War II aid was excessive repayment of that debt. The Soviet Union challenged the Marshall Plan as against their interests, and they waged a political and psychological warfare campaign to disrupt European recovery along democratic lines. According to a report to the Soviet Politburo by Andrei Zhdanov, the main theme of the Soviet attack of falsification and of distortion against the Marshall Plan was that the "American economic 'assistance'" plan pursued "the broad aim of bringing Europe into bondage to American capital" with "harsher" terms dictated for the more economically

Ten posters to highlight goals of the Marshall Plan. In 1950 artists from 13 Marshall Plan countries took part in a competition to create posters that captured the goals and spirit of the Marshall Plan; these 10 are a sample of the 25 winning entries. (*Source:* The Marshall Plan, Washington, DC: U.S. Information Agency, 1997)

unstable countries. The invitation to the Soviet Union to participate in the Marshall Plan was given "to mask the hostile nature of the proposals" and "to lure the countries of East and Southeast Europe into the trap of economic restoration of Europe and American assistance," so Soviet attempts were made to doom the Marshall plan to "failure." Efforts included well-placed stories in Communist newspapers, overt and covert, in every ERP country and criticism of the Marshall Plan atlas, with the assisted countries highlighted, as a "shameless adulation of American imperialism" that was used by "naive" educators to teach geography to their children. The Marshall Plan expired on December 31, 1961, after distributing more than $12 billion in foreign aid. On June 5, 1972, West German Chancellor Willy Brandt (1913–1992), while delivering an address at Harvard commemorating the twenty-fifth anniversary of Marshall's 1947 speech, created the German Marshall Fund of the United States.

See also World War II

FURTHER READING: Michael Beschloss, *The Conquerors: Roosevelt, Truman and the Destruction of Hitler's Germany, 1941–1945* (New York: Simon and Schuster, 2002); "Communist Attacks on US Aid to Europe," in *Psychological Warfare Casebook*, ed. William E. Daugherty (Baltimore: Johns Hopkins; published for Operations Research Office, Johns Hopkins University, 1958); Notes from 'Marshall Plan' exhibition at the Library of Congress, June 2–August 31, 1997.

MARSHALL PLAN ATLAS. *See* Marshall Plan

MARTIN-BITTMAN, LAWRENCE. *See* Ladislav Bittman

MARXIST PROPAGANDA. Karl Marx wrote books, articles, and brochures with the intent of overthrowing existing institutions, but he was a more successful propagandist after his death, when the Soviet Union used his writings as the basis for their doctrine. In 1842, he became a journalist and editor of Cologne's *Rheinische Zeitung*. In 1862, he wrote his last article as London correspondent of the *New York Daily Tribune* and the *Vienna Presse*. After this, his newspaper articles were published only sporadically. His major work was the *Communist Manifesto*. His concepts were used as the basis for Soviet propaganda in foreign countries, including the United States.

FURTHER READING: Saul K. Padover, "Karl Marx, the Propagandist as Prophet," in *Propaganda and Communication in World History*, v. 2, ed. Harold D. Lasswell, Daniel Lerner, and Hans Speier, (Honolulu: Published for the East-West Center by the University of Hawaii, 1979–1980).

MASON, JOHN MURRAY. *See* Civil War Propaganda

MASSACHUSETTS GAZETTE AND BOSTON NEWS-LETTER. *See Boston News-Letter*

THE MASSES. Socialist weekly founded in New York in January 1911 to propagandize "for the cooperatives movement" with political discussions supplemented by mostly European fiction; many of its contributors were prominent left-wing intellectuals. With sharp, critical reportage and pointed cartoons, the magazine started slowly but soon found direction when Max Eastman became editor in 1912. One of its targets, the Associated Press (AP), sued for slander but quietly dropped its suit rather than go to court for a possibly embarrassing trial that could have revealed AP's unsavory business practices. After it published "The Ballad of Joseph the Nazarene" (1916), which portrayed Joseph as a man who saved Mary from becoming an unwed mother, *The Masses* was banned from New York subway stands. In 1918, the magazine was suppressed by the federal government for its opposition to World War I; the editors were twice tried under the Espionage Act, but the government failed to obtain a conviction. Almost immediately after the suspension of *The Masses*, Eastman established *The Liberator*, which became increasingly radical and associated itself with the

Communist Party in 1922. It ceased publication in 1924. *The New Masses* was established by the Communist Party in 1926. In 1948 it merged with another periodical and continued as *Masses and Mainstream* for the next several years but finally stopped publication in 1953.

FURTHER READING: Joseph North, *New Masses: An Anthology of the Rebel Thirties* (New York: International Publishers, 1969).

MATTHEWS, JOSEPH BROWN. *See* U.S. Congressional Investigations of Propaganda

McCARTHYISM. The term *McCarthyism* came from the Republican U.S. senator from Wisconsin, who alleged that Communists had infiltrated the federal government. McCarthyism came to define tactics that used the powers of government investigations, such as those by the FBI or the U.S. Congress; it was an extremely successful propaganda term for anticommunism invented by the American left but widely accepted as a term even today. As with all slogans, its purpose was to end discussion by applying a pejorative term to opponents.

See also Books; *Counterattack*; Libraries; *Red Channels*; U.S. Congress. House. Committee on Un-American Activities; U.S. Congressional Investigations of Propaganda; United States Information Agency; Voice of America

FURTHER READING: Ted Morgan, *Reds: McCarthyism in Twentieth-Century America* (New York: Random House, 2003).

McCORMACK-DICKSTEIN COMMITTEE. *See* House Resolution 199; U.S. Congressional Investigations of Propaganda

MECKLIN MEMORANDUM. *See* Vietnam. Joint United States Public Affairs Office (JUSPAO)

MEIN KAMPF. Adolf Hitler's political biography, *Mein Kampf* (translated as My Struggle or My Battle), was written as his pathfinder to what became the Nazi creed while he was serving a nine-month prison term in 1924. It was dictated to his cellmate, Rudolf Hess. It was originally published in two parts: A Reckoning (1925) and The National Socialist Movement (1926); later editions combined the two parts as one volume. In 1941, an English translation appeared in the United States. In his book, Hitler discussed the importance and the organization of propaganda, its objectives, and the types of tactics needed for its success. He analyzed the success of British war propaganda, promoted anti-Semitism and a white supremacy creed, and outlined the role propaganda would play in future warfare and observed how "the place of artillery preparation will be taken by propaganda, before the armies arrive" while "mental confusion, indecision, panic, these are the first weapons." The "intellectual level of the propaganda must be lower the larger the number of people who are to be influenced by it," and it does not need to be truthful but if falsehoods are used, they should be big ones (Big Lie).

FURTHER READING: David Welch, *The Third Reich: Politics and Propaganda* (London: Routledge, 2002).

MERRIAM, CHARLES EDWARD (November 15, 1874–January 8, 1953). Charles Merriam was born in Hopkinton, Iowa, the son of Charles Edward and Margaret Campbell Kirkwood Merriam. After graduating from Lenox College (1893) and from the State University of Iowa (B.A., 1895) with a law degree, he studied at Columbia University and in Germany, then began his academic career at the University of Chicago as a political scientist. He was heavily involved in Chicago politics as an alderman and was an unsuccessful candidate for mayor (1911). World War I ended his political career, but he took an interest in Chicago politics for the rest of his life. During the war, Merriam was head of President Wilson's propaganda mission to Italy, where he faced an Italian public that had grown restless under the reverses of its army. Merriam's job was to keep the Italian public's interest in the war at the highest possible level. He was trained in the propaganda of practical politics and was an effective public speaker, a priority in his Italian mission. He spoke only Italian phrases but was enthusiastically received when he mixed them in with his English language speeches. The progress of his Italian rhetoric was powerful propaganda of the deed designed to demonstrate his interest, conviction, and sincerity. After the war, Merriam became a prolific author of books on political theory, and he founded the Social Science Research Council (1923). He was a consultant to Presidents Hoover and Roosevelt, an appointee to the President's Committee on Administrative Management (1936), and a member of the National Resources Planning Board (1933–1945). He died in Rockville, Maryland.

FURTHER READING: "Language Idiom and Accent in Psychological Warfare," in *Psychological Warfare Casebook*, ed. William E. Daugherty (Baltimore: Johns Hopkins; published for Operations Research Office, Johns Hopkins University, 1958); Barry D. Karl, *Charles E. Merriam and the Study of Politics* (Chicago: University of Chicago, 1974).

MEXICO. *See* American Republics; Buenos Aires Convention for Promotion of Inter-American Cultural Relations; Coordinator of Inter-American Affairs: Libraries; Zimmermann Telegram

MIDDLE EAST. *See* Anti-Semitic Propaganda; *Changing Minds Winning Peace*; Gulf War Disinformation; Iraqi Propaganda; Operation Magic Carpet

MILITARY PROPAGANDA. Military propaganda, loosely defined, is the deliberate manipulation of information to promote the interests of armies, navies, or air forces; it may or may not be connected with warfare. It usually includes campaigns for military recruitment and increased military expenditure, or as often happens among South American governments, justifications for including the military in political decision making. Military propaganda is sometimes considered an extension of war propaganda, which encourages public support of the war effort on the home front, such as fund-raising, war work, recruitment, and personal sacrifice. It promotes public morale at home and in enemy-occupied countries, undermines and demoralizes the enemy, encourages neutral countries and allies, and can help break the enemy's will to fight.

The first known instructions on military propaganda were included in *Art of War*, written during the fifth and third century B.C.E. and attributed to Sun Tzu, a mystic warrior– philosopher, who described dropping propaganda leaflets from kites to incite the enemy to surrender and the use of noise to paralyze and fool enemy soldiers. Then, between 1500 and 1600, the printing press opened the field of propaganda to mass communications.

Early American Conflicts

During the French and Indian War (1754), Benjamin Franklin drew a "**JOIN, OR DIE**" cartoon with a divided snake that appeared in the *Pennsylvania Gazette* urging British colonies to unite in the fighting. For the War of American Independence (1776–1783), both the Americans and the British used pamphlets, slogans, cartoons, and especially newspapers to generate public opinion to their side in what was a mostly ineffective propaganda campaign that was overshadowed by real events, such as the victory at Saratoga or Ethan Allen's assault on Fort Ticonderoga (1775), which gave an important opening to General Washington's forces. During the nineteenth-century wars, balloons were used to distribute **leaflets** during the Napoleonic wars, a stunt performed later by Union forces to reconnoiter Confederate positions in the Civil War. In the Mexican War of 1847, Mexican propaganda offered the appeals of land, honor, and common religious beliefs to American soldiers who doubted their cause.

Civil War

The American Civil War initiated propaganda campaigns from both the North and the South. President Lincoln imposed the first official U.S. government censorship of news media during wartime and issued an executive order, based on national emergency, that punished journalists for disloyalty, such as reporting unfavorable or inaccurate battle news. Lincoln also dispatched special agents to European countries to counter propaganda gains made by the Confederacy.

Spanish-American War

During the 1898 conflict, in which the United States sent troops and warships to Spanish territories in the Caribbean and in Asia, the U.S. Army provided daily bulletins to the press and highly patriotic films, such as *Tearing Down the Spanish Flag*, excited audiences while phony pictorial "news" accounts, typified by *The Campaign in Cuba* (actually filmed in New Jersey) showed a flagrant disregard for the truth. The use of films in a military exercise that was popularly known as the "Spanish-American War" was effective, but the most important propaganda tool was **newspapers**, the "yellow press," which brought the casualties down to the level of the average reader with lurid front page headlines and pictures. The efforts of William Hearst's *New York Journal* to promote the war with Spain are now regarded as classic propaganda; he used name-calling, atrocity stories, and appeals to American honor and sympathy for the underdog to inflame public opinion against Spain as a "cruel imperialist" and an "enemy of the United States."

World War I

World War I was the first international conflict in which full-scale use of propaganda was employed by all of the governments concerned. From its inception, both Germany and Great Britain tried to get the United States as its ally and geared much propaganda to that effect. From the beginning, all the warring nations organized campaigns to win the support of their own people for the war effort. In Germany, a group of staff officers at the High Command was assigned to generate propaganda on the home front. They began by issuing completely fictitious news bulletins about the alleged sabotaging of German water supplies by French, British, and Russian troops and managed to convince most German citizens that the German armies were acting in self-defense. Germany also attempted a few shortwave broadcasts in the new communication medium of radio.

Without the radio and television of later configurations, the **poster** was an important instrument of mass persuasion in World War I, especially in military recruiting, that combined both glamour and shame to eligible recruits. In Allied countries, the Germans were portrayed as rapacious Huns; the Allied soldier was depicted as fighting for home and country. The poster had a simple message; failure to enlist was akin to treason. Recruiting propaganda of the same sort found its way into popular music and vaudeville entertainment. Probably the most famous poster was American painter James Montgomery Flagg's "I Want You" (1917), which shows **Uncle Sam**, still a staple of military recruiting, pointing a finger directly at the viewer. This poster was used in both world wars, and eventually more than four million copies were distributed. However, French World War I posters set the standard for war poster design with their beautiful artwork and ardent messages, such as "On les aura" ("We'll get them") or "Sauvonsles" ("Let's save them"), which awakened citizens to the urgency of the war. Also effective were films about the war, exhibits of war art, and special gala evenings to gain support for the war.

American propaganda was coordinated by the **Committee on Public Information** (CPI), the first official propaganda agency in American history, created in April 1917 to guide and shape public attitudes about the war while avoiding direct censorship and interference with the press.

World War II

With World War II, military propaganda came into its own. Along with powerful programs in Nazi Germany and in Fascist Italy, the United States and Great Britain realized that they needed propaganda ministries to help them win the public opinion war as their countries entered the conflict. The Nazis were very effective propagandists with their filmed staged pieces of Nazi parades and rallies along with leaflet campaigns, such as the German "radio" leaflet, which invited Americans to surrender by promising them use of German radio to transmit word to their families that they were safe. Others questioned the loyalty of the women they left behind as well as questioning their reasons for fighting a war on a side that wasn't going to win.

The British government propaganda department, Ministry of Information, was established 1939 after the British government realized that propaganda had a profound impact on civilian morale during World War I, and it helped create pro-Allies sentiment in the United States before 1917.

To counter Nazi propaganda in Latin America, President Franklin Roosevelt created the **Office of the Coordinator of Inter-American Affairs** (CIAA), under Nelson Rockefeller and put all necessary tools at CIAA's disposal: publications, radio broadcasts, posters, and films. As pressure continued on the United States to enter the war that started in Europe in September 1939, Roosevelt decided to create a series of information agencies to excite public opinion on the home front. After Pearl Harbor, the president wanted a propaganda agency to coordinate all these information activities but without the power that Wilson delegated to the **Committee on Public Information**. The **Office of War Information** (OWI) was established in June 1942 under the direction of Elmer Davis. Along with its publications and radio broadcasts over the Voice of America, OWI and the War Department worked out agreements with the media about the control of battlefront news, especially statistics on the dead and the wounded, and created psychological warfare outposts around the world. They also struck up an agreement with Hollywood studio heads on the types of films that could be made to support the war effort.

Japanese propaganda used some of the same themes as the Germans. One was a leaflet dropped on Australia troops stationed in remote Pacific Islands while American troops were stationed in Australia. The point was to arouse bad feelings between the Australian and American forces by promoting Australian fears of what was happening to their women "back home." Meanwhile, Allied forces dropped seeds on Asian countries, such as Burma, to show the population that the Japanese forces brought destruction and ruin while the Allies brought prosperity. Information was included on how to sow the seeds.

Korea

Five years after World War II ended, North Korean Communist troops crossed into South Korea, and the Korean Conflict began with U.S. troops assisting the South Korean forces. North Korean propaganda used quotes from American sources to support statements aimed at destroying American soldiers' willingness to fight and directed appeals to their fears of being victimized and dying for profiteers in the United States. In a divide-and-conquer approach, American leaflets showed the North Korean soldier being pushed to the war front by the Chinese and Russian Communists. Another leaflet pictured a Chinese military hand over a North Korean soldier's eyes to prevent him from seeing United Nations facts on the Korean situation. The leaflets were aimed at splitting up the Chinese and North Korean alliance. Most effective were the baseless accusations that the United States initiated germ warfare, charges that were still being debated in 1999. During the Malayan Emergency (1948–1960), the British established the Emergency Information Service (1952); by 1954, it distributed more than 100 million leaflets.

Vietnam

The **Vietnam Conflict** (1954–1975) drew on the troop strengths of some of America's allies, especially the British and the Australians. The propaganda campaign was fought on two sides: the American military establishment as it tried to sell a very unpopular situation to the people and the antiwar activists, who used sometimes violent methods to show their dissatisfaction with a conflict they were against and to win public opinion for their side. Posters were especially symbolic, such as the one of the daisy sticking out of the bayonet. On the pro-government side, the military went all the way in exhorting young men to sign up for military duty, despite the draft, which brought in thousands of men to the service every month. Particularly well known was the Marine Corps slogan: "We never promised you a rose garden." However, the most lasting and powerful images from Vietnam were the live battle scenes and the death tolls that appeared every night on television.

Although it promotes the interest of the various services (Air Force, Army, Coast Guard, Marine Corps, and Navy), military propaganda is not always about warfare. It most often is used for military recruitment, notably in the U.S. Marine Corps posters ("Marines are looking for a few good men"; "We never promised you a rose garden"), or as an appeal for bigger military budgets.

Compared to other propaganda campaigns and the incredible amount of literature that they have generated, the Vietnamese Conflict has not been adequately addressed. World War II was the exception, but the Korean conflict generated little evaluation. Since Vietnam, a social science effort has started to evaluate the psychological warfare methods and activities in future U.S. armed conflicts, such as the Gulf War and Iraq.

See also Gulf War Disinformation; Iraqi Propaganda

FURTHER READING: Edward W. Barrett, "Psychological Offensive in the So-Called Cold War," November 13, 1951 (Unpublished; U.S. Dept. of State memorandum); Robert Cole, *Propaganda in Twentieth Century War and Politics: An Annotated Bibliography* (Lanham, MD: Scarecrow; Pasadena, CA: Salem, 1996); William E. Daugherty, *Psychological Warfare Casebook* (Baltimore: Johns Hopkins; published for Operations Research Office, Johns Hopkins University, 1958); Daniel Lerner, *Psychological Warfare Against Nazi Germany: The Skyewar Campaign, D-Day to VE-Day* (Cambridge, MA: MIT 1971).

MILITARY RECRUITING. *See* **MILITARY PROPAGANDA**

MILLER, CLYDE. *See* **Institute for Propaganda Analysis**

MILLER, GLENN (March 1, 1904–December 15, 1944?). Born in Clarinda, Iowa, Glenn Miller was a successful bandleader when he disbanded his swing orchestra in September 1942 and enlisted in the armed forces as a major in the U.S.

Air Corps for morale building, but the military decided to also use him for propaganda against German morale. During World War II, the U.S. government, through its **Office of War Information**, enlisted the talents of musicians as propagandists to demoralize the enemy's troops. Swing music was recorded and broadcast over the airwaves of occupied countries to convince the enemy that, despite the difficult wartime conditions, the Allies were having a wonderful time. These tapes were officially known as the OWI recordings and were recently discovered after 50 years.

Miller directed the Army Air Forces Training Command Band, which played popular music with anti-Nazi commentaries interjected in his comments between pieces. Seventy-four of these recordings, which were taped from March to June 1944, are now available from RCA Victor as *The Secret Broadcasts*. His Armed Forces Network broadcasts included propaganda playlets that dramatized the Four Freedoms, outlined the official goals of the war, and equated American music with free expression and American culture.

On the night of December 15, 1944, Miller left an air base in England to entertain U.S. troops in Paris. His plane disappeared in fog, and Miller was never seen again. There is no indication it was deliberate or "friendly fire," and it remains an enduring mystery in entertainment history. Hollywood turned his life into a film, *The Glenn Miller Story* (1954) with James Stewart and June Allyson.

FURTHER READING: Cover notes, *Glenn Miller: The Secret Broadcasts* (RCA Victor); Lewis A. Erenberg, "Swing Goes to War: Glenn Miller and the Popular Music of World War II," in *War in American Culture: Society and Consciousness During World War II*, ed. Lewis A. Erenberg and Susan E. Hirsch (Chicago: University of Chicago, 1996).

MINCEMEAT (OPERATION). *See* Operation Mincemeat

MISSION TO MOSCOW. Communist propaganda film that was based on the book by Joseph E. Davies, former U.S. Ambassador to the Soviet Union (1936–1938). This 1943 Warner Bros. film, which starred Walter Huston as Davies and Ann Harding as his wife, was controversial upon its release. The blatantly propagandist film attempted to show how smart Davies was in his book of the same name and how the Russians were our friends. It was an interesting film that seems to feature almost every character actor in 1940s Hollywood that had an accent, but many of the scenes depicting Soviet life were considered ludicrous and inaccurate, a feeling shared by Moscow moviegoers; these included factory sequences and other attempts to humanize life behind the Iron Curtain, most famously a re-creation of the 1937 Moscow purge trials, in which the film accepted the false charges leveled against the defendants as accurate. In 1958, Nikita Khrushchev's secret speech denouncing Stalin exposed the trials as frame-ups.

The film rationalized Moscow's participation in the Nazi-Soviet Pact and its invasion of Finland and portrayed the Soviet Union as a nontotalitarian state that was moving toward the American model, committed to internationalism. The film was pro-Russian at the time of its release but later Cold War developments made the film both a curiosity piece and a fairy tale.

Since its release, *Mission to Moscow* has been attacked by contemporaries and scholars alike, beginning with congressional hearings by the House Committee on Un-American Activities, *Hearings Regarding the Communist Infiltration of the Motion Picture Industry* (Washington, DC: Government Printing Office, 1947), held October 20–30, 1947. Historians, who more recently researched the film's production history, argued that *Mission to Moscow* was a well-intentioned but unsuccessful attempt by President Franklin Roosevelt, Ambassador Davies, Warner Bros. Studios, and the **Office of War Information** (OWI), whose staff reviewed various editions of the film's script before production began, to counter American distrust of their Soviet ally. Others have determined that the film reopened the market for American movies in the Soviet Union because it was one of the first American motion pictures seen by Soviet viewers in well over a decade, and it was used as a diplomatic tool by Roosevelt and Davies to persuade Soviet premier Joseph Stalin of American support for the Stalinist regime and to impress on Americans the idea that the Soviet Union was a dependable ally.

FURTHER READING: Todd Bennett, "Culture, Power, and 'Mission to Moscow': Film and Soviet-American Relations During World War II," *Journal of American History* 88, no. 2 (September 2001): 489–518; Jay R. Nash and Stanley R. Ross, *The Motion Picture Guide, L-M: 1927–1983*; v. 5 (Chicago: Cinebooks, 1986); U.S. Congress. Senate. Committee on Government Operations, *Congressional Investigations of Communism and Subversive Activities: Summary-Index, 1918–1956, United States Senate and House of Representatives* (Washington, DC: Government Printing Office, 1956).

MONK, MARIA. *See* Catholic Church

MORGENTHAU PLAN. Officially, the Morgenthau Plan, named for its originator, U.S. Treasury Secretary Henry Morgenthau, Jr., was drafted in 1944 as a "top-secret" plan for the pastoralization of Germany by dismantling the defeated nation's industrial facilities and mines, turning the nation into an agricultural state. Otherwise, an industrialized Germany would always be a threat to world peace. Formulated as the policy thinking of Morgenthau, the themes of the plan were actually drafted by his deputy, Harry Dexter White (1892–1948), an expert in international financial affairs who was a Soviet agent. The plan included the idea that Germany would be turned into a pasture after World War II and thus rendered incapable of waging war again ("hard peace"), and it was to be a major cornerstone of the Allies psychological warfare effort when the war ended. After Roosevelt and Churchill discussed it in secret, they decided that it should be rejected. It was leaked to the press from the Treasury Department, where White worked, as if it were an official U.S. government policy, and it became a major theme of the Nazis' anti-American propaganda. By shoring up the resolve of the German soldiers to fight against the Western allies, the Morgenthau Plan benefited only the Soviet Union.

FURTHER READING: William E. Daugherty, "Unconditional Surrender," *Psychological Warfare Casebook* (Baltimore: Johns Hopkins; published for Operations Research Office, Johns Hopkins University, 1958); U.S. Congress. Senate. Committee on the Judiciary.

Subcommittee to Investigate the Administration of the Internal Security Act and Other Internal Security Laws, *Interlocking Subversion in Government Departments (The Harry Dexter White Papers)* (Washington, DC: Government Printing Office, 1956); U.S. Dept. of State, *Foreign Relations of the United States: The Conference at Quebec* (Washington, DC: Government Printing Office, 1972).

MORONIC LITTLE KING INCIDENT. On Sunday, July 25, 1943, the **Office of War Information** (OWI) received the news of Dictator Benito Mussolini's resignation, King Victor Emmanuel's appointment of Marshal Pietro Badoglio as his successor, and the latter's statement reaffirming Italy's alliance with Nazi Germany. In a broadcast that evening by OWI's radio service, the **Voice of America** announcer Samuel Grafton referred to King Victor Emmanuel III of Italy as "the moronic little king" who was a "puppet" to his prime minister, Marshall Pietro Badoglio, described as a "one of the best Fascists." President Roosevelt was particularly outraged at this insult to a fellow head of state, and the U.S. government took immediate steps to apologize to the king and to his government. However, the *New York Times* criticized Roosevelt's rebuke to OWI as U.S. policy that served the interests of the Communists and endangered the lives of American soldiers.

FURTHER READING: James P. Warburg, *Unwritten Treaty* (New York: Harcourt, Brace, 1946; reprinted in William E. Daugherty, *Psychological Warfare Casebook* (Baltimore: Johns Hopkins; published for Operations Research Office, Johns Hopkins University, 1958).

MOSCOW EXHIBITION. *See* **American National Exhibition, Moscow**

MOTION PICTURES. Motion pictures by their very nature are propaganda, but they are especially effective during wars and conflicts when it is essential to rally a group to a common cause. They were first used as part of a military action in the Spanish-American War to stir up American feelings against the Cubans. Since then, the motion picture has remained one of the most effective propaganda tools. As many Americans were relatively uninformed about the specifics of a conflict, in part because the war was being fought on another continent, a lack of information made it more difficult to motivate soldiers to enlist and to rally the home front citizens to support the war effort. They were used to even greater effect during World War I, when films were used by all the warring parties. Official filmmakers carefully cut in scenes shot in training or staged after battles to make sure that the public saw only positive images. The American film industry produced silent films whose message was blatant: the German or the Hun was the villain and the American, British, or French soldier always was the good guy protecting the innocent victim from the ravages of the hated enemy.

The medium came into its own as propaganda during World War II when Hollywood studios actively cooperated with the U.S. government by producing hundreds of racist anti-German and anti-Japanese war epics. Mystery stories involved Nazi spies, and gangster movies used Nazis for the bad guys while the heroes were fighter pilots and Resistance fighters. By 1943, 30 percent of all Hollywood films had war-related themes, whereas documentaries conveyed wartime messages and influenced large audiences. Probably the best known of these was Frank Capra's Why We Fight series. During World War II, both the American and British film industries devoted their resources and manpower to the war effort, producing documentaries, newsreels, recruiting films, and war sagas.

In the post–1945 Cold War environment, some pro-Soviet films also made during wartime proved controversial while American films were distributed to foreign audiences in the post–WWII years through the Korean Conflict to Vietnam movies on to the 2003 war on terrorism in the Mideast. Hollywood was seen as a vital weapon in the battle for European minds. In 1988, under court order, USIA created new interim rules that certified documentaries that want duty-free distribution status in foreign markets and allowed government officials to still impose propaganda warnings on unacceptable films.

See also *Birth of a Nation*; Documentaries; *I Was a Communist for the FBI*; Lorentz, Pare; *Mission to Moscow*; *Mrs. Miniver*; *The Plow That Broke the Plains*; *The River*

FURTHER READING: David Culbert, Lawrence Said, and Richard Wood, eds., *Film and Propaganda in America: A Documentary History*, 4 vols. (New York and Westport, CT: Greenwood, 1990); David W. Ellwood and Rob Kroes, eds., *Hollywood in Europe: Experiences of a Cultural Hegemony* (Amsterdam: VU University, 1994); Lee A. Gladwin, "Hollywood Propaganda, Isolationism, and Protectors of the Public Mind, 1917–1941," *Prologue* (Winter 1994): 235–47; Richard D. MacCann, *People's Films: A Political History of U.S. Government Motion Pictures* (New York: Hastings House, 1973); K. R. M. Short, ed., *Film and Radio Propaganda in World War II* (Knoxville: University of Tennessee, 1983).

MOTION PICTURES IN WARTIME. *See* Motion Pictures

MOVIES. *See* Motion Pictures

MRS. MINIVER. Film that was used for propaganda, but it was not originally created for that purpose. *Mrs. Miniver* was a 1942 MGM film directed by William Wyler that starred Greer Garson and Walter Pidgeon as a British couple enduring the hardships at home during World War II. The film became one of the top grossing films of the year. At a screening, President **Franklin D. Roosevelt** was so moved by the vicar's (Henry Wilcoxon) sermon about suffering, loss, and remembrance of the dead that he requested that it be broadcast over the Voice of America in Europe, translated into several languages, and air-dropped in millions of printed leaflets over German-occupied territory. The speech, like the film, was intended as **home front propaganda**; at the end, the vicar exhorted his congregation from the pulpit of a bombed-out church "to free ourselves and those who come after us from the tyranny and terror that threatens to strike us down! Fight it, then! Fight it with all that is in us! And may God defend the right." Wyler described the film as propaganda used to coax the United States into joining forces with Great Britain.

FURTHER READING: Jan Herman, *A Talent for Trouble: The Life of Hollywood's Most Acclaimed Director* (New York: G. P. Putnam's Sons, 1995).

MÜENZENBERG, WILLI (August 14, 1889–June 20, 1940?). Major propagandist who developed techniques that influenced post–World War I propaganda. Willi Müenzenberg was a German Communist, publisher, and entrepreneur who created a network of international front organizations, starting in 1922. His organizations and publications were spread worldwide. They were particularly effective in the United States in propagandizing for Soviet policies. He was considered Nazi propagandist Joseph Goebbels's equal in creating totalitarian propaganda methods, especially the technique of exploiting "fellow travelers," such as writers, artists, scientists, and other intellectual non-Communist party members as ardent Communist supporters.

Müenzenberg was born in Erfurt, Thuringia, Germany, apprenticed as a barber and a shoemaker, and became an active Socialist at an early age. During World War I, he supported the antiwar faction of the European Socialist movement. After the Bolshevik Revolution, he became head of the Young Communist International and a high official on the Communist International (Comintern). He attracted the attention of Vladimir Lenin, who instructed him to establish an International Communist front called Workers' International Relief (Mezhrabpom), which he directed for at least 10 years, to aid the starving people in Russia. This became the basis of a whole network of Communist front organization, including the **Anti-Imperialist League** and the League Against War and Fascism, which functioned through the 1920s and 1930s. He was considered the best propagandist of the Comintern. In 1938, Müenzenberg broke with Stalin, and when World War II started, he helped the French develop their German language propaganda broadcasts against the German army. Still, the French interned him. After the fall of France he escaped from the internment camp to avoid the Nazis. A few days later, his body was found hanging from a tree near Charmes, France. His widow and others believed that the Soviet secret police had him murdered.

Müenzenberg was considered a genius at organization and was the party fundraiser for Communist congresses, campaigns, and causes of the 1920s and 1930s. As a German entrepreneur, his interests ranged from newspaper publishing to cigarette manufacturing to film producing. In Germany and throughout the Communist world, he was called the "red millionaire" without actually being one. The Nazis accused him of being the mastermind of the 1933 Reichstag fire.

FURTHER READING: Babette Gross, *Willi Müenzenberg: A Political Biography* (Lansing: Michigan State University Press, 1974); Stephen Koch, *Double Lives: Stalin, Willi Müenzenberg and the Seduction of the Intellectuals* (New York: Welcome Rain, 2001).

MURAL ART. *See* **Federal Arts Project**

MURROW, EDWARD [EGBERT] ROSCOE (April 25, 1908–April 27, 1965). Edward (born Egbert) Roscoe Murrow was born in Greensboro, North Carolina, and graduated from Washington State College (1930). After working for a short time in the timber industry in the Northwest, Murrow became assistant director of the International Institute of Education (1932–1935) before joining the Columbia Broadcasting System as a reporter, where he recruited William L. Shirer, Eric Sevareid, and others for the CBS staff. From 1937 to 1945, Murrow went to

Europe for CBS, where he gained his fame as a wartime broadcaster and journalist; he broadcast from London during many of the most heroic events (e.g., Battle of London), in which he became known for his dramatic yet calm broadcasts in an understated style and in language described by a fellow commentator as "metallic poetry." He was one of the best-known World War II correspondents. His depiction of British courage was effective in pushing American opinion toward joining the war on the Allied side; he was also influential in changing British attitudes toward the eventuality of American participation. From December 1940, he urged American military intervention against Germany. After the war, Murrow was vice-president and director of public affairs for CBS. When he tired of administrative duties in 1947, he returned to the air as a radio and television commentator and host of highly regarded stories such as *Person to Person* and *See It Now* and became one of the pioneers in documentary television. Murrow was a figure of integrity and one of the few broadcasters to oppose Senator Joseph R. McCarthy (R-Wisc.). During the Kennedy administration, he became the nation's premier official propagandist as director of USIA; he brought television fame with him to USIA, and he tried to professionalize the operation and to maintain the **Voice of America**'s objectivity. His most important accomplishment at USIA was to heighten the well-being and the morale of employees, a not inconsiderable achievement after the dangers of the McCarthy years and its almost devastating impact on both staff and programs. Murrow married Janet Huntington Brewster in 1934; they had one son. He died of lung cancer on April 27, 1965. In his honor, the Murrow Center of Public Diplomacy, Tufts University, annually honors a senior Foreign Service Officer from the **Bureau of Public Diplomacy, U.S. Department of State**, with its Murrow Award.

FURTHER READING: Alexander Kendrick, *Prime Time; the Life of Edward R. Murrow* (Boston: Little, Brown, 1969); Murrow, Edward R. *In Search of Light: The Broadcasts of Edward R. Murrow, 1938–1961*; ed. with an introduction by Edward Bliss, Jr. (New York: Da Capo, 1997); Ann Sperber, *Edward R. Murrow: His Life and Times* (New York: Freundlich, 1986).

MUSIC. American music started as a combination of patriotic songs, children's ditties, drinking ballads, and folk songs. Popular music has always reflected political and cultural attitudes. The U.S. national anthem, "Star Spangled Banner," combines a stirring text by Francis Scott Key (1780–1843) with the popular drinking song, "Anacreon in Heaven," by John Stafford Smith. It was written during the War of 1812 and has one of the most stirring musical scores of any of the national anthems, but its notes are difficult to sing. In 1942, Aaron Copland (1900–1990) wrote "Fanfare for the Common Man," a short piece for brass and percussion, which is considered a form of civil religion. It sells products (advertisers), communicates ideas, and expresses protests from folk to Christian to heavy metal (rock- and-roll performers), whereas overtly partisan music is confined to more specialized recordings. These include record companies, such as Brass Tacks Music, New Haven, Connecticut, which produces records and cassettes with radical political messages. In the 1930s, the U.S. government created the Federal Music Project to help unemployed composers and musicians, but with the advent of World War II, music became stirring and emotional. A good example is the German song, "Uber, Uber Deutschland Alles" based on Austrian anthem, "Austria" ("Glorious Things of Thee are Spoken"), still used by white supremacist groups in the United States.

U.S. Department of State

Beginning in the 1940s, the **U.S. Department of State** began to use music in cultural exchanges when it sent well-known performing artists, such as Louis Armstrong and Duke Ellington, abroad where their particular type of music was especially popular. This program was continued by the U.S. Information Agency.

See also National Anthems

FURTHER READING: John Y. Cole, "Amassing American "Stuff," *Quarterly Journal of the Library of Congress* (Fall 1983): 356–89; Michael Denning, *The Cultural Front: The Laboring of American Culture in the Twentieth Century* (London and New York: Verso, 1997); David K. Dunaway, "Music and Politics in the United States," *Folk Music Journal* 5, no. 3 (1987): 268–94.

MUSLIMS. *See* **Iraqi Propaganda**

MUTUAL EDUCATIONAL AND CULTURAL EXCHANGE ACT. Public Law 87-256, approved September 21, 1961, is better known as Fulbright-Hays Act for its two sponsors, Senator J. William Fulbright (D-Ark.) and Congressman Wayne Hays (R-Ohio). The legislation strengthened certain provisions of the Smith-Mundt Act relating to educational and cultural exchanges and added authority for U.S. participation in international fairs and expositions abroad, including trade and industrial fairs; book translations; establishment and maintenance of schools abroad; support of American studies; promotion of medical, scientific, cultural, and educational research and development; and modern foreign language training.

See also Domestic Dissemination; United States Information and Educational Exchange Act

FURTHER READING: *Legislation on Foreign Relations Through 1999* (Washington, DC: Government Printing Office, 2000).

N

NATIONAL ANTHEMS. A hymn or praise of allegiance, these songs are characteristic or peculiar to the people of a nation, stir an emotional reaction, and create a patriotic response in the listener. In most countries the audience is expected to stand while their national anthem is being played, such as "Star Spangled Banner" (United States) or "God Save the Queen" (Great Britain). A famous example of an emotionally stirring national anthem was "Deutschland Uber Alles" for Germany, which used the music of Josef Haydn's "Austria" (whose tune later became the hymn, "Glorious Things of Thee are Spoken"). "The Star-Spangled Banner," symbolizes good citizenship and patriotism, not wartime propaganda, but the Veterans of Foreign Wars (VFW) and other patriotic societies have become committed to generate respect for the national anthem as an ideal important to them.

FURTHER READING: John Y. Cole, "Amassing American "Stuff," *Quarterly Journal of the Library of Congress* (Fall 1983): 356–89; Michael Denning, *The Cultural Front: The Laboring of American Culture in the Twentieth Century* (London and New York: Verso, 1997); David K. Dunaway, "Music and Politics in the United States," *Folk Music Journal* 5, no. 3 (1987): 268–94.

NATIONAL COMMITTEE FOR A FREE EUROPE. *See* Radio Free Europe

NATIONAL ELECTRIC LIGHT ASSOCIATION. The National Electric Light Association (NELA) was a trade group representing private power companies established in the late 1870s. After World War I, it subsidized textbooks and college courses on power generation. Investigations of the NELA campaign by the National Education Association (1929) and the American Association of University Professors (1930) widely publicized the general problem of propaganda in the schools. NELA believed that schools could help spread its views; it provided pamphlets for use in civic and education classes. These materials infiltrated a one-sided propaganda debate into the classroom. NELA was able to persuade publishers to submit some drafts of textbooks for their comment, to provide retainers to professors for study and for consultation, to establish college courses about utilities in which company speakers did some or all of the teaching, and to try to squelch any ideas of government regulation. In the late 1920s, the Federal Trade Commission (FTC) investigated efforts of the electrical power industry, in the authority of NELA, to manipulate public debate on power-plant ownership (privately owned plants were best whereas city-owned plants were "socialistic"). The FTC, which found that national and state representatives of NELA provided retainers to a number of college faculty members for study and for consultation, believed that covert contacts between scholars and industrial organizations were inherently detrimental because politically motivated support could be expected to generate biased research findings.

FURTHER READING: Ernest Gruening, *The Public Pays: A Study of Power Propaganda* (New York: Vanguard Press, 1931); J. Michael Sproule, *Channels of Propaganda* (Bloomington, IN: EDINFO/ ERIC Clearinghouse on Reading, English, and Communication, 1994).

NATIONAL RECOVERY ADMINISTRATION (NRA). *See* New Deal

NATIONAL SOCIALIST WHITE PEOPLE'S PARTY. *See* American Nazi Party

NATIVISM. *See* Anti-Semitic Propaganda; Catholic Church

NAZISM. *See* American Nazi Party

NETHERLANDS. *See* Occupied Countries and Territories

NETWORK ALLOCATION PLAN. *See* Home Front Propaganda

NEUE ZEITUNG. Die Neue Zeitung (The New Daily) was a newspaper launched in the fall of 1945 by OMGUS (U.S. Office of the Military Governor for Germany) in Munich that became an extremely influential barometer of public opinion by early 1946 with a circulation of 1.6 million and some 8 to 10 million readers. However, many observers in the military government considered it a political disaster that should never have been established. The purpose of the newspaper was to inform the locals of American policy, features, viewpoints, and the American way of life. It was distributed in all four occupation zones as well as in Austria under the official masthead "An American Newspaper for the German Population." *Die Neue Zeitung* ceased publication in January 1955 after the U.S. Congress stopped its funding.

FUTURE READING: Jessica C. E. Gienow-Hecht, "Art is Democracy and Democracy Is Art: Culture, Propaganda, and the *Neue Zeitung* in Germany, 1944–1947," *Diplomatic History* 23, no. 1 (Winter 1999): 21–43; Jessica C. E. Gienow-Hecht, *Transmission Impossible: American Journalism as Cultural Diplomacy in Postwar Germany, 1945–1956* (Baton Rouge: Louisiana State, 1999).

NEUTRAL COUNTRIES IN WARTIME. *See* Occupied Countries and Territories

NEW DEAL. Roughly, the years 1933–1939, which coincided with the first two terms of Franklin Roosevelt's presidency. When the social upheavals of the Great Depression led to the installation of an activist Democratic administration promising a "New Deal," official U.S. propaganda was reborn after the inactive years following World War I, although privately originated propaganda increased during this same period as numerous pressure groups attempted to influence individual actions as well as government policies. The expansion of government powers and the introduction of new social security, public works, labor, housing, agricultural, military, and other policies required unparalleled peacetime publicity; federal authorities were committed to generate public support. An important tool was motion picture advertising, which was extended and commissioned to produce documentary films with strong social messages. *The Plow That Broke the Plains* (1936) and *The River* (1937), for example, both highlighted the need for government intervention in conserving natural resources; their success led to the creation of a federally controlled **U.S. Film Service.**

The most controversial New Deal propaganda campaign was probably the one involving the **National Recovery Administration.** Their methods included the enforced display of the blue NRA eagle emblem by "cooperating" businesses; NRA was later declared unconstitutional and nullified by the Supreme Court, partially on the basis of its supporters' excesses.

FURTHER READING: Richard W. Steele, *Propaganda in an Open Society: The Roosevelt Administration and the Media, 1933–1941* (Westport, CT: Greenwood, 1985).

NEW MASSES. Published by the Communist Party from May 1926 to January 13, 1948, *New Masses* started as an attempt to provide a broad left forum for radical thought. Publication soon became more doctrinaire Marxist, and by the 1930s it grew in intellectual influence as a source of Communist revolutionary literature, but it merged with *Mainstream* in 1947 to form *Masses and Mainstream.* A selection of poetry, stories, and essays from *New Masses* was compiled by Joseph North as *New Masses: An Anthology of the Rebel Thirties* (1969).

FURTHER READING: Mari Jo Buhle, Paul Buhle, and Dan Georgakas, eds., *Encyclopedia of the American Left*, 2nd ed. (New York and Oxford: Oxford University, 1998), with additional comments by Herbert Romerstein.

NEW YORK JOURNAL. *See* Spanish-American War

NEWSPAPERS. One of the earliest and most important instruments of American propaganda, newspapers were established in the United States on the English model, but they operated from the very beginning on the principle of press freedom, without fear of prior restraint and with little fear of lawsuits resulting from coverage of governmental issues or public officials.

The first newspaper in what became the United States was *Publick Occurrences, Both Foreign and Domestic*, which appeared in Boston on September 25, 1690; its publisher was Benjamin Harris, and its lead story was about Massachusetts Native Americans celebrating a day of thanksgiving for a successful harvest. However, the newspaper only survived one issue. The revolutionary period in America began with the Stamp Act of 1765, which imposed a special tax on newspapers, books, and legal documents. Opposition to the tax in the colonies was widespread, and it was accompanied by inflammatory patriot propaganda, represented by **Benjamin Edes** and John Gill's *Boston Gazette*, Isaiah Thomas' *Massachusetts Spy*, and others. The Whig position, supporting self-government but opposed to independence, was represented by John Dickinson's "Letters from a Farmer" in the *Pennsylvania Chronicle*. The best-known Tory editor was James Rivington, who published the *New York Gazetteer*. With the outbreak of the Revolutionary War, the *Gazette* and *Spy* were forced to flee Boston. The Whigs withdrew. Rivington renamed his paper the *Royal Gazette*, which the patriots called "Rivington's Lying Gazette," and published it under the protection of the British. **Thomas Paine** contributed his first Crisis paper to the *Pennsylvania Journal* (December 19, 1776) and wrote additional numbers of the Crisis throughout the Revolution.

At a later period of unrest, newspapers serialized (1852) Harriet Beecher Stowe's **Uncle Tom's Cabin**, the novel that Abraham Lincoln believed was one of the causes of the Civil War in the fictionalized but powerful picture it depicted about slavery. For Northern readers, especially, the newspaper serialization of Stowe's novel was their first exposure to this way of life. During the Civil War, newspaper coverage and the emerging war correspondent brought the battle casualties to the home front, but wartime censorship was more strictly enforced in the South than in the North.

Joseph Pulitzer and William Randolph Hearst perfected yellow journalism (scare headlines, sensationalism, faked stories and pictures, jingoistic propaganda) at the time of the Spanish-American War when Pulitzer's *New York World* and Hearst's *New York Journal* campaigned for war as they competed for circulation. Yellow journalism was soon taken up by other papers, and today it is promoted on the Internet.

Each succeeding decade of the twentieth century saw improvements in the speed that news was transmitted but the post–World War II period initiated more press freedom and challenges to censorship. In the 1960s, the emerging underground and alternative press targeted a growing minority of radical readers who expressed an opposite viewpoint from the closed, buttoned-down thinking of the 1950s and more of the alternate news. This coincided with the antiprotest movement against the **Vietnam Conflict**. These newspapers, often free weeklies and newssheets produced on shoestring budgets, were never competition for the major newspapers, but they were adept at exposing corruption and ridiculing the establishment sacred cows. By the end of the twentieth century, there were also more libel suits and libel laws for private individuals and corporations that were less favorable to newspapers. However, the press continues to enjoy broad protection that allows aggressive reporting, and the federal government, along with many state governments, has passed freedom of information laws that require public meetings to be open and public documents to be available to citizens, including reporters. Many states have also passed shield laws that protect journalists from having to divulge their notes or information about their sources, even when under a court order.

FURTHER READING: William E. Daugherty, *Psychological Warfare Casebook* (Baltimore: Johns Hopkins; published for Operations Research Office, Johns Hopkins University, 1958); Amanda C. Quick, ed., *World Press Encyclopedia: A Survey of Press Systems Worldwide*, 2d ed. (Farmington Hills, MI: Gale Group, 2003).

NEWSREELS. *See* Documentaries

NORDEN, COMMANDER ROBERT LEE. In an attempt to set up a **psychological warfare** unit in the U.S. Navy (**OP-16W**) similar to NID-17 Zed and to cooperate with the British in a psychological warfare attack on the enemy, an American intelligence officer in London, Lieutenant Commander Ralph G. Albrecht, with nearly perfect facility in German and experience as an international lawyer, was asked by NID-17 Zed to make two radio broadcasts to German seamen. To mask his background, Albrecht became the fictional Commander Robert Lee Norden, USN ("Fregattenkapitan Robert Lee Norden der Amerikanischen Kriegsmarine"). To lend credibility to his operation, the U.S. Navy downgraded and released significant intelligence data to make him appear more knowledgeable than the Germans on any matter relating to their navy. Between the first broadcast on January 8, 1943, and V-J Day, Norden delivered 309 broadcasts in which he successfully incorporated details of German campaigns as well as the names of officers promoted to flag rank (Admiralinflation). There are indications that Norden's work was a propaganda success, for in September 1943 the Germans discontinued publishing lists of promotions to flag rank. German prisoners of war were familiar with the Admiralinflation and Norden's broadcasts in reference to it; one remarked that Norden's quip that more admirals had been launched than submarines was often quoted by German naval personnel.

FURTHER READING: "Commander Norden and the German Admirals," in *Psychological Warfare Casebook*, ed. William E. Daugherty (Baltimore: Johns Hopkins; published for Operations Research Office, Johns Hopkins University, 1958); Ken Ringle, "War and Ambivalence," *Washington Post*, April 22, 2001: F1, F4–F5.

NORMANDY INVASION. Along with the military campaign, there was a propaganda campaign to confuse the enemy on where the landing would take place. On June 6, 1944 (D-Day), General Dwight Eisenhower launched the greatest military invasion in history (3.5 million men, 5,000 ships, 13,000 aircraft) against Hitler's Atlantic Wall. Its official name was Operation Overland. Both the Allies and the Germans waged propaganda campaigns on the French population prior to the invasion. The Germans emphasized Churchill's promise to liberate France "before the leaves fall" with these words mounted on leaves. There were also leaflets questioning why the Allies were planning to invade France while pointing out the tremendous destruction of Allied bombings. The Allies dropped leaflets on specific towns warning of imminent air bombardments and warning the inhabitants to go into the fields away from any potential targets. French townspeople were also given copies of Eisenhower's announcement of the landings in France and the liberation of all European nations but asking them to await his orders.

FURTHER READING: William E. Daugherty, *Psychological Warfare Casebook* (Baltimore: Johns Hopkins; published for Operations Research Office, Johns Hopkins University, 1958).

NORTH AMERICAN SERVICE. *See* U.S.A. Zone of the Overseas Service (North American Service)

NORWAY. *See* Occupied Countries and Territories

NUCLEAR DISARMAMENT. *See* Atoms for Peace

NUCLEAR POWER PRODUCTION. *See* Atoms for Peace

NUCLEAR WEAPONS. *See* Atoms for Peace

O

OMGUS (U.S. OFFICE OF MILITARY GOVERNOR FOR GERMANY). *See Neue Zeitung*; Occupied Countries and Territories

OCCUPIED COUNTRIES AND TERRITORIES. The occupation of a country by an enemy force during wartime provides one of the most important uses of propaganda as both sides of the conflict appeal to the occupied territory. During World War I, German forces invaded Belgium, and the British used it to stir up support of its American, French and Russian allies by reporting alleged German atrocities toward Belgian citizens, such as the rape and mutilation of children and the execution of nurse Edith Cavell for assisting British soldiers in Belgium. The most effective methods were poster art, photographs, and films.

World War II

With World War II, propaganda became more important than in any previous war, and the radio and motion pictures, both highly effective communication tools, became two of the most influential types of propaganda used to influence citizens in occupied countries. In France, propaganda campaigns were produced by the prearmistice government, the Vichy regime, the Free French forces of General Charles de Gaulle, the political parties, and other groups. In the occupied zone, the German Military Command maintained its own propaganda section to promote its belief that German dominance over the new Europe was inevitable, with rigid controls over the press, radio, and cinema. This policy was followed in all German-occupied territories, most notably Belgium, Denmark, Luxembourg, the Netherlands, Norway, and Poland. On the fringes were the Balkans (Albania, Bulgaria, Greece, Romania, and Yugoslavia).

The neutral countries (Portugal, Spain, Sweden, and Switzerland) were targeted with vigorous propaganda campaigns by the belligerent countries to recruit them to their side or at the very least to stay neutral. The two major protagonists at the beginning of the war in 1939 were Germany and Great Britain, but the United States made a major propaganda effort after **Pearl Harbor**, with its methods a combination of German bombast and British subtly. The neutral countries did not maintain extensive propaganda campaigns; instead they used censorship to protect their neutrality by limiting the flow of external information, but their support of the Allied cause wavered, dependent on political realities, until the eminent defeat of Germany made it practical to favor the winning side.

For many occupied countries, their governments-in-exile successfully used the radio to encourage and to rally their citizens. Queen Wilhelmina of the Netherlands and Haakon VII of Norway broadcast to their countrymen from exile and became heroes for the efforts they made to stand up to the Axis, a sad counterpart to Leopold III of the Belgians, who was branded a traitor for cooperating with the Nazis when they invaded his country. In 1951, he was forced to abdicate in favor of his son, so strong was the bitterness by the Belgian people for what they perceived as his wartime cowardice. In Greece, Queen Frederika was the granddaughter of Kaiser Wilhelm II.

Along with radio broadcasts, occupation propaganda used pamphlets and leaflets, that were distributed to the populace; **posters**; and **clandestine radio stations**, which appeared after Hitler came to power in Germany; these were operated by anti-Nazi dissidents. During World War II, clandestine radio stations became routine with both the Allied and the Axis powers to complement other propaganda campaigns. One was Radio 1212, which claimed to be a German-based and German-operated anti-Nazi station, but was actually transmitted behind Allied lines by the Psychological Warfare Bureau, U.S. Army. Most of these World War II clandestine stations disappeared by the end of the war. Finally, there was confiscation of property, especially a country's cultural heritage. Museums, libraries, and archives were looted, and paintings, sculpture, and other priceless artifacts were destroyed or stolen; 60 years later, some governments have begun efforts to reclaim their cultural property.

Once the United States entered the war, it conducted its own propaganda efforts to occupied countries. Along with the **Office of War Information** activities, the **Office of Strategic Services** (OSS) conducted clandestine anti-Axis psychological warfare or black propaganda programs as well as more conventional spy missions. OSS parachuted agents into Occupied Europe to organize and train resistance forces. A variety of weapons were developed that could not be easily found if the agent was arrested. One such tool was a cigarette lighter that functioned as a camera and as a single-shot gun. Special operations were employed in organizing and assisting resistance movements in Europe during World War II and for morale operations or **black propaganda**.

In 1942, the **Voice of America** (VOA) began shortwave broadcasts in German, French, Italian, and English; the first VOA broadcast to Germany took place the evening of February 24/25. During World War II, the VOA established other broadcast services in several languages to countries under Axis occupation (Albanian, Danish, Dutch, French to Europe, Greek, Italian, Japanese, Norwegian, Polish, Portuguese to Portugal, Romanian, Russian, Serbo-Croatian, Slovene, Spanish to Spain, Swedish), but ended them after the war ended.

General Robert A. McClure, an intelligence officer on the staff of Lieutenant General Dwight D. Eisenhower, was appointed chief of the Information and Censorship Section, Allied Force Headquarters (AFHQ), Psychological Warfare

Division (PWD) of Supreme Headquarters Allied Expeditionary Force (SHAEF) to plan and to execute propaganda and related activities during combat and to devise a de-Nazified information control program to be used in the Allied zones in Germany after World War II ended. PWD prepared and distributed millions of leaflets to influence enemy troops and civilians, broadcast appeals and announcements, cooperated with the French underground, and trained units to operate militarily licensed "clean" press, films, music, and theater in the occupied areas.

Resistance to the German Army was feeble and ineffective in the early days of occupation. For example, in Norway, many confused Norwegians joined or collaborated with the Nazis; defiance to party dogma and military presence gradually built over the years as the powerful counterforce of people's humor emerged. Against overwhelming odds, anti-Nazi jokes began raising consciousness and changing minds. As momentum grew, Norwegians made full use of available ideas and the material culture to undermine the enemy: symbolic clothing, subversive children's books, mock stamps, underground Christmas cards and posters, typographical tricks, sly poetry, and double-meaning personal ads. Most important for morale was the role humor played as a form of psychological warfare, with cartoons and satirical verses and posters against the Nazis. The Hollywood film *The Moon Is Down* (1943), based on John Steinbeck's novel, related the German occupation of a Norwegian village during World War II. The screenplay was by playwright Arthur Miller.

Post–WWII Occupied Zones

Perceptions in the United States during wartime and then after peace was declared, and in countries occupied by American forces, saw a shift in sympathies when countries were no longer at war with the United States. Austria, Italy, Japan, and Germany were occupied by American forces, but the primary source of foreign assistance for rebuilding was the United States, which provided economic development through the **Marshall Plan**, the Economic Recovery Program (ERP), which covered 18 countries in Europe and reconstructed a war-devastated Europe. Films about postwar reconstruction were prepared by the federal government. In Europe, many governments produced materials to explain the Marshall Plan to their citizens, but not every American supported the Marshall Plan.

Germany

This was the country in which the United States expended much of its funds and efforts. On April 16, 1945, after the fall of the Third Reich, the Chief of Staff, Supreme Headquarters, Allied Expeditionary Forces (SHAEF), released two documents dealing with the upcoming U.S. occupation Army Groups: *Manual for the Control of German Information Services* and *Directive for Psychological Warfare and Control of German Information Services.*

At the time these documents were released, it was difficult to determine the length of time that the U.S. forces would be responsible for the country. Three phases of occupation were planned, with provision made for the British Control

Commission. The directive forbade Army Groups from relaying any radio programs from a station other than Radio Luxembourg, and all broadcasting stations operating in Germany would carry the same material, with restrictions on all broadcasts to relays from a common point. There would be five minutes of local news with military instructions at the end of every relay period, and radio stations operating in the SHAEF zone would only relay specified programs from Radio Luxembourg or at a later date from Deutschlandsender, if the Americans were successful in arranging for multipartite control of that transmitter.

In 1946, the Office of Military Governor of United States (OMGUS) was established in occupied Germany. One of its mandates was to provide cultural and informational programs (books, libraries, film showings, distribution of pamphlets). In 1949, U.S. Office of High Commissioner for Germany (HICOG) replaced OMGUS. Among its efforts was an American radio outlet in Berlin, **Radio in the American Sector** (RIAS), which proved to be a valuable adjunct to the American effort in the propaganda struggle against the Communist forces of East Germany.

Between 1948 and 1953, multimedia information programs were presented to promote and document European Recovery Program conducted by the Marshall Plan agencies (Economic Cooperation Administration and Mutual Security Agency). One of the first was the Informational Media Guaranty (IMG) program in which producers of various informational media (books, magazines, films, musical recordings) could sell their products in countries short of hard-currency foreign exchange. There were also massive reorientation and reeducation programs. Major resources were spent in Germany and in Japan, but Austria and Italy were also the beneficiaries of U.S. information programs.

The **U.S. Department of State** funded millions of dollars for cultural and educational programs. U.S. information officers were advised to set up cultural programs that would have an impact on the occupied country. In Austria and in Germany, one of the most long lasting was a series of libraries and cultural centers, designated as Amerika Hausers (America Houses), that were used for cultural activities, such as lectures and film showings, for English-language classes, and as libraries and binational centers.

Later Occupations

In 1956, the Hungarian Revolution proved the effectiveness of VOA and of Radio Free Europe in bringing a balanced message to captured Hungarians of events going on in their country. During the Reagan administration, an expensive USIA TV production, ***Let Poland Be Poland***, hosted by Frank Sinatra, was televised on January 31, 1982, to support Polish people under martial law. Fifteen world leaders, among them British Prime Minister Margaret Thatcher, came together to offer courage and concern. Under H.J. Resolution 382, Congress allowed the film to be shown in the United States. The next year, **Radio Marti** was created by the Radio Broadcasting to Cuba Act (Public Law 98-111), signed October 4, to provide Spanish-language news and programming to Cuba; its first broadcast was May 20, 1985. Then, in 1990, TV Marti was created under Section 241 (Television Broadcasting to Cuba) of the Foreign Relations Authorization

Act, Fiscal Years 1990 and 1991 (Public Law 101-246), on February 19. Fidel Castro denounced TV Marti and its "propaganda broadcasts" as unlawful interference in Cuban domestic affairs and jammed it from its first broadcast on March 27, 1990.

Another 1985 initiative was the **Afghan Media Project**, which was funded by USIA but administered through Boston University's School of Media and Communications. It was appropriated $500,000 from Supplemental Appropriations Act of 1985 (Public Law 99-88) to focus world attention on the Soviet invasion of Afghanistan; it included VOA broadcasts and editorials, publications, and TV programs distributed by USIA.

The most recent development was in the Gulf War. Voice of the Gulf radio network, operated by members of the U.S. Special Forces psychological operations (PSYOPS), began broadcasting in 1991 as part of a propaganda effort that also included loudspeaker operations and leaflet drops. There was also a disinformation campaign that originated with the Gulf military operation. It began when a South African minister was speaking to the media about the "genocide" caused by depleted uranium. In 2003, American presence in Iraq had to deal with, among other things, the bombing of archives and libraries and the destruction of artworks, the aftermath of any occupation.

See also **Iraqi Propaganda**

FURTHER READING: James J. Carafano, *Waltzing into the Cold War: The Struggle for Occupied Austria* (College Station: Texas A&M University, 2002); Gerd Horten, *Radio Goes to War: The Cultural Politics of Propaganda during World War II* (Berkeley and Los Angeles: University of California, 2002); Henry P. Pilgert, *History of the Development of Information Services Through Information Centers and Documentary Films* (Bonn?: Historical Division, Office of the Executive Secretary, Office of the U.S. High Commissioner for Germany, 1951); "Communist Attacks on U.S. Aid to Europe," in *Psychological Warfare Casebook*, ed. William E. Daugherty (Baltimore: Johns Hopkins; published for Operations Research Office, Johns Hopkins University, 1958); Kathleen Stokker, *Folklore Fights the Nazis: Humor in Occupied Norway, 1940–1945* (Madison, NJ: Fairleigh Dickinson University; London: Associated University Presses, 1995); Eiji Takemae, *Inside GHQ: The Allied Occupation of Japan and Its Legacy*, trans. and adapted by Robert Ricketts and Sebastian Swann (New York: Continuum, 2002).

OFFICE OF FACTS AND FIGURES. One of the early information agencies that President Franklin D. Roosevelt established in December 1941 as a propaganda monitoring agency under the leadership of poet Archibald MacLeish, it was first the Bureau (then the Office) of Facts and Figures (OFF). One of his first recruits was communications expert **Wilbur Schramm**. With the establishment of the **Office of War Information** (OWI) in June 1942, Congress forced the merger of OFF into OWI and cut OFF's budget in half.

FURTHER READING: Richard W. Steele, *Propaganda in an Open Society: The Roosevelt Administration and the Media, 1933–1941* (Westport, CT: Greenwood, 1985).

OFFICE OF STRATEGIC SERVICES. American intelligence agency established by President **Franklin D. Roosevelt** in World War II (June 1942) to coordinate the United States' covert or secret propaganda activities and spying in World War II. It was headed by **William J. Donovan**. OSS was the predecessor of the **Central**

Intelligence Agency (CIA). As Europe edged closer to World War II, President Franklin D. Roosevelt called on World War I hero Donovan to help improve the quality of intelligence reaching Washington. Over the strong objections of FBI director J. Edgar Hoover and the heads of military spy groups fearful of losing power, the president in 1941 appointed Donovan to head the new office of the **Coordinator of Information**, which was to collect and analyze all data of interest to national security. In 1942, after the U.S. entry into the war, Donovan's fledgling group was renamed the **Office of Strategic Services** (OSS), with responsibility for both military and diplomatic intelligence. The agency received valuable help in perfecting its methods from the respected British secret service, MI-6.

Despite its successes during the war, President Harry S Truman bowed to public pressure from Hoover and congressional critics and disbanded the OSS in 1945, but less than a year later, Truman reversed his OSS decision to deal with the sudden onset of the **Cold War**. Closed out of the Soviet Union in the aftermath of World War II, American policy makers had no reliable information on which to base U.S. policy toward the wartime ally turned adversary. By contrast, covert action had been an integral part of Soviet foreign policy since the USSR was founded in 1922. To counter Stalin's KGB, Truman decided the United States needed a permanent, peacetime intelligence capability. The CIA formally began in 1947.

OSS conducted clandestine anti-Axis **psychological warfare** and black propaganda programs as well as more conventional spy missions through its Morals Operations Branch (MO), which Donovan created to fight subversive propaganda operations, popularly called **fifth column** activities. He believed that softening up enemy populations with propaganda was a first step in a psychological warfare offensive. The first major effort was in Italy after the July 1943 invasion of Sicily. MO agents created the Wie Lange Noch? (How Much Longer?) campaign and, in June 1944, distributed leaflets, stickers, and music throughout the country, southern France, and the Balkans. When the bulk of leaflets made distribution difficult, MO agents placed programmed stickers on walls. Another campaign was the use of special transmitters that facilitated MO "black" radio operations, which were aimed at "the enemy homeland, the enemy-occupied territories, and enemy troops." OSS also parachuted agents into Occupied Europe to organize and to train resistance forces. A variety of weapons were developed that could not be easily found if the agent was arrested. One such tool was a cigarette lighter that functioned as a camera and as a single-shot gun.

The long-classified U.S. War Department's *War Report of the O.S.S.* (1976), written by Kermit Roosevelt, Jr., provides an incisive look at the organization's clandestine psychological operations. Special operations were employed in organizing and in assisting resistance movements in Europe during World War II and for morale operations.

FURTHER READING: Clayton D. Laurie, "Black Games, Subversion, and Dirty Tricks," *Prologue* (Fall 1997): 258–71; U.S. Dept. of State. *Foreign Relations of the United States, 1945–1950: Emergence of the Intelligence Establishment* (Washington, DC: Government Printing Office, 1996).

OFFICE OF THE COORDINATOR OF INTER-AMERICAN AFFAIRS. *See* Coordinator of Inter-American Affairs

OFFICE OF WAR INFORMATION. President Franklin D. Roosevelt established the Office of War Information (OWI) in June 1942 to coordinate the
United States' overt propaganda activities in World War II. It was formed by the
merger of the overseas functions of the **Coordinator of Information, Office of
Facts and Figures** and an overseas component called the U.S. Information Service
(USIS), the name still used outside the United States for **U.S. Information Agency**
posts. Its mandate was to make the war understandable to Americans, and it utilized the services of hundreds of people in government public relations work
under the direction of veteran radio journalist **Elmer Davis.** It was responsible
for both internal (domestic or home front) and external (overseas) information.

During World War II, OWI and other U.S. government agencies produced
thousands of posters, billboards, radio spots, and newspaper ads to mobilize citizens in support of the war effort. Negative images of the enemy were often used
to promote patriotism in the basest of ways, a not-so-pleasant part of the WWII
home front. A Coordinator of Government Films, 1941–1942 worked with the
Hollywood community in preparing movies that sold the war effort on the domestic front. A Division of Public Inquiries and a Division of Press Intelligence
issued summaries and digests of radio and press comments. Less well known
was the crucial role OWI played in mobilizing black support and by interpreting
U.S. race relations to an international audience through its publications and
broadcasts.

Working under the premise that citizens of a democracy distrust propaganda,
Congress limited OWI to nondomestic activities, but it still did an effective job
of supporting the war effort. Also, President Roosevelt, who was Assistant Secre-
tary of the Navy in World War I, was determined that he was not going to give
Elmer Davis the power and authority that **George Creel** and his **Committee on
Public Information** had wielded during the earlier war.

An important part of OWI's work was the posters that very effectively communicated the message: "Someone Talked!" (1942), Norman Rockwell's **Four Freedoms** (1943), "This is the Enemy" (1943), "Bits of Careless Talk . . ." by Stevan
Dohanos (1943), and "Save Waste Fats for Explosives . . ." by H. Koerner (1943)
along with the classic "Loose Lips Sink Ships." The **poster** campaign, inexpensive, colorful, and immediate, was the ideal medium for delivering messages
about Americans' duties on the home front during World War II; they were seen
in schools, in workplaces, and in other public spaces. The posters touched on all
aspects of wartime life, from the factory, where workers were instructed to take
shorter cigarette breaks and focus on increased production ("KILLING Time Is
KILLING Men"), to the home, where conserving scarce resources was essential
("We'll have lots to eat this winter, won't we Mother? Grow your own"), to the
farm, where eggs and meat were wartime weapons in their own right ("Our Allies
Need Eggs" and "Grow It Yourself—Plan a Farm Garden Now"). Its publication,
Victory magazine, 1943–1946, similar in format to *Life* magazine, was translated
into at least six languages.

OWI Assam Psywar team were members of a psychological warfare operation
against the Japanese forces in Burma. They made effective use of a group of
Japanese prisoners of war (POWs) as a consultative panel to pretest leaflets and
to discuss propaganda ideas. When World War II ended, President Truman abolished OWI but retained the Office of Public and Cultural Affairs, headed by

Archibald MacLeish. That unit was merged into the U.S. Department of State under advertising executive William Benton, named by Truman as undersecretary for public and cultural affairs.

FURTHER READING: William L. Bird and Harry R. Rubenstein, *Design for Victory: World War II Posters on the American Home Front* (Princeton, NJ: Princeton Architectural, 1998); William E. Daugherty, *Psychological Warfare Casebook* (Baltimore: Johns Hopkins; published for Operations Research Office, Johns Hopkins University, 1958); Gerd Horten, *Radio Goes to War: The Cultural Politics of Propaganda during World War II* (Berkeley and Los Angeles: University of California, 2002); U.S. Office of War Information, *Combat Propaganda in Burma* (Washington, DC: OWI, 1945); Allan M. Winkler, *Politics of Propaganda: The Office of War Information, 1942–1945* (New Haven, CT and London: Yale, 1978).

OFFICIAL BULLETIN. See **Committee on Public Information**

OP-16W (DIRECTIVE). The Navy Department established a highly secretive Special Warfare Branch (OP-16W) within the Office of Naval Intelligence (ONI) to plan and to assist with the conduct of special operations in the area of psychological warfare comparable to NID 17-Zed, the psychological warfare unit of the British Naval Intelligence Service. Captain (later Admiral) **Ellis M. Zacharias** was one of the movers in this organization. In addition to Zacharias's broadcasts to Japan (1945), another noteworthy operation of this small psychological warfare staff was the **Commander Norden** appeals to the Nazis. OP-16W worked closely with the **Office of War Information** (OWI) and assisted that agency in the preparation of propaganda directives, especially those related to naval warfare. It did not attempt to compete for outlets for its propaganda releases; instead it prepared broadcast recordings and carefully documented intelligence information to release to enemy forces through OWI or related channels. It initiated a program, *Prisoner-of-War Mail*, that it turned over to OWI radio desks in which letters were solicited from German and Italian prisoners of war held in the United States with the knowledge that their messages would be broadcast to their homelands. ONI collected, assembled, and downgraded all types of detailed information, such as scandals, petty gossip, and romantic entanglements and friction of German naval officers to use in propaganda releases and in other OP-16W efforts, such as Commander Norden's broadcasts.

FURTHER READING: William E. Daugherty, *Psychological Warfare Casebook* (Baltimore: Johns Hopkins; published for Operations Research Office, Johns Hopkins University, 1958).

OPERATION ANNIE. Operation Annie, also known as Radio 1212 because of its broadcasting frequency, the second most powerful commercial transmitter in Europe (1212 meters), the home of Radio Luxembourg, was a strategic clandestine Allied propaganda station operated by the Psychological Warfare Branch, U.S. 12th Army Group, from December 19, 1944, to April 25, 1945, to develop an audience among German troops by broadcasting news with a pro-German bias. The program ran from 2:00 A.M. to 6:30 A.M. and purported to come from a

Rhineland resistance group from Annie, a supposedly secret German radio station operated within German territory by a small group of Rhinelanders loyal to the German cause. The voice of Radio 1212 was Lt. Benno Frank, its principal broadcaster, who put together the distinct broadcast segments, and what made the station completely believable was the fact that Frank, a former Rhinelander who became an American citizen, had an unmistakable Rhenish accent.

Annie initially concentrated on providing detailed and truthful news to build up audience trust and then begin to insert false reports, orders, and rumors to create chaos in front of the Allied advance. Reports from POWs and civilians indicated that "1212" had a wide audience. Annie ceased broadcasting after General Eisenhower concluded that it had outlived its usefulness; its death signaled the end of World War II in Europe.

FURTHER READING: Berrin A. Beasley, "Hier 1st 1212 Operation Annie, Psychological Warfare and the Capture of the Rhineland," Paper presented at the Popular Culture Association/American Culture Association Joint National Conference, New Orleans, LA, April 20, 2000; Clayton D. Laurie, "Black Games, Subversion, and Dirty Tricks," *Prologue* (Fall 1997): 258–271; Lawrence C. Soley and John S. Nichols, *Clandestine Radio Broadcasting: A Study of Revolutionary and Counterrevolutionary Electronic Communication* (New York and Westport, CT: Praeger, 1987).

OPERATION CORNFLAKES. During World War II, the American **Office of the Strategic Services** (OSS) and the British SOE counterfeited German stamps for use on letters containing Allied propaganda. Some mailbags filled with such letters bearing Hitler head stamps were dropped by British planes on a bombed German mail train. The bags were recovered by the German post office, and thinking they were authentic, they were placed in the German mail system. This high-level clandestine plan, Operation Cornflakes, was supposed to undermine the morale of the average German citizen. The Allies determined that if many Germans started receiving anti-Nazi propaganda in their morning mail delivered promptly at breakfast ("cornflakes") time by the mailman, they would feel that their German Empire was falling apart.

The stamps were printed by OSS operations in Switzerland then smuggled into the regular German postal system by bombing the mail trains. The standard 6-pfennig and 12-pfennig Hitler Head stamps were forged in sheets of 50 instead of the sheets of 100 of the originals, and an additional forgery on the 12-pf stamp was made, with the inscription altered to read "Futsches Reich" ("Ruined Empire"). However, these were not used in Operation Cornflakes.

In addition to dropping bombs to possibly wreck the trains, they dropped sacks of mail containing anti-Nazi propaganda. In the confusion of cleaning up the wreck, the false mail sacks were mixed with the damaged German mail. The OSS re-created all aspects of the German postal system from real business return addresses to many thousands of names and addresses pulled from the telephone directories. They replicated the mail bags, postal markings, and every other detail of the postal system. Every letter was franked with a 12-pf stamp or two 6-pf. On opening the letter, the recipient would find it filled with anti-Nazi propaganda.

The first mission was on February 5, 1945, when a mail train on its way to Linz in Austria was attacked, and the engine was destroyed. Eight mail bags, each with about 480 letters, were dropped on target. The mail was carefully prepared to coincide with towns on the route of the target train. Envelopes were franked immediately prior to takeoff to ensure the current date appeared.

See also Forgeries

FURTHER READING: Brian Moynahan, "Our Poison Pen War Against the Nazis," in American Institutes for Research, *Art and Science of Psychological Operations: Case Studies of Military Application*, vol. 2; ed. Ronald De McLaurin et al. (Washington: Headquarters, U.S. Dept. of the Army, 1976): 763–65.

OPERATION MAGIC CARPET. In mid-August 1952, about a week before the city gates to Mecca (Holy City) were to be closed on August 27 by Saudi Arabian authorities, more than 9,000 Muslims found themselves stranded in major air transfer points in the Middle East. Of these, 4,000 were left in Beirut, Lebanon, 800 miles from Mecca; all had tickets but they lacked reservations and the regular commercial airlines were unable to provide passage for more than a few hundred of those who had reached Beirut. Because most were elderly and undertaking a lifetime dream of going to Mecca, they needed to reach the Holy City before the closing of the gates deprived them of one of the chief goals of their earthly existence. The **U.S. Department of State** and the U.S. Air Force rescued them under the direction of the American Minister in Lebanon, Harold B. Minor, who quickly arranged the airlifting of the stranded pilgrims from Beirut to Jidda, Saudi Arabia, 40 miles from Mecca. After a flurry of diplomatic cable traffic among the involved U.S. agencies, the mass movement by air began on August 25 in the early morning; no traveler was left behind. Media coverage of this event, along with the gratitude of the stranded pilgrims when they returned home, was quite laudatory and did much to counteract Russian anti-American propaganda of the event. In telling their story of the modern "Magic Carpet," the pilgrims were able to say that it bore the label "Made in the USA."

FURTHER READING: "Operation Magic Carpet," in *Psychological Warfare Casebook*, ed. William E. Daugherty (Baltimore: Johns Hopkins; published for Operations Research Office, Johns Hopkins University, 1958).

OPERATION MINCEMEAT. The British used a bizarre technique that deceived the location where the Allies would make the 1943 assault on the European continent. Evan Montagu, then a naval intelligence officer but later Judge Advocate of the Fleet, devised "the man who never was" (also known as Major William Martin of Britain's Royal Marines). A corpse that was actually a young man who had just died of pneumonia would be dressed as a British officer and dropped off the coast of Spain, where it would wash ashore. The officer would carry papers indicating that an attack on Sicily would not be the real thing but that the real objective was Sardinia and Greece. How would the Germans hear about it? The Spaniards who would tip them off.

Montagu had complete respect for his German opposite numbers, so he planned his bluff with consummate skill and named it Mincemeat. "Major William Martin" got a complete identity, including an identity card and a "fiancee" with love letters. In the wee hours of April 30, 1943, the submarine

Seraph surfaced about a mile off the estuary of the Huelva River and dropped its cargo. Prime Minister Winston Churchill, in Washington, D.C., with President Franklin D. Roosevelt, was notified that "Mincemeat swallowed whole." Hitler believed it for almost two weeks after the invasion, and Sicily began to mobilize considerable German manpower in preparation for the expected invasion of Greece. In Sicily, forces were shifted from the south, where the actual attack began, to the north. "Major Martin" did his job well and was buried in the Huelva cemetery on orders of the British vice-consul. His name, but not his rank, is on the gravestone. Operation Mincemeat is now considered one of the most bizarre stories of deception in recent military history.

FURTHER READING: Ian G. Colvin, *The Unknown Courier* (London: W. Kimber, 1953); Ewen Montagu, *The Man Who Never Was* (Philadelphia: Lippincott, 1954); "Operation Mincemeat," in *Psychological Warfare Casebook*, ed. William E. Daugherty (Baltimore: Johns Hopkins; published for Operations Research Office, Johns Hopkins University, 1958).

OPERATION OVERLORD. *See* **Normandy Invasion**

OPERATION VETO. First sustained effort to reach the population of an Iron Curtain country by both printed and spoken word on a closely coordinated, saturation basis. Operation Veto was to be a long-term campaign in which the message, rather than the ingenuity of the means (balloons, radio broadcasts) was paramount. It started April 29, 1954, and extended to that autumn. More than 100,000 hydrogen-filled neoprene rubber balloons, over four feet in diameter, fell over Czechoslovakia disseminating approximately 50 million antiregime leaflets, stickers, manifestos, mock election ballots, posters, and newssheets. At the same time, **Radio Free Europe** transmitters in Munich beamed explanatory broadcasts to the Czech and Slovak people.

FURTHER READING: "Free Europe Committee" and "Operation Veto," in *Psychological Warfare Casebook*, ed. William E. Daugherty (Baltimore: Johns Hopkins; published for Operations Research Office, Johns Hopkins University, 1958).

OPERATIONS COORDINATING BOARD. The Operations Coordinating Board (OCB) was created in 1953 after President Eisenhower dissolved the **Psychological Strategy Board** and the **Psychological Operations Coordinating Committee** and combined their functions into this new entity. Chaired by a ranking State Department official, OCB reported to the National Security Council. Its September 2, 1953, charter charged OCB with coordinating all "overseas information and psychological warfare activities" of the U.S. government. Two of its major functions were interdepartmental sources and the implementation of decisions.

In November 1960, the National Security Council Political Committee prepared a report on issues with national security implications. One of these was OCB, which was considered a "great generator of useless paper work." It was abolished by President John F. Kennedy by Executive Order No. 10920 (February 18, 1961) and became part of the National Security Council (NSC) Secretariat along with "other special projects within the White House" under Special Assistant for National Security Affairs, McGeorge Bundy.

FURTHER READING: William E. Daugherty, *Psychological Warfare Casebook* (Baltimore: Johns Hopkins; published for Operations Research Office, Johns Hopkins University, 1958); U.S. Dept. of State, *Foreign Relations of the United States, 1961–1963; vol. VII: National Security Policy* (Washington, DC: Government Printing Office, 1996).

OPINION POLLS. *See* Public Opinion

ORGAN PARTS TRAFFICKING. *See* Baby Parts

ORPHAN ANNIE. *See* Tokyo Rose

OVERMAN COMMITTEE (U.S. SENATE). *See* U.S. Congressional Investigations of Propaganda

OVERT PROPAGANDA. *See* White Propaganda

P

PAINE, THOMAS (January 29, 1737–June 8, 1809). Political radical and propagandist of the American Revolution who was considered a master of persuasion rather than an original or a profound thinker. Thomas Paine was a major revolutionary pamphleteer in both America and France. He was born in Thetford, England, attended grammar school until the age of 13, then worked at various occupations, including ladies corset maker. He published his first pamphlet, *The Case of the Officers of Excise: with remarks on the qualifications of officers and on the numerous evils arising to the revenue from the insufficiency of the present salary, humbly addressed to the Hon. and Right Hon. the members of both houses of Parliament* (S.l: s.n., 1772), which appealed to Parliament to raise the wages of excisemen. In London, he met **Benjamin Franklin**, and two years later, he arrived in Philadelphia with letters of introduction from him. Soon, he contributed articles to *Pennsylvania Magazine* and to the newspapers. In one of his submissions, he supported the abolition of slavery. In January 1776, Paine published *Common Sense*, which advocated America's immediate independence from Great Britain; within three months, it sold more than 120,000 copies. On December 19, 1776, the first of Paine's Crisis papers appeared in the *Pennsylvania Journal* in which he inspired his readers that "these are the times that try men's souls." Paine's rebellious and equalitarian nature emerged. He opposed monarchism as a corrupt and vicious form of government. After the Declaration of Independence, he enlisted in the Revolutionary army and took part in its retreat through New Jersey. His first Crisis paper was read to Washington's troops before the Battle of Trenton. In 1777, Paine was appointed by Congress as secretary of its committee on foreign affairs; two years later, he became clerk of the Pennsylvania Assembly. He departed for England at the age of 50, where he published *The Rights of Man* (1791–92) urging the English to overthrow their monarch and establish a republic. He was forced to flee to France (1787), where he became a French citizen, was elected to the National Convention, and, as a Girondist, was imprisoned for a time. In 1794–1796, Paine wrote *The Age of Reason*, in which he accepted the existence of God and of immortality but rejected the Bible, revelation, and Christianity. He returned to America (1802) but was attacked and ostracized as an atheist. Paine died in New York. Foner has suggested that Paine's influence was not only propagandistic but also economic. As an innovative political communicator, he truly believed in the utopian vision of an egalitarian American society.

FURTHER READING: Alfred O. Aldridge, *Man of Reason: The Life of Thomas Paine* (Philadelphia: Lippincott, 1959); John Keane, *Tom Paine: A Political Life* (New York: Grove, 2003).

PAMPHLETS. One of the earliest forms of American propaganda and one of the easiest to produce. Because of its compact size, it can be dropped from airplanes or distributed on the ground. Many effective pieces of public opinion started as pamphlets, such as **Thomas Paine's** *Common Sense.*

See also Abolitionist Propaganda; Adams, Samuel; Civil War Propaganda; Committee on Public Information; Four Freedoms; Iraq; Leaflets; Office of War Information; Propaganda Collections; *Protocols of the Learned Elders of Zion;* War of American Independence Propaganda; Vietnam Conflict

FURTHER READING: William E. Daugherty, *Psychological Warfare Casebook* (Baltimore: Johns Hopkins; published for Operations Research Office, Johns Hopkins University, 1958).

PANEL ON INTERNATIONAL INFORMATION, EDUCATION, AND CULTURAL RELATIONS. This panel, chaired by Frank Stanton, studied the public diplomacy of the United States at the joint initiative of the U.S. Advisory Commission on Information and the U.S. Advisory Commission on International Educational and Cultural Affairs. It began its investigation in April 1974 and issued its final report on May 6, 1975. The panel recommended that the so-called slow media functions of the **U.S. Information Agency** (i.e., magazines, libraries, exhibits, cultural presentations, and films) be merged with State Department's Bureau of Educational and Cultural Affairs to form an Information and Cultural Affairs Agency, which would relate to the State Department in the same way as what existed with the Arms Control and Disarmament Agency; that an Office of Policy Information be established under a Deputy Under Secretary of State that would combine all foreign policy information and advisory functions within the Department at a level where these functions could be properly carried out; and that the **Voice of America** be established as a separate organization controlled by an independent Board of Directors, whose majority would be presidential appointees.

Three years after the report was issued, President Jimmy Carter merged USIA with the Bureau of Educational and Cultural Affairs as the independent U.S. International Communication Agency but in 1982 the former name, U.S. Information Agency, was restored. However, on October 1, 1999, USIA was abolished and all its functions but international broadcasting were integrated into the **U.S. Department of State,** whereas the Voice of America remained in the International Broadcasting Bureau, created in 1994, as an independent agency. The Stanton Panel report continues to be a blueprint for all proposed reorganizations of the U.S. cultural and educational programs.

FURTHER READING: Panel on International Information, Education and Cultural Relations. *International Information Education and Cultural Relations: Recommendations for the Future* (Washington, DC: Center for Strategic and International Studies, 1975).

PEARL HARBOR. The poster, "Remember Dec. 7th," by Allen Saalburg for the **Office of War Information** (OWI), with quotations from Abraham Lincoln's Gettysburg address, ignited popular opinion against the Japanese and led, the next day, to the declaration of war by Congress against the Axis Powers. The attack on the American fleet changed public opinion dramatically. Twisted or little-known truths were enhanced by real footage of the attack on Pearl Harbor, which was taken by a Navy photographer during the actual bombing; it was later incorporated into the John Ford-Gregg Toland documentary, *December 7*, which won an Oscar.

Another movie, *Pearl Harbor*, opened in May 2001 as popular depiction of the story that combined factual storytelling with fictional characters. Prior to the movie's opening, there were well-placed stories about the actual bombing and interviews with survivors of the bombing and their families. The actual event was once again in people's minds, but it became chillingly real on September 11, 2001, when the World Trade Center towers in New York and the Pentagon outside Washington, D.C., were bombed by terrorists. The similes between the 1941 event and the 2001 tragedy, both designated as a "day of infamy" by the media, brought the horrors of the Pearl Harbor attack home to a new generation.

FURTHER READING: James M. Skinner, "December 7: Filmic Myth Masquerading as Historical Fact," *Journal of Military History* (October 1991): 507–16.

PETER PORCUPINE. *See* **Cobbett, William**

PHILBRICK, HERBERT ARTHUR. *See I Led Three Lives*

PICKETT, JOHN T. *See* **Civil War Propagandists**

THE PLOW THAT BROKE THE PLAINS. **Pare Lorentz**'s documentary film, *The Plow That Broke the Plains* (Resettlement Administration, 1936), promoted natural resource conservation and was considered an innovative piece of propaganda for the **New Deal**. It contained some powerful footage that highlighted how production overuse of the land in World War I caused the disastrous effect of "high winds and sun" in the 1930s. An emotional musical score by Virgil Thompson (1896–1989) heightened the dramatic tension of the visual images of the Dust Bowl, many featuring children from the region. However, the film's impact was undercut by low production values.

FURTHER READING: Pare Lorentz, *FDR's Moviemaker: Memoirs and Scripts* (Reno: University of Nevada, 1992); Richard T. MacCann, *The People's Films: A Political History of U.S. Government Motion Pictures* (New York: Hastings House, 1973); Robert L. Snyder, *Pare Lorentz and the Documentary Film* (Reno: University of Nevada, 1968).

POLAND. *See* **Katyn Forest Massacre;** *Let Poland Be Poland*; **Occupied Countries and Territories**

POLITICAL CARTOON ART. *See* **Cartoons**

POLITICAL PROPAGANDA. *See* Foreign Agents Registration Act; Front Organizations; Postal Regulations (Communist Political Propaganda); Propaganda Collections; U.S. Congress. House. Committee on Un-American Activities; U.S. Congressional Investigations of Propaganda

POSTAL DELIVERY OF PROPAGANDA. *See* Postal Regulations (Communist Political Propaganda)

POSTAL REGULATIONS (COMMUNIST POLITICAL PROPAGANDA). Section 305(a) of the Postal Service and Federal Employees Salary Act of 1962 (39 U.S.C. Section 4008-A) provided that "mail matter, except sealed letters, which originates or which is printed or otherwise prepared in a foreign country" and which is determined by the Secretary of the Treasury to be "Communist political propaganda" can be detained by the Postmaster General when it arrives in the U.S. domestic mails. The propaganda had to list country of origin and be properly labeled. The addressee had to be notified that this material was received and could be delivered only if the addressee requested it by returning an attached card; otherwise the mail would be destroyed. The statute further defined "Communist political propaganda" in similar terms to the **Foreign Agents Registration Act** by outlining what constituted political propaganda and by noting an exemption from its provisions for such mail addressed to governmental agencies and educational institutions or sent pursuant to a reciprocal cultural international agreement.

To implement the statute, the U.S. Post Office established 11 screening points through which all nonexempt communist political propaganda from designated foreign countries was routed and examined by U.S. Customs officials before the addressee was notified. The Supreme Court found this governmental censorship unconstitutional in *Lamont v. Postmaster General*; it ruled the entire process a violation of First Amendment rights because the addressee had to perform a positive action (i.e., return an attached reply card, before receiving mail). Also, the Court was opposed to the government's interference in what a person wanted to read in publications from other countries.

FURTHER READING: Dorothy G. Fowler, *Unmailable: Congress and the Post Office* (Athens: University of Georgia, 1977); James C. N. Paul and Murray L. Schwartz, *Federal Censorship: Obscenity in the Mail* (Westport, CT: Greenwood, 1977).

POSTER ART. *See* Posters in Wartime

POSTERS IN WARTIME. Drawings to incite a population during wartime were used as propaganda from the earliest times. In the United States, there were broadsides with slogans during major conflicts, such as the **War of American Independence** and the Civil War. During the **Spanish-American War** (1898), posters and films served the purpose most effectively but it was during World War I that posters were used for the first time as a primary tool of propaganda.

Without the radio and television of later configurations, the poster was an important instrument of mass persuasion in World War I, especially in military recruiting, which represented both glamour and shame to eligible recruits. In Allied countries, the Germans were portrayed as rapacious Huns; the Allied soldier was depicted as fighting for home and country. The poster had a simple message—failure to enlist was akin to treason. Recruiting propaganda of the same sort found its way into popular music and vaudeville entertainment. Probably the most famous poster was American painter James Montgomery Flagg's "I Want You" (1917), which shows **Uncle Sam,** still a staple of military recruiting, pointing a finger directly at the viewer. This poster was used in both world wars, and eventually more than four million copies were distributed. However, French World War I posters set the standard for war poster design with their beautiful artwork and ardent messages such as "On les aura" ("We'll get them") or "Sauvonsles" ("Let's save them"), which awakened citizens to the urgency of the war. Also effective were films about the war, exhibits of war art, and special gala evenings to gain support for the war. Looking at these posters, the viewer can trace the war's causes and crises in poignant messages conveyed by each image. The pleas were effective not only in mobilizing citizens to serve but also in mobilizing those on the home front to produce supplies for the soldiers in the trenches.

One of the most effective and popular posters of World War I that played on anti-German hysteria in the United States was "Spies and Lies," which was produced by the **Committee on Public Information** as a warning to Americans about "loose lips" and the damage they could cause national security if speaker was not careful because foreign enemy agents were everywhere, "eager to gather scraps of news about our men, our ships, our munitions" and listening to every word. The poster gave specific directives on what to avoid ("Do not become a tool of the Hun" by passing on gossip; "Do not wait until you catch someone putting a bomb under a factory" or "spreads pessimistic stories") and advised Americans to immediately contact the Justice Department with this information because "you are in contact with the enemy today, just as truly as if you found him across No Man's Land."

By 1941, the poster was one of several media in a landscape of commercial promotion that had hardly existed 20 years before. Much of this was due to an increasingly mobile audience that was shaped by commercial radio, motion pictures, magazines, and billboards that populated this environment. During World War II, posters helped to mobilize a nation as government agencies, businesses, and private organizations issued an array of poster images linking the military front with the home front, calling on every American to boost production at work and at home. Posters produced by the United States differed from the British by placing much greater emphasis on motivation for fighting and for encouraging the purchase of war bonds. Similar themes were the need to maintain secrecy, to save everything salvageable (even though the American public suffered less than other countries), to conserve fuel and food, to maintain one's health, and to produce more and better quality for the soldiers. Advertising staff at the **Office of War Information** created posters that conveyed many messages, especially pride and confidence, though there were also images that spread a mild paranoia about enemy spies ("Loose Lips Might Sink Ships"). In factories, they encouraged production and quality ("GET HOT—keep moving, DON'T WASTE A PRECIOUS MINUTE" and "Your Job Is Your Gun—Give the Enemy Hell!") and linked the worker with the front line soldier ("Never Late Is Better, Better Late Than Never—Let's Start on Time to Finish the Axis!" and "The Jap Way—Cold Blooded Murder. We'll make them pay if you keep up PRODUC-TION"). Absenteeism was equated with helping the Nazis. "Careless Talk" posters urged caution and secrecy; others solicited support for the Red Cross, for recruitment for the various military services, and for war bond drives.

With the Korean Conflict (1950–1953), the function of posters was replaced by the emerging medium of television, which brought home to the American people the actual events on the daily news. This reached its peak during the coverage of the Vietnamese Conflict during the 1960s and 1970s.

See also Home Front Propaganda

FURTHER READING: William L. Bird and Harry R. Rubenstein, *Design for Victory: World War II Posters on the American Homefront* (New York: Princeton Architectural Press, 1998); Stacey Bredhoff, *Powers of Persuasion: Poster Art From World War II; Based on an Exhibition at the National Archives, Washington, DC, February 1994–February 1995* (Washington, DC: National Archives Trust Fund Board; published for the National Archives, 1994); Elena G. Millie, "Posters; a Collectible Art Form," *Quarterly Journal of the Library of Congress* (Summer 1982): 146–64; Tod Olson, "The Power of Persuasion," *Scholastic Update* [Teacher's Edition] (March 24, 1995): 16–19; *Paper Bullets: Great Propaganda Posters, Axis and Allied Countries WWII* [with an essay on psychological warfare by **Daniel Lerner**] (New York: Chelsea House; distributed by Whirlwind Books, 1977); Poster, "Spies and Lies," U.S. Committee on Public Information; Walton Rawls, "Wake Up, America!" *American History Illustrated* (September 1988): 32–45.

POUND, EZRA LOOMIS (October 30, 1885–October 30, 1972). Poet and critic Ezra Pound was born in Hailey, Idaho, and graduated from Hamilton College. He taught languages at Wabash College, Crawfordsville, Indiana, for the fall semester (1907), was fired, then left for Europe. Pound finally settled in London, where he published his poems, taught literature, and became an art and music critic. In 1920 he settled in France, then moved to Italy in 1924, where he became an ardent admirer of Italian dictator Benito Mussolini.

A supporter of Fr. **Charles Coughlin,** who inspired him to do radio broadcasts, Pound offered his services to the Axis Powers, especially to Mussolini's government; he contracted to make regular propaganda broadcasts on Rome Radio (1941–1943) in which he offered his views on world events and attacked American politicians and policies (e.g., he believed **Franklin D. Roosevelt** was a tool of Jewish financial interests). Many of these broadcasts, which contained Pound's vehement anti-Semitic commentaries and his attacks on the U.S. war effort, were taped by the **Office of Strategic Services.**

His propaganda broadcasts from Italy favorably compared Mussolini to Thomas Jefferson and were later held by the victorious Allies as clear proof of his insanity. He was captured by the Allies (1945) and charged with treason against the country of his birth. Pound was tried for treason in February 1946 in the U.S. District Court for the District of Columbia, where he was judged legally insane and held as a patient at St. Elizabeth's Hospital, Washington, D.C., where he saw the psychiatrists as instruments of a Jewish conspiracy but continued work on his *Pisan Cantos*, which he began as early as 1912 but which appeared in 1948. The next year, he generated much controversy, mostly due to his political attitudes, especially his anti-Semitism, when the poems won the Bollinger Prize in Poetry. After his release (1958), generated by pressure from influential persons such as Robert Frost, Ernest Hemingway, and T. S. Eliot, Pound returned to Italy, where he died in Venice.

FURTHER READING: Humphrey Carpenter, *A Serious Character: The Life of Ezra Pound* (Boston: Houghton Mifflin, 1988); Wendy S. Flory, *The American Ezra Pound* (New Haven, CT: Yale University, 1989); Paul Hendrickson, "Fighting Words," *Washington Post*, May 3, 1997, C1, C5.

POWS (PRISONERS OF WAR). *See* Prisoners of War

PRESIDENT'S ADVISORY COMMITTEE ON GOVERNMENT ORGANIZATION.
The Advisory Committee on Government Organization, first chaired by Nelson Rockefeller (until 1958) and then by Arthur Flemming, was established by President Eisenhower on January 24, 1953, to assist him in finding ways to improve the organization and the management of the Executive Branch. In its April 7, 1953, report, *Foreign Affairs Organization, Memorandum 14*, the Committee recommended the establishment of a new foreign information agency that would consolidate the most important foreign information, cultural, and educational exchange programs then being carried out by the U.S. State Department's International Information Administration, by the Mutual Security Agency, and by the State Department in the occupied areas. The Advisory Committee also called for the term *Voice of America* to be used only to refer to official U.S. policy positions. These recommendations were approved by President Eisenhower and led to his issuance of Reorganization Plan No. 8 of 1953, which created the U.S. Information Agency.

On November 20, 1958, the Committee issued another report, *Organization for National Security-International Affairs* (Flemming Report), that called for the return of the information program to the State Department.

FURTHER READING: U.S. President's Advisory Committee on Government Organization, *Foreign Affairs Organization, Memorandum 14* (Washington, DC: Unpublished, 1953); U.S. President's Advisory Committee on Government Organization, *Organization for National Security-International Affairs* (Washington, DC: Unpublished, 1958).

PRESIDENT'S COMMITTEE ON INFORMATION ACTIVITIES ABROAD.
Also called the Sprague Committee after its chairman, Mansfield D. Sprague, the President's Committee on Information Activities Abroad was an outgrowth of the series of recommendations made in spring 1959 by the U.S. Advisory Committee on Government Operations. It was established that December by President Eisenhower to review the findings and recommendations of the President's Committee on International Information Activities in its 1953 report and to update

the changes in the international situation that affected the validity of the findings and recommendations in that report. The committee's report, issued on January 9, 1961, was reviewed by the incoming Kennedy administration. The new president rejected the recommendation concerning the continuance of the **Operations Coordinating Board** but accepted the others, including more resources to carry out international information activities. Overall, the committee found that the U.S. informational system and its efforts to integrate psychological factors into policy with the growing role of international public opinion were very effective and that there was little need to alter its organizational framework.

FURTHER READING: U.S. President's Committee on Information Activities Abroad, *Conclusions and Recommendations of the President's Committee on Information Activities Abroad* (Washington, DC: Unpublished, 1960).

PRESIDENT'S COMMITTEE ON INTERNATIONAL INFORMATION ACTIVITIES. Chaired by William H. Jackson, the President's Committee on International Information Activities investigated how the United States could best respond to the psychological offensive undertaken by the Soviet Union. It reported to President Eisenhower in 1953 after his decision to establish the **U.S. Information Agency** (USIA). The Committee's recommendations included the merger of all information programs within the State Department and the identification of a "psychological" element to "every diplomatic, economic, or military policy and action." That August, the president issued Reorganization Plan No. 8, which established USIA. Besides Jackson, other committee members included Charles D. Jackson, Robert Cutler, Sigurd Larmon, Gordon Gray, Barklie McKee Henry, John C. Hughes, and Abbott Washburn.

FURTHER READING: U.S. President's Committee on International Information Activities, *International Information Activities* (Washington, DC: Unpublished, 1953).

PRESIDENT'S TASK FORCE ON U.S. GOVERNMENT INTERNATIONAL BROADCASTING. This task force was convened by President George H. W. Bush in early 1991 to review the international broadcasting structure in a post–Cold War environment, to look at the possibility of creating a single entity, to examine the new technology, to offer comments about how U.S. Government International Broadcasting should cooperate with the private sector, and to make recommendations for future direction. The task force had a six-month deadline to issue its report, popularly called the Hughes Report, after its chairman, former VOA director John Hughes. Other members were Stuart Eizenstat and Abbott Washburn, USIA's first deputy director.

The task force was able to come to agreement on its positions on all issues except the proposal to establish a new Asia broadcasting service, which resulted in a new commission that oversaw the creation of **Radio Free Asia**. The most important recommendation, the consolidation of certain radio services, came about with the United States International Broadcasting Act, Title III of the Foreign Relations Authorization Act, Fiscal Years 1994 and 1995 (Public Law 103-236), which established the International Broadcasting Bureau (IBB) within the **U.S. Information Agency** (USIA) and created a presidentially appointed Broadcasting

Board of Governors (BBG) with jurisdiction over all civilian U.S. government international broadcasting. The law consolidated the **Voice of America, Worldnet TV, Radio Marti, Television Marti,** and the Office of Engineering and Technical Services with the new **Radio Free Asia.** On October 21, 1998, President Clinton signed the Foreign Affairs Reform and Restructuring Act (Public Law 105-277), perhaps the single most important legislation affecting U.S. government international broadcasters. This law placed all U.S. publicly funded, nonmilitary overseas broadcasting into a new entity called the Broadcasting Board of Governors, abolished USIA, merged all but its broadcasting functions into the State Department, and inaugurated the independence of U.S. government civilian international broadcasting.

FURTHER READING: U.S. Congress, *Legislation on Foreign Relations Through 2000* (Washington, DC: Government Printing Office, 2001); U.S. Congress. House. Committee on Foreign Affairs, *Report of the President's Task Force on U.S. Government International Broadcasting* (Washington, DC: Government Printing Office, 1992).

PRESTIGE PROJECT. Report prepared in 1953 by the Operations Coordinating Board in response to the National Security Council directive to the **Psychological Strategy Board** contained in NSC Action 867 that surveyed the "reported decline in American prestige abroad" in each of the general regions of the globe (actually "Free World"): Europe and Canada, Far East and Western Pacific, Near East and South Asia, and Latin America. One of the factors recommended to produce a more favorable trend of opinion in Europe was "action by the United States government to avoid the appearance of lecturing or 'preaching' to allied nations in official announcements or through United States propaganda media."

Overall, the report painted a pessimistic picture of the United States that conveyed the impression that the fall in U.S. prestige overseas, coinciding with "McCarthyism" on the domestic political front, was solely the fault of the United States at a time when it was taking a position of world leadership.

FURTHER READING: U.S. Dept. of State, *Foreign Relations of the United States, 1952–1954, vol. 1: General and Political Matters* (Washington, DC: Government Printing Office, 1984): 1480–1551.

PRETESTING MATERIALS. *See* **Public Opinion**

PRINCETON CONFERENCE ON PSYCHOLOGICAL WARFARE. High-level meeting at Princeton University May 10–11, 1952, organized by Charles D. Jackson, to produce a political warfare blueprint that presidential candidate Dwight Eisenhower could use, presuming he won the November election. Representatives came from government agencies, such as the **U.S. Department of State, Psychological Strategy Board,** and the **Central Intelligence Agency,** along with radio enthusiasts and academic specialists. The conference attendees agreed at the meeting that "political (psychological) warfare, properly employed, can win World War III . . . without recourse to arms" but "the Russians have had it all over us in this department." The conferees also determined that the U.S. needed "a more dynamic and positive policy" as American foreign policy failed to "clearly enunciate a policy of determination to work for the liberation of the captive peoples of Eastern and Central Europe, without which our propaganda to this area has been handicapped." Eisenhower promised Jackson his "full endorsement" to initiate a more aggressive propaganda strategy to penetrate the Iron Curtain and thanked the conferees for "the extremely interesting material on the Psychological Warfare Conference at Princeton," which Eisenhower considered to be of the "utmost significance."

FURTHER READING: Walter L. Hixson, *Parting the Curtain: Propaganda, Culture, and the Cold War, 1945–1961* (New York: St. Martin's, 1997).

PRINCETON RADIO PROJECT. *See* **Cantril, Albert Hadley**

PRISONER-OF-WAR MAIL. See **Prisoners of War**

PRISONERS OF WAR. According to Winston Churchill, a prisoner of war (POW) is "a man who tries to kill you and fails, and then asks you not to kill him." The use of prisoners of war (POWs) in **psychological warfare** goes back to earliest days. The first 1929 Convention Between the United States of America and Other Powers, Relating to Prisoners of War (Geneva Convention) mandated the decent treatment of POWs while captors were responsible for the protection of those rights, including such amenities as decent food, medical care, and weekly Red Cross parcels. During World War II, numerous countries violated the guidelines of the 1929 convention that protected POWs, especially the Japanese, who forced prisoners to dig their own graves then shot them in the head, as punishment for trying to escape, an action that was repeated by the Koreans. POW mistreatment by the Germans and by the Japanese has been the subject of several films, including *So Proudly We Hail* (1943), *Three Came Home* (1950), the Oscar-winner, *The Bridge on the River Kwai* (1957), and *Paradise Road* (1997).

Because of the massive numbers of violations of these statutes during World War II, a new Geneva Convention Relative to the Treatment of Prisoners of War was passed in 1949 to protect POWs from all forms of torture with more detailed and concise directions to countries at war, including mistreatment of prisoners, forced marches (e.g., Bataan Death March), starvation and torture by the Japanese, who did not recognize the 1929 Convention. The situation did not change as the POW situations that followed in Korea and in Vietnam proved. In 1977, there was a Diplomatic Conference on International Humanitarian Law Applicable in Armed Conflicts that addressed how prisoners were to be removed from a battlefield.

Korean War

World War II used POWs in posters and other publications to heighten the importance of home front support. A good example was one that promoted defense production with captured American nurses unrealistically depicted in full regalia complete with caps, capes, white stockings, and pumps with the caption: Work! To Set 'Em Free! Work! To Keep' Em Firing! The Navy's Special Warfare Branch provided an especially significant contribution with a program called *Prisoner-of-War Mail*, which was prepared and turned over to the **Office of War Information** radio desks. Letters were solicited from German and Italian POWs held in the U.S. with the knowledge that the messages would be broadcast to their homelands.

Television was just in its infancy during the Korean Conflict (1950–1953), so not every American household owned one, but television broadcasts were especially effective with the Vietnamese conflict when the television medium brought the war home every night. This made Vietnam and subsequent military engagements more personal, most recently with the abuse of Iraqi prisoners at the Abu Ghraib prison in Baghdad. Revelations in early May 2004 that at least seven U.S. soldiers from the 372nd Military Police Company based in Cumberland, Maryland, were torturing Iraqi prisoners under American protection sent shockwaves around the world after the news reports relayed the images continuously through the media.

See also **Katyn Forest Massacre;** *Pueblo* **Film**

FURTHER READING: Tom Bird, *American POWs of World War II* (Westport, CT and London: Praeger, 1992); Lewis H. Carlson, *We Were Each Other's Prisoners* (New York: HarperCollins, 1997); Gavan Daws, *Prisoners of the Japanese* (New York: William Morrow, 1994); William E. Daugherty, *Psychological Warfare Casebook* (Baltimore: Johns Hopkins; published for Operations Research Office, Johns Hopkins University, 1958); Barbara Haber, *From Hardtack to Home Fries: An Uncommon History of American Cooks and Meals* (New York and London: Free Press, 2002); Harley O. Preston, James L. Monroe, and Alan L. Raffa, "U.S. Vulnerabilities as Portrayed in the East German Television Film, *Pilots in Pajamas*," in *The Art and Science of Psychological Operations: Case Studies of Military Application*, vol. 2, ed. American Institutes for Research (Washington, DC: Headquarters, U.S. Dept. of the Army, 1976); PSYOP Group, "The Pueblo Film," in *The Art and Science of Psychological Operations: Case Studies of Military Application*, vol. 2, ed. American Institutes for Research (Washington, DC: Headquarters, U.S. Dept. of the Army, 1976); "Treatment of American Prisoners of War in North Vietnam," *Department of State Bulletin*, December 22, 1969: 596–599.

PROBLEMS OF COMMUNISM. Until its demise in 1992 with the end of the Cold War, *Problems of Communism* was a bimonthly publication that provided "analyses and significant information about the contemporary affairs of the Soviet Union, China, and comparable states and political movements." The magazine was started in 1952 in response to a continuing demand from the field for high-quality, well-documented materials on communism and was intended for overseas distribution to a relatively small number of persons especially concerned with the problems posed by communism. It was patterned after the German-language periodical, *Ost-Probleme*, issued under the auspices of the U.S. Office of the High Commissioner for Germany (HICOG), which was highly effective. *Problems of Communism* provided a forum for the serious analysis of all issues, political, economic, cultural, and philosophical, relating to Communism. Its articles were signed, and its authors included scholars from all over the world. Although produced by the **U.S. Information Agency**, it was one of the two (the other was *English Teaching Forum*) agency-produced publications that was excepted from the domestic dissemination ban and allowed to be sold in the United States through the Government Printing Office. With its dispassionate and analytical tone, the magazine attempted to prove that the U.S. government could sponsor a sober, careful, nonpolemical discussion of the Communist issue that had more impact than conventional anti-Communist propaganda, but with the end of the Cold War, *Problems of Communism* lost much of its impact. Its January–April 1992 issue highlighted the proceedings of the 40th Anniversary Conference, "Toward a Postcommunist World," held October 22–23, 1991, in Washington, D.C. The last issue was a special edition (Spring 1992) with the correspondence between President John F. Kennedy and Russian Premier Nikita S. Khrushchev during the 1962 Cuban Missile Crisis.

FURTHER READING: Howard Oiseth, *Way It Was: USIA's Press and Publications Service, 1935–77* (Washington, DC: USIA, 1977); Issues of *Problems of Communism*.

PROJECT TROY. Special report the State Department commissioned from the Massachusetts Institute of Technology (MIT) on "the broad problem of how to get information into Russia." The group was composed of 21 scholars from Harvard and MIT to study technical means of circumventing Soviet jamming of the **Voice of America** and analyzed communications theory, psychology, and other aspects of information through radio transmission, leaflet-filled balloons, and other propaganda programs. Drawing on expert reports, the panel produced a Ring Plan for a series of high-powered, strategically located transmitters. On April 4, 1950, NSC 66 directive called for maximum support of efforts to overcome Soviet jamming with new facilities. That September, Congress allocated funds for the Ring Plan.

Project TROY directly influenced the establishment of the **Psychological Strategy Board,** and one of its initiatives led directly to the creation of the Center for International Studies at the Massachusetts Institute of Technology.

FURTHER READING: Walter L. Hixson, *Parting the Curtain: Propaganda, Culture, and the Cold War, 1945–1961* (New York: St. Martin's, 1997); Allan A. Needell, "'Truth is Our Weapon': Project TROY, Political Warfare, and Government-Academic Relations in the National Security State," *Diplomatic History* 17, no. 3 (summer 1993): 399–420.

PROPAGANDA (ANALYSIS). *See* Propaganda Analysis

PROPAGANDA, ANTI-COMMUNIST. *See* Advancing American Art; *Amerika Illustrated*; American National Exhibition, Moscow; Baby Parts; Biological and Chemical Weapons; Books; Cartoons; Comics and Comic Strips; Disinformation; Forgeries; Front Organizations; McCarthyism; Motion Pictures; Postal Regulations (Communist Political Propaganda); President's Advisory Committee on Government Organization; President's Committee on Information Activities Abroad; *Problems of Communism*; Propaganda Committees; Radio Free Europe; Radio Liberty; U.S. Congress. House. Committee on House Un-American Activities; U.S. Congressional Investigations of Propaganda; United States Information Agency; Voice of America

PROPAGANDA, CULTURAL. *See* **Cultural Diplomacy; Cultural Exchanges**

PROPAGANDA: THE FORMATION OF MEN'S ATTITUDES. In his very important book, *Propaganda: The Formation of Men's Attitudes*, first published in 1965, Jacques Ellul argued that propaganda generally aims at influencing the political and social behavior of groups or of publics, which he divided into two broad categories: political propaganda and social propaganda, both with broad and inclusive definitions and applications, and both disseminated by either official or unofficial agencies. Ellul regarded propaganda as a sociological phenomenon rather than as something made by certain people for certain purposes; it exists and thrives as the Siamese twin of our technological society. Only in the technological society can there be anything of the magnitude of modern propaganda, which rejects the lies of past and outmoded forms of propaganda but cannot work without education.

FURTHER READING: Introduction and notes in Jacques Ellul, *Propaganda: The Formation of Men's Attitudes* (New York: Vintage Books, 1973/1965).

PROPAGANDA ANALYSIS. During the 1920s and the 1930s, propaganda research was largely impressionistic, pacifist, and aimed at educating a broad public about the continuing dangers of the persuasion industries. This revisionist line of questioning, which drew on rhetorical scholarship and progressive ideology, was designated "propaganda analysis." With a more precise definition of the social sciences after World War II, those in the competing schools considered themselves "empirical communication researchers." Still later, an emphasis on quantifiable documentation became the dominant approach to research resulting in much contemporary writing about power groups and propaganda using qualitative historical-critical research methods prepared by Marxist, libertarian, and other ideologically motivated researchers.

Propaganda Analysis was also a monthly periodical published by the Institute for Contemporary Analysis that attempted to stimulate critical thinking in an educational curriculum by using case studies of various forms of propaganda.

FURTHER READING: Institute for Propaganda Analysis, *Propaganda Analysis* (New York: The Institute, 1938).

PROPAGANDA COLLECTIONS. Generally, a library of sample propaganda material or an archive holding the papers or records of individuals and organizations who engaged in propaganda activities. Such a library collection used to exist in the **U.S. Information Agency**, Washington, D.C.; it was a sampling of Free World books, pamphlets, posters, and periodicals received from Communist bloc countries (USSR, People's Republic of China, Albania, Bulgaria, Czechoslovakia, East Germany, Hungary, Poland, Romania, Yugoslavia, North Korea, North Vietnam, Cuba). The aim of the collection, started after World War II when the Cold War was just beginning, was to provide a primary source of Communist propaganda intended for foreign readership and to make such material available for use in agency lectures, budget hearings, and exhibits. The kinds of material included in the collection included new publications offered by Communist countries, international front organizations, local Communist groups; bibliographic material on bloc publications; and sample publications of bloc countries in bloc languages.

The Propaganda Collection, as the library was designated, was first part of the International Information Administration, U.S. Department of State, then it was transferred to the newly created USIA in 1953, where it was maintained by the Agency Library; it was probably the most extensive, if not the only one, of its kind. Along with USIA staff members, the USIA Propaganda Collection served other government agencies as well. However, the material had to be scrutinized through the Bureau of Customs, U.S. Treasury Department, when it entered through New York. Because it was designated as political propaganda sent from the Soviet bloc countries to the United States with its source in the Soviet government and in Soviet bloc countries' governments, this material came under the provisions of the **Foreign Agents Registration Act** (FARA). For years, Irving Fishman, Assistant Deputy Commissioner, Bureau of Customs, in the U.S. Customhouse, New York City, screened and monitored the bags of books, newspapers, pamphlets and films of propaganda that entered through the Port of New York en route to Washington, under special contract with USIA.

Another major collection, more archival, is in the Hoover Institution on War, Revolution and Peace Library and Archives, Stanford University, Stanford, California. Along with the personal papers of propagandists such as **George Creel, Martin Herz, Daniel Lerner**, and Paul M. A. Linebarger, there are the papers of such propaganda organizations as **Radio Free Europe/Radio Liberty** broadcast archives and corporate records and the **America First Committee**. These are only two of the many libraries and archives. See also the research sources at the back of the book.

FURTHER READING: Files on the USIA Propaganda Collection, Public Diplomacy Historical Collection, Bureau of Public Diplomacy, U.S. Department of State; *Hoover Institution Finding Aids* (Stanford, CA: Sanford University, 2002; online: http://www.hoover. org/hila); Charles G. Palm and Dale Reed, *Guide to the Hoover Institution Archives* (Stanford, CA: Stanford University, Hoover Institution Press, 1980); Joseph J. White, *Sino-Soviet Bloc Periodicals Published in Free World Languages* (MSLS, Catholic University, 1964).

PROPAGANDA COMMITTEES. During World War II, at the Third Washington [D.C.] Conference, May 12–25, 1943, attended by both President **Franklin D. Roosevelt** and British Prime Winston S. Churchill, one of the points of discussion was the necessity for a central agency to coordinate all propaganda by the Allied powers. This discussion came about from a perceived lack of clear understanding between theater commanders and the Combined Chiefs of Staff concerning the propaganda to be used. In a directive on the subject (August 31, 1943), it was ordered that all propaganda aims and themes had to be effective before and during the operation, and changes in approved themes had to meet the situation. Everything had to be cleared through the Combined Chiefs of Staff. At other discussions, Anglo-American committees of equal membership, especially from the **Office of War Information** and its British counterpart, the Political Warfare

Executive, to coordinate propaganda were to be established in Washington for the Pacific Theater, in London for the European Theater, and in New Delhi for the South East Asian Theater. To handle emergency situations, it was proposed that an Anglo-American Emergency Propaganda Committee for Pacific, European and South-East Asian Theatres be set up.

FURTHER READING: U.S. Dept. of State, *Foreign Relations of the United States: The Conferences at Washington and Quebec 1943* (Washington, DC: Government Printing Office, 1970).

PROPAGANDA IN JAPAN. *See* Japan; Occupied Countries and Territories; Pearl Harbor; Tokyo Rose; Zacharias, Ellis Mark

PROPAGANDA JOURNALS. *See Amerika Illustrated; Covert Action Information Bulletin; The Hour; The Index; New Masses; Official Bulletin; Problems of Communism*

PROPAGANDA LIBRARIES. *See* Propaganda Collections

PROPAGANDA OF THE DEED. The use of direct action, including violence, to make a political point, usually because the organization employing terror cannot attract sufficient support for their cause through open political processes. To many terrorists and armed anarchists, a single decisive deed is better propaganda than a thousand pamphlets. The term was borrowed from social revolutionaries, who emphasized the importance of assassinating or the taking of emotionally significant cities or the importance of surprise and the cultivation of revolutionary aims against enemy governments. It is more potent than propaganda of the word. Early use was in 1882, when Johan Most, a German radical, arrived in the United States to preach "the propaganda of the deed" and communist anarchism. It was used by the Communists only when it did not interfere with the implementation of an efficient control system.
See also Terrorist Propaganda

FURTHER READING: William E. Daugherty, *Psychological Warfare Casebook* (Baltimore: Johns Hopkins; published for Operations Research Office, Johns Hopkins University, 1958).

PROTOCOLS OF THE LEARNED ELDERS OF ZION. No country has used forgeries as extensively as the Soviet Union; they developed them to a level unparalleled in previous times. For the Soviets, forgeries are a weapon of active measures (i.e., influence operations) that support propaganda themes. The KGB has the responsibility for carrying out active measures and producing forgeries. Describing the role of the KGB in influencing attitudes in the West, Yuri Andropov, then head of KGB, said in 1967: "The state security bodies are also actively participating in the fulfillment of this task. The workers of these bodies are aware that peaceful coexistence is a form of class struggle; that it is a bitter and stubborn battle on all fronts, economic, political, and ideological. In this fight, the state security bodies are obliged to carry out their specific duties efficiently and faultlessly." These Soviet state security bodies built on the activities of the czarist secret police (Okhrana), who produced one of history's classic forgeries.

Among the most widely circulated propaganda **forgeries** and one of the center-pieces of anti-Semitic literature, the *Protocols of the Learned Elders of Zion* appeared shortly before the 1905 uprising against Nicholas II of Russia. It was authorized by Pyotr Ivanovich Ratchkovski, the head of the czarist secret police (Okhrana), who circulated it, although authorship is now given to Mathieu Golovinski. The forgery derived from a French political pamphlet, "Dialoque aux Enfers entre Montesquieu et Machiavel," by Maurice Joly, which was first published in 1864 as an attack on Napoleon III's ambitions for world domination. In the *Protocols*, the Jews were substituted for the French emperor.

The *Protocols of the Learned Elders of Zion* purported to be the minutes and proceedings of a Jewish conclave led by the Grand Rabbi and held during the first Zionist Congress in Basel, Switzerland, in 1897. The purpose of this secret meeting of the "innermost circle" of worldwide Jewish leadership was to structure a "blueprint" for world domination of all non-Jews to slavery and then to set the schedule for subsequent gatherings every 100 years by an endless succession of "autocrats of the House of David." It fabricated an international Jewish conspiracy, in league with Freemasons, to seize world power. These forgeries were continually reprinted and circulated by the Nazis and other extremist groups, despite being discredited by scholars. The document is an example of **disinformation** that serves the purpose of prejudice, but significant parts of the *Protocols* are virtual copies of an obscure French satire, John Robison's *Proof of a Conspiracy*, which popularized the role of Freemasons in causing the French Revolution. Since its publication, it has been used by both the gullible and the cruel to terrorize the Jews. After the Russian Revolution (1917), anti-Semitic monarchists circulated translations of the *Protocols* in other countries, including the United States and Great Britain, and they were used as a key source in Hitler's *Mein Kampf*. Henry Ford was among those who believed in their authenticity; he published it in the 1920s as a series of untitled articles, "The International Jew" in his newspaper, *Independent Dearborn*, but later recanted his actions (1927) and tried to make amends. In 1938, Fr. **Charles Coughlin** introduced the *Protocols* as an extensive series of articles in his newspaper, *Social Justice*, by invoking the authority of Henry Ford in the authenticity of the writings. When questioned about his actions, Coughlin replied that the *Protocols* "fit with what is going on," but his actions were bitterly criticized by Jewish and other groups. Today, evangelist Pat Robertson's accusations of conspiracies by European bankers has overtones of the *Protocols*' language.

In 1967, Norman Cohn wrote *Warrant for Genocide: The Myth of the Jewish World Conspiracy and the Protocols of the Elders of Zion* (New York: Harper, 1967), which studied the impact of the *Protocols* on anti-Semitic thought and traces the origins of the myth of the Jewish world conspiracy and its psychological roots.

See also Anti-Semitic Propaganda

FURTHER READING: Neil Baldwin, *Henry Ford and the Jews: The Mass Production of Hate* (New York: Public Affairs, 2001); Norman R. C. Cohn, *Warrant for Genocide: The Myth of the Jewish World Conspiracy and the Protocols of the Elders of Zion* (New York: Harper and Row, 1967); Sergiei A. Nilus, *The Protocols of the Meetings of the*

Learned Elders of Zion, trans. Victor E. Marsden (Houston: Pyramid Book Shop, 1934); Binjamin W. Segal, *A Lie and a Libel: The History of the "Protocols of the Elders of Zion"* (Lincoln: University of Nebraska, 1995).

PSYCHOLOGICAL OPERATIONS COORDINATING COMMITTEE. Interdepartmental Psychological Operations Coordinating Committee (POCC) assigned peacetime role, in name, in psychological warfare as part of President Truman's **Campaign of Truth.** It was composed of the members of the original **Psychological Strategy Board** (PSB), but its line of authority with PSB was never clearly defined. Generally, its mission was the direction and determination of current psychological operations and policies. Both POCC and PSB were headed by former Assistant Secretary of State for Public Affairs Edward W. Barrett. The Psychological Operations Coordinating Committee was dissolved in October 1953 at the recommendation of the President's Committee on International Information Activities, and its functions were merged with those of PSB into the **Operations Coordinating Board.**

FURTHER READING: William E. Daugherty, *Psychological Warfare Casebook* (Baltimore: Johns Hopkins; published for Operations Research Office, Johns Hopkins University, 1958).

PSYCHOLOGICAL STRATEGY BOARD. The Psychological Strategy Board (PSB) was created by presidential directive on June 20, 1951, and was responsible to the National Security Council. Its mission was to plan long-term psychological approaches to the nation's problems and to help influence opinions, attitudes, and behavior abroad in support of national objectives. Regular members were the Under Secretary of State, Deputy Secretary of Defense, and the Director of the Central Intelligence Agency (CIA). Other agencies, such as the Mutual Security Agency and the **U.S. Information Agency,** participated as needed. A representative of the Joint Chiefs of Staff was principal adviser, and the board's director was appointed by the president. The Psychological Strategy Board was dissolved in October 1953 at the recommendation of the President's Committee on International Information Activities as not meeting "the real need which exists in government" for psychological strategy. It was replaced by the **Operations Coordinating Board.**

FURTHER READING: William E. Daugherty, *Psychological Warfare Casebook* (Baltimore: Johns Hopkins; published for Operations Research Office, Johns Hopkins University, 1958); U.S. Department of State, *Foreign Relations of the United States, 1951: vol. 1: National Security Affairs; Foreign Economic Policy* (Washington, DC: Government Printing Office, 1980): 58–60.

PSYCHOLOGICAL WARFARE. Type of propaganda that aims to weaken the enemy's will to fight or believe in their government. A related technique, brainwashing, is used against prisoners. Psychological warfare, an important element of military propaganda, is designed to influence enemy personnel, including political leaders, to serve the manipulator's purposes. The tools of psychological warfare include the presentation or distortion of images, the coordination of military or diplomatic action to create certain images, and the exploitation of existing tensions within the enemy camp to affect morale, decision making, or discipline.

Official sources and publicists lack agreement on the proper terminology and scope of "psychological warfare" but it has proved a handicap when used in reference to peacetime international communications. One of the best definitions was formulated by Paul M. A. Linebarger, who called it propaganda used against the enemy, together with "such other operational measures of a military, economic, or political nature as may be required to supplement propaganda." The term has definite negative connotations, both in the United States and abroad, and was never popular with the American people; warfare of all kinds should be left to the military.

On February 16, 1953, President Eisenhower appointed **Charles D. Jackson** as his personal adviser on psychological warfare, an executive action that placed the coordinated direction of psychological factors in U.S. foreign affairs at the highest level of government. Jackson resigned in April 1954.

One of Eisenhower's first acts as Chief Executive was to appoint an eight-member committee (President's Committee on International Information Activities) chaired by W. H. Jackson to study the problem of psychological warfare. The committee's startling conclusion was that *psychological warfare* and *cold war* were unfortunate terms that do not describe efforts to build world peace and should be discarded in favor of other terms that better describe the United States' true goals. It also recommended that the **Psychological Strategy Board** be abolished and clarified that there are no psychological warfare instruments distinct from traditional instruments of policy except for propaganda. One of the effects of the committee was the establishment of the **U.S. Information Agency** in August 1953 to handle the overseas information program.

See also **American National Exhibition, Moscow; Atoms for Peace; Brussels Universal and International Exposition (Expo 58); Cold War; Disinformation; Forgeries; Iraq; Psychological Warfare Branch, Allied Forces Headquarters (PWB/AFHQ); Psychological Warfare Division, Supreme Headquarters Allied Expeditionary Forces (PWD/SHAEF); Soviet Active Measures; Vietnam Conflict**

FURTHER READING: Edward W. Barrett, "Psychological Offensive in the So-Called Cold War," November 13, 1951 (Unpublished; U.S. Dept. of State memorandum); William E. Daugherty, *Psychological Warfare Casebook* (Baltimore: Johns Hopkins; published for Operations Research Office, Johns Hopkins University, 1958); Daniel Lerner, *Psychological Warfare Against Nazi Germany: The Skyewar Campaign, D-Day to VE-Day* (Cambridge, MA: MIT, 1971/1949).

PSYCHOLOGICAL WARFARE BRANCH, ALLIED FORCES HEADQUARTERS (PWB/AFHQ). Established by General Dwight Eisenhower to organize propaganda for the upcoming TORCH operation (invasion of North Africa) during World War II, the Psychological Warfare Branch (PWB) was formed with the **Office of War Information** (OWI) and the British propaganda arm, Political Warfare Executive (PWE), as well as those from the U.S. **Office of Strategic Services** and the British Ministry of Information. Its chief was Colonel Charles B. Hazeltine, a cavalry officer with no experience with propaganda activities when he was appointed. His group required "a thorough understanding of the prejudices, the emotional enthusiasms, the likes and dislikes" of their particular audience.

PWB was an important development in the conduct of Allied propaganda. It established the principle that such operations in the war theaters were subject to military control and started the organized **psychological warfare** campaign. When the North African campaign began in November 1942, PWB members landed with the Allied troops along the Mediterranean coast in Morocco and in Algeria, using radio and megaphone requests for surrender, while the crew aboard USS *Texas* tried to encourage surrender by local military leaders with broadcasts over medium wave until a radio blast jammed the delicate equipment. PWB "psychological warriors" attempted to control all North African media facilities (newspapers, radio stations, film theaters) that could help Allied publicity and quickly established propaganda plants that contained publications and pictorial displays that praised the Allies.

FURTHER READING: William E. Daugherty, *Psychological Warfare Casebook* (Baltimore: Johns Hopkins; published for Operations Research Office, Johns Hopkins University, 1958); Allan Winkler, *Politics of Propaganda: The Office of War Information, 1942–1945* (New Haven, CT and London: Yale, 1978).

PSYCHOLOGICAL WARFARE DIVISION, SUPREME HEADQUARTERS, ALLIED EXPEDITIONARY FORCES (PWD/SHAEF). Organized by Charles Douglas (C. D.) Jackson, in association with Brigadier General Robert A. McClure, an intelligence officer on the staff of Lieutenant General Dwight D. Eisenhower, the Psychological Warfare Division (PWD) of Supreme Headquarters Allied Expeditionary Force (SHAEF) planned and executed propaganda and related activities during combat and devised de-Nazified information control programs to be used in the Allied zones in Germany after World War II ended. It started as the Publicity and Psychological Warfare Division, SHAEF, then shortly was called the G-6 Division. On April 13, 1944, G-6 was discontinued, and PWD was established along with a parallel Public Relations Division.

At its inception, PWD was given three phases of operation: all media of public expression were to be shut down; overt operation of certain selected instruments of public information, such as radio transmitters and newspapers, by the Allied Forces; and the gradual turning over of the various instruments by means of licenses to carefully selected anti-Nazi, democratic-minded Germans.

PWD prepared and distributed millions of leaflets to influence enemy troops and civilians. Along with the Safe Conduct leaflets dropped behind enemy lines, a widely disseminated one was in the form of an autumn leaf with a facsimile headline from an edition of the *Muenchner Neueste Nachrichten*, which quoted an empty Hitler promise that 1941 would be the year of Germany's final victory. PWD also broadcast appeals and announcements, cooperated with the French underground, and trained units to operate militarily licensed "clean" press, films, music, and theater in the occupied areas. PWD operated from April 13, 1944, when it was created under Brigadier General McClure, to July 13, 1945, when it was dissolved. PWD's successor was designated the Information Services Control Branch, Control Commission for Germany, and the Information Control Service, U.S. Group Control Council, with McClure as chief of both these American organizations.

FURTHER READING: Daniel Lerner, *Psychological Warfare Against Nazi Germany: The Skyewar Campaign, D-Day to VE-Day* (Cambridge, MA: MIT, 1971/1949); Psychological Warfare Division, Supreme Headquarters Allied Expeditionary Force, *An Account of Its Operations in the Western European Campaign, 1944–1945* (Bad Homburg, Germany: SHAEF, 1945).

PSYCHOLOGICAL WARFARE SECTION. *See* **Psychological Warfare Branch, Allied Forces Headquarters (PWB/AFHQ)**

PSYCHOLOGY OF RADIO. Book (1935) by **Hadley Cantril** and Gordon W. Allport that has been used as a guidebook for radio propaganda. In it, the authors analyzed the factors, both cultural and psychological, that influence radio programming and audience response. In a chapter on radio propaganda, Cantril and Allport found that the nature of a country's control and ownership of the airwaves determines the type of propaganda (e.g., in the United States, where radio is subsidized by the sale of air time, commercial propaganda is a dominating factor). However, the effectiveness of the radio message still depends heavily on program scheduling and its accessibility to the targeted audiences.

FURTHER READING: Introductory material in Hadley Cantril and Gordon W. Allport, *Psychology of Radio* (New York and London: Harper and Brothers, 1935).

PSYOPS. *See* **Psychological Warfare**

PUBLIC DIPLOMACY. The term *public diplomacy* is relatively new, but it is credited to Dean Edmund Guillion (1913–1998) of the Fletcher School of Law and Diplomacy, Tufts University, Medford, Massachusetts, in connection with the establishment of the school's Edward R. Murrow Center for Public Diplomacy in 1965. At that time, Tufts University defined the term as "the cause and effect of public attitudes and opinions which influence the formulation and execution of foreign policy." Since then, there have been various definitions of "public diplomacy." Other nations have public diplomacy activities that try to influence the U.S. government.

During the Reagan administration, it became popular as the overall function and mandate of the **U.S. Information Agency** (USIA) and referred to government-sponsored programs intended to inform or to influence public opinion in other countries. It was a more refined way to say propaganda, which was undoubtedly then USIA Director Charles Wick's intention. Its chief instruments are publications, motion pictures, cultural exchanges, and radio and television. For example, the United States uses shortwave radio to provide information to closed societies. USIA was responsible for the U.S. government's overseas information and cultural programs, including the **Voice of America.** In 1999 it was abolished, and the public diplomacy function was transferred to the newly created Bureau of Public Diplomacy in the **U.S. Department of State.**

After the September 11, 2001, terrorist attacks on the World Trade Center and on the Pentagon, the role of public diplomacy achieved a new importance as the U.S. government, led by the Office of International Information Programs in the bureau, attempted to counterattack anti-U.S. opinion with pamphlets (*Network of Terrorism*), Web pages, speeches, VOA broadcasts (in the newly independent International Broadcasting Bureau), and other media instruments as part of its Response to Terrorism campaign.

In October 2001, hearings were held on the effectiveness of public diplomacy in handling the U.S. response in countering negative opinion toward the terrorism attacks. One of its key witnesses was Charlotte Beers, new Undersecretary of Public Diplomacy and Public Affairs, who resigned her post in March 2003, after several public diplomacy missteps, including criticism of a high-profile campaign of television advertisements in the Middle East featuring Arab Americans. Another witness was Nick Nathanson, chairman, Broadcasting Board of Governors, International Broadcasting Bureau.

In October 2003, President Bush nominated Margaret Tutwiller as Charlotte Beers's successor, the same month that the U.S. Advisory Group on Public Diplomacy for the Arab and Muslim World issued its report, *Changing Minds Winning Peace: A New Strategic Direction for U.S. Public Diplomacy in the Arab and Muslim World.*

FURTHER READING: Kenneth Adelman, "Speaking of America: Public Diplomacy in Our Time," *Foreign Affairs* (spring 1981); David Hoffmann, "Beyond Public Diplomacy?" *Foreign Affairs* 81, no. 2 (March-April 2002): 83–95; Stephen Johnson and Helle Dale, "How to Reinvigorate U.S. Public Diplomacy," *Heritage Foundation Backgrounder*, no. 1645 (April 23, 2003); Frank Ninkovich, "U.S. Information Policy and Cultural Diplomacy," *Headline Series* (Foreign Policy Association) no. 308 (fall 1996): 3–63; Peter G. Peterson, "Public Diplomacy and the War on Terrorism," *Foreign Affairs* 81, no. 5 (September/October 2002): 74–94; U.S. Dept. of State, *Dictionary of International Relations* (Washington, DC: The Department, 1987); Christopher Ross, "Public Diplomacy Comes of Age," *Washington Quarterly* 25, no. 2 (spring 2002): 75–83; U.S. Advisory Commission on Public Diplomacy, *Diplomacy in the Information Age* (Washington, DC: The Commission, 1993); U.S. Advisory Commission on Public Diplomacy, *Consolidation of USIA Into the State Department: An Assessment After One Year* (Washington, DC: The Commission, 2000).

PUBLICK OCCURRENCES, BOTH FOREIGN AND DOMESTIC. *See* **Newspapers**

PUBLIC OPINION. Swaying public opinion is the primary role of propaganda. Despite considerable research by social scientists, public opinion has yet to be adequately defined; some 50 different definitions have been cited. However, scholars generally agree that it exists. In a democracy, it may be a force of considerable power, setting limits within which government policy must operate. In a totalitarian country, it is not permitted expression. Is public opinion rational? How well informed is it? And what constitutes a public? These questions resist explanation because public opinion is as difficult to ascertain as the world of affairs on which it supposedly reflects. Journalists are concerned about public opinion and frequently the most influential group for molding it. Public opinion may coalesce about an idea or a leader or respond to an event or campaign. It can be exploited or it may be instinctively correct in its judgment of an issue or of an individual. Public opinion continues to be polled and persists in demonstrating its presence, for example, antiabortion rallies and antinuclear protests. Everyone is entitled to an opinion, and others are often interested in it. A pioneer work was Walter Lippmann's *Public Opinion* (1922), which discussed themes that were revolutionary for its time but became standard later.

FURTHER READING: William Bollinger and Daniel M. Lund, "Mixing Polls and Propaganda," *Nation* 246, no. 18 (May 7, 1988): 635–38; George H. Gallup, *The Gallup Poll: Public Opinion, 1935–1971* (New York: Random House, 1972); Bob Garfield, "I Hear America Yakking," *Washington Post* Magazine (November 5, 1995): 10–13, 30–35; Bernard Hennessy, *Public Opinion* (Monterey, CA: Brooks/Cole, 1985); Walter Lippmann, *The Phantom Public* (New York and London: Macmillan, 1953); U.S. Congress. House. Committee on Un-American Activities, *Manipulation of Public Opinion by Organizations Under Concealed Control of the Communist Party (National Assembly for Democratic Rights and Citizens Committee for Constitutional Liberties)*; Report (Washington, DC: Government Printing Office, 1961).

PUBLIC RELATIONS. Public relations creates goodwill, visibility, and morale; negotiates crisis and news management; and uses images to create symbolic relationships ("You don't sell steak, you sell the sizzle"). Public relations developed in early twentieth-century America as businessmen responded to the criticism of reformers. An early practitioner was **Ivy Lee**, an ex-newspaperman, who advised the Pennsylvania Railroad, John D. Rockefeller Sr., and the Bethlehem Steel Co. During World War I, **George Creel** directed the **Committee on Public Information**, a "plain publicity proposition, a vast enterprise in salesmanship," as Creel later remembered it. After the war the field expanded rapidly. **Edward L. Bernays** enlisted clients, formulated techniques, and polled **public opinion**.

Government agencies began to hire publicity people in the 1920s and 1930s, such as top-flight public relations people like Ben Sonnenburg and Earl Newsom. With World War II, the profession came into its own, with every branch of government and the armed services practicing public relations. By the 1960s, public relations became a significant characteristic of American life, with everyone aware at least of publicity, the need for it, and the value of it.

Is public relations propaganda? Its critics reply affirmatively and attack its methods and its ethics (artificial buildup, exploitation of contacts, manipulation of opinion), whereas its supporters disagree. Ivy Lee claimed that it was humanly impossible to state an absolute fact ("all I can do is give you my interpretation of the facts"). William L. Safire said it was a matter of leverage with a number of different groups having a vested interest in any number of causes with imagination the real "fulcrum."

FURTHER READING: Scott M. Cutlip, *Unseen Power: Public Relations, a History* (Hillsdale, NJ: Lawrence Erlbaum Associates, 1994); Richard W. Steele, *Propaganda in an Open Society: The Roosevelt Administration and the Media, 1933–1941* (Westport, CT: Greenwood, 1985).

PUBLIC UTILITIES. *See* **National Electric Light Association**

PUBLICITY BUREAU. A popular name with various organizations established to promote any number of causes. The Publicity Bureau was in the U.S. Department of the Treasury during World War I, where it publicized the liberty loan campaign in 1917. The Publicity Bureau was also the first public relations firm. It was founded in Boston in 1900 by George V. S. Michaelis, Herbert Small, and Thomas O. Marvin "to do a general press agent business." One of its most prominent cases was an issues management case for the railroad industry (1906–1908) as it fought the attempts by President Theodore Roosevelt to impose regulatory legislation on the industry. Another type was the Publicity Bureau for the Exposure of Political Romanism, which organized opposition to "progress destructive of free institutions including present-day uprising against political Romanism" and the reform program, and there was a Publicity Bureau for South China.

FURTHER READING: Scott M. Cutlip, *Unseen Power: Public Relations, a History* (Hillsdale, NJ: Lawrence Erlbaum Associates, 1994).

PUBWATCH. *See* Books

PUEBLO FILM. Event was propaganda to a certain extent. On January 23, 1968, the USS *Pueblo*, an intelligence-gathering ship, was seized in the Sea of Japan by North Koreans, who claimed the ship violated its territorial waters. The *Pueblo* crew remained captured until December 1968. Although not actually POWs, American coverage described them not actually as prisoners of war, but as hostages. They were constantly photographed with the results disseminated for public consumption, and there were constant press conferences with prearranged answers to prearranged questions.

North Korea made much propaganda use of this incident through radio broadcasts on the "intrusion of the U.S. imperialist armed spy ship" almost daily, and the domestic daily newspapers gave it extensive coverage as well, but the highlight of the North Korean propaganda effort was a film produced by "2.8 Studio" of the North Korean People's Army (KPA) entitled *Pueblo, Armed Spy Ship of the U.S. Imperialist Aggressors*, which was shown around the world. The English-language film, with narration by the North Koreans and the voices of various *Pueblo* officers and crewmen, emphasized that the *Pueblo*, under direct orders from the U.S. government, intruded into North Korean territorial waters for espionage activities; now the United States must apologize for this activity. The film stressed that the crewmen were being treated well.

See also Prisoners of War

FURTHER READING: PSYOP Group, "The Pueblo Film," in *The Art and Science of Psychological Operations: Case Studies of Military Application*, vol. 2, ed. American Institutes for Research (Washington, DC: Headquarters, U.S. Dept. of the Army, 1976).

PULITZER, JOSEPH. *See* Yellow Journalism

Q

QUANTICO VULNERABILITIES PANEL. Meeting that originated with Nelson Rockefeller, who replaced **C. D. Jackson** as President Eisenhower's **psychological warfare** adviser in December 1954, to assess Soviet weaknesses and possible U.S. initiatives at the upcoming Geneva Conference. The special panel of experts convened June 5–10, 1955, at Quantico, Virginia. It was chaired by MIT's Walt Rostow. In its report, the panel concluded that the United States, operating "from a position of strength," should present the USSR "with heavy demands for major concessions"; rejected negotiations with Moscow; and agreed that the combination of Soviet vulnerabilities and Western strengths would allow the Allies to "transcend the area of negotiations" to effect "a rollback of Soviet power in Eastern and Central Europe and in Asia."

FURTHER READING: U.S. Dept. of State, *Foreign Relations of the United States, 1955–1957, vol. 24: Soviet Union; Eastern Mediterranean* (Washington, DC: Government Printing Office, 1989); Walter L. Hixson, *Parting the Curtain: Propaganda, Culture, and the Cold War, 1945–1961* (New York: St. Martin's, 1997).

R

RADIO 1212. *See* Operation Annie

RADIO AMERICAS. *See* Radio Swan

RADIO BROADCASTING BY THE U.S. GOVERNMENT. During World War II, many government agencies, including the U.S. Department of the Treasury, broadcast highly patriotic radio programs, such as *Treasury Star Parade* (1943–1944) to sell war bonds and to maintain enthusiasm for continuing the fight. America's favorite radio characters were also pressed into service to help the war effort after **Pearl Harbor**. Radio quickly became the central wartime propaganda instrument because it provided a daily and continuous link with many people and because it was a commercial medium, but it has often been overshadowed by print and by film propaganda.

In February 1942, the U.S. government's radio broadcasting service, the **Voice of America**, went on the air with the first broadcast to Germany at the same time the **Coordinator for Inter-American Affairs** started a series of radio broadcasts to Latin America. In the immediate post–World War II period, **Radio Free Europe** (RFE) and **Radio Liberty** (RL) were created by CIA funding then incorporated under the Board for International Broadcasting in 1974 by Congress with oversight responsibility for both radio services. In 1982, **Radio Marti** was established under the Radio Broadcasting to Cuba Act (Public Law 98-111) but in 1994, the United States International Broadcasting Act, Title III of the Foreign Relations Authorization Act, Fiscal Years 1994 and 1995 (Public Law 103-236), established the International Broadcasting Bureau (IBB) within the United States Information Agency (USIA) and created a presidentially appointed Broadcasting Board of Governors (BBG) with jurisdiction over all civilian U.S. government international broadcasting. The law consolidated VOA, **Worldnet** TV, Radio and **Television Marti,** the Office of Engineering and Technical Services, along with RFE/RL and a new **Radio Free Asia**. On October 21, 1998, President Clinton signed the Foreign Affairs Reform and Restructuring Act (Public Law 105-277), perhaps the single most important legislation affecting U.S. government international broadcasters.

This law placed all U.S. publicly funded, nonmilitary overseas broadcasting into a new entity called the Broadcasting Board of Governors, abolished USIA, merged all but its broadcasting functions into the U.S. Department of State, and inaugurated the independence of U.S. government civilian international broadcasting.

See also Clandestine Radio Broadcasting; Debunk (Radio Station); Lorient; Radio Caiman; Radio in the American Sector; Radio Swan; Soldatensender Calais

FURTHER READING: Donald R. Browne, *International Radio Broadcasting: The Limits of the Limitless Medium* (New York: Praeger, 1982); Gerd Horten, *Radio Goes to War: The Cultural Politics of Propaganda during World War II* (Berkeley and Los Angeles: University of California, 2002); International Broadcasting Bureau. *U.S. International Broadcasting Chronology* (IBB Web site: http:// www.ibb.gov); Michael Nelson, *War of the Black Heavens: The Battles of Western Broadcasting in the Cold War* (London: Brassey's, 1997); Nancy L. Street and Marilyn J. Matelski, eds., *Messages from the Underground: Transnational Radio in Resistance and in Solidarity* (Westport, CT: Praeger, 1997); Philo C. Wasburn, *Broadcasting Propaganda: International Radio Broadcasting and the Construction of Political Reality* (Westport, CT: Praeger, 1992).

RADIO CAIMAN. Radio Caiman was a CIA clandestine radio station that targeted young Cubans. Its transmitter was in Central America. It began broadcasting in summer 1985 but was terminated in December 1994 when President William Clinton terminated most CIA covert operations against Cuba.

FURTHER READING: Nancy L. Street and Marilyn J. Matelski, eds., *Messages from the Underground: Transnational Radio in Resistance and in Solidarity* (Westport, CT: Praeger, 1997); Jon Elliston, ed., *Psywar on Cuba: The Declassified History of U.S. Anti-Castro Propaganda* (Melbourne, Victoria, Australia and New York: Ocean Press, 1999).

RADIO DEBUNK. *See* Debunk (Radio Station)

RADIO FREE ASIA. In 1994, the United States International Broadcasting Act, Title III of the Foreign Relations Authorization Act, Fiscal Years 1994 and 1995 (Public Law 103-236), merged Radio Marti, along with Television Marti, with the **Voice of America** and recommended the creation of a third broadcasting service, Radio Free Asia, Inc.; all were consolidated in the International Broadcasting Bureau (IBB) under the direction of a Broadcasting Board of Governors. The proposal for RFE was also discussed in the report of the Task Force on U.S. International Broadcasting, chaired by former VOA director John Hughes, in 1989. RFE started in March 1996 to broadcast domestic news and information in nine languages (Mandarin, Tibetan, Burmese, Vietnamese, Korean, Lao, Khmer, Cantonese, and Uyghur) to listeners in Asia who do not have access to full and free news media.

FURTHER READING: International Broadcasting Bureau, *U.S. International Broadcasting Chronology* (IBB Web site: http://www.ibb.gov); Handouts from IBB Public Liaison Office.

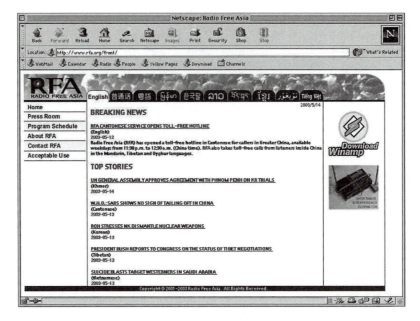

Radio Free Asia's Web page.

RADIO FREE EUROPE. In the United States, front organizations under the guise of dummy corporations have been used by the Central Intelligence Agency (CIA). The most notable purpose was to provide cover for the CIA funding that established and enlarged Radio Free Europe (RFE) and a sister network, **Radio Liberty**, both uncovered in a 1967 *Ramparts* magazine article that exposed RFE's longtime CIA financing.

Radio Free Europe was established by former **Office of Strategic Services**' officers with secret CIA funding. Unlike the **Voice of America**, it appeared to be funded and operated by the National Committee for a Free Europe (NCFE), which was a CIA front organization. It created the Crusade for Freedom to erect "a spontaneous movement" to promote the idea of freedom and "to build up the prestige" of Radio Free Europe, NCFE's most important operation. Crusade for Freedom, a fund-raising project of the American Heritage Foundation, and once headed by **C. D. Jackson,** was a cover for NFCE activities that enabled it to appear as a popular movement. Both NCFE ("To Halt Communism and Save Freedom") and Crusade for Freedom ("The Struggle for the Souls of Men") were organized "to liberate" central Europe. RFE was considered the most important part of the NCFE operation. Its objective was to begin where VOA stopped with no official limitations. It broadcast to Communist-dominated East Europe, and its principal objective was to reveal the Communist regimes (Albania, Bulgaria, Czechoslovakia, Hungary, Poland, and Romania) in the worst possible light. RFE started broadcasting in Munich on May Day 1951 with the first international transmitter broadcast only to Czechoslovakia; by the end of that summer, there were additional transmitter broadcasts to Hungary and to Poland. RFE featured music and news, skits, satires, and talks by exiled leaders; monitored the broadcasts of all central and eastern Europe; and managed the use of information compiled from the intelligence community.

The Committee for a Free Europe developed a full-scale plan for the liberation of East Europe. Between April 1954 and November 1956, Radio Free Europe's predecessor, Free Europe Committee, Inc., through its Free Europe Press, conducted a program of regular deliveries of printed matter by balloon from West Germany to Czechoslovakia, Hungary, and Poland. The materials delivered were leaflets and informational booklets; the purpose was to help amend the lack of free exchange of information that these Communist countries tried to control. The balloon program of Free Europe Press aimed at providing news and information not otherwise available in printed form to peoples of Soviet-dominated Eastern Europe.

RFE and **Radio Liberty** continued to be supported by the CIA until June 1971, when its undercover involvement was exposed. In August 1972 President Richard Nixon appointed a Presidential Study Commission on International Broadcasting that found that RFE and Radio Liberty, with their flow of "free and uncensored information to peoples deprived of it" actually contributed to a

Radio Free Europe/Radio Liberty Web page.

climate of détente. In 1973, the two radio stations were placed under the jurisdiction of the Board for International Broadcasting.

Clinton administration officials wanted to save $210 million annually by
closing Radio Free Europe and Radio Liberty, but the two stations felt they still
provided a service, even though Communism's threat was diminished, by broadcasting news services that formerly Communist countries would transmit if they
could. The administration consolidated U.S. international broadcasting operations with Public Law 103-236 under USIA's new Broadcasting Board of Governors (BBG), which included the VOA, Radio Free Europe, and Radio Liberty. The
law maintains RFE/RL's status as a private corporation funded by grants from
the BBG. Presently, RFE broadcasts in three East European languages (Bulgarian,
Romanian, Slovak), three Baltic languages (Estonian, Latvian, Lithuanian) and
since 1994, in Serbian and in Croatian. Sig Mickelson, a former RFE/RL director,
argued that such broadcasts were not propaganda but "free information" to censored societies behind the former Iron Curtain.

FURTHER READING: William E. Daugherty, ed., *Psychological Warfare Casebook*
(Baltimore: Johns Hopkins; published for Operations Research Office, Johns Hopkins
University, 1958); Sig Mickelson, *America's Other Voices: Radio Free Europe and Radio
Liberty* (New York: Praeger, 1983); Arch Puddington, *Broadcasting Freedom: The Cold
War Triumph of Radio Free Europe and Radio Liberty* (Lexington: University of Kentucky,
2000); U.S. Presidential Study Commission on International Radio Broadcasting, *The
Right to Know; a Report* (Washington, DC: Government Printing Office, 1973?); George
R. Urban, *Radio Free Europe and the Pursuit of Democracy: My War within the Cold
War* (New Haven, CT and London: Yale University, 1997).

RADIO IN PROPAGANDA. *See* **Clandestine Radio Broadcasting; Debunk
(Radio Station); Lorient; Radio Broadcasting by the U.S. Government; Radio
Caiman; Radio in the American Sector; Radio Sawa; Radio Swan; Soldatensender
Calais; U.S.A. Zone of the Overseas Service (North American Service)**

RADIO IN THE AMERICAN SECTOR. Radio in the American Sector (RIAS)
began in February 1946 as a U.S. military government-supported radio service for
the U.S. occupation sector in Berlin, largely as a means of supplying the German
population of that sector with information on daily living, such as stocks available at food distribution centers, and education on the evils of the Nazi regime.
RIAS proved to be a valuable adjunct to the American effort in the propaganda
struggle against the Communist forces of East Germany and within 10 years, the
station became one of the larger radio operations in Western Europe, with three
separate broadcast services over long wave, medium wave, shortwave, and PM.
RIAS was placed under the authority of the **U.S. Information Agency** through a
cooperative arrangement with the Federal Republic of Germany in 1974. With
the fall of the Berlin Wall and its significance as the end of a divided Germany,
RIAS plays a less important role than it did at its creation. There are now more
diverse radio and television stations, both domestic and foreign, for the listener,
that offer both entertainment and informational programming.

FURTHER READING: Henry P. Pilgert, *Press, Radio and Film in West Germany,
1945–1953* (Bonn: Historical Division, Office of the Executive Secretary, Office of the

U.S. High Commissioner for Germany, 1953); K. R. M. Short, ed., *Western Broadcasting over the Iron Curtain* (London and Sydney: Croom Helm, 1986); Edmund Taylor, "RIAS: The Story of an American Psywar Outpost," in *Psychological Warfare Casebook*, ed. William E. Daugherty (Baltimore: Johns Hopkins; published for Operations Research Service, Johns Hopkins University, 1958); U.S. Information Service, Bonn, *Four Decades of Broadcasting: RIAS Berlin, 1946–1986* (Bonn, FRG: USIS, 1986); Harold Zink, *United States in Germany, 1944–1955* (Princeton, NJ: Van Nostrand, 1957).

RADIO LIBERATION. *See* Radio Liberty

RADIO LIBERTY. Radio Liberation, later renamed Radio Liberty, was formally conceived, organizationally, in Delaware on January 18, 1951, with the incorporation of the "American Committee for Freedom of the Peoples of the USSR, Inc." (sometimes called the American Committee for Liberation from Bolshevism, Inc.), the forerunner of the Radio Liberty Committee, Inc., which was established by the CIA to run a broadcasting service to the Soviet Union that was independent of the **U.S. Information Agency**. Like **Radio Free Europe**, it was created by former **Office of Strategic Services**' officers with secret CIA funding. Broadcasts began on March 1, 1953, in Munich, on a very small scale. Basic policy called for the "liberation" of the Soviet Union from the "tyranny of Bolshevism," a policy that changed in later years from "liberation" to "liberalization" as conditions in the Soviet Union improved under the impact of de-Stalinization.

RFE and Radio Liberty continued to be supported by the CIA until June 1971, when its alleged undercover involvement was exposed during protests against secrecy and covert operations that accompanied American involvement in Vietnam. In August 1972 President Richard Nixon appointed a Presidential Study Commission on International Broadcasting that found that RFE and Radio Liberty, with their flow of "free and uncensored information to peoples deprived of it" actually contributed to a climate of détente. In 1973, the two radio stations were placed under the jurisdiction of the Board for International Broadcasting.

Clinton administration officials wanted to save $210 million annually by closing Radio Free Europe and Radio Liberty, but the two stations felt they still provided a service, even though Communism's threat was diminished, by broadcasting news services that formerly Communist countries would transmit if they could. The administration consolidated U.S. international broadcasting operations with Public Law 103-236 under USIA's new Broadcasting Board of Governors (BBG), which included the VOA, Radio Free Europe, and Radio Liberty. The law maintains RFE/RL's status as a private corporation funded by grants from the BBG. Presently, Radio Liberty broadcasts to Russia and to the New Independent States (NIS) 24 hours a day in Russian and in other languages of the NIS republics, including Belarus, Kazakhstan, Kyrgyzstan, Tajikistan, and Turkmenistan.

In 1994, the United States International Broadcasting Act, Title III of the Foreign Relations Authorization Act, Fiscal Years 1994 and 1995 (Public Law 103-236), established the International Broadcasting Bureau (IBB) within the United States Information Agency (USIA) and created a presidentially appointed Broadcasting Board of Governors (BBG) with jurisdiction over all civilian U.S. government international broadcasting. The law consolidated VOA, **Worldnet**

TV, Radio and **TV Marti,** the Office of Engineering and Technical Services, along with RFE/RL and a new **Radio Free Asia.**

FURTHER READING: James Critchlow, *Radio Hole-in-the-Head/Radio Liberty: An Insider's Story of Cold War Broadcasting* (Washington, DC: American University, 1995); William E. Daugherty, ed., *Psychological Warfare Casebook* (Baltimore: Johns Hopkins; published for Operations Research Office, Johns Hopkins University, 1958); Sig Mickelson, *America's Other Voices: Radio Free Europe and Radio Liberty* (New York: Praeger, 1983); Arch Puddington, *Broadcasting Freedom: The Cold War Triumph of Radio Free Europe and Radio Liberty* (Lexington: University of Kentucky, 2000); Gene Sosin, *Sparks of Liberty: An Insider's Memoir of Radio Liberty* (University Park: Pennsylvania State University, 1999); U.S. Presidential Study Commission on International Radio Broadcasting, *The Right to Know; a Report* (Washington, DC: Government Printing Office, 1973?).

RADIO MARTI. The Office of Cuba Broadcasting, which operates Radio Marti and **Television Marti,** was created by the Radio Broadcasting to Cuba Act of 1983 (Public Law 98-111) to focus on Cuban domestic and international news and information that is not reported by the government-controlled media. According to the legislation, Radio Marti programming with its mixture of Spanish-language news, features, cultural, and entertainment programming to its Cuban audience, must follow all **Voice of America** standards; programs must be objective, accurate, and well balanced.

Radio Marti went on the air on May 20, 1985, but it is now considered virtually a Cuban exile propaganda organ paid for by U.S. taxpayers with its programming

Office of Cuba Broadcasting's (OCB) youth-oriented program, *High Voltaje,* with hosts Miguel Vazquez (left) and Victor Gonzalez. OCB incorporates both Radio and TV Marti. (*Source:* IBB publication, Broadcasting Board of Governors, 2002)

allegedly controlled by the Cuban-American Foundation. In 1994, Radio Marti introduced "live coverage of special events in the U.S. and around the world that directly affect Cuba and its citizens," such as hearings held by Congressman Charles B. Rangel (D-NY) to lift the U.S. embargo against Cuba and speeches by Latin American heads of state at the Summit of the Americas in Miami.

In 1996, it was announced that Radio Marti was moving from Washington, D.C., to Miami, Florida, without congressional hearings and in contravention of the station's original mandate, despite accusations of mismanagement that bordered on criminal misconduct. Radio Marti broadcasts seven days a week, nonstop, and broadcasts more than 70 programs weekly.

FURTHER READING: International Broadcasting Bureau, *U.S. International Broadcasting Chronology* (IBB Web site: http://www.ibb.gov); Handouts from IBB Public Liaison Office; Wayne S. Smith, "Pirating Radio Marti," *Nation* 264, no.3 (January 27, 1997): 21–22; U.S. Congress. Senate. Committee on Foreign Relations, *Radio Broadcasting to Cuba;* hearings, 97th Congress, 2d Session (Washington, DC: Government Printing Office, 1982–1983); Kyu Ho Youm, "The Radio and TV Marti Controversy: A Re-Examination," *Gazette* 48 (1991): 95–103.

RADIO SAWA. Arabic language service created by the **Voice of America** in the aftermath of the September 11, 2001, terrorist attacks; it made its debut in spring of 2002, targeted to 18- to 30-year-old listeners. Radio Sawa replaced

Radio Sawa's Web page.

VOA's former Arabic Service as an AM/FM station that combines sanitized American and Arab pop songs with pro-American news broadcasts from Beirut to Kuwait City, but the station will not play hard rock, country, or anything that is considered "political music." Sawa means "together" in Arabic, and it is seen by the Bush administration as its principal means of communicating with the Arab world.

FURTHER READING: Michael Dobbs, "America's Arabic Voice," *Washington Post*, March 24, 2003: C1, C2; International Broadcasting Bureau, *U.S. International Broadcasting Chronology* (IBB Web site: http://www.ibb.gov); Handouts from IBB Public Liaison Office; Eli Lake, "Pop Psychology," *Washington Post*, August 4, 2002: B3.

RADIO SWAN. Radio Swan was CIA's first major anti-Castro radio station; it began broadcasting on May 17, 1960, to Cuba and the Caribbean. The broadcasting station was part of a covert action program approved by President Eisenhower to replace the Castro regime. Within the propaganda framework of that program, an important objective was to create and to utilize a high-powered medium- and short-wave radio station. The CIA was asked to provide such a station within 60 days and outside the continental United States. The station was located on Swan Island off the coast of Honduras and was fronted by a private U.S. company. Fidel Castro denounced Radio Swan in a speech before the United Nations General Assembly on September 26, 1960, and alleged that the United States was behind the station. The next month, the U.S. Department of State publicly denied any official involvement with the station. In 1961, it was renamed Radio Americas as the Kennedy administration made a renewed effort to overthrow Cuba's revolutionary government; it kept up the pressure with continued propaganda operations. The station ceased operations in May 1968, but limited broadcasts to Cuba continued with the **Voice of America**.

FURTHER READING: Jon Elliston, ed., *Psywar on Cuba: The Declassified History of U.S. Anti-Castro Propaganda* (Melbourne, Victoria, Australia and New York: Ocean Press, 1999).

REAGAN, RONALD WILSON (February 6, 1911–June 5, 2004). Ronald Wilson Reagan was born in Tampico, Illinois, the son of John Edward Reagan and Nelle Wilson. After he graduated from Eureka College (1932) with a B.A., he was hired as sports announcer for the University of Iowa over WOC, a small radio station in Davenport, Iowa, then with WHO, in Des Moines, where he announced Chicago Cubs baseball games. While covering the Cubs at spring training on Catalina Island, he was discovered by a Warner Bros. scout and signed to a film contract. He appeared in several films, most notably *Brother Rat* (1938), *Dark Victory* (1939) *Knute Rockne, All-American* (1940), and *Kings Row* (1941). In 1940, he married actress Jane Wyman, who divorced him in 1948. Four years later, he wed Nancy Davis. Reagan's political instincts sharpened during his terms as president of the Screen Actors' Guild (1947–1952, 1959–1960) and as host and performer for *General Electric Theater*, as he shifted from liberalism to conservatism. He turned Republican in 1962. Reagan was elected governor of California in 1966; he served two terms (1967–1975), then made his first unsuccessful attempt for the presidency in 1976. He lost the nomination to incumbent Gerald R. Ford, but he was quite successful four years later, winning a landslide victory over incumbent Jimmy Carter.

As president, Reagan was dubbed the "Great Communicator" from his knowledge and experience with radio, film, and television media. His ability to communicate with an audience was one of his greatest strengths as president, and he enjoyed the best press coverage of any president since John F. Kennedy. The Reagan administration was especially notable for bringing down the Soviet Empire. Helped by his immense popularity at home, Reagan took full advantage of U.S. propaganda overseas, beginning with the appointment of his friend, Charles Z. Wick (1917–), as director of the **U.S. Information Agency** and initiating or supporting **Radio Marti** broadcasts to Fidel Castro's Cuba, **Worldnet** television satellite network, which linked U.S. embassies globally and permitted interactive discussions between Washington policy makers, *Let Poland Be Poland* to support the Solidarity movement in Poland, and programs to counter **Soviet active measures, disinformation**, and **forgeries**. Reagan's Strategic Defense Initiative (SDI), nicknamed "Star Wars" by the Democrats, had a large propaganda component to it as did Reagan administration efforts to aid anti-Communist regimes and guerrilla movements in Central America. An interagency committee was the **Active Measures Working Group**. After Reagan left office in 1989, he returned to California, but in 1994 he announced publicly that he was suffering from Alzheimer's disease. He died in Los Angeles.

See also **Voice of America**

FURTHER READING: Lou Cannon, *President Reagan: The Role of a Lifetime* (New York: Simon and Schuster, 1991); Nicholas J. Cull, David Culbert, and David Welch, *Propaganda and Mass Persuasion: A Historical Encyclopedia, 1500 to the Present* (Santa Barbara, CA and Denver, CO: ABC-Clio, 2003); Robert Dallek, *Ronald Reagan: The Politics of Symbolism* (Cambridge, MA: Harvard University, 1999).

RED CHANNELS. *Red Channels: The Report of Communist Influence in Radio and Television* was first published in June 1950 by the same group, American Business Consultants, former FBI agents, that published the anti-Communist newsletter, *Counterattack*. The paperback book, with its graphic cover of a red hand behind a microphone, listed persons employed in the entertainment industry who had lent their names to fronts for the Communist Party. The information was taken from publicly available sources, and the purpose of the compilation was threefold. First, it was to show how the Communists have been able to carry out their plan of infiltration of the radio and television industry; second, to indicate the extent to which many prominent actors and artists have been inveigled to lend their names, according to these public records, to organizations espousing Communist causes, whether they actually believe in, sympathize with, or even recognize the cause advanced; and last, to discourage actors and artists from naively lending their names to Communist organizations or causes in the future. Coincidentally, the book was published the same month as the North Korean invasion of South Korea. Strong anti-Communist feelings among the American people resulted in many entertainers losing their jobs without the differentiations made by the editors of the book, who also wrote that "in screening personnel every safeguard must be used to protect innocents and genuine liberals from being unjustly labeled." Only five years before, entertainers from Germany and the occupied countries were similarly blacklisted. The "political screening" lasted for years, and the accused were further blacklisted by advertisers, by advertising agencies, and by broadcasters.

FURTHER READING: Mark Goodson, "'If I'd Stood Up Earlier...'," *New York Times Magazine* (January 13, 1991): 22–23, 39–40, 43; *Red Channels: The Report of Communist Influence in Radio and Television* (New York: American Business Consultants, 1950).

REED, JOHN (October 22, 1887–October 19, 1920). Journalist, poet, and revolutionist, John Reed was the author of an eyewitness account of the Russian Revolution, *Ten Days That Shook the World* (1919). He was born in Portland, Oregon, the son of a prosperous businessman who was also a (Theodore) Roosevelt liberal, and graduated from Harvard (1910). He wrote for *American Magazine*, published poetry, joined the staff of **The Masses**, worked with the International Workers of the World to support the silk workers' strike in Paterson, New Jersey (1913), for which he was jailed, then organized a "strike pageant" in New York City's Madison Square Garden. He went to Mexico to cover its revolution for *Metropolitan Magazine*, where he rode with Pancho Villa for four months; his articles were collected as *Insurgent Mexico* (1914). He was next dispatched to Europe by *Metropolitan* to cover the front during World War I; his reports were published as *The War in Eastern Europe* (1916). In 1917, Reed was in Petrograd when the Bolsheviks seized power; he attended all the meetings, talked with everyone he could, and befriended Lenin. He was working for the Russian bureau of propaganda when he died of typhus in Moscow; he was buried in the Kremlin. His wife was Louise Bryant, another journalist, whom he married in 1917. The couple were the subject of the 1981 film *Reds*. Reed's uncollected articles, speeches, and letters were compiled as *John Reed and the Russian Revolution* (1992). In his honor, **John Reed Clubs**, affiliated with the Communist Party, were established in many major American cities.

FURTHER READING: David C. Duke, *John Reed* (Boston: Twayne, 1987); Barbara Gelb, *So Short a Time: A Biography of John Reed and Louise Bryant* (New York: Norton, 1973); Richard O'Connor and Dale L. Walker, *Lost Revolutionary* (New York: Harcourt, Brace and World, 1967).

REED, REBECCA. *See* **Catholic Church**

REGIONAL SERVICE CENTERS. To ensure more prompt and efficient production of American printed material, a regional production center (RPC), later called regional service centers (RSC), was established in Manila (1950) to serve the needs of the many Far East outposts of the U.S. information program; RPCs were later opened in Beirut, Mexico City, New Delhi, and Vienna by the U.S.

Information Agency (USIA). Administrative practice after World War II favored decentralizing propaganda while concentrating printing establishments in a few centers (London, Paris, Manila, Washington) not too far from the areas where the leaflets, pamphlets, and booklets were produced and where they would be disseminated after they were printed. Contract officers dealt with commercial printers and, to a lesser extent, with the Government Printing Office (GPO). In 1950, the drive for mass leadership, President Truman's **Campaign of Truth,** and the onset of the Korean Conflict changed the service's printing needs because the United States planned to distribute quantities of material in the Far East and needed suitable printing facilities. The outbreak of war caused the United States. Information Service to change from showing "a full and fair picture of America" to a hard-hitting psychological offensive against communism.

The information service already had authority to print abroad under the Smith-Mundt Act (1948), which provided exemption from a 1919 law requiring that all federal printing be done through GPO. Authority for an overseas printing operation was implicit in the annual legislative appropriations. One month after the Korean war began, State requested a $200,000 supplemental appropriation from Congress to open a printing plant in Bombay. Because it was wartime, Congress approved the funding for a center in Manila, not Bombay, and the Far East Regional Production Center, as the new Manila operation was called, soon opened. Forty-five days after the first training class, planes dropped leaflets on Huk hideouts in the Philippine mountains, which guaranteed safe passage to those who surrendered. Other leaflets, explaining the U.S. role in the Korean War, were spread throughout Asia. The success of Manila led to another operation in Beirut (1953), which provided editorial and printing services to USIS posts in Africa, in the Near East, in Europe, and in all French language countries. In 1962, a third RSC was opened in Mexico City to serve USIS installations in the American Republics, in Spain, and in Portugal.

During the **Vietnam Conflict,** RSC Manila ran an around-the-clock operation that produced millions of leaflets, magazines, and pamphlets, many for the Defense Department. By 1977, Manila and Mexico City were producing almost all USIA publications; the Beirut plant was closed by the civil war in Lebanon and its printing transferred to Manila, which remains the most important RSC. Cost comparisons for specific printing jobs reflected substantial savings at RPCs over local GPO printing costs. In addition to overseas posts, all Agency domestic elements now utilize the cost-saving advantages of RSC Manila's printing services, no matter where the material will eventually be distributed. Today, budget cuts have forced the Bureau of Public Diplomacy, U.S. Department of State, which replaced USIA in 1999, to combine some of its regional production centers; they are now in Vienna and Manila.

FURTHER READING: Handouts from USIA and the U.S. Department of State; Howard Oiseth, *Way It Was: USIA's Press and Publications Service, 1935–77* (Washington, DC: USIA, 1977); Earl J. Wilson, "The Far East Regional Production Center," in *Psychological Warfare Casebook*, ed. William E. Daugherty (Baltimore: Johns Hopkins; published for Operations Research Office, Johns Hopkins University, 1958).

RELIGIOUS PROPAGANDA. *See* Anti-Semitic Propaganda; Catholic Church; Holocaust Denial; Iraq

REVISIONISM AND PROPAGANDA. *See* Barnes, Harry Elmer

REVOLUTIONARY WAR, AMERICAN. *See* War of American Independence Propaganda

RIEGEL, OSCAR WERTHOLD (1902–August 22, 1997). Born in Reading, Pennsylvania, Oscar Riegel was a graduate of the University of Wisconsin (1924) and had a master's degree in American literature from Columbia University. He was a journalist with the Paris bureau of the *Chicago Tribune* and the *New York Daily News* and taught English at Dartmouth College. Riegel was considered an authority on propaganda, an interest he acquired in Europe between the two world wars, and continued this as a journalism professor at Washington and Lee University (1930–1973). By World War II, Riegel was already a nationally known propaganda expert and took a leave from teaching to become the principal propaganda analyst for the **Office of War Information**. He was acknowledged as one of the first people to foresee propaganda as a dominant force in the twentieth century. Riegel collected propaganda materials from Asia and from Europe, including over 2,500 political posters from both World Wars, and German posters of the Hitler-Goebbels period and from postwar election campaigns. In 1992, a set of **posters** from his World War II collection was produced and distributed as a line of trading cards by Tuff Stuff. Riegel's publications include "The Editorial Writer as Propagandist," *Masthead* (Winter 1980–81); *Analysis of the Contents of Some Virginia Daily Newspapers* (1932), a report for the Committee on Public Opinion, Virginia Social Science Association, that he chaired; and *Mobilizing for Chaos; the Story of the New Propaganda* (1934). Riegel married Jane Butterworth; he died in Lexington, Virginia.

FURTHER READING: Obituary, *New York Times* (August 26, 1997); U.S. Information Agency, *Manual for the Members of the Executive Reserve of the U.S. Information Agency* (Washington, DC: USIA, 1962).

THE RIVER. **Pare Lorentz** made his second film, *The River* (Farm Security Administration, 1937), about the Mississippi and the havoc it could wreak. Its working title was originally, *Highway to the Sea* but this was later simplified. Unlike his earlier experience with *The Plow That Broke the Plains*, *The River* was considered Lorentz's masterpiece and a "documentary film poem" for its breathtaking images, which included floods, levee building, and a Tennessee Valley Authority sequence. Upon its general release, it was well received, and it won the top award in the documentary category at the International Cinema Exposition (1938), but some critics still labeled the film "**New Deal** propaganda."

FURTHER READING: Pare Lorentz, *FDR's Moviemaker: Memoirs and Scripts* (Reno: University of Nevada, 1992); Richard T. MacCann, *The People's Films: A Political History of U.S. Government Motion Pictures* (New York: Hastings House, 1973); Robert L. Snyder, *Pare Lorentz and the Documentary Film* (Reno: University of Nevada, 1968).

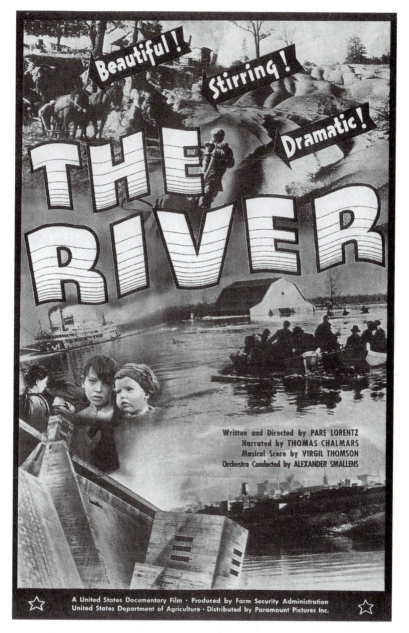

Poster for *The River*, a film by the Resettlement Administration, produced by the Farm Security Administration, U.S. Department of Agriculture. (*Source:* National Archives; reproduced in Bruce I. Bustard, *A New Deal for the Arts* [Washington, DC: National Archives and Records Administration, in association with University of Washington Press, 1997])

ROBESON, PAUL LEROY (April 9, 1898–January 23, 1976). African-American actor and singer who became a prominent American propagandist for the Soviet Union as well as a sharp critic of American racism. He graduated from Rutgers and the Columbia University law school. After briefly practicing law, he turned to acting and singing professionally. After various roles, Robeson performed the leads of *All God's Chillun Got Wings* and Eugene O'Neill's *The Emperor Jones*. He starred in a film version of the O'Neill play (1933), which was denounced by the African-American press when it was released for its portrayal of the protagonist who rises from Pullman porter to dictator of a Caribbean island. This was considered the first instance of an African American getting top billing in an American film. Another motion picture success was *Showboat* (1936), which Robeson performed in several productions. He was proud of his roles in *Song of Freedom* (1936) and *The Proud Valley* (1940), but Robeson resented the stereotyping and racial slights suffered by blacks in the film industry, and he demanded more-positive acting roles.

During the 1930s, Robeson lived most of the time abroad to avoid racial discrimination, and he returned to the United States only for film roles and concert appearances. After a concert tour in the Soviet Union (1934), Robeson began to spend extended periods of time in Moscow, where he became politically active in opposing fascism, imperialism, and racism. In return, he allowed his image to be used by Stalin for propaganda purposes.

When World War II started, Robeson was forced to return to the United States, but he continued to fight racism and promote the Soviet Union. When he tried to travel to the Soviet Union in 1950, the State Department revoked his passport, but he successfully sued to have it restored, which the State Department did in 1958; after that, he freely traveled abroad. While living in Russia, a country with which he claimed a strong allegiance, he won the Stalin Prize (1952) and had a mountain named after him. In later concerts and public appearances, he was accused of putting Communist propaganda into his songs and speeches.

On June 12, 1956, he was summoned before the House Committee on Un-American Activities but refused to cooperate and to admit any Communist affiliations; he constantly invoked the Fifth Amendment and was not allowed to read his prepared statement. He was heavily criticized for his actions, blacklisted by the entertainment industry, denounced by the black and white press, repudiated by civil rights organizations, and attacked by congressional committees and government agencies. Robeson's autobiography, *Here I Stand* (1958), reaffirmed his admiration for the Soviet Union. After his death, the Communist Party announced that Robeson had been a secret party member.

FURTHER READING: Eric Bentley, ed., *Thirty Years of Treason: Excerpts from Hearings Before the House Committee on Un-American Activities, 1938–1968* (New York: Viking, 1971); Sheila T. Boyle and Andrew Bunie, *Paul Robeson: The Years of Promise and Achievement* (Amherst: University of Massachusetts, 2001); Ann Hornaday, "Worthy or Not, 'The Emperor' is Restored," *Washington Post*, August 31, 2002: C1, C5; U.S. Congress. House. Committee on Un-American Activities, *Investigation of the Unauthorized Use of United States Passports*; hearings; 84th Congress, 2d Session [85th Congress, 1st Session] (Washington, DC: Government Printing Office, 1956).

ROBISON, JOHN. *See Protocols of the Learned Elders of Zion*

ROCKEFELLER, NELSON. *See* Coordinator of Inter-American Affairs; Rockefeller Letter

ROCKEFELLER COMMITTEE. *See* President's Advisory Committee on Government Organization

ROCKEFELLER LETTER. Extensive forgery presented as a private letter from Nelson A. Rockefeller to President Dwight D. Eisenhower in which Rockefeller was portrayed as the advocate of a "bolder program of aid to under-developed countries," as a cover for what the East Germany press called "supercolonialism" ("superkolonialismus"). Its aim was to discredit the U.S. commitment to the removal of the old colonial powers from their involvements in Africa and in Asia. The document first appeared on February 15, 1957, in the East German daily, *Neues Deutschland*, and circulated throughout the world during what was termed the "Camp David" period of East–West cordiality (1959–1960); it later appeared on Radio Moscow, in *Pravda* (Soviet party organ), on Radio Hanoi, on Radio Beijing, in the Czechoslovak domestic press, and in the official news agency of the People's Republic of China. The letter was exposed as a fake by its use of language considered totally inappropriate for a Republican politician, especially one with Rockefeller's background and education.

FURTHER READING: Herbert Romerstein, "Disinformation as a KGB Weapon in the Cold War," paper prepared for a Conference on Germany and Intelligence Organizations: The Last Fifty Years in Review, Akademie fur Politische Bildung Tutzing [Germany] (Washington: Unpublished, 1999).

ROCKWELL, GEORGE LINCOLN (1918–August 25, 1967). World War II Navy veteran and a strong anti-Communist, Rockwell was a natural showman with a background in advertising. By 1959, Rockwell was an overt Nazi who organized a following of storm troopers (World Union of National Socialists) from his headquarters, Hatemonger Hill, Arlington, Virginia. He popularized the insidious anti-Semitic propaganda tool of Holocaust denial and other Nazi atrocities within the racist right and introduced its precepts to the American public. Rockwell believed that Jews were behind the Communist conspiracy in the United States and that the world was under Jewish control, two constant themes at the public rallies he organized on the National Mall in Washington, D.C., but he soon added Negroes and Catholics to this theory. Rockwell preached "white power" and advocated a confrontational style that alienated many people. In 1966, Rockwell and his supporters challenged Martin Luther King in Chicago, but he was assassinated the next year by a fellow **American Nazi Party** member. Rockwell was succeeded by Frank Collin, who led the American Nazi Party until he was jailed for child molestation.

FURTHER READING: Notes from *Nazi America: A Secret History* (TV documentary on The History Channel, 1/21/00); Frederick J. Simonelli, *American Fuehrer: George Lincoln Rockwell and the American Nazi Party* (Urbana and Chicago: University of Illinois, 1999).

ROCKWELL, NORMAN PERCEVAL (February 3, 1894–November 8, 1978). One of the best-known American artists who has been critically jeered but enormously popular for his renditions of common people and situations. Rockwell was born in New York City, where he studied at the Art Students League. He began his professional career illustrating children's books and began painting covers for the *Saturday Evening Post* (1916); by 1929 he was the magazine's premier illustrator, and his covers caused magazine sales to increase. In 1925, Rockwell started illustrating his annual picture for the Boy Scouts of America, at no fee, that were published as *Boys' Life* covers and other Scout materials regularly until 1976. Norman Rockwell's "reverent portraits of America's youthful ideal" included his 1944 patriotic, "We, Too, Have a Job to Do" and the 1973 "From Concord to Tranquility," in which Boy Scouts were highlighted with a Revolutionary War figure and with astronaut Neil Armstrong, a former Boy Scout and the first man to walk on the moon.

During World War II, the *Post* published Rockwell's series, **The Four Freedoms** (Want, Worship, Fear, Speech), inspired by President Franklin Roosevelt's 1941 speech, and perhaps his best-known and most reproduced work. Its heavy propaganda value promoted "all the American virtues" in an enormously successful government War Bond drive that was built around The Four Freedoms after their publication in the *Post* (February and March 1943).

A November 24, 1951 cover, "Saying Grace," depicting a grandmother and her grandson bowing their heads in a restaurant, was voted by *Post* readers as the most popular of Rockwell's covers, but by the early 1960s, his cover ideas were no longer acceptable to new *Post* editors, who wanted to refocus it as a "sophisticated, muckraking magazine." Rockwell's last cover was Jacqueline Kennedy inside the October 26, 1963 issue. He followed this with an assignment from *Look* magazine that resulted in the powerful portrait, "The Problem We All Live With," of an African-American child being escorted to school by four U.S. marshals in the 1950s, but he had few opportunities to repeat this success although he remained well paid and active. His last published work was the cover of *American Artist* (July 1976). Rockwell, who married three times, died in Stockbridge, Massachusetts, the site of the Norman Rockwell Museum. His publications include his autobiography, *My Adventures as an Illustrator* (1960), and *How I Make a Picture* (1979).

FURTHER READING: Henry Allen, "Brave, Trustworthy, Loyal, Obedient," *Washington Post*, April 26, 1996: BI, B6; Sandy Coleman, "Seeing Rockwell, Seeing Yourself," *Boston Globe*, December 25, 1994: A25, A31–A32; "Norman Rockwell: An American Portrait" [Video, 1987].

ROMAN CATHOLIC CHURCH. *See* **Catholic Church**

ROOSEVELT, FRANKLIN (January 30, 1882–April 12, 1945). Franklin Delano Roosevelt was a master propagandist, with considerable rhetorical skills, who led the American people through the Great Depression of the 1930s and World War II. Roosevelt was born in Hyde Park, New York, the son of James Roosevelt and Sara Delano. After he graduated from Harvard, he entered Columbia Law School but never practiced. In March 1905, he married his cousin, Anna Eleanor Roosevelt, the niece of President Theodore Roosevelt, a personal idol of the young Franklin. During **World War I**, Roosevelt served as Assistant Secretary of the Navy.

Roosevelt was elected governor of New York State in 1928; four year later, he won election as the 32nd president of the United States. His first important propaganda initiative was the **New Deal** programs he created under the National Industrial Recovery Act (1933), such as the Works Progress Administration, with its controversial Federal Arts Project and Federal Theater Project. He encouraged **Pare Lorentz** in his controversial work as a New Deal documentary filmmaker (*The Plow That Broke the Plains, The River*) but the New Deal was never a coherent propaganda effort; it moved in many directions and attempted many things.

With the beginning of World War II in Europe, Roosevelt utilized propaganda more effectively. An early effort was the **Four Freedoms** speech (1941) he gave at the opening of the 77th Congress on January 6, 1941, which later became a pamphlet and a series of famous paintings by **Norman Rockwell**. With the approach of U.S. involvement in the war, Roosevelt established several information-gathering agencies, such as the **Coordinator of Information** (later the **Office of Strategic Services**, a predecessor to the **Central Intelligence Agency**) and the **Office of Facts and Figures**, to make war intelligence available to officials who needed it. To counter Nazi propaganda efforts in the American Republics, he created the **Coordinator of Inter-American Affairs** (CIAA) in 1940. As Assistant Secretary of the Navy, he saw the control that **George Creel** had as director of the **Committee on Public Information** and the zeal with which CPI carried out its World War I mission. For this reason, he was hesitant about establishing a full-scale wartime propaganda agency but when he did create the **Office of War Information** (OWI), he considerably weakened the authority he gave to OWI and to its director, **Elmer Davis**.

President Franklin D. Roosevelt (1933–1945), who created the World War II proaganda agencies, Office of War Information, and Coordinator of Inter-American Affairs and established the Voice of America. (*Source:* Voice of America)

Roosevelt was a superb proponent of the radio, which he used quite successfully to bring his ideas to the American people. His "fireside chats" were intimate and comforting. With the outbreak of the war in Europe, Roosevelt told the American people that if England were defeated, America would confront a united Nazi Europe as her enemy and that Germany would start to conquer South America. To strengthen the "war of words," he established the **Voice of America** in February 1942 as the U.S. government's international broadcasting medium; it complemented the lesser known U.S. government broadcasting efforts, which were already transmitting to the American Republics under CIAA guidance. Roosevelt was also effective in his use of the major Hollywood studios to produce propaganda films, such as *Mission to Moscow* and *Mrs. Miniver*, and documentaries, most notably the **Why We Fight** series, to support the war effort and to gain public support for his policies. Roosevelt died in Warm Springs, Georgia.

See also **Buenos Aires Convention for Promotion of Inter-American Cultural Relations; Goebbels and His Propaganda Efforts Against the Allies; Home Front Propaganda; Libraries; Rosie the Riveter**

FURTHER READING: Ernest B. Furgurson, "Back Channels," *Washingtonian* 31, no. 9 (June 1996): 56–59, 102–105, 110–114; Richard W. Steele, *Propaganda in an Open Society: The Roosevelt Administration and the Media, 1933–1941* (Westport, CT: Greenwood, 1985).

ROSIE THE RIVETER. Classic propaganda symbol and slogan during World War II when it was used for the representation of women who took up men's jobs while they were in the armed forces. Jobs were supposed to be temporary; when war was over and men came home, women were to return to their traditional homemaking roles as wives and mothers. The original drawing, titled "We Can Do It" by Howard Miller, was done for the War Production Coordinating Committee. As a poster, it was heavily used in the World War II effort and figured prominently in **Office of War Information** (OWI) output. It also became a famous drawing by **Norman Rockwell**, which first appeared on a *Saturday Evening Post* cover in 1943. Decades after the war ended, Rosie the Riveter has become one of the most memorable images of World War II home front propaganda.

See also **Home Front Propaganda; Women as Propaganda Images in Wartime**

FURTHER READING: "A Long Road Home: Remembering World War II," *Washington Post* (July 26, 1995): H7; Leila J. Rupp, *Mobilizing Women for War: German and American Propaganda, 1939–1945* (Princeton, NJ: Princeton University, 1978).

ROYAL AMERICAN MAGAZINE. Royal American Magazine; or, American Monthly Museum, was founded by **Isaiah Thomas** in Boston in January 1774, in a period when no magazine had been published in the American colonies for almost two years. It was discontinued in March 1775 on the eve of the Battle of Lexington, as "all Ranks of men" were thrown into confusion. It was a general magazine (miscellany) that offered articles on agriculture, medicine, education, and religion, as well as fiction, essays, and selections from English publications.

Royal American Magazine totally supported independence ("Huzza! huzza! huzza! huzza! for free America") and among its engravings were three political cartoons by Paul Revere, one showing a half-nude figure of America with restrained wrists and forced to swallow a "bitter draught" (military law, the Boston Port Bill).

FURTHER READING: Amy Janello and Brennon Jones [for the] Magazine Publishers of America [and] American Society of Magazine Editors, *The American Magazine* (New York: Abrams, 1991); Edward W. R. Pitcher, compiler, *The Royal American Magazine, 1774–1775: An Annotated Catalogue* (Lewiston, NY: E. Mellen Press, 2001).

RUMOR. Rumor is very useful in propaganda because its source is not obvious, and it does not depend on a formal communication system for its dissemination. It is very effective if the communicator has an understanding of how the message is likely to be received by members of the target audience. Someone tells the original story but details are omitted as it goes from person to person. Rumors are closely allied with superstitions and whispering campaigns.

During World War II, rumors were part of **psychological warfare** campaigns devised by both sides for the same purpose. As an example, the Germans used rumor in connection with psychological warfare, to discredit Allied propaganda, in connection with intelligence, and to encourage their own population. Specific rumor uses were as divisive propaganda, to induce fear, to engender overconfidence, to enhance the effect of a war of nerves, to discredit Allied propaganda, to increase the credibility of enemy sources, and to aid deception.

See also Baby Parts; Disinformation

FURTHER READING: "The Use of Rumor in Psychological Warfare," in *Psychological Warfare Casebook*, ed. William E. Daugherty (Baltimore: Johns Hopkins; published for Operations Research Office, Johns Hopkins University, 1958).

RUSES. *See* Deception; Disinformation

RUSSIA. *See* **American National Exhibition, Moscow; Brussels Universal and International Exposition (Expo 1958); Cold War; Disinformation; Forgeries; Soviet Active Measures**

S

SABRE FOUNDATION. *See* Books

SAFE CONDUCT PASSES. *See* Leaflets

SCHRAMM, WILBUR LANG (1907–December 27, 1987). Educator, author, and a leading researcher in the field of mass communications, Schramm received his Ph.D. in American history from the University of Iowa (1932), where he taught; other teaching positions were at the University of Illinois and at Stanford before he joined the East-West Center's Institute of Culture and Communication, Honolulu. He was among the first to volunteer to work in the propaganda monitoring agency, **Office of Facts and Figures**. In World War II, he was an editorial director for the **Office of War Information**. In 1947, he became director of the newly created Institute of Communications Research, University of Illinois, the world's first behavioral and social science communication research center. The institute later relocated to Stanford University. Schramm's appointment as the first professor of communications led to the awarding of doctoral degrees in this new field.

In the early 1950s, Schramm was a consultant to the **Voice of America** and its parent agency, the International Information Administration, later the **U.S. Information Agency** (USIA), and he was asked by the U.S. government to study firsthand the North Korean invasion of the South from a propaganda perspective; it resulted in *The Reds Take a City*, with John Riley (1950), along with several articles and book contributions on psychological warfare. He continued this theme in *Four Working Papers on Propaganda Theory* ([Urbana: Institute of Communications Research, University of Illinois] under contract to United States Information Agency, 1955); *Four Theories of the Press* (1952); and essays on **psychological warfare**. For USIA, Schramm prepared *The Process and Effects of Mass Communication* (1954), which was considered a landmark in mass communication theory.

Between 1948 and 1977, Schramm produced almost a book a year (edited or reedited and authored) in addition to articles, book chapters, conference papers, and reports. He was the author of numerous books and articles on communications theory and practice, including *Science of Human Communication* (1963); *Men, Messages, and Media* (1973); and co-author, *The Nature of Psychological Warfare* (1953). He edited *Communications in Modern Society* (1948), *Mass Communications* (1949), and *Communication and Change* (1976).

FURTHER READING: Daniel Lerner and Lyle M. Nelson, eds., *Communication Research: A Half Century Appraisal* (Honolulu: Published for the East-West Center by University Press of Hawaii, 1977); Emile G. McAnany, "Wilbur Schramm, 1907–1987: Roots of the Past, Seeds of the Present," *Journal of Communication* 38, no. 4 (Autumn 1988): 109–122.

SCHWEITZER-PINOCHET LETTER. In July 1985, an Italian journalist received a copy of a letter signed with the name of General Robert Schweitzer, the head of the Inter-American Defense Board. The letter was a forgery addressed to

INTER-AMERICAN DEFENSE-BOARD
2600 - 16th Street, N.W.
Washington, D.C. 20441

25 de febrero de 1985

Su Excelencia
Augusto Pinochet Ugarte
Presidente de la República de Chile
Cap. Gral. del Ejército
Palacio de la Moneda
Santiago

Estimado Sr. Presidente:

Me complace informar a Su Excelencia que la entrega a Chile del nuevo armamento solicitado será decidida en el más corto plazo. Me ha causado agrado el saber, a través del Sr.Motley, que usted ha mostrado vivo interés por ampliar nuestra cooperación en el terreno militar. Estimamos su profunda comprensión de las particularidades de la nueva situación internacional y de las iniciativas del presidente Reagan, encauzadas a fortalecer nuestra capacidad defensiva común.

Quisiera asegurar a Su Excelencia que seguirá usted contando con nuestro decidido apoyo en sus esfuerzos por fortalecer la libertad y la democracia en Chile.

Con respecto a nuestras acciones conjuntas en América Central, quisiera sugerirle la conveniencia de que las primeras unidades chilenas sean trasladadas a El Salvador y Honduras ya en marzo. Nuestros representantes en dichos países recibirán instrucciones dentro de dos semanas. Junto con su representante trataremos los demás problemas de nuestra cooperación en una de las próximas reuniones de la JID.

Con los mejores testimonios de mi más alta consideración y estima personal hacia Su Excelencia, saluda a usted

Muy atentamente,

Robert L Schweitzer
ROBERT L. SCHWEITZER
Lieutenant General, U.S. Army
Presidente

(Continued)

```
                    C-XX 8 (NOTE:  FIRST TWO NUMBERS NOT LEGIBLE)
 INTER-AMERICAN DEFENSE BOARD
 2500 16TH STREET, N.W.
 WASHINGTTON, D.C., 20441
 YOUR EXCELLENCY
 AUGUSTO PINOCHET UGARTE
 PRESIDENT OF THE REPUBLIC OF CHILE
 CAP. GRAL. OF THE ARMY
 PALACIO DE LA MONEDA
 SANTIAGO
 ESTEEMED MR. PRESIDENT:

     I AM HAPPY TO INFORM YOUR EXCELLENCY THAT THE DELIVERY
 TO CHILE OF THE NEW ARMAMENT REQUESTED WILL BE DECIDED VERY
 SHORTLY.  IT HAS PLEASED ME TO KNOW, VIA MR. MOTLEY, THAT YOU
 HAVE SHOWN A STRONG INTEREST IN BROADENING OUR COOPERATION IN
 THE MILITARY AREA.  WE ESTEEM YOUR PROFOUND UNDERSTANDING OF
 THE PECULIARITIES OF THE NEW INTERNATIONAL SITUATION AND
 THE INITIATIVES OF PRESIDENT REAGAN, WHICH AIM AT STRENGTHENING
 OUR COMMON DEFENSIVE CAPACITY.

     I WOULD LIKE TO ASSURE YOUR EXCELLENCY THAT YOU WILL
 CONTINUE TO HAVE OUR DECIDED SUPPORT IN YOUR EFFORTS TO

 STRENGTHEN LIBERTY AND DEMOCRACY IN CHILE.

     WITH RESPECT TO OUR JOINT ACTIONS IN CENTRAL AMERICA, I
 WOULD LIKE TO SUGGEST TO YOU THAT IT WOULD BE CONVENIENT THAT
 THE FIRST CHILEAN UNITS BE TRANSFERRED TO EL SALVADOR AND
 HONDURAS BY MARCH.  OUR REPRESENTATIVES IN SAID COUNTRIES WILL
 RECEIVE INSTRUCTIONS WITHIN TWO WEEKS.  TOGETHER WITH YOUR
 REPRESENTATIVE WE WILL DEAL WITH THE OTHER PROBLEMS OF OUR
 COOPERATION IN ONE OF THE NEXT MEETINGS OF THE JID.

     WITH THE GREATEST OATH OF MY HIGHEST CONSIDERATION AND
 PERSONAL ESTEEM TOWARDS YOUR EXCELLENCY, YOU ARE GREETED

             VERY ATTENTIVELY BY

             (SIGNATURE:  ROBERT L. SCHWIETZER)
             ROBERT L. SCHWIETZER
             LIEUTENANT GENERAL, U.S. ARMY
             PRESIDENT
```

Copy of alleged communication to Chilean President Augusto Pinochet Ugarte from the Inter-American Defense Board president, Lt. Gen. Robert Schweitzer, regarding a proported movement of Chilean troops to El Salvador and Honduras. Two versions are shown: the original in Spanish with the English translation. (*Source:* U.S. Department of State, *Active Measures: A Report on the Substance and Process of Anti-U.S. Disinformation and Propaganda Campaigns* [Washington, DC: The Department, 1986])

President Pinochet of Chile asking him to provide troops to fight on behalf of the United States in Central America. The journalist contacted the U.S. Embassy and within the day received evidence that the letter was a forgery. He did not write a story based on the letter. A few days later, however, another Italian press service ran a story datelined Mexico City based on the letter. When they were advised it was a forgery, they investigated and discovered that the letter had been provided to one of their writers by the public relations man for the Guatemalan insurgency, which is supported by Cuba and Nicaragua. The news service ran an expose of the forgery, attributing it to the Cubans and Nicaraguans. This incident points to a problem the Soviets have in surfacing forgeries. On the one hand, the common technique of using a plain, unmarked envelope to surface the forgery creates suspicion in the mind of the recipient. On the other hand, the use of a human being to pass on the forgery provides a trail leading back to the forger.

Former USIA Soviet disinformation officer Herbert Romerstein wrote a letter to General Schweitzer on August 16, 1985, providing background on the forgery, then sent a copy of this letter to the U.S. Senate Committee on Foreign Relations, where he testified, for printing in a congressional report on Soviet active measures. Romerstein wrote the word *copy* on the top of the letter then, at the request of a Czech diplomat, Vaclav Zluva, provided him with a copy of this letter. As a precaution, Romerstein drew a line under the word *copy* on the original from which all subsequent copies were made, which made Zluva's letter unique and identifiable.

In August 1986, the *Washington Post* and *U.S. News and World Report* received a forgery in a plain white envelope signed with Romerstein's name. The *Washington Post* called him in; he looked at it, explained the forgery, and the newspaper carried a story on it (August 19, 1986). The forgery was on the letterhead of the U.S. Information Agency and was signed with Romerstein's name. At the top of the forgery was the word "copy" with no line under it. This made it clear that the exemplar for the forgery was the letter Romerstein had given to the Czech. When Romerstein confronted Zluva about this, he admitted sending the exemplar to Prague.

In the forgery, Romerstein was made to appear as if he had organized a USIA effort to spread false stories around the world after the Chernobyl disaster. In fact, the stories were generated by Soviet reluctance to reveal information about the accident. On April 26, 1987, the Soviet publication *Moscow News* admitted, "The formulation: Not for the press, is being used more and more often. Why cannot our press use what is being regularly reported to the International Atomic Energy Agency? There are some who do not understand that rumors and hearsay are generated not by summaries and figures, but by their absence."

FURTHER READING: Herbert Romerstein, "Disinformation as a KGB Weapon in the Cold War," paper prepared for a Conference on Germany and Intelligence Organizations: The Last Fifty Years in Review, Akademie fur Politische Bildung Tutzing [Germany] (1999).

SEVEN ARTS. *See New Masses*

SHANGHAI INCIDENT. *See* Borah-Simpson Letter

SHORT NARRATIVE OF THE HORRID MASSACRE IN BOSTON. In the immediate aftermath of the **Boston Massacre**, the people feared a hostile British reaction. At a town meeting March 12, 1770, James Bowdoin, Joseph Warren, and Samuel Pemberton were appointed as a committee to prepare a particular account of the Boston Massacre. *Short Narrative of the Horrid Massacre in Boston: Perpetrated in the Evening of the Fifth Day of March, 1770, by Soldiers of the XXIXth Regiment, Which, With the XIVth Regiment Were Then Quartered There: With Some Observations on the State of Things Prior to That Catastrophe* was prepared from the report's introduction and 96 depositions taken from eyewitnesses, accepted at a town meeting held March 19, and ordered immediately printed (by Edes and Gill). It was published in England as a propaganda piece that proved highly effective in minimizing the affair in British eyes.

FURTHER READING: Philip Davidson, *Propaganda and the American Revolution, 1763–1783* (New York: Norton, 1973); Thomas I. Fleming, "Verdicts of History I: The Boston Massacre," *American Heritage* 13, no. 1 (1966): 6-11, 102-111.

SIMPLICITY AND REPETITION. One of the common-sense techniques of effective propaganda. It must be easy to understand and to remember. The propagandistic appeal is simple, catchy slogans that are constantly repeated. Hitler wrote that "the intelligence of the masses is small [but] their forgetfulness is great [and] they must be told the same thing a thousand times."

SIX MONTHS IN A CONVENT. See **Catholic Church**

SKYEWAR. *See* **Psychological Warfare**

SLAVERY. *See* **Abolitionist Propaganda**

SMEDLEY, AGNES (February 23, 1892–May 6, 1950). Journalist and author, well known for her books and articles on China and on the Far East, Agnes Smedley was born in Campground, Sullivan County, Missouri, and was largely self-educated. After an early marriage that ended in divorce and various menial jobs, she moved to New York City, where she became interested in the Indian revolutionary cause. In 1918, Smedley was accused of "aiding German espionage," because one of the German societies sent money to the Indian nationalists and was briefly imprisoned before going to Europe, where she lived for nine years working for Indian independence. She published her semiautobiographical novel, *Daughter of Earth* (1927), and in the next year, Smedley began her journalist career as the correspondent for the *Frankfurter Zeitung* in China. Her experiences resulted in *Chinese Destinies*, published in 1933, the same year she visited the Soviet Union, where she wrote her next book, *China's Red Army Marches* (1934) followed by *China Fights Back* (1938). These books were compiled from information covertly supplied by Chinese Communist Party (CCP) agents, which gave Smedley's writing a certain notoriety.

From 1938 to 1941, Smedley was a publicist and a field worker for the Chinese Red Cross Medical Corps and a special correspondent for the *Manchester Guardian*, then she returned to the United States (1941) to recover from illness she acquired in China. Her book, *Battle Hymn of China* (1943), was an account of her experiences. In a November 1943 radio program, "Author Meets Critic," she attacked the United States and Great Britain as largely responsible for the backward conditions in China. A 1949 report issued from General Douglas MacArthur's intelligence staff accused Smedley of being a Soviet secret agent, but the Secretary of the Army withdrew the accusation after she threatened legal action. Documents found in Soviet archives after the fall of the Soviet Union found that she was, in fact, working for Communist International and for the

Soviet intelligence service. Smedley died in Oxford, England; her ashes were placed in Peking's National Memorial Cemetery of Revolutionary Martyrs.

FURTHER READING: Janice R. MacKinnon and Stephen R. MacKinnon, *Agnes Smedley, the Life and Times of an American Radical* (Berkeley: University of California, 1988).

SMITH, GERALD LYMAN KENNETH (February 27, 1898–April 15, 1976). Editor, lecturer, and clergyman who was known for his extreme right-wing views, his anti-Semitic bigotry, and his hate mongering, Gerald Smith was born in Pardeeville, Wisconsin, into a family of fundamentalist preachers, graduated from Valparaiso University (1918), and worked as an unordained minister in several churches, finally settling in Shreveport, Louisiana, where he became a paid organizer for the state's senator, Huey P. Long, in the 1930s. Smith supported Long for president and founded the Christian Nationalist Crusade. He was considered to be a spellbinding orator, one of the more famous in the United States, who preached "true Americanism": the rights of private property, upholding the Constitution, glorifying the flag, and expelling Communists from the United States. Smith campaigned for the Share-Our-Wealth Society and Long as "the Kingfish," and after Long's 1935 assassination, he fought President Franklin D. Roosevelt and labor unions and supported Father **Charles E. Coughlin.** In 1937, Smith founded the Committee of One Million, which was succeeded first by the America First party, then by the Christian Nationalist party, and finally by the Christian Nationalist Crusade. In 1939, he ran unsuccessfully for the U.S. Senate in Michigan and for president (1944, 1948, 1956) and started a political-religious journal, *The Cross and the Flag* (1942), for a "white, Christian America," which became his mouthpiece.

Smith's crusades covered a wide spectrum: politics (1930s), anti-Semitism (1940s), anti-Communism (1950s), and religious fundamentalism (1960s), but he was notorious for his blatant hostility to the Jews, whom he blamed for all of the problems in the world, in his speeches and in the pages of *The Cross and the Flag*, where he printed *Protocols of the Learned Elders of Zion*. In his later years, he supported younger anti-Semites with articles and information for their publications.

With the popularity of television in the 1950s, Smith turned from radio to the written word instead of to the new medium and became a wealthy man from his very effective direct-mail solicitations for money. In the 1960s, he developed a religious shrine in Eureka Springs, Arkansas, Christ of the Ozarks, where he staged a passion play, built a religious art gallery, and opened a Bible museum. Smith died in Glendale, California.

FURTHER READING: Glen Jeansonne, *Gerald L. K. Smith: Minister of Hate* (New Haven, CT: Yale University, 1988).

SMITH-MUNDT ACT. *See* **United States Information and Educational Exchange Act**

SOCIAL JUSTICE. See **Coughlin, Charles Edward**

SOLDATENSENDER CALAIS. [Soldiers' Radio, Calais]. Soldiers' Station, Calais, was an Allied station that broadcast without identifying itself as Allied. It counseled sabotage, among other things, and even gave detailed instructions on how to make explosives and bombs and how to use incendiary packets dropped by Allied planes. However, little sabotage by Germans ever resulted; a few foreign workers made some attempts but nothing much resulted from them. In its sabotage broadcasts, the Soldiers' Sender broke its rule and adhered to what was probably the truth; it carried "news" of extensive sabotage that never took place. This was later verified by the widespread German belief that part of their defeat was the result of sabotage. It was ordered in the midst of a highly successful black propaganda operation to go tactical. It was to broadcast in such a manner as to get the German population out on the roads with the objective of hampering the retreat of the German army.

FURTHER READING: Howard Becker, "Nature and Consequences of Black Propaganda," *American Sociological Review* 14 (1949): 221–35; reprinted in: William E. Daugherty, ed., *Psychological Warfare Casebook* (Baltimore: Johns Hopkins; published for Operations Research Office, Johns Hopkins University, 1958).

SOLDIERS' SENDER, CALAIS. *See* Soldatensender Calais

SOLDIERS' STATION, CALAIS. *See* Soldatensender Calais

SONS OF LIBERTY. One of the propaganda conduits (the other was the **Committees of Correspondence**) during the War of American Independence, they were radical organizations formed in the American colonies after Parliament's passage of the Stamp Act (1765). Societies sprang up simultaneously, with two of the largest and most active chapters in Boston and in New York, all working for colonial self-government. Members circulated petitions, tarred and feathered violators of patriotic decrees, intimidated British officials and their families, and stimulated a consciousness of colonial grievances by propaganda.

The name was resurrected during the Civil War for a secret organization of Copperheads, strongest in the Northwest, to oppose unconstitutional acts of the federal government and to support states' rights principles. Confederate agents in Canada attempted unsuccessfully to promote a so-called Northwest Conspiracy, which involved using the Sons of Liberty to form a Northwest Confederacy, but members of the organization were arrested and tried for treason in 1864.

FURTHER READING: Philip Davidson, *Propaganda and the American Revolution, 1763–1783* (New York: Norton, 1973/1941).

SOUTH AMERICA. *See* Coordinator of Inter-American Affairs (CIAA)

SOVIET ACTIVE MEASURES. Soviet active measures refer to the influence operations organized by the Soviet government. These include black, gray, and white propaganda, as well as **disinformation.** **White** (overt) **propaganda** was created by the Information Department of the Communist Party and included those publicly identified Soviet channels as Radio Moscow, *Novosti*, pamphlets, and magazines as well as official Soviet government statements. **Gray** (lightly concealed) **propaganda** was organized by the International Department of the Communist Party and used such channels as the foreign Communist Parties and the network of international Soviet fronts. **Black** (covert) **propaganda** was prepared by the KGB and included agents of influence, covert media placements, and until 1959 assassinations. Forgeries and disinformation were used by the Soviets in all modes.

FURTHER READING: U.S. Information Agency, *Soviet Active Measures in the Era of Glasnos*, prepared at the request of the U.S. House of Representatives, Committee on Appropriation, for presentation at a hearing on March 8, 1988, by Charles Z. Wick, Director, U.S. Information Agency. Washington, 1988; U.S. Congress. Senate. Committee on Foreign Relations. Subcommittee on European Affairs, *Soviet Active Measures*, hearings; 99th Congress, 1st Session (Washington, DC: Government Printing Office, 1985).

SOVIET NATIONAL EXHIBITION OF SCIENCE, TECHNOLOGY AND CULTURE, NEW YORK. *See* American National Exhibition, Moscow

SOVIET PROPAGANDA. *See* Active Measures Working Group; Baby Parts; Biological and Chemical Weapons Warfare; Disinformation; Forgeries; Soviet Active Measures.

SOVIET UNION. *See* Active Measures Working Group; Baby Parts; Biological and Chemical Weapons Warfare Disinformation; Forgeries; Soviet Active Measures

SPAIN. *See* Spanish-American War

SPANISH-AMERICAN WAR. The *Maine* was a second-class battleship, launched in 1885, that became an emotional precursor to the Spanish-American War when it was blown up in Havana harbor on February 15, 1898. The *Maine* arrived in Havana on January 25 on an alleged goodwill visit. The explosion killed 260, and the incident became a sensation in the American press, who laid the blame on the Spanish, with whom the United States was then having bad relations, and it served as a rallying point to the American people to "remember the *Maine*," a highly effective propaganda slogan. Admiral Hyman Rickover later argued that the *Maine* exploded because of sporadic internal combustion but further investigations never conclusively placed the blame on any one party. The destruction of the battleship accelerated the pace toward war.

The most important propaganda tool was newspapers, the yellow press, which brought the casualties down to the level of the average reader with lurid front-page headlines and pictures. The efforts of William Hearst's *New York Journal* to promote the war with Spain are now regarded as classic propaganda; he used name-calling, atrocity stories, and appeals to American honor and sympathy for the underdog to inflame public opinion against Spain as a "cruel imperialist" and an "enemy of the United States." One of the major factors given for the initiation of U.S. hostilities against Cuba were the propagandistic efforts of Pulitzer and Hearst which encouraged the United States jingoistically to go to war with Spain. *The World* and the *New York Journal*, along with other newspapers that published material from these two New York City newspapers, exerted a strong influence on America's decision to go to war by stirring up interventionist enthusiasm. Often overlooked is the role of Cuban nationalists in encouraging U.S. involvement in the conflict, but the publishers' primary concern was increased circulation rather than human rights.

During the 1898 conflict in which the United States sent troops and warships to Spanish territories in the Caribbean and in Asia, the U.S. Army provided daily bulletins to the press, and highly patriotic films, such as *Tearing Down the Spanish Flag!* (1898) electrified U.S. audiences when the hated European emblem was replaced by Old Glory, a dramatic, crowd-rousing hit. J. Stuart Blackton directed the scene in a 10 ft. × 12 ft. room with the building next door as background. While an operator managed the camera, Blackton raised the flag. The tremendous popularity of this film, which was actually filmed on a New York City rooftop, produced a host of imitators once war began. Phony pictorial "news" accounts were typified by *The Campaign in Cuba*, which showed a flagrant disregard for the truth. Because cameramen were often prohibited from gaining access to authentic battleground footage due to military censorship, much of the visual "reportage," such as the series released as *The Campaign in Cuba* (1898), was secretly filmed in the New Jersey wilderness. The use of films, in a military exercise that was popularly known as the "Spanish-American War," was effective, as this was the first U.S. military conflict that was documented on film; these were used effectively for propagandistic purposes.

The power of film in this war with its "actuality" and "documentary" effects freed propagandists for the first time from nearly complete reliance on publications and on the printed word.

FURTHER READING: George W. Auxier, *The Propaganda Activities of the Cuban Junta in Precipitating the Spanish-American War, 1895–1898* (Durham, N.C., 1939; reprinted from the *Hispanic American Historical Review*, v. XIX, no. 3 (August, 1939); Karen C. Lund, "The Motion Picture Camera Goes to War," *Library of Congress Information Bulletin* 57, no. 3 (March 1998): 48–49, 53; Peggy Samuels and Harold Samuels, *Remembering the Maine* (Washington, DC: Smithsonian Institution Press, 1995); Joseph E. Wisan, *The Cuban Crisis as Reflected in the New York Press, 1895–1898* (New York: Columbia University; London: P. S. King and Son, 1934); Marcus M. Wilkerson, *Public Opinion and the Spanish-American War: A Study in War Propaganda* (Baton Rouge: Louisiana State University, 1932).

SPANISH-AMERICAN WAR FILMS. *See* Spanish-American War

SPECIAL COMMITTEE TO INVESTIGATE COMMUNIST PROPAGANDA IN THE UNITED STATES (FISH COMMITTEE). *See* U.S. Congressional Investigations of Propaganda

SPECIAL INTEREST LOBBYING. *See* Foreign Agents Registration Act

SPIES AND LIES. *See* Posters in Wartime

SPONSORED FILMS. *See* Documentaries

SPRAGUE COMMITTEE. *See* President's Committee on Information Activities Abroad

SPREADING GERMS OF HATE. Important book in the field of propaganda ("primary weapon of the world's invisible government"), written by **George Sylvester Viereck**; the first edition had a forward by Colonel Edward M. House, one of President Wilson's closest advisers during World War I and Viereck's friend, who noted that the book would "remind us how foolish and partisan we can be in times of high emotional tension." The insightful book was written after World War I while Viereck continued his activities as a major propagandist for Germany, a country he believed in. During World War II, Viereck incorporated many of these same ideas for the Nazis. The book is a detailed, straightforward account of how an important propagandist worked. In the introduction, Viereck notes his intent to make the reader "propaganda-conscious" and to narrate "for the first time, the part played by propaganda in the United States during and after the War."

FURTHER READING: George S. Viereck, *Spreading Germs of Hate* (New York: Horace Liveright, 1930).

STAMP ACT. On March 22, 1765, Parliament passed the Stamp Act, the first direct tax on its American colonies. It demanded payment of revenue to defray the cost of maintaining royal troops. The Act's unpopularity through the colonies caused it to be repealed in 1766 but resentments toward British rule continued to escalate. The repeal was attributed to heavy newspaper coverage in British America of the Act and highlighted the news medium as an important opinion-making force able to unite people for political action.

FURTHER READING: Philip Davidson, *Propaganda and the American Revolution, 1763–1783* (New York: Norton, 1973/1941); Frederic B. Farrar, *This Common Channel to Independence: Revolution and Newspapers, 1759–1789* (Garden City, NY: Farrar Books, 1975).

STANTON PANEL. *See* Panel on International Information Education and Cultural Relations

THE STARS AND STRIPES. Famous newspaper of the American Expeditionary Force (AEF) in World War I, the eight-page paper was started February 8, 1918, and continued for 16 months until June 1919. It evolved from the complaints of almost two million soldiers for reliable news from home. It was published in France and raised a fund of two million francs from AEF members for war orphans. When the AEF discovered it could print an eight-page paper by selling subscriptions

First page of the first issue of the official U.S. Army newspaper, *The Stars and Stripes*. (*Source:* Kay Murray and Georgia Higley, "The Stars and Stripes: The Next Best Thing to Receiving a Letter from Home, *Information Bulletin* [September 2003]: 211)

and advertisements, it began publishing its own newspaper. Harold Ross, longtime editor of the *New Yorker*, headed its editorial board. The paper's journalists included famous names such as Alexander Woolcott, Franklin P. Adams, and Grantland Rice. Originally a soldiers' newspaper, it eventually was dominated by the brass, who controlled and even censored its contents but also saw the paper as an opportunity to publish information about military decorum and orders and to keep morale high among the troops. The stories tried to present a favorable opinion of U.S. efforts, but its quality writing made it more than a propaganda tool.

It disseminated useful information on subjects as varied as baseball, hygiene, and politics. Doughboy doggerel covered everything from beer to death. There were also verses on the difficulties of living in France and the problems of deferring to officers. Doughboys and officers praised the paper as contributing something human in the dreary trenches, an excellent morale booster that made American soldiers feel closer to home. Newspapers in the United States praised it for its high standards and its service to the fighting soldier. A weekly *Stars and Stripes*, edited in Washington, D.C., was published for a few years after the armistice. During World War II, the name was revived to denote a dozen publications for units worldwide, and the paper was published in both European and Pacific editions.

FURTHER READING: Alfred E. Cornebise, *The Stars and Stripes: Doughboy Journalism in World War I* (Westport, CT: Greenwood, 1984); Bud Hutton and T. A. MacMahon, "Brass Hats and Blue Pencils: How *Stars and Stripes* Became an Organ of Propaganda," *Collier's* 117 (May 18, 1946): 24, 67–71; Oram C. Hutton and Andy Rooney, *The Story of the Stars and Stripes* (Westport, CT: Greenwood, 1970/1946); Ken Zumwalt, *Stars and Stripes: World War II and the Early Years* (Austin, TX: Eakin, 1989).

STATE-ARMY-NAVY-AIR COORDINATING COMMITTEE. The State-Army-Navy-Air Coordinating Committee (SANACC) was created to initiate steps toward the conduct of covert psychological operations designed to counteract Soviet and Soviet-inspired activities and to ensure that all overt foreign information activities were effectively coordinated. At its inception, it was called the State-War-Navy Coordinating Committee (SWNCC) but the name was changed to better reflect the military agencies that were members after their post–World War II creation.

In 1946, its Subcommittee on Special Studies and Evaluations was charged with developing a plan for wartime psychological warfare and for making whatever peacetime preparations were required to move quickly to a wartime footing in this field. Their paper proposed a Psychological Warfare Organization to direct and to coordinate all national **psychological warfare** activities and operations.

FURTHER READING: U.S. Dept. of State, *Foreign Relations of the United States, 1945–1950: Emergence of the Intelligence Establishment* (Washington, DC: Government Printing Office, 1996).

STATE-WAR-NAVY COORDINATING COMMITTEE. *See* **State-Army-Navy-Air Coordinating Committee**

STATE DEPARTMENT. *See* **U.S. Department of State**

STATION DEBUNK. *See* **Debunk (Radio Station)**

STEICHEN, EDWARD. *See* **The Family of Man**

STIMSON–BORAH LETTER. A published letter was employed as a psychological warfare technique to influence at least five separate target groups on behalf of at least three major political objectives. The cause was an international conflict that happened on the night of September 18, 1931 when Japanese troops of the Kwantungarmy drove out the Chinese garrisons and seized Mukden, Changchun, and several other Manchurian cities (Mukden Incident) and destroyed a section of the South Manchurian Railroad track. By early 1932, the Japanese had conquered northern Manchuria, despite protests from the United States and the League of Nations.

Secretary of State Henry L. Stimson wrote an open letter to Senator William E. Borah, chairman of the Senate Foreign Relations Committee, dated February 23, 1932, that was "intended for the perusal of at least five unnamed addresses" with the knowledge that such a letter would be transmitted around the world and translated into many languages. In the open letter, Stimson outlined the doctrine of nonrecognition of conquests by aggression, emphasized the 1922 Nine-Power Treaty, and proposed the imposition of economic sanctions on China, but he drafted it so that the implied message for one of the groups would not be canceled out by the implied message to any of the others.

By releasing the letter, Borah hoped to incite American public opinion to the dangers inherent in a continuation of the Far East controversy and to unnamed foreign powers: the League of Nations, and the peoples of China, of Japan, and of Great Britain. Drafting the message for one of the groups required that the implied message to this group not be canceled out by the implied message to any of the others; the letter had to be prepared with great care.

It is hard to ascertain what effect the message had on Japan and on China as the two countries signed peace terms shortly after the release of the letter and the last of the invading Japanese troops left the Shanghai sector on May 31, 1932.

FURTHER READING: William E. Daugherty, ed., *Psychological Warfare Casebook* (Baltimore: Johns Hopkins; published for Operations Research Office, Johns Hopkins University, 1958); U.S. Department of State, *Foreign Relations of the United States: Diplomatic Papers, 1932; vol. 3: The Far East* (Washington, DC: Government Printing Office, 1948); Henry L. Stimson and McGeorge Bundy, *On Active Service in Peace and War* (New York: Octagon Books, 1971/1948).

STOUT, REX TODHUNTER (December 1, 1886–December 27, 1975). The mystery writer who created Nero Wolfe, Rex Stout was born in Noblesville, Indiana. He attended the University of Kansas then joined the U.S. Navy. Upon his discharge, he wandered the country doing odd jobs before he settled in New York, where he began a productive career as a novelist. After he married Fay Kennedy (1916), he joined his brother in business. He moved to Europe in 1927, where he published *How Like a God* (1929) then returned to Connecticut. The Stouts divorced in 1931; the next year the writer married Pola Hoffmann and published four more novels. In 1934, he published the first Nero Wolfe novel, *Fer-de-Lance*, which began Stout's fame. There were 30 three more in the series written before Wolfe's death.

During World War II, Stout was an active propagandist for the war effort with his efforts directed at the Nazis. Between 1938 and 1945, he cut back on his fiction writing for this purpose. He helped to establish the **Fight for Freedom Committee** and Freedom House (both in 1941), and he was elected president of the Society for the Prevention of World War III. With a talent for broadcasting, Stout became a master of ceremonies on *Speaking of Liberty* (1941); the next year he was elected president of Friends of Democracy, became the voice in *Voice of Freedom* (1942), and wrote the broadcast scripts for *Our Secret Weapon* countering Nazi propaganda. Stout also helped organize the Writers' War Board (later the Writers' Board).

After the war, Stout fought for writers' economic rights, served as president of Vanguard Press (1925–1928), helped bring out leftist books that otherwise were unlikely to be published, became president of the Authors' Guild (1945), founded the Writers' Board for World Government (1949), and was appointed president of the Mystery Writers of America (1958). He died in Connecticut.

FURTHER READING: David Anderson, *Rex Stout* (New York: F. Ungar, 1984); John McAleer, *Rex Stout* (San Bernardino, CA: Brownstone Books: Distributed by the Borgo Press, 1994).

STOWE, HARRIET BEECHER (June 14, 1811–July 1, 1896). Harriet Beecher Stowe, born into a strong northern abolitionist family in Litchfield, Connecticut, was the daughter of the famous preacher Lyman Beecher and his wife, Roxana. On January 6, 1893, she married Calvin Stowe, a biblical scholar, and wrote intermittently as family finances demanded. A collection of her stories was published as *The Mayflower* (1843).

Stowe wrote ***Uncle Tom's Cabin*** in 1851, a powerful indictment of slavery that was heavily attacked by southerners who argued that Stowe distorted plantation life, but President Lincoln allegedly called her "the little woman who wrote the book that started this great war" when she visited the White House in 1862.

In response to her critics, Stowe published *A Key to Uncle Tom's Cabin* (1853). Other books included *Sunny Memories of Foreign Lands* (1854), an account of her travels in England, another antislavery novel, *Dred* (1856), *The Minister's Wooing* (1859), *Agnes of Sorrento* and *Pearl of Orr's Island* (both 1862), *Oldtown Folks* (1869), *Lady Byron Vindicated* (1870), *Pink and White Tyranny* (1871), *We and Our Neighbors* (1875), and *Poganuc People* (1878). Stowe died in Hartford, Connecticut.

FURTHER READING: Charles Foster, *Rungless Ladder: Harriet Beecher Stowe and New England Puritanism* (Durham, NC: Duke University, 1954); *Notable American Women, 1607–1950*, vol. 3 (Cambridge, MA: Belknap Press of Harvard University Press, 1971–1980); Forrest Wilson, *Crusader in Crinoline* (Westport, CT: Greenwood, 1972/1941).

STRONG, ANNA LOUISE (November 24, 1885–March 29, 1970). Journalist, author, lecturer, and Communist propagandist, Anna Strong was born in Friend, Nebraska, and received her Ph.D. from the University of Chicago in 1908. After several years doing reform work, Strong went to Washington, D.C., to work for the Children's Bureau as director of exhibits (1914–1915) before joining the Anti-Preparedness League. During World War I, she anonymously wrote antiwar and anticapitalistic articles for the socialist *Seattle Daily Call* and under the pseudonym Anise became a feature editor for a labor paper, *Seattle Union Record*.

In 1921, Strong went to Poland to do publicity for the American Friends Service Committee then headed to Russia to be part of the revolution, where she became the Moscow correspondent for Hearst's *International* and befriended Lenin and Trotsky. Her book, *First Time in History* (1924), was a defense of Lenin's economic policy, and she organized the first English newspaper (1930) in Russia, the *Moscow Daily News*. After World War II, Strong had difficulties with the Soviet Union. Her travels subsequently took her to Communist China. She wrote many books, including her best-selling autobiography, *I Change Worlds: The Remaking of an American* (1935), and she edited a newsletter, *Letter from China*, which became a regular information source about Chinese positions in the Sino-Soviet debate while it gave Western readers a glimpse of Chinese life and served as a propaganda vehicle for her friend, Mao Tse-Tung. Strong was a frequent contributor to periodicals. In a famous interview with her in Yenan, Mao Tse-tung observed that "American reactionaries are merely a paper tiger [impotent United States]" and in appearance, "the reactionaries are terrifying, but in reality they are not so powerful" and "it is not the reactionaries but the people who are really powerful." In 1949, Strong was deported from Moscow on charges of espionage and returned to the United States but went back to China (1958), where she lived for the last twelve years of her life. She died in Beijing and was buried in its National Memorial Cemetery of Revolutionary Martyrs, near the grave of **Agnes Smedley**.

FURTHER READING: *Notable American Women: A Biographical Dictionary, 1607–1950*, vol. 3 (Cambridge, MA: Belknap Press of Harvard University Press, 1971–1980); Robert W. Pringle, "Anna Louise Strong: Propagandist of Communism" (Ph.D. diss., Univ. of Virginia, 1972); Tracy B. Strong and Helene Keyssar, *Right in Her Soul* (New York: Random House, 1983).

SUN TZU. *See* **War Propaganda**

SUPERSTITIONS. The effectiveness of superstitions in **psychological warfare** requires the most detailed and intimate knowledge of a targeted people by the planner or operator wherever superstitions are to be exploited by the propagandist. They have been used since the beginning of recorded time to outmaneuver the enemy and to influence the thoughts and actions of actual and potential allies. During World War II, an actual operation was planned in Burma in which an officer with excellent knowledge of the country's folklore proposed that the death of the popular British commander, General Wingate, be represented as a suicide rather than as the result of Japanese military action because Burmese historical tradition had leaders in times of crises frequently taking their own lives to free their spirits from their bodies to oversee the welfare of the country.

FURTHER READING: William E. Daugherty, "The Exploitation of Superstitions in Psychological Warfare," in William E. Daugherty, ed., *Psychological Warfare Casebook* (Baltimore: Johns Hopkins; published for Operations Research Office, Johns Hopkins University, 1958).

SYMBOLS. This technique requires words and illustrations that bring strong responses from people. Individuals react not only to the actual meaning of the words and the pictures but also to the feelings aroused by such symbols. Example: Nearly all cultures have favorable reactions to a picture of mother and child or to words like *homeland* and *justice*. Propagandists create an association in people's minds between symbols and messages they are trying to spread. Powerful negative images are often used to increase prejudice, hostility, and hatred toward the propaganda target. The dove, international symbol of peace, has been used in various ways by the world's peace groups. Modes of presentation include portraiture, allegory or metaphor, illustration, "heraldic collocation," and caricature.

FURTHER READING: Gary Yanker, *Prop Art: Over 1000 Contemporary Political Posters* (New York: Darien House; distributed by New York Graphic Society, Greenwich, CT, 1972).

SZYK, ARTHUR (1894–September 13, 1951). Arthur Szyk, born in Lodz, Poland, when it was part of the Russian empire, was one of the foremost caricaturists of World War II. He acquired his art training in Paris and in Cracow. He married Julia Liekerman in 1916; there were two children. Between 1919 and 1920, during Poland's war against the Soviet Bolsheviks, he was artistic director of the Department of Propaganda for the Polish army regiment quartered in Lodz. In 1921, Szyk moved to Paris, then came to the United States in 1934 for exhibitions of his work, including one at the Library of Congress. After living in England, he immigrated to the United States in 1940, where he embraced the patriotic and democratic spirit of his adopted country. His works during this period included "The United States of America," with its diverse portrayals of American society, "The Declaration of Independence," "Four Freedoms Prayer," and "Bill of Rights." Between 1940 and 1941, Szyk toured the United States and Canada, where he exhibited his work to heighten awareness of the war in Europe. During World War II, Szyk devoted his talents solely to make propaganda against the Axis. He produced hundreds of anti-Axis illustrations and cartoons that showed corpulent Nazis and vile Japanese, and he rendered Hitler, Goring, Goebbels, Himmler, Mussolini, and Hirohito as buffoons, inflating their features into indictments of evil but in images that were precisely detailed. In fact, Szyk took the racist stereotype of the evil Japanese farther than most official propaganda. His work appeared in popular magazines as *Collier's* and *Time* and there were two published contributions, *The New Order* (1941) and *Ink and Blood* (1946). Szyk's work reflected the moods and the attitudes of the United States in wartime.

After World War II, Szyk continued his work for a Jewish state in Palestine and returned to the art of illumination and book illustration, including *Andersen's Fairy Tales, Pathways Through the Bible, The Ten Commandments,* and several commissions for the Limited Editions Club and from the United Nations. He became an American citizen in 1948.

FURTHER READING: Catalog of Szyk exhibition, Library of Congress; exhibit, "The Art and Politics of Arthur Szyk," U.S. Holocaust Memorial Museum, Washington, D.C.; Stephen Luckert, *The Art and Politics of Arthur Szyk* (Washington, DC: United States Holocaust Museum, 2001); Irvin Ungar, *Justice Illuminated: The Art of Arthur Szyk* (Chicago: Spertus Museum, Spertus Institute of Jewish Studies, 1998).

T

TABLOID JOURNALISM. *See* **Yellow Journalism**

TANAKA MEMORIAL. In 1929, a different form of Soviet forgery appeared when a document, purporting to be a memorandum from the Japanese Prime Minister Tanaka to the Emperor Hirohito, found its way into the Western press. This document supposedly laid out a Japanese plan for world conquest. According to the introduction to a 1941 publication of the document by the American Communist Party, "The Tanaka Memorial . . . was written in 1927 as a confidential document. It first came to light in 1929 after it had been purchased from a Japanese by Chang Hsueh-liang, then the Young Marshal of Manchuria." He was a warlord who frequently collaborated with the Chinese Communists. In late 1936, he kidnapped Chiang Kai-shek and demanded that he cooperate with the Communists in the war against Japan.

The Tanaka document was clearly a forgery. It contained errors of fact about Japan and even about Baron Tanaka, but it was widely circulated until the end of World War II. An insight into its Soviet origin was provided in 1941 by Leon Trotsky, who argued that it was authentic. According to an article by Trotsky, written shortly before his death, Felix Dzerzhinsky, the head of Cheka, secured the document in 1925 through a spy in the Japanese Ministry of Foreign Affairs. The document was photographed and then translated for Trotsky, who was still an important Soviet official. Trotsky did not explain how the Soviets came into possession in 1925 of a document not written until 1927, the year Tanaka became Prime Minister. It is possible that the Soviets created the forgery based on an authentic document stolen in 1925.

Trotsky revealed that the document was put into circulation in the United States through Amtorg, the Soviet trading corporation, headed by Bogdanov. Because Bogdanov did not arrive in the United States until 1930, Trotsky's knowledge of the method of surfacing could only have come through his contacts in the GPU, which he maintained after being ousted from the Soviet leadership. This date would be consistent with the forgery's original surfacing in China in 1929 and its replay in the United States in 1930.

The most recent replay of the Tanaka forgery was a reference to it in a Kuwaiti newspaper in January 1987. The unsigned article, in Arabic, which showed substantial evidence of Soviet authorship, accused the United States of developing an "ethnic weapon," a biological weapon that would supposedly affect only black or brown-skinned people. This bizarre allegation has been repeated in both official Soviet media and in publications influenced by the Soviets for years. The article was also accompanied by a purported picture of the "ethnic weapon" being fired, which carried the caption, "The germ bomb is fired from regular tanks looking like regular bombs and spreading the germs." The opening paragraphs of the article accused the United States of taking over biological weapons research from the Japanese, who were supposedly carrying out the plans revealed by Tanaka in his letter to the Emperor.

FURTHER READING: Herbert Romerstein, "Disinformation as a KGB Weapon in the Cold War," paper prepared for a Conference on Germany and Intelligence Organizations: The Last Fifty Years in Review, Akademie fur Politische Bildung Tutzing [Germany] (1999).

TEARING DOWN THE SPANISH FLAG! See **Spanish-American War**

TELEVISION BROADCASTING. Television is a powerful, visually perceptive image maker that has become one of the most important transmitters of propaganda images, with lasting mental imprints that can be dramatic and provocative. Not always as fast as radio or the Internet, which gets the news or the first bulletin on the air faster, television transports the viewer to the local disaster story, to the international crisis, to the political debate, to the sports event, and even to the moon ("living room" wars).

After the limitations on private broadcasters in World War II, when television was still in its infancy, the prosperous 1950s saw an increase in the popularity of television, as more Americans had one in their homes. There was a move to commercial sponsorship and the power of TV advertising that also saw the emergence of public interest regulatory bodies co-opted by the industry.

Official government propaganda included such efforts as the Armed Forces Radio and Television Service and **Television Marti** to Cuba. In 1951, the **U.S. Department of State** established a television service in recognition of the new medium, which was transferred to the **U.S. Information Agency** in 1953, where the fledgling operation needed cheap programs and access to newsmakers. State Department agencies with film units included the Mutual Security Agency, the Federal Security Agency, and the Economic Cooperation Administration. They produced films for propaganda use in nations receiving foreign aid and lent these films to broadcasters for free. Many of these were loaned to the television networks (ABC, CBS, NBC, and Dumont), which used them in little-watched portions of their broadcast schedules. Dumont showed several films about **psychological warfare** under the series title, *Our Secret Weapon—The Truth*, and ABC gathered Federal Security Agency films into a series called *Everybody's Business*. As late as 1954, the least financially secure network, ABC, continued to air State Department films as summer replacement series. In addition, the State Department exerted control over the independent production companies that produced these films by lending selective assistance and access to personnel and to contacts abroad and use of its film archives. Officials helped filmmakers they considered reputable who would make films consistent with their policy interests.

During the Reagan administration, there was *Let Poland Be Poland* (1982). In September 1983, U.N. Ambassador Jeane Kirkpatrick used a tape produced by USIA's Television and Film Service to provide conclusive evidence in the U.N. Security Council that the Soviets destroyed an unarmed civilian airliner, the first time a videotape was used in the Security Council. Two months later, Kirkpatrick was linked via satellite with the prime ministers of Barbados and of St. Lucia and journalists in five capitals to clarify the U.S. rescue missions in Grenada. From this initial merger of satellite television with public diplomacy, USIA's live, global satellite television network, **Worldnet**, grew.

Another distribution means is through "interactives" (one-way video, two-way audio telepress conferences), specialized dialogues that allow foreign journalists, scholars, political leaders and others access to prominent in U.S. politics, military, business, and other areas (e.g., science, economics, and culture). Each interactive resembles a long-distance press conference with audio and video transmitted from a Worldnet studio in Washington to a post overseas, with individuals at the post asking questions via telephone. These programs have become very popular and have been excerpted on both foreign television and radio stations. In contrast, production costs for U.S. government broadcast television programs are high and placement is difficult.

In the 1990s, USIA began digital video conferences (DVCs) with hookups from Washington, D.C., headquarters with participants in other parts of the globe but around-the-clock programming by CNN, C-Span. and other television services have brought home events as soon as they happen. This has impacted public opinion, most recently seen with the incessant coverage of the Iraq war. Like the situation during the Vietnam coverage, the casualties came right into American living rooms.

The Foreign Scene

The globalization of American television has provided both negative and positive images. The tragedy of the terrorist attacks of September 11, 2001, brought support and sympathy from around the world as viewers were transfixed by the towers falling, the rescue efforts, and the overwhelming support that followed. The negative is the image of pro-America that corporate giants, such as Disney, offer along with a diversity of translated programs. For example, the international television activities of The Walt Disney Company, a recognizable brand name globally, were reorganized into a newly formed division within the Walt Disney Television and Telecommunications Group, Walt Disney Television (International). The first regional office was in Hong Kong to oversee the Asian and the Pacific markets, including Japan, India, Australia, and New Zealand. In early 1995, Disney launched Super RTL in Germany and a Disney Channel in the United Kingdom followed by similar channels in Taiwan. The company has also explored program offerings in other European, Asian, and Latin American markets, and it has expanded its programming to Eastern Europe in Russia, Hungary, Poland, Bulgaria, and the Czech Republic. As a copartner, Disney is a 50 percent

Cover: USIA-TV. Montage
with 12 TV sets, each with
a different image of USIA-
TV productions. (*Source:*
USIA, 1985)

shareholder in Super RTL along with Compagnie Luxembourgeoise de Telediffu-
sion (CLT), one of Europe's leading media companies, and is seeking a joint venture with The Modi Group in India. There are now more than 35 Disney programs
airing weekly around the world. In Japan, Disney is the only U.S. production company with an ongoing series on a network, *Team Disney*.

In Canada, the Canadian Broadcasting Corporation (CBC) has eliminated several hours of prime-time American network television programming to protect
its own culture despite the fact that at least 90 percent of Canadians live within
100 miles of the Canada–U.S. border ("undefended border").

For Worldnet, strict government control of the media limits its ability to be
carried over local cable stations in the region. Direct placement of individual
programs is currently the only way to reach much of the East Asian audience.
The signal is presently carried on systems in New Zealand, the Philippines, and
Singapore. Worldnet is carried on cable in Romania, Bulgaria, and the Czech
Republic and is available to 1.5 million people in these countries. In Western
Europe, Worldnet is beamed on more than 90 cable systems, including systems
in Denmark, France, Luxembourg, Norway, Spain, Switzerland, and the United
Kingdom, and can be seen by 1.8 million viewers.

FURTHER READING: Nancy E. Bernhard, "Clearer Than Truth: Public Affairs, Television
and the State Department's Domestic Information Campaigns, 1947–1952," *Diplomatic
History* 21, no. 4 (Fall 1997): 545–67; Anne Cooper-Chen, *Games in the Global Village*
(Bowling Green, OH: Bowling Green State University, 1994); Anna E. Sweeney, *Worldnet
Television: Audience Reach via Cable Systems Worldwide* (Washington: Office of Research
and Media Reaction, U.S. Information Agency, 1996); Christian W. Thomsen, ed., *Cultural
Transfer or Electronic Imperialism?: The Impact of American Television Programs on
European Television* (Heidelberg: C. Winter Universitatsverlag, 1989).

TELEVISION IN PROPAGANDA. *See I Led Three Lives*; Television Broadcasting; Television Marti; Worldnet

TELEVISION MARTI. The Office of Cuba Broadcasting, which operates **Radio Marti** and Television Marti, was created by the Radio Broadcasting to Cuba Act of 1983 (Public Law 98-111) to focus on Cuban domestic and international news and information that is not reported by the government-controlled media. According to the legislation, it must follow all **Voice of America** standards and programs and must be objective, accurate, and well balanced.

TV Marti has been jammed by the Castro government since its first broadcast on March 27, 1990, and its critics feel that the television station is a waste of taxpayers' money whose programs no one ever sees, a wasteful relic of the Cold War. The antenna and transmitter for TV Marti are mounted aboard a balloon tethered 10,000 feet above Cudjoe Key, Florida, but its programs now originate in Miami. Also aboard the balloon is radar used to track incoming drug flights. When TV Marti goes on, the radar goes off, a schedule well known to drug smugglers, who know the best time to operate. The station is on the air seven days a week, four and a half hours a day and includes half-hour nightly newscasts, a weekend news summary of the preceding week's major events, and special programs (public affairs, culture, music, sports, entertainment).

In 1994, the United States International Broadcasting Act, Title III of the Foreign Relations Authorization Act, Fiscal Years 1994 and 1995 (Public Law 103-236), established the International Broadcasting Bureau (IBB) within the **U.S. Information Agency** (USIA) and created a presidentially appointed Broadcasting Board of Governors (BBG) with jurisdiction over all civilian U.S. government international broadcasting. The law consolidated VOA, Worldnet TV, Radio and TV Marti, the Office of Engineering and Technical Services, along with RFE/RL and a new **Radio Free Asia**.

FURTHER READING: International Broadcasting Bureau, *U.S. International Broadcasting Chronology* (IBB Web site [http://www.ibb.gov], 2001); Peter Kornbluh and Jon Elliston, "Will Congress Kill TV Marti?" *Nation* 259, no. 6 (August 22, 1994): 194–96; U.S. Advisory Board for Cuba Broadcasting. *Annual Reports*, 1991– (Washington, DC: The Board, 1992–).

TERRORISM. Terrorism propaganda is often called **propaganda of the deed**, a strategy used by activists when socially acceptable information efforts are ineffective to change. The term *terrorism* did not officially exist until 1970, when it first appeared in the *New York Times Index*, that arbiter of American usage, instead of other options, such as "freedom fighter," "member of a liberation front," "resistance leader," and "guerrilla." The implication is an illegitimate or criminal activity. The alternatives suggest a particular incident, such as kidnapping, bombing, or killing, as legitimate and attention-getting tactics for social justice.

At the height of the Cold War, a popular theory found terrorism movements globally interlocked and manipulated by KGB agent provocateurs to support Soviet aims indirectly. Opponents disputed this U.S.-government-supported "official" account as **Cold War** disinformation to direct attention away from American-backed activities, such as state terrorism in Latin America, in Israel, in South Africa, and in other countries.

On September 11, 2001, the bombing of World Trade Centers in New York City and of the Pentagon, outside Washington, D.C., became a double attack on the financial center and the military fortress of the United States. After these terrorist attacks, a **disinformation** campaign originated as a conspiracy theory that 4,000 Jews did not show up for work on that day. Was this a harmless conspiracy theory or a virulent new anti-Semitism? This was the first recorded account of an urban legend that has swept the Arab world. Not a single fact in it has ever been substantiated. It appears to be based on concern expressed by the Israeli government for the fate of 4,000 Israelis resident in New York, a small number of whom worked at the World Trade Center. Within a matter of days it was no longer 4,000 Israelis who were supposed not to have turned up to work, but 4,000 Jews; then reports appeared that "not a single Jew" died on September 11. It was easy to rebut as the list of victims was printed on many reputable Web sites. A quick scan showed about one out of every dozen names was Jewish. That matched U.S. Census Bureau data, which showed 9 percent of New York's population is Jewish. If 4,000 Jews didn't go to work that day, far fewer than 1 out of 12 would be on the lists. In fact, many American Jews died in the attack, as well as four Israeli citizens, two in the World Trade Center and two on hijacked planes, according to the Israeli Foreign Ministry. President Bush's erroneous assertion in his September 20 speech to Congress that "more than 130 Israelis" had perished has yet to be explained, but the source was most likely not the intelligence agents in Tel Aviv but overwhelmed authorities in New York.

The first order of business was getting a grasp on the number of Jews potentially missing. Mordecai Dzikansky, a New York City police detective assigned to the Manhattan South homicide squad and an Orthodox Jew, pored over the missing-persons reports. Roughly 1,700 people listed the religion of the missing person; of those, some 10 percent were Jewish. The evidence for this widely circulated view was a rumor that on the day before the attacks, Israeli intelligence warned 4,000 American Jews working in the World Trade Center not to go to work. Missing from the story: The contradictory facts that the list of victims includes many Jewish names, that more than 130 Israeli nationals perished in the attacks, and that the hijackers were all Arabs.

Counterterrorism Campaign

The U.S. government developed four enduring policy principles that guide its counterterrorism strategy:

First, make no concessions to terrorists and strike no deals.

Second, bring terrorists to justice for their crimes.

Third, isolate and apply pressure on states that sponsor terrorism to force them to change their behavior.

Fourth, bolster the counterterrorist capabilities of those countries that work with the United States and require assistance.

The Web site Response to Terrorism was already in place before the attacks, but the day after, the Office of International Information Programs (IIP), U.S. Department of State, expanded it (http://usinfo.state.gov/is/international_security/terrorism.html). Two months after the attack, IIP issued a special electronic journal, *Terrorism: Threat Assessment, Countermeasures and Policy* (http://usinfo.state.gov/journals/itps/1101/ijpe/ijpe1101.htm). This 20th issue of U.S. Foreign

Policy Agenda, planned well before the tragic events of September 11 in New York, the Washington, D.C. area, and Pennsylvania, was rushed into publication right after the attacks; it explored major themes in international terrorism and its increasingly violent nature through a series of articles, fact sheets, and references from experts within the U.S. government and from the academic and private sectors. The introduction was by President George W. Bush. Among the special publications released in this period, *The Network of Terrorism*, a report on the United States and the international campaign to end global terrorism, was one of the most requested abroad.

The annual *Patterns of Global Terrorism* report for 2001, released in early 2002, by the Secretary of State and the Coordinator for Counterterrorism in compliance with Title 22 of the United States Code, Section 2656f(a), took on special significance in its 2001 edition; it was expanded and translated into five languages. This report requires the Department of State to provide Congress a full and complete annual report on terrorism for those countries and groups meeting the criteria of Section (a)(1) and (2) of the Act. Electronic version: http://www.state.gov/s/ct/rls/pgtrpt/2001

An unexpected side effect of the terrorism attacks was the increase in the speaker program as IIP tried to keep up with post-9/11 requests for experts on terrorism. IIP sends out nearly a thousand speakers annually to discuss with foreign audiences issues that have been identified by U.S. embassies. Although most speakers travel abroad to meet with government officials, journalists, academics, and other key opinion leaders, many also participate electronically through digital videoconferencing (DVC). There are more than 125 facilities around the world.

Also responsive was the **Voice of America**, which created a new type of Arabic language service that made its debut in spring 2002 and targeted 18- to 30-year-old listeners. **Radio Sawa** replaced VOA's former Arabic Service as an AM/FM station that combined sanitized American and Arab pop songs with pro-American news broadcasts from Beirut to Kuwait City, but the station will not play hard rock, country, or anything that is considered "political music." Sawa means "together" in Arabic, and it is seen by the Bush administration as its principal means of communicating with the Arab world.

FURTHER READING: Michael Dobbs, "America's Arabic Voice," *Washington Post*, March 24, 2003: C1, C2; Edward S. Hermann, *Real Terror Network: Terrorism in Fact and Propaganda* (Boston: South End Press, 1982); Eli Lake, "Pop Psychology," *Washington Post*, August 4, 2002: B3; Claire Sterling, *Terror Network: The Secret War of International Terrorism* (New York: Holt, Rinehart, and Winston, 1981). Other related Web sites: Library of Congress (http://thomas. loc.gov/home/terrorleg.htm); U.S. Department of State, Diplomacy and the Global Campaign Against Terrorism (http://www. state.gov/coalition/); U.S. Department of State, Office of Counterterrorism (http://www. state.gov/s/ct/).

THEATER. *See* **Federal Theater Project**

THEMES. Themes are topics or subjects of discussion whose employment in propaganda output should support the achievement of the **psychological warfare**

objectives or goals undertaken; must be carefully selected, timely, and appropriate to the objectives sought and to the target audience or audiences addressed; and need to be suitable for conveyance by the media of dissemination available. The selection of appropriate themes depends on a number of factors: psychological warfare objectives, policy directives, and available intelligence. To be effective, themes need to be reasonable, timely, logical, and in accord with existing conditions. **Daniel Lerner** wrote about the experiences of Americans engaged in psychological warfare operations in Europe during World War II and considered the formulation of themes as "possibly the most critical step in the whole Skyewar process."

FURTHER READING: American Institutes for Research, *Art and Science of Psychological Operations: Case Studies of Military Applications*, vol. 1; ed. Ronald De McLaurin, Carl F. Rosenthal, Sarah A. Skillings et al. (Washington, DC: Headquarters, U.S. Dept. of the Army, 1976); William E. Daugherty, ed., *Psychological Warfare Casebook* (Baltimore: Johns Hopkins; published for Operations Research Office, Johns Hopkins University, 1958).

THEODORE ROOSEVELT AND THE "GREAT WHITE FLEET." *See* World Cruise of the U.S. Navy (1907–1909)

THOMAS, ISAIAH (January 19, 1749–April 4, 1831). Patriot printer, publisher, author. He was born in Boston, Massachusetts and apprenticed at six to a printer, Zechariah Fowle. Thomas claimed later that the only education he received was from the books for which he set type. When he was 16, he had a dispute with Fowle and left for Halifax, Nova Scotia, where he worked on the *Halifax Gazette* and got into trouble for opposing the Stamp Act. He returned to Boston, gained his release from his apprenticeship, and started the *Massachusetts Spy* in 1770 with Fowle. Its earliest motto was "A Weekly Political and Commercial, Open to All Parties but Influenced by None" but Thomas ignored this; he was a radical leader of the patriot underground. He soon changed his motto to "The Massachusetts Spy, or American Oracle of Liberty," whose contributors advocated independence. Thomas printed his paper carefully, targeted the workingman, and generated the largest circulation in New England. On April 16, 1775, Thomas escaped with his press and type to Worcester, Massachusetts, where he covered the events of the next days, including an account of the battles of Lexington and Concord, with a dramatic front-page banner and a masthead designed by Paul Revere. After the Revolution, Thomas became a leading publisher, employing 150 persons and operating seven presses, a paper mill, and a bindery. He published magazines, more than 400 books, the first Greek grammar in America, and the first printed music. He wrote the two-volume *History of Printing in America* (1810), a standard reference for the period, and founded the American Antiquarian Society.

Thomas, a superb printer, was called the "Baskerville of America" by **Benjamin Franklin.** Historians now consider him the greatest newspaperman of the American Revolution.

FURTHER READING: Annie R. Marble, *From 'Prentice to Patron* (New York and London: D. Appleton-Century, 1935); Clifford K. Shipton, *Isaiah Thomas: Printer, Patriot and Philanthropist, 1749–1831* (Rochester, NY: Hart, 1948).

THOMPSON, DOROTHY (July 9, 1893–January 30, 1961). Journalist and political commentator, Dorothy Thompson was born in Lancaster, New York. She was a fervent anti-Nazi who became a crusader for alerting Americans to the Nazi threat. During World War II, Thompson turned propagandist for the Allied cause. Based on her intimate acquaintance with the nation, she prepared materials on Nazi Germany for President Roosevelt, the **U.S. Department of State**, and the **Office of Strategic Services** and asked **Elmer Davis** for an assignment with the **Office of War Information**. She received a role in a project that used the shortwave facilities of the Columbia Broadcasting Company (CBS) to broadcast anti-Nazi propaganda.

In 1942, she helped the American war effort by making propaganda broadcasts that were transmitted to Germany by shortwave radio. These anti-Nazi speeches, delivered to "Hans," a hypothetical friend (actually Count Helmuth von Moltke), asked him to rise up against Hitler, to stop the mounting atrocities, and to accept the Allied victory. In her broadcasts, Thompson did not vilify the German nation as a whole but instead tried to create a context in which rational adults could agree on certain important ideas. These broadcasts were published as *Listen, Hans* (Boston: Houghton Mifflin, 1942).

Thompson's postwar activities were less effective than in the 1930s, but Thompson adopted an anti-Zionist, pro-Arab position. In 1951, she founded American Friends of the Middle East (AFME), partly financed by the Arabian American Oil Company and the Central Intelligence Agency, a fact apparently unknown to Thompson. She died in Lisbon, Portugal. Thompson's second husband, who she married in 1928, was Nobel-winner Sinclair Lewis. They divorced in 1942.

FURTHER READING: Barbara Sicherman and Carol H. Green, eds., *Notable American Women: The Modern Period; A Biographical Dictionary* (Cambridge, MA and London, England: Belknap Press of Harvard University, 1980); Nancy Signorielli, ed., *Women in Communication: A Biographical Sourcebook* (Westport, CT: Greenwood, 1996).

THOMPSON, JOHN REUBEN. *See* **Civil War Propaganda**

THOMSEN, HANS (1891?–19??). Hans Thomsen was an important Nazi propagandist in the United States who devised several propaganda campaigns to support American isolationism to counter growing American sympathy for the Allies, including "literary countermeasures," which was to use famous authors to write pieces against intervention. As German Charge D'Affaires in the United States, he urged support of American isolationism and directed German efforts to defeat President Franklin Roosevelt's reelection efforts in 1940. To ensure American neutrality, Thomsen listed several themes he considered most effective for Nazi propaganda because the American people were much more hostile to Germany than during World War I. These included the senseless and useless loss of lives and wealth that the United States had sustained in the First World War, the large public debt the previous war caused, economic disintegration, role of the munitions industry as war profiteer, Great Britain's "cynical" role as a debtor and its double-dealing in 1916 when it allegedly concealed a secret treaty with her allies, and America's refusal to ratify the Versailles Treaty, which conceded the justice of the German cause. Thomsen circulated copies of the speeches of Hitler and other leading Nazi spokesmen.

FURTHER READING: Alton Frye, *Nazi Germany and the American Hemisphere, 1933–1941* (New Haven, CT and London: Yale, 1967); Morris Schonbach, *Native American Fascism During the 1930s and 1940s: A Study of Its Roots, Its Growth and Its Decline* (New York and London: Garland Publishing, 1985).

TOGURI, IVA. *See* Tokyo Rose

TOKYO ROSE. Name that U.S. servicemen gave to female Japanese propaganda broadcasters in World War II, who gave their American and British listeners the impression that Japanese intelligence was better than it really was. During World War II, Japanese radio propaganda operated under the direction of the War Information Bureau, and all English-speaking workers were screened by the security police. One of these women was Iva Ikuko Toguri d'Aquino, a Japanese-American born in Los Angeles and a graduate of the University of California at Los Angeles. She later claimed she was visiting Japan during the **Pearl Harbor** attack and was forced to make the broadcasts under duress, as were the others that the Japanese recruited.

The first broadcast went on the air as "Ann" (short for "announcer") but later became "Orphan Annie—your favorite enemy." The propaganda broadcasts used information picked up from U.S. commercial radio stations, especially from American newscasts of disasters, that could be inserted among the recordings of dance bands and classical music. The women, all called Tokyo Rose, announced false casualty figures, sometimes mentioning specific military units; tales of infidelities from the wives and girlfriends back home; and "prophetic" reports of upcoming operations.

When the war ended, the Japanese identified d'Aquino as Tokyo Rose, but others also did the broadcasts. She was tried in the United States (1949) for treason and for undermining American troops' morale but continually insisted that she was forced to make the broadcasts and was one of at least 20 "Tokyo Roses." D'Aquino was acquitted of treason but convicted of undermining troop morale; she served 10 years in prison on the lesser charge until President Ford pardoned her in 1977, after it was discovered that that the broadcasts were actually written by two POWs, an American and an Australian, whose secret intention was to subvert the propaganda process.

FURTHER READING: Masayo Duus, *Tokyo Rose: Orphan of the Pacific* (Tokyo: Kodansha International, 1979); Russell W. Howe, *The Hunt for "Tokyo Rose"* (Lanham, MD and London: Madison, 1990).

TRUST. One of the most important techniques in propaganda. Propagandists must be believable, and their audience must consider them reliable authorities. One method to gain an audience's trust is to report unfavorable news that the audience knows or will discover. Another way is to agree with their existing opinions; people most trust speakers and writers whose ideas are similar to their own. Successful propaganda agrees with what people already know or believe and only a little of it is news.

FURTHER READING: William E. Daugherty, ed., *Psychological Warfare Casebook* (Baltimore: Johns Hopkins; published for Operations Research Office, Johns Hopkins University, 1958).

TUCCI, NICCOLO (May 1, 1908–December 10, 1999). Niccolo Tucci was born Bartolomeo Strabolgi in Lugano, Switzerland, but he was raised in Florence, Italy, where he studied with private tutors. After receiving a doctorate in political science from the University of Florence, Tucci joined Mussolini's press and propaganda ministry and became head of the German-language radio station, where he invited Jews to air their political views; he was reprimanded for this but not fired because his allegorical fairy tales in German were popular with audiences. He resigned in 1936, the same year he married Laura Rusconi, and moved to New York (1937), where he was a propagandist and Dante lecturer at the Italy-American Society, a cultural organization, where he devoted his efforts to producing anti-fascist propaganda, translating and ghostwriting.

In 1941, Tucci was appointed assistant director of the Bureau of Latin American Research in Nelson Rockefeller's **Office of the Coordinator of Inter-American Affairs** and in the **U.S. Department of State**, where he wrote anti-fascist articles and uncredited stories for Walt Disney. In 1944, he became a freelance writer for magazines, and in 1965 Nucci was a writer-in-residence at Columbia University. He published novels, plays, several autobiographies, and short stories, many for the *New Yorker*. He died in New York.

FURTHER READING: *Contemporary Authors*, vols. 81–84 (Detroit, MI: Gale Research, 1979); obituary, *Washington Post*, December 18, 1999: B8.

U

UNCLE SAM. Symbol of the United States that has been recruited for many causes. The most lasting image was created by James Montgomery Flagg, who drew the original poster of Uncle Sam that became one of the most popular American images as the July 6, 1916, cover of *Leslie's Illustrated Weekly* with its "I Want You for U.S. Army" slogan; it was based on a 1914 British military recruiting poster. It was reprinted for World War II then used by advertisers to sell real estate and household products in the 1950s. During the Vietnam era, Uncle Sam was reborn as a combination of antiestablishment sentiment, the civil rights movement, and the influences of a pop-art poster craze bowdlerized his once patriotic image. One of the most shocking was a skeleton in top hat and tatters bursting through a traditional Uncle Sam war poster while the most harrowing was probably that of a bandaged Uncle Sam with a crumpled hat under one arm and the second one stretched in supplication with the words, "I Want Out." Since then, it has been used to promote political agendas, such as Uncle Sam as the wounded soldier and 1972 Uncle Sam as skeleton, posters protesting the Vietnam War. Other images were followed by expressions such as "I Want You To End the Military Ban" (campaign for military service), "Have You Had Your Pill Today?" (sexual revolution), and "Who Needs You?" (*MAD Magazine*).

Uncle Sam as propaganda represented movements from the radical right to the far left. It began with a real person, Sam Wilson, who ran a meatpacking plant in Troy, New York. During the War of 1812, he shipped meat to the troops in crates stamped "U.S.," and soldiers said it came from Uncle Sam. Contemporary portrayals by printmakers and cartoonists depicted Wilson as an honest man, although Thomas Nash drew him as a gaunt figure with long legs.

Uncle Sam's historical symbolism has become a popular icon for protest art, the underground press, and guerrilla art.

FURTHER READING: Yvonne French, "'Everybody's Uncle Sam': Poster Has Been Recruited for Many Causes," *Library of Congress Information Bulletin* 54, no. 10 (May 15, 1995): 220–23.

UNCLE TOM'S CABIN. Written by New Englander **Harriet Beecher Stowe,** this powerful propaganda novel that attacked slavery was a major mouthpiece of the abolitionist movement, a powerful indictment of slavery, that was first serialized in the *National Era* between June 5, 1851 and April 1, 1852. It was considered the outstanding American propaganda novel of the century after it was published in 1852; it drew on the familiar genre of the slave narrative cast in a fictional tale with regional types and racy slang. The story was originally written as installments in the Washington, D.C., antislavery newspaper, *National Era*. It sold an unprecedented 300,000 copies during its first year of publication and contributed significantly to the abolitionist movement.

The book was an antislavery tract, with a rather sentimental plot, that provoked strong attitudes, both positive and negative, toward the slavery question, and it had propaganda value to both sides in the Civil War as well as abroad. It introduced characters such as Tom, George, Eliza, Topsy, "the angelic little Eva," and the slavemaster, Simon Legree. It was heavily attacked by Southerners who argued that Stowe distorted plantation life, but President Lincoln allegedly called her "the little woman who wrote the book that started this great war" when she visited the White House in 1862.

Stowe had no experience with plantation life, and her book was strongly influenced by Lydia Child's *An Appeal in Favor of That Class of Americans Called Africans* (1933) and **Theodore Weld's** classic work, *American Slavery As It Is* (1839), with their attacks on the atrocities of the slave system. The novel was later condemned by African-American groups as tokenism and "Uncle Tom" became a derogatory term for a black man who helped the white cause. It had propaganda value to both sides in the Civil War as well as abroad. As a response to her critics, Stowe published *A Key to Uncle Tom's Cabin* (1853). Today *Uncle Tom's Cabin* is considered a period piece with its quaint story and characters.

  See also Abolitionist Propaganda

FURTHER READING: Charles Foster, *Rungless Ladder: Harriet Beecher Stowe and New England Puritanism* (Durham, NC: Duke University, 1954); *Notable American Women, 1607–1950,* vol. 3 (Cambridge, MA: Belknap Press of Harvard University Press, 1971–1980); Forrest Wilson, *Crusader in Crinoline* (Westport, CT: Greenwood, 1972/1941).

UNCONDITIONAL SURRENDER. Policy formulated by President Roosevelt and British Prime Minister Winston Churchill at the Casablanca Conference (1943) that, with the **Morgenthau Plan** for Germany, anticipated the defeat of Germany and how it was to be treated as a conquered country with a "hard peace." There were to be no "escape clauses" such as Woodrow Wilson's Fourteen Points for Germany after World War I. It was conceived for bolstering home-front morale and to stiffen inter-Allied determination to fight World War II through to a successful and decisive end, but it posed problems for Allied propagandists, whose major responsibility was to convince the enemy that it was advantageous to lay down their arms short of complete or near annihilation. Also, the policy was altered after Roosevelt's death by President Harry Truman.

Although the policy of "unconditional surrender" delayed the end of the war by several months, the propagandists were able to salvage something from it for effective use in propaganda warfare that relied on two themes: the inevitability of Allied victory and the integrity and decency of the democratic world compared to the corruption and untrustworthiness of the Nazis.

FURTHER READING: William E. Daugherty, "Unconditional Surrender," in *Psychological Warfare Casebook*, ed. William E. Daugherty (Baltimore: Johns Hopkins; published for Operations Research Office, Johns Hopkins University, 1958); U.S. Senate. Committee on the Judiciary. Subcommittee to Investigate the Administration of the Internal Security Act and Other Internal Security Laws, *Interlocking Subversion in Government Departments (The Harry Dexter White Papers)*; hearing, August 30, 1955, pt. 30. (Washington, DC: Government Printing Office, 1956).

UNFINISHED BUSINESS (EXHIBIT). *See* Brussels Universal and International Exposition (EXPO 1958)

UNION LEAGUE BOARD OF PUBLICATIONS. *See* Civil War Propagandists

UNION OF SOVIET SOCIALIST REPUBLICS (SOVIET UNION). *See* Brussels Universal and International Exposition (EXPO 1958); Disinformation; Forgeries; Soviet Active Measures

UNITED KINGDOM. *See* Hotze, Henry; Norden, Commander; War of American Independence Propaganda

U.S. ARMY FIELD MANUAL. U.S. Army Field Manual, FM 30-31B, also known as "Stability Operations-Intelligence," was the most ubiquitous forgery of recent years. In September 1976, a photocopy of this forgery appeared on the bulletin board of the Philippine Embassy in Thailand together with a letter addressed to President Marcos. The forgery said that the United States planned to use leftist terrorist groups in Western countries to promote U.S. objectives. It reappeared in 1978 in two Spanish publications, where it had been planted by a Spanish Communist and a Cuban intelligence officer. The next year, copies of a Portuguese language translation were circulated by the Soviets among military officers in Lisbon.

The forged field manual had worldwide distribution in the late 1970s. In January 1979, *Covert Action Information Bulletin*, published in the United States by CIA defector Philip Agee, reproduced the forgery as if it was an authentic document. Whereas the original forgery was a typescript, the magazine reset it in font that gave the impression that it was a printed document.

In 1983, the Soviets began to replay the story. In the new version, the manual had been discovered in the possession of the Italian Masonic organization P2, which was involved in an important scandal at the time. This was an attempt both to link the U.S. government to the scandal and to authenticate the forgery.

FURTHER READING: Herbert Romerstein, "Disinformation as a KGB Weapon in the Cold War," paper prepared for a Conference on Germany and Intelligence Organizations: The Last Fifty Years in Review, Akademie fur Politische Bildung Tutzing [Germany] (1999).

U.S. BUREAU OF CUSTOMS (TREASURY DEPARTMENT). *See* **Postal Regulations (Communist Political Propaganda)**

U.S. CENTRAL INTELLIGENCE AGENCY. *See* **Central Intelligence Agency**

U.S. COMMITTEE ON PUBLIC INFORMATION. *See* **Committee on Public Information**

U.S. CONGRESS. HOUSE. COMMITTEE ON INTERNAL SECURITY. *See* **U.S. Congressional Investigations of Propaganda**

U.S. CONGRESS. HOUSE. COMMITTEE ON UN-AMERICAN ACTIVITIES. The most famous committee of Congress was created in June 1938 as a temporary investigating committee to deal with the growing concern over propaganda activities of both Nazi and Communist sympathizers in the United States in the late 1930s. The House Special Committee on Un-American Activities existed until 1945. After that, it became a regular House committee, the House Un-American Activities Committee (HUAC); its first chairman was John S. Wood (D-GA). The committee was charged with the resolution that created it to investigate "the extent, character, and objects of un-American propaganda activities in the United States" and "the diffusion within the United States of subversive and un-American propaganda that is instigated from foreign countries or of a domestic origin and attacks the principle of the form of government as guaranteed by our Constitution." In the course of its existence, HUAC primarily investigated Communist activities and propaganda, did extensive investigations, and issued reports on Nazi activities and propaganda, as well as on Nazi and Soviet espionage. It was popularly called the Dies Committee after its chairman, Martin Dies (D.-Texas), who used the committee to attack **New Deal** programs of the Roosevelt administration.

In its first year of operation, J. Parnell Martin (R-NJ) called for an investigation of propaganda by the **Federal Theater Project** and the Federal Writers projects, which were sponsored by the Works Progress Administration created by President Franklin Roosevelt. Although the projects gave employment for many writers and performers, Congress was not inclined to champion the arts when the needs of the rest of the country seemed more pressing and basic. In July 1939, an amendment to save the programs was defeated, and the Federal Theater and Federal Writer projects were voted out of existence.

After the attack on **Pearl Harbor**, Joseph B. Matthews, the special committee's chief investigator and staff director, advocated retaliation for the sneak attack in a speech that marked the first congressional radio broadcast. J. Parnell Thomas succeeded Wood as committee chairman. From October 20 to October 30, 1947, the committee conducted hearings on the Communist infiltration of the motion picture industry. One of the "friendly" witnesses was actor **Ronald Reagan**. The hearings discussed specific examples of Communist propaganda, such as *Mission to Moscow* (1943), *North Star* (1943), and *Song of Russia*, all produced when the Soviet Union was still a U.S. ally. Among the many witnesses subpoenaed to testify, the least cooperative were designated the "Hollywood Ten," who claimed First Amendment protection. HUAC returned to an investigation of the motion picture industry from May to November 1951, when the committee held extensive hearings. From 1952 through 1958, HUAC turned from films to the rest of the entertainment industry, particularly radio, television, and publishing. Thomas remained HUAC chairman until the Democrats regained control of Congress in January 1949. Woods returned as chairman and in 1951–1952, reopened hearings on the motion picture industry with witnesses such as Larry Parks, Elia Kazan, Lillian Hellman, Clifford Odets, and Budd Schulberg.

In subsequent years, HUAC conducted investigations of Communist influence in the field of publications (*March of Labor*), (July 8–15, 1954); Communist propaganda among prisoners of war in Korea, including **front organizations**, such as the American Peace Crusade Save Our Sons Committee (June 18–19, 1956); international Communist propaganda activities (January 30, 1957); Communist propaganda in the United States (February–March, October 1957); Communist infiltration and propaganda activities in basic industry, in areas such as Gary, Indiana (February 10–11, 1958); pro-Castro propaganda activities in the United States (1963–1964); and activities of the **Ku Klux Klan** (1965–1966).

In 1969, HUAC became the House Committee on Internal Security, but the committee was abolished in 1975. However, the Senate also conducted investigations on Communist propaganda.

See also McCarthyism; U.S. Congressional Investigations of Propaganda

FURTHER READING: U.S. House. Committee on Un-American Activities, *Cumulative Index to Publications of the Committee on Un-American Activities, 1938–1954* (Washington, DC: Government Printing Office, 1962); ibid., *Supplement to the Cumulative Index to Publications of the Committee on Un-American Activities, 1955–1968* (Washington, DC: Government Printing Office, 1970); U.S. Senate. Committee on Government Operations, *Congressional Investigations of Communism and Subversive Activities: Summary-Index, 1918 to 1956* (Washington, DC: Government Printing Office, 1956).

U.S. CONGRESS. HOUSE. SPECIAL COMMITTEE ON UN-AMERICAN ACTIVITIES. *See* U.S. Congress. House. Committee on Un-American Activities; U.S. Congressional Investigations of Propaganda

U.S. CONGRESSIONAL INVESTIGATIONS OF PROPAGANDA. The first Congressional hearings on propaganda activities in the United States were held immediately after World War I when the subcommittee of the Senate Committee on the Judiciary, chaired by Lee S. Overman, investigated German and Bolshevik (Russian) propaganda in September 1918. This committee did not resume its hearings on subversive activities until 1948.

More hearings on Russian propaganda were held (January 12, 1920 through March 29, 1920) by the Senate Committee on Foreign Relations. These were chaired by Senator George H. Moses. Four years later, the same committee scheduled testimony on the recognition of Russia in which propaganda carried on in the United States but directed from Russia was investigated. Like Judiciary, this committee held hearings sporadically until the late 1940s.

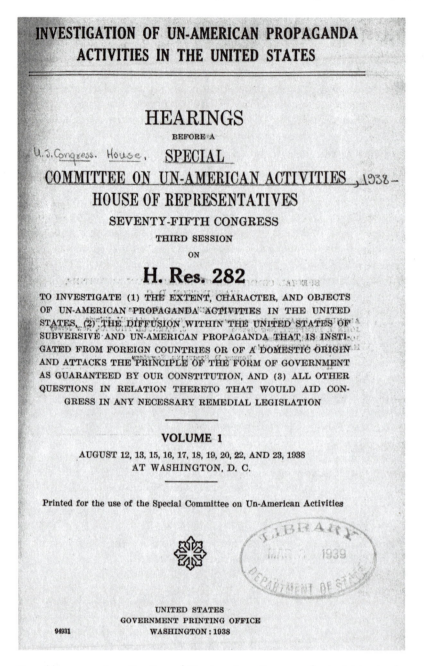

Pamphlet cover: *Investigation of Un-American Propaganda Activities in the United States*; hearings before a Special Committee on Un-American Activities, House of Representatives, 1938.

However, most of the Congressional investigation of propaganda was carried out on the House side, beginning with the House Special Committee to Investigate Communist Activities in the United States, designated the Fish Committee, for its chairman, Hamilton Fish, Jr. (R-NY), which was created in 1930. It did an extensive investigation of Soviet and Communist operations and propaganda in the United States, including espionage.

House Resolution 199, the legislation introduced by Representative Samuel Dickstein on January 3, 1934, to provide for the investigation of Nazi propaganda activities in the United States, resulted in the House Special Committee on Nazi Propaganda, an investigative committee chaired by John McCormack (D-MA), which produced two laws: the compulsory registration of foreign agents disseminating propaganda in the United States (**Foreign Agents Registration Act**), and the empowering of congressional committees holding hearings outside of Washington, D.C., to issue subpoenas.

The most famous committee was created in June 1938 as a temporary investigating committee to deal with the growing concern over propaganda activities of both Nazi and Communist sympathizers in the United States in the late 1930s. The House Special Committee on Un-American Activities existed until 1945. After that, it became a regular House committee (**U.S. Congress. House Committee on Un-American Activities [HUAC]**).

After the Senate Foreign Relations Committee hearings in 1920, the Senate Judiciary Committee resumed its investigative activities in 1948 with its Subcommittee to Investigate the Administration of the Internal Security Act and Other Internal Security Laws, chaired by Patrick McCarran (D-NV). In 1953, the subcommittee held hearings on Communist underground printing facilities and illegal propaganda and on Communist propaganda from June 22 to October 14, 1954.

McCarthy Committee

In 1953, Senator Joseph McCarthy chaired the Senate Government Operations Committee and its Permanent Investigations Subcommittee. He conducted hearings on waste and mismanagement in U.S. government agencies as well as on Communist propaganda. In 1955, the Democrats resumed control of the Senate, and Senator John McClellan became chairman of the committee; he continued the same investigations that had been started by McCarthy.

See also **McCarthyism**

FURTHER READING: Both the House and the Senate committees produced voluminous sets of hearings and reports on their investigations into Communist propaganda and other subversive activities in the United States. The most complete set is probably at the Library of Congress but other institutions may also prove useful. See also: U.S. House. Committee on Un-American Activities. *Cumulative Index to Publications of the Committee on Un-American Activities, 1938–1954* (Washington, DC: Government Printing Office, 1962) and the HUAC annual reports; ibid. *Supplement to the Cumulative Index to Publications of the Committee on Un-American Activities, 1955–1968* (Washington, DC: Government Printing Office, 1970); U.S. Senate. Committee on Government Operations, *Congressional Investigations of Communism and Subversive Activities: Summary—Index, 1918 to 1956* (Washington, DC: Government Printing Office, 1956).

U.S. CONTINENTAL CONGRESS. COMMITTEE OF SECRET CORRESPONDENCE. *See* **Committee of Secret Correspondence**

U.S. COORDINATOR OF INFORMATION. *See* Coordinator of Information

U.S. CULTURAL AND INFORMATION PROGRAMS. On October 1, 1999, the educational exchange programs, **libraries**, Washington File, foreign press centers, and speaker programs were transferred to the **U.S. Department of State. Voice of America, Radio Marti, Radio Free Asia, Radio Liberty,** and **Radio Free Europe** were kept in the International Broadcasting Bureau under a Broadcasting Board of Governors as an independent agency. Between 1945 and 1953, all of these programs were directed by the State Department. When USIA was abolished, its various programs again became part of the State Department, and they are still mandated by the **U.S. Informational and Cultural Exchange Act** of 1948 (Smith-Mundt Act), the act under which all the cultural, informational and educational programs still operate.

Milestones

1918—**Committee on Public Information** (CPI), World War I predecessor to the present program, represented the U.S. government's first large-scale information program. CPI distributed publications, supplied articles to the foreign-language press, opened offices in major capitals, established reading rooms in foreign countries, and brought foreign journalists to the United States.

1927—First **Binational Center** (BNC) established in Buenos Aires at same time U.S. government was conducting unofficial cultural exchanges in Latin America.

1935—First "Radio Bulletin," a direct precursor of the Washington File, transmitted via Morse Code by the State Department.

1938—Buenos Aires Convention that established an official U.S. government exchange program.

1939–1945—U.S. government programmed American speakers for overseas engagements.

1940—Office of the **Coordinator of Inter-American Affairs** (CIAA), headed by Nelson Rockefeller, to counter Nazi propaganda in Latin America. CIAA initiated exchange programs, established libraries and **binational centers**, and started a broadcasting service.

1942—Voice of America, the U.S. international broadcasting service, began its service with broadcasts to Europe. **Office of War Information** (OWI) created to coordinate U.S. information activities during World War II.

1946—Information programs handled by Office of War Information (OWI) during World War II are placed in the State Department. In that same year, the Fulbright Act was signed by President Truman.

1953—President Eisenhower signs Reorganization Plan No. 8 (1953) that creates the **U.S. Information Agency** (USIA) as a Cold War propaganda agency to "tell America's story abroad." It became, in effect, a ministry of American culture with chief responsibility for organizing an American cultural offensive worldwide that created sympathy and understanding among foreign audiences for U.S. foreign policy objectives. The educational exchanges remain in the State Department. In many overseas posts, USIA is known as the U.S. Information Service.

1961—Mutual Educational and Cultural Exchange Act (Fulbright-Hays) consolidated various U.S. international educational and cultural exchanges and established government operation of cultural and educational centers abroad.

1978—State's Bureau of Educational and Cultural Affairs, including the Fulbright program, was combined with USIA as a new agency: U.S. International Communication Agency (USICA). This name was abolished in August 1982 and the agency became USIA again.

1990—Amendment to Smith-Mundt Act of 1948 authorized USIA to make certain materials available for domestic distribution.

1994—International Broadcasting Act of 1994 established the International Broadcasting Bureau (IBB) within USIA and consolidated U.S. government broadcasting, including Voice of America, Radio and TV Marti, Radio Free Asia and **Worldnet**, under a Broadcasting Board of Governors.

1998—President Clinton signed the Omnibus Authorization Act (Public Law 105-277) that abolished the foreign affairs agencies, including USIA, and integrated all agency elements except the International Broadcasting Bureau (which became an independent agency) into the State Department on October 1, 1999.

U.S. cultural offensive takes many forms: performances of American music, exhibitions of American artists, well-stocked libraries of American books and periodicals, and representations at international expositions. Through its Binational Centers (BNCs), it has furthered the study of English (as a second language) and supported American studies. Through Voice of America programming, such as its country music and jazz broadcasts, the United States transmits a range of American cultural forms to the world. It also operates the U.S. government's educational exchange program of which the best known is the Fulbright scholarship program, which operates in over 140 countries. Today, it is involved in public diplomacy, government-sponsored programs intended to inform or influence public opinion in other countries through its chief instruments of publications, motion pictures, cultural exchanges, foreign press centers (New York, Los Angeles, Washington), international visitors programs, university partnerships, Freedom Support Act grants, parliamentary exchanges, media internships and in-country workshops, business programs, local and regional government exchanges, radio (VOA), and television (Worldnet). It now maintains more that 212 posts in 147 countries.

FURTHER READING: Allen C. Hansen, *USIA: Public Diplomacy in the Computer Age*, 2nd ed. (Westport, CT: Praeger, 1989); Hans N. Tuch, *Communicating with the World: U.S. Public Diplomacy Overseas* (New York: St. Martin's Press, 1990); "The United States Information Agency, 1953–1993," *USIA World* 12, no. 4 [Entire issue, 1993]; Bureau of International Information Programs, U.S. Department of State Web site (http://usinfo.state.gov).

U.S. CUSTOMS SERVICE. *See* Postal Regulations (Communist Political Propaganda)

U.S. DEPARTMENT OF AGRICULTURE. The U.S. Department of Agriculture is an example of one of the many U.S. government agencies that uses propaganda. Its Motion Picture Service went through various phases of expansion after the time of Secretary James Wilson and secret operations in an 8-by-12 attic room. For a year during World War I, the office did work for the Committee on

Public Information. Under the long and prosperous directorship of Raymond Evans, its growing demands required its own sound stage and its studios taken over by Office of Strategic Services during World War II for the preparation of visual reports for the president and the chiefs of staff. USDA produced films like *The Tree of Life*, which showed unplanned lumbering operations resulting in abandoned communities and "sustained yield" experiments resulting in controlled natural resources and stable communities. Its most notable filmmaker, **Pare Lorentz**, was not a propagandist by choice. He produced and directed ***The Plow That Broke the Plains*** (1936) and ***The River*** for the Resettlement Administration with the Department of Agriculture under its undersecretary, Rexford G. Tugwell; both films were considered New Deal propaganda.

FURTHER READING: Richard D. MacCann, *The People's Films: A Political History of U.S. Government Motion Pictures* (New York: Hastings House, 1973).

U.S. DEPARTMENT OF STATE. The U.S. Department of State is the oldest department in the U.S. government. It started as the Department of Foreign Affairs in 1781, five years after the Declaration of Independence and its respect for the "opinions of mankind." Although the department's primary mission is diplomacy, it has engaged in certain propaganda (or public diplomacy, as it was later designated) activities. Although it did not officially create them, the State Department authorized such early activities as the pro-Union campaign President Lincoln sent to Europe to counter the more effective propaganda activities of **Henry Hotze** for the Confederacy. During World War I, State was overshadowed by the first official U.S. propaganda agency, the **Committee on Public Information,** in the promotion of the war effort, but during Roosevelt's **New Deal**, it issued the first "Radio Bulletin" (1935), precursor to the present "Washington File," sent via Morse Code to key diplomatic posts abroad. This was followed by the Interdepartmental Committee for Scientific and Cultural Cooperation and Division of Cultural Cooperation formed (1938) to counteract German and Italian propaganda in Latin America.

During World War II, the cultural and the information programs were handled by various propaganda agencies, culminating in the **Office of War Information,** which lacked the authority of its World War I predecessor. In 1946, the information and cultural programs were absorbed into the Office of International Cultural Affairs and the International Press and Publication Division under advertising executive William Benton, named by Truman as undersecretary for public and cultural affairs. In a speech that same year, Benton insisted that the office's function was to conduct "a dignified information program, as distinguished from propaganda," a comment echoed by Secretary of State John Foster Dulles in his "no propagandists in State Department" comment, made at the time that President Eisenhower decided to create a separate **U.S. Information Agency** (USIA) to handle U.S. propaganda while the exchange programs stayed in the State Department, where they remained until 1978, when they were placed in USIA. In October 1999, USIA was abolished and both its educational exchange programs and its information activities, unique to the State Department, became part of a new **Bureau of Public Diplomacy** under the direction of an assistant secretary of public diplomacy and public affairs, who answered directly to the

USIS poster production, Shanghai, with seven sample documents, each in a different language: Indonesian, Siamese, Turkish, Chinese, Tagalog, Cebuano, and English. These were produced by the U.S. Department of State. Note: There is no date on this photo, but the pictures of President Harry Truman (1945–1953) and Secretary of State George Marshall in the Siamese poster indicate that this was produced during the years the U.S. Information program was part of State (1945–1953); USIA was established under Eisenhower, and his picture would have replaced Truman. (*Source:* USIA-Regional Publication Center, Manila)

Secretary of State. The International Broadcasting Bureau, which includes the **Voice of America,** became an independent agency.

FURTHER READING: Materials on the history of the U.S. Department of State (U.S. Dept. of State Web site: http://www.state.gov).

U.S. DEPARTMENT OF THE TREASURY. PUBLICITY BUREAU. *See* Publicity Bureau

U.S. DIVISION OF CULTURAL RELATIONS (DEPARTMENT OF STATE). *See* Division of Cultural Relations (Department of State)

U.S. FILM SERVICE. After the success of *The Plow That Broke the Plains* (1936), made for the Resettlement Administration, and *The River*, produced for its successor, Farm Security Administration, President Franklin Roosevelt decided to improve the quality and expand the distribution of government films. In September 1938, he created the U.S. Film Service within the National Emergency Council "to acquaint Federal and State agencies, educational institutions, and interested civic organizations and groups with the availability of silent and sound motion pictures produced by various Government bureaus." **Pare Lorentz** was the director. Richard MacCann, in his book, *People's Films: A Political History of U.S. Government Motion Pictures* (New York: Hastings House, 1973) claims that the decline of the documentary movement within the U.S. government began with the beginnings of the U.S. Film Service because funding was cut within a year by the House Committee on Appropriations, and the U.S. Film Service had to prove that, even without a direct appropriation, it could continue operations from allocations for filmmaking received from other agencies, especially the Works Progress Administration (WPA) and the Farm Security Administration (FSA).

Conservative criticism of the U.S. Film Service focused on its New Deal agenda and the films that were created around New Deal themes. These included *The Fight for Life* (1940), an attempt by Lorentz to impress the film world as well as Congress; *The Land* (1941), which was produced by Robert Flaherty, who is still considered the inventor of the American documentary film; and *Power and the Land* (1940) by Joris Ivens, the Dutch exponent of realistic photography, filmed in cooperation with the Rural Electrification Administration (REA).

On July 1, 1939, Reorganization Plan No. 11 abolished the National Emergency Council and placed its film and radio services in the U.S. Office of Education where it was administered by the Federal Security Administrator. The U.S. Film Service lasted until June 1940, when Congress cut its funds and effectively ended the project. It was silenced by a House Appropriations Committee subcommittee (House, 76th Congress, 3d Session, Department of Labor-Federal Security Agency Appropriation Bill for 1941) and a single Senate debate (Senate, 76th Congress, 3d Session, Department of Labor-Federal Security Agency Appropriation Bill for 1941).

The U.S. Film Service marked a great new development in government responsibility for public information, and it was the perfect **New Deal** agency, which also proved to be its strongest negative in Congress with its need to generate peacetime publicity to support New Deal programs. As soon as **Pare Lorentz**'s group came out in the open, they were marked for attack, and the political strength of Lorentz and his associates could not offer a successful counterattack.

See also Documentaries; *Plow That Broke the Plain*; *The River*

FURTHER READING: Richard MacCann, *People's Films: A Political History of U.S. Government Motion Pictures* (New York: Hastings House, 1973); Richard W. Steele, *Propaganda in an Open Society: The Roosevelt Administration and the Media, 1933–1941* (Westport, CT: Greenwood, 1985).

U.S. GOVERNMENT. Many U.S. government departments and agencies are responsible for information gathering and/or communication. Today the federal government, more than any Madison Avenue advertising firm or corporate entity, is perhaps the single greatest propaganda machine in the United States. Despite cutback attempts by successive administrations, there are specialists in some 47 different federal agencies who spend over three billion annually to influence American thinking. Uncle Sam is the nation's leading publisher and film producer, distributing thousands of magazines and books, hundreds of motion pictures and videocassettes, and innumerable press releases. Example: The Treasury Department continues to underwrite production of special video episodes for internal government (e.g., using top Hollywood stars to promote the purchase of savings bonds by federal employees).

The official government public relations organization was the **U.S. Information Agency**, which designated its functions as **public diplomacy** during the 1980s. When USIA was abolished in 1999, its activities became part of a new **Bureau of Public Diplomacy** in the **U.S. Department of State** but the authorizing legislation continued the **domestic dissemination** ban of the Smith-Mundt Act (1948), which limits its audience to overseas countries only. Its books, films, radio broadcasts, libraries, and information offices are forbidden by the Act's domestic dissemination ban from being distributed within the United States. Taxpayers are also supporting the American military as one of the country's largest advertisers, with its messages to young people to enlist, especially the effective Marine Corps and their search for "a few good men."

Government broadcast advertising developed the public service announcements that still try to solicit public support for various causes, usually in the middle of a popular television event. There is also broadcast deregulation by agencies such as the Federal Communications Commission, which still retains powerful authority over electronic communicators with its fairness doctrine.

See also Black Propaganda; Central Intelligence Agency; Committee of Secret Correspondence; Committee on Public Information; Coordinator of Information; Division of Cultural Relations (Department of State); Federal Arts Project; Federal Theater Project; Gray Propaganda; Office of Strategic Services; Office of the Coordinator of Inter-American Affairs; Office of War Information; President's Advisory Committee on Government Organization; President's Committee on Information Activities Abroad; President's Committee on International Information Activities; Publicity Bureau; Uncle Sam; U.S. Congressional Investigations of Propaganda; White Propaganda; World Cruise of the U.S. Navy; Why We Fight Series

U.S. INFORMATION AGENCY. The U.S. Information Agency (USIA) was the information service of the federal government. On August 1, 1953, as part of an executive branch reorganization (Reorganization Plan No. 8) by the Eisenhower administration, the USIA was created to consolidate programs formerly run by the International Information Administration, the Mutual Security Agency, the Technical Cooperation Administration, programs financed in connection with government in occupied areas, and the **Voice of America**. The Office of Educational Exchange stayed in the **U.S. Department of State** (until 1978), but its overseas administration was transferred to USIA, which was created as a weapon in America's arsenal against international Communism. Its mission was to make the case for the superiority of American values and to unmask and counteract hostile attempts to frustrate U.S. policies. It was the first ongoing peacetime propaganda program.

From 1953 until 1999, USIA operated information services, most notably its radio broadcasting service in VOA, as well as a wide variety of cultural and educational exchanges. It was funded independently of the **U.S. Department of State** but worked closely on policy coordination with the department. Its first director was Theodore C. Streibert (1953–1956), former chairman of the Mutual Broadcasting System, but one of the most important directors was George V. Allen (1958–1961), who took over the agency at a time of considerable disarray caused by its inability to favorably portray the civil rights movement in the

Montage of USIA scenes. (*Source:* U.S. Information Agency: A Commemoration [Washington, DC: USIA, 1999])

United States or to respond persuasively to the dramatic Sputnik voyage of the USSR. Under Allen, USIA initiated a policy of gentle persuasion in information programming and renewed U.S.–USSR cultural exchanges, including the **American National Exhibition** in Moscow in 1959. The agency's most famous director was **Edward R. Murrow** (1961–1964), who brought a distinguished broadcasting and journalism background to the position and distinction to USIA.

In October 1998, the Foreign Affairs Reform and Restructuring Act (Public Law 105-277) abolished USIA and consolidated its functions into the State Department. The following October when the merger took place USIA ceased to exist. The educational exchange programs and those in the Bureau of Information were placed in a newly created **Bureau of Public Diplomacy** headed by an under secretary. The first was Evelyn Lieberman.

Vice President Richard Nixon and Soviet Premier Nikita Krushchev inspect the Moscow Exhibition grounds on July 24, 1959. Note: This was the beginning of the walk that resulted in the "kitchen debate" later that day between the two men. (*Source:* "Review of the American National Exhibition in Moscow, July 25–September 4, 1959" [Washington, DC: USIA, 1959])

See also Advancing American Art; Art Exhibitions; Domestic Dissemination; Public Diplomacy; U.S. Information and Educational Exchange Act

FURTHER READING: Allen Hansen, *United States Information Agency: Public Diplomacy in the Computer Age*, 2d ed. rev. (Westport, CT: Praeger, 1989); David I. Hitchcock, *U.S. Public Diplomacy* (Washington, DC: Center for Strategic and International Studies, 1988); Hans Tuch, *Communicating with the World: U.S. Public Diplomacy Overseas* (New York: St. Martin's Press, 1990); Dick Kirschten, "Restive Relic," *National Journal* (April 22, 1995): 976–80; News Releases from USIA, VOA, and State Department; Shawn J. Parry-Giles, *Rhetorical Presidency, Propaganda, and the Cold War, 1945–1955* (Westport, CT: Praeger, 2002).

U.S. INFORMATION AND EDUCATIONAL EXCHANGE ACT. Public Law 80-402, approved January 27, 1948, is popularly known as the Smith-Mundt Act. It came about due to Cold War concerns about Soviet **disinformation** efforts figured in the debates that led to the passage of this act, named for its cosponsors, H. Alexander Smith (R-NJ) and Karl Mundt (D-SD). The act authorized overseas information and cultural activities "to promote better understanding of the United States." Under Smith-Mundt, the **U.S. Department of State** divided public diplomacy operations into an Office of International Information and an

Office of Educational Exchange, whereas Section 501, the **domestic dissemination** ban, prohibited the use of program materials created by this information to be distributed in the United States without an act of Congress. In 1953, the information office became part of USIA. In 1977, under President Carter, the educational exchange office (Bureau of Educational and Cultural Affairs) was reorganized with USIA as the U.S. International Communication Agency (USICA). In 1983, this name was abolished and the agency retained USIA again. With the consolidation of USIA and its information functions into the State Department again, Smith-Mundt was closely studied to determine how much of the original legislation was still applicable under its new organization in State, but the authorizing legislation made all public diplomacy functions still obligated by the act.

FURTHER READING: U.S. Congress. Joint Committee Print. Senate Committee on Foreign Relations and House Committee on International Relations. *Legislation on Foreign Relations Through 1999: Current Legislation and Related Executive Orders* (Washington, DC: Government Printing Office, 2000); Dick Kirschten, "Restive Relic," *National Journal* (April 22, 1995): 976–80.

UNITED STATES MAGAZINE. The *United States Magazine*, edited by Henry Brackenridge, assisted by **Philip Freneau**, appeared after the adoption of the Declaration of Independence. It included essays about the war, satirical poems, accounts of battles and of British atrocities, and sermons. Later issues lacked enough contributions to carry the satire; instead, it relied on military news and state constitutions, which were printed in later issues, but the magazine ceased publication after only 12 months. Brackenridge's statement when he stopped publication has tended to lessen the magazine's importance as propaganda.

FURTHER READING: Philip Davidson, *Propaganda and the American Revolution, 1763–1783* (New York: Norton, 1973/1941).

U.S. NAVY. *See* World Cruise of the U.S. Navy (1907–1909)

U.S. OFFICE OF INTER-AMERICAN COORDINATOR. *See* Office of Strategic Services; Office of the Coordinator of Inter-American Affairs

U.S. OFFICE OF STRATEGIC SERVICES. *See* Office of Strategic Services

U.S. OFFICE OF WAR INFORMATION. *See* Office of War Information

U.S. PRESIDENT'S ADVISORY COMMITTEE ON GOVERNMENT ORGANIZATION. *See* President's Advisory Committee on Government Organization

U.S. PRESIDENT'S COMMITTEE ON INFORMATION ACTIVITIES ABROAD. *See* President's Committee on Information Activities Abroad

U.S. PRESIDENT'S COMMITTEE ON INTERNATIONAL INFORMATION ACTIVITIES. *See* President's Committee on International Information Activities

UNITED STATES RELATIONS WITH CHINA. See China White Paper

U.S. WAR DEPARTMENT. *See* Why We Fight Series

U.S.A. ZONE OF THE OVERSEAS SERVICE (NORTH AMERICAN SERVICE). Established by German Propaganda Minister Paul Josef Goebbels as early as 1933 to house the foreign nationals who were broadcasting for the Nazis, the U.S.A. Zone was staffed with American expatriates ("foreign correspondents"). In February 1941, the U.S.A. Zone requested its North American listeners to forward broadcast requests through cost-free telegrams to Berlin, an action greeted with derision in the U.S. press. There were deliberate attempts to clog the German end of the telegram pipeline while U.S. intelligence agents argued that these large numbers of telegrams sent to Germany might contain potentially damaging information for the enemy. Over 10,000 telegrams were sent by the end of February; in the next month, the German propaganda ministry began *America Asks—Germany Answers*, a popular question-and-answer program that was a follow-up to the telegrams and that sparked an interest in American broadcasting personalities.

Germany was the first to employ foreign nationals as propagandists in their respective countries, and it recruited broadcasters from, among other nations, Egypt, France, Great Britain, Italy, Mexico, and South Africa, beside the United States. At the beginning of World War II, Goebbels staffed the U.S.A. Zone with broadcasters who were directed to cajole other Americans into supporting U.S. neutrality legislation. After Pearl Harbor, Goebbels ordered his American announcers to weaken the United States' resolve to fight and to raise Germany's credibility among Americans at Great Britain's expense. Broadcasters were expected to be patriotic but semidetached Americans who appeared motivated strictly by their country's best interests and an overall sense of fair play. Broadcasts were subjected to censorship, and the transmission of banned information had to be approved by Goebbels.

The U.S.A. Zone's campaign had two phases. The first, from the invasion of Poland to the German Blitzkrieg in the West, was to acquire a constituency and to consolidate its support. This was accomplished by reprinting selected excerpts from Nazi broadcasts in sympathetic German language newspapers throughout the United States and in literature distributed by Berlin's Library of Information. The second part of the campaign came after Hitler invaded the Low Countries and President Roosevelt hastened Lend-Lease aid to the Allied countries. Goebbels started a new campaign to unsettle the American public's faith in its leadership and in its democratic institutions. During both phases, Goebbels expected his American broadcasters to undermine the United States' ability to fight. Their compliance resulted in a U.S. federal grand jury indictment on July 26, 1943, which the "foreign correspondents" refused to obey.

The dean of the U.S.A. Zone repatriates was Frederick W. Kaltenbach (1895–1945), one of the first foreign-language broadcasters to join the German radio service. He started his propaganda broadcasts to the United States (1939) for the North American Zone as "Fred W. Kaltenbach." As a German radio propagandist, Kaltenbach's technique included a personal "Weekly Letter" to his friends in Iowa designed to embarrass them for their associations with him, and his "Friendly Quarrel between Fritz [played by Otto Koischwitz, Mr. O.K.] and Fred" [Kaltenbach]. Later, he provided material for the radio broadcasts to Great Britain and translated radio plays as he continued to advance the Nazi cause. According to William Shirer, then CBS's Berlin correspondent, Kaltenbach was the best of the radio broadcasters in the service of Nazi Germany who would die for Nazism, although, ironically, most Nazis found him a bit too American.

Other notable recruits included Jane Anderson, who was noticed by Joseph Goebbels and began broadcasting radio propaganda commentaries for the Nazis ("Voice of Europe") in February 1942 under the alias Georgia Peach; Robert H. Best (Mr. Guess Who), who first asked permission from the German authorities in Vienna to broadcast to the United States on the state-controlled radio, the Reichsrundfunk, part of Joseph Goebbel's propaganda machine, but nothing came of this, and he was fired by United Press, only to be hired the next year by Reichsrundfunk as a broadcaster to his native land with a program he called *Best's Berlin Broadcast*; Douglas Chandler (Paul Revere), who was considered America's last World War II radio traitor; and Donald Day, Edward Delaney, and Constance Drexel.

FURTHER READING: Horst J. P. Bergmeier and Rainer E. Lotz, *Hitler's Airwaves: The Inside Story of Nazi Radio Broadcasting and Propaganda Swing* (New Haven, CT: Yale, 1997); John C. Edwards, *Berlin Calling: American Broadcasters in Service to the Third Reich* (New York: Praeger, 1991).

USE OF PRISONERS OF WAR FOR PROPAGANDA. *See* **Prisoners of War**

V

VATICAN STATE. *See* Catholic Church

VICTOR EMMANUEL III. *See* "Moronic Little King" Incident

VIERECK, GEORGE SYLVESTER (December 31, 1884–March 18, 1962). German-American propagandist and strong advocate of any German government, George Viereck supported both Kaiser Wilhelm II's Germany in World War I and Hitler's Germany in World War II. During World War I, Viereck was employed by the German embassy to organize anti-British and pro-German propaganda. It was his eventually disastrous idea to put an advertisement in the American press (1915) signed by the German government warning Americans not to sail on British ships. The *Lusitania* was sunk a few days later, creating both strong anti-German feelings among Americans and the incorrect belief that the German embassy knew that the ship would sink. During the 1920s, Viereck wrote for the Hearst press. Before America's entry into World War II, he was employed by the German government again to edit the Nazis' news magazine and to organize covert propaganda. However, Viereck refused to write any anti-Semitic or anti-American propaganda. In fact, it was written into his contract with the Germans. He was convicted by the U.S. government for violation of the **Foreign Agents Registration Act** and sentenced (1943) to prison for one to five years for his wartime work for the Nazis; he served four years of his sentence. His books include *Confessions of a Barbarian* (1910); *My First Two Thousand Years: The Autobiography of the Wandering Jew* (1928); the classic **Spreading Germs of Hate** (New York: Horace Liveright, 1930), and *Men into Beasts* (1952). Viereck's publications emphasized four major propaganda themes: maintaining U.S. neutrality, promoting closer U.S.–German commercial and political ties, warning of the dangers of an entangling alliance with Great Britain, and exposing the pro-Allied bias of the U.S. news media. He married Margaret Edith Hein; they had two sons of whom one, George, was killed at the battle of Anzio fighting Germans while his father was in prison. Viereck died in Holyoke, Massachusetts.

FURTHER READING: Elmer Gertz, *Odyssey of a Barbarian: The Biography of George Sylvester Viereck* (Buffalo, NY: Promethus Books, 1978); Niel M. Johnson, *George Sylvester Viereck, German-American Propagandist* (Urbana: University of Illinois, 1972).

VIETNAM. *See* Vietnam Conflict; Vietnam. Joint United States Public Affairs Office (JUSPAO); Vietnam Movies

VIETNAM CONFLICT. The Vietnamese Conflict (1954–1975) drew on the troop strengths of some of America's allies, especially the British and the Australians. The propaganda campaign was fought on two sides: the American military establishment as it tried to sell a very unpopular situation to the people and the antiwar activists, who used sometimes violent methods to show their dissatisfaction with a conflict they were against and to win public opinion for their side.

American Friends of Vietnam (1955–1975) was a private lobbying group that attempted to rally support for South Vietnamese leader Ngo Dinh Diem in the late 1950s. It "preached to the converted" with its philosophy, held by many Americans, that anticommunist governments deserved support, but its impact seemed insignificant when President Lyndon Johnson channeled funds to the group to rally support for the escalation of the war effort, and it ceased in 1975. Antiwar **posters** were especially symbolic, such as the one of the daisy sticking out of the bayonet. On the pro-government side, the military went all the way in exhorting young men to sign up for military duty, despite the draft, which brought in thousands of men to the service every month. Particularly well known was the Marine Corps slogan: "We never promised you a rose garden." However, the most lasting and powerful images from Vietnam were the live battle scenes and the death tolls that appeared every night on television. This reliance on broadcasting for manipulation was particularly effective. Strategy was to break down the local communication structure and replace it with a tightly controlled new one. However, U.S. advisors underestimated competing propaganda strategies used by the insurgents, who successfully limited U.S.–South Vietnamese efforts. For propaganda purposes, the Soviet Union denounced U.S. military intervention. Trinh Thi Ngo ("Hanoi Hannah"), North Vietnam's radio propaganda queen, and her thrice-daily anti-American broadcasts that urged GIs to quit the "unjust and immoral war" between Elvis Presley and Herb Alpert records, played taped messages from Jane Fonda and other antiwar activists on the air, read stories about peace demonstrations in the United States, and recited the names of dead or captured Americans. Her major audience was captive: the POWs in the prison camps; many American servicemen didn't listen to her broadcasts.

In 1972, controversial film personality Jane Fonda broadcast a series of propaganda messages over Radio Hanoi denouncing the American military ("war criminals"), which proved to the North Vietnamese that there were Americans willing to broadcast for them and turn against their country, but it continues to shadow Fonda's career to date, as many veterans' groups refuse to see her movies or support her endorsements for what they consider treason. Since

Vietnam, a social science effort has started to evaluate its **psychological warfare** methods and activities.

See also Vietnam. Joint United States Public Affairs Office

FURTHER READING: Peter Braestrup, *Big Story! How the American Press and Television Reported and Interpreted the Crises of Tet 1968 in Vietnam and Washington* (Boulder, CO: Westview, 1977); Robert Chandler, *War of Ideas: The U.S. Propaganda Campaign in Vietnam* (Boulder, CO: Westview, 1981); Thomas W. Hoffer, "Broadcasting in an Insurgency Environment: USIA in Vietnam, 1965–1970" (Ph.D. dissertation, University of Wisconsin, Madison, 1972); Caroline Page, *U.S. Official Propaganda during the Vietnam War, 1965–1973: Limits of Persuasion* (London and New York: Leicester University, 1996).

VIETNAM. JOINT UNITED STATES PUBLIC AFFAIRS OFFICE. The Joint United States Public Affairs Office (JUSPAO), originally the United States Information Service, Saigon, was established in 1965 to coordinate propaganda activities (radio broadcasts, leaflets, pamphlets) during the American involvement in Vietnam. Along with headquarters in South Vietnam's capital, Saigon, there was an extensive field operation that produced public opinion survey reports. JUSPAO was staffed by the **U.S. Information Agency** but took its operational guidance from the U.S. Department of Defense. Earlier, John Mecklin, a USIA Foreign Service Officer, wrote a memorandum (September 10, 1963) to USIA director Edward R. Murrow concerning the U.S. situation in Vietnam in which he stated six assumptions, all controversial at the time, for a possible USIA public information operation:

1. A new Vietnamese government is essential;
2. Real power must go to a new man;
3. The odds are heavily against ousting the Ngo Dinhs without considerable bloodshed;
4. An unlimited U.S. commitment in Vietnam is justified;
5. U.S. forces could be used against Asian Communist guerrillas and win (And the stakes are so high that if unavoidable we must take the risk anyway);
6. The U.S. must accept the risks of covertly organizing a coup if necessary.

In Mecklin's opinion, "conditions in Viet-Nam [sic] have deteriorated so badly that the U.S. would be drawing to a three-card straight to gamble its interests there on anything short of an ultimate willingness to use U.S. combat troops."

When JUSPAO was established, its first director was Barry Zorthian, who maintained it as a strong presence in Vietnam, a stance that was often different from what the State Department wanted. He was replaced in 1968. Officially, he was appointed Special Assistant to the U.S. Ambassador with responsibility for policy direction and coordination of U.S. Mission relations with all media. Zorthian was succeeded as JUSPAO director in 1968, first by Ed Nickles then by Robert Lincoln, who closed JUSPAO down in 1975 when American troops evacuated the country.

See also Vietnam Conflict

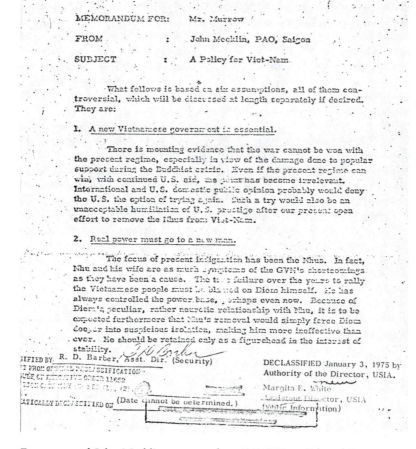

Front page of John Mecklin memorandum (9/10/63) to Edward R. Murrow re: "A Policy for Vietnam." (This is a copy; this has been declassified.)

FURTHER READING: Robert Chandler, *War of Ideas: The U.S. Propaganda Campaign in Vietnam* (Boulder, CO: Westview, 1981); Dennis J. Duncanson, Richard A. Yudkin, and Barry Zorthian, *Lessons of Vietnam; Three Interpretative Essays* (New York: American-Asian Educational Exchange, 1971); Caroline Page, *U.S. Official Propaganda during the Vietnam War, 1969–1973* (London and New York: Leicester University, 1996); Barry Zorthian oral history [USIA Alumni Association].

VIETNAM MOVIES. The Vietnam War was one of the most painful and divisive events in American history. The conflict, which took the lives of over 58,000 Americans and more than three million Vietnamese, became a subject of bitter and impassioned debate with the most dramatic, and often the best-remembered, efforts to define the U.S. involvement through the popular culture of literary

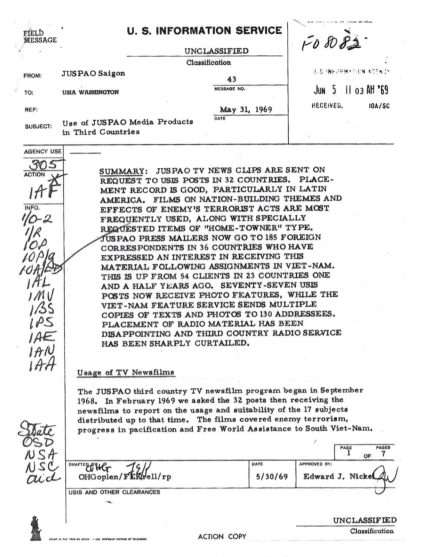

U. S. INFORMATION SERVICE

FIELD MESSAGE

UNCLASSIFIED
Classification

FROM: JUSPAO Saigon

TO: USIA WASHINGTON

REF:

SUBJECT: Use of JUSPAO Media Products
          in Third Countries

43
MESSAGE NO.

May 31, 1969
DATE

FO 8082

U.S. INFORMATION AGENCY

JUN 5 11 03 AM '69
RECEIVED,   IOA/SC

AGENCY USE

305
ACTION
IAF

INFO.
IO-2
IR
IOP
IOP/g
IOA/ES
IAL
IMV
IBS
IPS
IAE
IAN
IAA

State
OSD
NSA
NSC
aid

SUMMARY: JUSPAO TV NEWS CLIPS ARE SENT ON
REQUEST TO USIS POSTS IN 32 COUNTRIES. PLACE-
MENT RECORD IS GOOD, PARTICULARLY IN LATIN
AMERICA. FILMS ON NATION-BUILDING THEMES AND
EFFECTS OF ENEMY'S TERRORIST ACTS ARE MOST
FREQUENTLY USED, ALONG WITH SPECIALLY
REQUESTED ITEMS OF "HOME-TOWNER" TYPE.
JUSPAO PRESS MAILERS NOW GO TO 185 FOREIGN
CORRESPONDENTS IN 36 COUNTRIES WHO HAVE
EXPRESSED AN INTEREST IN RECEIVING THIS
MATERIAL FOLLOWING ASSIGNMENTS IN VIET-NAM.
THIS IS UP FROM 54 CLIENTS IN 23 COUNTRIES ONE
AND A HALF YEARS AGO. SEVENTY-SEVEN USIS
POSTS NOW RECEIVE PHOTO FEATURES, WHILE THE
VIET-NAM FEATURE SERVICE SENDS MULTIPLE
COPIES OF TEXTS AND PHOTOS TO 130 ADDRESSEES.
PLACEMENT OF RADIO MATERIAL HAS BEEN
DISAPPOINTING AND THIRD COUNTRY RADIO SERVICE
HAS BEEN SHARPLY CURTAILED.

Usage of TV Newsfilms

The JUSPAO third country TV newsfilm program began in September
1968. In February 1969 we asked the 32 posts then receiving the
newsfilms to report on the usage and suitability of the 17 subjects
distributed up to that time. The films covered enemy terrorism,
progress in pacification and Free World Assistance to South Viet-Nam.

PAGE 1 OF 7 PAGES

DRAFTED BY OHGoplen/FERrell/rp

DATE 5/30/69

APPROVED BY: Edward J. Nickel

USIS AND OTHER CLEARANCES

ACTION COPY

UNCLASSIFIED
Classification

First page of "Use of JUSPAO Media Products in Third Countries." Memorandum from JUSPAO Saigon to USIA Washington, May 31, 1969. (*Source:* USIA)

works, songs and films that created powerful, heartfelt works documenting thoughts and beliefs about the conflict. Of these, the most dramatic was undoubtedly the visual, especially those presented in the films. The conflict inspired a flood of movies noted for their depiction of the brutality of modern warfare and its effect on those forced to endure it.

Because of the passions that Vietnam stirred in Americans, few filmmakers wanted to address the conflict (1958–1975) while it was still going on. An exception was probably the most controversial film about this conflict, John Wayne's ***The Green Berets*** (1968), which was heavily criticized as propaganda for the U.S. government, especially the Lyndon Johnson administration, because Wayne was given the support and the use of U.S. military equipment and advisors. Its title song, "The Story of a Green Beret," recorded by Sgt. Barry Sadler, was one of the big hits of the 1960s.

Wayne's film attempted to support U.S. military involvement in the same way that World War II movies, many starring Wayne, gave total backing to the Allies. When the conflict ended, Hollywood decided to focus on Vietnam again. The pattern was set with Michael Cimino's Oscar winner, *The Deer Hunter* (1978), a powerful, violent film that dealt with the traumatic effect of the conflict on a small Pennsylvania community, especially the much-criticized scene in which Vietcong guards force American prisoners to play Russian roulette. More ambitious was Francis Ford Coppola's *Apocalypse Now* (1979), with its colonel who loved the smell of napalm and a story that contained parts of Joseph Conrad's *Heart of Darkness* transferred to the Vietnamese jungles.

The aftermath of the conflict when the veterans came home was displayed in another Oscar winner, Hal Ashby's *Coming Home* (1978), one of the most ironic Vietnam films in that it starred Jane Fonda, "Hanoi Jane" from her 1972 North Vietnamese broadcasts and still considered a traitor by many veterans. The film itself dealt with the experiences of veterans and their attempts to come to an understanding with their not-so-welcome return to the United States (coming home).

Other films with Vietnam as its main theme were often a mixture of violent action and psychological analysis, most notably in *Hamburger Hill* (1987); Stanley Kubrick's *Full Metal Jacket* (1987); Oliver Stone's *Platoon* (1987), about the men in the trenches; *Gardens of Stone* (1988), which showed the conflict from the viewpoint of the Old Guard at Arlington National Cemetery that had the burial details; and *Saigon* (1988). *Platoon* became the first part of a Vietnam trilogy by Vietnam veteran Stone, followed by *Born on the Fourth of July* (1989), which was based on the true experiences of paralyzed Vietnam veteran Ron Kovic, and *Heaven and Earth* (1993), which was unusual in that it tried to show the Vietnamese experience of the war.

However, despite with the praise these films received along with good box-office returns, there was just as much criticism that Hollywood glorified the Vietnam experience as fun. During the Reagan administration, especially, films appeared, such as *Rambo* (1982), *Rambo: First Blood, Part II* (1985), and *Missing in Action* (1984), in which U.S. forces actually refought the war with missions to rescue American POWs.

Overall, Hollywood and then television have presented real combat and POW films in an effort to provide realistic images of the conflict whereas superhero Vietnam veterans have provided material for the action and adventure films, and deranged veterans have provided the plots for thrillers and terrorist flicks. In the majority of these films, truth and accuracy have been ignored or manipulated, the veteran is more often the villain, and the disabled veteran becomes the hero because of his battlefield wounds.

Foreign Scene

War and movies, especially those churned out by the Hollywood studios, were always popular around the world, but that changed when American filmmakers tried to bring Vietnam to the screen. Much of this was due to the confusion and unpopularity of the conflict, but a more important factor was that it lacked clear objectives and easily identified enemies. As a result, attempts to distribute American films with Vietnam themes were not always successful in other countries, even though many of them were shot on foreign locations. A large number of Vietnam movies were filmed in the Philippines and in Thailand (and later in Vietnam) by Americans who erroneously thought one rice paddy or jungle was like any other. Some areas of the Philippines and other locations that stand in for Vietnam are quite realistic. Other countries attempted to make films about the American presence from their viewpoint, such as the Australian *Siege of Fire Base Gloria* with its cowardly captain and American soldiers who torture prisoners, whereas Stanley Kubrick filmed his *Full Metal Jacket* on British soundstages and sets, although he got the look and language right. Vietnam films have also been filmed in places such as Canada and Spain. In 1992, two French films, *The Lover* and *Indochine*, used Vietnam as part of the story; a year later, Tran Anh Hung's *The Scent of Green Papaya* became the first Vietnamese film about the conflict to find an audience in the United States.

FURTHER READING: Keith Beattie, *The Scar That Binds: American Culture and the Vietnam War* (New York: New York University, 1998); Jeremy M. Devine, *Vietnam at 24 Frames a Second: A Critical and Thematic Analysis of Over 400 Films about the Vietnam War* (Austin: University of Texas, 1999); Michael L. Lanning, *Vietnam at the Movies* (New York: Fawcett Columbine, 1994); Jonathan Law, ed. *Brewer's Cinema: A Phrase and Fable Dictionary* (London: Cassell, 1995).

VOICE OF AMERICA. On February 24, 2002, the Voice of America (VOA) celebrated its sixtieth anniversary in a wartime situation, the same circumstances in which it first went on the air on the evening of February 24, 1942, only weeks after World War II began. At the beginning of the 1940s, the United States had no plans to establish an official presence on the international airwaves; its shortwave resources consisted of a dozen low-powered, commercially owned and operated transmitters. In 1941, several of these transmitters were leased by the U.S. **Coordinator for Inter-American Affairs** (CIAA) to broadcast to Latin America, through the Pan American Union, to counter Nazi propaganda. In mid-1941, President Roosevelt established the U.S. Foreign Information Service (FIS), which, under the direction of playwright Robert Sherwood, began recruiting journalists and producing material for broadcast to Europe by the privately owned American shortwave stations and, if possible, over the facilities of the British Broadcasting Corporation (BBC).

In December 1941, FIS made its first direct broadcasts to Asia from a San Francisco studio, and on February 24, 1942, it beamed its first broadcast to Europe via BBC medium- and long-wave transmitters as the "Voices of America," in German, with "Yankee Doodle" as its theme song. The first VOA broadcast originated from New York City on February 24, 1942, just 79 days after the United States entered World War II. Speaking in German, announcer William Harlan Hale told his listeners, "Here speaks a voice from America. Every day at this time we will bring you the news of the war. The news may be good. The news may be bad. We shall tell you the truth." Its first broadcasts were in German, Italian, and French.

President Dwight D. Eisenhower at a VOA microphone, February 25, 1957, speaking during a program, *Freedom to Listen*. This was the first time a U.S. president spoke directly to a global audience of the U.S. government's international radio network.

FIS was part of the Office of the **Coordinator of Information**, the intelligence-gathering operation under William "Wild Bill" Donovan, then was transferred in June 1942 to the government's World War II propaganda agency, the **Office of War Information**. In 1953, VOA became the broadcasting bureau of the newly created **United States Information Agency**, the same year that the U.S. Senate Permanent Committee on Investigations, chaired by Senator Joseph McCarthy, held several weeks of televised hearings on VOA after alleged false charges of Communist influence at the radio station appeared. In November 1956, the Hungarian Revolution proved the effectiveness of VOA and of **Radio Free Europe** in bringing a balanced message to captured Hungarians of events going on in their country.

To protect the integrity of VOA programming and to define the organization's mission, the VOA Charter was drafted in 1960 and later signed into law (Public Law 94-350) on July 12, 1976, mandating that VOA broadcasts be "accurate, objective, and comprehensive" and "represent America, not any single segment of American society" but "present the policies of the United States clearly and effectively, and also present responsible discussions and opinion on these policies" and protect "the long-range interests of the United States," which are best served by "communicating directly with the peoples of the world by radio." In its charter, VOA was to "serve as a consistently reliable and authoritative source of news" that was to be "accurate, objective, and comprehensive." However, VOA does not broadcast within the United States. Section 501 of the Smith-Mundt Act of 1948 prohibits VOA from broadcasting into the United States. Still, many people in the United States tune into VOA on shortwave receivers or log onto VOA on the Internet.

VOA's New Sound was introduced by director John Chancellor in July 1966 when he discarded the traditional rigid format (news and commentaries followed by lengthy commentaries) and replaced it with a more diverse and flexible mixture (news, music, a variety of short pieces), a policy that is still effective.

In 1991, VOA's Office of Marketing and Program Placement, formerly the Office of Affiliate Relations and Audience Analysis, was created to maintain a network of affiliated AM and FM radio and TV stations around the world that will broadcast VOA and RFE/RL programs. Three years later, in 1994, President Clinton signed the International Broadcasting Act (Public Law 103-236), which established the International Broadcasting Bureau (IBB) within USIA. The IBB is under the jurisdiction of the Broadcasting Board of Governors, a nine-member bipartisan body that supervises the operations of the IBB with oversight authority over all civilian U.S. government international broadcasting and administers grants of congressionally appropriated funds to Radio Free Europe/Radio Liberty and Radio Free Asia, two nonprofit, grantee corporations. The act also consolidated VOA, Worldnet TV, **Radio Marti** and **Television Marti**, the Office of Engineering and Technical Services, along with **Radio Free Europe/Radio Liberty** and a new **Radio Free Asia**.

On October 21, 1998, President Clinton signed the Foreign Affairs Reform and Restructuring Act (Public Law 105-277), perhaps the single most important legislation affecting U.S. government international broadcasters. This law placed all U.S. publicly funded, nonmilitary overseas broadcasting into the Broadcasting Board of Governors, abolished USIA, merged all but its broadcasting functions into the **U.S. Department of State**, and inaugurated the independence of U.S. government civilian international broadcasting. Effective October 1, 1999, VOA became part of the independent International Broadcasting Bureau under the authority of the Broadcasting Board of Governors.

Through Voice of America programming, such as its country music, jazz, and rock broadcasts, USIA transmits a range of American cultural forms to the world. One of its most popular music broadcasters, recognized worldwide but little known in the United States, was Willis Conover, who started in the 1950s with a program, *Music USA*, that introduced jazz behind the Iron Curtain. When he died in 1996, Conover was eulogized from listeners all over the world. During the Fourth of July week 2001, the U.S. Embassy in Moscow, in conjunction with the Moscow Jazz Engagement, sponsored the Willis Conover Jazz Festival as part of its Independence Day celebration. In the late 1980s and early 1990s, VOA Music Director Judy Massa coordinated a series of country and western broadcasts from Nashville, hosted by country and western musician Charlie Daniels. On March 6, 2002, VOA started a series of classical music programs in its Washington, D.C., headquarters that were open to the public.

There are an estimated 83 million listeners of VOA's shortwave and medium-wave broadcasts weekly. A highly successful affiliates program has placed VOA-produced programming on more than 1,100 radio stations around the world, and in September 1994, VOA entered the world of television when it inaugurated "China Forum TV," a Mandarin-language TV program beamed by satellite to viewers in the People's Republic of China. Two years later, VOA's Arabic Service teamed up with Worldnet TV and the Middle East Broadcasting Centre (MBC) in London to launch *Dialogue with the West*. In 1996, a new television station was completed so VOA can now simulcast portions of some programs on radio and TV in such languages as Arabic, Bosnian, Chinese, English, Farsi, Serbian, and Spanish. VOA also puts audio and text on its Internet Web site and has begun an aggressive targeted e-mail program in countries where the Web site is blocked. In April 1998, President Clinton announced a new VOA service, Radio Democracy for Africa, that would operate under the VOA Charter. The broadcast languages for the new radio service include English, French, Hausa, Amharic, Afan Oromo, Tigrigna, Kinyarwando, Kirundi, and Swahili.

On September 11, 2001, VOA became one of the U.S. government's major weapons in the response to terrorism after the Taliban attacks on the World Trade Center and on the Pentagon. Along with an increase in the hire of Arabic broadcasters, President Bush increased the broadcasts of the Afghan service to an almost 24-hour programming schedule. Further controversy ensued over attempts by the State Department to censor a VOA broadcast to Afghanistan in October 2001 that included an interview with a top Taliban official, Mullah Mohammed Omar, but the VOA went ahead and broadcast Omar's comments in a story packaged with statements from other Afghan groups. It also approved a plan for a commercial-style radio channel consisting of music, talk, and news aimed at a young Arab audience, **Radio Sawa.**

Today the VOA broadcasts in 53 languages, including English, via medium-wave (AM) and shortwave broadcasts, and on local AM and FM stations, around the world, and on the Internet. It broadcasts over 900 hours of news, informational, educational, and cultural programs every week to an audience of some 91 million worldwide.

FURTHER READING: Materials on the International Broadcasting Bureau/Voice of America Web site: http://www.ibb.gov; Gerd Horten, *Radio Goes to War: The Cultural Politics of Propaganda During World War II* (Berkeley and Los Angeles: University of California, 2002); International Broadcasting Bureau. *U.S. International Broadcasting Chronology* (IBB Web site, 2001); Philomena Jurey, *A Basement Seat to History* (Washington, DC: Linus, 1995); Robert W. Pirsein, *The Voice of America: A History of the International Broadcasting Activities of the United States Government* (New York: Arno, 1979); Holly Shulman, *The Voice of America: Propaganda and Democracy, 1941–1945* (Madison: University of Wisconsin, 1990); U.S. International Broadcasting Bureau. Office of External Affairs, *Voice of America: A Brief History* (Washington: The Office, 1998); Philo C. Wasburn, *Broadcasting Propaganda: International Radio Broadcasting and the Construction of Political Reality* (Westport, CT: Praeger, 1992).

VOLLBEHR, OTTO HEINRICH FRIEDERICH (April 27, 1872 [some sources say 1869]–1946?). Confidential agent and propagandist who was very active for the Nazis in the United States. Otto Vollbehr was a German industrial chemist, born in Kiel, Germany, who became a noted antiquarian bookseller who sold millions of dollars in this country, but he was not an American citizen. At the close of World War I, he found himself with more assets than most. Either in his own collection or through consignment, Vollbehr had control of thousands of incunabula. In 1926, when he came to the United States; he brought with him a collection of 3,000 incunabula to be exhibited at the Eucharistic Congress in Chicago. After the exhibition, Vollbehr traveled by train to several other cities, ending in Washington, D.C., where over 100 of the books were exhibited in the Great Hall of the Library of Congress. He proposed that if a benefactor came forward to buy the collection for an American institution for half the asking price of $1.5 million, he would donate the other half and a complete copy of the Gutenberg Bible, printed on vellum. Congressman Ross A. Collins of Mississippi sponsored the necessary legislation in the U.S. House of Representatives to use public funds to acquire the Vollbehr collection for the Library of Congress and worked for its passage. In June 1930, Congress passed the bill, and President Hoover signed it into law. Vollbehr had previously given the library a collection of 11,000 printers' and publishers' marks and a collection of 20,000 wood engravings, which were exhibited in 1928.

Vollbehr was also a Nazi propagandist who issued "memoranda" on the political situation in Germany between October 1931 and April 1936. He argued for a more effective propaganda campaign to meet the increasingly hostile attitude in the United States, and he tried to stress more importance on greater secrecy in German operations. Vollbehr continued to send out his "memoranda" to influential Americans, but his propaganda efforts were seriously undermined by his poor command of the English language. Vollbehr was investigated by the House Special Committee on Nazi Propaganda; he gave testimony on November 30, 1934. His publications included *The Destroyers of International Goodwill Unmasked* (1933), *Is Pacifism Possible?* (1934), *A Statement of Principles* (1934), and *Message from Appomattox: Let's Have Peace!* (1936). He died in Baden-Baden, Germany.

FURTHER READING: Alton Frye, *Nazi Germany and the American Hemisphere, 1933–1941* (New Haven, CT: Yale University, 1967); U.S. Congress. Senate. Committee on Government Operations, *Congressional Investigations of Communism and Subversive Activities: Summary-Index, 1918–1956* (Washington, DC: Government Printing Office, 1956).

VON DAMM, HELENE. *See* Helene Von Damm Forgery Letter

W

WALKER, DAVID (September 28, 1785—June 28, 1830). David Walker was born in Wilmington, North Carolina, to a free mother and a slave father whose publications and antislavery rhetoric stirred up abolitionist sentiment. He witnessed slavery's vicious hold throughout the South, and he struggled vigorously to unite blacks against their bondage. In 1827, Walker went to Boston and started a clothing business. He published his famous pamphlet, *David Walker's Appeal, in Four Articles; Together with a Preamble to the Colored Citizens of the World, but in Particular, and Very Expressly, to Those of the United States of America* (1829; rev. ed; New York: Hill and Wang, 1995), essays that persuaded slaves to use violence to be free and had tremendous impact. It reflected Walker's ability to exhort African Americans to have more confidence in themselves and to transform their lives by collective action, and it became one of the most popular abolitionist tracts written by a black person but controversial in the South, where some state legislatures passed laws preventing its circulation and making it a crime punishable by death to distribute similar literature. Walker's efforts were part of a larger movement of resistance to slavery during the early years of the nineteenth century, and he had a unique grasp of the psychology of slaves. He was able to relate to blacks, to understand their exploitation, and to inspire them to resist. David Walker died three months after his controversial pamphlet was published in a third, revised edition; it was suspected he was poisoned because a group of southerners had put a price on his head after reading his appeal, but this has never been proved.

See also Abolitionist Propaganda

FURTHER READING: Donald M. Jacobs, ed., *Courage and Conscience: Black and White Abolitionists in Boston* (Bloomington, IN: Published for the Boston Athenaeum by Indiana University Press, 1993); Peter P. Hinks, *To Awaken My Afflicted Brethren: David Walker and the Problem of Antebellum Slave Resistance* (University Park: Pennsylvania State University, 1997).

WALL POSTERS. *See* Posters

WAR ADVERTISING COUNCIL. The War Advertising Council (WAC) was critical to this activity; its message was endorsed by its A War Message in Every Ad Campaign, which included the creation of **posters** as one of the most influential means of persuasion on the home front. The Council was a group of national advertisers who worked as liaison between advertising and government agencies. WAC was created before Pearl Harbor to cooperate with the government in the pending war effort. From this cooperation, the Network Allocation Plan was devised as a propaganda scheme in which the radio industry accepted OWI's Radio Division as the central clearing station for all government propaganda and as the authority on the types and priority of specific propaganda messages. In return, OWI provided every national radio advertiser with a schedule of propaganda themes at least a month in advance of the actual broadcasts.

The most important collaboration of WAC and the government was the national gas rationing effort after the Office of Price Administration (OPA) decided gas rationing was the best way to conserve rubber, a most essential commodity in wartime; there was not a shortage of fuel. Radio comedians, such as Fibber McGee and Molly, used their weekly NBC show to promote the government's message on gas rationing. Another was Jack Benny, whose comic reputation as a tightwad made him the perfect celebrity to defuse the public's growing resentment against rationing by exploiting its comic possibilities on his radio show. Networks had a pro-business program bias, and advertising played a crucial role. The government allowed businesses to write off up to 80 percent of their advertising costs as long as they participated in the propaganda effort. Advertising and commercial radio became an integral collaboration, helped immeasurably by images such as **Rosie the Riveter** and, most important of all, by Hollywood films. On a personal level, there were home front symbols, such as gold stars, for mothers who lost a child in the war, or flags on the lawn indicating that a family member was in the service.

The poster campaign, inexpensive, colorful, and immediate, was the ideal medium for delivering messages about an American's duties on the home front during World War II; they were seen in schools, in workplaces, and in other public spaces. The posters touched on all aspects of wartime life, from the factory, where workers were instructed to take shorter cigarette breaks and focus on increased production ("KILLING Time Is KILLING Men"), to the home, where conserving scarce resources was essential ("We'll have lots to eat this winter, won't we Mother? Grow your own"), to the farm, where eggs and meat were wartime weapons in their own right ("Our Allies Need Eggs" and "Grow It Yourself—Plan a Farm Garden Now").

See also Home Front Propaganda

FURTHER READING: William L. Bird and Harry R. Rubenstein, *Design for Victory: World War II Posters on the American Home Front* (Princeton, NJ: Princeton Architectural Press, 1998); Gerd Horten, *Radio Goes to War: The Cultural Politics of Propaganda During World War II* (Berkeley and Los Angeles: University of California, 2002).

WAR CASUALTIES. *See* **War Propaganda**

WAR DEPARTMENT. *See* **Why We Fight Series**

WAR OF AMERICAN INDEPENDENCE PROPAGANDA. During the French and Indian War (1754), **Benjamin Franklin** drew a political cartoon, "Join, or Die," a divided snake, that appeared in the *Pennsylvania Gazette* urging British colonies to unite in the fighting. For the War of American Independence (1776–1783), both the Americans and the British used pamphlets, slogans, cartoons, and especially newspapers to generate public opinion to their side in what was a mostly ineffective propaganda campaign that was overshadowed by real events, such as the victory at Saratoga or Ethan Allen's assault on Fort Ticonderoga (1775), which gave an important opening to General Washington's forces. The American Revolution was an ideological conflict in which both warring sides were convinced of the rightness of their cause. Not a spontaneous popular uprising, it was in reality the work of a small group of dedicated persuaders who created the first American propaganda and agitation campaign to overthrow a monarchial government. They started as the work of James Otis, **Samuel Adams**, Patrick Henry, Benjamin Franklin, and **Thomas Paine**, radical pamphleteers, who realized that effective propaganda requires: organization (the **Sons of Liberty** and **Committees of Correspondence** acted as propaganda conduits throughout the colonies); creative and identifiable emotive symbols (the Liberty Tree) and slogans ("Don't tread on me," and "Taxation without representation is tyranny") to simplify issues and arouse emotions; utilization of publicity and staged events (**Boston Tea Party**) to attract media attention and to enlist key supporters (religious leaders whose sermons were widely published and distributed); and exploitation of differences rather than similarities among targeted groups on a sustained, unrelenting basis through control of key public opinion tools (press, pamphlets, broadsides, songs). The early American patriots became expert at publicizing their grievances to establish a debate agenda while discrediting the Loyalist opposition. Both American and British propagandists were ineffective and largely unsuccessful in trying to convert, to persuade, or to intimidate people who at first seemed vulnerable. Events and real conditions were more persuasive than words. By 1777, most minds were made up despite actions aimed at such things as subverting the Hessian allies of Britain, fomenting slave insurrection, and winning the support of Indians; most of these attempts failed. Real events had more impact than propaganda (e.g., Canada was saved by British force, Indians stayed neutral or took sides based on solid economic or political motives, and the provocation of slave insurrection by the British merely embittered and fortified the slaveholders). The greatest impact came not from propagandists, such as Benjamin Franklin, but simply from the news of the war, such as the American victory at Saratoga. Neither persuasive appeals, nor threats, nor tricks could compare in influence with military victory or political and economic factors.

Propaganda events were made of the battle of **Lexington and Concord**, the battle of **Bunker Hill**, and Paul Revere's ride whereas Hessian soldiers were encouraged to desert with promises of free land by way of pamphlets distributed among them by the Army of the Revolution. Without newspapers, there would have been little chance of a revolution. With a uniformity of news resulting from the regular exchange of newspapers among printers, Americans read the same news and drew similar conclusions. According to R. A. Brown, "Whig leaders . . . were as appreciative of the importance of propaganda, and as adept at its use, as are any political and business leaders of this period." It is impossible to measure the effect newspaper propaganda had on readers, but several writers were prominent state leaders. The possibilities of a French–American war, possible peace proposals, war news, rebel cruelty stories, attacks on the currency of the new states, and "what appear to be conscious efforts to create the impression among the rank and file of the Whig adherents that their leaders were self-interested, tyrannical individuals, seeking to gain wealth and position at the expense of their followers" were some of the major types of propaganda. "[W]hether consciously or unconsciously selected they must have had some effect on the people who read them, especially on that large class of Americans who wavered with the changing tide of victory."

FURTHER READING: R. A. Brown, "New Hampshire Editors Win the War," *Rhode Island History* (1939): 35–51; R. A. Brown, "The Newport Gazette, Tory Newsheet," *Rhode Island History* (1954): 97–108, and (1955): 11–20; Carl Berger, *Broadsides and Bayonets: The Propaganda War of the American Revolution* (Philadelphia: University of Pennsylvania, 1961); Philip Davidson, *Propaganda and the American Revolution, 1763–1783* (New York: Norton, 1973/1941); Frederic B. Farrar, *This Common Channel to Independence: Revolution and Newspapers, 1759–1789* (Garden City, NY: Farrar Books, 1975).

WAR PROPAGANDA. War propaganda is an extension of military propaganda that encourages public support of the war effort, such as recruitment, and public sacrifice. One of the earliest works of war propaganda was *The Art of War*, the classic work by Sun-Tzu, a warrior and philosopher, written over 2,000 years ago between the fifth and third centuries B.C., which first mentioned the importance of wartime propaganda. The author encouraged deception along with the value of such battlefield actions as troop formation, maneuvering armies, and the importance of spies. Sun-Tzu considered warfare "the greatest affair of state, the basis of life and death" that must be "thoroughly pondered and analyzed." Later wars incorporated battlefield casualties into their propaganda campaigns, including inaccurate casualty figures, with sometimes effective results. Another important type of war propaganda is the balloon and leaflet campaigns into enemy territory, offering safe-conduct passes.

See also Civil War Propaganda; Gillars, Mildred; Leaflet Propaganda; "Moronic Little King" Incident; Occupied Countries and Territories; Tokyo Rose; U.S.A. Zone of the Overseas Service (North American Service); Vietnam; Joint United States Public Affairs Office (JUSPAO); War Advertising Council; War of American Independence Propaganda

WARBURG, JAMES PAUL (August 18, 1896–June 3, 1969). Writer, financier, and government official, James Warburg was born in Hamburg, Germany, but came to the United States (1901) and graduated from Harvard (1917). After naval service in World War I, he began his banking career with the National Metropolitan Bank (1918) and rapidly advanced through various positions in other financial institutions. In 1933, Warburg joined President Franklin Roosevelt's first "brain trust" as a financial adviser but resigned when the president rejected a return to the gold standard and criticized him in a series of syndicated newspaper columns and in two books. After a career as a freelance originator of industrial financing in New York City, Warburg supported Roosevelt's foreign policy in two more books and became a leading spokesman for the **Committee to Defend America by Aiding the Allies** as well as a founder of the **Fight for Freedom Committee**. In 1941, he debated Charles Lindbergh of **America First Committee** at Madison Square Garden. Warburg was appointed special assistant to the director, **Coordinator of Information**, where he worked in the development of propaganda and assembled a foreign-language staff for the Foreign Information Service. In July 1942, he became deputy director of the overseas branch, **Office of War Information** (OWI) in London to coordinate propaganda aimed at the Axis powers and at occupied European nations, but disagreed with the manner in which OWI carried this out. Warburg argued that the influence of the nation's top propagandists should reach into the counsel chambers where basic public policy is formulated and criticized OWI and its director, **Elmer Davis,** for his "timid indifference" to "serious consequences" and said Davis did not understand that he was managing "an important branch of modern warfare" and "deprived the **psychological warfare** agency" of a role in "the shaping of foreign policy." Warburg left government service in February 1944 and continued to support Roosevelt's policies, but was critical of President Harry S Truman and his Truman Doctrine. He helped to establish the United World Federalists (1947) that was skeptical of the United Nations' ability to maintain peace, supported John F. Kennedy for president (1960), and in the Kennedy administration assisted John McCloy in the formation of the Arms Control and Disarmament Agency. Warburg married three times and died in Greenwich, Connecticut. He was the author of several books, most notably *Unwritten Treaty* (New York: Harcourt, Brace, 1946) and *The U.S. in a Changing World* (1954).

FURTHER READING: Stephen Birmingham, *Our Crowd: The Great Jewish Families of New York* (Syracuse, NY: Syracuse University Press, 1996); Vincent P. Carosso, *Investment Banking in America, a History* (Cambridge, MA: Harvard University, 1970). William E. Daugherty, *Psychological Warfare Casebook* (Baltimore: Johns Hopkins; published for Operations Research Office, Johns Hopkins University, 1958).

WARRANTS FOR GENOCIDE. *See Protocols of the Learned Elders of Zion*

WASHINGTON, GEORGE. *See Farewell Address*

WELD, THEODORE DWIGHT (November 23, 1803–February 3, 1895). Antebellum reformer and educator Theodore Dwight Weld was considered one of the most effective of the early abolitionists. He was born in Hampton, Connecticut, and became a minister and an early temperance advocate. After 1830, he was influenced by the British Anti-Slavery Society, became an abolitionist, and worked with the American Anti-Slavery Society. In the 1840s, he advised the antislavery Whigs in Congress and encouraged them to break with their party on the slavery issue. Weld was editor of the *Emancipator*, in which he wrote many of the articles anonymously or under pseudonyms, and published several books, including his famous tract, *American Slavery As It Is* (1839), a compilation of firsthand descriptions of slave life in the South, which became the most widely distributed and most influential of all American antislavery tracts; it most certainly influenced **Harriet Beecher Stowe**'s portrayal of slavery, **Uncle Tom's Cabin**. Other works included *The Bible Against Slavery* (1837) and *Slavery and the Internal Slave Trade in the United States* (1841), published by the British and Foreign Anti-Slavery Society. Weld influenced many of the later abolitionists, such as the Beechers, the Grimke sisters (one of whom he married, Angelina), and Edwin Stanton. He shunned the limelight and prepared pamphlets rather than give speeches, but he was mainly responsible for igniting public opinion and support for the abolitionist movement throughout the United States. Weld died in Hyde Park (now part of Boston), Massachusetts.

See also Abolitionist Propaganda

FURTHER READING: Robert H. Abzug, *Passionate Liberator* (New York: Oxford University, 1980); Benjamin P. Thomas, *Theodore Weld: Crusader for Freedom* (New York: Octagon Books, 1973; reprint of the ed. published by Rutgers University Press, New Brunswick, NJ, 1950).

WHALEN DOCUMENTS. In 1930, the U.S. Congress was planning to establish a committee to investigate Communist propaganda. Shortly before it was formed, the New York City Police Department received copies of a set of documents purporting to be letters from the Communist International instructing Amtorg, a company organized in 1924 in the United States by the Soviet Union to serve as the buying and selling organization of the Soviet Union in trade between the two countries, to carry out Communist propaganda in the United States. Amtorg actually was deeply involved in Soviet espionage in the United States. The documents were released to the press on May 2, 1930, and appeared in print the next day. They were released by Police Commissioner Grover Whalen and came to be known as the Whalen Documents.

An examination of the documents reveals clearly that they are forgeries. For example, the letterhead reads "Ispolkom Kominterna" (Excom Comintern). An authentic document would spell out "Communist International," rather than using the nickname Comintern. The forgeries were exposed by journalist John L. Spivak, who provided the evidence to Congressman LaGuardia and wrote about the case in the *New York Evening Graphic*.

Spivak claimed that his editor gave him the assignment to trace the documents on May 3. After investigating type foundries and print shops, he said he discovered the identity of the printer of the letterheads on May 8. It took him four days to trace the printing. Spivak's story does not stand up to investigation. When the printer testified before a congressional committee, he revealed that he recognized the letterhead when he saw it reprinted on the front page of the Yiddish language daily newspaper, *The Jewish Daily Forward*. The same day, Spivak came into his store and accused him of being the printer of the letterheads. It is clear that Spivak knew the printer's identity as soon as he began his investigation. The printer, Max Wagner, signed an affidavit for Spivak acknowledging that had the printed the letterheads. The statement, read into the *Congressional Record* by Congressman Fiorello LaGuardia, states, "I printed this about four months ago and submitted two copies as a proof, but the man did not come back for the order, Signed, M. Wagner, printer."

The Communist Party newspaper, *Daily Worker* (May 13, 1930), reproduced a Photostat of the Wagner affidavit with a slightly different text leaving out the word "printer" and inserting the words "May 8, 1930." This appears to have been concocted to authenticate Spivak's claim that he confronted Wagner on May 8 rather than on May 3, when the incident actually took place.

In 1945, Elizabeth Bentley revealed to the FBI that she had worked as courier for a Soviet spy ring, and she identified Spivak as a member of the ring. The Communists used the forgeries to discredit the Congressional committee established to investigate Communist propaganda. The committee, headed by Congressman Hamilton Fish of New York, never authenticated the Whalen documents. However, Earl Browder, then head of Communist Party U.S.A., reported to a meeting of the Executive Committee of the Communist International held in Moscow in April 1931 that, "the notorious forged 'Whalen Documents,' produced by the Czarist 'General' Djamgaroff, became the occasion for the United States Congress to set up the Fish Committee to investigate Communist activities in the United States. Behind the actions of this committee, which were the most vulgar farce considered in themselves, was the sinister and serious purpose of preparing 'public opinion' for the war of intervention against the U.S.S.R." Max Bedacht was later revealed by Whittaker Chambers as the man who recruited him as a Soviet spy. Bedacht was the contact between the leadership of the American Communist Party and the Soviet intelligence service.

FURTHER READING: Herbert Romerstein, "Disinformation as a KGB Weapon in the Cold War," paper prepared for a Conference on Germany and Intelligence Organizations: The Last Fifty Years in Review, Akademie fur Politische Bildung Tutzing [Germany] (1999).

WHISPERING CAMPAIGNS. *See* **Rumor**

WHITE, HARRY DEXTER. *See* **Morgenthau Plan**

WHITE, RALPH K. (December 9, 1907–). Psychologist who specialized in public opinion and the psychological causes of war, Ralph White was born in Michigan and educated at Wesleyan University (B.A., 1929) and Stanford University (Ph.D., 1937). He taught psychology at various colleges until 1946, when he became a research analyst, first for the **U.S. Department of State** and then at the **U.S. Information Agency**, where he was one of its Russian affairs experts. At the **American National Exhibition, Moscow** (Moscow Exhibition, 1959), White conducted public opinion surveys on the effectiveness of the many displays and analyzed the reactions of Russians to the first direct American propaganda effort inside the Soviet Union. He published his results as "Soviet Reactions to Our Moscow Exhibit: Voting Machines and Comment Books," *Public Opinion Quarterly* (Winter 1959– 1960). In 1961, Senator Thomas J. Dodd (D-Conn.) called for an investigation of USIA and the dismissal of White for statements he made at the American Psychological Association convention, in which he advanced the general theme that "we are not too different from the Communists after all." White retired from USIA in 1964 as chief of its Special Projects

Division, Research and Analysis Division, and became a professor of social psychology at George Washington University, a member of its Institute for Sino-Soviet Studies, and a participant on the Steering Committee, Psychologists for Social Responsibility.

White's publications include *The New Resistance to International Propaganda* (1952), in which he pointed out that "the world is more and more tired of 'propaganda'"; *Autocracy and Democracy* (1960); *Misperception and the Vietnam War* (1966), which originally appeared in the *Journal of Social Issues* (July 1966) for the Society for the Psychological Study of Social Issues, then published as *Nobody Wanted War: Misperception in Vietnam and Other Wars* (1968); and *Fearful Warriors: A Psychological Profile of U.S.–Soviet Relations* (1984). He also edited *Psychology and the Prevention of Nuclear War* (1986). Presently, White resides in a nursing home in Pookesville, Maryland.

FURTHER READING: "Dodd Asks U.S.I.A. to Dismiss Its Expert on Russian Affairs," *New York Times*, Sept. 9, 1961; Emma Harrison, "Psychologist Asserts U.S. and the Soviet Union Share Similar Illusions About Each Other," *New York Times*, Sept. 5, 1961; U.S. Department of State, *Biographic Register 1964* (Washington, DC: Government Printing Office, 1964).

WHITE COMMITTEE. *See* **Committee to Defend America by Aiding the Allies (CDAAA)**

WHITE HOUSE CONFERENCE ON CULTURE AND DIPLOMACY. *See* **Cultural Diplomacy**

WHITE PROPAGANDA. Propaganda from properly identified sources. White propaganda is open and straightforward and makes no pretense that it is anything but propaganda. It is also called overt propaganda. White propaganda is officially acknowledged by the government that disseminates it. Examples of white propaganda include **Radio Free Europe, Radio Liberty, Voice of America,** Radio Moscow, official government radios in World War II, and recruiting posters.

See also **Black Propaganda; Gray Propaganda**

FURTHER READING: Jacques Ellul, *Propaganda: The Formation of Men's Attitudes* (New York: Vintage, 1973); Garth Jowett and Victoria O'Donnell, *Propaganda and Persuasion* (London: Sage, 1992).

WHITEHOUSE, VIRA BOARMAN (September 16, 1875–1957). Vira Boarman, daughter of Robert and Cordelia Terrell Boarman, was educated at Sophie Newcomb College, New Orleans; she married Norman Whitehouse in April 1898. Whitehouse was chairman of the publicity council of the Empire State Campaign Committee (1913) and the New York State Woman Suffrage Party (1916). During World War I, Whitehouse was director of the Swiss office of the **Committee on Public Information** (1918) to organize publicity to combat German propaganda; she wrote a book, *A Year as a Government Agent* (1920) about her experience. Whitehouse was appointed by CPI director **George Creel,** in what was really the first important post held by a woman in the U.S. Foreign Service, but the appointment also generated considerable criticism. The propaganda program in Switzerland was opposed by the diplomatic community, who wanted it handled as secret operation. To get around this, Whitehouse's mission was stated as "studying conditions relating to women and children" rather than propaganda activities. She engaged the support of the Swiss press and skillfully employed German radical groups in Switzerland as a regular messenger service into Germany, often crossing the border herself to put U.S. material in the proper channels. After her government experience, Whitehouse was owner and majority stockholder of the Whitehouse Leather Company, 1920–1930, and active in state political campaigns and in women's clubs.

FURTHER READING: Gregg Wolper, "Woodrow Wilson's New Diplomacy: Vira Whitehouse in Switzerland, 1918," *Prologue* 24, no. 3 (Fall 1992): 226–239; *Who Was Who in America with World Notables*; vol. 5, 1969–1973 (1973).

WHY WE FIGHT SERIES. Film director Frank Capra, who popularized the image of small-town America in films such as *It's a Wonderful Life*, was commissioned by General George C. Marshall in 1942 to create a series of training films, produced by the U.S. Army, to prepare American soldiers for battle in World War II. Capra approached the project as an "informational" documentary film series with six specific themes for American military servicemen (GIs): the rightness of the cause, the difficulty of the job, confidence in their comrades and leaders to win the war, confidence in the integrity and fighting ability of the Allies, resentment of enemies, and a belief that military victory would result in a better world.

The U.S. Signal Corps worked with Capra to produce the orientation films, which became the most famous film achievement of the U.S. Department of War. The seven films, each approximately fifty minutes long, were entitled: *Prelude to War, The Nazis Strike, Divide and Conquer, The Battle of Britain, Battle of Russia, Battle of China*, and *War Comes to America*. Capra used existing footage from newsreels; created new film as needed; incorporated animation, multiple narrators, and recreations; and juxtaposed segments from Axis propaganda films, such as Leni Riefenstahl's National Socialist party rally films that were designed to glorify Hitler's regime, a classic example of powerful editing and distortion in propaganda. One of Capra's assistants on this series was Theodor Seuss Geisel ("Dr. Seuss"), who later created the well-loved children's books.

A typical comment on the first film, *Prelude to War*, was that it was propaganda, but "it's good propaganda." This was pertinent to the entire series. Unfortunately, Capra and the U.S. War Department accepted as authentic the **Tanaka Memorial** forgery and used it in the film. In 1985, Capra was featured in a television episode of *World War II: The Propaganda Battle*, in which he was interviewed by Bill Moyers.

FURTHER READING: David Culbert, ed., *Film and Propaganda in America: A Documentary History* ; vol. 3: World War II, Part 2 (New York and Westport, CT: Greenwood, 1990): 77–225; Richard D. MacCann, *The People's Films* (New York: Hastings House,

1973); Annalee Newitz, "It's Fun . . . But It Takes Courage: Remembering Frank Capra's America," *Bad Subjects*, no. 11 (January–February 1994).

WICK, CHARLES Z. (1917–). Charles Z. Wick was the U.S. Information Agency's longest serving director (1981–1989) and one of its most productive. Much of his success was due to the long friendship that Wick and his wife, Mary Jane Wick, enjoyed with President **Ronald Reagan** and his wife, Nancy, which Wick was able to direct into Reagan administration support for USIA programs. Wick was a Hollywood film producer and business executive who was closely associated with Reagan's 1980 presidential campaign. His appointment as USIA director was the beginning of a campaign Reagan started to revitalize USIA, which had not done well under the previous Carter administration; among other difficulties, it was renamed the U.S. International Communication Agency, which Congress abolished in August 1982 and restored the USIA designation.

The Reagan administration was especially notable for bringing down the Soviet Empire, and Reagan allowed Wick to take full advantage of U.S. propaganda efforts overseas. Wick built up the **Voice of America** and initiated **Radio Marti** broadcasts to Fidel Castro's Cuba, started a **Worldnet** television satellite network, which linked U.S. embassies globally and permitted interactive discussions between Washington policy makers, produced *Let Poland Be Poland* as a television special to support the Solidarity movement in Poland, and spearheaded programs to counter **Soviet active measures**, including an interdepartmental effort, **Active Measures Working Group**, to counter Soviet propaganda and **disinformation**. Wick retired to California.

FURTHER READING: Nicholas J. Cull, David Culbert, and David Welch, *Propaganda and Mass Persuasion: A Historical Encyclopedia, 1500 to the Present* (Santa Barbara, CA and Denver, CO: ABC-Clio, 2003); Alvin A. Snyder, *Warriors of Disinformation: American Propaganda, Soviet Lies, and the Winning of the Cold War; an Insider's Account* (New York: Arcade, 1995); [United States Information Agency], *United States Information Agency, 1981–1988: Years of Progress* (Washington, DC: Unpublished, 1989).

WILLIAM, JAMES. *See* Civil War Propaganda

WILSON, AUGUSTA JANE EVANS. *See* Civil War Propaganda

WILSON, THOMAS WOODROW. *See* Blankenhorn, Heber; Committee on Public Information; Creel, George; Four-Minute Men; Occupied Countries and Territories; Uncle Sam; Viereck, George Sylvester; Whitehouse, Vira Boarman; World War I; Zimmermann Telegram

WODEHOUSE, PELHAM GRENVILLE (October 15, 1881–February 14, 1975). British writer and lyricist who was accused of collaborating with the enemy in World War II, P. G. Wodehouse was a successful novelist and columnist who collaborated with American composer Jerome Kern, who in turn introduced him to fellow lyricist Guy Bolton. The team collaborated on several successful musicals. In

1934, Wodehouse moved to Le Touquet, the English playground in France near Boulogne. In September 1939, he and his wife, Ethel Newton Rowley, were unable to escape after the German occupation, and they ended up in a German prison camp. Bolton roused Americans to petition on his partner's behalf. In May 1941, Wodehouse wrote a humorous article on his experience as a civilian internee in 1940 in a series of German prison camps. He was advised by a camp official to prepare and record it as a series of broadcasts to the still-neutral United States. He was released from the prison camp and sent to Berlin, where he made the first of his five broadcasts on June 28, 1941. In his *Jeeves* tales, which he started in 1923, Wodehouse harpooned British Nazism. In his broadcasts, which used hyperbole, he portrayed his jailers as Wodehouseian buffoons. Not really political, P. G. Wodehouse was vilified in British propaganda broadcasts, and for a time, the British government believed his actions to be treason, although he was still being held in custody by the Germans. Wodehouse and his wife remained in Paris after the liberation in "preventive detention," but they returned to the United States in 1952 to Long Island, where they became neighbors of Bolton. Wodehouse died in Southampton, Long Island, shortly after he was knighted.

FURTHER READING: "The Humor That Backfired," *Washington Post* (October 1, 1996): D9.

WOMEN AS PROPAGANDA IMAGES IN WARTIME. During wartime, especially in such conflicts as the Civil War, World War I, and World War II, the image of American women as wives, mothers, and girlfriends left at the home front was used heavily in enemy propaganda to persuade the American fighting man to give up the battle and return home. While he was away, his wife or girlfriend was involved in unpatriotic activities, usually sexual, with the man left at home and not in uniform. Cartoons distributed by the enemy emphasized that the wife or sweetheart wouldn't wait for her fighting man to return and was involved with the guy left behind. Another type of portrayal of women was in popular magazines, newsreels, movies (*Conquer the Clock, Swing Shift Maisie*), and other media images as the sacrificing partner left behind on the home front to carry on while her man was fighting for his country ("Longing won't bring him back sooner . . . Get a war job!" "One woman can shorten this war! You're that woman. Yes, you!").

During World War II, a classic image was Norman Rockwell's **Rosie the Riveter,** with women proudly holding down jobs in factories and offices until the men returned from war, when it was expected they would gladly give the jobs up and return to home and hearth to raise children and be the supportive helpmate. Government posters and pamphlets, books, and articles, called on women to practice wartime housekeeping and take up volunteer work. Such propaganda was quite extensive in the United States and proved crucial in converting women to industrial work so that men could be freed to fight overseas. The reality was different: women held down jobs previously held by men and were reluctant to give them up when the war ended. After World War II, women in the workplace became a common occurrence, but media images still reverted back to the wife and mother stereotype. This quickly changed as the feminist movement took off in the 1960s.

FURTHER READING: Billie Melman, ed., *Borderlines: Genders and Identities in War and Peace* (New York: Routledge, 1998); Leila J. Rupp, *Mobilizing Women for War: German and American Propaganda, 1939–1945* (Princeton, NJ: Princeton University, 1978).

WOMEN AS STEREOTYPES. *See* Women as Propaganda Images in Wartime

WORKS PROGESS ADMINISTRATION. *See* Federal Arts Project; Federal Theater Project; New Deal

WORLD CRUISE OF THE U.S. NAVY (1907–1909). In February 1907, President Theodore Roosevelt dispatched the U.S. fleet on a world tour that emphasized U.S. interests in the Pacific and its willingness to defend them. As the grandest of naval expeditions undertaken by the United States in the early twentieth century, it was the final part of the tercentennial celebration of the Jamestown Exposition. Its itinerary included many exotic ports of calls and United States territories, one of which was the Philippines, and ended in Yokohama, Japan. The trip became a series of coordinated events, heavy as propaganda, that was used to deter the growing power of Japan from making additional martial gestures. The fleet left Hampton Roads for the Pacific Coast by way of Cape Horn with sixteen battleships comprising the U.S. Naval Fleet. During the cruise, jingo newspapers and the yellow press renewed their vitriolic attacks on the ships' movements. Westerners on the Pacific Coast hailed it as a momentous event, authorities in Eastern cities were concerned about their unguarded shores in case of European attacks, and other countries waited to see what the ships would do.

The fleet returned in February 1909, a success in its purpose; it was a decisive psychological warfare technique, well calculated as to its results and well executed in its endeavor.

FURTHER READING: Penelope Babcock, "The World Cruise of the U.S. Navy, 1907–1909," in William E. Daugherty, *A Psychological Warfare Casebook* (Baltimore: Johns Hopkins; published for Operations Research Office, Johns Hopkins University, 1958); "The Great White Fleet," Amy W. Yarsinske, *Jamestown Exposition: American Imperialism on Parade*, v.2. (Charleston, SC: Arcadia, SC, 1999): 95–112.

WORLD CRUISE OF THE "GREAT WHITE FLEET." *See* World Cruise of the U.S. Navy (1907–1909)

WORLD FAIRS. *See* International Expositions

WORLD WAR I. World War I was the first international conflict in which full-scale use of propaganda was employed by all of the governments concerned. From its inception, both Germany and Great Britain tried to get the United States as its ally and geared much propaganda to that effect. From the beginning, all the warring nations organized campaigns to win the support of their own people for the war effort. In Germany, a group of staff officers at the High Command was assigned to generate propaganda on the home front. They began by issuing completely fictitious news bulletins about the alleged sabotaging of German water supplies by French, British, and Russian troops and managed to convince most German citizens that the German armies were acting in self-defense. Germany also attempted a few shortwave broadcasts in the new communication medium of radio.

British and French propaganda highlighted "atrocities" committed by German soldiers in the early years of the war. From 1906–1915, the buildup of the Dreadnought fleet was helped by newspaper propaganda. One of the most effective was of German soldiers chopping off a baby's hands during the "rape" of Belgium. Another atrocity story was the shooting of a French boy, who had aimed his toy gun at Germans. Both of these stories were later proved to be exaggerations, if not complete inventions. Propaganda techniques became more sophisticated, and a wide variety of media were used. Carefully edited personal accounts of battle found their way into the popular press. The reports of war correspondents were also censored to present an optimistic picture of the progress of the war.

Without the radio and television of later configurations, the poster was an important instrument of mass persuasion in World War I, especially in military recruiting, which combined both glamour and shame to eligible recruits. In Allied countries, the Germans were portrayed as rapacious Huns; the Allied soldier was depicted as fighting for home and country. The poster had a simple message; failure to enlist was akin to treason. Recruiting propaganda of the same sort found its way into popular music and vaudeville entertainment. Probably the most famous poster was American painter James Montgomery Flagg's "I Want You" (1917), which shows Uncle Sam, still a staple of military recruiting, pointing a finger directly at the viewer. This poster was used in both world wars, and eventually more than four million copies were distributed. However, French World War I posters set the standard for war poster design with their beautiful artwork and ardent messages, such as "On les aura" ("We'll get them") or "Sauvonsles" ("Let's save them"), which awakened citizens to the urgency of the war. Also effective were films about the war, exhibits of war art, and special gala evenings to gain support for the war.

World War I, historically significant as the beginning of contemporary mass propaganda, failed to be the "war to end all wars," but it marked a significant break with the past. The public lies about national aims, the wasteful policy of attrition, and the breaking down of social barriers as the costly, bloody conflict continued helped explain the onset of postwar disillusionment as each side emphasized propaganda that differed in its approach toward the United States. Before the United States entered the war, the propaganda posters that raised men and money for the war effort in Europe began appearing in America. The Allies, including France, Great Britain, and Russia, sought American intervention as they fought the Central Powers, led by Germany. The warring nations conducted widespread propaganda operations, especially the pro-German reportage that appeared in books, films, pamphlets, periodicals, and newspapers; the last included the *New York Evening Mail*, secretly purchased by representatives of the Kaiser in 1915. German propaganda operations in the United States, aimed at keeping America out of the war, were helped considerably by **George S. Viereck.** The major United States propaganda effort was conducted by the **Committee on Public Information** (Creel Committee), established in 1917.

The organizational arrangements for foreign and domestic propaganda that emerged in England, France, Germany, and the United States during World War I differed in important respects. Interallied coordination of their separate propaganda efforts was virtually nonexistent. Hollywood studios practiced "practical patriotism" by making films that promoted the Allied war effort (and increased their profits).

See also Blankenhorn, Heber; Creel, George; Four-Minute Men; Occupied Countries and Territories; Whitehouse, Vira Boarman; Zimmermann Telegram

FURTHER READING: Nicholas J. Cull, David Culbert, and David Welch, *Propaganda and Mass Persuasion: A Historical Encyclopedia, 1500 to the Present* (Santa Barbara, CA and Denver, CO: ABC-Clio, 2003); William E. Daugherty, *Psychological Warfare Casebook* (Baltimore: Johns Hopkins; published for Operations Research Office, Johns Hopkins University, 1958); Stewart H. Ross, *Propaganda for War* (New York: McFarland, 1996).

WORLD WAR II. With World War II, military propaganda came into its own. Along with powerful programs in Nazi Germany and in Fascist Italy, the United States and Great Britain realized that they need propaganda ministries to help them win the public opinion war as their countries entered the conflict. Both the Allied and Axis powers waged a psychological battle that included radio broadcasts, movies, posters, and leaflets. Germany, Italy, and Japan fought Great Britain, the Soviet Union, the United States, and the other Allied countries. All the major powers spread far-reaching propaganda. The United States had two major propaganda agencies: **Office of War Information** (overt activities) and **Office of Strategic Services** (covert operations); both started as "Wild Bill" Donovan's Office of the **Coordinator of Information**. Most of the propaganda immediately after **Pearl Harbor** and the entrance of the United States into the war focused on Germany. Propaganda against the Japanese was dormant until the campaign in the Pacific, which witnessed some of the bloodiest fighting of World War II.

The Nazis were very effective propagandists with their filmed staged pieces of Nazi parades and rallies along with leaflet campaigns, such as those shaped like leaves and dropped over France in 1940 with the message, "If you fight England's battle, your soldiers will fall like autumn leaves," and the German "radio" leaflet, which invited Americans to surrender by promising them use of German radio to transmit word to their families that they were safe. Others questioned the loyalty of the women they left behind as well as questioning their reasons for fighting a war on a side "that wasn't going to win." The Nazi Propaganda Ministry, under the very capable Joseph Goebbels, has never been surpassed in the power that it wielded. Hitler used it completely to glorify his credo of a white superior race, and the films, radio broadcasts, newspapers, leaflets, and anything else Goebbels could devise were used.

The British government propaganda department, Ministry of Information, was established 1939 after the British government realized that propaganda had a profound impact on civilian morale during World War I, and it helped create pro-Allies sentiment in the United States before 1917. To prepare for the coming war, planning for a wartime Ministry of Information (MOI) was begun in the spring of 1939, and it assumed responsibility for all facets of British propaganda, domestic and foreign, once war actually began. Since 1945, the British army has incorporated propaganda specialists as part of its military campaigns.

To counter Nazi propaganda in Latin America, President Franklin Roosevelt created the **Office of the Coordinator of Inter-American Affairs** (CIAA), under Nelson Rockefeller, and put all necessary tools at CIAA's disposal: publications, radio broadcasts, posters, and films. As pressure continued on the United States to enter the war that started in Europe in September 1939, Roosevelt decided to create a series of information agencies to excite public opinion on the home front. After Pearl Harbor, the president wanted a propaganda agency to coordinate all these information activities, but without the power that Wilson delegated to the **Committee on Public Information**. The **Office of War Information** (OWI) was established in June 1942 under the direction of **Elmer Davis**. Along with its publications and radio broadcasts over the **Voice of America**, OWI and the War Department worked out agreements with the media about the control of battlefront news, especially statistics on the dead and the wounded, and created **psychological warfare** outposts around the world. They also struck an agreement with Hollywood studio heads on the types of films that could be made to support the war effort. Probably the best-known film series from World War II was **Why We Fight** series, training films produced by the U.S. Army to prepare American soldiers for battle in World War II.

Japanese propaganda used some of the same themes as the Germans. One was a leaflet dropped on Australian troops stationed in remote Pacific Islands while American troops were stationed in Australia. The point was to arouse bad feelings between the Australian and American forces by promoting Australian fears of what was happening to their women "back home." Meanwhile, Allied forces dropped seeds on Asian countries, such as Burma, to show the population that the Japanese forces brought destruction and ruin while the Allies brought prosperity. Information was included on how to sow the seeds. Prior to the Normandy Invasion, better known as D-Day (June 1944), half of all air-dropped propaganda went to the occupied countries (43 percent to France, 7 percent to the others); the other 50 percent of aerial propaganda was dropped over Germany. Up until D-Day, England and the United States dropped 1,760 million pieces of aerial propaganda; 3,240 million pieces were dropped from D-Day to the end of the war.

See also Braddock II; Darlan Interlude; Debunk (Radio Station); Donovan, William ("Wild Bill"); Four Freedoms; Frank, Benno; Geilenkirchen Salient; Gillars, Mildred Elizabeth (Axis Sally); Goebbels and His Propaganda Efforts Against the Allies; Joyce, William Brooke (Lord Haw Haw); Kobayashi Experiment; Leaflet Propaganda; Lorient (Radio Siege); Miller, Glenn; "Moronic Little King" Incident; Norden, Commander Robert Lee; Normandy Invasion; Occupied Countries and Territories; OP-16W (Directive); Operation Mincemeat; Pearl Harbor; Posters in Wartime; Pound, Ezra Loomis; Psychological Warfare Branch, Allied Forces Headquarters (PWB/AFHQ); Psychological Warfare Division, Supreme Headquarters Allied Expeditionary Forces (PWD/SHAEF); Rosie the

Riveter; Tanaka Memorial; Thompson, Dorothy; Thomsen, Hans; Tokyo Rose; U.S.A. Zone of the Overseas Service (North American Service); Viereck, George Sylvester; Warburg, James Paul; Wodehouse, Pelham Grenville; Women as Propaganda Images in Wartime; Zacharias, Ellis Mark

FURTHER READING: John M. Blum, *V Was for Victory: Politics and American Culture During World War II* (New York: Harcourt Brace Jovanovich, 1976); Nicholas J. Cull, David Culbert, and David Welch, *Propaganda and Mass Persuasion: A Historical Encyclopedia, 1500 to the Present* (Santa Barbara, CA and Denver, CO: ABC-Clio, 2003); William E. Daugherty, *Psychological Warfare Casebook* (Baltimore: Johns Hopkins; published for Operations Research Office, Johns Hopkins University, 1958).

WORLDNET. In September 1983, U.N. Ambassador Jeane Kirkpatrick used a tape produced by USIA's Television and Film Service to provide conclusive evidence in the U.N. Security Council that the Soviets destroyed an unarmed civilian airliner, the first time a videotape was used in the Security Council. Two months later, Kirkpatrick was linked via satellite with the prime ministers of Barbados and of St. Lucia and journalists in five capitals to clarify the U.S. rescue missions in Grenada. From this initial merger of satellite television with public diplomacy, USIA's live, global satellite television network, Worldnet, grew.

Worldnet reaches approximately eight million people every day on more than 700 cable systems around the world. It presents U.S. perspectives on important domestic and international events, explains U.S. government policies to a global audience, and transmits a visual image of American culture, history, and scientific and technological achievements. With six satellites carrying the signal, programming can be targeted to particular regions of the world and can be transmitted in regional languages. Foreign stations can obtain Worldnet programming through several different means to broadcast to their own country. One is distribution on a program-by-program basis ("placement"). Television broadcast stations can obtain programs on tapes sent from Worldnet studios in Washington or made at USIS posts in-country from the satellite transmissions.

Worldnet television is available in nearly every capital city in Latin America. Brazil is one of the largest commercial markets, whereas Argentina represents a good example of potential growth in cable television over a short period of time. Worldnet reaches Africa primarily by the placement system. Cable television is limited to South Africa, Botswana, Kenya, and major hotels in Senegal. In 1993, Worldnet launched a Ukrainian-language television broadcast, *Windows on America*, which provides an American perspective on U.S.–Ukrainian relations.

Another distribution means is through "interactives" (one-way video, two-way audio telepress conferences), specialized dialogues that allow foreign journalists, scholars, political leaders and others access to those prominent in U.S. politics, military, business, and other areas (e.g., science, economics, and culture). Each interactive resembles a long-distance press conference with audio and video transmitted from a Worldnet studio in Washington to a post overseas, with individuals at the post asking questions via telephone. These programs have become very popular and have been excerpted on both foreign television and radio stations. In contrast, production costs for U.S. government broadcast television programs are high, and placement is difficult.

In the 1990s, USIA began digital video conferences (DVCs) with hookups from Washington, D.C., headquarters with participants in other parts of the globe but around-the-clock programming by CNN, C-Span, and other television services have brought home events as soon as they happen. This has impacted on public opinion, most recently seen with the incessant coverage of the Iraq war. Like the situation during the Vietnam coverage, the casualties came right into American living rooms.

FURTHER READING: Alvin A. Snyder, *Warriors of Disinformation: American Propaganda, Soviet Lies, and the Winning of the Cold War: An Insider's Account* (New York: Arcade Publishing, 1995); Anna E. Sweeney, *Worldnet Television: Audience Reach via Cable Systems Worldwide* (Washington: Office of Research and Media Reaction, U.S. Information Agency, 1996). Also useful were press releases and other material distributed by USIA's Film and Television Service about the Worldnet operation.

Z

ZACHARIAS, ELLIS MARK (January 1, 1890–June 28, 1961). Ellis Zacharias was a U.S. naval officer, trained in the use of the Japanese language during the 1920s, who became an official spokesman of the United States in his 1945 broadcasts to the Japanese. He was born in Jacksonville, Florida, and graduated from the U.S. Naval Academy (1912), where he began a lifetime study of Japanese culture and language. In 1920, he became naval attaché in Tokyo, and for three years had a chance to learn Japanese and to meet and observe many of the men who later directed the Japanese war effort. He returned there in 1928, then headed the Far East Division of the Office of Naval Intelligence (ONI) in Washington. During World War II, Zacharias saw heavy military action and was able to establish a psychological warfare branch in ONI. Of special significance, the Special Warfare ("W") branch produced the successful **Commander Norden** broadcasts aimed at demeaning German U-boat crews.

In April 1945, Zacharias planned psychological operations (OP-16-W) intended to hasten Japan's surrender before the full-scale invasion planned for later that year. His operative included intense radio broadcasting. Because of his experiences in Japan, Zacharias knew many of the Japanese leaders, and he aimed his broadcasts directly to them, to their war-weariness, and to their vulnerability to propaganda. There were fourteen broadcasts from May 8 to August 4, 1945.

In his appeal to peacemaking forces among the Japanese leadership, it was essential that Zacharias's broadcasts appear as authentic and authorized representations of presidential policy and not merely "another propaganda campaign," although he worked from the **Office of War Information.** This was done by repeated designation of Zacharias as an "official spokesman" (which he dropped in the later broadcasts) and with quotes from presidential messages devised especially for the broadcasts. His previous official status was well known to the Japanese leadership, which gave reassurance of his reliability and his authority.

Zacharias received the Legion of Merit and retired as a rear admiral in 1946, the year he wrote his autobiography, *Secret Missions* , and *Behind Closed Doors: The Secret History of the Cold War* (1950), which advocated for a more aggressive psychological warfare campaign. After his retirement, he testified before a congressional committee that he warned Admiral Husband E. Kimmel in March 1941 that Japan's first war move would be a surprise attack, on a Sunday morning, against the fleet in Hawaii, but Kimmel denied it. In retirement, Zacharias supported an expanded psychological warfare program to combat communism. He died in West Springfield, New Hampshire.

FURTHER READING: U.S. Department of State, *Foreign Relations of the United States, Diplomatic Papers: The Conference of Berlin (The Potsdam Conference) 1945*, vol. 2. (Washington, DC: Government Printing Office, 1960); Maria Wilhelm, *Man Who Watched the Rising Sun; the Story of Admiral Ellis M. Zacharias* (New York: Franklin Watts, 1967).

ZIMMERMANN TELEGRAM. American use of this was propaganda. This telegram was written January 16, 1917, by German Under Secretary of State Arthur Zimmermann and sent to the German minister in Mexico, Heinrich von Eckhardt. It proposed that should the United States join the war against Germany, a German–Mexican alliance should be forged, with Mexico receiving financial aid and restitution of its lost territories (Texas, New Mexico, Arizona) in return for its aid to Germany against the United States. The telegram was intercepted and decoded on February 24 by British intelligence and passed on to the United States, where it had a great effect on President Woodrow Wilson and his administration, as the president was convinced of German treachery. Wilson arranged for the telegram to be released on March 1 by the Associated Press without information about how it was intercepted and deciphered. American pacifists considered it a hoax perpetrated by the British, but its authenticity was confirmed by Zimmermann himself at a March 3 press conference. After it was made public, the telegram damaged U.S.–German relations and accelerated U.S. entrance into World War I. When Wilson asked the U.S. Congress for a declaration of war on April 2, he mentioned the telegram as proof that Germany "means to act against our peace and security."

FURTHER READING: Patrick Beesley, *Room 40: British Naval Intelligence, 1914–1918* (Oxford [UK]: Oxford University, 1984); Michael Sanders and Philip M. Taylor, *British Propaganda During the First World War* (London: Macmillan, 1982); Barbara W. Tuchman, *The Zimmermann Telegram* (New York: Macmillan, 1966).

ZINOVIEV LETTER. On October 25, 1924, the British Foreign Office released to the press the text of an alleged document of the Communist International ordering the British Communist Party to carry out activities against the Labour government and to organize cells in the army. The document, signed with the name of the head of the Communist International, Grigory Zinoviev, is credited with bringing down the British Labour government, which was perceived as being too soft on the Soviet Union.

The Soviet government and Zinoviev denied the authenticity of the letter. However, it was quite consistent with instructions given to the British and other Communist parties by the Fifth World Congress of the Communist International held in Moscow in the summer of 1924. The instructions had been printed in the September 5, 1924, issue of the official Comintern publication, *International Press Correspondence*, published in German and English in Vienna.

Ruth Fischer, who later broke with communism, was an alternate member of the Executive Committee of the Comintern and had been a German delegate to the Fifth Congress. In her history of the German Communist Party, she claimed that Zinoviev had told her that the letter had indeed been a forgery but had been produced by the GPU (Soviet secret police) to undermine his position in the Party. The conventional wisdom on the origin of Zinoviev letter is found in a 1968 book written by three British authors. They quote Irina Bellegarde, the widow of a prominent White Russian émigré who had fought against the Bolsheviks, who claimed that the forgery was created by her husband and two other White Russians, one of whom, Druzhelovsky, had allegedly stolen a sheet of Communist International letterhead stationery from the Soviet embassy in Berlin. Another White émigré forged Zinoviev's signature.

However, this story does not stand up to scrutiny. Although the British government did not release a photographic copy of the original letter, only a translation, such a photographic copy has been found in the U.S. National Archives and was declassified in 1960. It is handwritten in Russian on a sheet of paper with no printed letterhead and does not carry the actual signature of Zinoviev. Mme. Bellegarde's Zinoviev letter may have existed, but it was not the one released by the British Foreign Office.

Druzhelovsky was well known to the Soviets as a notorious forger of alleged Soviet documents, and his activities were exposed in the Soviet book, *Anti-Soviet Forgeries*, published in Russian (1926) and in English (1927). After he went back to the Soviet Union, he was supposedly tried, convicted, and executed in 1927.

FURTHER READING: Herbert Romerstein, "Disinformation as a KGB Weapon in the Cold War," paper prepared for a Conference on Germany and Intelligence Organizations: The Last Fifty Years in Review, Akademie fur Politische Bildung Tutzing [Germany] (1999).

Appendix: Research Collections

The number of research collections in the United States with propaganda-related material is substantial. However, not all are readily available through Internet sites or published listings. The collections in this appendix have all been checked for accuracy of Web site, including its URL for the specific collection, when possible.

Research collections are essential for serious historical research of propaganda activities related to particular organizations, agencies, and individuals. Like most collections on a particular subject, important materials are widely scattered, often with incomplete or nonexistent finding aids and guides. Also, much of the material is ephemeral in nature: Leaflets, broadsides, banners, posters, pamphlets, broadcasts, commercials, and motion pictures.

UNITED STATES

U.S. National Archives and Records Services
8601 Adelphi Road
College Park, MD 20740-6001
Best place to start is the printed guide:
Guide to Federal Records in the National Archives of the United States, compiled by Robert B. Matchette and others (Washington, DC: NARA, 1995), which is also available online with additions.
Online: http://www.nara.gov

Note: The National Archives has the most substantial collection of propaganda materials in the United States. All its photographic and paper holdings are organized by government agency "Record Groups" (RG). A list of record groups is available on request from the archives; many RGs have printed "preliminary inventories" that are invaluable for locating specific documents, manuscripts, and other materials.
Web site: http://www.nara.gov
The National Archives now houses over 35,000 sound recordings, 50,000 reels of film, and more than 4.5 million photographic items. Among the more important RGs relating to federal propaganda and informational activities are the following.

RG 43—United States Participation in International Conferences, Commissions, and Expositions

RG 44—Office of Government Reports (OGR), which acted as a clearinghouse for government information and helped coordinate home-front aspects of the defense and war effort in World War II until being consolidated with other agencies to form the Office of War Information in 1942.

RG 59—U.S. Department of State

RG 63—Committee on Public Information (CPI)

RG 111—Office of the Chief Signal Officer includes propaganda and informational films and newsreels made by the Signal Corps since World War I, the immense bulk of production files for World War II releases, plus other related post-1945 material.

RG 131—Office of Alien Property has minutes, reports, pamphlets, press releases, periodicals, films, and other documents seized from German and Italian organizations operating in the United States (such as the German-American Bund) at the time of American entry into World War II collected in this record group. For a comprehensive introduction to the more general topic of "Germany and German Film, 1930–1945" and attempts to sway American audiences, see the comprehensive three-part research bibliography by Richard Alan Nelson published by the Journal of the University Film Association in 1977–1978.

RG 200—National Archives Gift Collection is a motion picture and newsreel treasure house covering the years from 1919 to 1967. Included in the collection are issues of the Official War Review, March of Time, Paramount News, Ford Animated Weekly (1914–1921), and commercial films investigated by a Senate subcommittee just prior to Pearl Harbor for their alleged war propaganda. The useful *Guide to the Ford Film Collection in the National Archives* by Mayfield Bray, documenting the auto manufacturer's motion picture interests, appeared in 1970.

RG 208—Office of War Information

RG 226—Office of Strategic Services

RG 229—Office of Inter American Coordinator [Coordinator of Inter-American Affairs (CIAA)]

RG 262—Foreign Broadcast Intelligence Service, with approximately 512 cubic feet of documents from the period 1940–1947, including English translations of monitored foreign broadcasts and actual recordings by U.S. citizens such as Edward Delaney, Douglas Chandler, and Fred Kaltenbach aired over German radio. Tokyo Rose broadcasts from Japan and speeches by Allied leaders are also preserved. Also, the Center for Research Libraries in Chicago has microfilm copies of the *Daily Report of Foreign Radio Broadcasts* (1941–) transcribed into English, Voice of America broadcast scripts in English (1953–present), foreign broadcasts monitored by CBS (1939–1945), and other related wide-ranging deposits of potential interest.

RG 306—United States Information Agency (USIA)

The National Audio-Visual Center, operated by the National Archives and Record Administration, rents and sells prints of motion pictures produced by the federal government since the 1930s. Included are many classic propaganda films from World War II, as well as more recent USIA productions.

Presidential Libraries

Herbert Hoover Library
211 Parkside Drive
P.O. Box 488
West Branch, IA 52358-0488
Web site: http://hoover.archives.gov

Franklin D. Roosevelt Library
511 Albany Post Road
Hyde Park, NY 12538-1999
Notes: Indispensable for research into the 1933–1945 New Deal period. A useful
pamphlet describing historical materials in the library is available on request.
Web site: http://www.fdrlibrary.marist.edu

Harry S Truman Library
500 West U.S. Highway 24
Independence, MO 64050-1798
Web site: http://www.trumanlibrary.org

Dwight D. Eisenhower Library
200 Southeast Fourth Street
Abilene, KS 67410-2900
Web site: http://www.eisenhower.utexas.edu

John F. Kennedy Library
Columbia Point
Boston, MA 02125-3398
Web site: http://www.jfklibrary.org

Lyndon B. Johnson Library
2313 Red River
Austin, TX 78705-5702
Web site: http://www.lbjlib.utexas.edu

Gerald R. Ford Library
1000 Beal Avenue
Ann Arbor, MI 48109-2214
Web site: http://www.ford.utexas.edu

Jimmy Carter Library
441 Freedom Parkway
Atlanta, GA 30307-1498
Web site: http://www.jimmycarterlibrary.org

Ronald Reagan Library
40 Presidential Drive
Simi Valley, CA 93065
Web site: http://www.reagan.utexas.edu

George Bush Library
1000 George Bush Drive West
College Station, TX 77845
Web site: http://bushlibrary.tamu.edu

William J. Clinton Presidential Materials Project
Little Rock, AR
Web site: http://clinton.archives.gov
[Library under construction]

Nixon Presidential Materials Staff
National Archives and Records Administration
8601 Adelphi Road
College Park, MD 20740-6001
Web site: http://www.archives.gov/nixon

The difficulty former President Nixon had in locating a home for his library, now in
Yorba Linda, California, including disputes over who owns what materials, further re-
stricted serious political communication research for several years. The Nixon Presidential
Materials Staff is part of the National Archives and Records Administration's (NARA)
Office of Presidential Libraries. The Nixon Staff is the custodian of the historical materials
created and received by the White House during the administration of Richard Nixon,
1969–1974. Following the Watergate controversy, Congress took possession of the records
with the Presidential Recordings and Materials Preservation Act of 1974 (PRMPA). The
Act mandates that the National Archives preserve and process these materials, and prepare
them for public access in the Washington DC area.
    The Richard Nixon Library and Birthplace in Yorba Linda, CA, is not affiliated with
the Presidential Materials Staff or NARA.

Richard Nixon Library and Birthplace
18001 Yorba Linda Boulevard
Yorba Linda, CA 92886
Web site: http://www.nixonfoundation.org

DISTRICT OF COLUMBIA

George Washington University
National Security Archive
Gelman Library
Suite 701
2130 H Street, NW
Washington, DC 20037

    Notes: The National Security Archive is an independent, nongovernmental research in-
stitute that collects and declassifies documents acquired through the Freedom of Information Act. As a result, much of this material is a duplicate of the originals in the National
Archives.
Web site: http://www.gwu.edu/~nsarchiv

Georgetown University
Lauinger Library
Special Collections Division
37 and O Streets, NW
Washington, DC 20057

    Notes: Collection has the papers of former U.S. Ambassador Martin Florian Herz
(1917–1983), containing correspondence, reports, memoranda, posters, propaganda
leaflets, and other material relating to psychological warfare in World War II and during
the Vietnam conflict.
Web site: http://www.library.georgetown.edu/dept/speccoll/cl134.htm

Library of Congress
101 Independence Avenue, SE
Washington, DC 20540

Notes: The Catalog of Holdings, the American Film Institute Collection and the United
Artists Collection at the Library of Congress lists the 14,124 motion pictures acquisi-
tioned through September 1977. Most of these are commercial features, but a number are
of interest for their political messages.

Motion Picture, Broadcasting, and Recorded Sound Division
Madison Building
LM 336
101 Independence Avenue, SE
Washington, DC 20540-4690

Notes: This Division has the German Speech and Monitored Broadcast Collection of
speech and broadcast recordings made in Germany in the 1930s and early 1940s and the
Office of War Information (OWI) Collection of broadcast recordings, photographs, and
research files assembled by the OWI in the early 1940s. [Portions of the collection are
also in the Prints and Photographs Division and the Archive of Folk Song]. Another
resource in this division is the Voice of America (VOA) Collection with broadcasts of
VOA music programs. [There is another substantial collection of VOA music broadcasts
in the National Archives, College Park, Maryland (RG 306)].
  Web sites:
  http://www.loc.gov/rr/mopic
  http://www.loc.gov/rr/record

Music Division (Performing Arts Division)
Madison Building
LM-11
101 Independence Avenue, SE
Washington, DC 20540-4710

Notes: This division has the papers of the Federal Theater Project (but see also the
entry on the FTP records at George Mason University, Fairfax, Virginia).
  Web site: http://www.loc.gov/rr/perform

Prints and Photographs Division
Madison Building
LM 339
101 Independence Avenue, SE
Washington, DC 20540-4730

Notes: The Prints and Photographs Division is rich with posters and political cartoons
of all periods, as well as World War II photos issued by the OWI and others. Also: Works
Progress Administration Poster Collection with over 750 silk-screened posters produced
in the 1930s; Gary Yonker Collection of political propaganda posters, late 1960s to the
present; and records and photographs of the American Colonization Society Collection,
also in the Manuscripts Division.
  Web site: http://www.loc.gov/rr/print/

Rare Book and Special Collections Division
Jefferson Building
LJ 239
101 Independence Avenue, SE
Washington, DC 20540-4740

Notes: This has a very large collection of early political broadsides (including over 250 relating to the Continental Congress and the Constitutional Convention of 1787) as part of its Early American Imprints and a similar collection of Confederate State Imprints. Also: Benjamin Franklin Collection with his papers and publications; portions are also in the Manuscript Division; Third Reich Collection of publications and photographs from the libraries of Nazi leaders. (Also in the Prints and Photographs Division).
Web site: http://www.loc.gov/rr/rarebook

Serial and Government Publications Division
Madison Building
LM 133
101 Independence Avenue, SE
Washington, DC 20540-4760

Notes: Two pertinent collections: Alternative Press Collection of American "underground" newspapers, mid-1960s to the present; and Comic Book Collection of over 2300 comic books acquired by copyright deposit, probably the largest in the United States, on the entire range of comic book subject matter.
Web site: http://www.loc.gov/rr/news

On deposit at the Library of Congress are many important collections of propagandists such as George Creel, Philip Freneau, Henry Hotze, Amos Kendall, Edward R. Murrow, and Herbert A. Philbrick. The library also houses the records of the National Board for Historical Service (which in World War I conducted an enemy press intelligence service), the Elmer Gertz Papers (with important materials relating to the career of George Viereck), and a series of bound volumes containing pamphlets issued by U.S. radical groups since the early 1900s.
Web site: http://www.loc.gov

The Library of Congress has produced guides to its collections. An early one was U.S. Library of Congress, *Special Collections in the Library of Congress: A Selective Guide,* compiled by Annette Melville (Washington, DC: Library of Congress, 1980). Guides are also available through the Library of Congress Web site, including finding aids to specific collections.

Smithsonian Institution
Cold War International History Project (CWIHP)
Woodrow Wilson International Center for Scholars
One Woodrow Wilson Plaza
1300 Pennsylvania Avenue, NW
Washington, DC 20004-3027

Notes: This project, established in 1991, had as its purpose the release of historical materials by governments on all sides of the Cold War, including previously unreleased archival records from former communist bloc countries.
Web site: http://cwihp.si.edu

Smithsonian Institution Archives
P.O. Box 37012
Arts and Industries Building
Room 2135
MRC 414
Washington, DC 20013-7012

Notes: After the success of the 1851 London Crystal Palace Exposition, the Smithsonian Institution was given responsibility for U.S. participation at all international expositions, also called world fairs, beginning with the event held in Philadelphia in 1876. The Smithsonian maintained this duty until World War II.

Guide: Joan Brownell, *Guide to the Exposition Records of the Smithsonian Institution and the United States National Museum, 1867–1939,* ed. by James A. Steed (Washington, DC: Smithsonian Institution Archives, 1991)

Web site: http://www.si.edu/archives/archives/finding aids/faru0070.htm

Smithsonian Institution Libraries
P.O. Box 37012
Natural History Building
Room 22
MRC 154
Washington, DC 20013-7012
National Museum of American History Library

Notes: With the 1876 Philadelphia Centennial Exhibition, Smithsonian Institution officials became active participants in fairs held in the United States as well as several held overseas. They returned with numerous books and pamphlets that by the late 1980s were brittle with age. To preserve them, the Smithsonian Institution Libraries initiated the Books of the Fairs Project to microfilm all material (books, reports, documents) relating to world's fairs and international exhibitions that were scattered throughout the Smithsonian's various libraries and offices. Upon the project's completion, the microfilmed set was placed in the NMAH library for use by researchers.

Microfilm collection: *The Books of the Fairs: A Microfilm Collection Drawn from the Holdings of the Smithsonian Institution Libraries* (Woodbridge, CT: Research Publications, Inc.) 174 reels of microfilm of almost 1,700 items in the SIL collections, 1834–1916, including major holdings of American and European fairs.

Published guides: Smithsonian Institution. Libraries, *The Books of the Fairs* (Chicago: American Library Association, 1992); Smithsonian Institution. Libraries, *Rare Books and Special Collections in the Smithsonian Institution Libraries* (Washington: Smithsonian Institution, 1995).

Web site: http://www.sil.si.edu

U.S. Department of State
Bureau of Public Diplomacy
Public Diplomacy Historical Collection
[formerly: USIA Historical Collection)
Room 135 SA-44
301 4th Street, SW
Washington, DC 20547
[formerly: United States Information Agency]

Notes: The USIA maintained its own historical collection, mentioned elsewhere in this text, that documented the persuasive efforts of the USIA and its predecessor organizations, back to World War I (Committee on Public Information).

Ralph J. Bunche Library
U.S. Department of State
Room 3239 Harry S Truman Building
2201 C Street, NW
Washington, DC 20520-2442
Web site: http://www.state.gov

Notes: This substantial collection, in the oldest federal library, has quite a bit on propaganda, including all the hearings and reports from both the House and the Senate on propaganda investigations and an extensive collection of documents created by the U.S. information and cultural programs, beginning in the late 1930s.
E-mail: library@state.gov
The library's direct link is classified.

United States Holocaust Memorial Museum
Archives
100 Raoul Wallenberg Place, SW
Washington, DC 20024-2126

Notes: The Archives Branch of the U.S. Holocaust Memorial Museum is one of the world's largest and most comprehensive repositories of Holocaust-related records. The collection, which consists of nearly twenty million pages of records, includes microform reproductions of materials held by state and private archival institutions in virtually every European country, including the countries of the former Soviet Union occupied by the German armed forces, as well as materials from the Dominican Republic, Argentina, Israel, Australia, China, Japan, Cuba, and the United States; personal papers, memoirs, and testimonies of Holocaust survivors, victims, liberators, historians, artists, and staff of the International Military Tribunal; video- and audiotapes of oral histories; film and video of historical moving images; and photographs.
Web site: http://www.ushmm.org/research/collections

STATE RESOURCES

Arkansas

University of Arkansas
University Libraries
Special Collections Division
Fayetteville, AK 72701

Notes: The Bureau of Educational and Cultural Affairs History Office Collection was sent to the University of Arkansas in 1983, with the permission of the U.S. National Archives, to complement the personal papers of former U.S. Senator James William Fulbright (D-AK). The collection covers roughly 1927–1980; it is substantial on educational exchanges and cultural diplomacy with much material on sports exchanges and performing artists sent abroad.
Guide: http://uark.edu/libinfo/speccoll/cuaid.html

Arizona

Arizona State University
ASU Libraries
Special Collections
Box 871006
Tempe, AZ 85287-1006

Notes: Agnes Smedley Collection, 1936–1949, consisting of her lecture notes, clippings, newspapers, periodicals, and photos.
Web site: http://www.asu.edu/lib/archives/archcoll.htm

California

California State University
Paulina June and George Pollak Library
P.O. Box 4150
800 North State College Boulevard
Fullerton, CA 92834-4150
PH: (714) 278-2633
FX: (714) 278-2439

Notes: Freedom Center of Political Ephemera, which has runs of over 800 labor publications dating from the late 1800s, election propaganda and campaign buttons from the twentieth century and a superb collection of world's fair materials.
Web site: http://www.calstate.edu

Walt Disney Company
Walt Disney Archives
500 S. Buena Vista Street
Burbank, CA 91521-3040

Notes: A virtual gold mine on Walt Disney's activities, with records on the characters, the films, and other Disney output.
Web site: http://disney.go.com/vault/archives

Southern California Library for Social Studies and Research
6120 South Vermont Avenue
Los Angeles, CA 90044

Notes: Left-wing propaganda of more than 15,000 volumes on Marxism, a like number of rare pamphlets dating back more than 85 years, over 2,000 tape recordings of contemporary antiestablishment leaders ranging from Angela Davis to Martin Luther King, Jr., plus 150,000 news clips broken down into 800 categories (including propaganda) and selected news films made in the 1930s are arranged for easy use. Also maintained are files documenting hundreds of labor, social, and political campaigns and groups active before World War I.
Web site: http://www.usc.edu/isd/archives/la/libraries/la_libraries_so_cal.html

Stanford University
Archives and Libraries
Hoover Institution Archives
Herbert Hoover Memorial Building
Serra and Galvez Streets
Stanford, CA 94305-6010

Hoover Institution Library
Herbert Hoover Tower
Galvez Street
Stanford, CA 94305-6010

Notes: The Hoover Institution on War, Revolution, and Peace Archives has one of the largest private repositories of propaganda-related material in the United States. Its library and archives has over 1.25 million book volumes dealing with all aspects of modern social, economic, and political change. It has a noteworthy collection of propaganda posters (more than 50,000), letters, leaflets, newspapers, rare photos, diaries, and personal records, including miscellaneous papers of George S. Viereck.
    Also:
Radio Free Europe/Radio Liberty (RFE/RL) Reference Library
Notes: According to a 2000 agreement, the Hoover Institution acquired the broadcast archives and corporate records of Radio Free Europe and Radio Liberty (RFE/RL), consisting of some 80,000 tapes and 10.5 million pages of documents, covering the period from the creation of the radios (1949 and 1951, respectively) to their move from Munich to Prague in 1995. Although its abundant holdings largely document current developments in the Soviet Union, there are also runs of RFE/RL publications and other pertinent materials detailing international broadcast propaganda. This is an exceptional research library that attracts scholars from across the globe interested in Soviet studies.
    Web site: http://hoorferl.stanford.edu

Poster Collection
Web site: http://www-hoover.stanford.edu/hila/posters.htm

Russian Collection
Web site: http://www.hoover.org/hila/ruscollection/home.htm

Several surveys of holdings and library catalogs have been published, indicating the importance of this research treasure house. For the posters, see:
    Hoover Institution on War, Revolution, and Peace, *War Revolution and Peace: Propaganda Posters From the Hoover Institution Archives, 1914–1945* (Stanford, CA: Hoover Institution, 1971?). For the published guide, see: Charles G. Palm and Dale Reed, *Guide to the Hoover Institution Archives* (Stanford, CA: Hoover Institution, 1980).
    Web site: http://www.hoover.edu/hila

University of California
UCLA Film and Television Archive Collections
P.O. Box 951575
11334 University—Young Research Library
Los Angeles, CA 90024

Notes: With over 220,000 films and television programs, and 27 million feet of newsreel footage, the UCLA Film and Television Archive is the world's largest university-held collection of motion pictures and broadcast programming.
    Web site: http://www.library.ucla.edu

Film
Material dates back to the 1890s. The motion picture holdings include major 35-mm collections from Paramount Pictures, Twentieth Century-Fox, Warner Bros., Columbia Pictures, New World Pictures, Orion Pictures, RKO, and Republic Pictures. In addition,

the archive's 16-mm film collection has more than 5,000 titles. Films have been received from hundreds of individuals, including William Wyler, Jean Renoir, King Vidor, George Pal, Stanley Kramer, Tony Curtis, and Robert Aldrich, among others.

News

The news collections, including the Hearst Newsreels and the News and Public Affairs collections, offer the researcher coverage of events from newsreels and national and local television news broadcasts.

Television

The television collection documents the entire course of broadcast history; it includes the Academy of Television Arts and Sciences/UCLA Collection of Historic Television, donations from the Hallmark Hall of Fame, Jack Benny, Milton Berle, and Loretta Young, and many milestones in the history of television technology.

Connecticut

Yale University
Beinecke Rare Book and Manuscript Library
Manuscripts and Archives
121 Wall Street
New Haven, CT 06520-8240
Mail: P.O. Box 208240

Notes: There are twentieth-century war posters plus the papers of Ezra Pound, whose propaganda broadcasts from Italy favorably comparing Mussolini to Thomas Jefferson were held by the victorious Allies to be clear proof of his insanity. Archives also has the papers of William Bayard Hale and the Robert O. Anthony collection of all known published writings by Walter Lippmann.
Web site: http://www.yale.edu/beinecke/blguide.htm

Public Opinion Collections
Web site: http://www.library.yale.edu/socsci/opinion/yaleresources.htmls24\

Florida

International Museum of Cartoon Art
201 Plaza Real
Boca Raton, FL 33432

Notes: The International Museum of Cartoon Art opened to the public on March 10, 1996, drawing crowds of people from all over the world. It is the only museum of its kind with cartoonists represented from over 50 countries. Its collection of over 160,000 original drawings includes every genre of the art: animation, comic books, comic strips, gag cartoons, illustration, editorial, cartoons, greeting cards, caricature, graphic novels, sports cartoons, and computer-generated art. The collection also includes over 10,000 books on cartoons and a thousand hours of film and tape of animated cartoons, interviews, and cartoon documentaries. There is material from more than 40 countries.
Web site: http://www.cartoon.org

Wolfsonian-Florida International University
1000 Washington Avenue
Miami Beach, FL 33139

Notes: The Wolfsonian is a museum and research center that promotes the examination of modern material culture, with the emphasis on political art and propaganda and world's fair memorabilia. It was originally the Wolfsonian Foundation of Decorative and Propaganda Arts until 2000, when it became the Wolfsonian-Florida International University. The Wolfsonian contains the country's largest collection of twentieth-century German, Italian, and United States political propaganda, including prints, posters, drawings, books and serial holdings, and objects that document the rise and demise of these nations' fascist movements. The museum's British and Dutch propaganda holdings are the most comprehensive in the United States. Graphic arts from Russia/USSR, middle Europe (particularly Czechoslovakia and Hungary), and Spain (Spanish Civil War posters) provide important and unusual documentation for the history of propaganda in the twentieth century.
Web site: http://www.wolfsonian.fiu.edu/collections

Georgia

University of Georgia
Libraries
Hargrett Rare Book and Manuscript Library
Athens, GA 30602-1641

Notes: There is a noted Confederate Imprint Collection with 80 broadsides and other persuasive documents (official and unofficial) issued between 1861 and 1865.
Web site: http://www.libs.uga.edu/hargrett/speccoll.html

World War I posters
Guide Web site: http://djvued.libs.uga.edu/wwpost

Indiana

University of Notre Dame
University Libraries
221 Hesburgh Library
Special Collections
Notre Dame, IN 46556

Notes: There are 69 microfilm reels of administrative records for the Congregatio de Propaganda Fide covering Catholic activities in the Americas and Great Britain from 1622 to 1865, housed, appropriately, at the University of Notre Dame Archives. A guide to these documents by Finbar Kenneally has been published.
Web site: http://www.archives.nd.edu/guide/476.htmcf1

Anti-Catholic Printed Material Collection
Web site: http://www.archives.nd.edu/findaids/ead/html/ANT.htm

Social Justice Papers
Web site: http://www.archives.nd.edu/findaids/ead/html/ZDJ.htm

Iowa

Iowa State University
Parks Library
Special Collections Department/University Archives
American Archives of the Factual Film (AAFF)
403 Parks Library
Ames, IA 50011-4120

Notes: The Center for the Preservation and Study of Business, Industrial, and Educational Film was established at Iowa State in 1975 and collected close to 7,000 corporate, government-sponsored, and institutional films. AAFF contains this collection and is a major repository of its kind for business, educational, and informational motion pictures prepared for private distribution.
Web site: http://www.lib.iastate.edu/spcl/collections

University of Iowa
Libraries
Special Collections
100 Main Library
Iowa City, IA 52242-1420

Notes: There are runs of more than 900 propaganda periodicals issued by right-wing groups since the 1920s. The basic collection is now available on microfilm for purchase by other research centers. The University of Iowa also holds the letters, papers, and legal documents of German-American propagandist George Sylvester Viereck. Nearly 1,300 items are included, covering the years 1896–1959, which reflect his long activist career.
Web site: http://www.lib.uiowa.edu/spec-coll/

Kansas

University of Kansas
Spencer Research Library
University Archives
1450 Poplar Lane
Lawrence, KS 66045

Notes: Encompasses strong holdings in radical ephemera from the United States, much of which is cataloged. The Leon Josephson Collection has pamphlets on modern socialism and on the Communist Party of America.
Web site: http://www.ukansas.edu

Maryland

University of Maryland
National Library of Broadcasting
Hornbake Library
College Park, MD 20742

Notes: This was formerly the Broadcast Pioneers Library, the oldest archive in the United States dedicated entirely to radio and television history; it was maintained first in New York City, then relocated to the National Association of Broadcasters (NAB) Building, Washington, DC; it was administered by the NAB's Public Affairs and Communications

Department. The collection includes an oral history collection of prominent broadcasters along with oral transcripts of film and television programs.
Web site: http://www.lib.umd.edu/LAB

Gordan W. Prange Collection
McKeldin Library
College Park, MD 20742

Notes: This is one of the most comprehensive collections of Japanese language publications issued in Japan during the post–WWII period, 1945–1949. There are more than 1.7 million items of pamphlets, news dispatches, documents, maps, photos, and posters, virtually everything published during the early years of the U.S. Occupation.
Web site: http://www.lib.umd.edu

Massachusetts

Boston University
BU Libraries
Mugar Memorial Library
Howard Gotlieb Archival Research Center
Historical Manuscript Collection
771 Commonwealth Avenue
Boston, MA 02215

Notes: Strong propaganda holdings including over 100 American, English and French propaganda posters from the First World War, which include work by the illustrators Howard Chandler Christy and James Montgomery Flagg.
Web site: http://www.bu.edu/archives/histman.htm

Harvard University
Radcliffe Institute for Advanced Study
Arthur and Elizabeth Schlesinger Library on the History of Women in America
10 Garden Street
Cambridge, MA 02138

Notes: Major research library on the history of women in the United States. It collects books, serials, manuscripts, photographs, oral histories, and other materials documenting the lives, activities, and concerns of women in the nineteenth and twentieth centuries.
Web site: http://www.radcliffe.edu/schles

Harvard College Library
Harry Elkins Widener Memorial Library
Cambridge, MA 02138

Notes: As the oldest university in the United States, Harvard has an overwhelming collection of Americana primary and secondary materials dating back to the seventeenth century. Its collections predate the Library of Congress. There is excellent material on propaganda in the period before the War of American Independence, but the collections are also substantial in other periods.
Web site: http://hcl.harvard.edu/widener
Web site: http://www.harvard.edu/libraries

Massachusetts Historical Society
Research Library
1154 Boylston Street
Boston, MA 02215

Notes: There are the papers of Samuel Adams and other revolutionary leaders.
Web site: http://www.masshist.org/welcome

Massachusetts Institute of Technology
Department of Political Science
News Study Group
Television Archives
77 Massachusetts Avenue
Cambridge, MA 02139-4307

Notes: Hundreds of commercials plus other political television materials. All of this is available on videotape for public inspection. In addition, a number of VHS compilations are beginning to appear for home and teaching use. Among the best is a 60-minute documentary hosted by former Senator Eugene McCarthy entitled *The Classics of Political Television Advertising* (Washington, DC: Campaigns and Elections, 1986). David Beiler has written a very informative accompanying viewer's guide to this outstanding collection.
Web site: http://www.mit.edu/polisci

Museum of Our National Heritage
P.O. Box 519
33 Marrett Road
Lexington, MA 02173

Notes: Justin Galford War Poster Collection of more than 750 posters believed to be one of the largest intact collections of WWII posters in existence. From December 1991 through May 1992, the museum hosted a major exhibition, With Weapons and Wits, of WWII propaganda artifacts from the collection of Kenneth W. Rendell. The published exhibition guide:
With Weapons and Wits: Propaganda and Psychological Warfare in World War II: Heroic Leaders and Heroic Unknown Warriors in Their Finest Hour; the Collection of Kenneth W. Rendell (Lexington, MA: Museum of Our National Heritage, 1992).
Web site: http://www.masonicinfo.com/musnatlh.htm

Tufts University
Fletcher School of Law and Diplomacy
Cabot Intercultural Center
Murrow Center of Public Diplomacy
160 Packard Avenue
Medford, MA 02155-7082

Notes: The papers of veteran newscaster Edward R. Murrow and his personal library. Along with personal items, such as Murrow's WWII passports and academic robes, there are scripts, research notes, and correspondence. These are also available on 50 reels from Microfilming Corporation of America, a New York Times company. [See the printed *Edward R. Murrow Papers, 1927–1965: A Guide to the Microfilm Edition* for more information. Murrow's papers as USIA director are in RG 306 (United States Information Agency) in the National Archives, College Park, MD]. Access to the Murrow Center is through the Edwin Ginn Library, Fletcher School of Law and Diplomacy; an appointment is required.
Web site: http://library.tufts.ed/ginn

Michigan

Henry Ford Museum and Greenfield Village
Benson Ford Research Center
20900 Oakwood Boulevard
Dearborn, MI 48121

Notes: Archives of the Ford Motor Company, including Henry Ford's papers.
Web site: http://www.hfmgv.org

University of Michigan
University Library
818 Hatcher Graduate Library
7th Floor
Special Collections
Ann Arbor, MI 48109-1205
Mail: P.O. Box 1970

Notes: The Labadie Collection forms part of the Special Collections Library at the University of Michigan, Ann Arbor. The Labadie is perhaps best known for its varied collections of anarchist materials and social protest literature whose scope includes civil liberties, socialism, communism, colonialism and imperialism, free thought, American labor history through the 1930s, the I.W.W., the Spanish Civil War, sexual freedom, women's liberation, gay liberation, student protest movements, and the counterculture. In addition to books, manuscripts, photographs, and ephemera, the Labadie also maintains a large and growing collection of posters. The posters, which number in the hundreds, document a variety of causes and movements worldwide. One of the areas that is well represented in this collection of posters is that of anarchism. In addition, there is a limited collection of World War I posters (320 items) and election advertisements dating from the 1950s (500-plus items from the United States, Canada, and Europe).
Web site: http://www.lib.umich.edu/spec-coll/labadie3\cf17

Wayne State University
Walter P. Reuther Library of Labor and Urban Affairs
Labor and Urban Manuscript Collections
5401 Cass Avenue
Detroit, MI 48202

Notes: Materials relevant to labor struggles as well as interesting collections. Most prominent are the papers of Heber Blankenhorn, a journalist and economist who played an important role in World War II army psychological warfare efforts.
Web site: http://www.reuther.wayne.edu/collections/hefa_294.htm

Nebraska

University of Nebraska
Don L. Love Memorial Library
Archives and Special Collections
Room 29
13th and R Streets
Lincoln, NE 68588-4100
Mail: P.O. Box 884100

Notes: The Rare Books and Special Collections Room has posters, pamphlets, clippings, and other fugitive propaganda issues from World War II numbering over 1,000 items.
Web site: http://www.unl.edu/libr/libs/spec/specar1.htmldtw-3\cf1

U.S. Wartime and Military Collection
Web site: http://www.unl.edu/libr/libs/spec/war.html3\cf1

New Jersey

Fairleigh Dickinson University
FDU Libraries
1000 River Road
Teaneck, NJ 07666

Notes: Harry "A" Chesler Collection consists of over 1,500 volumes of foreign and domestic monographs and periodicals dealing with comic art and illustration, satire, and caricature which support a collection of original comic art and illustrations predating 1939.
Web site: http://www.alpha.fdu.edu/library

Princeton University
Libraries
Seeley G. Mudd Manuscript Library
Department of Rare Books and Special Collections
One Washington Road
Princeton, NJ 08544

Notes: There are several major collections related to propaganda, including large holdings of right-wing political literature, documentation on controversial public relations pioneer Ivy Lee, and propaganda from World War I, including twelve file drawers of correspondence.

America First Committee

Notes: Files relating to the America First Committee and other organizations opposed to the entry of the United States into World War II. Contains mostly printed materials such as copies of the America First Bulletin, newspapers, and press releases.
Web site: http://libweb2.princeton.edu/rbsc2/aids/msslist/maindex.htm

Committee to Defend America by Aiding the Allies

Notes: Files relating to the political, educational, and fund-raising activities of the Committee to Defend America by Aiding the Allies with correspondence, such as that of Roger S. Greene, associate director of the Committee, daily reports, and subject files of the Committee's administrative management division at its national headquarters office in New York City; executive committee correspondence and minutes; state and local chapters material, with correspondence, field representatives files, chapter records; records of college, labor, and women's divisions; fund-raising files from the Committee's NYC headquarters; and published materials put out by the Committee, such as cartoons, Christmas cards, newsletters, pamphlets, press releases, radio transcripts, and speeches. Other Committee members who figure prominently in the collection are Ernest W. Gibson, national director

until the spring of 1941; Hugh Moore, chairman of the executive committee; Frederick C. McKee, treasurer; and Robert F. Duncan, assistant to the national director.
    Web site: http://libweb2.princeton.edu/rbsc2/aids/msslist/maindex.htm

Council on Books in Wartime

    Notes: Records of the Council on Books in Wartime (1942–1947) has subject files of correspondence on various other committees, book publishing projects with the Army, Navy, and Office of War Information, and book list plans (Imperatives and Recommended Books); radio program scripts for book dramatizations on "Words at War" and author interviews on "Fighting Words" and "Books are Bullets"; and financial statements.
    Web site: http://libweb2.princeton.edu/rbsc2/aids/msslist/maindex.htm

Lee, Ivy L. (Ivy Ledbetter), 1877–1934

    Notes: Personal papers of Lee (Class of 1898) and records (1916–1946) from the public relations firm he founded in 1916, Ivy Lee and Associates (now T. J. Ross and Associates, Inc.), documenting Lee's public relations theories and practice.
    Web site: http://libweb2.princeton.edu/rbsc2/aids/msslist/maindex.htm

Lockwood, William W. (William Wirt), 1906–1978

    Notes: Collection consists primarily of Lockwood's files concerning the Institute of Pacific Relations (IPR); he was research secretary (1935–1940) and executive secretary (1941–1943) of the American Council of the IPR, as well as a Princeton professor of politics and international affairs. IPR files contain correspondence, reports, minutes of meetings, memoranda, press releases, and conference data. Included are Lockwood's report "Studies of Relief and Rehabilitation Needs in China" (1943) and papers on the Senate investigation of the IPR on allegations by Senators Joseph McCarthy and Pat McCarran of communist activities. In addition, there are notes, articles, and printed matter on textile industries and economic planning in Asia and American foreign relation policies with Japan and China.
    Web site: http://libweb2.princeton.edu/rbsc2/aids/msslist/maindex.htm

New York

Alfred University
Herrick Memorial Library
One Saxon Drive
Alfred, NY 14802

    Notes: The H. Warner Waid Collection has over 700 titles, mostly published in Germany in the 1930s and 1940s, supplemented by periodicals and monographs about the occupation and rehabilitation of Germany collected from Allied and American High Commissions and U.S. State Department offices by Waid, who was editor-in-chief of the official U.S. Army of Occupation's *Information Bulletin*.
    Web site: http://www.herr.alfred.edu/special/index.asp

Hofstra University
Joan and Donald E. Axinn Library
Kroul Collection of Nazi Propaganda
West Campus Library
619 Fulton Avenue
Hempstead, NY 11549-1000

Notes: The Collection of Nazi Culture and Propaganda documents the rise of the National Socialist mentality in the Germany of the 1930s.

Web site: http://www.hofstra.edu/Libraries/Axinn/axinn_libdepts_spcoll_kroul_guide_rev.cfm

Museum of Public Relations
Reference Library
26 Broadway
22nd Floor
New York, NY 10004

Notes: Features one of the nation's largest collections on public relations, publicity and propaganda.

Web site: http://www.prmuseum.com

Museum of Television and Radio
25 West 52nd Street
New York, NY 10019

Notes: Collection of more than 60,000 television and radio shows as well as 10,000 commercials. The Museum of Television & Radio is a nonprofit organization founded by William S. Paley in 1975 to collect and preserve television and radio programs and to make these programs available to the public. The museum now includes more than 100,000 programs chosen for their artistic, cultural, and historical significance with news, drama, public affairs programs, documentaries, the performing arts, children's programming, sports, comedy, and advertising. This museum has also acquired copies of World War II Axis English-language propaganda programs and it has established a collection of landmark radio and television commercials. In 1996, the museum opened a branch in Los Angeles.

Los Angeles
Leonard H. Goldenson Building
465 North Beverly Drive
Beverly Hills, CA 90210
Web site: http://www.mtr.org

New York Historical Society
2 West 77th Street
New York, NY 10024

Notes: An excellent source for early Revolutionary and Civil War propaganda broadsides, the society also houses the Landauer Collection of American Advertising, more than 1 million pictorial items demonstrating the power and art of U.S. business propaganda.

Web site: http://www.nyhistory.org/library.html

New York Public Library
American History Division
Fifth Avenue and 42nd Street
New York, NY 10018-2788

Notes: Division has a substantial amount of political propaganda materials, including party pamphlets, presidential campaign buttons, posters, ribbons, and coins. Its research libraries also have a strong advertising collection and regular deposit of newer publications and materials from groups such as the Advertising Council. There are also Civil War enlistment posters and bound photographic volumes of over 2,000 World War I posters. The Bancroft Collection of original manuscripts from the American Revolution includes the papers of the Boston Committee of Correspondence and the papers of Samuel Adams and his grandson, Samuel Adams Wells. While considerable, these personal effects of Adams represent only a small portion of his total correspondence since much of what he wrote suffered from neglect or was destroyed in an effort to protect his reputation. Wells's papers consist of his manuscript notes and partial drafts for an unfinished biography of his grandfather, later utilized by subsequent writers. There are also antislavery materials, including runs of early abolitionist propaganda periodicals such as the *Anti-Slavery Reporter* and *Anti-Slavery Standard*, over 11,000 pamphlets from World War I; a number of psychological warfare leaflets distributed in Europe and Asia during World War II, and substantial holdings of press releases and other publications issued by various government information services, such as those of the U.S. Central Intelligence Group from the years 1942–1947. The papers of the Institute for Propaganda Analysis, long held privately by Alfred McClung Lee, have also been donated to the New York Public Library. The Jewish Division has a large collection of extremist literature.

Web site: http://www.nypl.org/research/chss/admin/collections.html

New York University
Elmer Holmes Bobst Library
Tamiment Labor History Collection
70 Washington Square South
New York, NY 10012

Notes: Radical literature. There are extensive holdings of AFL-CIO materials while the Oral History of the American Left Project serves as a repository for veterans of radicalism in unions, politics, and culture.

Web site: http://www.nyu.edu

St. John's University
Library
World War II Poster Collection
St. Augustine Hall
Room 430
8000 Utopia Parkway
Jamaica, NY 11439

Notes: A collection of posters displayed at St. John's College, Brooklyn, during the war years. The agency responsible for publication varied but most were distributed primarily by the Office of War Information. Artists represented in collection include James Montgomery Flagg and Norman Rockwell.

Web site: http://new.stjohns.edu/academics/libraries/archives

Syracuse University
E.S. Bird Library
George Arents Research Library for Special Collections
222 Waverly Avenue
Syracuse, NY 13244-2010

Notes: Dorothy Thompson Collection of manuscripts, scripts, and research materials.
Web site: http://www.syracuse.edu

Anti-Semitic and pro-Semitic propaganda is collected at:

American Jewish Committee
Blaustein Library
165 E. 56th Street
New York, NY 10022
Web site: http://www.ajc.org

Anti-Defamation League of B'nai B'rith
Rita and Leo Greenland Human Relations Library and Research Center
823 United Nations Plaza
New York, NY 10017
Web site: http://www.adl.org

YIVO Institute for Jewish Research
Library and Archives
15 W. 16th Street
New York, NY 10011
Notes: Nazi Collection
Web site:// http://www.yivoinstitute.org

Ohio

Bowling Green State University
University Libraries
204 William Jerome Library
Fourth Floor
Popular Culture Library
Bowling Green, OH 43403-0170

Notes: The Popular Culture Library, founded in 1969 and dedicated to the acquisition
and preservation of research materials on American popular culture (post-1876), is the
most comprehensive repository of its kind in the United States. Major subject strengths of
the Popular Culture Library include comic art and books; popular fiction in the romance;
mystery-detective, science fiction-fantasy and western genres; the performing arts and the
entertainment industry; graphic arts, film and mass communications; popular religion, the
occult and the supernatural; sports, recreation and leisure; hobbies, games and amuse-
ments; foodways and cookery; etiquette and advice; comedy and humor.
Web site: http://www.bgsu.edu/colleges/library/pcl/pcl.html

Hebrew Union College–Jewish Institute of Religion
Klau Library, HUC-JIR
Jacob Rader Marcus Center of the American Jewish Archives
(American Jewish Archives)
3101 Clifton Avenue
Cincinnati, OH 45220-2488

Notes: Archives includes the papers of important figures such as Jacob Schiff, Samuel
Untermeyer, Felix Warburg, and Isaac Wise. The records of the House Special Committee

on Un-American Activities, 1934–1939, focusing on Nazi propaganda in the United States, have been donated to the AJA by the family of Representative Samuel Dickstein.
   Web site: http://www.americanjewisharchives.org

Oberlin College
Archives
420 Mudd Center
148 West College Street
Oberlin, OH 44074-1532

   Notes: Microfilmed collection of abolition and antislavery materials. Guide: Oberlin College. Library. *A Classified Catalogue of the Collection of Anti-Slavery Propaganda in the Oberlin College Library*, compiled by Geraldine Hopkins Hubbard, edited by Julian S. Fowler (Oberlin: 1932).
   Web site: http://www.oberlin.edu/archive

Oklahoma

University of Oklahoma
Political Communication Center
Julian P. Kanter Political Commercial Archive
610 Elm Avenue
Norman, OK 73019-2081

   Notes: One of the largest collections of television and radio advertisements for national, state, and local political candidates in the United States, with more than 10,000 television spots and uncounted radio announcements. Rarities include a cartoon for Eisenhower, with a "We Like Ike" soundtrack song, the only animated commercial ever made by the Disney Studio for a political campaign. Material was collected over more than 30 years by Julian Kanter, come from all across the country and represent candidates for every office from president to city council member.
   Web site: http://www.ou.edu/pccenter

Libraries
Bizzell Memorial Library
Norman, OK 73019-2081

   Notes: Papers of Horace C. Peterson used in writing his book, *Propaganda for War: The Campaign against American Neutrality, 1914–1917* (Norman: University of Oklahoma, 1939), supplemented by reviews and other documentation of reaction to publication.
   Web site: http://libraries.ou.edu

Pennsylvania

American Philosophical Library
Library
105 South Fifth Street
Philadelphia, PA 19106-3386

   Notes: Houses the vast Richard Gimbel Collection, formerly at Yale University, of published and unpublished materials by and about Thomas Paine. Other documents have been added to make this the single best reference center for the study of Paine's life and work.
   Web site: http://www.amphilsoc.org/library/mole/p/paine.htmxpndtw-3\cf1

Haverford College
James P. McGill Library
Quaker Collection
370 Lancaster Avenue
Pennsylvania, PA 19041-1392

Notes: Records (1821–1858) of the Indian Society of Anti-Slavery Friends and the diary of William Charles Allen, which discusses at some length the effect of propaganda on American public attitudes in World War I.
Web site: http://www.haverford.edu/library

Historical Society of Pennsylvania
1300 Locust Street
Philadelphia, PA 19107

Notes: The World War II Collection is strong in broadsides, posters, and other forms of federal publicity and propaganda issued by U.S. government agencies.
Web site: http://www.hsp.org
The society inherited one of the country's largest collections of war posters and radical and racist literature when this collection was transferred from the Balch Institute for Ethnic Studies in Philadelphia. It has an online guide:
A Guide to Manuscript and Microfilm Collections of the Research Library of the Balch Institute for Ethnic Studies
Web site: http://www.hso.org/collections/Balch

Swarthmore College
Friends Historical Library
500 College Avenue
Swarthmore, PA 19081-1905

Notes: Material from World War I; it also holds propaganda materials issued by the Women's Information League for Peace and Freedom, the League of Nations Association, and the Emergency Peace Campaign of 1937.
Web site: http://www.swarthmore.edu/Library/friends

Swarthmore College Peace Collection
Web site: http://www.swarthmore.edu/Library/peace

Temple University
Temple University Libraries
Samuel Paley Library
Rare Books and Manuscripts Room
1210 W. Berks Street
Philadelphia, PA 19122-6088

Notes: Over 3,000 U.S. and foreign war posters dating from 1914 through the end of the Vietnam conflict. A card guide exists for World War I issues. The university's Contemporary Culture Center has equally impressive holdings of alternative and radical left- and right-wing press ephemera and polemical writings. These are supplemented by microfilm documents and taped interviews with neo-Nazi leaders and others.
Web site: http://www.library.temple.edu/speccoll

U.S. Army Military History Institute
Research Collection
22 Ashburn Drive
Carlisle Barracks, PA 17013-5008

Notes: Scrapbook of propaganda leaflets dropped over Japan in World War II. The U.S. Army Institute for Military Assistance Library, formerly the Special Warfare School Library, was transferred from Fort Bragg, North Carolina. It has more than 45,000 pamphlets and documents related to military strategy and counterintelligence, including propaganda leaflets from World War II and Korea and the William J. Donovan papers.
Web site: http://carlisle-www.army.mil/usamhi

Rhode Island

Providence Public Library
225 Washington Street
Providence, RI 02903-3283

Notes: Harris Collection on the American Civil War and Slavery includes propaganda pamphlets, books, periodicals, broadsheet music, and other eighteenth- and nineteenth-century materials reflecting both sides of the controversy, with more than 85 editions of *Uncle Tom's Cabin* in fourteen languages.
Web site: http://www.provlib.org

Tennessee

Vanderbilt University
Special Collections
Vanderbilt Television News Archive
419 21st Avenue S
Nashville, TN 37240-0007

Notes: Unique collection of nearly 10,000 hours of videotaped news and public affairs programs issued since August 1968.
Web site: http://www.vanderbilt.edu/speccoll/schome.html

Texas

Texas A&M University
James Gilliam Lee Library
2600 S. Neal Street
Commerce, TX 75429

Notes: Ku Klux Klan Collection of ephemera as well as over 300 monographs and serials illustrating the Reconstruction Klan and the Klan of the 1920s.
Web site: http://library.tamu.edu

Texas Tech University
The Vietnam Archive
18th and Boston
Box 41041
SW Collections 108
Lubbock, TX 79409-1041

Notes: Archive of the Vietnam Conflict Collection is a comprehensive collection of documents, including microfilms of the U.S. Military Assistance Command, books written about the fighting, letters from soldiers to loved ones at home, and the Douglas Pike records of books, monographs and slides.
Web site: http://www.vietnam.ttu.edu/vietnamproject/history.htm

University of Texas
Harry Ransom Humanities Research Center
P.O. Box 7219
Austin, TX 78713-7219

Notes: Collection includes the Frances Harvey papers, which discuss use of newspaper propaganda in the Southwest following the Civil War. The Edward A. Peden papers trace his work distributing U.S. propaganda materials in Germany after World War I.
Web site: http://www.hrc.utexas.edu

Utah

Brigham Young University
Harold B. Lee Library
2722 HBLL
P.O. Box 26800
Provo, UT 84602-6800

Notes: Richard Alan Nelson Mormon Film and Television Collection includes newspaper clippings, correspondence, film reviews, newsletters, promotional materials, essays, and photographs. Nelson is the author of *A Chronology and Glossary of Propaganda on the United States* (Westport, CT: Greenwood, 1996).
Web site: http://sc.lib.byu.edu

Virginia

Central Intelligence Agency
Historical Intelligence Collection
McLean, VA
Mailing address:
Center for the Study of Intelligence
History Staff
IG03 International Point
Washington, DC 20505

Notes: One of the primary intelligence collections in the world, a working repository of books and periodicals on all aspects of intelligence operations. The Historical Intelligence Collection is primarily an open-source library dedicated to the collection, retention, and exploitation of material dealing with the intelligence profession. Currently, there are more than 25,000 books and an extensive collection of press clippings on that subject. Not open to the public.
Web site: http://www.cia.gov/cia/information/tour/cia_library.html

George C. Marshall Research Foundation
Library and Archives
P.O. Drawer 1600
Lexington, VA 24450-1600

Notes: Along with General Marshall's private papers, there is a small but excellent twentieth-century war poster collection (nearly 700 issued in the United States, Germany, and France), over 6,000 uncataloged U.S. Signal Corps and OWI photos, and other military propaganda materials. A useful illustrated guide to the poster holdings written by Anthony Crawford, with an informed sixteen-page introduction by former OWI propaganda analyst O. W. Riegel, was published in 1979.

Web site: http://www.marshallfoundation.org/library_archives/library_archives.htm

George Mason University
Fenwick Library
Special Collections and Archives
4400 University Drive
Fairfax, VA 22030-4444

Notes: A collection of Federal Theater Project (FTP) materials, oral history interviews and research aids. Sources of donated materials include persons formerly employed in the FTP, various theater historians, the National Archives and Records Administration, and the Library of Congress. Types of materials include administrative records, billboard sheets, music, photograph prints and negatives, playbills, radio scripts and videotaped lectures. Contains over 130 linear feet of materials.

Web site: http://www.gmu.edu/library/specialcollections/federal.html
Guide to FTP Collection:
Web site: http://ead.lib.virginia.edu/vivaead/published/gmu/vivadoc.pl?file=vifgm00020.xml

Washington State

Tacoma Public Library
1102 Takoma Avenue S
Tacoma, WA 98402-2098

Notes: Collection of U.S. and French World War I propaganda posters (over 1,000) and pamphlets on file.

Web site: http://www.tpl.lib.wa.us

University of Washington

Libraries
Allen Library, Room 482
Seattle, WA 98195-2900
Mail: P.O. Box 352900

Notes: Anna Louise Strong papers; KIRO-CBS Collection of Broadcasts of the World War II Years and After Phonoarchive, which preserves inclusive sound recordings of one radio network's fare during the 1940s. A guide to this collection exists, prepared by Milo Ryan.

Web site: http://www.lib.washington.edu

Wisconsin

Wisconsin Historical Society
[formerly: State Historical Society of Wisconsin]
Library
Visual Materials Collections
816 State Street
Second Floor
Madison, WI 53706

Notes: Documents and audiovisual material, particularly in relation to communist propaganda in the motion picture industry. The collection keeps the records of the Pacifica Foundation, 1949–1976, of program guides, news scripts, correspondence, personnel lists, and financial information.

Web site: http://www.wisconsinhistory.org/library

The Wisconsin Historical Society maintains the Wisconsin Center for Film and Theater Research, one of the world's major archives of materials relating to the entertainment industry, with over 300 manuscript collections from outstanding playwrights, television and film directors, producers, writers, actors, and designers along with over 15,000 motion pictures, television shows and videotapes, two million still photographs and promotional graphics, and several thousand sound recordings. There are the papers of Dalton Trumbo, Albert Maltz, Melvyn Douglas, Samuel Ornitz, the Progressive Citizens of America/Hollywood Democratic Committee, plus Robert Morris and Robert Kenny (lawyers who defended the Hollywood 10). Other extensive film and television material is located there, including episodes of the controversial FBI-supported *I Led Three Lives* program aired during the McCarthy era of the 1950s. The papers of Frank Early Mason, also in the society's collections, contain private records of his radio propaganda activities as special assistant to the Secretary of the Navy in World War II. The Center is cosponsored by the Society and the University of Wisconsin-Madison.

Web site: http://www.wisconsinhistory.org/wcftr

University of Wisconsin
Communication Arts Department
6117 Vilas Hall
821 University Avenue
Madison, WI 53706

Notes: The university's School of Journalism and Mass Communication additionally operates a reading room with vertical file holdings on propaganda and public opinion.

Web site: http://commarts.wisc.edu

Wyoming

University of Wyoming
American Heritage Center
Dept. 3924
1000 E. University Avenue
Laramie, WY 82071

Notes: Several collections of papers, many relating to propaganda (such as those of Lyman Munson, Frank Capra's boss for the Why We Fight motion picture series).

Web site: http://ahc.uwyo.edu

INTERNATIONAL

Not all sources for the study of American propaganda, however, are to be found within the United States, as can be seen from the following resources

Canada

The Mackenzie Institute
P.O. Box 338
Adelaide Station
Toronto, Ontario
M5C 2J4
Canada

Notes: Publications on propaganda, many issued under institute's former designation:
The Mackenzie Institute for the Study of Terrorism, Revolution and Propaganda
Web site: http://www.mackenzieinstitute.com

England

Imperial War Museum
Lambeth Road
London, SE1 6HZ
England

Notes: A major propaganda research center. The museum's library is very strong in
twentieth-century pamphlets, film (with over 37 million feet from the two world wars and
an increasing collection of post-1945 footage, including Vietnam), artwork (the poster collection exceeds 50,000 items, among them significant U.S. issues), and photographs, as
well as standard book and clipping file materials.
Web site: http://www.iwm.org.uk

Psywar Society of England

Notes: Society publishes a fact-filled journal called *The Falling Leaf* and acts as a clearinghouse for psychological warfare memorabilia collectors. For example, Reginald Auck-
land, the present director, has a personal collection of over 9,000 items, including many
rare U.S. Army leaflets.
Web site: http://psywarsoc.psyborg.co.uk

Germany

Deutsche Bibliothek
Deutsche Bibliothek
Adickesallee 1,60322
Frankfurt am Main

Deutsche Bücherei
Deutscher Platz 1, 04103
Leipzig
Deutsches
Musikarchiv Berlin
Gärtnerstraße 25-32, 12207
Berlin

Notes: Die Deutsche Bibliothek is the national library and national bibliographic
information center for the Federal Republic of Germany. It is responsible for the collection, processing and bibliographic indexing of all German and German-language publications issued since 1913. Die Deutsche Bibliothek cooperates closely with all national and
international library institutions and organizations. Within this context, it has a leadership role in the development and application of common rules and standards for
Germany. Die Deutsche Bibliothek was established in 1990 on the basis of the Treaty of
Unification in a merger of the existing institutions the Deutsche Bücherei Leipzig (founded
in 1912) and the Deutsche Bibliothek Frankfurt am Main (founded in 1947), of which the
Deutsches Musikarchiv Berlin had been an integral part since 1970. Signed on September
23, 1990, the Treaty of Unification enabled the institutions to join together in fulfilling
the legally specified objectives of the national library.
Web site: http://www.ddb.de/index_e.htm

Hungary

Central European University
Open Society Archives
Research Center
1051 Budapest
Nador u.9
Budapest, Hungary

Notes: Material on communism, the Cold War, and Radio Free Europe/Radio Liberty publications.
Guide:
Web site: http://www.osa.ceu.hu/guide/research/index.shtml
Radio Free Europe/Radio Liberty
Web site: http://www.osa.ceu.hu/library/special_collections/

Russian Archives (Rosarchiv)

With the fall of the Soviet Union, it became easier to access one of the most important sources of historical documents in the world as more scholars have been able to use what is collectively called the Russian Archives; it comprises at least eleven archives. A good place to start is with the finding aid:

Archives and Manuscript Collections in Russia
Web site: http://www.idc.nl/catalog/faid/018English.html

Relevant archives important to the study of propaganda:

GARF: Gosudarstvennyj archiv Rossijskoj Federacii
Ul. B. Pirogovskaja 17, Moscow, Tel. 200 51 12
[Moscow State Archive, Russian Federation]
Web site: http://www.idc.nl/catalog/faid/497/B1findingaids.html

Rossiiskii gosudarstvennyi arkhiv kinofotodokumentov (RGAKFD)
[Russian State Archive of Documentary Films and Photographs]
143400, Moskovskaia oblast', Krasnogorsk, ul.Rechnaia, 1
Web site: http://www.idc.nl/catalog/faid/497/B11findingaids.html

Arkhiv vneshnei politiki Rossiiskoi Imperii (AVPRI)
[Archive of Foreign Policy of the Russian Empire]
Web site: http://www.idc.nl/catalog/faid/497/C3findingaids.html
Gosudarstvennyi fond kinofil'mov RF (Gosfil'mofond/GFF)
[State Fond of Motion Pictures]
Web site: http://www.idc.nl/catalog/faid/497/B11findingaids.html

Rossiiskii gosudarstvennyi arkhiv literatury i iskusstva (RGALI)
[Russian State Archive of Literature and Art]
Web site: http://www.idc.nl/catalog/faid/497/B7findingaids.html

Rossiiskii gosudarstvennyi voennyi arkhiv (RGVA)
[Russian State Military Archive]
125884, Moscow, ul. Admirala Makarova, 29
Web site: http://www.idc.nl/catalog/faid/497/B8findingaids.html

Rossiiskaia knizhnaia palata (RKP)
[Russian Book Chamber]
Russian Archive of Publications (RAP)
Web site: http://www.idc.nl/catalog/faid/497/C18findingaids.html

Others include: Russian Center for the Preservation and Study of Documents on Recent History [Rossiiskii tsentr khraneniia i izucheniia dokumentov noveishei istorii (RTsKhIDNI)] for pre-1953 Central Committee records; Center for the Preservation of Contemporary Documentation [Tsentr khraneniia sovremennoi dokumentatsii (TsKhSD)], for post-1953 Central Committee records; Archives of the Foreign Policy of the Russian Federation [Arkhiv vneshnei politiki Rossiiskoi Federatsii (AVPRF)] in the Ministry of Foreign Affairs (MFA); archives of the Ministry of Defense, the General Staff, and the KGB; Archive of the President of the Russian Federation [Arkhiv Prezidenta Rossiiskoi Federatsii (APRF)].

Notes: The Russian archives are a complex series of depositories that serves its own bureau, (e.g., AVPRF). This invaluable resource includes material on Party organizational, propaganda, and other activities. Beginning in 1995, Yale University Press started a major publication project that allows U.S. scholars the right to research and to publish the archives of the Soviet Union, 1917–1991, in its *Annals of Communism* series, with a minimum of twenty-five volumes. To date, thirteen volumes have been released.

English-language guide: Diane P. Koenker and Ronald D. Bachman (eds.), *Revelations from the Russian Archives: Documents in English Translation* (Washington, DC: Library of Congress, 1997).

PRINT RESOURCES TO FINDING PROPAGANDA COLLECTIONS

American Library Directory, 2003–2004: v.1: Libraries in the United States; 56th ed. (Medford, NJ: Information Today, 2003)

Index to Personal Names in the National Union Catalog of Manuscript Collections, 1959–1984 (Alexandria: Chadwyck-Healey, 1988), 2 v.

Richard A. Nelson, "Propaganda." In *Greenwood Guide to American Popular Culture*, ed. by M. Thomas Inge and Dennis Hall, vol. 3, 1327–1431 (Westport, CT: Greenwood, 2002).

National Historical Publications and Records Commission. *Directory of Archives and Manuscript Repositories in the United States*, 2nd ed. (Phoenix, AZ: Oryx, 1988).

This is a guide to over 3,200 archives and manuscript repositories in the United States, arranged by state and town. Additional access is provided by a name-subject index, as well as special lists of different types of repositories.

"Propaganda and Propagandists" [Propaganda Collections]. In *Subject Collections: A Guide to Special Book Collections and Subject Emphases as Reported by University, College, Public, and Special Libraries and Museums in the United States and Canada*, compiled by Lee Ash and William G. Miller, vol. 2, M–Z; 7th ed., rev. and enl. (New Providence, NJ: R. R. Bowker, 1876–1878).

Select Bibliography

This is not intended as an inclusive bibliography but as a general guide to basic works on the subject. The reader should also refer to the cited sources with each entry. The bibliography begins by providing sources listed by subject or formats. It continues with a list of general works, followed by relevant films and videos.

AMERICA FIRST COMMITTEE

Sarles, Ruth. *A Story of America First: The Men and Women Who Opposed U.S. Intervention in World War II*, edited by Bill Kauffman. Westport, CT: Praeger, 2003.

ANTI-SEMITISM

Adorno, Theodor W. "Anti-Semitism and Fascist Propaganda." In *Anti-Semitism: A Social Disease,* edited by Ernst Simmel, 125–37. New York: International Universities, 1946.
Dinnerstein, Leonard. *Anti-Semitism in America.* New York and London: Oxford, 1994.
Jaher, Frederic C. *A Scapegoat in the Wilderness: The Origins and Rise of Anti-Semitism in America.* Cambridge, MA: Harvard, 1994.
Wallace, Max. *The American Axis: Henry Ford, Charles Lindbergh, and the Rise of the Third Reich.* New York: St. Martin's, 2003.

ART

"American Art Abroad: The State Department Collection." *Art News* 45 (October 1946): 20–31.
Billington, Ray A. "Government and the Arts: The WPA." *American Quarterly* 13 (1961): 466–479.
Bustard, Bruce I. *A New Deal for the Arts.* Washington, DC: National Archives and Records Administration in cooperation with the University of Washington Press, Seattle, 1997.
Cole, John Y. "Amassing American 'Stuff': The Library of Congress and the Federal Arts Projects of the 1930s." *Quarterly Journal of the Library of Congress* (Fall 1983): 356–389.
"Cultural Diplomacy in the Post–Cold War World." *Journal of Arts Management, Law and Society* 29, no. 1 (Spring 1999) [Entire Issue].

Heger, Kenneth W. "Diplomats and the Depression: The Department of State and the New Deal." *Prologue: The Quarterly of the National Archives and Records Administration* (Summer 1998): 98–108.

Mathews, Jane de Hart. "Art and Politics in Cold War America." *American Historical Review* 81 (October 1976): 762–777.

O'Connor, Francis V., ed. *Art for the Millions: Essays from the 1930s by Artists and Administrators of the WPA Federal Arts Project.* Greenwich, CT: New York Graphic Society, 1973.

Park, Marlene and Gerald E. Mokowitz. *Democratic Vistas: Post Offices and Public Art in the New Deal.* Philadelphia: Temple University, 1984.

AUSTRIA

Wagnleitner, Reinhold. *Coca-Colonization and the Cold War: The Cultural Mission of the United States in Austria after the Second World War.* Chapel Hill: University of North Carolina, 1994.

BIBLIOGRAPHIES

Cole, Robert. *Propaganda in Twentieth Century War and Politics: An Annotated Bibliography.* Lanham, MD: Scarecrow/Salem, 1996.

Lasswell, Harold D., Ralph D. Casey, and Bruce L. Smith, eds. *Propaganda and Promotional Activities: An Annotated Bibliography.* Chicago: University of Chicago, 1969.

U.S. Congress. Senate. Committee on Government Operations. *Congressional Investigations of Communism and Subversive Activities: Summary-Index, 1918 to 1956, United States Senate and House of Representatives.* Washington, DC: Government Printing Office, 1956.

BIOGRAPHIES

Christians, Clifford G., and Michael R. Real. "Jacques Ellul's Contributions to Critical Media Theory." *Journal of Communication* 29, no.1 (Winter 1979): 83–93.

Johnson, Niel M. *George Sylvester Viereck: German-American Propagandist.* Urbana: University of Illinois, 1972.

Laurie, Clayton D. "'The Chanting of Crusaders': Captain Heber Blankenhorn and AEF Combat Propaganda in World War I." *Journal of Military History* 59, no. 3 (July 1995): 457–481.

Lee, Alfred McClung, and Elizabeth Briant Lee, eds. *The Fine Art of Propaganda: A Study of Father Coughlin's Speeches.* New York: Harcourt Brace and Company, 1939.

Oates, Stephen. "Henry Hotze: Confederate Agent Abroad." *Historian* 27, no. 2 (1965): 131–154.

Schapsmeier, Edward L., and Frederick H. Schapsmeier. *Walter Lippmann: Philosopher–Journalist.* Washington, Public Affairs, 1969.

Selwyn, Francis. *Hitler's Englishman: The Crime of "Lord Haw-Haw."* London: Routledge and Kegan Paul, 1987.

Tye, Larry. *The Father of Spin: Edward L. Bernays and the Birth of Public Relations.* New York: Crown Publishers, 1998.

Vaughn, Stephen. "Prologue to Public Opinion: Walter Lippmann's Work in Military Intelligence." *Prologue: Quarterly of the National Archives and Records Administration,* 15, no. 3 (Fall 1983): 151–163.

CARTOONS

Banta, Martha. *Barbaric Intercourse: Caricature and Culture of Conduct, 1841–1936.* Chicago: University of Chicago, 2003.

Gombrich, E. H. "The Cartoonist's Armoury." *South Atlantic Quarterly* 62 (Spring 1963): 189–227.

CHRONOLOGY

Nelson, Richard A. *Chronology and Glossary of Propaganda in the United States.* Westport, CT: Greenwood, 1996.

COMMITTEE ON PUBLIC INFORMATION

Creel, George. *How We Advertised America: The First Telling of the Amazing Story of the Committee on Public Information That Carried the Gospel of Americanism to Every Corner of the Globe.* New York: Arno Press, 1972.

Mock, James R., and Cedric Larson. *Words that Won the War: The Story of the Committee on Public Information, 1917–1919.* Princeton: Princeton University Press, 1939.

Vaughn, Stephen. *Holding Fast the Inner Lines: Democracy, Nationalism, and the Committee on Public Information.* Chapel Hill: University of North Carolina, 1980.

Whitehouse, Vira B. *A Year as a Government Agent.* New York and London: Harper, 1920.

Wolper, Gregg. "Wilsonian Public Diplomacy: The Committee on Public Information in Spain." *Diplomatic History* 17, no. 1 (Winter 1993): 17–34.

Wolper, Gregg. "Woodrow Wilson's New Diplomacy: Vira Whitehouse in Switzerland, 1918." *Prologue: Quarterly of the National Archives and Records Administration* 24, no. 3 (Fall 1992): 226–239.

CULTURAL DIPLOMACY

Berger, Peter L. "Four Faces of Global Culture." *National Interest* (Fall 1997): 23–29.

Cavaliero, R. E. "Cultural Diplomacy: The Diplomacy of Influence." *Round Table* (April 1986): 139–144.

Finn, Helena K. "The Case for Cultural Diplomacy: Engaging Foreign Audiences." *Foreign Affairs* 82, no. 6 (November/December 2003): 15–20.

Gregg, Donald P. "The Case for Continued U.S. Engagement." *Orbis* 41 (Summer 1997): 375–384.

Rothkopf, David. "In Praise of Cultural Imperialism?" *Foreign Policy* (Summer 1997): 38–53.

CULTURAL ACTIVITIES BY THE U.S. GOVERNMENT IN THE 1930S THROUGH 1940S

Espinosa, J. Manuel. *Inter-American Beginnings of U.S. Cultural Diplomacy, 1936–1948.* Washington, DC: Bureau of Educational and Cultural Affairs, U.S. Department of State; for sale by U.S. Government Printing Office, 1976 [i.e., 1977].

Fairbank, Wilma. *America's Cultural Experiment in China, 1942–1949.* Washington, DC: Bureau of Educational and Cultural Affairs, U.S. Department of State; for sale by U.S. Government Printing Office, 1976.

Kellermann, Henry J. *Cultural Relations as an Instrument of U.S. Foreign Policy: The Educational Exchange Program between the United States and Germany, 1945–1954.* Washington, DC: Bureau of Educational and Cultural Affairs, U.S. Department of State; for sale by U.S. Government Printing Office, 1978.

CULTURAL FRONT

Denning, Michael. *The Cultural Front: The Laboring of American Culture in the Twentieth Century*. London and New York: Verso, 1997.

DEFINITIONS

Doob, Leonard W. "Propaganda." In *International Encyclopedia of Communications*, edited by Erik Barnouw et al., vol. 4, 374–78. New York: Oxford University, 1989.

Johannesen, Richard L. "The Emerging Concept of Communication as Dialogue." *Quarterly Journal of Speech* 57 (December 1971): 373–82.

Kecskemeti, Paul. "Propaganda." In *Handbook of Communication*, edited by Ithiel de Sola Pool et al., 844–70. Chicago: Rand McNally, 1973.

Lasswell, Harold D. "Propaganda." In *Encyclopaedia of the Social Sciences*, edited by Edwin R. A. Seligman and Alvin Johnson, vol. 12, 521–28. New York: Macmillan, 1934.

Smith, Bruce L. "Propaganda." In *International Encyclopedia of the Social Sciences*, edited by David L. Sills, vol. 12, 579–89. New York: Macmillan, 1968.

DISINFORMATION

Bittmann, Ladislav. *The KGB and Soviet Disinformation*. Washington: Pergamon-Brassey's International Defense Publishers, 1985.

Bittman, Ladislav, ed. *Propaganda, Disinformation, Persuasion: Gorbachev's Glasnost: Challenges and Realities*. (Program for the Study of Disinformation Papers). Boston: Boston University, College of Communication, 1989.

Douglass, Joseph D. "The Growing Disinformation Problem." *International Security Review* 4 (1981): 333–353.

Kux, Dennis. "Soviet Active Measures and Disinformation: Overview and Assessment." *Parameters, Journal of the U.S. Army War College* 15, no. 4 (Winter 1985): 19–28.

Leventhal, Todd. *Iraqi Propaganda and Disinformation During the Gulf War: Lessons for the Future*. Abu Dhabi, UAE: Emirate Center for Strategic Studies and Research, 1999.

Romerstein, Herbert. "Disinformation as a KGB Weapon in the Cold War." Prepared for a Conference on Germany and Intelligence Organizations: The Last Fifty Years in Review, sponsored by Akademiefur Politische Bildung Tutzing, June 18–20, 1999.

Romerstein, Herbert. *Soviet Active Measures and Propaganda: "New Thinking" and Influence Activities in the Gorbachev Era*. Toronto, Canada: Mackenzie Institute for the Study of Terrorism, Revolution, and Propaganda; Washington, DC: National Intelligence Book Center, 1989.

Shultz, Richard H., and Roy Godson, *Dezinformatsia*. Washington: Pergamon-Brassey's International Defense Publishers, 1984.

U.S. Congress. House. Permanent Select Committee on Intelligence. *Soviet Active Measures;* hearings. 97th Congress, 2d Session. Washington, DC: Government Printing Office, 1982.

U.S. Congress. Senate. Committee on Foreign Relations. Subcommittee on European Affairs. *Soviet Active Measures;* hearings. 99th Congress, 1st Session. Washington, DC: Government Printing Office, 1985.

U.S. Department of State. *Active Measures: A Report on the Substance and Process of Anti-U.S. Disinformation and Propaganda Campaigns*. Washington, DC: The Department, 1986.

U.S. Department of State. *A Report on Active Measures and Propaganda, 1986–87*. Washington, DC: The Department, 1987.

U.S. Department of State. *A Report on Active Measures and Propaganda, 1987–1988*. Washington, DC: Department, 1989.

U.S. Information Agency. *Child Organ Trafficking Rumor: A Modern "Urban Legend,"* prepared by Todd Leventhal. Washington, DC: USIA, 1994.

U.S. Information Agency. *Soviet Active Measures in the Era of Glasnost*; prepared at the request of the U.S. House of Representatives, Committee on Appropriation, for presentation at a hearing on March 8, 1988, by Charles Z. Wick, Director, United States Information Agency. Washington, 1988.

ENCYCLOPEDIAS

Cole, Robert, ed. *The Encyclopedia of Propaganda*. Armonk, New York: Sharpe Reference, 1998.

Cull, Nicholas J., David Culbert, and David Welch. *Propaganda and Mass Persuasion: A Historical Encyclopedia, 1500 to the Present*. Santa Barbara, CA and Denver, CO: ABC-CLIO, 2003.

Lasswell, Harold D., Daniel Lerner, and Hans Speier, eds. *Propaganda and Communication in World History*. Honolulu: University Press of Hawaii for the East-West Center, 1979–1980. 3 vols. Contents: vol. 1: The Symbolic Instrument in Early Times; vol. 2: Emergence of Public Opinion in the West; vol. 3: A Pluralizing World in Formation.

EXHIBITIONS

They are commonly called "fairs" in the United States, "exhibitions" in Great Britain, and "expositions" in France. The terms are used interchangeably although they are actually different-sized events. The Bureau of International Expositions, the regulating body, designates them as "international expositions," which bridges the gap between fair and exhibition and is actually a larger, more extensive, and more formally organized event.

Allwood, John, Ted Allan, and Patrick Reid. *The Great Exhibitions: 150 Years*, edited by Jack Evans. 2nd ed. London: Exhibition Consultants, 2001.

Findling, John E. and Kimberly D. Pelle, eds. *Historical Dictionary of World's Fairs and Expositions, 1851–1988*. Westport, CT: Greenwood, 1990.

Haddow, Robert H. *Pavilions of Plenty: Exhibiting American Culture Abroad in the 1950s*. Washington and London: Smithsonian Institution, 1997.

Heller, Alfred. *World's Fairs and the End of Progress: An Overview*. Corte Madera, CA: World's Fairs, 1999.

Hixson, Walter L. *Parting the Curtain: Propaganda, Culture, and the Cold War*. New York: St. Martin's, 1997.

Krenn, Michael L. "'Unfinished Business': Segregation and U.S. Diplomacy at the 1958 World's Fair." *Diplomatic History* 20, no. 4 (Fall 1996): 591–612.

Landers, Robert K. "World's Fairs: How They Are Faring." *Editorial Research Reports* (April 18, 1986): 291–308.

Rydell, Robert W., and Nancy E. Gwinn, eds. *Fair Representations: World's Fairs and the Modern World*. Netherlands: University of Amsterdam Press, 1994.

FILMS. *SEE* MOTION PICTURES

FOREIGN COUNTRIES (AND U.S.)

Evans, Frank B. *Worldwide Communist Propaganda Activities.* New York: Macmillan, 1955.

Marlin, Randal. *Propaganda and the Ethics of Persuasion.* Peterborough, Ontario, Canada: Broadview, 2002.

Martin, L. John, ed. *Propaganda in International Affairs.* Philadelphia: American Academy of Political and Social Science, 1971.

GERMANY

Boelcke, Willi A., ed. *The Secret Conferences of Dr. Goebbels: The Nazi Propaganda War, 1939–43.* New York: E. P. Dutton, 1970.

Bruntz, George G. *Allied Propaganda and the Collapse of the German Empire in 1918.* Stanford, CA: Stanford University, 1938.

Bytwerk, Randall L. "Rhetorical Aspects of the Nazi Meeting: 1926–1933." *Quarterly Journal of Speech* 61 (1975): 307–18.

Doherty, M. R. *Nazi Wireless Propaganda: Lord Haw-Haw and British Public Opinion in the Second World War.* Edinburgh, Scotland: Edinburgh University, 2000. [Contains CD of Lord Haw-Haw's (William Joyce) German Broadcasts]

Doob, Leonard W. "Goebbels' Principles of Propaganda." *Public Opinion Quarterly* 14 (1950): 419–42.

Frye, Alton. *Nazi Germany and the American Hemisphere, 1933–1941.* New Haven, CT and London: Yale University, 1967.

Horne, John. "German Atrocities, 1914: Fact, Fantasy or Fabrication?" *History Today,* 52, no. 4 (April 2002): 47–53.

Laurie, Clayton D. *The Propaganda Warriors: America's Crusade Against Nazi Germany.* Lawrence: University Press of Kansas, 1996.

GREAT BRITAIN

Buitenhuis, Peter. *The Great War of Words: British, American and Canadian Propaganda and Fiction, 1914–1933.* Vancouver: University of British Columbia Press, 1987.

Cull, Nicholas J. *Selling War: The British Propaganda Campaign Against American "Neutrality" in World War II.* New York: Oxford University, 1995.

Squires, James D. *British Propaganda at Home and in the United States From 1914 to 1917.* Cambridge, MA: Harvard University, 1935.

GULF WAR

MacArthur, John R. *Second Front: Censorship and Propaganda in the Gulf War.* New York: Hill and Wang, 1992.

HISTORY

Bentley, Eric, ed. *Thirty Years of Treason: Excerpts from Hearings before the House Committee on Un-American Activities, 1938–1968.* New York: Viking, 1971.

Cutlip, Scott. *The Unseen Power: Public Relations, a History.* Hillsdale, NJ: Lawrence Erlbaum Associates, 1994.

Davidson, Philip G. *Propaganda and the American Revolution, 1763–1783.* Chapel Hill: University of North Carolina, 1941.

Ellul, Jacques. "An Aspect of the Role of Persuasion in a Technical Society." *Etc.* 36, no. 2 (Summer 1979): 147–52.

Ellul, Jacques. "Information and Propaganda." *Diogenes*, no. 18 (Summer 1957): 61–77.

Gordon, George N. *War of Ideas; America's International Identity Crisis.* New York: Hastings House, 1973.

Green, Fitzhugh. *American Propaganda Abroad.* New York: Hippocrene, 1988.

Jennings, Tom. "Chomsky, Propaganda, and the Politics of Common Sense." *Anarchist Studies* 3, no. 2 (1995): 121–44.

Keen, Sam. *Faces of The Enemy: Reflections of the Hostile Imagination.* San Francisco: Harper and Row, 1986.

Morrow, Glenn R. "Plato's Conception of Persuasion." *Philosophical Review* 62 (April 1953): 234–50.

Sproule, J. Michael. "The Institute for Propaganda Analysis: Public Education in Argumentation, 1937–1942." In *Proceedings of the Third Summer Conference in Argumentation*, edited by David Zarefsky, et al., 486–99. Annandale, VA: Speech Communication Association, 1983.

Sproule, J. Michael. "Progressive Propaganda Critics and the Magic Bullet Myth." *Critical Studies in Mass Communication* 6 (September 1989): 225–46.

Sproule, J. Michael. "Propaganda Studies in American Social Science: The Rise and Fall of the Critical Paradigm." *Quarterly Journal of Speech* 73 (February 1987): 60–78.

Taylor, Philip M. *Munitions of the Mind: A History of Propaganda from the Ancient World to the Present Era.* Manchester, England and New York: Manchester University; New York: Distributed by St. Martin's, 1995.

Wilke, Jurgen. *Propaganda in the 20th Century: Contributions to Its History.* Cresskill, NJ: Hampton, 1998.

LIBRARIES

Lincove, David A., "Propaganda and the American Public Library from the 1930s to the Eve of World War II." *RQ [Reference Quarterly]* (Summer 1994): 510–523.

Smith, Stewart W. "Propaganda and the Library." *Library Journal* (June 15, 1991): S28–S30.

U.S. Congress. Senate. Committee on Government Operations. *State Department Information Program: Information Centers;* hearing, 83d Congress, 1st Session. Washington, DC: Government Printing Office, 1954.

Wiegand, Wayne A. *Active Instrument for Propaganda: The American Public Library During World War I.* New York: Greenwood, 1989.

MEMOIRS

Carroll, Wallace. *Persuade or Perish.* Boston: Houghton Mifflin, 1948; reprinted Madison: University of Wisconsin Press, 1990.

Creel, George. *Rebel at Large: Recollections of Fifty Crowded Years.* New York: G. P. Putnam's Sons, 1947.

Snyder, Alvin A. *Warriors of Disinformation: American Propaganda, Soviet Lies, and the Winning of the Cold War; an Insider's Account.* New York: St. Martin's, 1995.

Viereck, George S. *Spreading Germs of Hate.* New York: Horace Liveright, 1930.

MILITARY PROPAGANDA. *SEE* PSYCHOLOGICAL WARFARE

MOTION PICTURES

USIA made films about many of its performing artists along with other subjects. Some were done at the time of performance at the post or embassy; others were documentaries put together by USIA film production teams or done by commercial filmmakers then bought by USIA. There are shorts, newsreels, and full-length documentaries. USIA also bought rights from Hollywood films to be shown overseas in its cultural centers as American films are very popular in other countries.

Film and Propaganda in America: A Documentary History. Editor-in-chief: David Culbert. Westport, CT and New York: Greenwood, 1990–1991. 4 vols. Contents: vol. 1: World War I; vol. 2: World War II, part 1; vol. 3: World War II, part 2; vol. 4: 1945 and After; vol. 5: Microfiche Supplement, 1939–1979.

Fyne, Robert. *Hollywood Propaganda of World War II.* Metuchen, NJ: Scarecrow, 1994.

Gladwin, Lee A. "Hollywood Propaganda, Isolationism, and Protectors of the Public Mind, 1917–1941," *Prologue: Quarterly of the National Archives and Records Administration* 26, no. 4 (Winter 1994): 234–247.

Koppes, Clayton R., and Gregory D. Black. *Hollywood Goes to War: How Politics, Profits, and Propaganda Shaped World War II Movies.* New York: Free Press; London: Collier Macmillan, 1987.

MacCann, Richard D. *People's Films: A Political History of U.S. Government Motion Pictures.* New York: Hastings House, 1973.

Pronay, Nicholas, and Spring, D. W., eds. *Propaganda, Politics, and Film, 1918–45.* London: Macmillan, 1982.

Short, K. R. M., ed., Film and Radio Propaganda in World War II. Knoxville: University of Tennessee, 1983.

Startt, James D. "American Film Propaganda in Revolutionary Russia." *Prologue: Quarterly of the National Archives and Records Administration*, 30, no. 3 (Fall 1998): 167–179.

Welch, David. "Powers of Persuasion." *History Today* 49, no. 8 (August 1999): 24–26.

MUSIC

Dunaway, David K. "Music and Politics in the United States." *Folk Music Journal* 5, no. 3 (1987): 268–294.

Perris, Arnold. *Music as Propaganda: Art to Persuade, Art to Control.* Westport, CT: Greenwood, 1985.

OFFICE OF WAR INFORMATION

Public Opinion Quarterly 7 (Spring 1943), entire issue. [Articles on the Office of War Information (OWI)]

Warburg, James P. *Unwritten Treaty.* New York: Harcourt, Brace, 1946.

Winkler, Allan M. *The Politics of Propaganda: The Office of War Information, 1942–1945.* New Haven, CT: Yale University, 1978.

POSTERS

Stanford University. Hoover Institution on War, Revolution and Peace Archives. *War, Revolution and Peace Propaganda Posters from the Hoover Institution Archives, 1914–1945; an Exhibition.* Organized by Paula Harper and Marcia C. Growdon. (Stanford, CA: Hoover Institution, 1971?).

PSYCHOLOGICAL WARFARE

American Institutes for Research. *The Art and Science of Psychological Operations: Case Studies of Military Application,* edited by Ronald De McLaurin, Carl F. Rosenthal, Sarah A. Skillings, et. al. Project Director: Daniel C. Pollock. Washington, DC: Headquarters, Dept. of the Army, 1976.

Daugherty, William E., and Janowitz, Morris. *Psychological Warfare Casebook.* Baltimore, MD: Johns Hopkins; published for Johns Hopkins University, Operations Research Office, 1958.

Holt, Robert T., and Robert M. van de Velde. *Strategic Psychological Operations and American Foreign Policy.* Chicago: University of Chicago, 1960.

McLaurin, Ronald D., ed. *Military Propaganda: Psychological Warfare and Operations.* New York: Praeger, 1982.

Roetter, Charles. *The Art of Psychological Warfare, 1914–1945.* New York: Stein and Day, 1974.

PUBLIC DIPLOMACY

Hitchcock, David I. *U.S. Public Diplomacy.* Washington, DC: Center for Strategic and International Studies, 1988.

International Information Education and Cultural Relations. *Recommendations for the Future.* Washington, DC: Center for Strategic and International Studies, 1975. (Stanton Panel Report)

Malone, Gifford D. *Political Advocacy and Cultural Communication: Organizing the Nation's Public Diplomacy.* Lanham, MD: University Press of America, 1988.

Ninkovich, Frank A. *The Diplomacy of Ideas: U.S. Foreign Policy and Cultural Relations, 1938–1950.* Cambridge [Eng.] and New York: Cambridge University, 1981.

RADIO

Bruner, Jerome S. "The Dimensions of Propaganda: German Short-Wave Broadcasts to America." *Journal of Abnormal and Social Psychology* 36, no. 3 (1941): 311–37. [Repeated in: Daniel Katz, et al., eds. *Public Opinion and Propaganda.* New York: Holt, 1954: 491–506.

Heil, Alan L. *Voice of America: A History.* New York: Columbia University, 2003.

Horten, Gerd. *Radio Goes to War: The Cultural Politics of Propaganda During World War II.* Berkeley and Los Angeles: University of California, 2002.

Jurey, Philomena. *A Basement Seat to History.* Washington, DC: Linus, 1995.

Krugler, David F. *The Voice of America and the Domestic Propaganda Battles, 1945–1953.* New York: Columbia: University of Missouri, 2000.

Pirsein, Robert W. *The Voice of America: A History of the International Broadcasting Activities of the United States Government.* New York: Arno, 1979.

Rawnsley, Gary D. *Radio Diplomacy and Propaganda: The BBC and VOA in International Politics, 1956–64.* New York: St. Martin's, 1996.

Savage, Barbara D. *Broadcasting Freedom: Radio, War, and the Politics of Race, 1938–1948.* Durham: University of North Carolina, 1999.

Shulman, Holly Cowan. *The Voice of America: Propaganda and Democracy, 1941–1945.* Madison: University of Wisconsin, 1990.

Shulman, Holly Cowan. "The Voice of America, U.S. Propaganda and the Holocaust: 'I Would Have Remembered.'" *Historical Journal of Film, Radio and Television* 17, no. 1 (March 1997): 91–103.

Soley, Lawrence C. *Radio Warfare: OSS and CIA Subversive Propaganda.* New York: Praeger, 1989.

TELEVISION

Doherty, Thomas P. *Cold War, Cool Medium: Television, McCarthyism, and American Culture.* New York: Columbia University, 2003.

UNITED STATES INFORMATION AGENCY/UNITED STATES INFORMATION SERVICE

Barrett, Edward W. *Truth Is Our Weapon.* New York: Funk and Wagnalls, 1953.

Bogart, Leo. *Cool Words, Cold War: A New Look at USIA's "Premises for Propaganda."* Rev. ed. Washington, DC: American University, 1995.

Dizard, Wilson P. *The Strategy of Truth: The Story of the U.S. Information Service.* Washington: Public Affairs Press, 1961.

Dizard, Wilson P. "Telling America's Story." *American Heritage* (August/September 2003): 41–47.

Elder, Robert E. *Information Machine: The United States Information Agency and American Foreign Policy.* Syracuse, NY: Syracuse University, 1968.

Goodfriend, Arthur. *The Twisted Image.* New York: St. Martin's, 1963.

Haefele, Mark. "John F. Kennedy, USIA, and World Public Opinion," *Diplomatic History* 25, no. 1 (Winter 2001): 63–84.

Hansen, Allen C. *USIA: Public Diplomacy in the Computer Age.* 2nd ed. New York: Praeger, 1989.

Sorensen, Thomas C. *The Word War: The Story of American Propaganda.* New York: Harper and Row, 1968.

Stephens, Oren. *Facts to a Candid World.* Stanford, CA: Stanford University, 1955.

Thomson, Charles A. H. *Overseas Information Service of the United States Government.* Washington, DC: Brookings Institution, 1948.

VIETNAM

Chandler, Robert W. *War of Ideas: The U.S. Propaganda Campaign in Vietnam.* Boulder, CO: Westview, 1981.

Page, Caroline. *U.S. Official Propaganda During the Vietnam War, 1965–1973: The Limits of Persuasion.* London and New York: Leicester University, 1996.

WAR PROPAGANDA

Hamlin, Charles H. *Propaganda and Myth in Time of War.* New York: Garland, 1973. Comprises: *War Myth in United States History* (1927) and *Educators Present Arms: The Use of the Schools and Colleges as Agents of War Propaganda, 1914–1918* (1939).

Holsinger, M. Paul, ed. *War and American Popular Culture: A Historical Encyclopedia.* Westport, CT: Greenwood, 1999.

Lavine, Harold. *War Propaganda and the United States.* New Haven, CT: Yale University, 1940.

Nelson, Derek. *The Ads That Won the War.* Osceola, MN: Motorbooks International, 1992.

WOMEN

Collins, Gail. *America's Women: 400 Years of Dolls, Drudges, Helpmates, and Heroines.* New York: Morrow, 2003.

Rupp, Leila J. *Mobilizing Women for War: German and American Propaganda, 1939–1945.* Princeton, NJ: Princeton University, 1978.

WORLD WAR I

Adler, Selig. "The War-Guilt Question and American Disillusionment, 1918–1928." *Journal of Modern History* 23, no. 1 (March 1951): 1–28.

Lasswell, Harold D. *Propaganda Technique in the World War.* New York: Peter Smith, 1938.

Lutz, Ralph Haswell. "Studies of World War Propaganda, 1914–33." *Journal of Modern History* 5, no. 4 (December 1933): 496–516.

Peterson, Horace C. *Propaganda for War; the Campaign Against American Neutrality, 1914–1917.* Port Washington, NY: Kennikat [1968, 1939].

Ross, Stewart H. *Propaganda for War: How the United States Was Conditioned to Fight the Great War of 1914–1918.* Jefferson, NC: McFarland, 1996.

Short, K. R. M., ed. *Film and Radio Propaganda in World War I: A Global Perspective.* Knoxville: University of Tennessee, 1983.

Welch, David. *Germany, Propaganda and Total War, 1914–1918: The Sins of Omission.* London: Athlone, 2000.

WORLD WAR II

Butow, R. J. C. "How Roosevelt Attacked Japan at Pearl Harbor: Myth Masquerading as History." *Prologue: Quarterly of the National Archives and Records Administration* 28, no. 3 (Fall 1996): 208–221.

Herz, Martin F. "Some Psychological Lessons from Leaflet Propaganda in World War II." *Public Opinion Quarterly* 13 (1949): 471–486. [Reprinted in Daniel Katz, et al., eds. *Public Opinion and Propaganda.* New York: Holt, 1954: 543–553].

Leff, Mark H. "The Politics of Sacrifice on the American Homefront in World War II." *Journal of American History* 77, no. 4 (March 1991): 1296–1318.

Rhodes, Anthony R. E. *Propaganda: The Art of Persuasion in World War I,* edited by Victor Margolin. New York: Chelsea House, 1976.

Roeder, George H. *The Censored War: American Visual Experience During World War II.* New Haven, CT: Yale University, 1993.

Shils, Edward A., and Morris Janowitz. "Cohesion and Disintegration in the Wehrmacht in World War II." *Public Opinion Quarterly* 12 (1948): 280–315. [Reprinted in: Daniel Katz, et al., eds. *Public Opinion and Propaganda.* New York: Holt, 1954. 553–582.]

With Weapons and Wits: Propaganda and Psychological Warfare in World War II: A Selection From the Exhibition. Museum of Our National Heritage, Lexington, Massachusetts. Wellesley, MA: Overlord, 1992.

GENERAL WORKS ON PROPAGANDA

Allen, George V. "Propaganda: A Conscious Weapon of Diplomacy." *Department of State Bulletin* 21, no. 546 (December 19, 1949): 941–943.

Alleyne, Mark D. *Global Lies?: Propaganda, the UN and World Order.* New York: Palgrave Macmillan, 2003.

Altheide, David L., and John M. Johnson. *Bureaucratic Propaganda.* Boston: Allyn & Bacon, 1980.

Barsamian, David. *Stenographers to Power: Media and Propaganda.* Monroe, ME: Common Courage, 1992.

Chomsky, Noam. *Letters from Lexington: Reflections on Propaganda.* Monroe, ME: Common Courage, 1993.

Choukas, Michael. *Propaganda Comes of Age.* Washington: Public Affairs, 1965.

Christenson, Reo M., and Robert O. McWilliams, eds. *Voice of the People: Readings in Public Opinion and Propaganda*. New York: McGraw-Hill, 1962.

Davison, W. Phillips. *International Political Communication*. New York: Published for the Council on Foreign Relations [by] F. A. Praeger, 1965.

Doob, Leonard William. *Propaganda: Its Psychology and Technique*. New York: Henry Holt and Company, 1935.

Dunham, Donald C. *Kremlin Target: USA; Conquest by Propaganda*. New York: Washburn, 1961.

Ellul, Jacques. *Propaganda: The Formation of Men's Attitudes*. New York: Knopf, 1965. (Reprinted Vintage, 1973)

Foulkes, A. Peter. *Literature and Propaganda*. London and New York: Methuen, 1983.

Fraser, L. M. *Propaganda*. London; New York: Oxford University Press, 1957.

Friedrich, Carl J. *The Pathology of Politics: Violence, Betrayal, Corruption, Secrecy, and Propaganda*. New York: Harper & Row, 1972.

Gary, Brett. *The Nervous Liberals: Propaganda Anxieties from World War I to the Cold War*. New York: Columbia University, 1999.

Gruening, Ernest. *The Public Pays: A Study of Power Propaganda*. New York: Vanguard, 1931.

Irwin, Will. *Propaganda and the News; or, What Makes You Think So?* New York and London: Whittlesey House [and] McGraw-Hill, 1936.

Jowett, Garth, and Victoria O'Donnell. *Propaganda and Persuasion*. 2nd ed. Newbury Park, CA: Sage, 1986.

Joyce, Walter. *Propaganda Gap*. New York: Harper and Row, 1963.

Lee, Alfred McClung. *How to Understand Propaganda*. New York: Rinehart, 1953.

Lee, John, ed. *The Diplomatic Persuaders: New Role of the Mass Media in International Relations*. New York: Wiley, 1968.

Lerner, Max. *Ideas are Weapons; the History and Uses of Ideas*. New York: Viking, 1939.

Lippmann, Walter. *The Phantom Public: A Sequel to* Public Opinion. New York: Macmillan, 1927.

Lippmann, Walter. *Public Opinion*. New York: Macmillan, 1950.

Meyerhoff, Arthur E. *The Strategy of Persuasion; the Use of Advertising Skills in Fighting the Cold War*. New York: Coward-McCann, 1965.

Mitchell, Malcolm G. *Propaganda, Polls, and Public Opinion: Are the People Manipulated?* Englewood Cliffs, NJ: Prentice Hall, 1970.

Murty, Bhagevatula S. *Propaganda and World Public Order; the Legal Regulation of the Ideological Instrument of Coercion*. New Haven, CT: Yale University, 1968.

Pratkanis, Anthony R., and Elliot Aronson. *Age of Propaganda: The Everyday Use and Abuse of Persuasion*. New York: W. H. Freeman, 1992.

Qualter, Terence H. *Opinion Control in the Democracies*. New York: St. Martin's, 1985.

Ross, Stewart. *Propaganda*. New York: Thomson Learning, 1993.

Rutherford, Paul. *Endless Propaganda: The Advertising of Public Goods*. Toronto, Ontario, Canada: University of Toronto, 2000.

Smith, Paul A. *On Political War*. Washington, DC: National Defense University, 1989.

Smith, Ted J., ed. *Propaganda: A Pluralistic Perspective*. New York: Praeger, 1989.

Society for the Psychological Study of Social Issues. *Public Opinion and Propaganda; a Book of Readings*, edited by Daniel Katz. New York: Dryden, 1954.

Speier, Hans. *The Truth in Hell and Other Essays on Politics and Culture, 1935–1987*. New York: Oxford University, 1989.

Sproule, J. Michael. *Channels of Propaganda*. Bloomington, IN: EDINFO Press and ERIC Clearinghouse on Reading, English, and Communication, 1994.

Sproule, J. Michael. *Propaganda and Democracy: The American Experience of Media and Mass Persuasion*. Cambridge, UK; New York: Cambridge University, 1997.

Steffens, Bradley. *Free Speech: Identifying Propaganda Techniques*. San Diego, CA: Greenhaven, 1992.

Thom, Gladys, and Marcella Thom. *The Persuaders: Propaganda in War and Peace*. New York: Atheneum, 1972.

Thomson, Oliver. *Mass Persuasion: An Historical Analysis of the Development of Propaganda Techniques*. Edinburgh: Paul Harris, 1977.

Whitton, John B., ed. *Propaganda and the Cold War*. Washington, DC: Public Affairs, 1963.

Whitton, John B., and Arthur Larson. *Propaganda Towards Disarmament in the War of Words*. Dobbs Ferry, NY: Published for the World Rule of Law Center, Duke University by Oceana Publications, 1964.

FILMS AND VIDEOS

The First Casualty. Heritage Visual Sales. [Propaganda and how it was used effectively in Great Britain by magazines, newspapers, posters, and animated cartoons to dominate the masses during World War I.]

Josef Goebbels. Sterling Educational Films, 1965. [Depiction of the German propaganda minister's life and the techniques he used to glorify the Nazi regime.]

Military Objectives of Axis Psychological Warfare. Washington: Office of Strategic Services, 1943. [Uses maps to illustrate the military objectives of psychological warfare as carried on by the Axis powers at thwarting the Allies—Casablanca policy of concentrating on Germany while containing Japan during World War II.]

The Moving Picture Boys in the Great War. Post-Newsweek Stations; Coronet/MTI Film and Video, 1975. [Changing attitudes from isolationism to involvement in World War I; film segments from commercial films, authentic military footage, and propagandistic use of newsreels.]

Project Gold Dust. Washington: Office of Strategic Services, 1944. [Psychological warfare techniques used by the OSS Morale Operations Unit and Kachin guerillas in Burma during World War II.]

Propaganda Parade. International Historic Films, Inc., 1957. [Study of American wartime propaganda films.]

The Propaganda Wars: Japan vs. the U.S. Arts and Entertainment (Time Machine Series); Moonbeam Publications, 1994. [Excellent propaganda footage.]

A Report on OSS Morale Operations in Italy. Washington: Office of Strategic Services, 1944. [Lt. Col. John Whitaker speaks before a map as he outlines OSS propaganda and psychological warfare operations during the Allied invasions of Sicily and Italy proper.]

The Uncounted Enemy: A Vietnam Deception. Columbia Broadcasting Service; Carousel Video, 1982. [Television documentary narrated by Mike Wallace that investigated the impact of intelligence reports that underestimated the size and strength that Vietcong forces had on the U.S. military, politics and public opinion.]

A Walk Through the 20th Century with Bill Moyers: World War II, the Propaganda Battle. Created and developed by the Corporation for Entertainment and Learning and Bill Moyers, in association with WNET/New York and KQED/San Francisco, 1982. Washington, DC: PBS Video, 1984. [Part of Moyers' series shown on the Public Broadcasting Service, video discusses the mass media and the psychological effects of propaganda in World War II.]

Why We Fight Series. U.S. Film Service/U.S. Department of War, 1942–1945. Distributor: Alpha Video Distributors. Director Frank Capra was commissioned by General George C. Marshall in 1942 to create a series of training films, produced by the U.S. Army, to prepare American soldiers for battle in World War II. There were six specific themes for American military servicemen (GIs): the rightness of the cause; the difficulty of the job; confidence in their comrades and leaders to win the war; confidence in the integrity and fighting ability of the Allies; resentment of enemies; and a belief that military victory would result in a better world. The seven films, each approximately 50 minutes long, were entitled: *Prelude to War; The Nazis Strike; Divide and Conquer; The Battle of Britain; Battle of Russia; Battle of China;* and *War Comes to America.*

World War II: The Propaganda Battle. Public Broadcasting Service, 1984. [The sophisticated propaganda of the modern mass media developed from the battle to "sell" World War II on the home front. There are interviews with Frank Capra (Why We Fight) and Nazi filmmaker Fritz Hippler.

Index

About the Authors

MARTIN MANNING is a research librarian in the in the Bureau of Public Diplomacy, the U.S. Department of State, which was formerly the United States Information Agency (USIA). There, among other duties, he maintains the Bureau's Public Diplomacy Historical Collection, which was created at the suggestion of the USIA director from 1961–1964, Edward R. Murrow, to answer questions on the history of USIA, its successors, and its functions. This book is an outgrowth of the knowledge the authors acquired from a combined total of over 70 years of research at USIA and in the U.S. Congress.

HERBERT ROMERSTEIN retired in 1989 as the Soviet Disinformation Officer of the USIA.